The **Rough Guide** to

Sicily

written and researched by

Robert Andrews and Jules Brown

ROUGH
GUIDES

NEW YORK • LONDON • DELHI

www.roughguides.com

Contents

Food and wine in Sicily
colour section
following p.184

Festivals and events
colour section
following p.408

◄◄ Palace of the Normans, Palermo ◄ Riserva Naturale dello Zíngaro

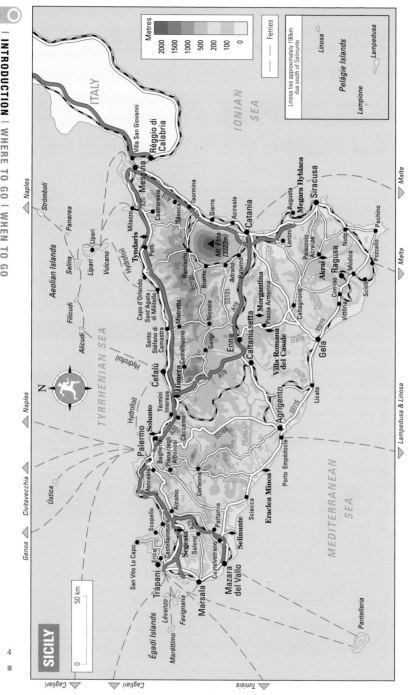

SICILY

0   50 km

Metres
2000
1500
1000
500
200
100
0

— — Ferries

Linosa lies approximately 190km
due south of Selinunte

Pelágie Islands

Linosa

Lampione

Lampedusa

ITALY

IONIAN
SEA

Villa San Giovanni
Réggio di
Calabria

Messina
A20

Strómboli
Panarea
Lipari
Vulcano
Salina
Filicudi
Alicudi
Aeolian Islands

TYRRHENIAN
SEA

Ustica

N

Naples
Naples
Civitavecchia
Genoa

Égadi Islands
Maréttimo
Lévanzo
Favignana

San Vito Lo Capo
Érice
Trápani
Scopello
Castellammare
Segesta
Alcamo
Salemi
Castelvetrano
Mazara
del Vallo
Marsala
Partanna
Selinunte
Sciacca
Eraclea Minoa
Porto Empédocle

Monreale
Palermo
Bagheria
Piana degli
Albanesi
Corleone
Caccamo
Términi
Imerese
Solunto
Cefalù
Himera
Castelbuono
Santo
Stéfano di
Camastra
Sant'Agata
di Militello
Capo d'Orlando
Patti
Milazzo
Tyndaris
Castroreale
Savoca
Taormina
Giarre
Acireale
Catania

Randazzo
Bronte
Adrano
Paternò
Mt. Etna
(3323m)

Gangi
Nicosia
Mistretta
Enna
Caltanissetta
Morgantina
Piazza Armerina
Villa Romana
del Casale
Caltagirone
Agrigento
Licata
Gela

Lentini
Augusta
Megara Hyblaea
Siracusa
Palazzolo
Acreide
Akrai
Ragusa
Módica
Comiso
Scicli
Vittoria
Noto
Pachino
Pozzallo

Monreale
Agrigento

MEDITERRANEAN
SEA

Pantelleria

Cagliari
Cagliari
Tunisia
Lampedusa & Linosa
Malta
Malta

Hydrofoil

SS120
SS113
A20
A19
SS121
SS117
SS189
SS115
A19
A18

Introduction to
Sicily

At the centre of the Mediterranean but on the periphery of Europe, the island of Sicily is a distinct entity from the rest of Italy. A mere 3km from the mainland across the Straits of Messina, it's much further away in appearance, feel and culture. A hybrid Sicilian dialect is still widely spoken, and many place names are tinged with the Arabic that was once in wide use on the island. The food is noticeably different, too: spicier and with more emphasis on fish, fruit and vegetables in the daily diet than in the north. The flora also echoes the shift south – oranges, lemons, olives, almonds and palms are ubiquitous. Above all, though, it's the nature of day-to-day living that separates Sicily from the rest of Italy – experienced outdoors with an operatic exuberance in markets, piazzas and alleys, and reflected in the unique festivals, ceremonies and processions that take place throughout the year.

The people certainly have a separate quality, seeing themselves as Sicilians first and Italians a very firm second. The island's strategic importance meant it was held by some of the western world's richest civilizations, among them the Greeks, Romans, Arabs, Normans and Spaniards. While bequeathing many fine monuments, that made Sicily the subject of countless foreign wars, and left it with little economic independence. Centuries of oppression have bred insularity and resentment, and the island was probably the most reluctantly unified Italian region, with Sicilians almost

Fact file

• Sicily is the largest and one of the most densely populated islands in the Mediterranean, with extensive areas of **mountains** in the north and east, the highest being Mount Etna (3323m) – Europe's largest active volcano. Apart from Etna's sporadic eruptions, Sicily is also prone to seismic upheavals – massive **earthquakes** destroyed Messina in 1908, and rocked the western part of the island in 1966.

• Sicily has a semi-autonomous status within the Italian republic, with its own **parliament** and **president**, and limited legislative powers in such areas as tourism, transport, industry and the environment. There is no **separatist movement** to speak of, though suspicion of central government runs deep.

• Compared to north Italy, the **economy** has remained relatively underdeveloped. Though there are pockets of oil-refining and chemical-industrial activity, Sicily is mainly **agricultural**, devoted to the cultivation of wheat, barley, corn (maize), olives, citrus fruit, almonds, wine grapes and some cotton. Tuna and sardine fishing are also important, while the last thirty years or so have seen **tourism** playing an increasingly crucial role.

• The **population** – mainly concentrated in the two main cities of Palermo and Catania, on the northern and eastern coasts – is something over five million.

▼ Piazza Duomo, Cefalù

instinctively suspicious of the intentions of Rome. Even today, relations with the mainland are often strained. For many Sicilians, their place in the modern Italian state is illustrated every time they look at a map to see the island being kicked – the perpetual football.

And Sicilians do have a point. There's much that remains unchanged since Unification in the nineteenth century, and what modernization there is has brought associated ills. Pockets of the island have been disfigured by bleak construction projects and unsightly industry, and despite Sicily's limited political autonomy, little has really been done to tackle the more deep-rooted problems: emigration (both to the mainland and abroad) is still high, poverty seemingly endemic, and there's an almost feudal attitude to business and commerce. Both European and central government aid continues to pour in, but much has been siphoned off by organized crime, which, in the west of the island at least, is still widespread. For visitors, however, these matters rarely impinge upon their experience. Mafia activity, for example – almost a byword for Sicilian life when viewed from abroad – is usually an in-house affair, with little or no consequence for travellers.

First-time visitors and regular returnees alike all remark on the island's astonishingly all-encompassing appeal. Its dramatic landscapes range from a mountainous interior and rugged coastlines to remote outlying islands and the volcanic foothills of Mount Etna. Sicily's diverse history,

Catacombs, caves and holes in the ground

Sicily is home to some of the world's creepiest tourist destinations, in the form of its catacombs and caves, used as burial places for thousands of years and accessible to anyone with a flashlight and a strong nerve. The oldest, the rock-cut tombs of the great necropolis at Pantálica, were first used in the thirteenth century BC. Another huge swathe of tombs is on view below the Greek temples at Agrigento, while catacombs riddle the ground in the city of Siracusa. But for sheer hands-in-the-air horror, there's no beating the infamous preserved bodies that line the catacombs of Palermo's Convento dei Cappuccini, or the smaller-scale show in the little village of Sávoca, near Taormina. Bodies were placed here as late as the nineteenth century, and the locals used to pay daily visits, often standing in the adjacent niches to accustom themselves to the idea of the great ever-after.

▼ Lipari, Aeolian Islands

meanwhile, has left it with an amazing abundance of archeological remains and architectural marvels. The island was an important power-base during the Hellenistic period, and its Greek relics, especially, are superb, standing comparison with any ruins in Greece itself. The Arab and Norman elements of Sicilian history are vividly manifest on the west and north coasts, while Baroque architecture shows its face in the elegantly restrained cities of the southeast. And if the history leaves you cold, you could simply come – as many do – for the food, the sun, the sea and the beaches. The coastal settlements soak up most of the summer-holiday trade, either at fashionable resorts or simple fishing villages fronted by long swathes of sand, though a number of offshore islands – some quite remote – offer a real chance to escape the crowds.

Where to go

Set in a wide bay at the foot of a fertile valley, the capital, **Palermo**, is among Italy's most visually striking cities, boasting some of the island's finest churches, markets, museums and restaurants. It gets hot and stuffy here in summer, though, which makes escapes out of the city all the more tempting: to the fashionable beach at Mondello, the sanctuary on Monte Pellegrino or to see

▲ Ceramics, Caltagirone

On location

Setting out on the movie trail in Sicily throws up some interesting cinematic bedmates. Francis Ford Coppola's *Godfather* trilogy is the obvious heavyweight – village scenes in *Part II* (1974) were filmed in Sávoca near Taormina, while *Part III*'s finale (1990) splatters gore across the steps of Palermo's Teatro Mássimo. There couldn't be more of a contrast to the gentilities of *Cinema Paradiso* (1989), filmed by Giuseppe Tornatore in the island's interior, or Michael Radford's *Il Postino* (1994), which used locations on offshore islands Salina and Pantelleria to great effect. These last two films, in particular, were amazing crossover successes, highlighting what many Italian directors had known for years – namely that the glories of the Sicilian landscape offered a unique hinterland for the expression of emotion. To best appreciate the relation of location and mood, see the great Roberto Rossellini's appreciation of the dramatic possibilities of the volcano in *Strómboli: Terra di Dio* (1949), starring a young Ingrid Bergman.

the extraordinary church mosaics at **Monreale**. East of Palermo, the Tyrrhenian coast provides the first opportunity to climb into the hiking and skiing grounds of the Monti Madonie, and it's along here that you'll find one of Sicily's premier resorts, **Cefalù**, handily situated just an hour from Palermo.

Ferries and hydrofoils depart from various points on the Tyrrhenian coast to the **Aeolian Islands**, a stunning chain of seven volcanic islands – including Vulcano, Panarea and Strómboli – that attract sun-worshippers, celebrities and adventurous hikers alike. Assorted seasonal holiday towns stretching between **Messina** – crossing-point to mainland Italy – and the fashionable resort of **Taormina** make up the island's Northern

The Normans in Sicily

In a long history of invasion and occupation, Sicily's most brilliant period belongs to the **Normans**, the swashbuckling "men from the north" who seized Messina from the Arabs in 1061, and captured Palermo eleven years later. In just over a century, four Norman kings – from Roger I to William II – changed the island's social and political landscape, and bequeathed a lasting legacy of **art and architecture**.

Whether in the small, gloriously decorated chapels of Palermo or the vibrant mosaics in the cathedrals of Monreale and Cefalù, the evidence of the glittering wealth and quasi-imperial certainty of the Norman invaders is clear. And by streamlining administration, imposing the French and Italian languages on what had been a largely Arabic island, and ruling absolutely from a position of strength, the Normans set the framework for the next seven hundred years of foreign domination.

Ionian coast, while Sicily's second city, east-coast **Catania**, broods under the graceful cone of **Mount Etna**, Europe's largest and most active volcano.

The finest concentration of historical and architectural sites is arguably in **Siracusa**, where classical ruins and stunning Baroque buildings decorate Sicily's most attractive city. In the southeast region beyond, beautiful towns

▼ Mount Etna at dawn

like **Noto** and **Ragusa** were rebuilt along planned Baroque lines after a devastating earthquake in the seventeenth century, though the unique Neolithic cemeteries of **Pantálica** survived to provide one of Sicily's most atmospheric backwaters.

After the richness of the southeast towns, many find the simple, isolated grandeur of the interior a welcome change. This is the most sparsely populated region, hiding gems like the well-preserved mosaics at **Piazza Armerina**, which recall the lavish trappings of Sicily's Roman governors, and the historic mountain stronghold of **Enna**. Away from the few interior towns, remote roads wind north, back towards Palermo, through little-visited destinations like Prizzi or Corleone whose names chime with the popular image of Sicily as a nest of Mafia intrigue.

Along the south coast, only the ancient temples of **Agrigento** and the Greek city and beach at Eraclea Minoa attract visitors in any numbers. Further around the coast, **Trápani** anchors the west of the island, a great base for anyone interested in delving into the very different character of this side of Sicily. The Arabic influence is stronger here than elsewhere, especially in Marsala and Mazara del Vallo, while **Selinunte** and **Segesta** hold the most romantic sets of ancient ruins on the island. It's from ports on the south and west coasts, too, that Sicily's most absorbing

outlying islands are reached. On Lampedusa and Linosa, on the Égadi Islands and, above all, on distant Pantelleria, the sea is as clean as you'll find anywhere in the Mediterranean, and you truly feel you're on the edge of Europe.

When to go

Sicily can be an extremely uncomfortable place to visit at the height of summer, when the dusty *sirocco* winds blow in from North Africa. In **July and August**, you'll roast – and you'll be in the company of tens of thousands of other tourists all jostling for space on the beaches, in the restaurants and at the archeological sites. Hotel availability is much reduced and prices will often be higher. If you want the heat but not the crowds, go in May, June or September, while swimming is possible right into November.

Spring is really the optimum time to come to Sicily, and it arrives early: the almond blossom flowers in February, and there are fresh strawberries in April. **Easter** is a major celebration, a good time to

▼ Hiking on Vulcano, Aeolian Islands

▲ The beach at Cefalù

see traditional festivals like the events at Trápani, Érice and Piana degli Albanesi, though again they'll all be oversubscribed with visitors.

Winter is mild by northern European standards and is a nice time to be here, at least on the coast, where the skies stay clear and life continues to be lived very much outdoors. On the other hand, the interior – especially around Enna – is very liable to get snowed under, providing skiing opportunities south of Cefalù, at Piano Battáglia, or on Mount Etna, while anywhere else in the interior can be subject to (often considerable) blasts of wind and torrential downpours of rain.

Daytime temperatures (°C)

	Jan	Feb	Mar	Apr	May	Jun	Jul	Aug	Sep	Oct	Nov	Dec
Palermo												
Average	10.3	10.4	13	16.2	18.7	23	25.3	25.1	23.2	19.9	16.8	12.6
Taormina												
Average	11	10.6	13.1	16.2	20.1	24.1	27.1	27.1	23.7	20	16	12.6

27

things not to miss

It's not possible to see everything Sicily has to offer in one trip – and we don't suggest you try. What follows is a selective taste of the island's highlights – architecture, dramatic landscapes, and exciting experiences. They're arranged in five colour-coded categories, so you can browse through to find the very best things to see and do. All highlights have a page reference to take you straight into the guide, where you can find out more.

01 Diving in Ústica Page **116** • The best place in Italy for undersea exploration, with exceptionally clear waters.

02 Beach, Eraclea Minoa Page **341** • This sweeping south-coast beach, backed by pine trees and chalky cliffs, is a magnet for locals and visitors during the summer.

03 Mount Etna Page **232** • Europe's greatest volcano – still very active – is the ultimate Sicily adventure trip.

04 The Villa Romana del Casale, Piazza Armerina
Page **311** • Uncovered at a Roman hunting lodge near Piazza Armerina, these brightly coloured mosaics are unrivalled in the Roman world in their quality and extent.

15

05 **Aeolian Islands** Page **156** • Island-hopping, Sicilian-style – jump on a ferry or hydrofoil to see the seven Aeolians, each with a distinct flavour of its own.

06 **Ortigia, Siracusa** Page **251** • Ortigia's seafront is the ideal place to enjoy the traditional early-evening *passegiata*.

07 **Morgantina** Page **315** • Typical of Sicily's hidden gems, the ancient ruins of Morgantina spread across an isolated hillside.

08 **San Giorgio, Ragusa** Page **273** • The restorers have been to work in Ragusa Ibla, now one of the best-looking Baroque old towns on the island.

09 **Pescheria, Catania** Page **224** • The city's vibrant fish market is the best of its kind on the island.

10 **Valle dei Templi, Agrigento** Page **334** • Agrigento's "Valley of the Temples" is a stunning series of ancient Greek temples lining the ridge below town.

11 **Erice** Page **376** • Wander the medieval lanes of western Sicily's most intimate, attractive town.

12 Pantálica Page **266** • This high ravine would be spectacular even without the thousands of prehistoric tombs that honeycomb its sheer walls.

13 Castello di Lombardia, Enna Page **293** • Enna's mighty castle guards the steep slopes of this ancient fortified town.

14 Gola di Alcántara Page **211** • Prepare to get wet as you wade the dramatic deep Alcántara gorge.

15 **The Duomo, Siracusa** Page **254** • Siracusa's ancient cathedral flanks one side of Sicily's finest piazza.

16 Museo Archeológico Regionale, Palermo Page

83 • The capital's archeological museum contains western Sicily's finest remains and artefacts, bringing to life the island's major Carthaginian, Greek and Roman settlements.

17 La Scala, Caltagirone

Page **318** • Famous for its ceramics industry, Caltagirone's most dramatic artistic expression is La Scala, a flight of 142 steps decorated with hand-painted designs.

18 Mud baths, Vulcano Page

167 • Brave the smell and wallow in the sulphurous mud baths of the Aeolian island of Vulcano.

19 Cloisters at Monreale

Page **104** • The delicately sculpted columns here are immaculate examples of medieval craftsmanship.

20 **Museo delle Marionette, Palermo** Page **78** • Explore the history of Sicilian puppet theatre, or even catch a show, at Palermo's specialist puppet museum.

21 **Cappella Palatina in the Palazzo dei Normanni, Palermo** Page **75** • The chapel shows off a dazzling combination of Arab architecture and Byzantine mosaics.

22 **Pantelleria** Page **410** • The most chic of Sicily's islands, Pantelleria is closer to Africa than Italy, and its unique landscapes attract an increasing number of inquisitive visitors.

23 **Teatro Greco, Taormina** Page **205** • This magnificently located ancient theatre offers wonderful views towards Etna and down to the sea, and is still used to stage concerts and dramas.

24 **The ascent of Strómboli** Page **178** • The thrilling climb allows a close-up view of the fireworks at the crater.

25 **Selinunte** Page **402** • Sicily's most romantically sited Greek city lies in ruins in a remote corner of the west coast.

27 **Noto** Page **279** • The whole town is a marvel of Baroque building, filled with glorious honey-coloured palaces and churches.

26 **Riserva Naturale dello Zíngaro** Page **366** • Sicily's first and most beautiful nature reserve offers great walks and plenty of isolated cove beaches.

Basics

Basics

Getting there

Budget airlines fly direct to Sicily from all over Europe and, outside peak holiday periods, the taxes often cost more than the price of the ticket. The island has two main airports, at Palermo in the west and Catania in the east, though some airlines use the smaller Trápani airport in the far west, and there are also airports on the main outlying islands of Pantelleria and Lampedusa. No direct flights go to Sicily from the US, Canada, Australia or New Zealand: the main points of entry to Italy are Rome and Milan, from where it's easy to pick up a connection to any of the Sicilian airports. If you want to see some of France or Italy en route, or are taking a vehicle, various overland combinations of ferry, rail and road are possible, though these will nearly always work out pricier than flying direct. European rail passes will save you some money, but most need to be purchased before you leave. Finally, package holidays and tours can be good value – from beach holidays to escorted historical tours – while airlines, travel agents and specialist operators can all also provide car rental, hotel bookings and other useful services. Car rental, in particular, is usually best arranged before you leave.

Air fares are **seasonal**, at their highest at Easter (a big celebration in Sicily), Christmas and New Year (as Sicilian émigrés come home), and between June and August (when the weather is hottest and the island the busiest). The **cheapest flights** from the UK and Europe are usually with no-frills budget and charter airlines, especially if you're prepared to book several weeks in advance or chance a last-minute deal. Budget airline tickets are sold direct (by phone or online) on a one-way basis, so you may find the outward or return leg of your journey significantly more expensive depending on demand. Be aware too that **airport taxes** can be more expensive than the flight itself, while increasingly things like in-flight meals and luggage allowances are being charged as extra. Cheap flights also tend to have fixed dates and are non-changeable and non-refundable, while tickets with holiday charter airlines may limit your stay to one month.

Major **scheduled airlines** are usually (though not always) more expensive, but tickets remain valid for three months and usually have a degree of flexibility should you need to change dates after booking. You may be able to cut costs by going through a specialist **flight, discount or online agent**, who may also offer special student and youth fares, plus a range of other travel-related services.

Flights from the UK and Ireland

There are daily **direct flights to Sicily** with easyJet (London Gatwick to Palermo, ⓦwww.easyjet.com), Ryanair (Stansted to Palermo, ⓦwww.ryanair.com), British Airways (Gatwick to Catania, ⓦwww.britishairways.com) and Air Malta (Gatwick to Catania, ⓦwww.airmalta.com). Easyjet and Ryanair are usually the cheapest, but it's always worth checking the other two for good deals. Meanwhile, Thomsonfly (ⓦwww.thomsonfly.com) has a weekly seasonal service (May to Nov) from either Gatwick or Manchester to Catania. Prices on all routes can range from as little as £1 plus taxes each way to over £300 return.

From Ireland, Ryanair offers a weekly direct flight from Dublin to Trápani. Otherwise, you'll have to fly via the UK, or via Rome or Milan, either combining with Ryanair's other services or by using the scheduled services on airlines like British Airways, Aer Lingus (ⓦwww.aerlingus.com) or Alitalia (ⓦwww.alitalia.com).

The other alternative from the UK or Ireland is to fly to one of the many airports

Fly less – stay longer! Travel and climate change

Climate change is the single biggest issue facing our planet. It is caused by a build-up in the atmosphere of carbon dioxide (CO_2) and other greenhouse gases, which are emitted by many sources – including planes. Already, flights account for around 3–4 percent of human-induced global warming: that figure may sound small, but it is rising year on year and threatens to counteract the progress made by reducing greenhouse emissions in other areas.

Rough Guides regard travel, overall, as a global benefit, and feel strongly that the advantages to developing economies are important, as are the opportunities for greater contact and awareness among peoples. But we all have a responsibility to limit our personal "carbon footprint". That means giving thought to how often we fly and what we can do to redress the harm that our trips create.

Flying and climate change

Pretty much every form of motorized travel generates CO_2, but planes are particularly bad offenders, releasing large volumes of greenhouse gases at altitudes where their impact is far more harmful. Flying also allows us to travel much further than we would contemplate doing by road or rail, so the emissions attributable to each passenger become truly shocking. For example, one person taking a return flight between Europe and California produces the equivalent impact of 2.5 tonnes of CO_2 – similar to the yearly output of the average UK car.

Less harmful planes may evolve but it will be decades before they replace the current fleet – which could be too late to avoid climate chaos. In the meantime, there are limited options for concerned travellers: to reduce the amount we travel by air (take fewer trips, stay longer!), to avoid night flights (when plane contrails trap heat from Earth but can't reflect sunlight back to space), and to make the trips we do take "climate neutral" via a carbon offset scheme.

Carbon offset schemes

Offset schemes run by **climatecare.org**, **carbonneutral.com** and others allow you to "neutralize" the greenhouse gases that you are responsible for releasing. Their websites have simple calculators that let you work out the impact of any flight. Once that's done, you can pay to fund projects that will reduce future carbon emissions by an equivalent amount (such as the distribution of low-energy light bulbs and cooking stoves in developing countries). Please take the time to visit our website and make your trip climate neutral.

Ⓦ**www.roughguides.com/climatechange**

on the **Italian mainland**, and travel onwards from there. Ryanair alone flies to around twelve Italian airports, easyJet flies from Milan to Catania, while Alitalia and British Airways have decent connections from Rome, Milan and others to Palermo, Catania, Trápani, Lampedusa and Pantelleria. Meridiana (Ⓦwww.meridiana.it) has daily services from London Gatwick to Florence with onward connections to Palermo and Catania, and Air One (Ⓦwww.flyairone.it) connects London City to Milan and Rome, with onward connections for all Sicilian airports. Other Italian budget airlines also have connections to Sicily – including Volare (Ⓦwww.volareweb.com) from Milan to Palermo and Catania – as do the budget and holiday airlines of other countries (like Germany) with an established tourist connection to Sicily. In the end, you'll have to weigh up the extra travelling time flying via Italy, or elsewhere, with the savings you might make.

Flights from the US and Canada

There are no direct **flights from the US and Canada to Sicily**, so you'll have to fly first to Rome or Milan (9 hours from east coast US/Canada, 12 hours from Chicago, 15 hours from west coast US/Canada). For the connection to Sicily add on another hour and a half or so, plus any time spent waiting for the connection itself.

Alitalia (@www.alitalia.com) flies direct every day **between the US or Canada and Italy**, and their great advantage is the ease of making the connecting flight to Sicily with the same airline. But several other airlines – including Delta (@www.delta.com), Continental (@www.continental.com) and Air Canada (@www.aircanada.com) – fly to Rome or Milan, and can arrange an onward connection for you. Or you can fly to Italy with airlines like British Airways, Air France, Lufthansa and Iberia, which travel via their respective European hubs.

Generally, the cheapest round-trip **fare from the US** to Palermo or Catania, via Rome or Milan, starts at around US$600, rising to US$1000 during the summer. **From Canada**, low-season fares start at around Can$800, increasing to around Can$1400 in high season. The alternative option is to pick up a discounted flight to the UK, and then fly on to Sicily with one of the European budget airlines (see section above). It depends on how soon in advance you book, and the season, as to whether this will be a realistic way to save money.

Flights from Australia and New Zealand

Although there are no direct **flights from Australia or New Zealand** to Sicily, many airlines offer through tickets with their partners via European or Asian hubs. Round-trip **fares** from the main cities in Australia start from around A$1600 in low season, up to around A$2000 in high season; from New Zealand, fares cost from NZ$3000. Fares don't vary as much between airlines as you might think and, in the end you'll be basing your choice on things like flight timings, routes and possible stop-offs on the way. If you're seeing Sicily as part of a wider European trip, you might want to aim first for the UK in any case, since there's a wider choice of cheap options to Sicily once there – or consider a **Round-the-World** (RTW) fare, though note that these tend only to include Rome or Milan as standard stopovers.

Package holidays and tours

Most **package holidays** are to Taormina, Sicily's most chic resort, and its less glamorous beachside neighbour Giardini-Naxos (on the east coast), and to the historic beach town of Cefalù (north coast, near Palermo), though you'll also see holidays in the Aeolian Islands, and special tours of the major historical sights which take in overnight stops in several towns. It's obviously cheapest to go out of season, something we'd recommend anyway as the resorts and sights are much less crowded, and the weather warm without being oppressive.

From the UK, a flight and a week's self-catering apartment accommodation starts at around £350 per person. Staying in a three-star hotel on a B&B basis starts from around £450, and for four- and five-star properties you're looking at more like £800–1000. Obviously, special deals and last-minute offers can undercut these prices; for the best current deals consult any high-street or online travel agent. Some tour operators organize **specialist holidays** to Sicily, particularly walking tours, culinary trips, and art and archeology holidays, but they are usually more expensive as accommodation, food, local transport and the services of a guide are nearly always included. Walking tours tend to be cheapest, based in simple rural two- and three-star hotels, but a week's fully inclusive cultural holiday can easily cost £2000, and a ten-day cruise from around £3000. For more details check the specialist tour operator reviewed on p.31 and p.32.

From the US, dozens of companies operate group travel and **tours** in Italy, ranging from all-inclusive escorted bus tours to smaller specialized groups out biking and hiking. Although specifically Sicilian options are less common, most general operators usually offer tours at least partly based on the island. You can also, of course, simply book a hotel-plus-flight deal, or rent a villa or a farmhouse for a week or two. Prices vary wildly, so check what you are getting for your money (most don't include the cost of the airfare, though that can always be arranged for you). Reckon on paying at least US$2000 for a standard ten-day touring vacation without flight, and up to

US$6000 for a fourteen-day escorted specialist package.

Trains

It's a long journey from the UK **to Sicily by train** (2672km from London to Messina). The fastest route (via Paris, Rome and Naples) is scheduled to take 32 to 34 hours, but delays on the Italian stretch are not uncommon. Tickets include seat reservations, though for any degree of comfort it's also worth **reserving a couchette or sleeping car** for the overnight part of the journey. The easiest way is to take the **Eurostar** service (Ⓦwww .eurostar.com) from London to Paris (from £59 return), then the **overnight train from Paris to Rome** (from £52 return), followed by the direct Intercity express **from Rome to Sicily** (calling at Messina, Taormina, Catania and Siracusa, or to Palermo, from around £70 return). There's also an overnight Rome-to-Sicily service. You can book through tickets from London to Rome online with Rail Europe (Ⓦwww.raileurope .co.uk, Ⓦwww.raileurope.com), and then the Rome-to-Sicily section of the journey also online with Italian Railways (Ⓦwww.italiarail .co.uk or Ⓦwww.trenitalia.com, English-language version) – the Italian Railways sites also post fares and Italian train timetables.

The invaluable train travel website Ⓦwww .seat61.com tells you exactly how to book the entire journey, down to precise details about the various sleeper-train options. It also has a "Rail Shop" section which will help you decide whether or not buying a **rail pass** is a good idea. InterRail and Eurail are the best known of these, giving unlimited rail travel throughout Europe, as well as providing discounts on Eurostar and cross-Channel ferry crossings. For details of rail passes, including those for use solely within Italy, see "Getting around", p.33.

Buses

It's difficult to make any case for travelling to Sicily by bus, especially as there's no direct service from the UK. **Eurolines** (Ⓦwww .nationalexpress.com) has a service from London Victoria to Naples, but that takes at least 35 hours depending on connections in Paris and Milan, and then you'll have to take a second overnight bus with Italian bus

company SAIS (Ⓦwww.saistrasporti.it) on to Sicily (another 6 hours to Messina, 10 to Palermo). Even with book-in-advance promotional fares (up to thirty days in advance) you're looking at from £89 return for the London–Naples section, and another €35 each way for Naples–Sicily. It hardly compares with most budget airline fares, and you'll be half dead when you arrive.

By car and ferry

Driving to Sicily from the UK, using the standard **cross-Channel services** or **Eurotunnel** (Ⓦwww.eurotunnel.com) through the Channel Tunnel, takes at least two full days. From the France/Italy border, it's possible, with a bit of luck, to reach the Straits of Messina in a long day if you keep on the motorways (autostradas). While not a cheap option (factoring in the cross-Channel trip, tolls, overnight stops and meals), it is a good way of seeing something of France and Italy on the way.

The shortest crossing from the Italian mainland, over the Straits of Messina, is from **Villa San Giovanni by ferry**; or, fifteen minutes further south – at the end of the motorway – by **hydrofoil** or fast ferry from **Réggio di Calabria**. All the details are given in the box on p.189.

To cut the driving time in Italy, you could use one of the earlier **ferry or hydrofoil crossings from the Italian mainland** to Sicily, **from Genova** (to Palermo, 20hr), **Salerno** (to Palermo, 12hr) or **Naples** (to Palermo 11hr, Trápani 7hr, or Aeolian Islands 4–6hr). Non-drivers could even combine a cheap flight (say Ryanair to Genoa) with one of these ferry crossings. You can also approach Sicily by travelling **via Corsica or Sardinia**, though obviously this is a somewhat complicated route involving two lengthy crossings – it's not recommended for a short trip to Sicily. The Genova, Salerno and Naples crossing schedules are seasonal, and with several different operators, but there are daily sailings in summer and at least two or three per week throughout the year. The best places to check schedules and fares, and book tickets, are the exhaustive websites Ⓦwww.directferries.co.uk and Ⓦwww.viamare.com, which contain details about every Italian ferry service.

Booking flights and services online

ⓦwww.cheapflights.co.uk, ⓦwww
.cheapflights.com Price comparison on flights,
short breaks, packages and other deals.
ⓦwww.ebookers.com, ⓦwww.ebookers.ie
Flights, hotels, cars and holiday packages.
ⓦwww.expedia.co.uk, ⓦwww.expedia.com,
ⓦwww.expedia.ca Discount airfares, all-airline
search engine, and daily deals on hotels, cars and
packages.
ⓦwww.lastminute.com, ⓦwww
.us.lastminute.com Good last-minute flights,
holiday packages, hotel bookings and car rentals.
ⓦwww.skyscanner.net Flight search site that
covers lots of the budget and no-frills airlines.
ⓦwww.travelocity.co.uk, ⓦwww.travelocity
.com, ⓦwww.travelocity.ca, ⓦwww.zuji.com
.au, ⓦwww.zuji.com.nz Destination guides, hot
fares and good deals on car rental, rail passes and
accommodation.

Discount flight agents

Flight Centre Australia ☎133, ⓦwww
.flightcentre.com.au; Canada ☎1-877/967-
5302, ⓦwww.flightcentre.ca; New Zealand
☎0800/243544, ⓦwww.flightcentre.co.nz; South
Africa ☎0860/400727, ⓦwww.flightcentre.co.za;
UK ☎0870/499 0040, ⓦwww.flightcentre.co.uk;
US ☎1-866/967-5351, ⓦwww.flightcentre.us.
Specialist agent for budget flights, especially RTW and
European deals, and package holidays.
North South Travel UK ☎01245/608291,
ⓦwww.northsouthtravel.co.uk. Discounted fares on
scheduled flights to Sicily, as well as summer charters.
Profits are used to support projects in the developing
world, especially the promotion of sustainable tourism.
STA Travel Australia ☎134 782, ⓦwww.statravel
.com.au; US ☎1-800/781-4040, ⓦwww
.statravel.com; UK ☎0871/230 0040, ⓦwww
.statravel.co.uk. Worldwide specialists in low-cost
flights and tours for students and under-26s, though
other customers welcome. Also student IDs, travel
insurance, car rental and rail passes, etc.
Trailfinders Australia ☎1300/780 212, ⓦwww
.trailfinders.com.au; Republic of Ireland ☎01/677
7888, ⓦwww.trailfinders.ie; UK ☎0845/058 5858,
ⓦwww.trailfinders.com. One of the best-informed
and most efficient agents for independent travellers.

Tour operators

UK

Alternative Travel Group ☎01865/315678,
ⓦwww.atg-oxford.co.uk. Inclusive eight-day guided
walking holidays (April–June & Sept/Oct) in the Monti
Madonie, from Enna to Cefalù. Accommodation is two-
and three-star standard, and fully inclusive prices start
at around £1500.
Arblaster & Clarke ☎01730/263111, ⓦwww
.arblasterandclarke.com. Deluxe seven-night wine
tours, including flights, meals and tastings, plus an
expert guide, from £1899. There's also a wine cruise
of Italian islands, including Sicily and its offshore
islands.
Citalia ☎0871/200 2004, ⓦwww.citalia.com.
Italian holiday specialist, offering short breaks, resort
holidays, tailor-made island tours, villas and car rental.
Martin Randall Travel ☎0208/742 3355,
ⓦwww.martinrandall.com. Small-group cultural
tours, led by experts on art, history, archeology and
music, to the classic sites of Sicily. Tours depart two
or three times a year, from £2750 for thirteen days,
including flights, meals and transport.
Nautilus Yachting ☎01732/867445, ⓦwww
.nautilus-yachting.co.uk. Yacht holidays, operating
out of Sant'Agata di Militello (for the Aeolians) and
Marsala (Égadis). Prices start from £900 for the boat
for a week, though if you have no experience you can
add the services of a skipper from around another
£90 a day.
Ramblers Worldwide Holidays ☎01707/331
133, ⓦwww.ramblersholidays.co.uk. Eight-day
walking holidays based either in Francavilla (near
Taormina) for seeing eastern Sicily (from around

£550), or at various centres in western Sicily (from around £900). Weekly departures Feb, March–May, Sept, Oct & Dec.

Sunvil Holidays ☎ 0208/568 4499, 🌐 www .sunvil.co.uk. Holidays in the best of Sicily's resorts and historic cities, as well as island-based stays on Lípari (Aeolian Islands). Tailor-made routes and fly-drive holidays available.

Tabona and Walford ☎ 0208/767 6789, 🌐 www .tabonaandwalford.com. Cultural walking holidays (from around £1100) in Érice and the west or the Madonie and Lípari, with bike and market excursions, vineyard visits and other activities.

US and Canada

Adventure Center ☎ 1-800/228-8747, 🌐 www .adventurecenter.com. Worldwide adventure and hiking specialist has an eleven-day "Highlights of Sicily" walking tour that ranges across the entire island and out to the Aeolian island of Lípari, from US$1500.

Bike Riders ☎ 1-800/473-7040, 🌐 www .bikeriderstours.com. The Aeolians, Taormina and Etna by bike, cycling 15–35 miles a day, and sampling local cuisine as you go. It's four- and five-star standard, with April, September and October

departures, from around US$3900. Also "guest chef" gourmet biking trips, from US$4300.

The International Kitchen ☎ 1-800/945-8606, 🌐 www.theinternationalkitchen.com. Seven-night all-inclusive Sicilian culinary tours and cooking school holidays, from US$2000. Lessons and accommodation often based in restored farmhouses, with winery and market visits included.

Italian Connection Canada ☎ 1-800/462-7911, 🌐 www.italian-connection.com. The "Splendors of Sicily" walking and culinary tour (nine days, from US$4250) ranges across the island from east to west. But there are also more specialist cooking and cultural tours, all accompanied by local experts.

Italiatours ☎ 1-800/283-7262, 🌐 www .italiatours.com. Low-cost Italy tour specialist with a range of escorted bus-tour programmes, from three days to a week exploring the island highlights (from around US$1200). Also hotel bookings, flights and transfers.

Australia

CIT Holidays Australia ☎ 1300/361 500, 🌐 www.cittravel.com.au. Italian travel specialists, offering Sicily tours, hotel reservations, car rental and rail passes.

Getting around

You don't have to rent a car to see Sicily's major towns and sights, but getting around by public transport is not always as easy as it should be. The rail system is slow, few buses run on Sundays and route information can be frustratingly difficult to extract, even from the bus and train stations themselves. Sicily's geography makes it a push to get right across the island – say from Siracusa to Trápani – in a single day, though you'll be able to travel most of one of the coastlines easily enough. On the positive side, public transport prices are among the cheapest in Europe.

The "Travel details" section at the end of each chapter in this book gives the full picture on transport schedules and frequencies. Note that unless specified, these refer to regular working-day schedules, ie Monday to Saturday; services are much reduced, or even non-existent, on Sundays. Note also that comments such as "every 30min" are approximations – on the railways

in particular, there are occasional gaps in the schedule, typically occurring just after the morning rush hour, when the gap between trains may be twice as long as normal.

One thing to bear in mind is that travelling by train is not the best way to see all of the island. Some stations are located a fair distance from their towns – Enna and Taormina are two notable examples (though there are usually bus connections) – while much of the west and centre of Sicily is only accessible by bus or car.

By train

Italian State Railways, **Ferrovie dello Stato** (FS), operates the **trains** in Sicily (for details of Sicily's only **private railway**, the Ferrovia Circumetnea route around the base of Mount Etna, see p.237). The FS website ⓦwww .trenitalia.com has a useful English-language version, where you can view timetables and book tickets. Trains connect all the major Sicilian towns, but are more prevalent in the east of the island than the west. On the whole they *do* leave on time, with the notable exception of those on the Messina–Palermo and Messina–Catania/Siracusa routes that have come from the mainland. These latter can be delayed by up to three hours, though around an hour late is more normal.

Of the various **types of train**, the most expensive are the **Intercity** (IC) trains that link the main cities. **Diretto** and **Interregionale** trains are long-distance expresses, calling only at larger stations, while the **Regionale** services (also called Locale), which stop at every place with a population higher than zero, are usually ones to avoid. A **seat reservation** (*prenotazione*) is obligatory on Intercity services and advisable on other trains where possible, especially in summer when trains can get crowded. You can **buy tickets** and make reservations at any major train station, or buy online on the FS website (both regional and Intercity services). If you don't have time to buy a ticket at the station on the day of travel, you can simply pay the conductor, though that costs around thirty percent extra. **Fares** are very reasonable, with tickets charged by the kilometre – a typical journey, say Palermo to Catania, costs around €12. Children aged 4–12 pay half price, while the under-4s travel free provided they do not occupy a seat.

Information boards and **timetables** are displayed at stations. "Departures" are *Partenze*, "Arrivals" *Arrivi*, "Delayed" *In Ritardo*), while some services are seasonal (*periódico*) or only operate between certain dates (*Si effetua dal… al…*). *Feriale* is the word for the Monday-to-Saturday service,

Stamp it

All rail stations and platforms have validation machines in which passengers must stamp their ticket before embarking on their journey. Failure to **validate your ticket** may land you with an on-the-spot fine.

symbolized by two crossed hammers; *festivo* means that a train runs only on Sundays and holidays, with a cross as its symbol.

Unless you're visiting Sicily as part of a wider Italian or European tour, the major pan-European **rail passes** (InterRail and Eurail) are not worth considering. Both schemes do also have single-country Italy rail passes, but given the relative cheapness of local train tickets, and the restricted service in some parts of Sicily, buying one of these probably won't save you any money either. The **InterRail Italy pass** (ⓦwww.raileurope .co.uk/inter-rail) is only available to European residents, and allows three, four, six or eight days' train travel in one month (from £80 for three days, under - 26s from £52). For anyone else, Eurail (ⓦwww.raileurope.com) has various Italy passes available, typically offering three days' travel in two months (from US$196, under - 26s from $165). All passes have to be bought before you leave home, and you'll still be liable for supplements and seat reservations on Intercity trains.

By bus

Almost anywhere you want to go will have some kind of **regional bus** (*autobus* or *pullman*) service, usually quicker and more reliable than the train (especially between the major towns and cities), but generally more expensive.

Between them, four main **companies** – SAIS Trasporti (ⓦwww.saistrasporti.it), SAIS Autolinee (ⓦwww.saisautolinee.it), AST (ⓦwww.aziendasicilianatrasporti.it) and Interbus (ⓦwww.interbus.it) – cover most of the island. Other companies stick to local routes. Many routes are linked to school/ market requirements, which can mean a frighteningly early start, last departures in the afternoon, and occasionally no services during school holidays, while nearly everywhere services are drastically reduced, or non-existent, on **Sundays**.

The local **bus station** (*autostazione*) is often in a central piazza, or outside the train station, though in some towns different **bus companies have different bus terminals**. **Timetables** are available on the companies' websites, and also from company offices and bus stations. You usually buy **tickets** on the bus, though on longer routes (and to be sure of a place) you can buy them in advance from the companies' offices. On most routes, it's possible to flag a bus down if you want a ride. If you want to get off, ask "*posso scéndere?*"; "the next stop" is "*la próssima fermata*".

City buses usually charge a flat fare of around €1, and the tickets are often valid for ninety minutes allowing you to change services for free within that time. Invariably, you need a ticket *before* you get on. Buy them in *tabacchi*, or from the kiosks and vendors at bus stops, and then validate them in the machine in the bus. Checks are frequently made by inspectors who block both exits as they get on, though if you don't have a ticket you'll usually get off with an earful of Sicilian and be made to buy one; some inspectors might hold out for the spot fine.

By car

Driving in Sicily is almost a competitive sport, and although the Sicilians aren't the world's worst drivers they don't win any safety prizes either. However, with a car you'll be able to see a lot of the island quickly, and reach the more isolated coastal and inland areas.

Most **main roads** are prefixed SS (Strada Statale) or SP (Strada Provinciale), and are reasonably maintained and signposted. On the whole they are two-lane roads with passing places on hills, though some stretches near towns and cities are dual carriageway. Some roads provide spectacular cross-country driving routes (see the "best drives" box), as do the impressive Sicilian **motorways** (autostradas), which are carried on great piers spanning the island. These link Messina–Catania (A18), Catania–Palermo (A19), Palermo–Trápani/Mazara del Vallo (A29) and Messina–Palermo (A20), while work has begun on a stretch of

---

Sicily's six best drives

1. **SS120, Nicosia to Polizzi Generosa** – bare landscape punctuated by isolated hilltop villages, with Etna dominating the eastern horizon.
2. **SS185, Tyrrhenian coast to Giardini-Naxos** – across the Peloritani mountains to Etna and the sea.
3. **Ávola to Cava Grande** – winding up the mountain-side to where eagles dare.
4. **SP624 and SP5, Palermo to Piana degli Albanesi** – past jagged fangs and towers of rock, with glimpses of lakes and lingering views over fertile valleys.
5. **Trápani to Erice** – startling interplay of coast and mountain.
6. **SS118, Agrigento to Corleone** – remote western valleys and crags, rock tombs and Mafia towns.

---

autostrada between Gela and Siracusa. The Messina–Catania and Messina–Palermo autostradas are **toll-roads** (*pedaggio*, toll; *autostrada a pedaggio*, toll-motorway). Take a ticket as you come on, and pay on exit; the amount due is flashed up on a screen.

Rules of the road are straightforward: drive on the right; at junctions, where there's any ambiguity, give precedence to vehicles coming from the right; observe the speed limits (50kph in built-up areas, 110kph on country roads, 130kph on autostradas); and *don't* drink and drive. Speed cameras and traffic-calming humps are becoming more evident, but this doesn't seem to deter Sicilians from travelling at any speed they choose.

Italian **fuel prices** are roughly in line with those in the UK, with unleaded petrol (*senza piombo*) slightly cheaper than leaded (*super*). Blue lines in towns signify authorized **parking zones**, where you'll pay around €1 an hour, either in a meter or to an attendant hovering nearby. You can also often buy a *biglietto parcheggio*, a scratch card, from *tabacchi* or local bars, where you scratch off the date and time and leave it in the windscreen. However, if you've parked in a street that turns into a market by day, you'll be stuck until close of business, while if you park in a *zona di rimozione* (tow-away zone), your car will most likely not be there when you get back. Most cities and ports also have official **car parks** and **garages**, charging between €8 and €12 a day. **Never leave anything visible in the car** when you leave it, including the radio, and always depress your aerial and tuck in the wing mirrors.

To drive in Sicily, you need a valid **driving licence** and, if you are a non-EU licence holder, an international driving permit. It's *compulsory* to carry your car documents and passport while you're driving, and you'll be required to present them if you're stopped by the police – not an uncommon occurrence. You are also required to carry a portable triangular danger sign, which should be provided with rental cars. Many car insurance policies cover taking your own car to Italy; check with your insurer when planning your trip (you'll need an international green card of insurance). You'd also be advised to take out extra cover for motoring assistance in case you break down, and **motoring organizations** like the RAC (ⓦwww.rac.co.uk) or the AA (ⓦwww.theaa.co.uk) can help. Alternatively, by dialling ☎116 you can get 24-hour assistance from the Automobile Club d'Italia (ⓦwww.aci.it).

Car rental

Car rental in Sicily costs from around €250 per week for a three-door, air-con Fiat Punto, with unlimited mileage. It's usually cheaper arranged in advance through one of the large international chains (Avis, Budget, Europcar, Hertz, Holiday Autos, Thrifty, for example) – check websites for competitive Internet deals and special offers – or with your travel agent or tour operator. Otherwise, **rental agencies** – including local companies, like Maggiore (ⓦwww.maggiore.it) – are found in the major cities and at Palermo and Catania airports.

The Sicilian driving experience

If all you had to do was drive on Sicilian **motorways** – light traffic, fast travel, dramatic scenery – things would be fine. Unfortunately, you have to come off them sooner or later and drive into a town, and then all bets are off. The good news is that the swirling town **traffic** isn't as horrific as it first looks – the secret is to make it *very* clear what you're going to do, using your horn as much as your indicators and brakes. There are established **rules** of the road in force, though Sicilians, needless to say, ignore most, if not all, of them as a matter of principle. A character in Andrea Camilleri's Inspector Montalbano novels drives "like a dog on drugs", which is a pretty fair assessment of local driving skills, and if you go your entire holiday without being cut up on the inside, jumped at a junction or overtaken on a blind bend, you'll have done well. **One-way systems** – installed by traffic engineers with a sense of humour – play havoc with route-finding, reducing many through-town journeys to drive-and-hope marathons. Beware old-town areas particularly, where streets grow ever narrower until the point that you can't back out or turn round. It would help were it not accepted local **parking** practice simply to drive your car up on the pavement, or stop where it's most convenient for the driver – this can include the middle of the street, or pausing for a chat with a mate at a major road junction. Out in the **countryside** it's generally less of a hassle, though you do have to allow for shepherds and their sheep (and there aren't many places in Europe you can still say that about), idling around the next bend. **Pedestrians**, meanwhile, deal with the general mayhem by taking a deep breath, staring straight at the drivers and strolling boldly across the road. If in doubt, follow someone old and infirm, or put out your hand policeman-like, but *never* assume that you're safe on a pedestrian crossing – they're regarded by most drivers as an invitation to play human skittles.

Although the local companies might seem quite casual about such things, it's essential to check that you have adequate **insurance cover** for a rental car. Going by the dents and scratches on almost every car on the road, you want to make sure that your liability is limited as far as possible. Ensure that all visible damage on a car you're picking up is duly marked on the rental sheet. It's worth considering paying the extra charge to reduce the "excess" payment levied for any damage, but these waiver charges (charged by the day) soon add up. However, you can avoid all **excess charges** by taking out an annual insurance policy (from £49) with insurance4carhire.com, which also covers windscreen and tyre damage.

Bikes and scooters

Although **bicycle rental** on the Sicilian mainland is virtually unheard of, some of the offshore islands have bikes for rent. If you intend to bring your own bike, it's worth knowing that town and coastal traffic can be very off-putting, while heading inland and up into the mountains requires a decent machine and plenty of stamina: you can expect to be a real curiosity in some rural places. In the Madonie mountains, south of Cefalù, hiking itineraries published by the tourist office have brief notes for cyclists, though you should be prepared to push some of the way.

Mopeds and scooters are easier to find: virtually everyone in Sicily – kids to grandmas – rides these, although the smaller models are not suitable for any kind of long-distance travel. They're ideal for shooting around towns, and you can rent them in Taormina, Cefalù and other holiday centres – check the Guide for details. Crash helmets are compulsory, though you'll see many Sicilian youths just riding with one slung over one arm.

Ferries and hydrofoils

There are **ferries** (*traghetti*) and **hydrofoils** (*aliscafi*) to the Aeolians, the Égadi and Pelágie islands, and Pantelleria and Ústica, and there's also a summer hydrofoil service that runs along the northern Tyrrhenian coast, from Palermo to the Aeolians, stopping at a couple of towns on the way. The main **operators** are Siremar (⊛www .siremar.it), NGI (⊛www.ngi-spa.it) and Ústica Lines (⊛www.usticalines.it), and you'll find full details about services, schedules and fares in the relevant sections of the Guide. Timetables are also available online, pinned up at the dockside or are available from the ferry offices and tourist offices.

You can **island-hop** year-round in the Aeolians and Égadis. Services are heavily used in summer, making early booking advisable, though you should always get on a ferry if you just turn up. Both passenger and **car-ferry** services operate, though it's debatable how much you'll need a car on any of the islands – only Lípari, Pantelleria and Lampedusa are of any size, and in any case you can rent a vehicle there if you need to.

Internal flights

If you're short on time, consider flying to the **Pelágie Islands** or **Pantelleria** from Trápani or Palermo – otherwise, the alternative is an overnight ferry ride. Flights are with Air One (⊛www.flyairone.it) and Meridiana (⊛www .meridiana.it), and prices start at around €35 one-way – check the websites for timetables and the latest offers, or talk to a local travel agent. Other small airlines, including AlpiEagles (⊛www.alpieagles.com) and Volare (⊛www.volareweb.com), have regular services from Catania and Palermo to destinations on the Italian mainland, including Rome, Milan, Venice and Naples.

Accommodation

On the whole, accommodation in Sicily is slightly cheaper than in the rest of Italy, starting at around €50 a night for a basic double or twin room in either a private house or a simple family-run pension (though prices can double in summer in the most popular resorts). The only accommodation cheaper than this comes in the form of the very few youth hostels and the many campsites across the island. Hotels run across the entire range, from crumbling townhouses to five-star palaces, from restored country villas to resort hotels. There's also a growing number of "bed and breakfast" places and "agriturismo" rural properties, where the attraction is mixing with your hosts and experiencing something of Sicilian country life.

Accommodation is abundant in the main towns and tourist areas, but tends to thin out in remoter parts, especially inland, so it's often worthwhile calling ahead to book. All accommodation is officially **graded** and the tariffs fixed by law. In tourist areas, there's often a low-season and high-season price, but whatever it costs, the rate should be posted on the door of the room. However, in summer especially, hotels are prone to add a breakfast charge to the price, so make sure you know exactly how much you're going to be paying before you accept. Some places – especially in major resorts or on outlying islands – also insist on **half-board accommodation** (usually in August), when the price will include breakfast and either lunch or dinner, or you may even be asked to stay for a two- or three-night minimum. Few **single rooms** are available anywhere and, in high season especially, lone travellers will often pay most of the price of a double.

Hotels

Sicilian hotels are known by various titles (**pensione, albergo** – plural *alberghi* – or hotel) and are graded with one to five stars, though a star rating isn't always an exact guide to price or facilities. Some cheaper hotels, especially in town centres, are located in old mansion buildings or palaces, which can be characterful places to stay. However, not all have been modernized, so plumbing, heating and decor might occasionally be on the primitive side, and they probably won't take credit cards either.

A room in a one-star hotel starts at around €50 and there's usually a choice of rooms, with or without en-suite bath- or shower-room. Facilities in a one-star hotel tend to be minimal (there are exceptions), but once you're up to three-star level (€80–100) you can expect an en-suite room with satellite TV, air conditioning and, increasingly, Internet and Wi-Fi. Four-star hotels, plus hotels in resorts and on islands, can charge pretty

---

Accommodation price codes

All establishments listed in this guide have been coded according to price. The codes represent the cheapest available double/twin room in high season (Easter & June–Aug), though at other times you'll often be able to negotiate a lower price. Breakfast is usually included, with the common exception of the very cheapest places. For youth hostels we give a euro price for a dorm bed instead. The categories are:

❶ under €40	❹ €66–80	❼ €141–200
❷ €41–55	❺ €81–100	❽ €201–250
❸ €56–65	❻ €101–140	❾ over €251

Unusual places to stay

Alla Giudecca, Siracusa. Ancient Jewish houses, renovated as boutique hotel. See p.250.

L'Atelier sul Mare, Castel di Tusa. Extraordinary "art hotel" on the northern coast. See p.137.

Il Cavaliere, Módica. Stylishly restored Baroque B&B. See p.275.

Dammuso houses, Pantelleria. Native domed cube-houses, available for rent. See p.414.

Eremo della Giubiliana, Ragusa. Medieval feudal estate and hermitage, now five-star country retreat. See p.271.

Grand Hotel Villa Igiea, Acquasanta, near Palermo. Luxury Art Nouveau seaside villa. See p.68.

Hotel Orientale, Palermo. Atmospheric city-centre *palazzo*, budget prices. See p.67.

Ostello del Borgo, Piazza Armerina. Former Benedictine monastery, now backpackers' hostel and budget hotel. See p.310.

La Salina Borgo di Mare, Salina. Aeolian Island chic in an old saltworks. See p.171.

Tonnara di Bonagia, Bonagia, near Trápani. Stylish lodgings in a converted tuna-fishing village. See p.380.

much what they like, especially in August when room prices can top €250, while the dozen or so five-star hotels on the island (notably in Palermo, Taormina, Catania and Siracusa) charge international rates. There are some bargains around out of the summer season, when even the classier hotels drop their room rates by as much as forty percent, and in cheaper places you might be able to negotiate a lower rate for a longer stay (ask "*C'è uno sconto per due/tre/quattro notti?*").

In the cheaper places especially, you can always **ask to see the room** before you take it ("*Posso vedere?*") – and check if it's ensuite ("*La cámera ha un bagno privato?*") or air conditioned ("*C'è aria condizionata?*"). The latter can be a godsend in the summer, though many prefer the quieter option of a fan. It's worth noting that smaller, cheaper places don't have much in the way of **heating** in the winter – you can freeze in some of the older *palazzi*.

Private rooms and B&Bs

Private rooms (*cámere*) for rent are common in certain resorts, especially Taormina and other beach resorts, and on the Aeolian and Égadi Islands. Facilities vary, but the best are clean and modern, with private bathroom and often with a kitchenette. Breakfast isn't usually included, but is sometimes available for an extra charge. Prices start at about €50, with variations depending on the season and location – in August in Taormina and on the Aeolians you might pay as much as €100 a night for a room.

Recent years have seen the growth of "**bed and breakfasts**" (as they term themselves), where you'll usually get some contact with your hosts, at least at breakfast time. Some places going under the name are actually little different from private rooms, with the owners either not living on the premises or not always available throughout the day – often, you have to call a mobile phone number to summon attendance. The simplest B&Bs start at €30 or so per person per night, so they are not necessarily cheaper than an inexpensive hotel, but you will get a flavour of Sicilian home life. Some B&Bs, however, are magnificent, based in remarkable Baroque *palazzi* or country houses, and you can pay as much as €70 per person. The southeast particularly has lots of B&Bs, and tourist-friendly towns like Siracusa, Ragusa, Módica and Noto are awash with stylishly converted old homes. Touring Club Italiano publishes an annual "Bed and Breakfast" guide to Italy, available in local bookshops, or check the very useful websites Bed and Breakfast Italia

(⊛www.bbitalia.it) and Cafélletto (⊛www
.caffelletto.it), where you can view scores of
properties.

Self-catering villas and apartments

Private holiday **apartments** are available in
places like Taormina, Cefalù, Siracusa and
the Aeolians, and are generally rented for
anything from a couple of nights to a month.
Although these can be very expensive in the
peak summer season – when Italian families
come on holiday – real bargains can be
found in May or late September, and during
the winter. Ask in the tourist offices or a local
estate agency (*agenzia immobiliare*) and
keep an eye out for local advertisements.

Tour operators and villa companies also
have self-catering **villas, farmhouses and
apartments** available, located right across
the island, usually in beautiful locations, often
with swimming pools. Rates vary wildly, from
€600 a week (sleeps four) to thousands for a
place suitable for a house party. For an idea
of what's available, contact companies like
Think Sicily (⊛www.thinksicily.com), Bridge-
water (⊛www.bridgewatertravel.co.uk), Travel
Sicilia (⊛www.travelsicilia.com), Italian Breaks
(⊛www.italianbreaks.com), Holiday Rentals
(⊛www.holiday-rentals.co.uk) or Dolce Vita
Villas (⊛www.dolcevitavillas.com).

Rural accommodation

Rural tourism has expanded significantly in
Sicily in recent years, and every region now
holds a choice of interesting places to stay,
from working farms and wine estates to
restored palaces and architect-designed
homes. Accommodation is in private rooms
or apartments, and many establishments
also offer activities such as cooking
courses, horse-riding, mountain-biking,
walks and excursions. Hosts often speak
English or French, and sometimes offer
meals, or there might be a restaurant
attached serving home-produced food,
as is the case in many farmhouse-style
places. We've recommended some of
our favourites in the Guide, but many
others fall within various umbrella
schemes like Agriturist (⊛www.agriturist.it)
and Agriturismo (⊛www.agriturismo.com),
whose websites have sections on Sicily,

with links to the properties. Rooms usually
cost from €80–120, depending on the
establishment, and note that some places
will require a minimum stay of three nights.
Local tourist offices can also usually tell you
if there's anywhere suitable in the district.

Hostels, campsites and mountain huts

There are only seven or eight **youth
hostels** on the whole island, though they
do crop up in useful tourist destinations like
Palermo, Catania, Taormina, Noto,
Siracusa, Lípari and Piazza Armerina. Dorm
beds cost €15–20 a night, depending on
season, and all have some kind of self-
catering facility available. Some are official
IYHF hostels, others are independent
backpackers' (ie no membership required),
but the official ones at least are detailed on
⊛www.ostellionline.org (English-language
version available; online reservations) and if
you aren't already a member of your home
hostelling organization you can join upon
arrival at any hostel.

There are approximately ninety officially
graded **campsites** dotted around the
island's coasts, on a few of the outlying
islands, and around Mount Etna. Few are
open all year round; indeed, campsites
generally open or close whenever they want,
depending on business. If you want to be
sure, it's always worth a phone call; alternatively, check the comprehensive website
⊛www.camping.it. Camping isn't going to
save you a great deal of money, since most
of the sites are large, luxury affairs, often
complete with pools, bars, shops and sports
facilities. **Charges** are usually between €5
and €7 per person per day, sometimes the
same again for a tent and vehicle.

Staffed **mountain huts** (*rifugio*, plural *rifugi*)
are available in certain magnificent locations,
particularly in the Madonie and Nébrodi
ranges and on Mount Etna. They're used
mainly by hikers and outdoor enthusiasts,
and operated by the Club Alpino Italiano
(⊛www.cai.it) – non-members can use them
for around €20 a night, but advance reservations are essential. Local tourist offices have
all the contact details – we've listed some of
the best in the text, but you can also check
them out online.

Food and drink

There's much to be said for coming to Sicily just for the eating and drinking. Often, even the most out-of-the-way village will boast somewhere you can get a good lunch, while places like Catania, Palermo, Ragusa, Trápani and Siracusa can keep a serious eater happy for days. And it's not ruinously expensive either, certainly compared to prices in the rest of mainland Italy: a full meal with local wine generally costs around €30 a head, a pizza, drink and ice cream around half that.

Contemporary **Sicilian cooking** leans heavily on locally produced foodstuffs and whatever can be fished out of the sea, mixed with the Italian staples of pasta, tomato sauce and fresh vegetables. Red chillies, tuna, swordfish, sardines, olives, pine nuts and capers all figure heavily, while the mild winter climate and long summers mean that **fruit and vegetables** are less seasonal (and much more impressive) than in northern Europe: strawberries appear in April, for example, while oranges are available right through the winter. The **menu reader** in the "Language" section (p.464) covers all the basics, as well as including a full rundown of Sicilian specialities, some of which crop up in nearly every restaurant.

Breakfast, snacks and markets

For most Sicilians, **breakfast** (*prima colazione*) is an *espresso* or *cappuccino*, and the ubiquitous *cornetto* – a jam-, custard- or chocolate-filled croissant. Many bars and patisseries (a *pasticceria*) also offer things like an *iris* (a pastry ball stuffed with sweet ricotta cheese), an *arancino* (a deep-fried ball of rice, either *rosso*, filled with meat, or *bianco*, with butter and cheese) and *cannoli* (pastry tubes with sweet ricotta cheese and candied fruit). On the other hand, breakfast in a hotel will usually be a limp affair of bread rolls and bad coffee, though the better places make far more of an effort with cheese, eggs, salami, fruit and fresh pastries.

There are **sandwich** (*panini*) bars in the bigger towns, though alternatively, in most places, you can simply go into an *alimentari* (grocer's shop) and ask them to make you a sandwich from whatever they've got. Bakeries sometimes sell *panini* or *pane cunzati*, crusty bread rolls filled with pungent combinations such as tuna, tomato, anchovy and capers. *Tramezzini* are ready-made sliced white-bread sandwiches with mixed fillings, while toasted sandwiches (*toste*) tend to be a variation on cheese with ham or tomato.

You'll get most of the things already mentioned, plus small pizzas, ready prepared pasta, and full hot meals in a **távola calda** (literally, "hot table"), a sort of stand-up snack bar that's at its best in the morning when everything is fresh. In the larger cities, you'll occasionally come across an old-fashioned *focacceria* – takeaway establishments selling *focaccia* (an oven-baked flat bread, with a topping or filling) and other bread-based snacks. Or there's the ubiquitous **rosticceria** in every Sicilian town, a takeaway grill-house where the speciality is spit-roast chicken (*pollo allo spiedo*).

Meal prices

Restaurant reviews are graded according to the following scale:
Inexpensive: under €15
Moderate: €15–30
Expensive: €30–50
Very expensive: over €50
These prices reflect the cost of a full **meal per person**, including wine and cover charge, Obviously, you'll be able to eat for less than the upper price limit if you only have a couple of courses, and in pizzerias you'll rarely get into the Moderate category.

Ice cream

A cone (*un cono*) of famous Sicilian **ice cream** (*gelato*) – or perhaps a dollop in a brioche – is the indispensable accessory to the evening *passeggiata*. The best choice is at a **gelateria**, where the range is a tribute to the Italian imagination and flair for display. If they make their own on the premises, there'll be a sign saying "*produzione propria*"; sadly, however, this increasingly means they make the stuff from pre-packed commercial pastes and syrups. Anyhow, there's no trouble in locating the finest *gelateria* in town: it's the one that draws the crowds. And as it's hard to find decent ice cream in restaurants these days (it's mostly *confezionato*, ie mass-produced), many locals also head to the *gelateria* for dessert.

Grocers' shops and **markets** are the best places for fruit, veg and picnic food, and you'll usually be able to jazz up your picnic lunch with sweet peppers, olives, seafood salad, and pickled vegetables. Some markets also sell **traditional takeaway food**, loved by Sicilians, though perhaps a challenge for some visitors – usually things like boiled artichokes, cooked octopus, raw sea urchins and mussels, and fried offal sandwiches.

Pizzas

Outside its home of Naples, Sicily is the best place to eat pizza in Italy. It comes flat, not deep-pan, and the choice of toppings is often fairly limited – none of the pineapple-and-sweetcorn variations beloved of foreign pizzerias. However, you will see some more distinctively Sicilian combinations, using pecorino cheese instead of mozzarella, oregano instead of basil, and lots of anchovies, capers and hot peppers. It's also easy to find pizzas cooked in the traditional way, in **wood-fired ovens** (*forno a legna*), so that they arrive blasted and bubbling on the surface, with a distinctive charcoal taste. Unfortunately, because of the time it takes to set up and light the ovens, *forno a legna* pizzas are usually only served at night, except on Sundays and in some resorts in summer.

Restaurant meals

For a full meal, rather than just a pizza, you'll have to go either to a **trattoria** or a **ristorante**. A *trattoria* is usually the cheaper, more basic choice, offering good home cooking (*cucina casalinga*), while a *ristorante* is often more upmarket (tablecloths, printed menu and uniformed waiters). In small towns

and villages, the local trattoria is often only open at lunchtime – there probably won't be a menu and the waiter will simply reel off a list of what's available. In tourist resorts and larger towns you'll come across hybrid establishments (a *trattoria-ristorante*, say or *ristorante-pizzeria*) that cater to all tastes, while there are also more youthful pasta-orientated restaurant-bars called *spaghette-rias*. Signs or blackboards announcing "*pranzo turístico*" or "*pranzo completo*" are advertising a limited-choice **set menu** (usually at lunchtime), including wine, which can be pretty good value at €15–25.

Traditionally, lunch (*pranzo*) or dinner (*cena*) starts with an **antipasto** (literally "before the meal"); you'll only find this in restaurants, at its best when you circle around a table and help yourself to a cold buffet selection. If you're moving on to pasta and the main course you'll need quite an appetite to tackle the *antipasti* as well. Otherwise, the **menu** starts with soup or pasta, **il primo**, and moves on to **il secondo**, the meat or fish dish. Note that **fish** will either be served whole (like bream or trout) or by weight (usually per 100g, *all'etto*, like swordfish and tuna) so ask to see what you're going to eat and check the price first. The second course is generally

---

Sicilians are not hung up on restaurant formality. Asking for just pasta and a salad, or the main course on its own, won't outrage the waiter. Equally, asking for a dish listed as a first course as a second course, or having pasta followed by pizza (or vice versa), won't be frowned upon either.

The original fusion food

Historically, **Sicilian cuisine** has been held in high regard: one of the earliest of cookbooks, the *Art of Cooking* by Mithaecus, derived from fifth-century BC Siracusa, while in medieval times Sicilian chefs were much sought after in foreign courts. As the centuries passed, the intermittent waves of immigration left their mark, from the use of prickly pears (originally imported from Mexico by the Spanish) to the North African influence evident in the western Sicilian version of couscous or in orange salads. The **Arab influence** is also apparent in the profusion of sweets – marzipan is used extensively, while *cassata*, the most Sicilian of desserts, derives from the Arabic word *quas-at*, referring to the round bowl in which it was traditionally prepared. Indeed, virtually every dish – though apparently common-or-garden Italian/Sicilian – calls upon 2500 years of cross-cultural influences, from the Greeks and Romans to the Arabs, Normans and Spanish.

served unadorned, except for a wedge of lemon or tomato – **contorni** (vegetables and salads) are ordered and served separately, and often there won't be much choice beyond chips and salad. If there's no menu, the verbal list of what's available can sometimes be a bit bewildering, but if you don't hear anything you recognize just ask for what you want: everywhere should have pasta with tomato or meat sauce. Dessert (**dolci**) is almost always fresh fruit, fruit salad or ice cream, though restaurants may also have a choice of cakes, tarts and puddings – unfortunately, though, many of these are mass-produced (by such brands as Ranieri), and a restaurant *tiramisù* or *cassata*, say, can be a poor substitute for the real thing.

Although Sicily has hardly any specifically **vegetarian** restaurants, most pasta sauces are based on tomatoes or dairy products, and it's easy to pick a pizza that is meat- (and fish-) free. Pizzas are also available without cheese, though soups are usually made with a fish or meat broth.

In many places, **the bill** (*il conto*) doesn't amount to much more than an illegible scrap of paper so, if you want to be sure you're not being ripped off, ask for a receipt (*una ricevuta*). Nearly everywhere, you'll pay a small **cover charge** per person for the bread (*pane e coperto*); **service** (*servizio*) will be added as well in many restaurants, usually ten percent, though fifteen or even twenty percent isn't unheard of. If service isn't charged, leaving ten percent would do, though most pizzerias and trattorias won't expect it.

Coffee, tea and soft drinks

One of the most distinctive smells in a Sicilian street is that of fresh **coffee**. The basic choice is either an *espresso* (or just *caffè*) or a *cappuccino*. The latter is primarily a breakfast drink – no Italian would order a *cappuccino* after a meal. A watered-down *espresso* is a *caffè lungo*, with a drop of milk it's *caffè macchiato* ("stained"), while coffee with a shot of alcohol is *caffè corretto*. In summer you might want your coffee cold (*caffè freddo*), or try a *granita di caffè* – cold coffee with crushed ice that's usually topped with whipped cream (*senza panna*, without cream). **Tea**, too, can be drunk iced (*tè freddo*), usually mixed with lemon. Hot tea (*tè caldo*) comes with lemon (*con limone*) unless you ask for milk (*con latte*).

For a fresh **fruit juice** (usually orange, lemon or grapefruit), squeezed at the bar, ask for a **spremuta**. Fruit juice mixed with crushed ice is that Sicilian speciality, **granita**; a **frullato** is a fresh fruit shake, while a **succo di frutta** is a bottled fruit juice. As an alternative to Coke try the homegrown Italian alternative, Chinotto (Coke-like, but not so sweet, with a tamarind flavour). Tap **water** (*acqua normale*) is drinkable everywhere and you won't pay for it in a bar. But **mineral water** (*acqua minerale*) is the usual choice, either still (*senza gas* or *naturale*) or fizzy (*con gas*, *gassata* or *frizzante*).

Beer, wines and spirits

Beer (*birra*) – generally lager in Sicily – usually comes in 33cl (*piccolo*) or 66cl (*grande*)

Sicilian wine

Although they don't necessarily qualify for the strict Italian DOC and DOCG denomination systems, Sicilian wines have an increasing reputation (and the island often produces more wine in a year than any other Italian region, and as much as Australia). Typical of the wines making waves are those made from the local **Nero d'Avola** grape variety (a hearty red, similar to a Syrah/Shiraz) – it's well suited to the dry climate, and Planeta's Santa Cecilia (from Noto) is as good an example as you'll find. Other Sicilian regions produce very distinct tastes, too, like the dry reds and whites made from grapes grown on the volcanic slopes of **Etna**, the white **Bianco d'Alcamo** from Trápani province and **Cerasuolo di Vittória** (red and white) from vines in the area around Ragusa. Boutique wineries are springing up all over Sicily, perhaps just making a particular wine, though the major brands you'll see everywhere include Corvo, Donnafugata and Regaleali.

bottles. The Sicilian brand Messina, and the Italian Peroni and Dreher, are widely available – ask for *birra nazionale*, otherwise you'll be given a more expensive imported beer, and note that draught beer (*birra alla spina*) is usually more expensive than the bottled variety. So-called "dark beers" (*birra nera*, *birra rossa* or *birra scura*) are also available, which have a slightly maltier taste, and in appearance resemble stout or bitter.

Local **wine** (*vino locale*) is often served straight from the barrel in jugs or old bottles, and costs as little as €5 a litre. You may be flummoxed by the *vino locale* not being the colour you've ordered, but you'll get whatever they make – in the west, for example, it's often a tart but refreshing rosé, in Marsala it's amber. Bottled wine is more expensive, though still good value, from around €8–10 in a restaurant (though often much higher in tourist resorts).

The most famous Sicilian **dessert wine** is *marsala*, made in the western town of the same name – see the box on p.397 for more. If you're heading to the offshore islands, watch out for *malvasia* (from the Aeolians) and *moscato* (from Pantelleria), while around Taormina the local speciality is *vino alla mándorla*, almond wine, served ice cold. **Spirits** are known mostly by their generic names, except brandy which you should call *cognac* or ask for by name – again, for cheaper Italian brands, ask for *nazionale*. At some stage you should also try an **amaro** (literally "bitter"), a remarkably medicinal after-dinner drink supposed to aid digestion. The favourite brand is Averna (from Caltanissetta) but there are dozens of different kinds. Look out, too, for a feisty red liqueur called Fuoco dell'Etna, mostly sold on the east coast.

Where to drink

In most town and village **bars**, it's cheapest to drink standing up at the counter (there's often nowhere to sit anyway), in which case you pay first at the cash desk (*la cassa*), present your receipt (*scontrino*) to the bar person and give your order. There's always a list of prices (the *listino prezzi*) on display, and when you present your receipt it's customary to leave a small tip on the counter – though no one will object if you don't. It's more expensive to sit down inside than stand up (the difference in price is shown on the price list as *távola*) and it costs up to twice the basic price if you sit at tables outside (*terrazza*).

Although bars have no set **licensing hours**, outside the cities it's often difficult to find a bar open much after 9pm. Children are allowed in and bars, like restaurants, are smoke-free (strictly enforced), though if you're drinking or eating outside it's fine to smoke. Tourist bars and cafés are open later, but they're more expensive than the typical chrome-counter-and-Gaggia-machine local bar – any **stylish bar** that fancies itself tends to be called an "American Bar", a designation that you'll see all over Sicily.

Most Sicilians tend to drink when they eat, and young people especially don't make a night out of getting wasted. When they do go out on the town, it's to a **birreria** (literally "beer shop") or a "pub", although those bear little relation to their British namesakes. A little more recognizable are the **"Irish" pubs** that are springing up in the the cities and big resorts, where you'll be able to get a pint of Guinness and watch the big game.

Sports and outdoor activities

As a Mediterranean island, Sicily is well set up for water sports of all kinds, from scuba-diving to windsurfing, while many come in the cooler months either side of summer (April, May, September and October) for the hiking. The volcanoes of Etna and Strómboli offer more adventurous excursions – probably the most emblematic Sicilian outdoor activity is the climb up Strómboli to see the nightly volcanic light show.

Water sports

The best places for **snorkelling** and **scuba-diving** are the limpid waters of the offshore islands, principally Ústica, the Aeolians, Lampedusa and Pantelleria. Diving schools on each of these offer day trips and courses for beginners and experienced divers alike. Other areas are protected as marine and natural reserves, so even at far more touristed resorts like Mazzarò (Taormina) the water is often remarkably clear. **Windsurfing** gear is available for rent at most of the major resort beaches and lidos, and **kitesurfing** is increasingly popular at places like Mózia on the west coast. Almost wherever there's a harbour (and that's a lot of Sicily) you'll also be able to **rent a boat** of some kind, from a sailing dinghy to a fishing charter. It's not always an official set-up, more often a case of talking to people on the quayside and seeing what's possible.

Hiking

Hiking is growing in popularity, though it's nowhere near as established as in alpine Italy. If you're keen to do a lot of walking in a short time, your best bet is to join a **walking holiday** – several tour operators now offer this as an option (see "Getting there", earlier in this section) and the routes used have all been thoroughly tried and tested. The best walking is in the interior, around **Etna** in the east, and in the mountain regions of the **Monti Madonie** and **Monti Nébrodi** (between Etna and the Tyrrhenian coast), where a few marked trails have been laid out, making use of existing paths. Reliable hiking maps are not easily available (see "Travel essentials: Maps" on p.49), though we've featured a few good hiking routes in the text.

On the whole, though, given the paucity of information and services, unsupported hiking in interior Sicily is more for the experienced and well-equipped walker. If all you're looking for is a half-day stroll or short hike you're better off sticking to the coast or outlying islands. The Aeolians and Égadis in particular offer some lovely walking, while the protected coast between Scopello and San Vito Lo Capo (north of Trápani) has an excellent network of well-maintained paths.

Outdoor pursuits

The dramatic volcanic terrain around Mount Etna supports a whole **outdoor activities** industry, from guided summit hikes to four-wheel-drive safaris. Local tourist offices and travel agents as far away as Siracusa and Taormina are geared up to book visitors onto trips. The small mountain towns of Nicolosi and Linguaglossa are the centres for Etna's surviving **skiing** (ski lifts keep being destroyed by eruptions), and winter sports are also available in the Monti Madonie around Piano Battáglia, where you can rent ski gear. Really,

National game, national shame

Football (*calcio*) is the national sport – Italy won the World Cup for the fourth time in 2006. Both the two big Sicilian teams – Palermo (@www.ilpalermocalcio.it) and Catania (@www.calciocatania.it) – are currently in Serie A, the top domestic division. However, football in Italy is in crisis following a major match-fixing and corruption scandal and continuing violence at games, notably at a derby match between the Sicilian teams in 2007 that saw a policeman killed and hundreds of spectators injured during rioting. Matches were suspended at the time and many stadiums closed until they met more rigorous safety conditions, yet many now believe that Italian football continues on a downward spiral. Is it safe to go to a match in Sicily? Yes, probably, as there's little or no trouble at most matches, though you would want to avoid going to European cup games involving travelling British teams as such matches have witnessed violence in the past.

though, no one comes to Sicily just to ski. Volcanoes are a different matter, though, as few in the world are as active as Etna and **Strómboli** – the latter (the furthest flung of the Aeolian Islands) is another great base for guided crater treks (day and night), volcano-watching cruises and the like.

Don't miss the necropolis at Pantálica and the lesser-known example near Íspica, both in the southeast, where you can combine sightseeing with a spot of fantastic **gorge-walking**. There's also a great afternoon to be spent **gorge-wading** and waterfall-scrambling at the Gola di Alcántara, not far from Taormina. Finally, **horse-riding** and **pony-trekking** are available in some areas – sometimes offered by *agriturismo* (rural tourism) properties.

Travelling with children

Children are revered in Sicily and will be made a fuss of in the street, and welcomed and catered for in bars and restaurants. It's perfectly normal for Sicilian children to stay up until they drop, and in summer it's not unusual to see youngsters out at midnight, and not looking much the worse for it.

Pharmacies and supermarkets carry most **baby requirements**, from **nappies** to formula **food**. However, you may not see the brands you are used to at home, and don't expect there to be a full range of (or indeed any) organic food products, especially in smaller towns. Otherwise, **food** is unlikely to be a problem as most children eat pasta and pizza, and while specific children's menus are not common, many restaurants are happy to provide a smaller version of an adult meal.

Hotels normally charge around thirty percent extra to put an additional bed or cot in the room. However, **self-catering** apartments, or rooms with the use of a kitchen, are quite common and most Sicilian resorts offer such options. Generous **discounts** apply for children at most sights and attractions, and also when travelling on trains.

In high summer, the **heat and sun** can be exhausting for children. Make sure they are well covered with sun block, which can be bought in any pharmacy and many super-markets. Also, do as the Sicilians do and dress your children in bonnets or straw hats, available from most markets, and take advantage of siesta time to recover flagging energy. If you're using public transport, try and travel during the less busy periods – mornings and evenings – and make sure your children drink plenty of water.

Southern Mediterranean stereotypes certainly still apply in Sicily, with children firmly ensconced in their **gender roles** at an early age: the girls' clothes on sale are all frills and flounces, while the toy, candy and nut trolleys that you find in every piazza have one side devoted to guns and hammers, the other to dolls, tiaras and manicure kits.

Travel essentials

Beaches

You'll have to pay for access to many of the island's better beaches (referred to as *lidos*), with lounger, parasol and use of the showers often included in the price (usually €5–10 a day). Many lidos also have other facilities like pedalo- and windsurf-hire, bars and restaurants, and thus make a good bet for families. Elsewhere, beaches are free though not always clean – during the winter most look like dumps, as it's not worth anyone's while to clean them until the season starts at Easter.

Costs

Sicily isn't particularly cheap compared to other Mediterranean holiday spots, though it is usually better value than the popular tourist parts of mainland Italy. The single biggest cost is generally accommodation, with simple one-star hotels, private rooms and bed and breakfasts all starting at around €50 a night. A decent three-star hotel, on the other hand, will set you back up to €100. Of course, you'll pay a lot more in summer in the big tourist spots – Érice, Cefalù, Siracusa and Taormina – and more all year round on most of the offshore islands, particularly the Aeolians and Pantelleria. The interior, too, is not as cheap as you might expect – because it's little visited, there's no competition and rarely a choice of places to stay and eat.

Most other items are fairly inexpensive. The Sicilian staple, a pizza and a beer, costs around €10 just about everywhere, while a full restaurant meal can cost as little as €20 a head. Of course, there are some excellent Sicilian restaurants where the bill comes in much higher, up to say €50 a head, but even these are remarkably good value for the quality on offer. A carafe of local house wine rarely comes to more than €5, a bottle €8, and the same wine in a supermarket might be three times cheaper. Other snacks and drinks soon add up, especially in fancy resorts, and you should note that if you sit down in a café (rather than stand at the counter) it'll cost twice as much. Public transport, on the other hand, is very cheap, while even the island's showpiece museums, archeological ruins and attractions rarely cost more than €6 – and under-18s and over-65s usually get in for free.

Overall, apart from accommodation, you could reasonably expect to spend €50 a day – taking the train, eating picnics, cheap meals and pizzas, seeing the sights and so on. For a more comfortable daily experience (meals in better restaurants, plus taxis, evening drinks, concerts and the like) you're looking at €75 and upwards.

Crime and personal safety

Although Sicily is synonymous with the Mafia, you'll forget the association as soon as you set foot on the island. Cosa Nostra is as invisible to the average tourist as it is ingrained for the islanders, and the violence that sporadically erupts is almost always an "in-house" affair. Of more immediate concern is **petty juvenile crime**, mainly in crowded streets or markets, where gangs of *scippatori*,

Emergency phone numbers

Police (Carabinieri) ℡112
Emergency services (Soccorso Pubblico di Emergenze) ℡113
Fire brigade (Vigili del Fuoco) ℡115
Road assistance (Soccorso Stradale) ℡116

or bag-snatchers, strike on foot or on scooters, disappearing before you've had time to react. As well as handbags, they whip wallets, tear off visible jewellery and, if they're really adroit, unstrap watches. Don't flash anything of value, keep a firm hand on your camera, and carry shoulder bags, as you'll see many Sicilian women do, slung across your body. It's a good idea, too, to entrust most of your money and valuables to hotel managers. The vast majority of cases occur in Catania and Palermo, and at or on the way to and from the airports. On the whole it's common sense to avoid badly lit areas at night, or deserted inner-city areas by day.

If the worst happens, you'll be forced to have some dealings with the **police**. Most conspicuous are the **Carabinieri** – the ones with the blue uniforms – who are a branch of the armed forces and organized along military lines, dealing with general crime and public disorder. They are also the butt of most of the jokes about the police, usually on the "How many Carabinieri does it take to…?" level. They share a fierce turf rivalry with the **Polizia Statale**, or state police, to whom you're supposed to report any theft at their local HQ, the **Questura**. The **Polizia Urbana,** or town police, are mainly concerned with directing the traffic and punishing parking offenders. The **Guardia di**

Finanza, often heavily armed and screaming ostentatiously through the cities, are responsible for investigating smuggling, tax evasion and other similar crimes, and the **Polizia Stradale** patrol the autostrada.

Travellers with disabilities

Although most Sicilians are helpful enough if presented with a specific problem, the island is hardly geared towards accommodating travellers with disabilities. In the medieval city centres and old villages, few budget hotels have elevators, let alone ones capable of taking a wheelchair, and rooms have rarely been adapted for use by disabled visitors. Narrow, cobbled streets, steep inclines, chaotic driving and parking are hardly conducive to a stress-free holiday either. Crossing the street in Palermo is a major undertaking even if you're fully mobile, while Taormina, the most popular resort, poses great accessibility challenges for anyone in a wheelchair.

If the thought of negotiating your own way around the island proves too daunting, an **organized tour** may be the way to go. While that will cost more than planning your own trip, you can request accommodation in higher-category hotels that should at least have some facilities for disabled travellers, and you'll also have someone on hand who speaks Italian to help smooth the way. Accessible Italy (www.accessibleitaly.com) is an Italian organization offering tours and advice to foreigners, and though it's mainly useful for mainland Italy, you can ask for advice on travelling in Sicily. You can also contact one of the organizations in your own country dedicated to people with disabilities. Holiday Care

Women's safety

Although Italy has a reputation for **sexual harassment of women** that is well known and well founded, there's no reason to presume unwarranted intrusion at every turn. A woman travelling alone, or with another woman, can expect a certain amount of attention, including tooting and whistling, though bear in mind that local custom dictates that every friend and acquaintance is greeted with a toot. If you follow common-sense rules, the most that should worry you is the occasional try-on. Off the beaten track, you're more likely to be subjected to stares (from both sexes). For greater anonymity, dress smartly and, as a deterrent, flaunt a wedding ring.

(Ⓦwww.holidaycare.org.uk), for example, publishes an information pack about holidaying in Italy for disabled travellers.

Electricity

The supply is 220V, though anything requiring 240V will work. Most plugs are two round pins; a travel adaptor plug is useful.

Entry requirements

British, Irish and other EU citizens can enter Sicily and stay as long as they like on production of a valid **passport**. Citizens of the United States, Canada, Australia and New Zealand don't need a visa, but are limited to stays of three months. Most other nationals will have to apply for a visa from an Italian embassy or consulate.

Legally, you're required to register with the police within three days of entering Italy, though if you're staying at a hotel this will be done for you. Although the police in some towns have become more punctilious about this, most would still be amazed at any attempt to register yourself down at the local police station while on holiday.

Italian embassies abroad

Australia ☎02/6273 3333, Ⓦwww.ambcanberra .esteri.it.
Canada ☎613/232-2401, Ⓦwww.ambottawa .esteri.it.
Republic of Ireland ☎01/660 1744, Ⓦwww .ambdublino.esteri.it.
New Zealand ☎04/473 5339, Ⓦwww .ambwellington.esteri.it.
UK ☎0207/312 2200, Ⓦwww.amblondra.estri.it.
USA ☎202/612-4400, Ⓦwww.ambwashingtondc .esteri.it.

Gay and lesbian Sicily

Homosexuality is not illegal in Italy, and the age of consent is 16. That said, attitudes towards homosexuality are much less tolerant in Sicily than in Rome or the industrial north. Taormina is the only place in Sicily where there is any kind of gay scene, and even this is very low-key. Even so, physical contact between men is fairly common in Sicily, on the level of linking arms and kissing cheeks at greetings and farewells – though an overt display of anything remotely ambiguous is likely to be met with hostility. The main national gay organization, ArciGay (Ⓦwww.arcigay.it) has branches all over the country, including Sicily, and its English-language website is a good place to look for information. The Ⓦwww.gay.it website also has a wealth of information for gays and lesbians in Italy.

Health

Sicily poses few health problems for visitors; the worst that's likely to happen to you is suffering from the extreme **heat** in summer or from an **upset stomach**. Vaccinations are not required, but you should take insect repellent and strong sun protection. The **water** is perfectly safe to drink (though bottled water tastes better). You'll find public drinking fountains in squares and city streets everywhere, though look out for "*acqua non potabile*" signs, indicating the water is *not* safe to drink.

An Italian **pharmacist** (*farmacia*) is well qualified to give you advice on minor ailments, and to dispense prescriptions. There's generally one pharmacy open all night in the bigger towns and cities. A rota system is used, and you should find the address of the one currently open late/all night on any *farmacia* door or listed in the local paper.

As an EU country, Italy has reciprocal health agreements with other member states, and EU citizens can simply show their **European Health Insurance Card** (Ⓦwww.dh.gov.uk/travellers) and passport at a health centre or hospital. This basically entitles you to the same treatment as an insured person in Italy, but you're still advised to have a travel insurance policy as well.

Every town and village has a **doctor** (*médico*). To find one, ask at a pharmacy, or consult the local yellow pages (*Págine Gialle*) under "Azienda Unità Sanitaria Locale" or "Unità Sanitaria Locale Pronto Soccorso". If you're eligible, take your EHIC with you to the doctor's, which will enable you to get free treatment and prescriptions for medicines at the (much cheaper) local rate. For repeat medication, take any empty bottles or capsules with you to the doctor's – the brand names often differ.

In an **emergency**, dial ☎113 and ask for "*ospedale*" or "*ambulanza*". The nearest

hospital will have a **Pronto Soccorso** (casualty) section, while on smaller islands, or places with no hospital, there is usually a first-aid clinic known as the **Guardia Medica**.

Insurance

Although EU health care privileges apply in Italy, it's essential to take out a travel insurance policy to cover against theft, loss, illness or injury during your travels. A typical **policy** usually provides cover for the loss of baggage, tickets and – up to a certain limit – cash or cheques, as well as cancellation or curtailment of your journey. Most policies exclude so-called **dangerous sports**, unless an extra premium is paid: in Sicily this can mean things like scuba - diving, windsurfing and volcano trekking. With medical coverage, ascertain whether benefits will be paid as treatment proceeds or only after you return home, and whether there is a 24-hour medical emergency number. When securing baggage cover, make sure that the per-article limit – typically under £500/US$1000 – will cover your most valuable possession. If you need to **make a claim**, you should keep receipts for medicines and medical treatment, and in the event you have anything stolen, you must obtain an official statement from the police. This is sometimes easier said than done in Sicily, but persevere; without it, you'll not be able to claim your money back.

Rough Guides has teamed up with Columbus Direct to offer you **travel insurance** that can be tailored to suit your needs. Products include a low-cost **backpacker** option for long stays; a **short break** option for city getaways; a typical **holiday package** option; and others. Annual **multi-trip** policies cover those who travel regularly. Different sports and activities (trekking, skiing, etc) can usually be covered if required. See our website (ⓦwww.roughguides.com/website/shop) for eligibility and purchasing options. Alternatively, UK residents should call ☏0870/033 9988; Australians should call ☏1300/669 999 and New Zealanders should call ☏0800/55 9911. All other nationalities should call ☏+44 870/890 2843.

Internet

There are Internet places all over Sicily, with access costing around €5 an hour, though free Wi-Fi access is increasingly available in bars and hotels. Note that you may well be asked to show some form of ID to use a public Internet point.

Laundry services

Coin-operated laundries are very rare. More common is a *lavanderia*, a service-wash laundry, though these are fairly expensive. Although you can usually get away with it, washing clothes in your hotel room can be problematic – simply because the room's plumbing often can't cope with all the water. It's better to ask if there's somewhere you can wash your clothes.

Mail

Post office opening hours are usually Monday to Saturday 8.30am to 6.30pm; offices in smaller towns close on a Saturday, and everywhere else post offices close at noon on the last Saturday of the month. You can also buy stamps (*francobolli*) in some gift shops in tourist resorts, and in shops called *tabacchi*, recognizable by a sign displaying a white "T" on a black or blue background (these also sell cigarettes, sweets and stationery). The Italian postal service is among the slowest in Europe – if your letter is urgent, consider paying extra for the express service, or *posta prioritaria*.

Maps

The best large-scale **road map** of Sicily is published by the Touring Club Italiano (*Sicilia*, 1:200,000), available from map and travel bookshops or from online retailers like Stanford's (ⓦwww.stanfords.co.uk) or Rand McNally (ⓦwww.randmcnally.com). Rough Guides also has a Sicily map (1:200,000), printed on waterproof, untearable paper. Otherwise, the Automobile Club d'Italia issues a good, free 1:275,000 road map, available from the State Tourist Offices, while local tourist offices in Sicily often have free road maps of varying quality. Local tourist offices also hand out reasonable town plans and regional maps.

Hiking maps (scale 1:25,000 and 1:50,000) for the Monti Madonie and other areas can be ordered from the Istituto Geográfico Militare (Ⓦwww.igmi.org), or check what's available at the Palermo stationer's shop Cartoleria de Magistris, Via A. Gagini 23 (Ⓣ091.589.233). Note, however, that most of these maps were drawn up in the 1970s, and, particularly at altitudes above 1500m, many of the paths shown on them no longer exist. The Club Alpino Siciliano, Via A. Paternostro 43, Palermo (Ⓣ091.581.323, Ⓦwww .clubalpinosiciliano.it) or – sometimes – tourist offices in Palermo or Cefalù can supply you with 1:50,000 maps of the Monti Madonie, but again, these should be treated with caution. However, all national parks and nature reserves (Madonie, Nebrodi, Pellegrino, etc, see Ⓦwww.parks.it) have good English-language walking itineraries on their websites (though no actual maps), while the various park offices listed in the Guide can supply rudimentary hiking maps.

Media

The centre-left *La Repubblica* and authoritative and rather right-wing *Il Corriere della Sera* are the two most widely read national **newspapers**, based in Milan but published with local supplements. But Sicily also has its own **regional papers**, useful for transport schedules, reviews, film listings and suchlike. In Palermo, the best is *Il Giornale di Sicilia*; in Catania, *La Sicilia*; in Messina, *La Gazzetta del Sud*. The most widely read paper, though, is the pink *Gazzetta dello Sport*; essential stuff for the serious sports fan. **English-language newspapers** can be found in Palermo, Catania, Messina, Taormina and Cefalù, usually a day or two late.

Italian **television** is deregulated, with the three state-run channels, RAI 1, 2 and 3, suffering in the face of a massive downmarket independent onslaught. The output is pretty mainstream, with a heavy helping of Brazilian soaps, American sitcoms and films, and ghastly Italian cabaret shows, though the RAI channels have less advertising and mix some good reporting in among the dross. **Satellite and cable** TV is widely available, and at most bigger hotels

you'll often get a couple of foreign-language channels (BBC World, CNN, Eurosport, MTV) plus perhaps pay-for-movie channels.

The situation in **radio** is even more anarchic, with the FM waves crowded to the extent that you can pick up a new station just by walking down the corridor. Again, the RAI stations are generally more professional, though daytime listening is virtually undiluted, nonstop dance music.

Money

Italy's currency is the **euro** (€), though you may sometimes see prices also listed in *lire*, and many older people still mentally convert prices back into the former currency. Euro notes are issued in **denominations** of 5, 10, 20, 50, 100, 200 and 500 euros, and coins in denominations of 1, 2, 5, 10, 20 and 50 cents and 1 and 2 euros. At the time of writing, the **change rate** was around €1.35 to £1; (€1=74p) or €0.68 to US$1 (€1=$1.47). Up-to-the-minute rates are displayed at Ⓦwww.xe.com.

By far the easiest way to get money in Sicily is to use your bank debit card or credit card and a personal identification number (PIN) to withdraw cash from an **ATM** (known as *bancomat* in Italy). These are found even in the smallest towns and on some of the more remote islands, as well as on arrival at the two main airports. Instructions are available in English, and the daily withdrawal limit depends on your bank or credit card company, usually €200 a day. You'll need to check that you have a PIN number that's designed to work overseas, and whether you can use your debit card directly in shops as not all systems are available in Sicily. Amounts withdrawn from ATMs on a debit card are not liable to interest payments, though there is usually a transaction fee.

Credit cards can also be used for cash advances over the counter in banks and for payment in most hotels, restaurants, petrol stations and some shops. MasterCard and Visa are the most widely accepted cards. Cash advances on credit cards are treated as loans, with interest accruing daily from the date of withdrawal; there may also be a transaction fee on top of this. **Travellers' cheques** might be a useful back-up if your plastic is lost, stolen or swallowed by an ATM. In Italy, the most widely accepted brands are Thomas Cook and American Express. However, there's usually a fee charged by providers for issuing cheques, and another by the bank when exchanging them.

The main **banks** you'll see in Sicily are the Banco di Sicilia, the Banca Popolare Sant'Angelo, the Cassa di Risparmio, the Banca Nuova and the Banca Nazionale del Lavoro. **Banking hours** vary slightly from town to town, but generally banks are open Monday to Friday 8.30am–1.20pm and again around 3–4pm. Outside these times you can change travellers' cheques and foreign currency at large hotels, the airports at Palermo and Catania, and some main train stations.

Opening hours and public holidays

Basic opening hours for most **shops and businesses** are Monday to Saturday from 8am or 9am to around 1pm, and from around 4pm to 7pm or 8pm, though some offices work to a more standard European 9am to 5pm day. Everything, except bars and restaurants, closes on Sunday, though you might find cake shops, and fish shops in some coastal towns, open until lunchtime. Local religious holidays and festivals don't generally close down shops and businesses, but everything except bars and restaurants will be closed on the public holidays listed in the box.

Most **churches** open in the early morning (around 7am or 8am) for Mass and close around noon, opening up again at 4pm or 5pm, and closing at 7pm. More obscure ones will only open for early morning and evening services; some only open on Sunday and on religious holidays. One problem you'll face all over Sicily is that lots of churches, monasteries, convents and oratories are **closed for restoration** (*chiuso per restauro*). We've indicated the more long-term closures in the text, but even if there's scaffolding up you might be able to persuade a workman or priest/curator to show you around.

Museums are generally open daily from 9am to 1pm, and again for a couple of hours in the afternoon on certain days; likely closing day is Monday, while they close slightly earlier on Sunday, around 12.30pm.

Public holidays

January 1 *Primo dell'anno*, New Year's Day

January 6 *Epifania*, Epiphany

Good Friday *Venerdì Santo*

Easter Monday *Pasquetta*

April 25 *Giorno della Liberazione*, Liberation Day

May 1 *Festa dei Lavoratori*, Labour Day

June 2 *Festa della Repubblica*, Republic Day

August 15 *Ferragosto*, Assumption of the Blessed Virgin Mary

November 1 *Ognissanti*, All Saints Day

December 8 *Immaccolata*, Immaculate Conception of the Blessed Virgin Mary

December 25 *Natale*, Christmas Day

December 26 *Santo Stefano*, St Stephen's Day

Archeological sites are usually open from 9am until an hour before sunset (in practice until around 4pm from November to March, 7pm from April to October, though never bet against a custodian bunking off early on a slow day). Sites are also sometimes closed on Mondays.

Shopping

Sicilian street **markets** provide some of the best experiences on the island – the Vucciria in Palermo and Catania's fish market, for example, are sights in themselves, while any market can provide inexpensive souvenirs and gifts like stove-top coffee pots or espresso cups. You'll be taken for an imbecile if you don't haggle for everything except food – ask for "*uno sconto*" (a discount). Other day-to-day items, toiletries and basic supplies can be bought in local supermarkets. **Food and drink** souvenirs are almost endless – a bag of dried wild oregano or salted capers from the Aeolians, pistachios from Bronte, almonds from the Agrigento area, *frutta di martorana* from Palermo, marsala wine from Marsala. Taormina is probably the best single place on the island for clothes **boutiques**,

Visiting churches, museums and ruins

To visit **churches and religious buildings** you should dress **modestly** (which means no shorts, not even Bermuda-length ones, and covered shoulders for women), and avoid wandering around during a service. At otherwise free **chapels, museums and archeological sites**, if you're shown around by a custodian or caretaker it's customary to give a small tip – say €1 each.

while all the main Italian labels and brands have outlets in the three main cities of Palermo, Catania and Messina. Sicily has a reputation for its **ceramics**, widely available in tourist shops in the major resorts but best sourced if you're able at the production centres, like Santo Stéfano di Camastra (Tyrrhenian coast), Sciacca (south coast) and especially Caltagirone (southern interior). You'll see **lace and embroidery** in gift shops in places like Palermo, Taormina and Cefalù, and the quality isn't too bad, and the same tourist outlets usually sell gift versions of traditional Sicilian **theatre puppets** and **hand-painted carts**. Anywhere near Etna, you're also guaranteed to find things in shops fashioned from **lava**, paperweights to sculptures.

Telephones

Public **telephones** operated by **Telecom Italia** come in various forms, usually with clear instructions in English. Coin-operated phones are increasingly hard to find, so you will probably have to buy a **phonecard** (*schede telefóniche*), available in various denominations from €5 from *tabacchi* or newsstands. With it, you dial a special access number and key in the PIN number on the back of the card. Bars will often have a phone you can use: look for the yellow phone symbol. Alternatively, telephone offices in major towns have a *cabina a scatti*, a soundproofed and metered kiosk: ask to make the call and pay at the end. Phone **tariffs** are among the most expensive in Europe, especially if you're calling long-distance or internationally – it's always cheapest to buy a phonecard. Specifically, don't make any calls from hotel phones, which always have very high rates.

Dialling ☎170 or 176 will get you through to an English-speaking operator. You can **find numbers online** with the Italian Yellow Pages (🌐www.paginegialle.it) or White Pages (🌐www.paginebianche.it). To **call Sicily from abroad**, dial your international access number + 39 (Italy country code) + number.

Most **cellphones** bought in the UK and Ireland, Australia and New Zealand, will work in Sicily, though it's unlikely that a mobile bought for use in the US will work outside the States. Prices are coming down, but it's expensive to use your cellphone exclusively to make national and internationals calls in Sicily. You might simply be able to buy a replacement **SIM card** for your own phone, though this depends on the model, contract and service provider. Or, if you're coming for more than a couple of weeks, you could even **buy a mobile** in Sicily – basic models cost as little as €39.

Time

Sicily (and Italy) is always one hour ahead of the UK, except for one week at the end of October when the time is the same. Italy is seven hours ahead of Eastern Standard Time and ten hours ahead of Pacific Time.

Tourist information

The Italian State Tourist Office (🌐www.enit.it) has a useful website for general information, or you can contact the state tourist office organization in your own country. In Sicily, most towns, main train stations and the two principal airports have a **tourist office** (*ufficio di turismo*). Other than in the main tourist areas staff aren't likely to speak English, but you should at least be able to get a free town plan and a local listings booklet in Italian, and some offices will reserve you a room and sell places on guided tours.

Likely summer (April to Oct) **opening hours** are Monday to Friday 9am to 1pm and 4pm to 7pm, Saturday 9am to 1pm, though some offices in tourist areas open for longer. From November to March hours may be reduced. If the tourist office isn't open and all else fails, the local Sicilian telephone office and most bars with phones carry a copy of the local *Tuttocittà* (Ⓦ www.tuttocitta .it), a listings and information magazine which details addresses and numbers of most of the organizations you're likely to want to know about. It also has indexed street maps for local towns and adverts for restaurants and shops. The Palermo version (with an interactive map) is available online.

Plenty of other material about Sicily is available online. The following **websites** are a good place to start: Ⓦ www.bestofsicily .com (an informative site detailing history, the arts, books, food and wine, sights and travel); Ⓦ www.siciliaonline.it (some information in English, with details on everything from folklore and the weather to transport and festivals); and Ⓦ www.press. sicilia.it (mostly Italian, extracts from all sorts of articles about Sicily, plus news and reviews). All the major regions, towns, cities and islands have their own websites too, detailed where appropriate in the Guide.

Italian state tourist offices

Australia ☏ 02/9262 1666, Ⓔ Italia@italiantourism .com.au.
Canada ☏ 416/925 -4882, Ⓦ www.italiantourism .com.
UK ☏ 0207/408 1254, Ⓦ www.italiantouristboard .co.uk.
USA ☏ 212/245-5095, Ⓦ www.italiantourism.com.

Guide

Guide

1

Palermo and around

N

TYRRHENIAN SEA

MEDITERRANEAN SEA

0   50 km

CHAPTER 1 # Highlights

* **Frutta di Martorana** Artfully crafted from coloured almond paste, these fruit- and vegetable-shaped candies are a Palermitan tradition. See p.73

* **Cappella Palatina in the Palazzo dei Normanni** It's worth braving the scrum for the breathtaking beauty of the Byzantine mosaics, decorated marble floor and carved Arabic ceiling. See p.75

* **Museo delle Marionette** Catch a performance and admire the swashbuckling wooden Sicilian puppets in all their finery. See p.78

* **Museo Archeólogico Regionale** Palermo's archeological museum holds a superb collection of finds that range across every epoch of Sicily's ancient history. See p.83

* **The festival of Santa Rosalia** Mid-July sees the island's liveliest celebrations, with fireworks, processions and general merry-making. See p.86

* **The cloisters at Monreale** Don't miss the medieval columns with their intricate carvings. See p.104

* **Diving in Ústica** Gin-clear waters and lively underwater action make this one of the best places to dive in Sicily. See p.113

▲ Mosaics in the Museo Archeólogico in Palermo

Palermo and around

Unmistakably the capital of Sicily, Palermo is fast, brash, loud and exciting. Hub of the island since the ninth century AD, it borrows heavily from the past for its present-day look, showing a typically Sicilian fusion of foreign art, architecture, culture and lifestyle. In the narrow streets of Palermo's old town, elegant Baroque and Norman monuments exist cheek by jowl with Arabic cupolas, while Byzantine street markets swamp the medieval warrens, and the latest Milanese fashions sit in shops squeezed between Renaissance churches and Spanish *palazzi*. And, ricocheting off every wall, the endless roar of traffic and wail of police sirens

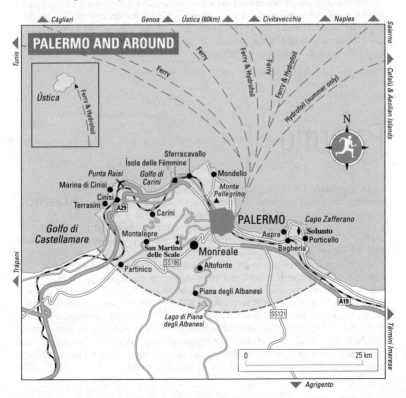

adds to the confusion. Palermo is probably the noisiest city in Italy, and there's pollution in the air, too – a pall of yellow smog hangs over the city, visible from the sea or from the mountains behind on bad days, and in the mottling of dust that covers every car.

It may not be the healthiest place in the world, but it's certainly not dull, with the oppressive summer climate and frenetic street scenes that are redolent of North Africa or the Near East. Indeed, there's little that's strictly European about Palermo, and its geographical isolation has forced the city to forge its own identity, distinct enough to demand that you devote a fair proportion of your stay in Sicily to the capital and its environs. Easily the most populous centre on the island, with around 700,000 inhabitants, it requires at least three or four days to fully explore. Palermo has some of the island's most intriguing sights; also some of its best food and markets, cheapest hotels, and easy access to one of Sicily's finest beaches, at **Mondello**. The other obvious quick retreat from Palermo's bustle is to the heights of **Monte Pellegrino**, the mountain that looms beyond the city to the north.

More substantial targets lie just outside the city's boundaries, most warranting a day-trip. If your enthusiasm has been fired by the city's great Norman heritage, you shouldn't miss the medieval cathedral of **Monreale** and its celebrated mosaics. The **Golfo di Carini**, the curving bay to the west of Palermo, sports a couple of low-key holiday resorts, all with beaches of varying attractiveness and local popularity. Or, heading east along the coast, you can spend an unhurried afternoon at **Bagheria** and its *palazzi*, and take in the nearby Roman site at **Solunto**. Further afield, around 25km south of Palermo, **Piana degli Albanesi** survives as an Albanian Orthodox enclave in a stridently Catholic island. If you feel the pull of the sea, you can always take a day-trip to the offshore island of **Ústica**, though you're likely to want to stay much longer, given the natural attractions of this craggy volcanic slab.

Palermo

In its own wide bay underneath the limestone bulk of Monte Pellegrino, and fronting the broad and fertile Conca d'Oro (Golden Shell) valley, **PALERMO** is stupendously sited. Originally a Phoenician colony, it was taken by the Carthaginians in the fifth century BC and became an important Punic bulwark against the Greek influence elsewhere on the island. It was named Panormus (All Harbour) after its obvious mercantile attractions, and it remained in Carthaginian hands until 254 BC. Long considered a prize worth capturing, the city then fell to the Romans, despite a desperate countersiege by Hamilcar Barca, which he directed from the slopes of Monte Pellegrino. Yet Palermo's most glorious days were still to come. In 831 AD the city was captured by the Arabs, under whose rule it thrived as an Islamic cultural and intellectual centre – the River Papineto that now flows beneath the city was said to speak with the Nile and abide by its tides. Two centuries later under the Normans, the settlement continued to flower as Europe's greatest metropolis – famed for the wealth of its court, and unrivalled as a nexus of learning.

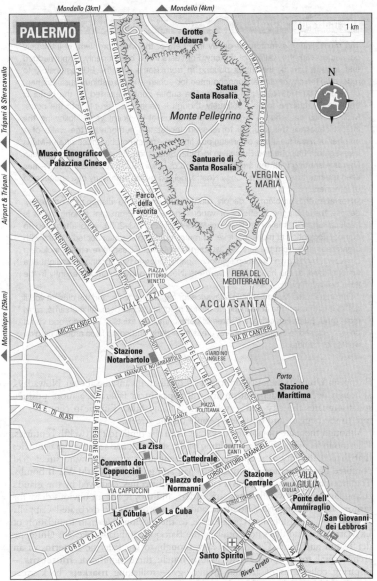

PALERMO

0   1 km

Mondello (3km) ▲   ▲ Mondello (4km)

Grotte
d'Addaura

Statua
Santa Rosalía

Monte Pellegrino

N

Museo Etnográfico
Palazzina Cinese

Santuario di
Santa Rosalía

VERGINE
MARIA

Parco
della
Favorita

PIAZZA
VITTORIO
VENETO

FIERA DEL
MEDITERRANEO

ACQUASANTA

Stazione
Notarbartolo

GIARDINO
INGLESE

Porto

Stazione
Maríttima

PIAZZA
POLITEAMA

La Zisa

QUATTRO
CANTI

Cattedrale

Convento dei
Cappuccini

Palazzo dei
Normanni

Stazione
Centrale

VILLA
GIULIA

Ponte dell'
Ammiraglio

La Cúbula   La Cuba

San Giovanni
dei Lebbrosi

Santo Spirito

River Oreto

Trápani & Steracavallo

Airport & Trápani

Montelepre (25km)

▼ Monreale (3km)   ▼ Piana degli Albanesi (25km)   Messina, Agrigento & Enna ▼

By way of contrast, social and economic decline has characterized much of
the last hundred years or so. Allied bombs during **World War II** destroyed
much of the port area and over seventy of the city's churches, turning parts of
the medieval town into a ramshackle demolition site – a state of affairs that is
now gradually being resolved. Regeneration has been due in no small measure
to the efforts of the former mayor, Leoluca Orlando, aided by funds from the

The Mafia in Palermo

The most glaring symptom of decay in Palermo, the Mafia problem, is intimately connected with the welfare of the city. For years it has been openly acknowledged that a large part of the funds pouring in from Rome and the EU, ostensibly to redevelop the city centre, are unaccounted for – channelled to dubious businessmen, or simply raked off by Mafia leaders. The subtle control exerted by the Mafia is traditionally referred to only obliquely, though it periodically erupts into the news. Mafia issues have had a higher profile than usual in recent years, following the intensification of the struggle to reassert the state's authority in the wake of a number of assassinations of prestigious figures – most notably those of anti-Mafia investigators Falcone and Borsellino in 1992. Since then, the arrest of leading Mafia figures – starting with the arrest of the *capo dei capi* Salvatore Riina in 1993 – has seen the tide turning against Cosa Nostra, helped by the testimony of a succession of informers.

However, the problem is deeply rooted and unlikely to disappear completely, despite the courageous efforts of various individuals. Prominent among these is Leoluca Orlando, mayor of Palermo 1985–90 and 1993–2000, who attempted to combat corruption at municipal level by removing companies suspected of links with organized crime from the tenders list for new contracts. Despite reversals, including disavowal by his own Christian Democrat party, Orlando has continued his fight at a national level, at the head of his own Rete (Network) party and more recently in the Italia dei Valori party.

Fortunately, the Mafia has little relevance for casual travellers, and the closest you'll get to it is through the screaming headlines of local newspapers. All the same, as in most other European cities, a degree of petty crime still exists in Palermo, and you'd be well advised to avoid back-street areas after dark, and not to flash around bulging wallets or cameras.

European Union (when not siphoned off by illicit means; see above). Nowadays, although decay and deprivation are still apparent in Palermo, a more positive spirit animates the city, and – unlike in so many other European centres – it's rare to see beggars and homeless people on the streets.

Although there are notable relics extant from the ninth to the twelfth centuries, Palermo in its prime, it's the rebuilding of the sixteenth and seventeenth centuries that shaped the city as it appears today: essentially a straightforward street-grid confused by the memory of an Eastern past and gouged by World War II bombs. Traditionally, Palermo has been a city of rich **churches**, endowed by the island's ruling families and wealthy monastic orders, and they're still an obvious draw for visitors, from the hybrid Cattedrale and the nearby mosaic-decorated Cappella Palatina, tucked inside the Royal Palace, to the glorious Norman foundation of La Martorana. And that's not counting the Baroque candidates, like San Giuseppe dei Teatini and Santa Caterina. Really, though, to see Palermo in terms of an architectural tour would be to ignore much: three significant **museums** – inspiring collections of art and archeology – rollicking **markets**, back-street puppet theatres, and a wealth of excellent restaurants.

Arrival

Palermo's Falcone Borsellino **airport** (T800.541.880, Wwww.gesap.it) is at Punta Raisi, 31km west of the city. From just outside the Arrivals terminal, regular Prestia & Comandè buses (1–2 hourly, 5am–11pm; 50min journey) run right into the centre, stopping by the Politeama Theatre on Piazza Ruggero Séttimo, and ending at Stazione Centrale, in front of the *Albergo Elena*; buy your ticket (€5) on the bus. Taxi fares for the same trip are around €50. Alternatively, you could take the regional train from the airport's Departures terminal, a five-minute walk from Arrivals, to Palermo's Stazione Centrale (roughly hourly, 5.30am–10.10pm; 40min–1hr journey). Note that though Catania rather than Palermo is the island's main airport, facilities here are good, including bars, a bank (Mon–Fri 8.30am–1pm & 2.45–3.45pm) with cash machine, an exchange office (daily 7am–9pm), a post office (Mon–Fri 8.30am–3.30pm) and an English-speaking **tourist office** (Mon–Fri 8am–midnight, Sat & Sun 8am–8pm; ☎091.591.698). All the **car rental offices** are about 400m to the left out of the Arrivals hall, connected by a free shuttle bus (*navetta*) leaving every eight minutes or so.

Trains all arrive at and leave from Stazione Centrale (☎892.021) in Piazza Giulio Césare, at the southern end of Via Roma. Some (from Trápani/Álcamo) stop first in the northwest of the city at Stazione Notarbártolo; sit tight and you'll end up at Stazione Centrale.

Local, provincial and long-distance, island-wide **buses** operate from a variety of terminals all over the city, of which there are full details in the box below. Handily, though, the **main bus arrivals** and ticket offices are in the streets around the train station – mainly Via Balsamo and Via Gregorio – while other major termini are Piazza Marina, down by the old port, and Piazzale John Lennon, near the intersection of Via Leonardo da Vinci with Via Regione Siciliana (bus #102 from Stazione Centrale) – the latter mostly used by AST

Palermo's bus terminals

AST Via R. Gregorio, near Stazione Centrale (☎091.617.5411, ⓦwww .aziendasicilianatrasporti.it), for Bagheria, Castelbuono, Corleone, Montelepre and Santa Flavia; Piazzale John Lennon, near Viale Regione Siciliana (☎091.685.8015), for Capaci, Carini and Partinico.

Camilleri Via R. Gregorio 38 (☎091.617.1861) for Agrigento.

Cuffaro Via P. Balsamo 13 (☎091.616.1510, ⓦwww.cuffaro.info) for Agrigento.

Interbus Via P. Balsamo 26 (☎091.616.7919, ⓦwww.interbus.it) for Catania and Siracusa.

Prestia & Comandè Stazione Centrale (☎091.580.457, ⓦwww.prestia-comande.it) for the airport and Piana degli Albanesi.

Randazzo Via P. Balsamo (☎091.814.8235, ⓦwww.autobusrandazzo.altervista.org) for Cáccamo and Términi Imerese.

Russo Piazza Marina (☎0924.31.364, ⓦwww.russoautoservizi.it) for Balestrate, Castellammare del Golfo and San Vito Lo Capo.

SAIS Autolinee Via P. Balsamo 16 (☎091.616.6028, ⓦwww.saisautolinee.it) for Caltagirone, Catania, Cefalù, Enna, Gela, Messina and Piazza Armerina.

SAIS Trasporti Via P. Balsamo 20 (☎091.617.1141, ⓦwww.saistrasporti.it) for Messina, Naples and Rome.

Salemi Via R. Gregorio 44 (☎091.617.5411, ⓦwww.autoservizisalemi.it) for Castelvetrano, Marsala and Mazara del Vallo.

Segesta Via P. Balsamo 26 (☎091.616.9039, ⓦwww.segesta.it) for Álcamo, Messina, Partinico, Trápani and Rome; Via Filippo Turati 3 for Álcamo and Trápani.

Virga Piazza Verdi, for San Martino delle Scale.

services to and from places west of Palermo. Some services (Russo and Segesta, for example) stop in Piazza Politeama.

Palermo is a grand place in which to arrive by sea. All **ferry** services – from Ústica, the Aeolians, Civitavecchia, Genoa, Naples and Cágliari (in Sardinia) – dock at the **Stazione Maríttima**, just off Via Francesco Crispi, from where it's a ten-minute walk (straight up Via Emerico Amari) to Piazza Castelnuovo and the modern city centre. The terminal building has a convenient, inexpensive left-luggage office (daily 7am–7.30pm; €1 per 12hr), great for stowing big bags if you're on a quick trip to the islands. There are also regular **hydrofoil** connections with Ústica and seasonal hydrofoil services (mid-June to Sept) to and from Cefalù and the Aeolian Islands, again docking at the Stazione Maríttima. "Listings" (p.98) has all the relevant ticket-office details.

Driving and parking

As **driving** into the city can be traumatic, it's something to avoid if you possibly can. Directional signs are confusing and the traffic unforgiving of first-time foreigners. Coming in on the A20 (from Cefalù), turn right at the first roundabout and keep straight on to reach Stazione Centrale. Otherwise, follow anything that reads "Centro" and aim/ask for Piazza Castelnuovo – a convenient area to leave your vehicle.

Finding a **parking space** can be a real problem at any time other than the early morning or late evening, though you might get lucky if you drive around for long enough. Parking meters are installed over a large part of the centre at a cost of €1 for one hour (maximum three hours); scratch cards (*schede gratta e parcheggia* or *biglietti parcheggio*) are available from nearby ticket machines and shops, and cost the same as meters – you simply scratch off the date and time of parking. In some areas, you will be ushered into a parking space by an attendant, whom you pay directly. There are always **garages** scattered about town, a wise option if you have to leave your car in Palermo's old quarter overnight; there's a list of some of the most central ones on p.98. *Never* leave anything of value, including the radio, visible in the car, and retract your aerial if you can or someone will probably snap it off.

Leaving the city by car, you need Via Oreto, behind Stazione Centrale, for the Palermo–Catania (A20) and Palermo–Messina (A19) autostradas; Corso Vittorio Emanuele (westbound) for Monreale; and Viale della Libertà (northbound) for the airport and Trápani.

Information

You'll be able to pick up **information** and free **maps** from the small tourist office at the airport (Mon–Fri 8am–midnight, Sat & Sun 8am–8pm; ☎091.591.698), though Palermo's main **tourist office** lies in the heart of the city – on the ground floor at Piazza Castelnuovo 34, hidden behind the trees across from the bandstand (Mon–Fri 8.30am–2pm & 2.30–6pm, Sat 9am–1pm; ☎091.605.8351, ⓦwww.palermotourism.com). Here, zealous staff provide a free map of the city and province, and a booklet (*Guida dell'Ospitalità*) containing full accommodation lists and prices for hotels, campsites, rooms to rent and mountain hostels throughout the province.

For complete **city listings** and a rundown of **what's on**, tourist offices can also provide the free twice-yearly *Agenda Turismo*, which lists useful addresses and telephone numbers, museum times, transport links, and cultural events in and around the city. For a more detailed rundown on arts and entertainments, look out too for *Lapis* (free), published fortnightly and widely available from cultural venues, bars and cafés, or online at ⓦwww.palermoweb.com/lapis. The local edition of the daily *Il Giornale di Sicilia*, available from newsstands all over the city, also details forthcoming events.

City transport

While Palermo is very much a city in which to **walk** when you can, you'll find getting around exclusively on foot exhausting and impractical, certainly for the peripheral sights. The **city buses** run by AMAT (Ⓣ 848.800.817 toll-free or 091.690.2690 from a mobile, ⓦwww.amat.pa.it) are easy to use, covering every corner of Palermo and stretching out to Monreale, Mondello and beyond; newer ones are air-conditioned, though the electronic signs that announce the next arrival aren't all that accurate. Most services run from around 4am until 11pm or midnight (sometimes earlier on Sundays). Flat-fare **tickets** cost €1, and are valid on any bus or buses for two hours; alternatively you can buy a ticket valid all day for €3.50; all tickets are available from AMAT's glass kiosks (outside Stazione Centrale, Piazza Politeama and Piazza Verdi), in *tabacchi*, or wherever else you see the sign "*Vendita Biglietti AMAT*" – validate one in the machine on the bus at the start of your journey (on just the first ride with an all-day ticket). You can also buy tickets on board from the driver for a small supplement (€0.40). **Fare dodging** – seemingly commonplace – is punishable by €52 spot fines from roving gangs of inspectors who board buses at random. Don't think that tourists are exempt, though in most cases you'll just be made to buy a ticket.

In addition to the regular buses, two circular **minibus** services, Linea Gialla (Yellow Line; Mon–Sat 7.45am–7.20pm, Sun 7.45am–1.30pm) and Linea

---

Useful bus routes

From the ranks outside Stazione Centrale

#101 and #102 to Piazza Politeama (Piazza Castelnuovo) and Viale della Libertà.

#109 to Piazza dell'Indipendenza (for Palazzo dei Normanni and buses to Monreale).

#139 to Piazza Marina/Corso Vittorio Emanuele and Stazione Maríttima.

Linea Gialla (circular minibus) to Orto Botanico, La Kalsa, Via Alloro, Quattro Canti, Ballarò and Corso Tukory.

Linea Rossa (circular minibus) to Via Roma, Vucciria, Piazza Politeama, Giardino Inglese, Via Libertà, Teatro Mássimo and Via Maqueda.

From Corso Vittorio Emanuele

#104 and #105 run along the corso.

From Via Roma

#101 to Via Príncipe di Belmonte and Giardino Inglese.

From Piazza Sturzo/Piazza Politeama

#806 to Parco della Favorita/Mondello.

Central taxi ranks

- Piazza Giulio Césare
  ☎091.616.2001
- Piazza Castelnuovo ☎091.588.133
- Piazza Giuseppe Verdi
  ☎091.320.184
- Piazza Indipendenza
  ☎091.422.703

- Piazza San Domenico
  ☎091.588.876
- Piazza Matteotti ☎091.303.237
- Via Malta ☎091.616.2000
- Via Roma ☎091.588.876

Rossa (Red Line; Mon–Sat 7.20am–7pm, Sun 7am–12.40pm), run from the train station and ply the most-frequented tourist destinations, including the markets, every twenty minutes or so: see box on p.65 for the routes. Tickets for these cost €0.52 for the day and are available from the AMAT ticket kiosks.

You'll find main **city bus ranks** outside the train station, in Piazza Castelnuovo, on Corso Vittorio Emanuele, and on the southern stretch of Viale della Libertà.

Taxis and other transport

With Palermo's efficient bus service, there's no particular need to take a **taxi** in the city, though they are useful for late-night trips across town or for when you're weighed down with luggage. There are ranks of gleaming white taxis all over the centre – call ☎091.513.311 or 225.455 for a 24-hour service – though don't count on flagging one down on a busy street. Few trips within the city will cost more than €15.

Taking a horse-drawn carriage, a **carrozza**, is a swanky way to see the city. They tout for business alongside Piazza Pretoria or by the cathedral: an hour-long trip costs around €60, though it's worth bargaining. Don't consider getting around the city **by car**: one short afternoon driving in congested Palermo could take years off your life. However, we've given details of car rental companies in "Listings" (see p.98), should you want to have your own transport once you're out of the city.

If you're adept on two wheels, **biking** presents an easier alternative: as long as you realize the rules of the road – he who hesitates is lost, and go for the gap – weaving your way in and out of the traffic can be an exhilarating way to save time and legwork. For the more adventurous, **scooter** rental is also available. Details of scooter and bike rental outlets are given in "Listings" (p.98).

Accommodation

Palermo is the easiest Sicilian city in which to find good, cheap **accommodation**. Prices here are among the lowest on the island. In the city itself, but not on the coast, July and August are counted as low season; in June and September, and also around the time of Palermo's annual festival (July 11–15), you'd be wise not to leave it too late in the day if you want the better rooms; turning up before noon is best, or ring ahead and reserve. Note that if you do go for a cheaper option, English-speaking staff are rare, and at night and in the early morning things can get very noisy (ear plugs are a help).

Hotels

Nearly all the reasonable budget **hotels** in Palermo – known variously as *alberghi*, *pensioni* or *locande* – are to be found on and around the southern ends of Via Maqueda and Via Roma, roughly in the area between Stazione Centrale and Corso Vittorio Emanuele. Here, there are often several separate places in the same block, usually cheaper the higher the floor. Beyond the corso, the streets begin to widen out and the hotels tend to get more expensive.

Stazione Centrale and around

Elena Piazza Giulio Césare 14 ℡091.616.2021, ℻091.616.2984. Not the smartest place in town, but it's cheap, opposite Stazione Centrale and right on the airport bus stop, so late-night arrivals need not fear walking the dark old-town streets. Three- and four-bedroom units are also available, and you'll save €15 if you forego a private bath. ❸

Orientale Via Maqueda 26 ℡091.616.5727, ⓦwww.albergoorientale.191.it. One of the most atmospheric old-town hotels, an eighteenth-century *palazzo* with a columned courtyard and marble staircase, a frescoed salon, and two cavernous, vaulted double rooms (nos. 6 and 7, where Mussolini once stayed) complete with a long balcony overlooking Via Maqueda. Other doubles – some en suite – are plainer and quieter, looking down onto the courtyard and the Albergheria market. Courtyard parking is available when space permits (€10). ❸

Rosalia Conca d'Oro 3rd floor, Via Santa Rosalia 7 ℡091.616.4543, ⓦwww.italiaabc.it/a/rosalia. Charming, fan-cooled rooms and a welcoming owner make this a sought-after choice, though it can be noisy. It's conveniently close to Stazione Centrale, and the seven rooms fill quickly. No credit cards. ❷

Sicilia Via Divisi 99 ℡091.616.8460, ⓦwww.hotelsiciliapalermo.it. Pleasantly run, this represents good value, with artistic touches in the air-conditioned rooms; those around the small downstairs courtyard are quieter. Parking available nearby (€8 per day). ❺

Corso Vittorio Emanuele and around

Centrale Palace Corso Vittorio Emanuele 327 ℡091.336.666, ⓦwww.centralepalacehotel.it. A few steps away from the Quattro Canti, this renovated *palazzo* makes a soothing base, overseen by courteous staff. Lovely rooms have high ceilings, quality furnishings and a choice of streetside, balcony or atrium view. Take breakfast in the cool Baroque salon, or dinner in the serene panoramic roof terrace-restaurant. Garage parking available for €16 a day. ❻

Cortese Via Scarparelli 16 ℡& ℻091.331.722. Buried within the web of lanes around the Ballarò market, this hotel offers great value, with friendly family management. The quiet, air-conditioned rooms are mostly en suite, and some have views over the market. The constant bustle hereabouts dispels any sense of menace in the dimly lit side streets at night. Follow the signs from Via Maqueda or Corso Vittorio Emanuele. ❷

Al Giardino dell'Alloro Vícolo San Carlo 8 ℡091.617.6904 or 338.224.3541, ⓦwww.giardinodellalloro.it. This B&B in the heart of the run-down Kalsa area has five boldly coloured, en-suite rooms full of contemporary Sicilian art. The old building and courtyard have been tastefully renovated, combining tiled floors and beamed roofs with modern designs, and a kitchen is available for guests' use. ❺

Letizia Via Bottai 30 ℡091.589.110, ⓦwww.hotelletizia.com. This attractive and friendly establishment is the best choice in the Piazza Marina area, with en-suite rooms full of character and period furniture. Four mini-suites are also available. There's Internet access for guests and free street parking or garage parking (€10 a day). ❻

Paradiso Via Schiavuzzo 65 ℡091.617.2825. The windows of this first-floor *pensione* (one of the cheapest in town) overlook the Piazza della Rivoluzione. It's pretty basic, but clean enough; all rooms share bathrooms. No credit cards. ❷

San Francesco Via Merlo 30 ℡091.888.8391 or 328.551.6242, ⓦwww.sanfrancescopalermo.it. Just steps away from the church of San Francesco d'Assisi, this B&B in an imaginatively restored old building has three en-suite rooms with wooden or arched ceilings, not very light, but cosy and full of character. You can have breakfast in your room if requested. Discounts on longer stays. No credit cards. Closed Oct & Nov. ❷

Le Terrazze Via Pietro Novelli 14 ℡091.652.0866 or 320.432.8567, ⓦwww.leterrazzebb.it. This upmarket B&B close to the cathedral offers two air-conditioned rooms – one accommodating up to four people – and boasts a total of five roof terraces, affording wonderful views of the city's roofs and towers. Breakfast is served outside in fine weather. Closed Nov. No credit cards. **⑤**

The modern city

Grand Hotel et des Palmes Via Roma 398 ☏ 091.602.8111, ⓦ www.hotel-despalmes.it. One of central Palermo's monuments, this magnificent building is where Richard Wagner stayed and finished composing *Parsifal* in 1882. Its tone is formal and its public rooms are glamorous, but some bedrooms are disappointingly basic and overpriced. Garage available for €18 a day. **⑧**

Joli Via Michele Amari 11 ☏ 091.611.1766, ⓦ www.hoteljoli.com. Classy rooms in a pleasant, quiet neighbourhood (right on Piazza Florio, handy for both the port and the modern city) make this a good choice. Frescoes and chandeliers adorn the Liberty-style interior, and there's parking (€10). **⑤**

Mercure Via Mariano Stabile 112 ☏ 091.324.911, ⓦ www.mercure.com. Palermo's most chic hotel, this is industrial minimalist design at its finest. The identical rooms all have sleek tiled baths, and some offer great views. It's popular with business travellers, which ensures full Internet facilities, and also makes weekends here refreshingly quiet. Garage available (€10). **⑥**

Politeama Palace Piazza Ruggero Séttimo 15 ☏ 091.322.777, ⓦ www.hotelpoliteama.it. An excellent location for this classy four-star, right opposite the Politeama Theatre. Behind the 1970s-style front, the spacious and fullye quipped rooms are soundproofed, which deals effectively with the manic traffic outside. Popular with older tour groups. **⑦**

Posta Via Gagini 77 ☏ 091.587.338, ⓦ www .hotelpostapalermo.it. Much favoured by actors, this courteously run, modern-city hotel has character, charm and a dash of 1970s styling. The archeological museum is just across the road. Garage parking and a private beach at Mondello available. **⑥**

Principe di Villafranca Via G. Turrisi Colonna 4 ☏ 091.611.8523, ⓦ www.principedivillafranca.it. Furnished to the hilt with antique Sicilian furniture and early twentieth-century art, this luxury hotel has a great location – it's far enough out of the centre to give some peace and quiet, and is a good, safe area to park in. **⑧**

Out of the centre

Grand Hotel Villa Igiea Salita Belmonte 43 ☏ 091.631.2111, ⓦ www.hilton.com/italy. At Acquasanta, 3km north of the city, this classic seaside Art Nouveau building, originally a villa of the Florio family (the first people to can tuna), was designed by Ernesto Basile in 1900. Now a five-star Hilton, it's still sumptuous and for the seriously wealthy; expect to pay over €300 per night in high season. **⑨**

Campsites and youth hostels

There are two **campsites** in the Palermo area, both at Sferracavallo, 13km northwest of the city, and reachable on bus #616 or #628 from the stadium at Piazzale De Gásperi, at the northern end of Viale della Libertà in the modern city (take #101 from the station or #106 from Piazza Sturzo to save a walk up this long avenue). If you're driving and heading out of town, other campsites within range are located along the Golfo di Carini, to the west of Palermo.

Palermo's official **youth hostel** also lies at Sferracavallo; a second, independent hostel lies closer to the centre, though it still requires a bus ride to reach.

Campsites

Campeggio degli Ulivi Via Pegaso, Sferracavallo ☏ 091.533.021, ⓦ www.campingdegliulivi.com. Five hundred metres from the sea, this is a small site and quite basic, though bungalows are available. **①**

Trinacria Via Barcarello, Sferracavallo ☏ 091.530.590, ⓦ www.campingtrinacria.it. Right across from the sea, with a pizzeria on the premises as well as sports facilities, this is pricier than the *Ulivi*, and offers bungalows that sleep two to four people. **②**

Hostels

Baia del Corallo Via Plauto 27, Sferracavallo ☏ 091.679.7807, ⓔ palermo@ostellionline.org.

Official youth hostel, open all year. At 30min or so from Palermo, it's convenient for the beach, but not much else. To get there, take bus #628 from Piazzale De Gásperi and get off at the Hotel Bellevue stop just after Sferracavallo. Dorm beds cost €17, rooms **①**

Casa Marconi Via Monfenera 140 ☏ 091.657.0611, ⓦ www.casamarconi.it. Spankingly modern and on the expensive side, this has en-suite private rooms only for two, three or four people, as well as singles; you'll need to book ahead as it fills quickly. It's a bit of a bus trek: take #246 from the station to the end of the line at the hospital, cross on to Via G. Basile and turn left into Via Monfenera. **③**

The City

Maintaining much of the medieval street system, historical Palermo sits compactly around one set of central crossroads, the **Quattro Canti**, the intersection of **Corso Vittorio Emanuele**, formerly "Il Cassaro", which runs from the old harbour, La Cala, southwest to both the Cattedrale and the Palazzo dei Normanni, and **Via Maqueda**, which runs northwest of the train station. Both streets date from the city's reconstruction in the sixteenth century. Parallel to Via Maqueda, and running north from Piazza Giulio Césare, **Via Roma** was a much later addition; together, the two streets now carry most of central Palermo's traffic, linking the old centre with the **modern city**. The central spine of this staid grid-network of shops, apartments and office blocks is **Viale della Libertà**, running from the double squares of **Piazza Castelnuovo** and **Piazza Ruggero Séttimo** – together known to Palermitans as **Piazza Politeama** – to the southern end of the **Parco della Favorita**. Piazza Politeama lies a lengthy 25- to 30-minute walk from the train station (there are frequent bus services), but is much closer to the **Stazione Maríttima**, where the ferries dock.

Four distinct quarters lie around Quattro Canti: the **Albergheria** and **Capo** districts lie roughly west of Via Maqueda, **Vucciria** and **La Kalsa** lie to the east, closest to the water. In the past there was little contact between the quarters, whose inhabitants had their own dialects, trades, palaces and markets – even intermarriage was frowned upon. Today these areas hold most of Palermo's most enduring monuments and buildings. It's a fairly undisciplined mess, with sixteenth- and seventeenth-century town planning conspiring with late nineteenth-century ambition and twentieth-century bombs to lend an eclectic look to the city – tight alleys, stately piazzas and contemporary office blocks mixed to distraction in a web-like system of streets. Often, the decaying buildings mask tranquil gardens or chapels containing outstanding works of art, or even stabling for a goat – a world away from the din of the urban assault course outside.

Given that cars, let alone buses, can't get down many of the narrow streets in the old city centre, you'll often have no choice but to walk around most of what is detailed below – although for certain specific sights, don't hesitate to jump on a bus. Certainly, you'll need some form of transport to reach Palermo's **outskirts**: it's no fun at all slogging up and down the long thoroughfares of the modern city.

If you want to cut down on **admission charges to museums**, go for the reduced-price tickets (€12), valid for two days and available from participating museums: one covers La Zisa, La Cuba, Monreale cloisters and San Giovanni degli Eremiti, the other the Museo Archeológico, Galleria Regionale and Palazzo Mirto. There are also versions encompassing fewer places for €7 and €10. Finally, bear in mind that information in English is scarce at most of the sights.

Around the Quattro Canti

In the heart of the old city – ten minutes' walk from the train station – is Piazza Vigliena, better known as the **Quattro Canti** or "Four Corners", the centre (if anywhere is) of the medieval town area. Erected in 1611, this is not so much a piazza as a set of Baroque crossroads that divide central Palermo into quadrants. It's worth strolling around to check the tiered statues – respectively a season, a king of Sicily and a patron of the city in each concave "corner", where, in

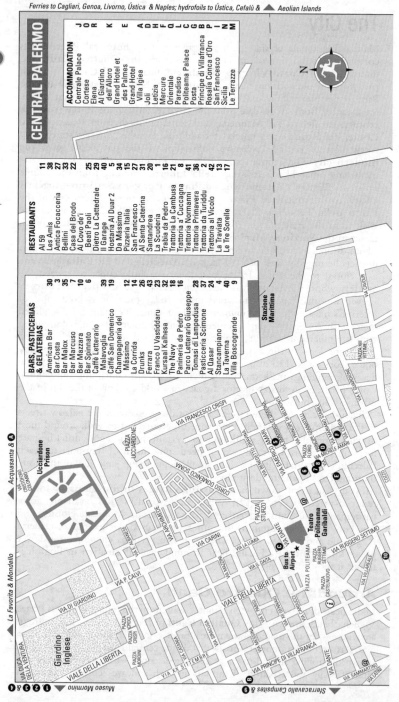

Ferries to Cagliari, Genoa, Livorno, Ústica & Naples; hydrofoils to Ústica, Cefalù & ▲ Aeolian Islands

CENTRAL PALERMO

ACCOMMODATION

Centrale Palace	J
Cortese	O
Elena	R
Al Giardino dell'Alloro	K
Grand Hotel et des Palmes	E
Grand Hotel Villa Igiea	A
Joli	D
Letizia	H
Mercure	F
Orientale	Q
Paradiso	L
Politeama Palace	C
Posta	G
Principe di Villafranca	B
Rosalia Conca d'Oro	P
San Francesco	N
Sicilia	M
Le Terrazze	

RESTAURANTS

Al 59	11
Les Amis	38
Antica Focacceria	27
Bellini	33
Casa del Brodo	22
Al Covo de'i	
Beati Paoli	25
Dietro La Cattedrale	29
Il Garage	40
Hostaria Al Duar 2	5
Da Mássimo	34
Pizzeria Italia	15
San Francesco	27
Al Santa Caterina	31
Santandrea	20
La Scuderia	1
Trabia da Pedro	16
Trattoria La Cambusa	21
Trattoria à Cuccagna	8
Trattoria Normanni	41
Trattoria Primavera	36
Trattoria da Turiddu	2
Trattoria al Vicolo	42
La Traviata	13
Le Tre Sorelle	17

BARS, PASTICCERIAS & GELATERIAS

American Bar	30
Bar Costa	3
Bar Malox	35
Bar Marcuso	7
Bar Mazzara	10
Bar Spinnato	6
Caffè Letterario Malavoglia	39
Caffè San Domenico	19
Champagneria del Mássimo	12
La Corrida	14
Ferrara	43
Franco U Vastiddaru	23
Kursaal Kalhesa	32
The Navy	18
Paninaria da Pedro	16
Parco Letterario Giuseppe Tomasi di Lampedusa	28
Pasticceria Scimone	37
Al Qasar	24
Stancampiano	4
La Taverna	40
Villa Boscogrande	9

Ucciardone Prison

Stazione Marittima

PIAZZA UCCIARDIONE

CORSO DOMENICO SCINA

VIA FRANCESCO CRISPI

PIAZZA EMERICO AMARI

VIA EMERICO AMARI

VIA BENEDETTO GRAVINA

VIA PRINCIPE DI BELMONTE

VIA MARIANO STABILE

VIA PRINCIPE GRANATELLI

PIAZZA FLORIO

VIA MICHELE AMARI

VIA GIARDINELLO

VIA TARANTO STABILE

VIA CERDA

VIA CAVOUR

VIA ARCHIMEDE

VIALE ARENE

VIA ALMAZION

PIAZZA STURZO

VIA DANTE

Teatro Politeama Garibaldi

PIAZZA POLITEAMA

PIAZZA RUGGERO SETTIMO

VIA RUGGERO SETTIMO

Bus to Airport

VIA CARINI

VIA LA LUMIA

VIA P. CALVI

VIA GIUSEPPE LA DAITA

VIA DI GIARDINO

Giardino Inglese

VIA DUCA DELLA VENTURA

VIALE DELLA LIBERTA

PIAZZA CRISPI

PIAZZA MORDINI

VIA MESSINA

VIA SIMONE CUZZONA

VIA PARISI

VIA WI GENNAIO

VIA CARDUCCI

PIAZZA CASTELNUOVO

VIA XX SETTIMBRE

VIALE DELLA LIBERTA

VIA PRINCIPE DI VILLAFRANCA

VIA DANTE

VIA SAMMARTINO

VIA VILLAREALE

PIAZZA XIII VITTIME

N

La Favorita & Mondello ▲

Acquasanta & Ⓐ

Museo Mormino ⬤ Ⓛ Ⓑ Ⓒ Ⓓ ▲

Sterracavallo Campsites & Ⓑ ▲

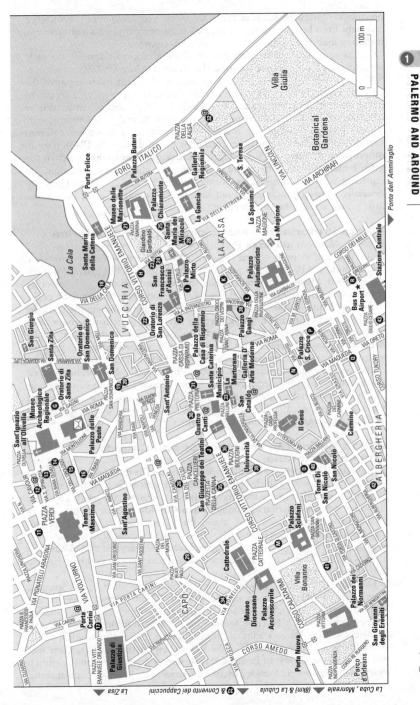

0

0   100 m

Ponte dell' Ammiraglio ▼

▲ *La Zisa*   ▲ *Convento dei Cappuccini* & (8km) ▲   ▲ *La Cuba & La Cubula*   ▲ *La Cuba, Monreale*

PIAZZA UNGHERIA
VIA VOLTURNO
Porta Carini
PIAZZA A. FRANCESCO DI PAOLA
VIA CARINI
Palazzo di Giustizia
Porta Nuova
CORSO AMEDO
PIAZZA INDIPENDENZA
CORSO RE RUGGERO
Parco d'Orleans
San Giovanni degli Eremiti
Palazzo dei Normanni
ALBERGHERIA
Villa Bonanno
Palazzo Arcivescovile
Museo Diocesano
Cattedrale
PIAZZA CATTEDRALE
Palazzo Sclafani
CORSO VITTORIO EMANUELE
CAPO
PIAZZA VERDI
Teatro Massimo
Sant'Agostino
Museo Archeologico Regionale
Sant'Ignazio all'Olivella
Palazzo delle Poste
VIA ROMA
VIA MAQUEDA
Sant'Antonio
Oratorio di Santa Zita
Santa Zita
San Giorgio
Oratorio di San Domenico
San Domenico
La Cala
Santa Maria della Catena
Porta Felice
FORO ITALICO
Palazzo Butera
VIA BUTERA
Museo delle Marionette
Palazzo Chiaramonte
Santa Maria dei Miracoli
Galleria Regionale
La Gancia
VIA DELLA VETRIERA
PIAZZA DELLA KALSA
S. Teresa
VIA LINCOLN
Botanical Gardens
Villa Giulia
Giardino Garibaldi
PIAZZA MARINA
San Francesco d'Assisi
Palazzo Mirto
Oratorio di San Lorenzo
Corso Vittorio Emanuele
VUCCIRIA
VIA DELLA CALA
Lo Spasimo
PIAZZA MAGIONE
La Magione
LA KALSA
Palazzo Aiutamicristo
VIA GARIBALDI
Palazzo Gangi
PIAZZA DELLA RIVOLUZIONE
Palazzo della Casa di Risparmio
Santa Caterina
La Martorana
Galleria D'Arte Moderna
San Cataldo
Palazzo S. Croce
Stazione Centrale
Bus to Airport ★
PIAZZA GIULIO CESARE
CORSO TUKORY
VIA ORETO
Quattro Canti
Municipio
PIAZZA PRETORIA
PIAZZA BELLINI
Il Gesù
PIAZZA CASA PROFESSA
San Giuseppe dei Teatini
Università
PIAZZA BOLOGNI
CORSO VITTORIO EMANUELE
Torre Di San Nicolò
San Nicolò
Carmine
VIA MAQUEDA
PIAZZETTA DELLA CANNA
71

previous centuries, the heads of convicted rebels were hung from poles. Only a few steps from here lie some of Palermo's most opulent piazzas and buildings, including four of the city's most extraordinary churches.

On the southwest corner (entrance on Corso Vittorio Emanuele), the early seventeenth-century **San Giuseppe dei Teatini** (Mon–Sat 7.30am–noon & 5.30–8pm, Sun 8.30am–12.30pm & 6–8pm) is the most harmonious of the city's Baroque churches. The misleadingly simple facade conceals a wealth of detail inside, from tumbling angels holding the holy water on either side of the door to the lavish side chapels and ceiling encrusted with writhing *putti*. There's plenty of contrasting space, though, with eight enormous columns supporting the dome (mostly restored after bomb damage in 1943), plus 26 others along the nave and side chapels. Outside, adjacent to the church, is the main building of the **Università**, a dull nineteenth-century restoration job replacing what was originally a convent adjoining San Giuseppe. There are generally plenty of students around here, and a couple of good bars in the little piazza across from the entrance.

Piazza Pretoria: the Municipio and Santa Caterina

Cross Via Maqueda to **Piazza Pretoria**, where you'll see the gleaming-white nude figures of its great central fountain, a racy sixteenth-century Florentine design, protected by railings to ward off excitable vandals. The piazza also holds the restored **Municipio**, now plaque-studded and pristine, and, towering above both square and fountain, the massive late sixteenth-century flank of the church of **Santa Caterina** (enter from Piazza Bellini), the antithesis of the quietly magnificent San Giuseppe over the road. This is Sicilian Baroque at its most exuberant: every inch of the enormous interior is covered in wildly decorative, pustular relief work, deep reds and yellows filling in between sculpted cherubs, Madonnas, lions and eagles. One marble panel (in the first chapel on the right) depicts Jonah about to be devoured by a rubbery-lipped whale, with a Spanish galleon above constructed from wire with string rigging. Given this overwhelmingly theatrical design, it's difficult to argue with Vincent Cronin's image of a " … frenzied mind … throwing out powerful and extravagant images before tumbling over the verge of madness".

Piazza Bellini: the churches of San Cataldo and La Martorana

Just around the corner from the Pretoria fountain, **Piazza Bellini** is largely a car park by day, with vehicles jammed together next to part of the city's old Roman wall, and beneath two more wildly contrasting churches. The little Saracenic red golf-ball domes belong to **San Cataldo**, a squat twelfth-century chapel on a palm-planted bank above the piazza (daily 9.30am–1pm, also April–Nov Mon–Sat 3.30–7pm; €1). Other than the crenellations around the roof, it was never decorated, and in the eighteenth century the chapel was even used as a post office: it still retains a good mosaic pavement in an otherwise bare and peaceful interior.

The understatement of this little chapel is more than offset by the splendid interior of **La Martorana** opposite (Mon–Sat 9.15am–1pm & 3.30–7pm, or 3.30–6.30pm in winter, Sun 8.30am–1pm), one of the finest surviving buildings of the medieval city. A Norman foundation, it was paid for in 1143 by George of Antioch, King Roger's admiral, from whom it received its original name, Santa Maria dell'Ammiraglio. After the Sicilian Vespers, the island's nobility met here to offer the Crown to Peter of Aragon, and under the Spanish the church was passed to a convent founded by Eloisa Martorana – hence its popular name.

Frutta di Martorana

When Palermo's religious houses were at their late medieval height, many supported themselves by turning out remarkable sculpted confectionery – fruit and vegetables made out of coloured almond paste. La Martorana was once famous for the quality of its almond "fruits", which were sold at the church doors, and today most Sicilian *pasticcerie* continue the tradition: in Palermo these creations are known as *frutta di Martorana*. It's always worth looking in cake-shop windows, which usually display not only fruit but also fish and shellfish made out of the same sickly almond mixture. The best time to see the displays is in October, before the festival of Ognissanti (All Saints).

It received a Baroque going-over and its curving northern facade in 1588, but happily this doesn't detract from the great power of the interior; enter through the slim twelfth-century campanile, an original structure that retains its ribbed arches and slender columns. A series of spectacular **mosaics** are laid on and around the columns supporting the main cupola – animated twelfth-century Greek works, commissioned by the admiral himself, who was of Greek descent. A gentle Christ dominates the dome, surrounded by angels, with the Apostles and the Madonna to the sides. The colours are still strong, a golden background enlivened by azure, grape-red, light-green and white, and, in the morning especially, light streams in through the high windows, picking out the admirable craftsmanship. Heavy Baroque marble and frescoes by the entrance do their best to dampen the effect, but even here there's some respite: on both sides of the steps, two more original mosaic panels (from the destroyed Norman portico) have been set in frames on the walls: a kneeling George of Antioch dedicating the church to the Virgin, and King Roger being crowned by Christ – the diamond-studded monarch contrasted with a larger, more simple and dignified Christ. The church is a popular location for Palermitan weddings, spectacular events that often culminate in newlyweds releasing a dozen white doves from the steps of the church. The church is closed to visitors during these occasions, and during Mass on Sunday from 10 to 11.45am.

The Albergheria

The district bounded by Via Maqueda and Corso Vittorio Emanuele, just northwest of Stazione Centrale – the **Albergheria** – can't have changed substantially for several hundred years. There are proud *palazzi* on Via Maqueda itself, notably the eighteenth-century **Palazzo Santa Croce**, on the corner of Via Divisi, but the real heart of the quarter is in the sprawling warren of tiny streets away from the main roads. It's a poor but highly atmospheric neighbourhood, its central core taken up by a lively street market, and there are several fine churches interspersed among the tall, blackened and leaning buildings.

The most spectacular of the churches is **Il Gesù**, or **Casa Professa** (daily 7–11.30am & 5–6.30pm), on Via Ponticello, the first Jesuit foundation in Sicily, topped by a green-and-white-patterned dome. It was begun in the mid-sixteenth century and took over a hundred years to complete, and was almost entirely rebuilt following bomb damage in World War II – there are still signs of the devastation in the surrounding streets. The reconstruction has been impressively thorough, and the church's awesome interior, a glorious Baroque swirl of inlaid marble, majolica, intricate relief work and gaudily painted ceiling, takes some time to absorb. Continuing down the road will lead you to **Piazza Ballarò**, the focus of a raucous daily fruit and vegetable **market**, alive with the

▲ Vegetable market in Palermo

cries of vendors from early in the morning. Here gleaming fish curl their heads and tails in the air, squashes come as long as baseball bats and vine leaves trail decoratively down from stalls. There are some very cheap snack and drinking places here, too, where you can sidle in among the locals and sample sliced-open sea urchins, fried artichokes, *arancini* and beer.

At one end of the piazza on Via Nasi, you can climb the 84 steps of the **Torre di San Nicolò** (Tues, Thurs, Sat & Sun 9.30am–1pm; €2 donation) for one of the best city views. The sturdy, square construction, with mullioned windows, started life as a watchtower in the thirteenth century and was joined to the adjacent church of San Nicolò in about 1518. The volunteers who manage the tower are mines of local information, and also run walking tours of the Albergheria quarter (see "Listings", p.98). At the southern end of Via Ballarò, the bright majolica-tiled dome of the seventeenth-century church of **Santa Maria del Cármine** (Mon–Sat 8.30am–noon) looms above Piazza del Cármine, a singular landmark amid the market stalls and rubbish-strewn alleys, with a spacious interior and adjoining cloister and convent.

San Giovanni degli Eremiti

Any of the long streets west of Piazza del Cármine lead to Via dei Benedettini, which marks the westernmost edge of the quarter. Over the busy road, behind iron gates, is the Alberghería's most peaceful haven, the deconsecrated church of **San Giovanni degli Eremiti** (Mon–Sat 9am–7pm, Sun 9am–1pm; €4.50) – St John of the Hermits. Built in 1132, this is the most obviously Arabic of the city's Norman relics, its five ochre domes topping a small church that was built upon the remains of an earlier mosque (part of which, an adjacent empty hall, is still visible). It was especially favoured by its founder, Roger II, who granted the monks of San Giovanni 21 barrels of tuna a year, a prized commodity controlled by the Crown. Apart from some worn frescoes, the interior reveals little of interest, though. A path leads up through citrus trees to the church, behind which lie some celebrated late thirteenth-century cloisters – perfect twin columns with slightly pointed arches surrounding a wilted garden. Note that much of the complex is currently under restoration, with restricted viewing, so call first if you want the full experience (℡091.651.5019).

Immediately behind the church, on Corso Re Ruggero, the **Palazzo d'Orleans** is also set in its own garden: home to the exiled Louis-Philippe, duke of Orleans (later the last king of France), between 1810 and 1814, it's now the official residence of Sicily's president.

The Palazzo dei Normanni

Turn left out of San Giovanni and it's a few paces to the main road, where, if you turn right and veer left up the steps, you'll climb out of the clamorous traffic to gaze on the vast length of the **Palazzo dei Normanni**, or Palazzo Reale. A royal palace has always occupied the high ground here, above medieval Palermo. Originally built by the Saracens in the ninth century, the palace was enlarged considerably by the Normans, under whom it housed the most magnificent of medieval European courts. Sadly, there's little left from those times in the current structure. The long front was added by the Spanish in the seventeenth century, and most of the interior is now taken up by the Sicilian regional parliament (hence the security guards and limited access).

Of the **Royal Apartments** (Mon, Tues & Thurs–Sat 8.30am–noon & 2–5pm, Sun 8.30am–12.30pm; €6, including Cappella Palatina) the showpiece is undoubtedly the **Sala di Ruggero**, one of the earliest parts of the palace and richly covered with twelfth-century mosaics of hunting scenes. Other rooms, such as the **Sala del Duca di Montalto**, are used for occasional exhibitions. The highlight of the visit, however, is the beautiful **Cappella Palatina** (Mon–Sat 8.30am–noon & 2–5pm, Sun 8.30–9.45am & 11.45am–12.30pm), the private royal chapel of Roger II, built between 1132 and 1143, and the undisputed artistic gem of central Palermo. Its intimate interior is immediately overwhelming, with cupola, three apses and nave entirely covered in **mosaics** of outstanding quality. The oldest are those in the cupola and apses, probably completed in 1150 by Byzantine artists; those in the nave are from the hands of local craftsmen, finished twenty-odd years later and depicting Old and New Testament scenes. The colours are vivid and, as at Monreale and Cefalù, it's the powerful representation of Christ as Pantocrator that dominates the senses, bolstered here by other secondary images – Christ blessing, open book in hand, and Christ enthroned, between Peter (to whom the chapel is dedicated) and Paul. Aside from the mosaics, the chapel has a delightful Arabic ceiling with richly carved wooden stalactites, a patterned marble floor and an impressive marble Norman candlestick (by the pulpit), 4m high and contorted by manic carvings.

The Cattedrale and the Capo

From the Quattro Canti, the busy southwestern stretch of **Corso Vittorio Emanuele** is dotted with secondhand bookshops and run-down eighteenth-century *palazzi*. There is no preparation for the sudden, huge bulk of the **Cattedrale** (Mon–Sat 9.30am–1.30pm & 2.30–5.30pm, Sun 7.30am–1.30pm & 4–7pm; closed during services; free; ⓦwww.cattedrale.palermo.it): set back in gardens on the right of the corso, it's a more substantial Norman relic than the

Royal Palace. Founded in 1185 by Palermo's English archbishop Gualtiero Offamiglio (Walter of the Mill), the Cattedrale was intended to be his power base in the city. Yet it wasn't finished for centuries, and in any case was quickly superseded by the glories of William II's foundation at Monreale.

The Cattedrale is an odd building in many ways, owing to the less-than-subtle late eighteenth-century alterations that added the dome – completely out of character – and spoiled the fine lines of the tawny stone. Still, the triple-apsed eastern end (seen from a side road off the corso) and the lovely matching towers are all twelfth-century originals; and, despite the fussy Catalan-Gothic facade and arches, there's enough Norman carving and detail to give the exterior more than mere curiosity value. The same is not true, however, of the overblown interior, which was modernized by Fuga, the Neapolitan architect responsible for the dome. It's grand enough, but cold and Neoclassical, and the main interest resides in the fine portal and wooden doors (both fifteenth-century) and the **Area Monumentale** (Mon–Sat 9.30am–1.30pm & 2.30–5.30pm; €2.50, or €4.50 including Museo Diocesano, see below), which is accessible during services. Here, you can view the royal **tombs** (€1), Palermo's pantheon of kings and emperors gathered together in two crowded chapels, including the mortal remains of some of Sicily's most famous monarchs, notably Frederick II (left front) and his wife Constance (far right), Henry VI (right front) and Roger II (rear left) – Roger's tomb was brought back shortly after he died from the cathedral at Cefalù, where he had requested that he be laid. In a reliquary chapel to the right of the choir, the remains of St Rosalia (see p.101) are housed in a silver casket, close to an urn containing the arm of St Agata. Also in the Area Monumentale is the **treasury**, or *tesoro*, holding such items as the twelfth-century jewel- and pearl-encrusted skullcap and three simple, precious rings removed from the tomb of Constance of Aragon in the eighteenth century, and the **crypt**, home to 23 impressive marble tombs (all numbered), many of which are Roman sarcophagi with interesting decoration – no. 12 is a Greek sarcophagus boasting an imposing effigy by Antonello Gagini, one of a prolific dynasty of talented medieval sculptors who covered Sicily with their creations, and no. 16 is the tomb of the founding archbishop.

Palazzo Arcivescovile and the Porta Nuova

Over the road, at the western end of the Cattedrale, stands the **Palazzo Arcivescovile**, the one-time archbishop's palace, entered through a fifteenth-century gateway. One wing of it is occupied by the **Museo Diocesano** (Tues–Fri 9.30am–1.30pm, Sat 10am–6pm, Sun 9.30am–1.30pm; €4.50), which brings together religious art from the cathedral and from city churches destroyed during World War II. There's some marvellous work here from the medieval and Renaissance periods, including a twelfth-century mosaic of the Madonna, a startling flagellation of Christ by Antonio Veneziano (1388), and a couple of lovely fifteenth-century triptychs, both showing the *Coronation of the Virgin* (one with angels blasting on trumpets). Sculpture by the Gaginis and Francesco Laurana is displayed downstairs.

A little way up Via Bonello (left out of the palace) there's usually some activity in the open-air **Mercato delle Pulci**, an antique/junk market in Piazza Peranni displaying chandeliers galore. Back on the corso, the road runs up to the Royal Palace, on the northern side of which lies the commanding **Porta Nuova**. Erected in 1535, it commemorates Charles V's Tunisian exploits, with suitably grim, turbaned and moustachioed figures adorning the western side. Through the gate, the long road, now Corso Calatafimi, heads southwest to Monreale.

Il Capo

Having circled around the apses of the Cattedrale, it's an easy stroll up into the **Capo** quarter, one of the oldest areas of Palermo. It's another labyrinthine web of run-down streets, unrelieved by space or greenery, save for the graceful **Piazza del Monte**, tree-planted and with a couple of restful neighbourhood bars. There's not much to see other than a few surviving sculpted portals in the decaying palaces, but it's an instructive tour if you've seen only grand buildings up to now. One alley, Via Porta Carini, climbs past shambolic buildings and locked, battered churches to reach the decrepit **Porta Carini** itself, one of the city's medieval gates. There are market stalls packed into Via Porta Carini, and the entire area is reminiscent at times of an Arab souk, though with a decidedly Sicilian choice of wares.

The market extends on either side of Via Porta Carini, west to the edge of the Capo district and east, along **Via Sant'Agostino** – the closer you get to Via Maqueda, the more it's devoted to clothes and shoes rather than food. Keep an eye out for **Sant'Agostino** (Mon–Sat 7am–noon & 4–6pm, Sun 7am–noon), built by the Chiaramonte and Scláfani families in the thirteenth century. Above the main door (on Via Raimondo) there's a gorgeous latticework rose window and, inside through the adjacent side-door, some fine seventeenth-century **stuccoes** by Giácomo Serpotta. Another door leads to a quadrangle of calm sixteenth-century cloisters. Otherwise, turn the corner, and along Via Sant'Agostino, behind the market stalls, the church sports a badly chipped, sculpted fifteenth-century doorway attributed to Domenico Gagini.

Up Via Roma to Corso Vittorio Emanuele

Running from the Stazione Centrale to Piazza Sturzo (below Piazza Ruggero Séttimo), **Via Roma** is a fairly modern addition to the city. Parallel to Via Maqueda, and connected to it by a series of narrow alleys, it's nothing like as interesting as its neighbour in its lower reaches, its buildings largely consisting of clothes and shoe shops interspersed by tall apartment blocks containing hotels. There are diversions on the intersecting lanes, however, such as **Via Divisi**, a narrow but busy thoroughfare whose pavements are chock-full of stacked bikes from a series of cycle shops. Other streets also group their commodities: ironmongery, wedding dresses, baby clothes and ceramics all have their separate enclaves. Off to the east, Via Divisi runs to **Piazza della Rivoluzione**, from where the 1848 uprising began, marked by an oddly elaborate fountain. From here, **Via Garibaldi** leads south, the route that Garibaldi took in May 1860 when he entered the city (he marched north, up Corso dei Mille and into Via Garibaldi). At Via Garibaldi 23, the immense, battered fifteenth-century **Palazzo Aiutamicristo** keeps bits of its original Catalan-Gothic structure.

North of Piazza della Rivoluzione, Via Aragona leads to Piazza Aragona, the first of a confusing jumble of squares. On the adjacent **Piazza Croce dei Vespri**, marked by a cross for the French who died in the 1282 Sicilian Vespers rebellion, stands the huge entrance to the **Palazzo Valguarnera Gangi**, where Visconti filmed the ballroom scene in *The Leopard*; you may be able to get a glimpse of the inside by smooth-talking the porter. East of Piazza Croce dei Vespri, towards Via Roma, Piazza Sant'Anna holds the church of Sant'Anna, whose attached, elegantly restored ex-convent now houses the city's **Galleria d'Arte Moderna** (Tues–Sun 9.30am–5.30pm; €7). There's some attractive work here, all Sicilian stuff from the nineteenth century onwards, best of which is the sculpture, including a small bronze study of an exhausted horse (by Enrico

Quattrociocchi) and Gerbino's sympathetic statuette of his greatcoated, heavily bearded father – though Michele Catti's autumnal scenes of Palermo are good, too. Watch out, as well, for the international touring exhibitions that often visit.

Along Corso Vittorio Emanuele: from Quattro Canti to the waterfront

A few steps up from Piazza Sant'Anna, Via Roma is intersected by **Corso Vittorio Emanuele**, stretching east towards the water. High narrow streets peel off to the left and right, mostly dark and forbidding. One, Via A. Paternostro, cuts away to the right to the thirteenth-century church of **San Francesco d'Assisi** (daily 8am–noon & 4–6pm), whose well-preserved portal, picked out with a zigzag decoration, is topped by a wonderful rose window – a harmonious design that is, for once, continued inside. All the Baroque trappings have been stripped away to reveal a pleasing stone interior, the later side chapels showing beautifully crafted arches – the fourth on the left is one of the earliest Renaissance works on the island, sculpted by Francesco Laurana in 1468. To the side of the church, at Via Immacolatella 5, the renowned **Oratorio di San Lorenzo** (Mon–Sat 9am–5pm; €2) contains another of Giácomo Serpotta's stuccoed masterpieces, intricately fashioned scenes from the lives of St Lawrence and St Francis.

Back on the main road, it's a straight run along the corso down to the water, with the old city harbour of **La Cala** to the left. This thumb-shaped inlet was once the main port of Palermo, stretching as far inland as Via Roma, but the harbour was in decline from the sixteenth century, when silting caused the water to recede to its current position. With all the heavy work transferred to new docks to the northwest, La Cala's present function as harbour to the few fishing-boats still working out of Palermo is now outweighed by its duty as marina for the yachts of the well-heeled. It's interesting to stroll around the maritime clutter at least once, and there are excellent views over to Monte Pellegrino in the distance. The little harbour is overlooked on one side by the church of **Santa Maria della Catena**, off Corso Vittorio Emanuele, named after the chain that used to close the harbour in the late fifteenth century. The corso ends at the Baroque **Porta Felice** gate, begun in 1582 as a counterbalance to the Porta Nuova, visible way to the southwest. From here, you can judge the extent of the late medieval city, which lay between the two gates.

Just before Porta Felice, make two quick rights onto Via Butera, then Piazzetta Niscemi, where you'll find the engaging **Museo delle Marionette** (Mon–Fri 9am–2pm & 3.30–6.30pm, Sat 9am–2pm; €5), Palermo's definitive collection of puppets and painted scenery. Puppet theatre is a traditional Sicilian entertainment and as well as the indigenous puppets, you'll see figures from Rajasthan, glittering dragons from Rangoon and full-frontal Korean nudes, together with the British Punch and Judy in their traditional booth. It's all great fun, and in summer the museum puts on **shows** (Spettácolo dei Pupi): tickets cost around €8 – check at the museum (☎091.328.060) or tourist office for times. There are also shows at a variety of other city theatres, for more on which, see the box on p.96.

Back on Via Butera, a little further down the street is **Palazzo Butera**, whose seventeenth-century facade faces out over the Foro Italico. Once the home of the Branciforte family, at one time the wealthiest family in Sicily, it was gradually partitioned and sold off, and is now only open for conferences or groups of visitors (call ☎091.611.0162 to arrange an appointment).

Numerous films have been shot here, including *The Talented Mr Ripley* and *The Godfather: Part III*.

The whole area beyond the Porta Felice was flattened in 1943, and has since been rebuilt as a fairly ugly promenade, the **Foro Italico** (also known as Foro Umberto I), complete with small amusement park, from where you can look back over the harbour to Monte Pellegrino. This is one of the liveliest places in the city on summer evenings, when the locals take to the street armed to the teeth with mobile phones and ice creams from one of the several *gelateria* palaces lined along here.

Piazza Marina and around

Double back through the gate and bear left into **Piazza Marina**, a large square that encloses the tropical **Giardino Garibaldi**, famed for its enormous banyan trees, laden with aerial roots. It's another popular venue for the city's elderly card-players, who gather around green baize tables at lunchtime for a game. Reclaimed from the sea in the tenth century, subsequently used for jousting tournaments and executions, and now surrounded by *palazzi* and pavement restaurants, every corner of the piazza is worth exploring. The second-largest of Palermo's palaces, the **Palazzo Chiaramonte**, flanks the east side of the square: dating from the fourteenth century, the palace was the home of the Inquisition from 1685 to 1782, before becoming the city's law courts – a function it only abandoned in 1972. Today, it is the administrative centre of the university and is open to the public for occasional art exhibitions only.

On the other side of Piazza Marina, the southwest corner is marked by the sixteenth-century church of **Santa Maria dei Mirácoli**, a lovely Renaissance structure. Just up from here, off the piazza, the narrow Vícolo della Neve all'Alloro holds the **Parco Culturale Giuseppe Tomasi di Lampedusa**, a cultural centre and wine bar with a small museum and bookshop dedicated to Lampedusa and his book *The Leopard*. The centre hosts concerts and readings, and runs two-hour **guided tours** of the area in Italian and English, focusing on places associated with the author, the book and the film (tours usually Wed 11am & Fri 5pm; ☏091.616.0796, ⓦwww.parcotomasi.it; €8). Even if you're not interested in Lampedusa, the centre makes a nice place to relax over a granita or a glass of red in its cobbled garden.

From Santa Maria dei Mirácoli, turn right off Via Lungarini to reach the **Palazzo Mirto** (daily 9am–7pm; €3) at Via Merlo 2, a late eighteenth-century building that's one of the few in the city to retain its original furniture and fixtures, thus giving a rare insight into *palazzo* life. Though nothing is labelled, it's worth going in for the exquisite ceilings, the intimacy of the Chinese Room, imposing *baldacchino* and the tapestries, still in good colour, in the Salone degli Arazzi. The second floor has the family's living quarters, consisting of smaller, though still richly furnished rooms, one displaying a collection of arms. You can also see the servants' kitchen (above the ticket office), a variety of carriages in the stables and an overblown Baroque fountain in the courtyard.

La Kalsa and the Galleria Regionale

Balarm, the immense city of beauty, the wondrous splendid sojourn, the world's vast metropolis, adorned in elegance… Balarm has buildings of such beauty that travellers come from afar for the well-known marvels of its architecture.

The "Balarm" in the laudatory above penned by al-Idrisi, court geographer to the Amir of Sicily, is of course Palermo, written at a time when **La Kalsa** (from the Arabic, *khalisa*, meaning "pure") was its cultural and intellectual heart. Planned and built by the Saracens, it is one of the oldest quarters in Palermo, brimming with history, though heavily bombed during World War II and now holding some of the poorest streets in the city. However, the area is showing some fruits of a gradual renovation, its centre grassed over and planted with trees to provide a welcome respite from the narrow confines of the surrounding streets and alleys. The programme of concerts, films, theatre and exhibitions of the summer Kals'Art festival, and at Lo Spasimo throughout the year (see p.95), has rejuvenated the area in the evenings, and on summer nights many of its historical buildings and monuments are open to the public, often with free tours (in English) guided by local students. Out of season, however, it's still an area where it pays to be cautious after dark.

The Galleria Regionale della Sicilia

For a daytime visual feast, the **Palazzo Abatellis**, Via Alloro 4, comes up trumps, a fifteenth-century building that still retains elements of its Catalan-Gothic and Renaissance origins, notably in its doorway and courtyard. Revamped since the war, it now houses the **Galleria Regionale della Sicilia** (daily 9am–1pm, Tues–Fri also 2.30–7pm; €6), with its excellent medieval art collection.

The **ground floor** contains sculpture, beginning with an intricately carved twelfth-century Arab doorframe that once adorned a Palermitan mansion. Beyond, room 4 holds works of the fifteenth-century sculptor **Francesco Laurana**: his white marble bust of *Eleonora d'Aragona* is a calm, perfectly studied portrait. Room 5 is devoted to the work of the Gagini clan, mostly statues of the Madonna, though Antonello Gagini is responsible for a rather strident *Archangel Michael*, with a distinct military manner. The only non-sculptural item is a magnificent fifteenth-century **fresco**, the *Triumph of Death*, by an unknown (possibly Flemish) painter. It's a chilling study, with Death cast as a skeletal archer astride a galloping, spindly horse, trampling bodies slain by his arrows. He rides towards a group of smug and wealthy citizens, apparently unconcerned at his approach; meanwhile, to the left, the sick and the old plead hopelessly for oblivion.

There are three further frescoes, this time thirteenth- and fourteenth-century Sicilian and rather crude, above the steps up to the **first floor**, which is devoted to painting. This section is unusually comprehensive, with no shortage of excellent Sicilian art, the earliest (thirteenth- to fourteenth-century) displaying marked Byzantine characteristics, including a fourteenth-century mosaic of the *Madonna and Child*, eyes and hands remarkably self-assured. Later fifteenth-century paintings and frescoes are all vivid and imaginative in their portrayal of the *Coronation of the Virgin*, a favourite theme. This floor also contains some notable highlights, not least a collection of works by the fifteenth-century Sicilian artist **Antonello da Messina**: three small, clever portraits of SS Gregory, Jerome and Augustine (with a rakish red hat); and an indisputably powerful *Annunciation*, a placid depiction of Mary, head and shoulders covered, right hand slightly raised in acknowledgement of the (off-picture) Archangel Gabriel. There's a second view – looking down – of the *Triumph of Death*, and some important Flemish works, too, such as a **Mabuse** triptych of the *Virgin and Child*, crammed with detail and surrounded by some extraordinarily ugly cherubs.

From La Gancia to La Magione

There's more work by the Gagini family (sculpted fragments and reliefs) in the fifteenth-century church of **La Gancia** – or Santa Maria degli Angeli – next door to the gallery on Via Alloro (Mon–Sat 9.30am–noon & 3–6pm, Sun 10am–12.30pm). The interior is covered in understated marble decoration and sports a ceiling of brown stars. From here, Via Alloro runs southwest, past a succession of ailing *palazzi*, towards Piazza Croce dei Vespri and Via Roma. Turning left off this axis of the Kalsa district, you'll come to a grassy open park popular with Palermo's young in the evenings: it's safe and well-lit and makes a good spot to sit down with a bottle of wine. To the southeast of the park, past Via della Vetriera (where the assassinated anti-Mafia judge Paolo Borsellino was born and bred), lies the former church and convent of Lo Spasimo, on Via dello Spasimo. The church itself, **Santa Maria dello Spasimo** (Mon–Sat 8am–8pm, Sun 9am–8pm), now roofless except for the Gothic apse, was variously used as a theatre, barracks, plague hospital and rubbish tip, and is now a popular concert venue, known Lo Spasimo (see p.95). Its most famous painting, *Lo Spasimo di Sicilia*, painted by Raphael and installed here in 1520, is now on show in the Prado in Madrid. To the side of the church is a small building (ask an attendant for the key if it's locked) which houses a large model of Palermo in wooden bricks; the garden above and beyond it on the bastions is a useful spot for listening in to concerts if the nave is full.

In the southern corner of the park, standing in isolation on Piazza Magione, the lovely church of **La Magione** (Mon–Sat 9.30am–7pm, Sun 9am–1.30pm; donation) is approached through a pretty palm-lined drive and garden. A fine example of Arab-Norman architecture, it was originally built in 1151 for the Cistercians, but given to the Teutonic knights as their headquarters by Henry VI in 1197. Its real treasures are housed in the **cloister** and adjacent corridor. The cloister itself was built in a similar style to the cathedral at Monreale, and houses a rare Judaic tombstone re-carved into a basin for holy water. In the room between the cloister and the chapel, there's a well-maintained fresco of the crucifixion which originally hung at the altar of the chapel, though far more interesting and rare is a plaster preparation of the fresco, opposite. The only example of a fresco model in Sicily, its near-mathematical sketch lines show the care and detailed planning that went into the creation of such works. Alongside, supporting two small stone arches, a small Arab-Norman column is carved with a Koranic inscription in Kufic Arabic, a first-millennium angular script used for inscribing on hard surfaces and extant throughout much early Islamic art. Several before-and-after photographs on the wall opposite the column show the facade of the church before it was restored to its original Arab-Norman design at the beginning of the 1900s.

Villa Giulia

A few minutes' walk from the piazza along Via Lincoln is Palermo's best central park, **Villa Giulia**, an eighteenth-century garden that provides a welcome escape from the traffic. Attractions include aromatic gardens, a children's train, bandstand, deer and ducks. There's also a botanical garden, the **Orto Botánico** (daily 9am–6pm; €4), next door to the park, which dates from 1795 and features tropical plants from all over the world – not a bad place to finish a tour of the city.

La Vucciria, San Domenico and around

North of Corso Vittorio Emanuele and east of Via Roma, one of Palermo's oldest and busiest markets, **La Vucciria**, is said to be named after the French *boucherie*, for butcher's shop. Winding streets radiate from a small enclosed piazza, wet from the ice and waste of the groaning fish stalls – swordfish heads stuck to

Shopping in Palermo

Palermo has western Sicily's widest array of shops, stores and boutiques for every pocket and taste. In the old city, especially, it sometimes seems as if the whole city is one big market.

Apart from the stalls of Capo, Vucciria and Ballarò markets, where a range of household items are on offer alongside the fruit and veg, the old city has several flea markets (*mercati delle pulci*) – with the occasional antique lurking amid the knick-knacks and curios – notably on Piazza Peranni (see p.76) and the Alberghería's Piazza San Francesco Saverio (on Sunday). You're more likely to find jewellery, watches – often convincing copies of branded products – and "designer" clothing on Via Sant'Agostino and the back streets of the Capo quarter.

Examples of Sicilian puppets and ceramics of varying quality are retailed along Corso Vittorio Emanuele, Via Divisi and around Piazza Marina, or, in the new city, around Piazza Castelnuovo and Via Libertà. You'll also find model Sicilian carts in abundance in all these areas – a typical, if rather corny, souvenir. If it's Frutta di Martorana you're after, look in the *pasticcerie* listed on p.91 – these are sold by weight, and do not need to be kept chilled. More upmarket boutiques are scattered along Via Roma and Via Ruggero Settimo, and on and around Via Libertà.

For everyday goods, including good-quality clothes at reasonable prices, there are supermarkets aplenty; one of the best chains is Oviesse, which has branches on Via Libertà (on the corner with Via Siracusa) and at Via Marco Polo 12 (northwest of the Palazzo di Giustizia), both open until 8pm including some Sundays. For food, the ubiquitous SISA, CRAI and GS supermarkets are perfectly adequate, though with considerably higher prices than the street markets; there's a GS on Piazza Marina, again open until 8pm.

marble slabs and huge sides of tuna from which fishmongers carve bloody steaks. There are a couple of excellent little trattorias tucked away in the alleys (best at lunchtime), some very basic bars where the wine comes straight from the barrel, and all manner of food (fresh octopus, for example) and junk on sale. This is also *the* place to buy porcelain pasta bowls, espresso cups and coffee-makers. Other than early morning, when the action is at its most frenzied, lunchtime is a good time for a wander, when the stallholders take a break for card-playing sessions conducted around packing cases, or simply fall asleep amongst their produce.

The northern limit of the market is marked by **San Domenico** (Tues–Fri 9am–11.30pm, Sat & Sun 5–7pm), a large church set back off Via Roma and fronted by a statue-topped marble column. The fine eighteenth-century facade, with its double pillars and slim towers, is lit at night to great effect, while inside a series of tombs contains a horde of famous Sicilians. Parliamentarians, poets and painters, they're of little interest to foreigners except to shed some light on Palermitan street-naming. The adjacent, slender-columned **cloister** is worth a quick whirl (Tues–Sat 9am–1pm), a section of it holding the **Museo del Risorgimento** (Mon, Wed & Fri 9am–1pm; free), dedicated to the nineteenth-century Italian anti-Bourbon revolt.

More worthwhile, however, is to head behind the San Domenico church along Via dei Bambinai to the **Oratorio del Rosario di San Domenico** (Mon–Sat 9am–1pm), one of many such small chapels in the old part of the city which contain the best of Palermo's Baroque decoration. This sixteenth-century oratory, built and still maintained by the Knights of Malta, was adorned by the acknowledged master of the art of stucco sculpture, **Giácomo Serpotta**, who lined the walls with allegorical figures. Born in Palermo in 1656, Serpotta devoted his entire life to decorating oratories like this, a tradition continued by his son, Procopio (some of whose work can also be seen in the Oratorio di Santa Caterina behind the main post office). Here, the figures of *Justice*, *Strength* and suchlike (resembling fashionable society ladies, who often served as models) are crowned by an accomplished and well-lit altarpiece by Van Dyck.

You'll find more stucco splendour further up Via Bambinai, behind the late sixteenth-century church of **Santa Zita** (or Santa Cita) on quiet Via Squarcialupo (Mon–Fri 9am–1pm & 3–5.30pm, Sat 9am–1pm) – the church itself was badly bomb-damaged during World War II, later restored, and reveals inside some flamboyant polychrome marbling and good sculpture by Antonello Gagini. Behind Santa Zita on Via Valverde, the marvellous **Oratorio del Rosario di Santa Zita** (Mon–Fri 9am–1pm & 2–7pm, Sat 9am–1pm) contains some of the wildest flights of Giácomo Serpotta's rococo imagination – a dazzling confusion of allegorical figures, bare-breasted women, scenes from the New Testament, putti galore, and, at the centre of it all, a rendering of the Battle of Lepanto. It's worth taking time to absorb the details of this tumultuous landscape, especially the loving care with which he depicted individual figures – the old men and women, melancholy boys perched on the ledge – and notice Serpotta's symbol on the left wall: the golden snake.

Via Squarcialupo continues down to **Piazza XIII Víttime**, where five tall V-shaped steel plates splinter out of the ground, commemorating the officials who lost their lives in Palermo's enduring struggle with the Mafia. It replaces a monument commemorating thirteen Palermitani shot by the Bourbons in the 1860 revolt, which now lies along Via Cavour. The whole of the area around is rather forlorn: to the south, the shored-up buildings just back from the water have ground floors given over to car repair workshops, the rooms open to the road and stuffed full of every kind of vehicular wreckage.

Continuing instead west along Via Valverde from Santa Zita, you'll end up back on Via Roma, and opposite Palermo's main post office, the gargantuan **Palazzo delle Poste**. Built by the Fascists in 1933, it's an oblong concrete block, with a wide swath of steps spreading up to a colonnade of ten unfluted columns that run the length and height of the building itself. The pink-coloured paint on the walls has somewhat softened the severe effect, especially at night when floodlights impart a rosy glow. But the empty pretension of the post office is put to shame by what hides behind it, around the corner in Piazza Olivella. Here, the church of **Sant'Ignazio all'Olivella** (Mon, Tues & Sun 9–10am, Thurs–Sat 9–10am & 5–6pm) displays an opulent Baroque touch in its great chandeliers, rich side chapels and paintings by Pietro Novelli; next door, the cloisters and surviving buildings of a sixteenth-century convent – once the property of the church – now house the city's excellent archeological museum.

Museo Archeológico Regionale

If you've been touring the best of western Sicily's ancient sites (or are intending to do so), the **Museo Archeológico Regionale** (Mon, Sat & Sun 8.30am–1.15pm, Tues–Fri 8.30am–1.15pm & 3–6.15pm; €6) is a must, gathering together artefacts found at all the major Neolithic, Carthaginian, Greek and Roman settlements in a magnificent collection that culminates with items from the site at Selinunte. The exhibits are displayed on two main floors, together with a top floor that is usually roped off, but can be visited in the company of a museum attendant. The main exhibits in the collection are labelled in English, and you can pick up a free illustrated booklet on them, also in English, on the way in.

The entrance to the **ground floor** is through the smaller of two cloisters, which displays anchors and other retrieved hardware from the sea off the Sicilian coast. There are **Egyptian and Punic** remains in rooms to either side, and beyond, the larger, thickly planted cloister is devoted to **Roman** sculpture, notably a giant Emperor Claudius on the left, enthroned in the style of Zeus. Rooms at the far end contain numerous early Greek carved stelae and assorted inscribed tablets (including one from Roman Taormina recording expenses charged by the town's magistrates).

Beyond here, the material is almost entirely **Greek**, beginning with the assembled stone **lion's-head water-spouts** from the fifth-century-BC Victory Temple at Himera – the fierce animal faces tempered by braided fur and a grooved tongue that channelled the water – and leading on to the high spot of the museum, the adjacent **Sala di Selinunte**. This gathers together the rich **stone carvings** (or metopes) from the various temples (known only as Temples A–G) at Selinunte on the southwest coast – a vital stop if you intend to visit the site itself; the sculpted panels from the friezes that adorned the temples are appealing works of art, depicting lively mythological scenes. The earliest and least impressive, single panels from the early sixth century BC, sit under the windows on the right and represent the gods of Delphi, the Sphinx, the rape of Europa, and Hercules and the Bull. The reconstructed friezes opposite, from Temples C and (more fragmentary) F, are more eye-catching: vivid works from the fifth century BC, like Perseus beheading Medusa with a short sword, his legs in profile but his head and torso facing directly out in archaic style. The most technically advanced tableaux are those in the frieze at the end of the room from Temple E, portraying a lithe Hercules fighting an Amazon, the marriage of Zeus and Hera, Actaeon savaged by three ferocious dogs, and Athena and the Titan. There's additional interest in the female heads, three on either side of the door, also taken from Temple E. The remaining rooms on the ground floor deal with mainly **Etruscan** funerary art, the most notable exhibits being several third- to second-century BC sarcophagi painted with graphic battle scenes.

You have to retrace your steps to the small cloister for the stairs up to the **first floor**, which also has plenty of interest: lead water pipes with stopcock retrieved from a site at Términi Imerese, some 12,000 votive terracotta figures, and a few delicately carved stone heads found at Solunto. There's more Greek sculpture (including a fragment of the frieze from the Parthenon) and a reconstructed Roman mosaic pavement as well. Worth a look are the Punic aedicules (mini-temples), from Lilybaeum (modern Marsala) gaily depicting funerary banquets, and a bronze fourth-century warrior's body armour and helmet from Greece. But pick of the lot here are two rich **bronze sculptures** – the naturalistic figure of an alert and genial ram (third century BC) from Siracusa, once one of a pair (the other was destroyed in the 1848 revolution), and a glistening, muscular study of Hercules subduing a stag, found near Pompeii.

The **second floor** holds a range of Neolithic items, including casts of the incised drawings from Addaura, on Monte Pellegrino, and Lévanzo, shelves full of Greek and Etruscan amphorae, and frescoes from Solunto. But the most impressive sight on this floor is the room full of beautifully preserved Roman mosaics – the largest of which measures nearly 10m in length – excavated from

Piazza della Vittória in Palermo: one, from the second century AD, depicts the triumph of Neptune; another, from the third century AD, shows Orpheus with a lyre, surrounded by amenable beasts.

Along Via Maqueda and Viale della Libertà: the modern city

It's a short walk west from the Museo Archeológico to **Via Maqueda**, which assumes an increasingly modern aspect as it progresses north from Quattro Canti. Barring the bustle of activity around **Via Candelai** – a busy shopping street by day, a hubbub of cafés at night – the interesting medieval alleys are gradually replaced by the wider and more nondescript streets around Piazza Verdi, site of the late nineteenth-century **Teatro Mássimo**. It's a monumental structure, all dome and columns, supposedly the largest theatre in Italy and originally envisaged as an emblem of the new Sicily, a monument to rival Europe's great opera houses in Paris and Vienna. Its construction was entrusted to Giovanni Battista Basile, whose strictly Neoclassical design was possibly influenced by Charles Garnier's contemporary plans for the Paris Opéra, and the first stone was laid in 1876. The architect did not live to see the end of the project, however, and the work was finished by his son, Ernesto Basile. After its inauguration, the opera house became the focus of high society, and saw an illustrious procession of musical performers grace its vast auditorium, with productions by the director (now senator) Franco Zeffirelli in the 1950s ranking among its greatest moments. Francis Ford Coppola shot the long climactic opera scene of *The Godfather: Part III* here, using the theatre's sweep of steps to great effect. You don't have to attend a performance to appreciate its majestic, heavily gilded interior, as **tours** with an English-speaking guide take place throughout the year (Tues–Sun 10am–3pm, every 30min; €5) except during rehearsals. There's an abundance of pink marble, rich reds, blues and golds in the echoing Sala Pompeiana where the nobility once foregathered and, in the auditorium, a domed ceiling, constructed in the shape of a flower head, which lifts its petals to the skies when things get too hot.

The theatre marks the dividing line between old and new Palermo. Beyond here there's little that's vital, though plenty that is grand and modern. Via Maqueda becomes **Via Ruggero Séttimo**, which cuts through gridded shopping streets and passes the enclosed Piazza Ungheria on its way to the huge double square that characterizes modern Palermo – known as **Piazza Politeama**, it's made up of Piazza Castelnuovo to the left and Piazza Ruggero Séttimo to the right. Dominating the whole lot is Palermo's other massive theatre, the late nineteenth-century **Politeama Garibaldi**, built in overblown Pompeiian style and topped by a bronze chariot pulled by four horses.

Along Viale della Libertà

Many of the city buses stop in Piazza Politeama, and you might want to hop on one if you're heading any further north, along the wide **Viale della Libertà**, as it's about 1km to the modern city's other attractions.

At Viale della Libertà 52, the **Museo Mormino** (Mon–Fri 9am–1pm & 3–5pm, Sat 9am–1pm; €4) houses a beautifully presented collection of artefacts and paintings in the sumptuous Banco di Sicilia building. On the **first floor**, there's a wide representation of colourful Italian majolica from the fifteenth to the eighteenth centuries, and an extensive collection of Greek vases. Look out, as you enter the gallery, for the splendid small Etruscan mirror with a relief of Silenus, and the third-century BC terracotta statue of a young boy in case B.

There are also maps and coins aplenty, but you'll probably get more from the horde of attractive nineteenth-century paintings in the second-floor rooms, including seascapes and tuna fishing as portrayed by Antonino Leto, and the charming paintings of women by Ettore de Maria Bergler.

From here, you're close to the **Giardino Inglese**, one of the city's few parks, though actually not much more than a palm-planted garden. For real expanses of parkland you'll have to take the bus a couple of kilometres further north to the Parco della Favorita.

A couple of blocks east of the Giardino Inglese is Palermo's notorious **Ucciardone prison**, connected by an underground passageway to the maximum-security bunker where the much-publicized *maxi processi* (maxi-trials) of Mafia suspects were held in the 1980s. The gloomy Bourbon prison has been called "the best-informed centre in Italy for gossip and intelligence about the operations of organized crime throughout the world", not least because it's been home to a good percentage of the biggest names in the Italian underworld. Supposedly, Mafia affairs were conducted here almost undisturbed, by bosses whose food was brought in from Palermo's best restaurants and who collaborated with the warders to ensure that escapes didn't happen – something that might increase security arrangements and hamper their activities. However, following the murders of Mafia investigators Falcone and Borsellino in 1992, many of the highest-risk inmates have been transferred to more isolated prisons in different parts of the country.

East to the water

On the east side of the prison, Via Cristóforo Colombo runs down to the water, past a selection of neglected Baroque *palazzi*, to the seventeenth-century **Arsenale** (closed to the public). The exterior – erected by Mariano Smirighio

La Festa di Santa Rosalia

An ebullient blend of devotion and revelry, Palermo's annual jamboree, La Festa di Santa Rosalia – "U Fistinu" in dialect – takes place during the second week of July, in honour of the city's patron saint. Next to nothing is known for sure about Rosalia, who was probably a member of the Norman court in the twelfth century, except that at some point she rejected her wealthy background and lived as a hermit, first on Monte Quisquina, then on Monte Pellegrino, outside the city. Since then, according to reports, she has manifested herself on several occasions, notably in 1624 and 1625, when she halted the plague that was then ravaging Palermo. By this act "La Santuzza" came to symbolize the city's inexhaustible capacity for self-renewal, though perhaps more important is her role as a unifying force in this complex and multi-faceted place. For locals, U Fistinu is the central event of the year; for tourists, it's an uproarious party, perhaps the most exhilarating you'll see anywhere in Italy.

The annual ritual includes both solemn processions and gaudy entertainments, with the passionate and vociferous participation of hundreds of thousands of Palermitani. The central event is a long parade through the centre of town, from the Palazzo dei Normanni along the old Cassaro (now Corso Vittorio Emanuele) to the seafront, headed by a candle-lit statue of the saint borne aloft on the "Carro Trionfale". Other attractions include puppet re-enactments of the saint's miracles, concerts, exhibitions, and a gastronomic feast on Foro Italico, where heaps of food are displayed and consumed – most famously, snails, nuts, watermelons and *dolci*. The celebrations culminate in a spectacular display of fireworks over the harbour. Note that accommodation should be booked well in advance if you're thinking of visiting Palermo during the Festa.

– is worth a look, if you fancy the stroll. To the north of here, 1km or so away, is the fairly attractive but foul-smelling port of **ACQUASANTA**, overlooking which is Ernesto Basile's **Villa Igiea**, an Art Nouveau building erected in 1899 for the wealthy Florio family. It's now a luxury hotel (see p.68), though if you have a drink in the bar you can poke around inside a little – the dining room, in particular, is a fantastic creation. Buses #721 and #731 from Piazza Crispi (near the Giardino Inglese and Ucciardone prison, and reachable on #101 from the train station or Piazza Politeama) run out as far as the villa.

Out from the centre

There are several targets beyond the old centre, on the outskirts of the modern city, that warrant investigation. Some, like the **ethnographic museum**, are of general interest; others have a low-key allure for fans of the **Norman** period; while one, the **Cappuccini monastery**, is decidedly ghoulish, and for the strong of stomach only.

The Parco della Favorita and Museo Etnográfico Pitrè

To the **north** of Palermo, around 3km from Piazza Castelnuovo, lies the city's grandest park, the **Parco della Favorita**: a long, wooded expanse at the foot of Monte Pellegrino, with sports grounds and stadiums at one end, and formal gardens laid out a couple of kilometres beyond. The grounds were originally bought in 1799 by the Bourbon king Ferdinand, during his exile from Naples, and for three years he lived here in the **Palazzina Cinese** (closed to the public), a small Chinese-style pavilion. This is just inside the main entrance, beyond Piazza Niscemi; to get here take bus #101 from the train station to the Stadio Partanna, where you change to the #614 or #645.

Next door is the **Museo Etnográfico Pitrè** (Tues–Sat 7.30am–7.30pm, Sun 7.30am–1pm; €5), which contains a wide-ranging exhibition on Sicilian folklore and culture, including the twin emblems of Sicilian folklore, puppets and brightly painted carts (*carretti*). In the past, people's status was judged by the skill and extent of the decorations on their carts, which could be any two-wheeled vehicles, ranging from barrows to horse-drawn wagons. Every available inch – sometimes including the spokes and undercarriage – was covered with intricate patterns and chivalrous historical scenes from the story of the Paladins. But no less fascinating are the less well-known aspects of Sicilian handicrafts and cultural life: a series of intricately sculpted and painted terracotta figures, ceramic holy-water stoupes; wooden *ex voto* (votive) tablets depicting the often gruesome death of the dedicatee; and sundry dolls, games, tapestries, tools, painted masks and costumes – particularly the nineteenth-century lace dresses. In a separate section, there's a well-lit display of *presepe* (nativity scenes); even non-admirers of this genre should appreciate the perky camels and dramatic killing of the innocents, and the vaulted room makes a great acoustic for the accompanying sound system. Note that the museum is currently being renovated, with the collection temporarily transferred to Palazzo Tarallo near Stazione Centrale, with entrances at Via delle Pérgole 74 and Via Chiáppara al Cármine 81, off Via Maqueda. Ask at the tourist office or call ☎091.617.7004 to check the exhibition's whereabouts and opening details.

Other remnants of Norman Palermo

Palermo's best Norman buildings are, with a couple of exceptions, in and around the old-town area of the city. But to be thorough in tracking down the rest of the Norman relics you'll have to poke around the **southern** and **western** outskirts – built-up areas that were once rolling parkland owned by successive kings.

La Zisa, La Cuba and La Cúbula

Bus #124 runs west from Piazza Sturzo and the Politeama to **La Zisa** (daily 9am–7pm; €4.50) – from the Arabic *al-aziz* or "magnificent" – a towering palace begun by William I in 1160, and later finished by his son William II. Built as a king's retreat along North African lines, La Zisa was at one time stocked with beautiful planned gardens and rare and exotic beasts. Apparently, a raid on the palace by disaffected locals in 1161 released some of the wild animals, something that probably came as a bit of a shock to William's neighbours.

Having languished for centuries within a great private estate, La Zisa is besieged by modern apartment blocks today, but has been thoughtfully restored to something approaching its former glory, fronted by an expanse of park planted with young trees. The building's centrepiece is the **Sala della Fontana**, comprising an elaborate fountain in a marble-sided chamber with glittering mosaic decoration. The incongruous frescoes and Corinthian columns were added later, as were those in the second-floor **Sala Centrale**. There are more Islamic mosaic designs within – appropriate surroundings for the modest collection of **Islamic art** and artefacts displayed here, mostly inscribed copper bowls from periods much later than when La Zisa was constructed, and from different parts of the Mediterranean. The latticed windows afford impressive views over the surrounding greenery.

To the south, about 1km beyond the Porta Nuova, at Corso Calatafimi 100 (opposite Via Quarto dei Mille), **La Cuba** is the remains of a slightly later Norman pavilion that formed part of the same royal park. Later occupied by a Bourbon cavalry unit, the shell still lies within a barracks, though it has a separate entrance (daily 9am–7pm, closes 11pm Thurs, Fri & Sat in summer; €2). Frankly, there's not a great deal to see: some blind arcading on the outside, an Arabic inscription, and the traces of a water gate, which would have been used when the royal pavilion stood in the middle of an artificial lake. A room to one side holds a good model showing how the palace must once have appeared, as well as the inscription that supplied the date of the building's foundation (1180), and there's a multimedia exhibition explaining its history and construction. You might catch a glimpse from the street, or from the #105, #309, #339 or #389 buses which run past it and continue up the corso to **La Cúbula** (on the right, at the end of Via Aurelio Zancla, between nos. 443 and 459 on the main road). This domed kiosk, once a summerhouse in the extensive grounds of La Zisa, now looks rather uncomfortable in the midst of the twentieth-century architecture that dwarfs it on all sides.

San Giovanni dei Lebbrosi and the Ponte dell'Ammiraglio

Around 1.5km southeast of Stazione Centrale is the well-restored domed church of **San Giovanni dei Lebbrosi** (Mon–Sat 9–11am & 4–6pm), reachable on buses #226, #227 or #231 from the northern end of Corso dei Mille. Just off the corso, at Via Cappello 38, this is one of the oldest Norman churches in Sicily, reputedly founded in 1070 by Roger I. The belltower was added in 1934. The church's name (St John of the Lepers) derives from a building nearby, which was once a leprosy hospital.

Back down the corso, the route Garibaldi and his "Thousand" (hence Corso dei Mille) took into the city in 1860, you reach the stranded **Ponte dell'Ammiraglio**, accessible on the same bus as San Giovanni. Built in 1113 by George of Antioch, founder of La Martorana, this slender bridge once straddled the River Oreto, though the water has since been diverted and it's now surrounded by a little garden. On the night of May 27, 1860, it figured as a brief stand of the Bourbon troops as Garibaldi marched into Palermo. If you don't want to make the trek out specifically to see it, the bridge is visible from the train to Cefalù/Messina.

The Chiesa dei Vespri

Last of the Norman attractions is the cemetery-surrounded church of **Chiesa dei Vespri** (daily 8am–2pm), also known as Santo Spírito. It's to the west of San Giovanni – take bus #246 from the station to the Cimitero Sant'Orsola. Founded in 1173, the church has been restored to its original, rather severe state. The **massacre of the Sicilian Vespers** began here in 1282, ostensibly sparked off when a French officer insulted a bride on her way to church. The ringing of the vesper (evensong) bell was the signal to drive the French out of Sicily; most were eventually slaughtered by the oppressed islanders.

The Convento dei Cappuccini

Of all the attractions on the edge of Palermo, the **Convento dei Cappuccini** (daily 9am–noon & 3–5pm; €1.50) is the most intriguing, reachable by taking bus #327 (or walking) from Piazza Indipendenza to Via Pindemonte, and following signposts for a couple of hundred metres. For several hundred years this monastery retained its own burial ground, placing its dead in catacombs under the church. Later, responding to requests and bequests from rich laymen, many others began to be interred here, right up until 1881. The bodies (some 8000 of them) were preserved by various chemical and drying processes – including dehydration, the use of vinegar and arsenic baths, and treatment with quicklime – and then placed in niches along various corridors, dressed in the suit of clothes that they had previously provided for the purpose. The rough-cut stone corridors are divided according to sex and status, with different caverns reserved for men, women, the clergy, doctors, lawyers and surgeons. Suspended in individual niches and pinned with an identifying tag, the bodies are vile, contorted, grinning figures, some decomposed beyond recognition, others complete with skin, hair and eyes, fixing you with a steely stare. Those that aren't arranged along the walls lie in stacked glass coffins, and, to say the least, it's an unnerving experience to walk among them. Times change, though, as Patrick Brydone noted in his late eighteenth-century *A Tour Through Sicily and Malta*:

Here the people of Palermo pay daily visits to their deceased friends ... here they familiarize themselves with their future state, and chuse the company they would wish to keep in the other world. It is a common thing to make choice of their nich, and to try if their body fits it ... and sometimes, by way of a voluntary penance, they accustom themselves to stand for hours in these niches ...

Of all the skeletal bodies, saddest are the many remains of babies and young children, nothing more than spindly puppets. Follow the signs for the sealed-off cave that contains the coffin of two-year-old Rosalia Lombardo, who

▲ In the catacombs of the Convento dei Cappuccini

died in 1920. A new process, a series of injections, preserved her to the extent that she looks as though she's asleep. Perhaps fortunately, the doctor who invented the technique died before he could tell anyone how it was done.

Eating

You can eat well and cheaply in Palermo, either snacking in bars and at market stalls or sitting down in a score of good-value pizzerias and restaurants throughout the old town. Basic foodstuffs are particularly good here: snacks like *arancini*, pastries and ice cream, as well as more substantial pizzas are among the best you'll taste in Sicily, if not Italy. Fish is a feature on menus in more expensive trattorias and restaurants that advertise *cucina casalinga* or *cucina siciliana*; the local speciality is *pasta con le sarde*: macaroni with fresh sardines, fennel, raisins and pine kernels. It's worth noting that eating places tend to close early, especially in the central old town, where if you turn up at 10pm the waiters are likely to be packing up around you. For the most popular places, go before 8pm, or be prepared to wait in line.

Breakfast and snacks

Almost any bar or *pasticceria* is a good bet first thing in the morning, with breakfast pastries fresh from the bakeries. But for something more substantial, a quick lunch or an afternoon snack, head for one of the following places:

Bar Costa Via G. d'Annunzio 15 (off Viale della Libertà, north of Piazza Boccaccio). High-class *pasticceria* in the north of the modern city, which specializes in lemon crème.

Ferrara Piazza Giulio Césare 46. Just to the left as you exit the train station, this has a good range of fast-food snacks as well as complete lunches.

Franco U Vastiddaru Piazza Marina 1. Though you pay for the location here, the pizzas, salads, burgers and fries are quite decent. Stand up to eat or sit in the square.

Bar Mazzara Via Generale V. Magliocco 15 (corner of Piazza Ungheria). Lampedusa is supposed to have written parts of *The Leopard* in this smart snack bar/*pasticceria*. Ice cream and *arancini* also available, as is a great array of marzipan goodies.

Panineria da Pedro Via Trabia 35 (off Via Maqueda, just south of Teatro Mássimo). Good toasted sandwiches and filled rolls; pizza slices, too. Closed Mon.

Caffé San Domenico Piazza San Domenico. Outdoor tables close to the Vucciria market for your early-morning coffee and *cornetto;* serves full meals, too.

Pasticceria Scimone Via Imera 8 and Via V. Miceli 18b (both north of Via Mosca). Excellent *pasticceria* whose goodies can also be eaten at *Trattoria La Cambusa* (see p.93).

Bar Spinnato Via Príncipe di Belmonte 115. Classy *pasticceria* and bar with great ice cream. Pianist plays outdoors in summer.

Ice cream

One of the city's prime glories is its *gelaterie* (ice-cream shops), and you might want to follow local custom and experiment with a morning *brioche con gelato* (ice cream in a bun). You can buy ice cream just about anywhere, but Palermo has some classic shops and cafés – famed all over Italy – especially in the newer, northern part of the city. Some places are only open between April and September.

Da Ciccio Corso dei Mille 73. Round the corner from the train station, this tiny, inexpensive place is usually packed.

Ilardo Foro Italico I 12 (at the end of Via Alloro towards the water). The *Ilardo* has been in business for decades and is well known for its very good (and luridly coloured) ice cream. Open from 4pm till late evening. Closed Oct–May.

San Francesco Piazza San Francesco. Just to the side of the *Antica Focacceria San Francesco* (see p.92) and run by the same people, this is a good old-town place with tables in the square, open till 4am. Closed Oct–March.

Stancampiano Via Notarbartolo 51. Not very central – in the modern north of the city – but well known for its award-winning ice cream.

Food markets

Some of the best snacks are on sale in Palermo's markets, mostly traditional takeaway food – chopped boiled octopus (*purpu* in Sicilian), *arancini*, cooked artichokes, as well as bread, fruit and vegetables. In every market, you'll also find stalls selling *pani cu' la meuza* – bread rolls filled with sautéed beef spleen or tripe, which either come unadorned (*schiettu*, meaning "nubile") or topped with fresh ricotta and caciocavallo cheese (*maritatu*, "married").

The best-known market is at Vucciria, off Via Roma between Corso Vittorio Emanuele and the San Domenico church, but there's also food on sale at the Ballarò market in Piazza del Cármine and along Via Sant'Agostino. The Ballarò market, in particular, has a few very basic *hosterie* – wooden tables scattered around the market stalls – where you can accompany your snack with a beer or two.

Restaurants and pizzerias

There are several budget eateries around Stazione Centrale, not all of them the tourist traps you might expect. Other **restaurants** are scattered all over the city, and many excellent local places serving *cucina casalinga* are hidden in gloomy old-town streets. At the other end of the scale, Palermo also has several top-notch restaurants worth considering if you want to taste the very best Italian food, and although prices in these are high, they're usually less expensive than equivalents elsewhere in Italy. **Non-Italian food** is becoming more common in Palermo, though some places have a mediocre menu and a short life; we've listed the best options below. Finally, it's worth bearing in mind that some of Palermo's best restaurants are way **out of the centre**, known to locals for their classic Sicilian cookery but fairly inaccessible for most visitors. If you've got a car, or someone to drive you, try one of those listed below; always ring first to check opening times.

The old city

Al 59 Piazza Giuseppe Verdi 59 ℡091.583.139. Alfresco dining opposite the Teatro Mássimo, in a large, covered bamboo terrace with a central fountain in which turtles wallow. Pizzas are the main choice; there are just five pasta dishes (€8–10) and a handful of main courses (€10–12) available. Open late. Closed Wed. Inexpensive–moderate.

Les Amis Piazza Rivoluzione ℡091.616.6642. Slightly off the beaten track, this friendly trattoria is a good bet for such tasty dishes as *fettuccine alla Lampedusa* (with shrimps, swordfish and tomatoes). Pasta dishes are €7–8, pizzas around €5. Gluten-free options are also available. Closed Tues. Inexpensive–moderate.

🏃 **Antica Focacceria San Francesco** Via A. Paternostro 58. Splendid old-time pizzeria opposite the church of San Francesco, open since 1834, with marble-topped tables and floor, cast-iron surroundings and authentic Sicilian fast food, from fresh pizza slices (€3) to other oven-baked snacks. Closed Tues Oct–May. Inexpensive.

Bellini Piazza Bellini ℡091.616.5691. Housed at the back of the Teatro Bellini, with outdoor tables underneath La Martorana church, this is one of the city's more romantic locations, and – inevitably – touristy. Pizzas, including the Bellini, with buffalo mozzarella and creamed asparagus, are €4–6, and there are also pastas and fresh fish for mains. Book for the best tables outside or upstairs by the window; queues develop after 8pm. Closed Mon. Inexpensive–moderate.

Casa del Brodo Corso Vittorio Emanuele 175. In business for over a century, this place attracts both locals and tourists to its two small rooms. *Bolliti di manzo* and *lingua in salsa verde* are the meaty specialities. First courses are €5–8, mains €7–12, and there are also good tourist menus (€16 and €18), which include a selection of antipasti but not drinks. Moderate.

Al Covo de'i Beati Paoli Piazza Marina 50 ℡091.616.6634. One of several restaurants on this piazza with outdoor tables, this place has a cave-like interior and brisk service. The pizzas (€6–8) are good, though you may have to wait for one, especially on weekend evenings. Closed lunchtime. Moderate.

Meal prices

The restaurants listed are graded according to the following price categories:

Inexpensive: under €15   **Moderate**: €15–30
Expensive: €30–50   **Very expensive**: over €50

These prices reflect the per person cost of a full meal including wine and cover charge.

Dietro La Cattedrale Piazza Santíssimi 40 Mártiri ☎347.573.7431. Smartish place with outdoor tables in a quiet piazza, not far from the cathedral (if not exactly "behind" it, as the name implies). First courses cost €10, mains €12–14. The good list of risottos includes one with sausage and pistachio, and the *ravioli di cernia* (with grouper fish) are also recommended. Closed Tues. Moderate.

Il Garage Piazza Ecce Uomo ☎333.490.6356. A great little hole-in-the-wall trattoria in the Ballarò market, whose affable Tunisian owner cooks very good fish, lamb and – on Wed – couscous dishes. Also makes a great beer or wine stop. It's quite hard to find, but ask anyone in the vicinity for "Mario" and they'll direct you. Closed lunchtime. Inexpensive.

Da Mássimo Piazza Papireto 15 ☎091.601.4528. This neighbourhood trattoria sits a few short blocks behind the cathedral, with tables in the piazza. The menu is almost exclusively seafood, with a great speciality of *tagliatelle alla Mássimo*, a filling pesto dish with fresh clam and shrimp (€8). Good pizzas are also available. Closed Mon. Moderate.

Pizzeria Italia Via Orologio 54 (off Via Maqueda, just before Teatro Mássimo). One of the best pizzerias in central Palermo, it gets crowded and noisy. Try the superb "Palermitana", made with anchovies, breadcrumbs, pine nuts, cheese and olive oil, or tasty creations using classic Sicilian ingredients like aubergine, pork sausage, capers and olives. Eves only. Closed Mon. Inexpensive.

Trattoria Normanni Piazza della Vittória 25 ☎091.651.6011. Close to the Palazzo dei Normanni, this reliable place attracts both locals and tourists. The speciality, *spaghetti ai Normanni*, is a terrific concoction of shrimps, aubergines, fresh tomatoes and grated peanuts. Expect to pay €25–35 for a full meal. Arrive early or book to be sure of a table outside. Closed Sun. Moderate–expensive.

Trattoria Primavera Piazza Bologni 4 ☎091.329.408. Excellent neighbourhood trattoria with a little terrace in the square, serving genuine Sicilian food. Numerous antipasti, a long list of risottos and pasta dishes (around €7) – including delicious *bucatini con le sarde* – and fresh fish and meat (including homemade sausage) are served up to enthusiastic locals and tourists. Reservations advised on weekend evenings. Closed Mon & Sun evening. Moderate.

Al Santa Caterina Corso Vittorio Emanuele 256–258 ☎338.808.2388. You can eat on a balcony overlooking the corso at this first-floor restaurant housed in a sixteenth-century *palazzo*. There's an extensive menu (firsts €8–10, mains €8–12, pizzas €5–7) and canned music. Booking advised for the best tables. Closed Wed. Moderate.

Santandrea Piazza Sant'Andrea ☎091.334.999. Chic and popular restaurant, a stone's throw away from Piazza San Domenico and the Vucciria market from which most of the ingredients are obtained. Dishes are seasonal, generally delicious and excellent value, with pasta dishes at €8–10 and main courses €12–14. The *antipasto misto* and *anciova* (pasta with anchovies, garlic, pine kernels and raisins) are recommended. The desserts are also fantastic, and there's a good wine list. Book early if you want to sit outside. Closed Sun & one wk Aug. Moderate.

Trabia da Pedro Via Trabia 35. This quick stop off Via Maqueda is more of an adjunct to the fast-food/sandwich/takeaway joint next door than a restaurant, but still a useful spot for *forno a legna* pizzas, mixed salads and house wine. Open till around 11pm. Closed Mon. Inexpensive.

Trattoria La Cambusa Piazza Marina 16. Excellent old-town restaurant specializing in fish – try *bucatini con le sarde* (pasta with sardines) – and also serving *semifreddo* (ice cream with brittle almond topping). Pasta dishes cost €7–9. Closed Mon. Moderate.

Trattoria al Vicolo Piazza San Francesco Saverio ☎091.651.4032. In this small but smart neighbourhood trattoria in the Albergheria, you can sit under arches and beams inside or at tables in the square. Among the abundant pastas, try the home-made *busiati* or *anciova*, followed by stuffed squid. First and second courses cost around €7 each. Closed Mon. Moderate.

The modern city

Hostaria Al Duar 2 Via Ammiraglio Gravina 31 ☎091.843.0786. There's regular Italian food here, but the best bet is the superb-value *Completo*

Tunisino (€14): a huge pile of Tunisian food, which comes as several different courses and ends with couscous. Alternatively, there are fixed-price menus for €10–20. Closed Wed. Moderate.

La Traviata Piazza Olivella 18. Nestled in a quiet alleyway just steps from the Museo Archeológico, with some tables under a canopy outside, this trattoria serves good pasta dishes for around €7.50 and a big selection of pizzas (€5–7). Service can be brusque. Moderate.

Le Tre Sorelle Via Volturno 110 ℡091.585.960. Friendly trattoria, not far from the Teatro Mássimo, whose menu includes such dishes as *bucatini con le sarde* and *casarecce allo lido* (fresh pasta with swordfish and aubergine) for around €8 (main courses are €8–10). Indoors there are check tablecloths, posters and pictures, and there are some tables outside. Closed Sun. Moderate.

Trattoria a' Cuccagna Via Príncipe di Granatelli 21a ℡091.587.267. This long-established restaurant, whose walls are crammed with paintings, photos and local memorabilia, serves authentic Sicilian food, including *sgaloppine al marsala* and *involtini*. A three-course meal should cost €25–40 excluding drinks. Moderate–expensive.

Restaurants out of the centre

La Scuderia Viale del Fante 9 ℡091.520.323. Classic Sicilian and Italian cuisine at a restaurant near the stadium at La Favorita, with dining in the garden in summer. The food is terrific, including such specialities as *gallinella con pomodorini* (local fish with fresh tomatoes, €16). Advance reservations are advised. Closed Sun & two wks Aug. Expensive.

Trattoria da Turiddu Via Ugo La Malfa 9150 ℡091.679.0317. This fantastic fish restaurant is a long ride north of the centre by taxi – on the road to the airport, before Sferracavallo. But the trip is rewarded by a set meal (€25) that encompasses plate after plate of marvellous fish and seafood. Closed Mon. Moderate.

Drinking, nightlife and entertainment

After dark and over much of the city, Palermo's frenetic lifestyle stops, pedestrians flit quickly through the shadows, and the main roads are given over to speeding traffic and screaming police sirens. You may find the empty streets off-putting if you're on foot, but keeping to the main thoroughfares should minimize the possibility of problems. The city centre's few **bars** tend to close at around 9pm, though **birrerias** stay open later, and in summer life continues unabated until the small hours at the near by of **Mondello**. Palermo's newer parts, around Viale della Libertà, see more street-life, with an energetic *passeggiata* and cruising cars blasting away like mobile discotheques. If none of this is your scene, then there is more cultural **entertainment** to be had back in the city centre, where music, theatre and dance performances, and arts events, are staged. Along with the larger mainstream venues, there are a good number of bars and clubs which put on live music and entertainment.

To find out **what's on** in Palermo, check the listings in *Lapis* or the daily newspaper, *Il Giornale di Sicilia* (see p.65).

Bars and birrerias

Places to **drink** in – as opposed to a coffee stop – drift in and out of fashion, and you'll have to follow the crowds to find the current favourite. Many of them are in the northern quarters of the city, some of them a bus- or taxi-ride away, and the only central street geared up to evening drinks is the traffic-free **Via Príncipe di Belmonte**, which has a glitzy selection of bars and *pasticcerie*. Worth checking, though, are the innumerable – and sometimes grungy – bars along Via Candelai, a favourite haunt of students.

American Bar Grande Albergo Sole, 5th floor, Corso Vittorio Emanuele 291 (near the Quattro Canti). Stunning roof-terrace bar, from where you can gaze across the rooftops to the city's church domes and the mountains behind. Excellent place for a sunset drink and well worth the slightly inflated prices.

Caffè Letterario Malavoglia Piazzetta P. Speciale. This small, backstreet place near Corso Vittorio Emanuele is easily missed. It has sofas, books and occasional exhibitions and live music. Cheap drinks 6 – 9pm, and open until late.

Champagneria del Mássimo Via S. Spinuzza 59. Charming wine bar with outdoor seating near the Teatro Mássimo; along with its neighbouring bars, it makes a lively spot on summer nights, and stays open till late. Closed Sun.

La Corrida Piazza Olivella 9. One of a line of bars opposite the archeological museum, this late-opening place is good for a snack and a sit-down. Closed Mon.

Drunks Via Candelai 28. An aptly named rock-n-roll pub humming with the local university crowd. Bottled beers are €1.50, and there's a long list of strong cocktails: try the deadly Nelson – bourbon, vermouth and crema cacao – but not on an empty stomach. Open until 2am.

Kursaal Kalhesa Foro Italico 21. Set deep in the rock of the *foro*, this café and wine bar (*enoteca*) is furnished with traditional Sicilian furniture and has a huge fire in winter, with English and European newspapers to browse through. There's also live music (see below). Closed Sun eve & Mon.

Bar Malox Piazzetta della Canna. Hidden away off an old-town alley, this convivial bar, popular with students, has plenty of tables outside, where the drinking continues till late. Closed Mon & alternate Sun.

Bar Marcuso Via Príncipe di Belmonte 84. Beer, ice cream, granitas, pizza slices and a good-humoured atmosphere, with seats outside. Closed Sun.

The Navy Via Cala 46. The only place for a beer on the harbour. The decor is rather staid, though reminiscent of an English pub, with a nautical theme and British beers.

Parco Letterario Giuseppe Tomasi di Lampedusa Vícolo della Neve all'Alloro Ⓦwww.parcotomasi.it. Between Piazza Marina and Via Alloro, this cultural centre dedicated to the Sicilian author offers a large wine list, with antipasti, panini and good granita as well. A cool and quiet place to stop, afternoon or evening, with outdoor seating.

Al Qasar Piazza Marina 6. Small and quiet drinking spot with tables outside in summer.

La Taverna Piazza Ballarò. This tiny place for beers and wines gets incredibly busy, with the mostly student crowd spilling out across the road. It's open late and has low prices.

Villa Boscogrande Via Tommaso Natale 91. Way out in the northeast of the city, towards Sferracavallo, this *palazzo* was the setting for parts of Visconti's film of *The Leopard*; part of it now houses a smart and expensive bar. Bus #628 or #677 from Piazza de Gásperi.

Music

The Teatro Mássimo on Piazza Verdi (☎091.605.3111, Ⓦwww.teatromassimo .it) is the first choice for performances of **classical music** (Oct–June), ranging from opera and ballet to concerts and recitals; in summer it moves to the Teatro del Parco di Villa Castelnuovo,Viale del Fante 70b (☎091.605.3301), for concerts and outdoor performances of ballet and operetta. The central Teatro Politeama Garibaldi on Piazza Ruggero Séttimo (☎091.588.001) also puts on a pretty decent programme of concerts throughout the year. In the Kalsa district, **Lo Spasimo**, on Via dello Spasimo (☎091.616.1486), runs an excellent series of concerts, both classical and jazz, many of them free, while the **Kals'Art** festival (Ⓦwww.kalsart.it) is a huge cultural extravaganza of live music, theatre and cinema events that take place at a number of venues between mid-July and mid-September.

Other **jazz** venues include *Kursaal Kalhesa* (☎091.616.2282, Ⓦwww .kursaalkalhesa.it) at Foro Italico 21, which has gigs on Thursday nights from about 10pm. For **folk music** and dance performances, the Teatrino Ditirammu del Canto Popolare, Via Torremuzza 6 in La Kalsa (☎091.617.7865, Ⓦwww .teatrinoditirammu.it), is an intimate venue with seating for just 52.

There's no major venue for live **rock music**, and top British and American bands rarely make it further south than Naples, though the *Comune* regularly stages open-air rock events in the summer, usually in the Giardino Inglese and other green spaces – watch out for posters around the city for details.You can catch local acts in the places listed below.

Palermo's **clubs** are almost exclusively found in the new, northern section of the city, especially on and around Viale Regione Siciliana. They're mostly expensive discos, chock-full of fashion victims and – unless you're very keen – rarely worth the long journey out there. Still, for anyone determined to party in Palermo itself, a list of the better places appears below, but check posters and newspapers for the current popular venues. In summer, the scene switches to Mondello and Isola delle Femmine, while the beach at Capo Gallo, between Mondello and Sferracavallo (about 30min north of the city), is popular with student groups for ad hoc weekend parties until dawn. Note that for the discos, you may have to pay to "join" the club before they'll let you in.

Agricantus Via XX Settembre 82a ☏091.309.636, ⓦwww.agricantus.org. Arts centre near Giardino Inglese, with regular live music and dance alongside theatre productions and readings. Closed Mon.

Biergarten Viale Regione Siciliana 6469 ☏091.754.1070. Long-established venue for rock, punk and metal acts.

Caffè 442 Piazza Don Bosco 1 ☏091.549.431. Lounge bar near Viale Lazio and La Favorita, with nightly DJ sets and dancing to house music.

I Candelai Via Candelai 65 ☏091.327.151, ⓦwww .candelai.it. Live rock and DJ sets on Fri & Sat.

Kursaal Tonnara Via Bordonaro 9, Vergine Maria ☏091.637.2267, ⓦwww.kursaaltonnara.it. Range of live music in this old tuna warehouse on the beach north of town (bus #139 from Stazione Centrale), with bars, restaurants and an outdoor stage.

Zsa Zsa Mon Amour Via Angelitti 32 ☏091.681.7516, ⓦwww.zsazsamonamour.com. Live rock, metal and funk bands. It's west of Stazione Notarbártolo, off Piazza Campolo. Closed July–Sept.

Theatre and cinema

Palermo and its surroundings have a stack of other **theatres**, worth checking out if you speak Italian; the season generally runs from November to May. Mainstream theatres include the Teatro Biondo, Via Teatro Biondo 11, off Via Roma (☏091.743.4311, ⓦwww.teatrobiondo.it), showing international and modern Italian plays, and Teatro Lelio, Via Furitano 5a (☏091.681.9122, ⓦwww.teatrolelio.it), which puts on its own productions as well as those by national drama companies. The Teatro Biondo also uses the stylish Teatro Bellini

Puppet theatre in Palermo

The best theatrical experience in Palermo is a visit to a puppet theatre. Based around French and Sicilian history and specifically the exploits of the hero Orlando (Roland), performances are rowdy affairs of battles and shouted dialect. The shows may be unashamedly touristy, but are no less entertaining for all that, and are often staged by backstreet puppet theatres run by the same families for generations. Many performances take place in outdoor venues. Look out for posters, and always confirm timings with the theatres listed below or at the tourist office.

Cuticchio Mimmo, Via Bara all'Olivella 95, close to the Museo Archeológico ☏091.323.400, ⓦwww.figlidartecuticchio.com.

Museo delle Marionette, Piazzetta Niscemi 5 ☏091.328.060, ⓦwww .museomarionettepalermo.it.

Teatro Argento, Via Pietro Novelli 1, near the Cathedral ☏091.611.3680 or 333.293.5028.

Teatro Carlo Magno, Via Collegio di Maria 17, behind the President Hotel at the port ☏091.814.6971, ⓦwww.mancusopupi.it.

Teatro Ippogrifo, Vicolo Ragusi 6, off Corso Vittorio Emanuele, not far from the Quattro Canti ☏091.329.194 or 333.897.9443.

▲ In the Museo delle Marionette, Palermo

in Piazza Bellini as a venue. The Teatro Franco Zappalà, at Via Autonomia Siciliana 123a (☏091.543.380), features traditional theatre productions in Sicilian dialect. For avant-garde theatre, there's the Teatro Libero, Salita Partanna 4, Piazza Marina (☏091.617.4040, ⓦwww.teatroliberopalermo.it).

Cinemas show the latest films dubbed into Italian – it's rare to find films in their original language with subtitles. The main central screens are right next to each other at Via Emerico Amari 160–166: ABC (☏091.329.246) and Imperia (☏091.611.3388).

Listings

Airlines All the following companies have desks at Falcone Borsellino airport; the addresses of city centre offices are given where these exist. Air Malta, c/o AST Travel, Via Trápani 1d ☏091.611.8452, ⓦwww.airmalta.com; AirOne ☏199.207.080, ⓦwww.flyairone.it; Alitalia ☏06.2222, ⓦwww.alitalia.com; Alpi Eagles ☏899.500.058, ⓦwww.alpieagles.com; British Airways ☏199.712.266, ⓦwww.britishairways.com; easyJet ☏899.678.990; Meridiana ☏892.928, ⓦwww.meridiana.it; Ryanair ☏899.678.910, ⓦwww.ryanair.com; Tunis Air, Piazza Castelnuovo 12 ☏091.611.1845, ⓦwww.tunisair.com.

American Express c/o Agenzia Ruggeri, Via Emerico Amari 38 ☏091.587.144 (Mon–Fri 9am–1pm & 4–7pm, Sat 9am–1pm).

Banks and exchange Banks are open Mon–Fri 8.30am–1pm; most branches also open for an hour in the afternoon, usually 2.45–3.45pm. There are banks on main streets throughout Palermo, as well as at the airport, Stazione Centrale and Stazione Maríttima. You can also exchange money at the main post office in Via Roma.

Bike rental Totò Cannatella, Via Papireto 14a ☏091.322.425, charges around €10 per day; you can also rent bikes from the *Kursaal Kalhesa* cultural centre at Foro Italico 21 ☏091.616.2828, and in Mondello (see p.100).

Bookshops There's a large selection of English books from Feltrinelli, Via Maqueda 395, close to the Teatro Mássimo (Mon–Sat 9.30am–8pm); from Mondadori, on the corner of Via Roma and Piazza

San Domenico (also open until 8pm); and Libreria Flaccovio, Via Ruggero Séttimo 37.

Bus companies See box, p.63.

Car rental Avis (Punta Raisi airport ☏091.591.684; Via Francesco Crispi 113–117 ☏091.586.940); Eurauto (for camper vans: Via Príncipe Paternò 119 ☏091.201.529); Europcar (airport ☏091.591.688); Hertz (airport ☏091.213.112; Via Messina 7e ☏091.323.439); Holiday Car Rental (airport ☏091.591.687; Via E. Amari 85a ☏091.325.155); Maggiore (airport ☏091.591.681; Stazione Maríttima ☏091.612.1415); Sicily By Car (airport ☏091.591.250; Via M. Stabile 6a ☏091.581.045).

Consulates UK, Via Cavour 117 ☏091.326.412 (Mon & Thurs 10am–noon); USA, Via Vaccarini 1 ☏091.305.857 (Mon & Fri 9am–12.30pm); Netherlands, Via E. Amari 8 ☏091.586.527 (Mon & Fri 10am–noon & 4–6pm); South Africa, Largo degli Abeti 16 ☏348.340.0219. Other major consulates are in Milan or Rome, including: Australia, Via Antonio Bosio, Rome ☏06.852.721; Eire, Piazza di Campitelli 3, Rome ☏06.697.9121; New Zealand, Via Zara 28, Rome ☏06.441.7171.

Emergency numbers Fire brigade ☏111; police ☏113; road accident ☏116; ambulance ☏118 or 091.666.5528.

Ferry and hydrofoil companies Grandi Navi Veloci, at the port at Calata Marinai d'Italia ☏091.587.404, ⊛www.gnv.it (for Civitavecchia – near Rome – Genoa and Tunis); Grimaldi, Via E. Amari 8 ☏091.611.4828, ⊛www.grimaldi-ferries .com (for Salerno and Tunis); Siremar, Via Francesco Crispi 118 ☏091.582.403, ⊛www .siremar.it (for Ústica); SNAV, Stazione Maríttima ☏091.601.4211, ⊛www.snav.it (for Civitavecchia and Naples); Tirrenia, at the port at Molo Vittorio Veneto ☏091.602.1111 (for Cágliari and Naples); Ústica Lines, Agenzia Pietro Barbaro, Via Príncipe di Belmonte 51 ☏091.333.333, or call ☏0923.22.200, ⊛www.usticalines.it (for Cefalù and the Aeolian Islands).

Hiking Club Alpino Italiano, Via Garzilli 59 ☏091.329.407, ⊛www.cai.it; Club Alpino Siciliano, Via A. Paternostro 43 ☏091.581.323, ⊛www.clubalpinosiciliano.it.

Hospital Ospedale Cívico, Via Carmelo Lazzaro (☏091.666.1111). For emergency first aid, see "Emergency numbers".

Internet Aboriginal Café, via S. Spinuzza 51 (daily 6pm–3am); Amstel Italia, Via Volturno 71 (daily 9am–9pm); Internet Point, Via Maqueda 179 (daily 10am–9pm); Internet@Point, Corso Vittorio Emanuele 304 (daily 9am–9pm); Ki Point, Via Ammiraglio Gravina 101b (Mon, Wed & Fri 9am–1pm & 3.30–7.30pm, Tues & Thurs 9am–7.30pm, Sat 9am–1pm); Kursaal Kalhesa, Foro Italico 21 (daily 11am–late).

Left luggage Stazione Centrale by track 8 (daily 7am–10pm; €4 for 5 hours, then €0.60 per hour); Stazione Maríttima (daily 7am–10pm; €2 for 12 hours).

Newspapers British, European and US newspapers and magazines are sold at kiosks at Stazione Centrale, Piazza Verdi and Piazza Castelnuovo, and at Kursaal Kalhesa, Foro Italico 21. Local listings are in the daily Giornale di Sicilia.

Parking Central, covered garages include: L'Oasi Verde, Corso Tukory 207, southwest of Stazione Centrale; Central Garage, Piazza Giulio Césare 43, in front of Stazione Centrale; Via Guardione 81, near Stazione Maríttima, behind Via Crispi; Via E. Amari 68, near Stazione Maríttima; Via Sammartino 24, town centre, off Via Dante. €10–18 per night to leave a car; usually less when arranged through your hotel.

Pharmacies All-night service at Lo Cascio, Via Roma 1; Di Naro, Via Roma 207; and Farmacia Inglese, Via Marina Stabile 177. Other chemists operate a rota system, with the address of the nearest open chemist posted on the door of each shop.

Post offices Main post office is in the Palazzo delle Poste at Via Roma 320 (Mon–Sat 8am–6.30pm), where there are poste restante (fermo posta) and money exchange counters.

Scooter rental Rent a Scooter, Via E. Amari 63 ☏091.336.804; Motorent, Via E. Amari 91 ☏091.602.3455; from €21 per day.

Tours City Sightseeing (☏091.589.429, ⊛www.palermo.city-sightseeing.it) operates a hop-on-hop-off open-top bus service around the sights with a multilingual commentary. Daily departures every 30–60min from Piazza Politeama; tickets on board (€20). CTG Angoli di Sicilia (☏091.652.6840, ⊛www.angolidisicilia.com) offers walking tours of the Albergheria quarter of Palermo; price negotiable.

Travel agents CTS, Via Garzilli 28g (off Via Dante, west of Piazza Castelnuovo) ☏091.332.209 (Mon–Fri 9am–1pm & 3.30–7pm, Sat 9am–1pm); Pietro Barbaro, Via Príncipe di Belmonte 51 ☏091.333.333 (Mon–Fri 9am–1pm & 4–7pm, Sat 9am–1pm).

Around Palermo

Any respite from Palermo's noise is welcome, and it's worth taking the time to get out of the city at least once. The easiest trips, to **Mondello** and **Monte Pellegrino**, can fill in a few spare hours whenever you like, though Palermitans tend to pack both destinations to the gills on summer Sundays. The other retreat, to the cathedral town of **Monreale**, demands more serious attention; you could see it in an afternoon, but consider a full day (and possibly a night) to get the most out of it and the surrounding valley. Less demanding is a jaunt west to the small family resorts that line the **Golfo di Carini**, a change in pace from the frenetic action at Mondello. Side-trips east, to **Bagheria** and **Solunto**, won't occupy more than half a day out from the city, and you could always see them as a stop on the route out of Palermo, along the Tyrrhenian coast. Travelling south from the capital, you can also make a stop at the Albanian settlement of **Piana degli Albanesi**, couched on an upland plain in thoroughly pleasant surroundings – the Easter celebrations here are justly renowned.

Bus and train services to all these places are good; details are given in the text and "Travel details", at the end of this chapter. For a real change of air, though, jump on a ferry or hydrofoil to the island of **Ústica**, as little as an hour and a quarter from the city. With its good, clean swimming and lazy feel, you may end up staying longer than planned.

Mondello

Regular buses run the 11km to **MONDELLO**, the most scenic route passing through Acquasanta and then skirting the coast below Monte Pellegrino as far as Valdesi. From here, a marvellous two-kilometre sandy **beach** curves round to the small resort, tucked under the mountain's northern bluff. The beach is the main attraction, though Mondello does have a tiny working harbour, a jetty from which you can try your luck fishing, and the remnants of a medieval tower. Come in the day and you can split your time nicely between the beach and **eating** on the seafront, a major occupation here. There's a line of trattorias – some with outdoor terraces – where the temptingly fresh fish is displayed in boxes. Or you can grab some excellent snack food from the waterfront stalls – *pasta con le sarde*, deep-fried vegetables, shrimps and whitebait – and then hit the **beach**. Here, you can rent parasols and loungers, and spend the afternoon windsurfing, diving or snorkelling, for which equipment is available at a number of outlets.

Summer **nights at Mondello** are fun, kicking off with the evening *passeggiata*. The bars in the main square, Piazza Mondello, are packed, the roads around blocked with cruising cars full of the local youth, and open-air discos add a bit of excitement. In winter it's more laid-back and rarely busy, but the restaurants and snack stalls are still open and it usually stays warm enough to swim until well past the end of the season.

Practicalities

From Piazza Sturzo or Viale della Libertà, buses #806 and #833 head to **Mondello**, a half-hour ride through the city's northwestern suburbs; the last

#806 back leaves 11.30pm–midnight, and the last #833 at 7–8pm. There's also a special "GT" summer coach service (mid-June to mid-Sept) plying between Piazza Sturzo and Mondello for which tickets (bought on board) cost €1.50; the last coach back leaves at 6.30pm. A taxi from or back to the centre costs about €35. Driving to Mondello, exit at the Tommaso Natale junction from the main road. There's a kiosk in the central piazza in summer, with scraps of **tourist information** to hand out (open daily until late). **Bike rental** is available from Ciclotour, Via Principe di Scalea 25a (℡091.454.798; €15–30 per day).

Hotels

With its higher room rates, there is no real reason to stay at Mondello rather than Palermo, and there's only a limited choice of **hotels**. All get impossibly full in summer, when bookings should be made well in advance.

Conchiglia d'Oro Viale Cloe 9 ℡091.450.032, ⊛www.hotelconchigliadoro.com. Some distance (600m) from the seafront, this 1960s-style family hotel is a quiet place, and has Wi-Fi Internet and a pool. ❻

La Torre Via Piano di Gallo 11 ℡091.450.222 or 800.236.118, ⊛www.latorre.com. At the end of the beach road, this huge modern establishment is set apart from the beach and harbour, with good-sized rooms and a terrace bar with views straight out to sea. Sea-facing rooms cost extra. There's a tennis court and pool. ❻

Restaurants

None of the seafront **restaurants** is particularly cheap, but they have plenty of boisterous seaside atmosphere, and the food is usually good and fresh. Alternatively, you can put together inexpensive meals by eating from the snack stalls or buying portions of sliced *pólipo* (octopus) from stand-up counters at the front of several restaurants.

Da Calógero Via Torre 22 ℡091.684.1333. Close to Mondello's tower, this trattoria serves plates of mussels and other seafood dishes from €6, including *ricci di mare* – black, prickly sea urchins – which you can have with spaghetti. Moderate.

Charleston Viale Regina Elena ℡091.450.171. You don't need to spend a fortune at the area's swankiest restaurant, a Disneyesque Art Nouveau structure on an offshore platform, offering one of the best dining experiences in Sicily. First courses cost €11–16, mains €12–18. *Risotto ai sapori di Sicilia* is a signature dish, and there's a copious wine list. Delicious desserts (€4) include *parfait di mándorla* (almond parfait). Opt for a table on the terrace right over the sea. Expensive.

Siciliando Via Mondello 98 ℡091.454.422. Just off the central piazza, this place with red-check tablecloths has a huge selection of pizzas and reasonably priced pasta dishes. The best tables on the upstairs terrace are usually reserved, so call ahead. Closed Wed except July & Aug. Inexpensive–moderate.

Sympathy Via Piano di Gallo 18 ℡091.454.470. Located beyond the piazza on a continuation of the lungomare, this fancy restaurant attracts a local, well-heeled crowd. The house speciality is *fettuccine alla Michele* (with clams, prawns, garlic and parsley) at €12. The passing traffic may be bothersome if you're seated outside. Closed Tues. Expensive.

Totuccio Via Torre 28 ℡091.684.1333. Slightly grander than some of its neighbours, this has a first-floor balcony overlooking the sea, and serves such fresh seafood dishes as *spaghetti di vóngole* and *fettuccine all'aragosta*. There are fixed-price menus for €25 and €30, and pizzas are available. Closed Tues in winter. Moderate.

Monte Pellegrino: mountain and sanctuary

North of the city and a clear landmark visible from the port area, the massive bulk of **MONTE PELLEGRINO** splits Palermo from the bay at Mondello. The mountain was occupied as far back as 7000 BC: Paleolithic incised drawings were found in the Grotta d'Addaura on Pellegrino's northern slopes and there are casts of some of the best in Palermo's Museo Archeológico. Today, the mountain is a nature reserve, with paths and **guided excursions** available (book at ☎091.671.6066, or online ⓦwww.riservamontepellegrino.palermo .it). For most locals, though, Monte Pellegrino is primarily a venue for Sunday picnickers and, as the site of the shrine of the city's patron saint, **St Rosalia**, a place of pilgrimage. William II's pious niece, Rosalia, renounced worldly things and fled to the mountain in 1159; nothing more was heard of her until the early seventeenth century, when a vision led to the discovery of her bones on Pellegrino. Pronounced sacred relics, the bones were processed around the city in a successful attempt to stay the ravages of a terrible plague, a ceremony that is re-enacted every July 15 and September 4, with a torchlight procession to the saint's sanctuary (for the Festa di Santa Rosalia, see the box on p.86).

The half-hour **ride to the mountain** is extremely impressive (bus #812 from Piazza Sturzo or Teatro Politeama every one or two hours), providing wide views over Palermo and its plain. The **Santuario di Santa Rosalia** (daily 7am–7pm) lies at the end of the road, part of a ramshackle collection of huts and stalls, and entered through a small chapel erected over the deep cave in the hillside where the saint's bones were discovered in 1624. Inside, a bier contains a reclining golden statue of the saint. Goethe thought the statue "so natural and pleasing, that one can hardly help expecting to see the saint breathe and move". Certainly the saint's expression is realistic, though she seems rather smug, too – an effect perhaps induced by the huge pile of banknotes stacked up beside her, offerings from the faithful. The water trickling down the walls is supposedly miraculous.

A small road to the left of the chapel leads to the cliff-top promontory – a half-hour's walk – where a more restrained statue of St Rosalia stares over the sprawling city. Another path, leading up from the Santuario to the right, takes you to the top of the mountain – 600m high, and around a forty-minute walk. Elsewhere, the trails that cover Monte Pellegrino are dotted with families picnicking, while kids play on rope swings tied to the trees. Heading back, wait until the heat drops and descend by the **Scala Vecchia**, a stepped path that twists from the road by the sanctuary all the way down to Le Falde, near the site of the city's exhibition ground, the Fiera del Mediterraneo. On the way, you can make a short diversion to the Castello Utveggio (built in 1932, now a management school) for more marvellous views, and regain the road at the bottom to pick up a bus back to the city centre.

Monreale and around

Beach and mountain are all right for a couple of hours' escape from the city, but the major excursion is to **MONREALE**, a small hill-town 8km southwest of Palermo that commands unsurpassed views down the Conca d'Oro valley, with the capital shimmering in the distant bay. The travel writer Norman Lewis called the valley "the greatest and most glorious orchard and market garden in the world", noting that although "there was nothing of gold about it except the roofs of houses on nearby slopes, it frothed, bubbled and exploded with the voluptuous greenery of millions of trees and plants". This panorama from the "Royal Mountain" alone is worth making the trip for, though the real draw is not this, but the mighty Norman cathedral, hidden further in among the houses.

Bus #389 runs frequently from Piazza dell'Indipendenza (outside the Porta Nuova, reached by bus #109 from Stazione Centrale) through the western suburbs and up the valley, taking around twenty minutes. A **taxi** costs €25–30 each way.

The Duomo

Flanking one side of the town atop a sea-facing shelf of land, the **Duomo** (daily: mid-April to Oct Mon–Sat 8am–6.30pm, Sun 8am–12.30pm & 3.30–7pm; Nov to mid-April 8am–12.30pm & 3.30–6.30pm; Ⓦwww .cattedraledimonreale.it) presides magisterially over the town and Conca d'Oro valley. The rather severe, square-towered exterior, though handsome enough, gives no hint of what's inside: one of the most extraordinary and extensive areas of Christian medieval mosaicwork in the world, the apex of Sicilian-Norman art. Keep €1 coins handy to switch on the lights inside if they aren't already on, though the chances are you won't be the only visitor here, as it's a regular coach stop. Bear in mind that, despite the continual influx of tourists, the same rules apply as in other Italian churches: miniskirts, shorts and bare shoulders are frowned upon, and you may not be allowed in if dressed inappropriately.

The cathedral and the town that grew up around it in the twelfth century owe their existence to young King William II's rivalry with his powerful Palermitan archbishop, the Englishman Walter of the Mill. Work had started on Walter's fine cathedral in the centre of the city in 1172. Determined to quickly break the influence of his former teacher, William endowed a new monastery in his royal grounds outside the city in 1174, and its abbey church – this cathedral – was thrown up in a matter of years. Already exempt from taxes and granted other privileges, the church consolidated its position when Monreale was made an archbishopric in 1183, two years before Walter's cathedral was finished. This unseemly haste had two effects. A highly personal project, Monreale's power lasted only as long as William did: though he wanted to create a royal pantheon, he was the last king to be buried there; and later, when Roger II's tomb was removed from the cathedral at Cefalù, it went to Walter's cathedral in Palermo. But the speed with which the Duomo at Monreale was built assisted the splendid uniformity of its most famous feature, its interior art – a galaxy of coloured mosaic pictures bathed in a golden background.

The **mosaics**, almost certainly executed by Greek and Byzantine craftsmen, are a magnificent achievement, thought to have been completed in just ten years. Despite the sheer size of the decorated interior (102m by 40m), the gleaming mosaics form a circular and reinforcing picture from which it's possible to read the Testaments straight from the walls. Once inside, your eyes are drawn immediately over the wooden ceiling to the all-embracing half-figure of Christ in benediction in the **central apse**. It's an awesome and pivotal mosaic, the head and shoulders alone almost 20m high, face full of compassion, curving arms with outstretched hands seemingly encompassing the whole beauty of the church. Underneath sits an enthroned Virgin and Child, attendant angels and, below, the ranks of saints – each subtly coloured and identified by name. Interesting here is the figure of Thomas à Becket (marked "SCS Thomas Cantb", between Silvester and Laurence), canonized in

▲ The Duomo at Monreale

1173 (just before the mosaics were begun), and presumably included as a political show of support by William for the papacy – an organization for which Walter of the Mill's lay supporters, the nobility, held no brief. The two **side-apses** are dedicated to SS Peter (right) and Paul (left), the arches before each apse graphically displaying the martyrdom of each – respectively, an inverse crucifixion and a beheading. The **nave mosaics** are no less remarkable, an animated series that starts with the Creation (above the pillars to the right of the altar) and runs around the whole church, while the darker **aisle mosaics** depict the teachings of Jesus. Most scenes are instantly recognizable: Adam and Eve; Abraham on the point of sacrificing his son; positively jaunty Noah's-ark scenes showing the ship being built, recalcitrant animals being loaded aboard, Noah's family peering out of the hatches; the Feeding of the Five Thousand; and the Creation itself, a set of glorious, simplistic panels portraying God filling His world with animals, water, light … and Man.

It's difficult to keep your eyes off the walls, but it's worth roaming the whole building. Above the two thrones (royal and episcopal) are more mosaics: William receiving the crown from Christ (less graceful than a similar picture, of Roger, in La Martorana; and the king offering the cathedral to the Virgin. Both William I and William II are buried here in side chapels, the cathedral's progenitor in the white marble sarcophagus to the right of the apse.

The southwest corner of the cathedral gives access to the **tower** (Mon–Sat 9.30am–5.30pm, Sun 8am–10pm & 3.30–5.30pm; €1.50), well worth the entry fee. One hundred and eighty steps take you up to the roof, for views of the cloisters, from where you continue around the church and upwards, leaving you standing right above the central apse – an unusual and precarious vantage-point. Back inside, tickets for the collection of reliquaries in the **treasury** (same times as tower; €2) are sold at the end of the left aisle.

The apse and cloisters

Although all the major artistic attractions lie inside, the cathedral's exterior merits a closer look too, particularly the enormous triple **apse** (signposted "*absidi*") – a polychromatic jumble of limestone and lava, supported by slender columns and patterned by a fine series of interlacing arches. You have to circle the cathedral to see this, down a street to the left of the entrance. And it's certainly worth visiting the **Chiostro dei Benedettini**, or cloisters (daily 9am–7pm; €6), part of William's original Benedictine monastery. The formal garden is surrounded by an elegant arcaded quadrangle, 216 twin columns supporting slightly pointed arches – a legacy of the Arab influence in Sicilian art. Look closely at the carved capitals of the twelfth-century columns and you'll see that no two are the same: on one, armed hunters do battle with winged beasts; another has two men lifting high a casket of wine; elsewhere are flowers, birds, snakes and foliage; while around the whole facade of the arches, geometric shapes dip and dance from column to column. A single column in the southwest corner even forms a little fountain, in its own quadrangle. Entrance to the cloisters is from Piazza Gugliemo, in the corner by the right-hand tower of the cathedral.

The rest of town

After you've seen the cathedral, there's a lot to be said for just strolling the dense latticework of steep streets – especially in the early afternoon when few people are about. Several Baroque churches (mostly locked) are hidden here and there; the **Chiesa del Monte**, in Via Umberto I, has stuccoes by Serpotta. At some point, wander into the grounds of the new convent (built in 1747) behind the cathedral cloisters for the fine views from the **belvedere**, straight down the valley. The convent itself displays Pietro Novelli's fine seventeenth-century painting of St Benedict handing out bread to assorted monks and knights. Elsewhere, the modern **Istituto Statale d'Arte per il Mosaico** (200m south of the car park to the right, past the Carabinieri barracks) is open during term time for anyone interested in watching mosaic-restorers at work. Otherwise, it's easy to while away time in the couple of bars in Piazza Vittorio Emanuele, overlooking a fountain and palm trees.

If you're in Monreale on a summer evening, stop by the Sanicola theatre, Via D'Aquisto 33 (☎091.640.9441), for one of its frequent **puppet shows**.

Practicalities

There's limited **accommodation** in town, but a good selection of **places to eat** in the streets just off the Piazza Duomo and further afield. These can be pricey, though fixed-price menus help to keep the bill down.

Hotels & B&Bs

Carrubella Park Via Umberto I 233 ☎091.640.2187. Pleasant, if somewhat old-fashioned, family-run hotel with large rooms (some with balconies), big breakfasts and great views over the Conca d'Oro from its east side. It's a 10min walk uphill from the centre. ❺

La Ciambra Via Sanchez 23 ☎091.640.95.65 or 335.842.58.65, ⓦwww.laciambra.com. Quaint B&B wedged into a web of leafy alleys behind the Duomo's apse, which is visible from its windows. There are just two rooms, with a separate entrance. No credit cards. ❹

Messina Via della Regione 108 ☎091.418.149. On the road to San Martino delle Scale, halfway between the abbey and the Castellaccio, this modest place makes a useful place to stay, with en-suite bedrooms. Pizzas and other cheap meals are also available here. ❷

Restaurants

Dietro L'Angolo Via Piave 5 ☎091.640.4067. Just a minute's walk from the Duomo (towards the belvedere), this boasts spectacular views of the valley from its terrace. Spaghetti dishes cost around €8, and there are tourist menus for €20–25. Closed Tues. Moderate.

La Fattoria Via Circonvallazione. Out of town on the Palermo road, "The Farm" is a large garden restaurant, that is a favourite with families on Sundays and with coach parties all week. Its prices are very low (most dishes range €5–10) and the house speciality, *maccheroncelli allo Caruso*, is particularly good. It's 3km by road from the centre, a stop on the bus route from Palermo, but far closer if you walk down the hill from the Duomo, below the main town car park. Closed Mon. Moderate.

Mizzica Via Cappuccini 6. On a side street below the cathedral's apse, this is a popular choice, with an outdoor seating area and a good-value tourist menu for €13. Closed Tues. Moderate.

Peppino Via B. Civiletti 12 ☎091.640.7770. Close to the cathedral, this is tucked away down on a side street off Via Roma and Piazzetta Giuseppe Vaglica, with some outdoor tables. Decent meals with a range of antipasti and fresh pasta cost around €15, and pizzas are always available. Closed Tues. Moderate.

Around Monreale: San Martino delle Scale and Báida

Seven kilometres out of Monreale, on a hill above the road to San Martino, you'll see the finely preserved twelfth-century Norman castle on the right, known as the **Castellaccio**. Once a fortified monastery built by William II, it's now run by the Club Alpino Siciliano as a mountain refuge, though if there's anyone at home they'll let you in to look around the castle. You could reach it on foot from Monreale – it's a full morning or afternoon's walk – but in any case it's worth the twenty-minute scramble from the road for the views. Easily visible is the impressive white monastery at nearby **SAN MARTINO DELLE SCALE**, an ancient religious settlement that has been taken over in recent years as a summer hill resort – holiday homes and Sunday-trippers are much in evidence. The Benedictine monks are still here, however, and you can visit their **Abbazia di San Martino** (Mon–Sat 9am–noon & 4.30–6.30pm, Sun 9–11am & 5–6.30pm) – supposedly founded by Gregory the Great in the sixth century – to see frescoes by Pietro Novelli, a grand fountain and sculptures by Marabitti, and the eighteenth-century marble staircase, all in the abbey; the church itself is monumental but rather bland.

You can reach San Martino from Monreale on the local #2 **bus**, or on the Virga buses that run three to four times a day from Palermo's Piazza Verdi (by the Teatro Mássimo), running through the wooded "Paradise Valley". At the eastern end of the valley, a road leads from the village of Boccadifalco (about 5km out of the capital) 2km north to **BÁIDA**, a tenth-century Saracen village (*baidha* is Arabic for "white"). Here, you'll find a convent built in the fourteenth century by monks from the Castellaccio, and an interesting church, which retains an ochre facade from its fifteenth-century construction, together with an earlier apse, and a statue of St John the Baptist, wrought by Antonello Gagini; ask for the custodian at Via del Convento 41. Báida is a pretty village, ringed by hills, and again there are direct buses from Palermo, most convenient of which is the #462 from Piazza Príncipe di Camporeale (itself reached by #122 from Stazione Centrale, or #110 from Piazza dell'Indipendenza).

West: the Golfo di Carini and inland

If you're looking for a **beach** to while away a few hours, then the small fishing ports and holiday resorts along the **Golfo di Carini** are perfectly adequate, and certainly less intense than Mondello. In fact, given their proximity to the capital, they're surprisingly undeveloped – better still, they're sheltered by the huge mass of Monte Gallo to the east and protected from the waste ejected into the sea from the city by virtue of their location, tucked safely around the corner of the headland.

The coast: Sferracavallo to Terrasini

The nearest, adjacent towns of **SFERRACAVALLO** and **ISOLA DELLE FÉMMINE** are the best bet for an easy getaway, and while the latter is uncomfortably close to a cement factory on one side, it's quickly forgotten once you're inside the town. The *isola* in question is a tiny offshore islet. Both towns run to pricey hotels, and **campsites** – the closest official camping spots to Palermo: the two in Sferracavallo are listed on p.68; in Isola delle Fémmine (actually 1km west of town), *La Playa* (☎091.867.7001, ⓦwww.campinglaplaya.net; closed mid-Oct to Feb), lies close to a sandy beach and has caravans to rent (❷). For a decent **restaurant**, you need only head to the beach road where you'll have your pick from nearly a dozen places. *Ristorante Cutino*, Via Palermo 10 (☎091.867.7062; closed Tues), in Isola delle Fémmine, is highly recommended, specializing in seafood with a €27 menu; sit outside or at tables on the pavement. There's similar good food at *La Scogliera Azzurra*, Via Nazionale 13, right on the seafront, with set-price menus for

€33–45. It's also a small hotel that's popular with families, with access to a pool and private beach (☎091.867.7874, ⓦwww.scoglieraazzurra.it; ❹).

Regular local **trains** stop in Isola delle Fémmine, which is also served by bus #628 from Piazzale De Gásperi, near the stadium and La Favorita (bus #101 or #107 from Stazione Centrale). The train stops at other resorts on or just in from the **Golfo di Carini**, including **Capaci**, where's there's another campsite: *Aria Aperta* (☎091.867.1042; closed mid-Sept to mid-June), which has good sports facilities. The western promontory of the gulf, **Punta Raisi**, is home to Palermo's airport.

Further west, **TERRASINI**, forty minutes out of Palermo, is typical of the small ports along the gulf, with a sandy beach, several trattorias and a clutch of expensive tourist hotels. On the waterfront west of the centre, on Lungomare Peppino Impastato, the **Palazzo d'Aumale** (Mon–Sat 9am–1pm & 2.45–6.45pm, Sun 9am–1pm; €5) holds collections of Sicilian painted carts, ethnographic items and archeology. In August, the *palazzo* remains open until midnight, and between July and September theatrical and musical performances are held in the courtyard: call ☎091.881.0989 for details. *Turiddu*, opposite, is a good local trattoria for fresh seafood and pizzas.

Inland: Carini, Montelepre and Partinico

The arc of villages to the southwest of Palermo are not exactly scenic, though they are separated by occasionally grand landscapes of dry, bare hills with distant views out to sea. For centuries, poverty, desperation and outlawry have been ingrained in the local culture, evident not just in the romanticized tales of banditry still popular here, but in the more sinister network of mutual interests and organized criminality that continue to bind politicians and mafiosi together. You won't see outward signs of either phenomenon in the villages of **Carini** or **Partinico** today, though **Montelepre** now trades on its outlaw links, and its museum is well worth a look. The road connecting Montelepre and Partinico would make an interesting alternative to the much busier coastal route for those heading west from Palermo.

Carini

Five kilometres from the coast, and reachable from Palermo either by train or by AST bus from Piazzale John Lennon, **CARINI** is distinguished by a clutch of sixteenth-century churches, and a first-rate **castle** (Tues–Sun: May–Sept 9am–1pm & 4–8pm; Oct–April 9am–1pm & 3–7pm; €4). The battlemented fortress dates from Norman times and was subsequently held by some of Sicily's leading feudal dynasties: in 1508 a famous murder occurred here when the local count killed his errant daughter and her lover, immortalized in an anonymous contemporary poem considered to be the highest example of Sicilian popular versifying, *La Baronessa di Carini*. Inside you can see grand courtyards and a series of restored chambers, some holding period furniture, with wooden ceilings, frescoes and coats of arms. Occasional exhibitions are held here.

Montelepre

A very minor road climbs 11km south of Carini to the small town of **MONTELEPRE** (direct AST bus from Palermo), notable only for its history. To Sicilians, Montelepre is instantly familiar as the birthplace and home of the notorious bandit **Salvatore Giuliano**, who hid out in the hills and caves around here, slipping into town at night to see family and friends. The house in which he lived, **Casa Giuliano**, Via Pietro Merra 189 (daily 9am–1pm & 3.30–7pm; €2 donation), is now a museum run by Giuliano's nephew,

Salvatore Giuliano

Salvatore Giuliano (1922–50) was Sicily's most dashing anti-establishment hero – and villain. Known to his comrades as Turiddu, he embodied the hopes and frustrations of the Sicilian people more than any other individual in recent history. Part of his charm lay in his long defiance of the government. Starting out as a petty criminal and black-marketeer, he was a hunted man after his murder of a Carabiniere who had challenged him as he transported stolen grain in 1943. Gathering a band of followers in the mountains around his home in Montelepre, he was not only pursued by the Carabinieri but by platoons of hand-picked soldiers who combed the maquis for him. As his ambitions and legend grew, so did his charisma, enhanced by such madcap gestures as writing to President Truman and offering the annexation of Sicily to the United States, in a last-ditch attempt to sever the island from the Italian State.

Giuliano's separatist ambitions led him into some disreputable alliances, and his fall from grace occurred when he was shown to be behind the massacre of villagers at Portella della Ginestra in 1947 (see p.112). Just three years later, he was betrayed and killed, his body found in a courtyard in Castelvetrano, in the south. No one knows exactly what happened or who was responsible for his death, though his deputy, Gaspare Pisciotta, chose to confess to the crime. Many doubt that he was the one who pulled the trigger, and Pisciotta himself was on the verge of making revelations at his trial that would have implicated high-ranking Italian politicians, when he too was assassinated in his cell at Ucciardone prison. Whatever the truth, there's a pungently Sicilian flavour to the affair, full of corruption, betrayal and counterbetrayal, and Giuliano's legend has since grown to Robin Hood dimensions, nowhere more so than in his home territory around Montelepre. As his biographer Gavin Maxwell was told: "They should change the name of that village, really – anything else but Montelepre would do. No one can look at it straight or think straight about it now – it just means Giuliano."

showing a wealth of personal effects including the various musical instruments that he played, the bike he rode, and the bed he was born and slept in. You can also see the room belonging to his sister, who headed the women's section of Giuliano's "army", and, in the attic, a collection of farming tools and other agricultural items of the period. If the museum is closed, you can usually gain entry by asking up the road at the **hotel** and **restaurant** run by his nephew, ⚔ *Castello di Giuliano*, Via Pietro Merra 1 (☎091.894.10.06, 🌐 www.castellodigiuliano.it; ❹). This eccentric construction built to look like a castle has more Giuliano memorabilia on display, and would make a fine place to spend the night – with solid, rustic/medieval-style rooms. The restaurant serves a plentiful menu of good seafood dishes, including *pesce fantasia allo chef* (€10). There's a tourist menu for €18, and pizzas available in the evenings.

Partinico

As gripping a story as Giuliano's is that of **Danilo Dolci** and his campaign for relieving some of the burden weighing down the people of **PARTINICO**. Around 10km southwest of Montelepre on the SS113 (and 1hr by train from Palermo), this dreary and distressingly poor town is primarily known for its connections with this social reformer, the "Sicilian Gandhi", who founded his first self-help and education centre here and campaigned tirelessly to have a dam built locally – something that was resisted at every turn by the Mafia and their political clients, who controlled the existing water supplies. For more on Dolci, and the villages along the Golfo di Castellammare – with which Partinico properly belongs – see p.361.

If you're driving this way, you might relish a break at the *Mamma Rosa*, at Piazza Stazione 5 (℡091.890.3331; closed Tues), a surprisingly good pizzeria-**restaurant** with veranda seating, located outside the village next to the train station. Main courses, including a choice of grills, cost €8–12.

East: to Bagheria and Solunto

You're likely to see both **Bagheria** and the ancient ruins at **Solunto** as easy half-day trips from the capital; regular **buses** (AST from Stazione Centrale) and frequent local **trains** swing out of Palermo and cut eastwards, across Capo Zafferano, stopping in both towns. It's a considerably more pleasant journey than it was in the eighteenth century, when the road – as described by Dacia Maraini in her memoir *Bagheria* – was not only foully potholed, but lined "with the heads of bandits impaled on pikestaffs ... dried by the sun, infested by flies, often with chunks of arms and legs with blackened blood sticking to the skin ..."

Bagheria

It's **BAGHERIA** that provides the first spark of interest on the run out through Palermo's uninspiring eastern suburbs. Just 14km from the city, it quickly established itself as a seventeenth- and eighteenth-century summer retreat, the Palermitan nobility sitting out the oppressive heat in a series of Baroque

▲ The Villa Palagonia in Bagheria

country villas scattered across town. The whole, in the words of Maraini, evoked "the atmosphere of a summer garden enriched by lemon groves and olive trees, poised between the hills, cooled by the salt winds". Most of the villas are still privately owned, however, and you'll need to find someone in the grounds (or ring the bell) to be allowed in.

Access to the notorious **Villa Palagonia** (daily 9am–1pm & 4–7pm, or 3.30–5.30pm Nov–March; €4; ⓦ www.villapalagonia.it) is easier: it's on Piazza Garibaldi, at the end of Via Palagonia, a good ten minutes' walk from the train station (left out of the station onto Corso Butera, then left onto Via Palagonia). Buses drop you in Corso Umberto, from where it's a straight walk. Known for its eccentric menagerie of grotesque gnomes, giants, gargoyles and assorted mutants, the villa was the brainchild of Ferdinand, Prince of Palagonia, a hunchback who – in league with the architect Tommaso Napoli – took revenge on his wife's lovers by cruelly caricaturing them. The garden walls are still amply furnished with the deformed monsters, though only 64 of the original 200 statues remain, and now in a rather deteriorated state. Nonetheless, they add entertainment to a wander around the well-stocked garden. Climbing an impressive stairway watched over by a menacing eagle that surmounts the pediment, the villa itself holds the **Salone degli Specchi** – its ceiling covered with mirrors, sadly in want of repair – and some good marbling. Only one wing is currently visitable, though it is possible that the whole of the first floor will be accessible in future.

From Corso Umberto, on the south side of Villa Palagonia, Via Trabia brings you to the more restrained Villa Trabia and **Villa Valguarnera** (also by Napoli), which comes as something of a relief after this madness, the latter displaying Bagheria's most sumptuous facade, pink and festooned with a royal coat of arms, Attic statues by Marabitti, and views out towards the sea. Villa Valguarnera's oval courtyard was one of the settings used in the Taviani Brothers' film *Kaos*. Just when you thought you'd left the weirdness behind, **Villa Butera**, at the end of Corso Butera, has within its grounds a collection of wax figures in Carthusian apparel. Legend has it that their creator, Ercole Branciforti, had promised the erection of a Carthusian abbey in return for the granting of a prayer, and took the crafty way out when the prayer was answered. Contact the tourist office (see below) for the latest information on whether any of these *palazzi* are currently open to the public.

One Baroque villa that is always open lies a little further out from the centre (back to the train station and over the level crossing, 300m to the right), the **Villa Cattólica** at Via Consolare 9 (Tues–Sun 9am–1.30pm & 2.30–7pm; €2), which contains a good gallery of twentieth-century art and has regular exhibitions and a permanent exhibition of Bagheria's most famous son, Renato Guttuso (1912–87). The latter's brilliant use of colour and striking imagery made him one of Italy's most important modern artists; his tomb, designed by his friend, the sculptor Giacomo Manzù, is in the garden.

Practicalities

There's a tourist office close to Villa Palagonia at Corso Umberto 171 (Tues & Fri 5–7pm; ☎091.9090.20). If you fancy **staying the night** here, you could book into *Da Franco Il Conte* (☎091.966.815, ⓦ www.dafrancoilconte.it; ❸), a comfortable, modern lodging with a decent **pizzeria** attached (closed Fri), signposted on Via Vallone de Spuches. For food nearer Villa Palagonia, try the atmospheric *Osteria Zza Maria*, off Via Goethe at Via Paternò 11 (closed Mon) – walk 100m up the corso, turning right at Via XX Settembre. With black-and-white photos and a dismantled Sicilian cart on the walls, it's the oldest restaurant in town, and a bit rough and ready (there's no menu), but it has inexpensive dishes, homemade bread and wine from the cask. On the corso itself at no. 145, *Sam* has wholesome hot snacks to eat in or take away, while, at the beginning of the corso on Piazza Vittorio Emanuele, the *New Oasi* has **ice cream** and granitas and tables in the square.

Solunto

One train stop beyond Bagheria (get out at Santa Flavia–Solunto–Porticello station), you can view the remains of an important Greco-Roman settlement at **SOLUNTO**. Cross over the tracks and walk down the main road towards the sea; after 300m there's a signposted left turn up the hillside, a twenty-minute walk. Beautifully stranded on top of Monte Catalfano, ancient Solus, a Phoenician settlement, was originally founded in the eighth century BC, resettled in the fourth century BC, and later Hellenized, finally surrendering to Rome after the First Punic War, when its name was changed to Solentum. The **site** (Mon–Sat 9am–7pm, Sun 9am–2pm, last entry 1hr before closing; €2) holds a museum and a scattered collection of ruins, mostly dating from the Roman period. Notable among these are the impressive remains of wealthy houses lining the hillside; one, with a standing column, was built on two floors, the stairs still visible, and retains a complete geometric mosaic floor. The main street, Via dell'Agora, leads past more houses and shops to the *agora* itself, a piazza with nine clay-red-coloured recessed rooms at the back. Above it sit the fragmentary ruins of a theatre and a smaller odeon, deliberately sited so as to give marvellous views away to the coast. Beyond the *agora* are the remains of a water cistern and storage tanks – necessary, as Solentum had no natural springs. It was, and is, a glorious spot: the fishing villages below are split by a small bay, and guarded at one end by the medieval **Castello di Sólanto**.

Porticello and Aspra

With your own transport you can return to Palermo along the coastal route from Santa Flavia, through **PORTICELLO** village, where there's a decent **hotel**, the *Baia del Sole*, close to the beach at Via Raffaello Sanzio 39 (☏091.957.590; ❸), with some rooms enjoying sea views; ring ahead, as it's popular. There are also several fine trattorias and **restaurants** on the seafront, including the renowned *La Muciara*, Via Roma 103 (☏091.957.868; closed Mon in winter), which offers a wide range of fresh fish, impeccable service and a rather grand wine list. There's a fixed-price three-course menu for €40, and tables inside and out; booking is advised.

Past the stuck-out thumb of Capo Zafferano, it's about another 5km to **ASPRA**, from where you can see the whole of the Gulf of Palermo ahead of you. From here, one road runs the 2km or so south to Bagheria; another goes west, back into the city.

South: Piana degli Albanesi

Less than an hour's bus ride south of the capital is the upland plain where **PIANA DEGLI ALBANESI**, founded by fifteenth-century Albanians uprooted from their homes in flight from the Turkish invasions, sits placidly above a pleasant lake, a million miles from the manic goings-on in Palermo. The six thousand inhabitants here follow the Orthodox rite (though they acknowledge the authority of the pope), and proudly retain many of their old traditions – signs here are in Albanian as well as Italian, and on Sunday mornings you can attend traditional Orthodox services in one of the three churches lining the steeply sloping main street, **Via Giorgio Kastriota**. Piana is most spectacular at Easter, when the small town is full to the brim with people here to admire the handsome costumes – black with gold brocade on Good Friday, brightly coloured on Easter Sunday. You can see examples of these in the **Museo Cívico** on Via Guzzetta (Tues–Sat 9am–1pm & 3–7pm, Sun 9am–1pm; free), just a few steps from the main Piazza Vittorio Emanuele, an ethnographical museum illustrative of former rural life and displaying a range of traditional costumes and jewellery. There are also sections on local history, including exhibits on the massacre of Portella della Ginestra (see below).

Apart from the museum and the Easter celebrations, there's little else to spark your interest in the town itself – the main attraction is in the immediate surroundings. Three kilometres south of the town, the artificial **lake** lies in a beautiful setting, surrounded by mountains, a good venue for a picnic and a lazy siesta. If you want a decent walk, you should carry on (4km from Piana, to the right of the lake) to the mountain pass southwest of town, **Portella della Ginestra**, scene of one of the most infamous episodes in recent Sicilian history. On May 1, 1947, when the Albanians and villagers from neighbouring San Giuseppe Jato had assembled for their customary May Day celebrations, gunfire erupted from the crags and boulders surrounding the plain, killing eleven and wounding 55, many of them children. This massacre was the work of the bandit Giuliano, whose virulent anti-Communist feelings were exploited by more sinister figures high up in the political and criminal hierarchy: only two weeks previously, the people of Piana degli Albanesi, together with most other Sicilians, had voted for a Popular Front (left-wing) majority in the regional parliament. The cold-blooded killings erased at one stroke the bandit's carefully nurtured reputation as defender of the poor and friend to the oppressed. The spot is marked today by a sculptural memorial of inscribed rocks. From the car park opposite, tracks radiate out into the surrounding hills of the **Serre della Pizzuta**, inviting a country ramble.

Practicalities

There are several **buses** (Mon–Sat), run by Prestia & Commandé, from Stazione Centrale in Palermo; the last one back leaves at 4pm. Buses stop at the top of Piana, 500m from Piazza Vittorio Emanuele, at the Villa Comunale: from here, cross the road viaduct to reach Via Kastriota and the centre of town. You can get local information from the **Pro Loco** at Via Kastriota 207 (Tues–Sat 9am–1pm & 4–8pm, Sun 9am–1pm; ℡091.857.4504, ⓦ www.pianalbanesi.it).

For **food**, the best choice is _Trattoria San Giovanni_, Via G. Matteotti 34 (℡091.857.1070; closed Tues), a pleasant, yellow-walled place whose windows overlook the town, with pasta and main dishes for €6–7 each; it's right by the bus stop and the Villa Comunale. _Bar Elena_, opposite, is a great stop for _pizzette_, _arancini_, granitas and ice cream (closed Fri).

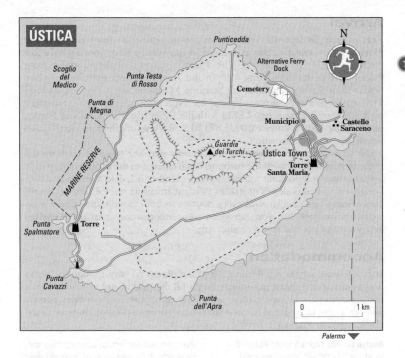

Ústica

A turtle-shaped volcanic island, a lonely 60km northwest of Palermo, **ÚSTICA** is one of the most appealing destinations for trips out from the capital, ideal for putting your feet up for a few days. Colonized originally by the Phoenicians, the island was known to the Greeks as Osteodes, or "ossiary", a reference to the remains of six thousand Carthaginians they found here, abandoned to die on the island after a rebellion. Its present name is derived from the Latin *ustum* – "burnt" – on account of its blackened, lava-like appearance. Exposed, isolated and never a particularly attractive place to live, Ústica had a rough time throughout the Middle Ages, its sparse population constantly harried by pirates who used the island as a base. In the Bourbon period the island was commandeered as a prison for political enemies, and even as late as the 1890s the few inhabitants were nearly all exiled prisoners: Antonio Gramsci, the great theorist of the Italian Communist Party, was once interned here.

Today, tourism has rescued Ústica, even at the risk of spoiling its charms – its population of 1,330 rises to 5000 in the summer months, and you'll see it at its best if you can avoid coming in August. The island's fertile nine square kilometres are just right for a day's ambling, and though it lacks sandy beaches, its greatest draw is the surrounding limpid waters, ideal for **snorkelling** and **skin-diving**. These activities attract an international meeting of scuba enthusiasts every summer, and there are ample opportunities to have a go. Part of the coastline has been designated Italy's first **Natural Marine Reserve**, where "fish-watching" is a popular activity (since "fish-catching" is forbidden): **boat trips** to tour the many grottoes that puncture the rugged coastline are plentiful.

Arrival

Ferries and **hydrofoils** operate daily from Palermo (from the Stazione Maríttima), the cheapest passage being €14 one way by ferry (journey time 2hr 30min), or €20 by hydrofoil (1hr 15min); summer departure times from Palermo are currently 8.15am, 3.30pm and 7pm (but check first). You can buy tickets from Siremar, opposite the Stazione Maríttima at Via Francesco Crispi 118 (℡091.582.403, Ⓦwww.siremar.it). Note that there's also a summer hydrofoil service connecting Ústica with the Égadi Islands, Trápani and Naples, operated by Ústica Lines (℡0923.873.813, Ⓦwww.usticalines.it); see "Travel details" for more information.

You arrive at **Ústica Town**, the island's only port: the town centre is up the flight of steps leading from the harbour. You'll emerge in the main square, which is really three interlocking squares – piazzas Umberto I, della Vittoria and Vito Longo. From Piazza della Vittoria, an efficient **minibus** service (pay on board) plies Ústica's one circular road every hour or so until around 7pm. There is no tourist office here, but you can glean some information from the **websites** Ⓦwww.ustica.net and Ⓦwww.ustica.org.

Accommodation

Ústica Town is where you'll find most of the **places to stay**, though the island is not particularly cheap; in summer hotels fill up quickly, and in winter only a few remain open. However, there are plenty of opportunities to **rent rooms** (*cámere*): a couple are listed below – for others, ask around in the shops or at the *Bar Centrale*, in Piazza Umberto.

Ariston Via della Vittória 5 ℡091.844.9042. A smart, central hotel with eleven rooms and impressive sea views. Diving trips and scooter rental can be arranged. Sizeable reductions in winter. No credit cards. ❺

Caminita Vittorio Via Tufo 1 ℡091.844.9212. The friendly couple at this address rents out three attractive self-contained mini-apartments, each with kitchenette, bathroom, terrace and separate entrance. One has a sweeping view down over the town to the sea, another has three floors. It's just a few minutes from the square: at the church, turn right along Via Calvario and Via Tufo is the sixth on the left. No credit cards. ❸

Hotel Clelia Via Síndaco 29 ℡091.844.9039, Ⓦwww.hotelclelia.it. This smart little place has well-equipped rooms, a roof-terrace restaurant with sea views and Internet access for guests. Rates drop considerably out of season. ❼

Hotel Giulia Via San Francesco 16 ℡091.844.9007, Ⓦwww.giuliahotel.net. Open year-round, with ten perfectly acceptable, two-star rooms right off the main piazza (single rooms also available). There's a good restaurant downstairs. No credit cards. ❻

Grotta Azzurra Località San Ferlicchio ℡091.844.9048, Ⓦwww.framonhotels.com. Part of the elite *Framon* chain, this luxurious four-star hotel sits over its own bay, with a pool and sun terraces cut into the rocks below. It's a 5min walk from the centre: as you climb from the port, follow the road around to the left. You may find bargains here outside the peak season. Open June–Sept only. ❾

Tranchina *Da Umberto* restaurant, Piazza della Vittória 7 ℡091.844.9542, Ⓦwww.isoladiustica .com. Gigi Tranchina rents out rooms in over thirty apartments and houses around Ústica, some with great sea views, others more rustic in the middle of the island overlooking a few grazing cattle. He also rents out scooters and can arrange boat tours. ❹

Around the island

ÚSTICA TOWN is a small, bright place, built on a steep slope, many of its low buildings covered in murals. Most of what passes for entertainment here – chatting in the open air, having a coffee in the couple of bars, impromptu games of soccer – takes place in and around the three central squares, which merge into each other, tumbling down the hill from the church. Historical interest can be found at the **Museo Archeológico**, housed in the Torre Santa Maria to the south of the town (usually May–Sept daily 9am–1pm & 3–8pm; €2.50); it's a low-key assortment, mostly comprising crusty anchors, amphorae, oddments from shipwrecks in the area and Bronze Age objects from Faraglioni.

What you don't get from the town centre, however, is a view of the water and, consequently, a sense of Ústica as an island, so perhaps the first thing you should do is climb up to the remains of the **Castello Saraceno**, above the town: from the top of the square to the right of the church, the path runs left of the fancy cross at the end of Via Calvario. This easy twenty-minute walk leads to an interesting old fort, pitted with numerous cisterns to catch the precious water, and provided with rock-cut steps, which give you a good initial view of the island's layout.

From here you can see Ústica's highest point, the **Guardia dei Turchi** (244m), at the summit of a ridge that cuts the island in two, and topped by what looks like a giant golf ball – in fact a meteorological radar system. You can also climb up here from the town, in about an hour or so: take Via B. Randaccio to the right of the church, turn left at the top and then right, and you'll come to the Municipio, where you turn left along Via Tre Mulini for the summit – keep straight ahead on the cobbled path, cutting off to the left when you reach the stepped path.

Once you've exhausted the possibilities in town, exploring the **rest of Ústica** is easily accomplished. You could make use of the minibus service or rent a scooter, or, with more time, walk – it wouldn't take much more than two or three hours to walk round the entire island. There's a **coastal path** for at least half of the route, which you pick up by keeping straight on past the Municipio and then bearing off the road to the right, down past the cemetery. The path hugs the cliffs along the island's north side as far as the **Marine Reserve**, whose northernmost point is at **Punta di Megna** (where the path and road converge). If you're equipped, you can enjoy excellent snorkelling at Punta di Megna and at the offshore rock of **Scoglio del Médico**, where the clear water is bursting with fish, sponges, weed and coral. The road then keeps to the west coast as far as the old *torre* (tower) at **Punta Spalmatore**, where you'll find some of the island's best bathing spots; try below the *torre*, or – below the nearby lighthouse – at **Punta Cavazzi**, where there's a *piscina naturale*, a perfect, sheltered pool of seawater that can get uncomfortably crowded in high season.

The more cultivated southern coast is best seen by boat, as the road runs inland here. If you're walking, veer away from the coast at Spalmatore, following the inland road past the Punta Spalmatore tourist village. After about twenty minutes you'll rejoin the main road leading back across the eastern half of the island to the port.

Eating and drinking

There are several places to eat on and around the central squares, and most of the hotels have **restaurants**, often with roof terraces and sea views. Most restaurants not attached to hotels close during the winter. Of the **bars**, the *Oasi Bar*, serving snacks as well as drinks, is dead central in Piazza Vito Longo, as is the *John Bar* in Piazza Umberto I. *Kiki's Bar*, overlooking the harbour on Via Colombo, is a cool place to hang out of an evening, with tables outside and panini and other snacks for sale. Close by, *Il Faraglione* (℡091.844.9752) is another good nightspot above the harbour, with food, an outdoor lounge and dance area, and occasional live music.

Hotel Giulia Via San Francesco 13. The simple trattoria attached to this *hotel* specializes in fish couscous (€30 for two). No credit cards. Moderate.

Mario & Giapè Piazza Umberto I 21. In this small and simple, box-like restaurant on the square, with tables outside in summer, you'll find such dishes as the excellent *pesto all'Usticese*:

spaghetti with fresh tuna, *peperonici*, tomatoes, pine kernels, almonds and pictachios (€8). Closed Dec–Feb. Moderate.

Da Umberto Piazza della Vittoria. Central eatery with tables on the terrace and a standard menu chiefly consisting of spaghettis (€8–10) and seafood main courses (€12–15). Moderate.

Listings

Bank Monte dei Paschi di Siena, Via Cap. V. di Bártolo, on the left-hand side of the church, with ATM (Mon–Fri 8.20am–1.20pm).

Bike, boat and car rental Usticamare Noleggio, Via C. Colombo 40 (☎091.844.9548 or 339.218.5630), has bikes, boats and cars to rent. *Tranchina* (see "Accommodation") also rents out scooters.

Boat tours Round-the-island and other boat excursions from the quay should cost around €15 per person for three hours, though be sure to agree a price beforehand. Tranchina (see "Accommodation") also arranges tours.

Diving Alta Mare (☎091.625.4096 or 347.175.7255, Ⓦwww.altamareaustica.it) and Tortuga

(☎338.788.6948 or 335.833.2020, Ⓦwww.tortugadiving-ustica.com) organize snorkelling and diving trips and packages. Profondo Blu (☎091.844.9609 or 349.672.6529, Ⓦwww.ustica-diving.it) arrange diving courses and accommodation in their own self-contained resort outside town.

Ferries and hydrofoils The R&S Militello ticket agency, Via Cap. di Bártolo 15 (☎091.844.9002), dispenses all tickets; there's also a ticket kiosk at the harbour, open just before sailings.

Pharmacy Piazza Umberto I 30 ☎091.844.9382 (Mon–Sat 8.30–1pm & 5–8.30pm). Closed Wed afternoon Nov–April.

Post office Largo Ameria (Mon–Fri 8am–1.30pm, Sat 8am–12.30pm).

Festivals

January
6 Orthodox Epiphany procession at **Piana degli Albanesi**; traditional costumes and the distribution of oranges. Similar goings-on at **Mezzojuso** to the southeast.

Easter
Holy Week Traditional Orthodox processions and celebrations at **Piana degli Albanesi**, best on Good Friday and Easter Sunday; and also at **Mezzojuso**.

April
23 Costumed processions at **Piana degli Albanesi** to celebrate St George's Day.
Last week Annual World Windsurfing Festival at **Mondello**; races, food, drink and entertainment.

July
11–15 The festival of St Rosalia – who saved the city from plague – in **Palermo**. A procession of the saint's relics, fireworks and general mayhem.

August
21 A colourful horseback parade, *la cunnatta*, at **Marineo**, on the Corleone road.

September
4 Pilgrimage to Monte Pellegrino in **Palermo** in honour of St Rosalia, patron saint of the city.
Last week Annual International Tennis Tournament in **Palermo**.

October/November
Last week in October and first week in November A week of ecclesiastical music concerts at **Monreale** cathedral.

Travel details

Trains

Palermo to: Agrigento (11 daily Mon–Sat, 7 daily Sun; 2hr); Bagheria (2–3 hourly; 10min); Caltanissetta (6 daily Mon–Sat, 2 daily Sun; 2hr); Capaci (hourly; 40min); Carini (hourly; 45min); Castellammare del Golfo (hourly; 1hr 30min); Castelvetrano via Álcamo (5–6 daily; 2hr 25min); Catania via Caltanissetta (3 daily Mon–Sat, 1 daily Sun; 3hr 30min–4hr 30min); Cefalú (hourly; 45min–1hr); Enna via Caltanissetta (3 daily; 2hr 10min–3hr 15min); Isola delle Fémmine (hourly; 30–45min); Marsala via Trápani (5–6 daily; 2hr 50min–3hr 40min); Mazara del Vallo via Álcamo (5 daily; 2hr 30min–3hr); Milazzo (hourly; 2hr 30min–3hr); Messina (13 daily; 3–4hr); Solunto (1–2 hourly; 15min); Términi Imerese (2–3 hourly; 25–40min); Trápani (7 daily; 2hr 15min–3hr 40min).

Buses

Palermo to: Agrigento (hourly Mon–Sat, 5 daily Sun; 2hr 15min); Bagheria (1–2 hourly Mon–Sat; 1hr 15min); Cáccamo (4 daily Mon–Sat; 1hr); Caltagirone (1 daily except Sat; 3hr); Caltanissetta (7–10 daily Mon–Sat, 5 daily Sun; 1hr 40min); Capaci (Mon–Sat 1–2 hourly; 1hr); Carini (Mon–Sat 1–2 hourly; 1hr–1hr 30min); Castelbuono (5 daily Mon–Sat, 1 daily Sun; 1hr 40min–2hr 30min); Castellammare del Golfo (6 daily Mon–Sat, 1–3 daily Sun; 50min); Catania (hourly; 2hr 40min); Cefalú (3 daily Mon–Sat, 1 daily Sun; 1hr); Corleone (hourly Mon–Sat; 1hr 30min); Enna (5–7 daily; 1hr 35min–1hr 50min); Gela (3–4 daily; 2hr 45min–3hr); Messina (5–9 daily; 2hr 45min); Piana degli Albanesi (6 daily Mon–Sat; 1hr); Piazza Armerina (3–6 daily Mon–Sat, 4 daily Sun; 2hr–2hr 20min); San Martino delle Scale (2 daily Mon–Sat; 30min); San Vito Lo Capo (2–4 daily Mon–Sat, 1–3 daily Sun; 2–3hr); Siracusa (2–4 daily Mon–Sat, 2 daily Sun; 3hr 15min); Términi Imerese (6 daily Mon–Sat; 40min); Trápani (hourly Mon–Sat, 11 daily Sun; 2hr).

Ferries

Palermo to: Cágliari (1 weekly; 14hr 30min); Civitavecchia (2–13 weekly; 12–13hr); Genoa (5–7 weekly; 20hr); Naples (2–3 daily; 10hr 30min); Salerno (1–2 weekly; 9hr); Tunis (1–2 weekly; 10–11hr); Ústica (1 daily; 2hr 30min).

Hydrofoils

Palermo to: Aeolian Islands (June to mid-Sept 2 daily; mid-Sept to May 3 weekly; 2hr–5hr 45min); Cefalú (June to mid-Sept 1 daily; mid-Sept to May 3 weekly; 1hr 10min); Ústica (June–Sept 2–3 daily; Oct–May 1–2 daily; 1hr 15min).
Ústica to: Favignana (June–Sept 3–4 weekly; 2hr); Lévanzo (June–Sept 3–4 weekly; 2hr 25min); Naples (June–Sept 3 weekly; 4hr); Palermo (June–Sept 2–3 daily; Oct–May 1–2 daily; 1hr 15min); Trápani (June–Sept 3–4 weekly; 2hr 50min).

Planes

Palermo to: Lampedusa (2–4 daily; 1hr); Milan (10 daily; 1hr 35min); Naples (5 daily; 50min); Pantelleria (1–3 daily; 40min); Rome (22 daily; 1hr).

2

The Tyrrhenian coast

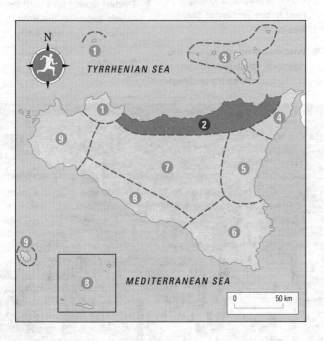

CHAPTER 2 # Highlights

✳ **Castello at Cáccamo**
Perched high on a spit of land, this impressive Norman castle can be seen for miles and offers great inland views.
See p.125

✳ **Gibilmanna** Stupendous view from the sanctuary over the lush countryside and snaking road to the Tyrrhenian sea.
See p.134

✳ **Wild mushrooms** Sample the delicious varieties of funghi cooked up at the *Nangalarruni*

restaurant in Castelbuono.
See p.135

✳ **Monti Madonie** Walks in the mountains are especially beautiful in spring, when wild flowers are superabundant, and in autumn when the leaves turn. See p.136

✳ **Tíndari** Spend time with the lizards exploring the Roman remains of Tyndaris, loftily located by the sea.
See p.142

▲ The magnificent hill-town of Cáccamo

The Tyrrhenian coast

P ractically the whole of Sicily's northern shore, the **Tyrrhenian coast**, is dedicated to holidaying. At its best it's an eye-catching succession of cliff and cove, sandy strips and citrus groves, but all too often these are eclipsed by a monotonous ensemble of new villas and hotel developments. In summer, the beaches can get as congested as the road that runs through the numerous small coastal towns and villages, but out of season, you'll find that there's plenty of room to breathe.

At any time of year, the major distraction is **Cefalù**, a beach resort *par excellence*, whose medieval cathedral contains some of the best mosaicwork you'll find on the island. Its fine beach and rocky setting provide the sort of views that attract coach parties and package tours in droves. Consequently, you'll find hotel space difficult to come by in summer, though it's worth battling with the crowds to spend at least a day here. Cefalù aside, the attractions of the Tyrrhenian coast are best enjoyed en route to Palermo or Messina. A good half-day's wandering can be spent in and around the old spa town of **Términi Imerese**, including a trip out to the blustery hill-top stronghold of **Cáccamo**, which holds the biggest and best-preserved of Sicily's Norman castles. Everywhere, too, the Tyrrhenian coast is dotted with ancient archeological remains, the most complete of which is the cliff-top site of Greco-Roman **Tyndaris** in the east.

If it's **beaches** you're after, then some of the best lie beyond the off-putting industrialization around the fortified town of **Milazzo**, or just below Tyndaris at **Oliveri**; other more crowded swathes lie around small resorts like **Sant'Agata di Militello** and **Capo d'Orlando**, which also make lively stopovers. Away from the coast, you soon leave the crowds behind in the dramatic **Madonie** and **Nébrodi** mountains. There are some good hikes in the hills between **Castelbuono** and **Piano Battáglia**, while further east you can make other inland excursions to some venerable old hill-towns, especially **Mistretta**, **San Fratello** and **Castroreale**, little touched by the mayhem on the coast.

The Tyrrhenian coast is more accessible than much of the Sicilian seaboard. There's a good **train** service all the way along, making it easy to stop off in any of the seaside resorts that take your fancy, or at places from which regular **buses** link inland destinations, though a car is useful for continuing into Sicily's interior. **Driving** can be slow on the coast itself, along which traffic files at a snail's pace on the twisting SS113, but runs much faster on the A20 autostrada (a toll-road), which features some outstanding feats of road-engineering – in the form of miles of tunnels and soaring viaducts – as well as impressive views over mountain and sea. It's also work knowing that Ústica Lines operates a useful (though limited) summer **hydrofoil** service between Palermo and the Aeolian Islands, taking in Cefalù.

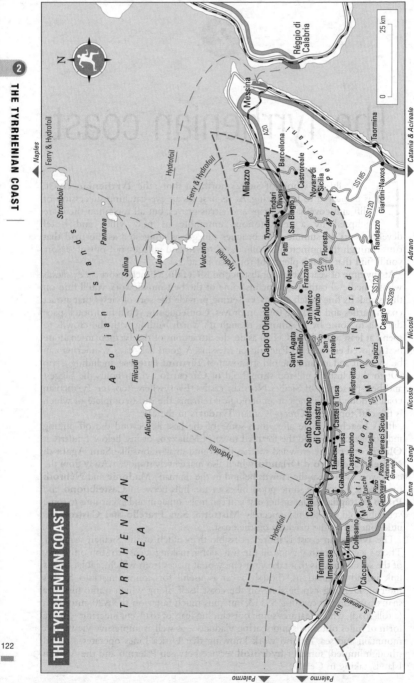

THE TYRRHENIAN COAST

TYRRHENIAN SEA

Aeolian Islands

Alicudi

Filicudi

Salina

Lipari

Vulcano

Panarea

Strómboli

Naples — Ferry & Hydrofoil

Hydrofoil

Ferry & Hydrofoil

Hydrofoil

Hydrofoil

N

25 km

0

Messina

Réggio di Calabria

A20

Milazzo

Barcellona

Castroreale

Novara di Sicilia

SS185

Taormina

Giardini-Naxos

SS120

Randazzo

Adrano ▶

SS289

Cesarò

SS120

Nicosia ▶

Capizzi

Mistretta

Monti Nébrodi

San Fratello

Floresta

Monti Peloritani

Tyndaris Oliveri

Patti

San Biagio

Naso

Frazzanò

San Marco d'Alunzio

Sant' Agata di Militello

Capo d'Orlando

SS116

Castel di Tusa

Santo Stéfano di Camastra

Halaesa Tusa

Gibilmanna

Castelbuono

Pizzo Zucchi

Pizzo Carbonara

Pizzo Antenna Grande

Monti Madonie

Piano Battáglia

Piano Zucchi

Geraci Sículo

SS117

Nicosia ▶

Gangi ▶

Enna ▶

Cefalù

Términi Imerese

Himera

Collesano

Cáccamo

S. Leonardo

A19

Palermo ▶

Palermo ▶

Catania & Acireale ▶

Términi Imerese, Cáccamo and ancient Himera

The first stop east out of Palermo is **Términi Imerese**, though if you're driving keep an eye open for the **Chiesazza** on the left, after the exit for Altavilla Milicia. Built by Robert Guiscard in 1077, this ruin of a Norman church was once annexed to a Basilian monastery. The autostrada is the best vantage point from which to view the remains, which appear stranded by the side of the road – don't bother working your way round to take a closer look.

Términi Imerese

Fifteen kilometres further on, **TÉRMINI IMERESE** has the magnificent backdrop of Monte Calógero, and a seafront marred by some of the only industry you'll see this side of Milazzo. Términi was originally settled by Greeks from Zancle (Messina) in the seventh century BC, and subsequently grew in importance as it absorbed the influx of survivors from the destroyed city of Himera, 13km to the east. Later, as Therma Himeraia, it flourished under the spa-loving Romans, and today the town is still famous for its waters, reputed to be good for arthritis and pasta-making. Otherwise, the main attractions are some noble Baroque churches, and a good museum holding finds from the site of ancient Himera. Términi makes a useful base for trips to this site, and inland to Cáccamo – both easy bus rides away.

Términi is split between its lower town, where the train station is located, and the more scenic upper town, about a fifteen-minute climb. The narrow streets of the **lower town** have less of specific interest, though plenty of atmosphere, the narrow lanes a congested mix of traffic, people and grocery stores. This is where you'll find the only accommodation in Términi (see below), including the *Grand Hotel delle Terme* in Piazza delle Terme, now housing the town's famous **thermal spa**, where the waters issue forth at a constant 42°C. Non-residents can stop in and have a look at the stone and mosaic thermal baths beneath the hotel, where some of the original Roman structure is still visible, and use the modern spa facilities (from €10 for facials, mud baths and massages).

If you're not here to take the waters, head for the **upper town**, which holds Términi's main sights, a few laid-back eateries and the town's centre. At the top of the steep cobbled steps and lanes sits a spacious and sleepy piazza, dominated by the pink-fronted **Duomo**, a monumental seventeenth-century creation that's been heavily restored over the years. The inside reveals some eighteenth-century sculptures by **Marabitti**, best of all his *Madonna del Ponte* in the fourth chapel on the right, and – unusually – there's plenty of information in English.

Beyond the Duomo extends the palm-fringed **belvedere**, which offers an extensive panorama over the lower town, port and sea that's partly disfigured by the industrial tangle below. A few metres below the Piazza Duomo, the excellent **Museo Cívico** (Tues–Sat 9am–1pm & 4.30–6pm, Sun 9am–12.30pm; free) is housed in a building that contains elements dating back to the fourteenth century. Look out for the marble bust of an elegant second-century Roman matron in room 4 and, in a restored chapel upstairs, work by Antonello Gagini and a triptych of the *Madonna with Child and Saints* attributed to Gaspare da Pésaro. There are more paintings on the top floor, including a fine sixteenth-century Flemish *Annunciation* and some grisly scenes of martyrdom, while other

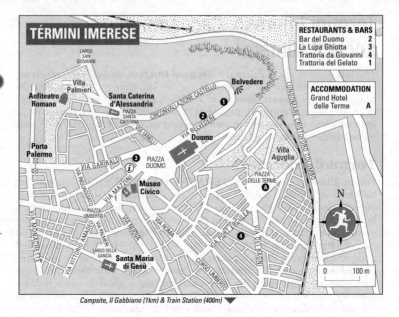

Campsite, Il Gabbiano (1km) & Train Station (400m) ▼

rooms in this well-displayed collection hold prehistoric and archeological material, notably coins and ceramics from Himera and ancient Arabic inscriptions from the Castello area of Términi.

Back across the piazza and down Via Iannelli, the small fifteenth-century church of **Santa Caterina d'Alessandria** has a pointed arched doorway surmounted by a crude relief. The church is generally locked up, but if you're lucky you'll get to see some frescoes of the saint's life inside, with captions written in the local dialect. A few steps around the corner from here, the shady vegetation of **Villa Palmieri** shelters the remnants of a public building from the Roman era, and there are the remains of an **Anfiteatro Romano** at the far end of the park, off Via Garibaldi – just up from the Porta Palermo, the former entrance to the city.

Although there's not much else to detain you, the steep, cracked streets below the Duomo are pleasant to explore. Below Piazza Umberto I, on Largo della Gancia, there is a fine Renaissance wooden panel hidden behind the altar in **Santa Maria di Gesù**. Dating from around 1400, it shows St George slaying the dragon.

Practicalities

The **train station** is 400m southeast of the town centre, and sells tickets either at the station newsstand or at the machines in the waiting room (they'll cost a few euros more on the train). To reach the centre, turn right outside the station, walk past Piazza Crispi and down Corso Umberto e Margherita to Via Roma, the stepped street that climbs to the upper town. Local and long-distance **buses** arrive at and depart from immediately outside the station, with a stop in the upper town. The **tourist office** (Mon–Fri 8am–2pm, plus Mon & Wed 3–6pm; ☎091.812.8500) is situated in the upper town, close to the main piazza, just off Via Mazzini at Cortile Maltese 18. **Hotels and restaurants** in Términi are few and far between, though will meet your needs for an overnight stop.

Accommodation

Il Gabbiano Via Libertà 221 ☎091.811.3262, ⓦwww.hotelgabbiano.it. A business-travellers' stop, this is a pricey choice with well-equipped rooms, though more basic ones in the annexe (some with shared facilities) are available (❷). The main downside is the distance to town – about 1km east of the train station. Turning left out of the station, follow the road running parallel to the lines; the hotel is on the right. ❻
Grand Hotel delle Terme Piazza delle Terme ☎091.811.3557, ⓦwww.grandhoteldelleterme.it.

With its alluring rooftop pool, the hotel dominates Términi's lower town. Prices for the elegant rooms are steep, but are especially good value in winter months, when prices drop and guests can take advantage of the various therapies on offer. ❼
Villagio Himera Buonfornello ☎091.814.0644, ⓦwww.villaggiohimera.com. The nearest campsite to town lies 15km east, with an Olympic pool, a disco and small apartments for rent. To get there, take a bus from outside the train station.

Eating and drinking

Bar del Duomo Via Belvedere ☎091.811.2978. This old-fashioned bar in the upper town has upstairs seating under a colourful wooden roof, where you can have set meals featuring meat (€15) or fresh fish (€23). Pastries and granitas are on offer downstairs and at outdoor tables. Moderate.
Da Giovanni Vico Nogara 4 ☎091.814.4362. Search out this welcoming trattoria in the lower town (signposted), buried within the network of alleys off Piazza Terme. There's no menu, but the owner will reel off the options – the stuffed

swordfish are a good bet. No credit cards. Inexpensive.
La Lupa Ghiotta Piazza Duomo ☎091.811.2435. A range of snacks and full meals, from panini and crepes to pasta dishes (try the *funghi porcini*, €7) and mains (€9–12), are served at tables in the square. No credit cards. Inexpensive–moderate.
Trattoria del Gelato Via Belvedere. At the far end of the promenade in the upper town, this *gelateria*, with ice cream in all shades and flavours, is the perfect place to break your *passeggiata*.

Cáccamo

Randazzo buses from Términi's train station run regularly to **CÁCCAMO**, 10km south. Set amid green hills, it's worth visiting chiefly for its remarkable **castello** (daily 9.30am–1pm & 3–7.30pm, 4–8.30pm in summer; €2), a chalk-white array of towers and battlements dominating the town and commanding the heights above the deep San Leonardo river valley. Built in the twelfth century, but much modified, the castle has some 130 rooms, though only about 25 are open to the public. Nonetheless, the heavily restored interior, accessed by a steep path leading through three gateways, merits a wander, and there's usually a multilingual guide on hand, able to point out various features of the building with some colourful background stories (there's little in the way of labelling or explanation) for a few euros. The highlight is the grand Sala della Congiura, where the barons' plot against William I ("the Bad") was hatched in 1160; it has a fine painted wooden ceiling and walls festooned with arms. Other rooms hold more weapons, costumes, coats of arms and reproductions of period furniture. There's also a photo exhibition showing how Cáccamo once appeared (including the castle before its restoration), and a terrace allows you to savour the glorious views.

When you've had your fill of the castle, take time to stroll around the jumble of houses and squares that make up the town. It's not much more than an overgrown village, disturbed only by the weight of traffic along the one main street, Corso Umberto I. By turning right off the corso, you'll wind up at the secluded Piazza del Duomo behind the castle crag. Here sits an enclave of faded buildings presided over by Cáccamo's **Chiesa Madre** (Mon–Sat 8am–1pm & 4–7pm), dating in part from 1090, though rebuilt during the fifteenth century, and now heavily Baroque in character. The reliefs around the sacristy door are attributed to Francesco Laurana, the Renaissance sculptor who has left his mark all over the region, particularly in Palermo. Look out, too, for the seventeenth-century tablet depicting St George and the Dragon over the main portal. To the right of the cathedral as you enter the piazza, the **Chiesa dell'Anime del Purgatorio** (erratic hours) is a more compelling attraction. Its walls are covered with pretty blue, white and gilded stucco decoration, but the *pièce de résistance* is the **catacombs**, revealed when the custodian peels away part of the floor in front of an altar. Follow him down the crumbling steps to view the fully clothed and collapsing bodies lying in niches in the walls, topped by a row of white skulls. Nobles and clergy of the town made their last journey here between the seventeenth and mid-nineteenth centuries. When the church is closed, ask around for the custodian, who will generally expect a tip for letting you into the catacombs. If you can't get in, you can get a glimpse of the niches and skulls by peering through the grate beneath the front entrance.

For a **meal** right by the castle, there's the medieval-looking *A Castellana* (closed Mon), a pizzeria-*ristorante* housed in its old grain store, with a long list of meat dishes and pizzas, and reasonably priced tourist menus. There's a less touristy alternative at the top of the town, *La Spiga d'Oro*, Via Margherita 74 (℡091.814.8968; closed Tues), with a fairly standard menu of regional dishes; it's a ten-minute walk up Corso Umberto from the *castello*, then a left turn at the bar.

If you're heading **for Palermo**, there's a handy early-afternoon bus to the capital from Cáccamo, and there's also a 12.35pm departure **for Cefalù**; otherwise the last bus back to Términi leaves at around 6pm (Mon–Sat) – buy tickets on board.

Ancient Himera

The site of Greek **Himera** (Mon–Sat 9am–6.30pm, Sun 9am–1pm; €2) is a short train ride from Términi Imerese – if you're driving, take the Buonfornello exit from the autostrada. Himera was the first Greek settlement on Sicily's northern coast, founded in 648 BC as an advance post against the Carthaginians, who controlled the west of the island, and allegedly dedicated to Athena. The town inevitably became a flashpoint, and in 480 BC the Carthaginian leader Hamilcar landed a huge force on the coast nearby, with the intention of taking Himera and very probably the rest of Sicily at the same time. Pitted against the combined armies of Akragas (Agrigento), Gela and Syracuse, the invading force was demolished and Hamilcar himself perished – either assassinated by Greek spies before the battle, or killed when he threw himself onto the pyre afterwards, depending on whose version you read. The outcome of the battle marked a significant upheaval of the classical world – and, in the case of Sicily, a new balance of power, with the Greeks in the ascendant. But their glory was short-lived: in 409 BC Hamilcar's nephew, Hannibal, wreaked his revenge and razed the city to the ground, forcing the surviving citizens west to what is now Términi Imerese.

All that's left of the important Chalcidinian settlement that once stood here is one ruined monument: a massive **Tempio della Vittória** erected to commemorate the defeat of the Carthaginians. It's a conventional Doric construction, with six columns at the front and back, and fourteen at the sides. Interestingly, the two stairwells on either side of the entrance to the *cella*, or sanctuary, suggest the involvement of craftsmen from Akragas in its construction, though it's known that the physical labour was carried out by the captured Carthaginians themselves. Despite the paucity of the actual remains, and the proximity of the modern road and rail network, the solitary ruin does have a powerful appeal. It's said to stand on the very site of the 480 BC battle, and after the victory some of the rich Carthaginian spoils were pinned up inside.

The acropolis lay to the south of the temple, inland, and, though excavations have uncovered a necropolis and some smaller temples, much work remains to be done at the site. Only the western area is open, below which is an extensive, well-designed **museum** (same hours and ticket), housing some of the items dug up from the area. The collection is repetitive, consisting mostly of large, cracked vessels, though there are good plans of the site as you come in and, on a lower floor, a big well-maintained mosaic and a few of the striking lion's-head water-spouts that drained the temple's roof. One strangely moving window displays the grave of a married couple, the wife sleeping curled up next to her husband's skeleton, her leg resting on his, their mouths agape. The Museo Cívico in Términi and the Museo Archeológico Regionale in Palermo also house a number of assorted findings from the Himera site. Moderately priced **meals and refreshments** are available at *Baglio Himera*, opposite the temple (closed Mon).

Cefalù

Despite the barrage of modern building outside the town centre, **CEFALÙ**, 35km east of Términi Imerese, remains a fairly small-scale fishing port, partly by virtue of its geographical position – tucked onto every available inch of a shelf of land underneath a fearsome crag, **La Rocca**. Roger II founded a mighty cathedral here in 1131, and, as befitting one of Sicily's most influential rulers, his church still dominates the skyline: the great twin towers of the facade rear up above the flat roofs of the medieval quarter, and the whole structure is framed by the looming cliff. Naturally, it's the major attraction in town, but visitors are also drawn to Cefalù's fine sands, and it is the combination of these two factors – the historical and the picturesque – which have made the town the major tourist resort on this coast. It's still not quite as developed as Sicily's other package resort, Taormina: the crowds are manageable, even in summer, and outside July and August you could do worse than make Cefalù your base for a few days, especially if you're attracted by the hiking possibilities in the hills to the south. Palermo, too, is less than an hour to the west by train.

Arrival and information

The **train station** is south of the centre, ten minutes' walk from the main Corso Ruggero; **buses** pull into the square outside the station. Drivers will find **parking** spaces by the sea, either on the street (€1 for 1 hr) or in a nearby car park (€4 for 1–5 hr). The summer **hydrofoil** service to and from Palermo and the Aeolian Islands operates from the port east of town, a twenty-minute walk around the headland; the boat leaves Cefalù for the Aeolians at around 8.15am and calls again for Palermo at around 8.10pm. The **tourist office** is at Corso Ruggero 77 (Mon–Sat: summer 8am–8pm; winter 8am–7pm; ☏0921.421.050, Ⓦwww.cefalu-tour.pa.it), where you can pick up free maps, accommodation lists and bus timetables, as well as **listings** of daily summer concerts and theatre performances: for more information on cultural events, check Ⓦwww .cefaluinforma.it. The **websites** Ⓦwww.cefaluonline.com and Ⓦwww.cefalu.it are also useful for accommodation, restaurants and local services.

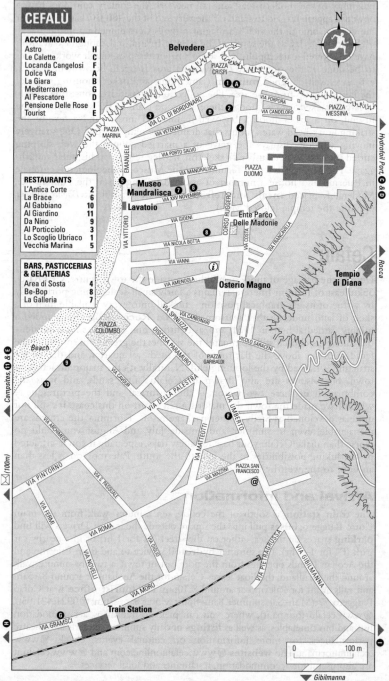

CEFALÙ

ACCOMMODATION
Astro   H
Le Calette   C
Locanda Cangelosi   F
Dolce Vita   A
La Giara   B
Mediterraneo   G
Al Pescatore   D
Pensione Delle Rose   I
Tourist   E

RESTAURANTS
L'Antica Corte   2
La Brace   6
Al Gabbiano   10
Al Giardino   11
Da Nino   9
Al Porticciolo   3
Lo Scoglio Ubriaco   1
Vecchia Marina   5

BARS, PASTICCERIAS
& GELATERIAS
Area di Sosta   4
Be-Bop   8
La Galleria   7

Belvedere

PIAZZA CRISPI

VIA PORPORA
VIA CANDELORO
PIAZZA MESSINA

Hydrofoil Port

VIA C.O. DI BORDONARO
PIAZZA MARINA
VIA VETERANI
VIA PORTO SALVO
VIA MANDRALISCA

Duomo
PIAZZA DUOMO

Museo Mandralisca
Lavatoio
VIA XXV NOVEMBRE
VIA GIOENI

CORSO RUGGERO
Ente Parco Delle Madonie
VIA COSTA
VIA FRANCAVILLA

Rocca

Tempio di Diana

VIA NICOLA BOTTA
VIA VANNI
VIA AMENDOLA
Osterio Magno

PIAZZA COLOMBO
Beach

VIA CARBONARI
VIA SPINUZZA
DISCESA PARAMURO
PIAZZA GARIBALDI
VICOLO SARACENI

Campsites,

(100m)

VIA VITTORIO EMANUELE

VIA CAVOUR
VIA DELLA PALESTRA
VIA ARCHIMEDE
VIA PINTORNO
VIA FERMI
VIA S. PASQUALE

PIAZZA GARIBALDI

VIA MATTEOTTI
VIA UMBERTO

PIAZZA SAN FRANCESCO
VIA MAZZINI

VIA ROMA
VIA GIGLIO
VIA NOVELLI
VIA MORO

VIA PIETRAGRUSSA
VIA GIBILMANNA

Train Station
VIA GRAMSCI

0   100 m

N

Gibilmanna

Accommodation

Staying over can prove expensive in summer, and prices rocket in peak season, July and August, when vacancies are hard to find. Outside this period, though, it's easy enough to find accommodation. If you're staying for a few days, you can cut costs by renting self-catering **apartments**, though there's usually a minimum stay of seven nights. Try the website Ⓦwww.casevacanzecefalu.it or ask for a list of local agencies at the tourist office. Most of the places recommended below are officially open all year, but may close with no notice if there's no business. The nearest **campsites** are next to each other 3km west of town; both are closed in winter.

Hotels & B&Bs

Astro Via Nino Martoglio 8 ℗0921.421.639, Ⓦwww.astrohotel.it. Close to the beach, where it has its own private stretch, this hotel is modern and pleasantly furnished, though the rooms are rather bland. It's a few minutes' walk west of the train station, reachable from Via Moro/Via Gramsci or Via Roma. Rates halve outside August. ❼

Le Calette Via Vincenzo Cavallaro 12 ℗0921.424.144, Ⓦwww.lecalette.it. On the eastern side of the headland, overlooking the hydrofoil port, this villa-style hotel is beautifully sited in its own little cove. All rooms face the sea and those on the second floor have large balconies, though the proximity of the rail-line can mean rude dawn awakenings. Otherwise, facilities are top-notch. Half-board weighs in at €130 per person in peak season. ❼

Locanda Cangelosi Via Umberto I 26 ℗0921.421.591. Also known as *Chez Franco*, this is the cheapest place in town by some way, with very basic facilities. There are four rooms here – two with balconies overlooking the noisy street – with a shared bathroom, but the better bet is to book one of the four small self-catering apartments available in a quieter position nearby for €5 per person extra. No credit cards. ❶

🏃 **Dolce Vita** Via Bordonaro 8 ℗0921.923.151, Ⓦwww.dolcevitabb.it. Located in the heart of the old town, with the sea below, this B&B offers five tasteful, well-equipped rooms, each with bathroom, a/c and Internet connection. Best of all, though, is the terrace, a perfect haven with grand views and barbecue facilities. Sea-facing rooms are best. Breakfast is taken in a bar in the piazza. ❻

La Giara Via Veterani 40 ℗0921.421.562, Ⓦwww.hotel-lagiara.it. *La Giara* is very central, close to the Duomo, and offers clean rooms and a handsome terrace. Street-facing rooms can be noisy, and service is sometimes offhand. Outside of Aug, when half- or full-board may be necessary, it's reasonably priced. ❻

Mediterraneo Via Gramsci 2 ℗0921.922.573, Ⓦwww.htlmediterraneo.it. Handily placed right opposite the train station, this modern hotel lacks character, but represents good value and offers friendly service. There's no restaurant. ❻

Al Pescatore Località Caldura ℗0921.421.572, Ⓦwww.hotelalpescatore.it. Around the headland via the SS113, this is excellent value, with amenable service, but no restaurant. The ceramic-floored rooms with sea-facing balconies are simply furnished. Watch for the sign: it's a little difficult to spot. ❻

Delle Rose Via Gibilmanna ℗0921.421.885, Ⓦwww.dellerosebb.it. Good-value B&B with its own parking and functional rooms, some with views and spacious terraces (worth the supplement). Breakfast includes cheese and salami as well as rolls and jam. The main drawback is its distance from the centre, a 15–20min walk along the continuation of Via Umberto I. ❹

Tourist Viale Lungomare ℗0921.421.750, Ⓦwww.touristhotel.it. Though it's a bit of a walk (15min) along the shore road, this holiday hotel is a good bet if you're looking for peace and quiet away from central Cefalù. The rooms are somewhat soulless, but many have small balconies and enviable sea views, and there's a good beach in front. Bookings are normally taken by the week only, but it's always worth trying for shorter periods. Rates plummet in low season. ❼

Camping

Costa Ponente Località Ogliastrillo ℗0921.420.085. Well-equipped site with a swimming pool and nearby beach, located a short drive or bus ride (Sommatinese buses stop outside) west of town, just off the SS113 (and behind the Club Med complex). April–Oct.

San Filippo Località Ogliastrillo ℗0921.420.184. Adjacent to the *Costa Ponente*, much smaller and with fewer facilities (though there is a shop), and cheaper. Mid-April to mid-Oct.

The Duomo

It's worth making a beeline for the **Duomo** (daily: summer 8am–7pm; closes
5.30pm in winter) first thing in the morning if you want to avoid the coach
parties. Apocryphally, it was built in gratitude by Roger 11, who found refuge at
Cefalù's safe beach in a violent storm, though it's more likely that the cathedral
owed its foundation to his power struggle with Pope Innocent II. Shortly after
his coronation, Roger had allied instead with Anacletus, the anti-pope, whose
support enhanced the new king's prestige. Roger's cathedral benefited from
Anacletus's readily granted exemptions and privileges, its conception at once rich
and showy, something that's obvious over 850 years later. Quite apart from the
massive, fortress-like exterior, with twin towers linked by a double row of arches,
inside (covering the apse and presbytery) are the earliest and best preserved of all
the Sicilian church mosaics, dating from 1148.

Most of the rest of the Duomo's interior is thoroughly plain, with all the
former Baroque decoration finally stripped away after years of "restoration",
which enhances the impact of the **mosaics**. They follow a familiar pattern:
Christ Pantocrator, right hand outstretched in benediction, open Bible in the left,
dominates the central apse; underneath is the Madonna flanked by archangels;
then the twelve Apostles, in two rows of six. Forty years older than those at
Monreale, these mosaics are thoroughly Byzantine in concept: Christ's face is
elongated, the powerful eyes set close together, the outstretched hand flexed and
calming; the archangels have their heads tilted towards the Madonna. Check out
the Gagini statue of the Madonna in the chapel to the right of the sanctuary,
then head back outside for an exterior view of the triple apse – hemmed in by
the soaring cliff. Next door, the twelfth-century cloister is worth a look for its
original twin columns, carved with anthropomorphic figures.

The rest of town

Cefalù's ageing, tangibly Arabic tangle of central streets provides an immediate
incentive for some strolling around. Piazza Duomo itself is always lively, especially
in the early evening. Just around the corner, at Via Mandralisca 13, the **Museo
Mandralisca** (daily 9am–7pm; €5) houses a small collection of quality objects.
On the first floor you'll find its most famous exhibit, the wry and inscrutable
Portrait of an Unknown Man by the fifteenth-century Sicilian master **Antonello
da Messina**; however, it suffers from a lack of sensitive framing and presentation,
and a rope keeps you well at a distance. Look out, too, for the quirky Greek *krater*
(fourth century BC) showing a robed tuna-fish salesman, knife in hand, disputing
the price of his fish. Shell devotees should head for the top floor, where you'll
find 26 cases of them, brought here from around the world.

From the museum, walk down towards the water and the little harbour off
Piazza Marina. When it's quieter, say at lunchtime, this part of Cefalù repays
long dawdles through its alleys with views of rows of washing stretched between
houses, and fishermen mending nets in the high-vaulted boathouses along Via
Vittorio Emanuele. At the latter, you'll also see a relic of Saracen occupation –
the **lavatoio**, a wash-house at the bottom of a curving staircase, with cold water
pouring forth into the basins. Back past Piazza Marina, a left turn off Via C. di
Bordonaro brings you to Piazza Crispi, where a **belvedere** gives onto the old
Greek walls of Cefalù, mostly covered and incorporated into a sixteenth-
century bastion. Frankly, though, these sights are no more than excuses to poke
around this atmospheric area: each of the parallel streets off narrow Corso
Ruggero is lined with attractive buildings in various stages of well-tended decay.
One of the most impressive is the **Osterio Magno**, on the corner of

▲ The waterfront at Cefalù

Via Amendola and the corso, the surviving part of a medieval palace, now renovated with wood and steel and regularly used for art exhibitions (free). Meanwhile, the long sandy **beach** beyond the harbour beckons. It's one of Sicily's best, though jam-packed in summer, and offers marvellous views over the red roofs of the town and sheltered swimming in clear waters. The best swimming spots are west of town, where there are free showers.

If you have time, it's also worth walking east, around the headland beyond the Duomo, to the port where the summer hydrofoils dock. It's a pretty bay, full of fishing-boats and with some strange rock stacks inviting a clamber on the far side of the port.

La Rocca

A much more energetic pastime is to climb the mountain above town, **La Rocca**, following the steps at the side of the Banco di Sicilia in Piazza Garibaldi. There's a kiosk selling tickets for access to the path between Easter and October (8am–8pm; €3.50), but it's always open and free the rest of the time.

A steep twenty-minute climb takes you to the so-called **Tempio di Diana**, a megalithic structure adapted in the fifth century BC by the addition of classical doorways, their lintels still in place. Keep to the left of the temple and a path continues upwards, right around the crag, through pinewoods and wild fennel. Further on, it dips in and out of a surviving stretch of medieval wall to the sketchy **fortifications** at the very top, which look down to the coasts on either side of the headland. You can then cut down to the temple and rejoin the path back into town, the whole walk taking a little over an hour – much longer if you stop and stare at the extensive views. Take water with you, as it's a strenuous climb.

Eating and drinking

Of the dozens of **places to eat** scattered around town, many are overpriced and mundane; the best are detailed below, most offering good-value tourist menus. Anyone on a tight budget, and vegetarians could do worse than to sample the self-service *antipasto al buffet* in the restaurants along the waterfront – you get a plateful for around €7. Note that most places may close or have reduced opening in winter.

Restaurants

L'Antica Corte Corso Ruggero 193 ☎0921.423.228. A simple, elegant restaurant with seating in a quaint, cobbled alley. Pizzas are on offer as well as a full menu: try the li*nguine Antica Corte* (with lobster, prawns, tomatoes and cream) or the fish couscous. There's a tourist menu for €13.50, otherwise count on €15–20 for two courses. Moderate.

La Brace Via XXV Novembre 10 ☎0921.423.570. You dine here to classical music in a room formed by three stone arches. Most of the pasta dishes are vegetarian. The *involtini di melanzane* (stuffed aubergine), *spiedini di pesce spada* (swordfish kebabs) and tournedos (fillet steak) are all worth sampling; main courses cost around €12. It fills up quickly, and you'll need to book in summer at weekends. Dutch and English spoken. Closed Mon, Tues lunch & mid-Dec to mid-Jan. Expensive.

Al Gabbiano Lungomare G. Giardina. One of the best of a row of seafront restaurants, this place with terraces to front and back has a good *antipasto al buffet*, spicy *zuppa di cozze* and pizzas in the evening. Service is brisk but polite. Only bottled wine available. Closed Wed in winter. Moderate.

Al Giardino Lungomare G. Giardina. A 15min walk west along the seafront, this lively restaurant has a summer terrace, huge pizzas and pasta dishes including a zesty spaghetti with clams (both €7–9). Closed Thurs lunch. Inexpensive–moderate.

Da Nino Lungomare G. Giardina. Similar food and prices to neighbouring *Al Gabbiano*, but pizzas are also served at lunchtime. Tourist menus are available for €14 and €16.50. Closed Tues in winter & Nov. Inexpensive–moderate.

Al Porticciolo Via C. O. di Bordonaro 66 (☎0921.921.981) and 90 (☎0921.423.151). Two atmospheric, low-vaulted little ristoranti attracting a smart crowd, with outdoor seating: no. 90 is slightly more upmarket, but both have surprisingly reasonable prices, with first courses in no. 66 at €5–6. Fixed-price menus at no. 90 are €18–35 for three courses, and pizzas are also available. No. 66 closed Wed, no. 90 closed Mon, both mid-Sept to mid-July only. Moderate–expensive.

Lo Scoglio Ubriaco Via C.O. di Bordonaro 2–4 ☎0921.423.370. At the bottom of the corso, this slick place adorned with photos and messages from stars and VIPs has a sea-facing terrace and serves pizzas (in the evening) as well as pasta (€6–8) and main dishes (€9–11). The name means the "Drunken Rock". Closed Tues Sept–June. Moderate.

Vecchia Marina Via Vittorio Emanuele 73 ☎0921.420.388. Good fish restaurant, one of whose walls incorporates a mighty fish tank. Sicilian dishes served, and a decent wine list, too. Set menu at €26, otherwise a three-course meal will cost €25–35. No credit cards. Closed Tues & Jan. Moderate–expensive.

Bars and birrerias

You could spend a lot of money in Cefalù's **bars**, either as refreshment stops during the day or whiling away an evening. Summer nights here can be fun, with a proliferation of cool wine bars and boisterous **birrerias**, though obviously things slow right down outside the season.

Area di Sosta Corso Ruggero 158. For a quick fill-up, you can try out a range of healthy yoghurts, including fruit salads and brioches, and there are also crepes, frappés and ice cream. Closed Oct–Easter.

Be-Bop Via Nicola Botta 4. A pub-like joint with a courtyard, that serves decent hot and cold snacks, sandwiches, crepes and ice cream. Live jazz and South American music at weekends.

La Galleria Via XXV Novembre 22–24. Trendy modern bar and "literary café", incorporating bookshop, cultural centre and Internet point. The large courtyard provides atmosphere for late drinking and occasional live music, but it can get crowded. Pricey meals are available. Closed Wed mid-Sept to mid-July.

Listings

Bike rental See Scooter rental.
Car rental Autoeuropa, Via Roma 123
⊤800.334.440, ⓦwww.autoeuropa.it; Meditravel,
Via Vittorio Emanuele 57 ⊤0921.420.441,
ⓦwww.meditravel.it; Siciltravel, Piazza Garibaldi 9
⊤0921.420.090, ⓦwww.siciltravel.it.
Hiking Regular excursions around Castelbuono and
in the Monti Madonie. For details, contact the local
branch of the Club Alpino Italiano, Vicolo alle
Falde 4, ⓦwww.caicefalu.it, or the Ente Parco delle
Madonie, Corso Ruggero 116, ⊤0921.923.327,
ⓦwww.parcodellemadonie.it.
Hospital Contrada Pietrapollastra ⊤0921.920.111.
Hydrofoils There's a ticket kiosk at the tourist
port; in town, you can buy tickets from Pietro
Barbaro: see Travel agents, below.
Internet Kefaonline, Piazza San Francesco 1
(Mon–Fri 9am–1pm & 3.30–7.30pm, Sat
9am–1pm). You can also log on at La Galleria
(see "Bars, birrerias" above).
Pharmacies Battáglia, Via Roma 13,
⊤0921.421.789; Cirincione, Corso Ruggero 144,
⊤0921.421.209 (both roughly Mon–Fri 9am–1pm
& 4.30–8.30pm). There's a rota system for evening
and late-opening pharmacies posted in the window.
Police Carabinieri Discesa Paramuro
⊤0921.421.412.
Post office Via Vazzana 2 (between Via Roma and
the seafront). Changes foreign currency (cash only).
Mon–Fri 8am–6.30pm, Sat 8am–12.30pm.

Scooter rental Scooter for Rent, Via G. Matteotti
13 ⊤0921.420.496 or 338.230.9008,
ⓦwww.scooterforrent.it; €25–35 per half-day,
€35–45 per day. Mountain bikes available for €10
per day. Meditravel (see Car rental) also rents
scooters.
Shopping Cefalù has endless souvenir and gift
shops. Most peddle the same goods, though some
have a better range – Capriccio Siciliano at Via
Umberto I 1, for example, where local wines and
foods are sold, and there are free wine tastings.
There's a supermarket, Ipersidis, on Via Vazzana,
between Via Roma and the seafront, open daily.
Taxis Rank at Piazza Stazione ⊤0921.422.554;
try also ⊤0921.424.200, 338.690.5894 or
338.650.5952.
Tours Half- or full-day daily boat excursions in
summer with SMIV, Corso Ruggero 83
⊤800.077.822, either along the coast (€30) or to
the Aeolian Islands (€60). Half-day or evening
fishing expeditions (€45) with Coop Nettuno, Via
Pietragrossa 32 ⊤338.230.9141. Coach tours
available from Meditravel (see Car rental) and
Barranco, Via Vittorio Emanuele 27
⊤0921.923.877.
Travel agents Pietro Barbaro, Corso Ruggero 82
⊤0921.421.595; Turismez, Via Umberto 1
⊤0921.420.601, ⓦwww.turismezviaggi.it.

Into the hills: Gibilmanna, Castelbuono and the Monti Madonie

South of Cefalù, there are some invigorating excursions to be made into the leafy, green and flower-filled **Monti Madonie**, and for once the public transport services make them easily accessible. The area has been designated a regional park, the **Parco Regionale delle Madonie**, which ensures there is a decent infrastructure of waymarked paths and information offices – including one in Cefalù (see Listings, "Hiking") – where you can pick up hiking itineraries and a useful map of the area. The **websites** ⓦwww .parcodellemadonie.it and ⓦwww.madonie.it are also good resources for accommodation, transport links, fauna and flora, and detailed itineraries (though all in Italian).

Driving to the park from Palermo or Términi, take the Buonfornello autostrada exit, continue east on the coastal SS113 and head south at Campofelice di Roccella. By **bus** you can get as far as Munciarrati, beyond which you have to hitch or walk. There are numerous **accommodation** possibilities in and around Castelbuono, as well as a handful of rather remote hostels, or *rifugi*, for which advance booking is essential.

Gibilmanna

Coming from Cefalù, your first stop might be the **Santuario di Gibilmanna** (daily: summer 7.30am–1pm & 3.15–7.30pm; winter 8am–1pm & 3.15–5.30pm; free), just 14km from town (buses from Cefalù's train station) in a spot made sacred by the Arabs, who recorded miraculous deeds by the Madonna on the hillside. The sanctuary is the goal of pilgrimages, which culminate on September 8 each year, though there are usually people around throughout the summer, picnicking amid the cypress trees, praying, or admiring the superb view from the belvedere. There's a **museum** beside the sanctuary (daily 10.30am–12.30pm & 3.30–6.30pm, closes 5pm in winter; €1.50), containing artefacts from churches, convents and monasteries in the area, and a restaurant and bar nearby. The only **accommodation** lies 1km beyond the shrine at the *agriturismo Fattoria Pianetti*, surrounded by mountain and woodland walks (℡0921.421.890, ⓦwww.fattoriapianetti.com; no credit cards; ❸): half-board or full-board are also possible and may be compulsory in high season. You stay in little cottages beyond the farmhouse; the dining room is open to non-residents at weekends (book ahead), and pony treks are available in spring and summer. Meditation courses are also held here over weekends in April–July and September–October.

Castelbuono and Geraci Sículo

Further into the mountains, the comely town of **CASTELBUONO**, self-styled "capital" of the Monti Madonie, owes its origins to the Ventimiglia family, who made the town something of a cultural centre in the fifteenth century, a role it retained until well into the eighteenth century. The squat **Castello Ventimiglia** (May–Sept Tues–Sun 8.30am–2pm & 4–9pm; Oct–April Tues–Sun 9am–1pm & 3–8pm; €2) dates from around 1316, inside which you can view a small stuccoed chapel of **Sant'Anna**, from the Serpotta workshop. Spread across the lower reaches of the mountains, Castelbuono's steep, crooked streets – dotted with elaborate fountains and shady piazzas – encourage a stroll. Best of the churches is the fourteenth-century **Matrice Vecchia** (daily 11am–1pm & 5–7pm), fronted by a pretty loggia and containing extensive sixteenth-century frescoes of the *Passion of Christ* in the crypt.

Beyond Castelbuono there's good **hiking** country: head up the road (SS286) towards Geraci Sículo, and half an hour's walk gives you splendid views back over the town and castle. There's a superb hike from Castelbuono to Piano Battáglia (see box on p.136), or you could keep on the road as far as **GERACI SÍCULO** itself, 25km from Castelbuono, sitting under the brow of its hill and marked by a ruined eleventh-century castle. Buses connect the village with Cefalù twice a day (once on Sun), passing through Castelbuono, and you can complete the transmountain route by staying on until Gangi, another 25km.

Practicalities

Castelbuono lies on a regular **bus** route from outside Cefalù's train station. By car, it's a forty-minute ride, a signposted route that turns inland about 8km east of Cefalù, running up the green valley and dipping over the first range of hills; from Gibilmanna, continue south to Isnello, where a road leads another 8km east to Castelbuono. The local **tourist office** at Via Umberto I 79 (May–Sept Mon–Sat 9am–1pm & 4–7pm, Sun 9am–1pm; Oct–April Mon–Sat 9am–1pm & 3–6pm; ℡0921.671.124, ⓦwww.comune .castelbuono.pa.it) can supply maps and information on facilities and activities in the area, for example pony trekking. The **Internet**, a rare luxury in these parts, can be surfed at Planet Web, Via Vittorio Emanuele 46 (Mon–Sat 9am–1pm & 4–8.30pm, Sun 10am–1pm).

There are a few good **accommodation** options hereabouts: the *Ariston*, Via Vittimaro 2 (☎0921.671.321; no credit cards, ❷), is a rather basic choice in town, while 2km south of town on the SS286, the *Bergi agriturismo* ranch (☎0921.672.045, ⓦwww.agriturismobergi.com; ❺) has spacious accommodation and a cavernous room for meals. For a luxurious – but ovepriced – splurge, there's the five-star *Relais Santa Anastasia*, 15km towards Cefalù (☎0921.672.233, ⓦwww.santa-anastasia-relais.it; ❽), a restored tenth-century abbey with pool, sauna and fitness centre.

For **meals**, don't miss the wild-mushroom dishes at the highly recommended ⚞ *Nangalarruni*, Via delle Confraternite 5 (☎0921.672.045; closed Wed in winter), with its brick decor. It offers good-value tasting menus from €32, and the sweet, local *digestivo*, Elisir di Fontana, is definitely worth a sip or two.

Piano Zucchi and Piano Battáglia

The heart of the Madonie lies southwest of Castelbuono, the slopes filled with skiing Palermitani in winter but increasingly popular in spring and autumn for picnics, country strolls and mountain hikes. Without a car, you could get as far as Munciarrati (also known as Mongerati, between Collesano and Isnello) by bus from Palermo, Términi Imerese or Cefalù, beyond which you have to hitch or walk the 10km south to **Piano Zucchi**. If you want more than a few hours in the hills around here you can **stay** at the *Rifugio Orestano* (☎0921.662.159, ⓦwww.rifugiorestano.com; ❹), which has en-suite single and double rooms, and **meals** available to all. For this and the *Merlino* listed below, it's always wise to book ahead. Ten kilometres further south, **Piano Battáglia** is the best base for visiting the highest of Sicily's peaks after Mount Etna, and is reachable on foot from Castelbuono (see below). As the only other resort (apart from Etna) equipped for winter sports, it's a very un-Sicilian-looking place, with Swiss-type chalets and even alpine churches. In addition to hikes to the two highest peaks, Pizzo Antenna Grande (or Pizzo della Principessa, 1977m) and Pizzo Carbonara (1979m), there's a good choice of less ambitious walks along the numerous paths hereabouts. The website ⓦwww.pianobattaglia.it has **information** on accommodation, itineraries, weather conditions and skiing facilities – a number of outlets around here rent out **skiing equipment**. You can pick up **food and refreshments** from the shop and bar-restaurant at *Rifugio Piero Merlino*, which also offers en-suite **accommodation** (☎0921.649.995, ⓦwww.rifugiopieromerlino.it; ❸); close to the ski slopes and mountain trails, it's a welcoming place, with small, pine-clad rooms and dormitories. There's also *Rifugio Marini* here (☎0921.649.994), which is currently being renovated – call to check if it's reopened. The large, cheerful *Hotel Pomieri* (☎0921.649.998, ⓦwww.pomierihotel.com; no credit cards; ❹) offers a more upmarket alternative, located 4km southeast of Piano Battáglia, towards Petralia Sottana – and there are other good accommodation choices in this village at the southern edge of the Madonie. Otherwise, there are plenty of **freelance camping** possibilities in these hills during the summer.

From Piano Battáglia you can continue south along good minor roads to Polizzi Generosa or Petralia Sottana, 16km and 25km respectively; alternatively, you can head back down towards the coast, bypassing Collesano and following the minor road due north for Cefalù.

From Castelbuono to Piano Battáglia

To manage this strenuous seven-hour, twelve-kilometre hike easily in a day, you'll have to base yourself at the snug Club Alpino Siciliano refuge, the *Francesco Crispi* (☎0921.672.279; €35 half-board or €40 per person full-board), two hours' strenuous walk above Castelbuono, in the Milocca forest; follow the steep winding road out of town for half an hour beyond the *Hotel Milocca* (☎0921.671.944, ⓦwww .albergomilocca.com; ⑤), a fully equipped three-star with a pool and gym. Ask here about ponies for hire.

From the refuge, keep on the jeep path, leaving the woodlands after half an hour to reach Piano Pomo. Carry on to a small plain surrounded by four minor peaks, with crosses on each of the summits. There's a wire fence on the left, which you should climb over, and then continue over stony ground in the same direction for fifteen minutes until the large rounded peaks appear: 1km ahead (due west) is Pizzo Antenna Grande (1977m), topped with an antenna; further away to the left (southwest) is conical Monte Ferro (1906m). Take the wooded Zotofonda Valley between these two and you'll reach Piano Battáglia in around three hours.

If you're intent upon other serious walks in the hills, the national park office in Cefalù has details of the local refuges, as well as contoured 1:50,000 maps of the region; alternatively, try the tourist office in Castelbuono. For campers, there's no shortage of places to pitch a tent.

From Piano Battáglia to Pizzo Carbonara

This fairly demanding walk (4–5hr there and back) takes you through contrasting countryside of beechwoods and bare, limestone peaks, with rewarding views whether you make the summit or not. From *Rifugio Merlino*, cross the plain to come out onto the road; turn right and immediately left, winding uphill to reach a small footpath ascending steeply along the main valley. Continue for an hour and round the spur, turning into the river valley. The level path enters a small wood; on leaving this you'll see a zigzag path rising on the opposite bank. Continue along this for twenty minutes and you'll find yourself looking down on Piano Zucchi; otherwise, leave the path and cut up the head of the valley to reach the open uplands, dotted with deep depressions and beechwoods. Continue in the same direction until wooden crosses mark the rounded summit of Pizzo Carbonara – head for it by any convenient route. On a very clear day you can see Etna's peak from here.

East to Capo d'Orlando: more routes inland

East of Cefalù stretches a series of modern seaside resorts fronted by clean sand and stony beaches, many backed and interspersed by extensive groves of orange and lemon trees. There's decent hotel accommodation at several of these holiday centres – **Castel di Tusa**, **Sant'Agata** and **Capo d'Orlando** – which are connected by the coastal train line. If you're driving, you can easily park on the SS113 highway and make your way down to the more remote beaches, though motoring along this road can be frustratingly slow in summer, especially as the railway intersects the road at several points, bringing traffic to a standstill for up to fifteen minutes while trains pass. There are also roads and bus routes from various points on the coast into the **Monti Nébrodi** – short runs worth making if only for the leafy views and for a breath of fresh air away from the popular beaches.

Castel di Tusa

Some 25km east of Cefalù, across the Palermo-Messina provincial boundary, the village of **CASTEL DI TUSA** is smaller and quieter than most along this stretch, with the remnants of a defensive castle and some good rocky beaches. In recent years, however, the place has become better known for its modern art, largely owing to the efforts of one man, **Antonio Presti**, who in the late 1980s and early 1990s invited artists from around the world to create a group of large-scale sculptures to be arrayed along the river bed (*fiumara*) of the Tusa River, which flows from the Nébrodi mountains to the sea just east of the village. After a protracted legal battle with the authorities, the sculptures were saved from demolition and formally inaugurated as the **Fiumara d'Arte** sculpture park in 2006. It's worth a sortie up the Tusa Valley to view these bold, mainly concrete constructions, though you'll need time to visit them on foot, as they're scattered over a wide area – a car is an asset, as all lie near roads. Closest to Castel di Tusa, and the earliest of the commissions, is *La Materia Poteva Non Esserci*, a structure resembling two giant hands joined in prayer, located off the road leading south from the SS113 towards the village of Pettineo, a couple of kilometres out of town. One of the most beautiful works is situated a winding 6km east of Pettineo, outside Motta d'Affermo: *Energia Mediterranea*, representing a graceful curving wave in mottled blue. Another cluster lies 10km south of Pettineo, outside the hamlet of Castel di Lucio, where works include *Il Labirinto di Aretusa*, a striking concrete spiral, and *Una Curva Gettata alle Spalle del Tempo*, a tall, undulating, brick-red monolith. The works are signposted, and you can pick up a map from the "art **hotel**" in Castel di Tusa that was founded by Presti, and which itself has become something of a local tourist attraction: ☆ *L'Atelier sul Mare*, close to the sea on Via C. Battisti (☎0921.334.295, ⊛www.ateliersulmare.com; ❻). Fifteen of its forty rooms have been designed by different artists: one is adorned with Arabic and Italian poetry and sports a mammoth window looking onto the sea, with a shower that works like a car wash, while another has furnishings that emanate a red glow at night. Other rooms are more conventionally styled, but still spacious, and cost considerably less than the "art rooms" (sea-facing rooms also cost more). All in all it's a unique place to stay; non-residents can see round the rooms on a guided tour daily at noon (call to check). For those who prefer more low-key – and cheaper – accommodation, there's a **campsite** 1.5km west of here, signposted off the SS113 coast road: Lo Scoglio (☎0921.334.345, ⊛www.loscoglio.net; April–Sept), right above a rocky beach, part of which has been reserved for naturists. The site has B&B rooms, apartments to rent and a pool.

Three kilometres up the road (there's no bus), on the way to the inland village of **TUSA**, are the sparse ruins of **Halaesa** (daily 9am–1hr before sunset; €2), a fifth-century BC Sikel settlement that enjoyed some success under Rome until despoiled by the Praetor Verres. The name derives from the Greek *alaomai*, meaning to wander aimlessly, and refers to the original settlers here, the peripatetic Alesini, who had tried settling just about everywhere else. You can just about make out the chequered layout of the streets, remains of the *agora*, and – at the highest point – foundations of two third-century BC temples, with lofty views down over the Tusa Valley.

Santo Stéfano and Mistretta

Frequent trains from Palermo/Cefalù stop at **SANTO STÉFANO DI CAMASTRA**, a coastal resort renowned for its colourful ceramic work. Santo Stéfano is awash with gift shops, with plates, jugs and decorative pottery piled high along the sides of the roads – haggle hard for the best bargains. There's an

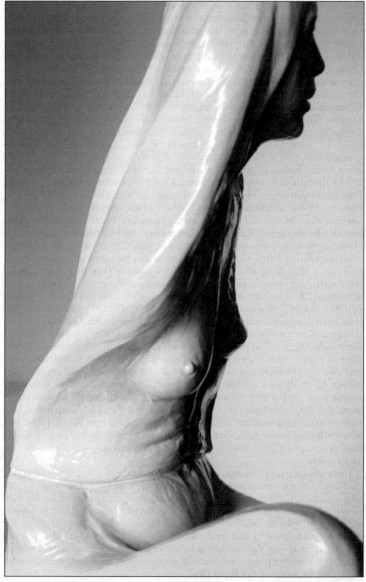

▲ Ceramic statue in Santo Stéfano

eclectic range of mostly modern ceramics displayed in the spacious **Museo della Ceramica** (Tues–Sun 9am–1pm & 4–8pm, or 3.30–7.30pm in winter; free), towards the sea in the Palazzo Trabia, Via Palazzo; it's all a bit random, with no labelling or explanation, but there are some handsome pieces here, and upstairs you can admire the restored rooms with colourful ceilings. If you need a **place to stay**, the best central option is *Girasole*, a B&B at Via Antonio Garofalo 19 (T0921.339.586, Wwww.girasole.me.it; ❹), with airy, majolica-tiled rooms. If you prefer to be near the sea, seek out *La Playa Blanca* (T0921.331.248, Wwww.laplayablancahotel.com; ❺), a family-oriented place in Contrada Fiumara, signposted off the road just west of town; there's a pool and the water is right below. There's a swish **pizzeria** next door, *Approdo del Duca* (T0921.339.852), wood-built with a modern interior and outdoor tables, offering a €16 tourist menu – you'll also find a small selection of pizzerias and fish restaurants in Santo Stéfano's centre.

West of the village, a high viaduct flies off 16km inland to one of the biggest of the **Nébrodi** hill-villages, **MISTRETTA** – reached by bus from Santo Stéfano. The handsome old centre of eighteenth- and nineteenth-century buildings is unspoiled by modern construction; a seventeenth-century cathedral has the hoary look of a medieval monument; and the population is largely composed of brown-suited pensioners milling around their veterans' associations. If you can, visit during the Saint's Day's **festivities** (the Festa della Madonna) on September 7–8, when the Madonna delle Luci is paraded around accompanied by figures of Mytia and Kronos, allegedly the founders of the village.

Mistretta also holds a couple of rare **accommodation** options in the Nébrodi hills, an alternative in high season to the noisy coast. The sole hotel is the *Sicilia*, at the top of the main corso at Via Libertà 128 (T0921.381.463; closed ten days in Sept; ❷), but if you're looking for a touch more luxury, head for ✣ *Agriturismo*

The Monti Nébrodi

Covering a wedge of land between Santo Stéfano di Camastra and Nicosia in the west to Etna and the Monti Peloritani in the east, the Monti Nébrodi are a sparsely populated expanse of forest and remote rocky peaks. Much of it is now protected as a national park, though the area is less coherent and the infrastructure not so well developed as the Parco delle Madonie. Unless you're hiking long distances, most of the area is only accessible from the coast or from the SS120, with few roads connecting the scattered villages. The highest peak is Monte Soro (1847m), between San Fratello and Cesarò and reachable from the SS289, from which extensive views spread out encompassing the Aeolian Islands to the north and Etna to the southeast.

You can pick up maps and itineraries from the **visitor centres** at Via Cosenz 149, Sant'Agata di Militello (Mon, Tues, Thurs & Fri 7.30am–2pm, Wed 7.30am–6pm, plus some weekends; T0941.705.934) and Via Umberto 1, Santo Stéfano di Camastra (Mon–Fri 9am–2pm, Sat 9am–2pm & 4–7pm, Sun 9am–1pm & 4–7pm; reduced hours in winter; T0921.331.199); in the mountains, the village of Cesarò also has a visitor centre, and there are others in San Fratello and San Marco d'Alunzio – most are open during weekday mornings only. The **websites** Wwww .parcodeinebrodi.it and Wwww.parks.it/parco.nebrodi list accommodation options and have walking itineraries, points of interest, background on the landscape, and the history and fauna and flora of the park. There's also a museum dedicated to the region in Sant'Agata di Militello, currently closed and due to reopen in a new location that has yet to be confirmed – check at the local visitor centre.

Santa Sofia, Via Nazionale 1 (☎0921.383.032 or 338.584.2635, ⓦwww
.agriturismosantasofia.it; ⓪), which offers robust country furnishings, tiled floors,
extensive grounds and stupendous views. Whether or not you stay here, it's
well worth stopping at its **restaurant** to feast on the *Pranzo della mamma Lidia*,
a four-course meal of traditional local dishes for €22. The *Sicilia* also runs a
ristorante-pizzeria with outside seating (closed Fri mid-Sept to mid-July). For
snacks, call in at the *Gran Bar*, halfway up the corso – it's an old-fashioned place
perfectly in keeping with Mistretta's prevailing sepia tone.

The road from here rolls on over the mountains to Nicosia, 28km south,
accessible by a regular daily bus (not Sun), which afterwards doubles back
into the mountains to the small village of **CAPIZZI**, isolated amid vernal
woods and meadows. You can **eat** inexpensive and nourishing local fare here
at *Trattoria Da Piro*, Via Roma 34 (☎0935.933.881) – worth booking ahead
as it gets busy.

Sant'Agata and San Fratello

Back on the coast, **SANT'AGATA DI MILITELLO** is one of the livelier
Tyrrhenian resorts, busy and noisy in summer with mainly Italian tourists. Its
wide landscaped promenade supports a little funfair, there's a very long pebbled
beach, and the remains of a dumpy castle now house a pizzeria. The small
fishing fleet working off these shores means you get excellent fish in the local
restaurants; for somewhere **to stay**, there's the ageing two-star *Parimar*, Via
Médici 1 (☎0941.701.888; ③), a ten-minute walk east of the centre of town, or
the sprucer *Roma Palace*, about the same distance on the main road west of the
centre, at Via Médici 443 (☎0941.723.815; ④). There is an occasional summer
hydrofoil service connecting Sant'Agata with the Aeolian Islands, though this
does not operate every year; for information, contact the Chidas agency at Via
Médici 383 (☎0941.701.318), which sells tickets – alternatively, there are
departures from Capo d'Orlando, along the coast.

A regular daily bus service – leaving from the central piazza and Via Médici (by
the Banco di Sicilia) – connects Sant'Agata with **SAN FRATELLO**, 15km south.
This large village was once populated by a Lombard colony, introduced to Sicily
by Roger II's queen, Adelaide di Monferrato, and still retains Gallic-Italian traces
in the local dialect. The best time to come here is on the Thursday and Friday of
Holy Week, before Easter, for the **Festa dei Giudei** (Feast of the Jews) – a unique
Carnevale-type celebration in the post-Lent period, when locals adorn themselves
in red devils' costumes, masked and hooded, complete with black tongues and
horses' tails (a reminder of their traditional trade of horse-raising), to the cacophonic
accompaniment of trumpets, bells and drums. Needless to say, the ecclesiastical
authorities take a dim view of these proceedings, but have to make do with having
the Easter Sunday church congregations in suitably contrite and sober mood.

For a pleasant picnic spot, head for the Norman church of **Santi Alfio,
Filadelfio e Cirino**, isolated on top of a hill at the entrance to the village
(follow the rough track from the cemetery). The church is dedicated to three
brothers horribly martyred by the Romans: the first had his tongue torn out,
the second was burnt alive, and the third hurled into a pot of boiling tar.

From Sant'Agata and San Fratello, one early-morning bus (not Sun) meanders
over the mountains to Cesarò, 30km south, en route to Catania.

San Marco d'Alunzio and Frazzanò

Seeing any more of the coast between Sant'Agata and Capo d'Orlando, or
the hills beyond, isn't really on without your own transport. Buses are too

few and far between to be much good for day-trips, although regular services do leave Sant'Agata for **SAN MARCO D'ALUNZIO**, 8km away. An impressively sited inland village, called Aluntium by the Romans, San Marco had already been established in Greek times, and its principal point of interest, the **Tempio di Ércole**, recalls that era – an evocative shell that was converted into a Norman church by Robert Guiscard. It has since been deconsecrated, though something of its mystique remains, thanks to its imposing position high above the coast. Later religious monuments, many built from the local red marble, particularly the **Chiesa di Santa Maria della Grazie**, with a *Madonna* attributed to **Domenico Gagini**, and the **Chiesa Matrice** with an unusual triumphal arch, make San Marco somewhere you could easily spend a couple of hours roaming around; there are also the fragmentary remains of a **castle** where members of the Hauteville family (Sicily's Norman rulers) once resided.

A short drive east along the coastal road brings you to the turnoff for **FRAZZANÒ**, 14km up in the mountains, beyond which lies the Basilian church and monastery of **San Filippo di Fragalà**, a fortress-like structure built by Count Roger in the eleventh century. With high walls enclosing a courtyard, this is sadly abandoned and falling apart, but you can tiptoe over the crumbling floors and peer into the narrow cells, examine the faded Byzantine frescoes on the walls of the church, and enjoy the views from the ramparts. If there's no one around to let you in, try round the back for an open door.

Capo d'Orlando and Naso

Occupying a headland that was the site of a historic defeat for the Aragonese king, Frederick II, at the hands of a group of rebellious barons in 1299, **CAPO D'ORLANDO** is a slick holiday town today, surrounded by good rocky and sandy beaches. If you're sufficiently charmed by the **swimming**, which is best on its eastern side (around the San Gregorio area), you might well want **to stay**. The cheapest accommodation choice is the 1960s-style *Nuovo Hotel Faro*, Via Libertà 7 (℡0941.902.466, ⓦwww.nuovohotelfaro .com; ❸), with spacious rooms and balconies fronting the beach; half-board is usually compulsory in August, at €65 per person. Turn right out of the station and walk along Via Crispi, head for the sea at Piazza Matteotti, and the hotel's a few blocks to the right. The town has plenty of restaurants, bars and *birrerias*, with a choice of discos open in summer. There are also daily **excursions to the Aeolian Islands** between June and September, with departures at 8am, returning at 6.30pm: contact any travel agency in town for further information and bookings, for example Agatirso Viaggi, Via Consolare Antica 332 (℡0941.912.756) or La Rosa, Via Piave 67 (℡0941.904.045). For general tourist **information**, ask at the kiosk on the seafront (summer daily 9am–1pm & 5–8pm, weekdays with reduced hours the rest of the year; ℡0941.918.134) or at the regular **tourist office**, Via Améndola 20, on the corner of Via Volta (Mon–Fri 8am–2pm & 4.30–7.30pm; ℡0941.912.784, ⓦwww.aastcapodorlando.it).

Inland from Capo d'Orlando, the oddly named town of **NASO** ("Nose") sits at the end of a twelve-kilometre bus ride, where you can see (just before entering the town, up a steep lane on the left) the partly ruined **Convento dei Minori Osservanti** – fifteenth-century, with an interesting tomb of the same period decorated with allegories of the six virtues. The road continues up, another 33km, to **FLORESTA**, lying on a grassy plain and, at 1275m, claiming the distinction of being Sicily's highest village, then down to Randazzo and the

foothills of Mount Etna. If you need a break, you can **eat** well for €15–20 at
Floresta's *Trattoria Il Fienile*, Via Vittorio Emanuele (☎0941.662.313), good for
antipasti and meat dishes.

Roman remains at Patti, Tíndari and San Biagio

East of Capo d'Orlando, the coast is more built-up, the unremarkable towns in
places merging into featureless conurbations. Along the way lie a scattering of
Roman remains which merit brief stops; most impressive is the Greco-
Roman site at **Tíndari**, sharing a high promontory with a popular pilgrimage
spot. Lacking the physical splendour of Tíndari's site, the villas at **Patti** and **San
Biagio** are less enticing, though neither requires a great effort to visit if you're
travelling under your own steam.

Patti

Thirty kilometres east of Capo d'Orlando, **PATTI** has more charm than
many of the centres on this coast. At the top of the town, Patti's **Cattedrale**
has a powerful *Madonna* by Antonello de Saliba and, in the right transept, the
tomb of Adelasia, much-loved first wife of Roger I, with the date of her
death inscribed at the bottom, 1118. East of the town, close to the train
station and under an autostrada viaduct, lie the remains of a fourth-century
AD **Roman villa** (daily 9am–1hr before sunset; €2, or €3 for a combined
ticket with Tyndaris), where you can view a few poorly maintained mosaics
and the ruins of a bathhouse; a small **antiquarium** (same ticket) shows finds
from the site.

Tíndari

The area's most complete collection of classical remains is at **TÍNDARI**, 11km
to the east (two–three buses from Patti's main square, also one daily departure
from Messina and one from Milazzo, all Mon–Sat). Originally founded in 396
BC, **Tyndaris**, as it was known, was one of the last Greek settlements in Sicily,
built and fortified by settlers from ancient Syracuse as a defence against
Carthaginian attacks along this coast. Almost impregnable on its commanding
height, the town prospered even under Rome, when it was given special
privileges in return for its loyalty.

Climbing the hill to the site, however, the first thing you see, glistening from
its cliff-top position, is the **Santuario di Tíndari** (Mon–Sat 6.45am–12.30pm
& 2.30–7pm, Sun 6.45am–12.45pm & 2.30–8pm; closes 1hr earlier in winter;
ⓦwww.santuariotindari.it), a lavishly kitsch temple erected in the 1960s to
house the much-revered *Madonna Nera*, or Black Madonna. A plaque underneath this Byzantine icon boasts *Nigra sum, sed hermosa* ("I am black, but
beautiful"), a reference to the esteem in which she has been held for a thousand
years since the icon appeared from the east to perform a series of miracles, such
as producing a soft mattress in the nick of time to save a child who was hurtling
to the rocks below. Pilgrims throng to the sanctuary to pay their respects,
especially around the Black Madonna's feast day on September 8. Buses stop in
the car park over 1km from the sanctuary, from where minibuses leaving every
ten minutes or so shuttle up to the litter of cabins and stalls at the foot of the

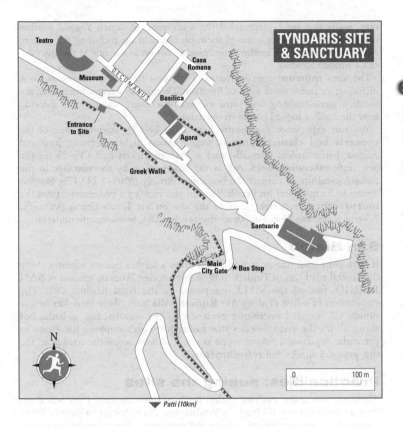

TYNDARIS: SITE & SANCTUARY

Teatro

Casa Romana

Museum

DECUMANUS

Basilica

Entrance to Site

Agora

Greek Walls

Santuario

Main City Gate ★ Bus Stop

N

0   100 m

▼ Patti (10km)

church (return tickets €1). There's a great view from the sanctuary, overlooking a long tongue of white sand and the Marinello lagoons below.

The **archeological site of Tyndaris** (daily 9am–7pm; €2, or €3 including Roman villa at Patti) lies at the end of a path that starts in front of the sanctuary. Most of the visible remains are Roman, including some houses and shops along the main street, the *decumanus* – one of them (probably a *caldarium*, or bathhouse) with traces of plumbing still surviving – and an impressive **basilica** at the eastern end. The basilica would have been the entrance to the *agora* lying beyond (now covered by tourist shops). It was restored in the 1950s, using modern materials, though it still retains a certain grandeur. You can just about make out the manner of its construction, bridging Greek and Roman building techniques, and designed in such a way that the central gallery could be shut off at either end and used for public meetings, with the market traffic diverted along the side passages.

The *decumanus* has streets running off it, and at the bottom of one is the **Casa Romana**, a Roman house in good condition, with mosaic floors. At the other end of the main street, the **teatro**, cut into the hill, boasts a superb view over the sea, as far as the distant Milazzo promontory. A part of the stage remains from the original third-century BC Greek edifice, but most of the rest is Roman, dating from the Imperial Age when the theatre was converted for use as a gladiatorial arena. Later, it was partly dismantled to furnish stone for the city walls that once surrounded the settlement, of which a good portion remain. You'll have seen some of them on the road up, including the ancient city's main gate, built to the same "pincer" design as the one at the Euryalus castle outside Siracusa.

The site's museum contains some of the best finds from the excavations, including a massive stone head of Augustus. There's also a reconstruction of the theatre's scene-building, and some eighteenth-century watercolours showing how the basilica looked before its overhaul.

You can experience the theatre here at its best by attending one of the concerts and classical dramas staged almost nightly between June and August; performances normally start at 9.15pm, tickets cost €15–25 for the best seats, otherwise €6–15. Ask at the ticket office by the entrance to the archeological site or contact the box office directly (℡0941.243.176, ⓦwww .teatrodeiduemari.net) for details. You can also pick up a programme from the tourist office here, right next to the site on Via Teatro Greco (Mon–Fri 7.30am–2pm, also Wed 3–6.30pm; ℡0941.369.184, ⓦwww.pattietindari.it).

San Biagio

If have your own transport, you could drive a further twenty minutes along the coastal road east of Tíndari to the more modest Roman remains at SAN BIAGIO, just off the SS113 (signposted to the right heading east). The excavations of a first-century AD Roman villa here (daily 9am–1hr before sunset; €2) revealed interesting evidence on the construction of baths, but above all it's the vivid mosaics that make this worth stopping for – one in particular depicting a fishing scene at sea. *Il Ritrovo*, across the road from the site, provides snacks and refreshments.

Practicalities: seeing the sites

There are two train stations within reach of the main sites: Patti–San Piero Patti station is the stop for Patti; for Tyndaris you can either take a bus from Patti station direct to the site, or stay on the train for a few more kilometres to Oliveri-Tíndari, from where it's about a three-kilometre (uphill) walk.

Without a vehicle, it's easy to get stranded in these parts. If you do stay, you can enjoy plenty of decent and peaceful swimming, and there's a well-equipped campsite at Patti, the *Marinello* (℡0941.313.000), within a few steps of a good sandy beach and with bungalows available; it's located off the coast road east of town at Località Marinello, at the end of a track. There's another, smaller site at Oliveri: *Baia del Príncipe* (℡0941.313.302). There are also some decent beachside hotels in and around Patti; *Villa Romana*, a few metres from the sea on Via Playa (℡0941.361.268, ⓦwww .hotelvillaromanapatti.com; ➌), offers the best value; at least half-board is required in peak season (€58 per person).

Inland: to Castroreale

From San Biagio, the SS185 branches inland into the mountains, the only road connecting the Tyrrhenian and Ionian coasts, ending at Giardini-Naxos. This is one of the finest routes on the island, climbing gently into the hills through some handsome countryside to NOVARA DI SICILIA, whose main street is dotted with bars selling ice cream and other nibbles. The dense woods above, with expansive views over the sea, are a favourite spot for the locals, who come out here on a Sunday, armed to the teeth with picnic hampers and portable stoves, though there are enough shady nooks and glades to find your own space. Soon after Novara, the road climbs to 1270m before descending, in sight of Etna's dramatic slopes, to Francavilla and Castiglione.

Castroreale

Back on the coast and heading east, you can make a detour at the uninspiring town of Barcellona to the Peloritan hill-village of **CASTROREALE**, 8km to the south and one of the oldest cities in Sicily. Favoured by Frederick II of Aragon, who came here for the hunting, the town enjoys magnificent views over the hills and out to sea. At its highest point is a tower, the one remaining fragment of Frederick II's fort, built in 1324 and subsequently ruined by earthquakes.

The rest of Castroreale is creakingly medieval, and it's enough just to stroll along the quiet, sloping streets, dropping in at the couple of basic bars for a drink. The village hosts the annual festival **Castroreale Jazz** over ten days in late July and early August (Ⓦ www.castrorealejazz.it), featuring evening performances by international jazz musicians in Piazza Peculio.

There's an excellent **place to stay** just outside town on Via Porticato – ⚐ *Green Manors agriturismo* (Ⓣ 090.974.6515, Ⓦ www.greenmanors .it; ❼), run by a Belgian-Italian family and dishing up some of the best meals around. Guests can make use of a swimming pool, a "tropical garden" and a library. If you just want to eat here, phone first. Cheaper accommodation includes an attractive, friendly, if rather rudimentary, **youth hostel**, located in the highest part of the village next to the old Aragonese tower: *Ostello delle Aquile* (Ⓣ 333.900.3308 or 373.6535, Ⓦ www.ostellodelleaquile.com). Each of the male and female dormitories holds ten beds (€13.50 each, less in low season); the minimal facilities include a kitchen (there's no restaurant), washing-room and luggage deposit, and there are organized excursions into the Nébrodi mountains.

To get to Castroreale by **public transport**, take a bus from the bus station at Ponte Longano, in the centre of Barcellona (4 daily Mon–Sat; last departure at 1.35pm); if you're arriving by train, buses connect Barcellona's train station, some way north of the centre, with the bus station (6 daily Mon–Fri; last departure at 2.20pm; tickets from the bar in the station). Alternatively, it would not be inconceivable to walk up, by following the Longano River valley inland for about three hours – the steep bit's at the end.

Milazzo

If it weren't for the industry besieging **MILAZZO** – the first major town on this coast after Términi – it wouldn't be a bad-looking place. A long plane- and palm-tree-lined promenade looks across the sparkling sea, while behind the town a rambling old castle caps Milazzo's ancient acropolis. Most people, though, are put off by the unsightly oil refinery that occasionally produces a yellow smog overhead, and only stop long enough to get out again, taking the first ferry or hydrofoil to the Aeolian Islands (see Chapter Three), for which Milazzo is the major point of embarkation. But Italian tourists know the town well, and regularly crowd the beaches and campsites strung along **Capo Milazzo**, the finger of land behind the town.

The Town

If you're in a hurry, Milazzo is easy enough to handle. You could be on an outward-bound ferry or hydrofoil within an hour of arriving; see below for all the details. But there's enough in and around town to make it an enjoyable overnight stop, before or after your Aeolian trip, with one major sight – the castle – that stands comparison with any in Sicily.

Historically, the site's strategic importance made it one of the most fought-over towns in Sicily. The Greeks arrived in 716 BC, after which the town was contested by successive armies, from the Carthaginians to the Aragonese. It even became a base for the British during the Napoleonic Wars, while fifty years later Garibaldi won a victory here that set the seal on his conquest of Sicily. None of this is evident from the fairly nondescript modern streets behind the port, but a fifteen-minute walk north along Lungomare Garibaldi and up through the **old town** offers a pleasing change in aspect. Here, the views open out over bay and plain, while the higher you climb, the older and more decrepit the buildings become – some churches and *palazzi* on the approach to the castle are little more than precariously balanced shells.

To appreciate the citadel's size, walk round to the north side, where the formidable defences erected by the Spanish still stand almost in their entirety. The massive walls are magnificent, pierced by a suitably imposing tunnelled gateway. The **castello** itself (guided tours hourly Tues–Sun: March–May 9.30–11.30am & 3–5pm; June–Aug 9.30–11.30am & 5–7pm; Sept 9.30–11.30am & 4–6pm; Oct–Feb 9.30–11.30am & 2.30–3.30pm; €3.10) is steeped in military history: built by Frederick II in the thirteenth century on the site of the Greek acropolis and on top of Arab foundations, it was enlarged by Charles V, and restored by the Spanish in the seventeenth century. Inside the castle walls is the **Duomo Antico**, a central Norman keep, the old Sala del Parlamento and the remains of the Palazzo dei Giurati, later used as a prison.

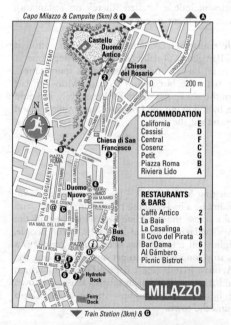

Milazzo has a couple of other churches worth looking at. Directly opposite the castle's entrance, the Dominican **Chiesa del Rosario**, together with its convent, was formerly a seat of the Inquisition, while below, in the new town, the silver-domed **Duomo Nuovo** has some excellent Renaissance paintings in the apse: four panels of SS Peter, Paul, Rocco and Thomas Aquinas; between the last of these, an *Adoration of the Child* by Antonello de Saliba, and an *Annunciation* by Andrea Giuffrè above that. Large, graceful chandeliers adorn the nave.

Capo Milazzo

The thin promontory north of town is the focus of most of the summertime activity.

A couple of fine hotels, three or four well-equipped campsites and a decent restaurant or two are grouped around the headland of **Capo Milazzo**, 6km out of town; it's a twenty-minute bus ride away on #6 from the port. There are plenty of good **beaches** all around here, but the sandiest is close to the centre of town, on Milazzo's western, less-developed side (at the end of Via Colombo).

Practicalities

Buses (including the Giuntabus service from Messina) stop right on the quayside. The **train station** is a good 3km south of the centre, but local buses run into town every 15–30 minutes during the day, dropping you on the quayside or further up in Piazza della Repubblica. Buy tickets (€0.85) aboard, or take a taxi (around €10).

Milazzo's **tourist office** is at Piazza Duilio 20 (Mon 8.30am–1.30pm & 3.30–6.30pm, Tues–Sat 8.30am–1.30pm; ℡090.922.2865), just back from the harbour. There's **Internet** access at Redac, Via Cosenz 29c (Mon–Sat 8.30am–1pm & 4–8pm).

For **ferries** and **hydrofoils** to and from the Aeolian Islands, see p.156; shipping agencies in Milazzo are listed below.

Getting to the Aeolians from Milazzo

Sailings to the Aeolians from Milazzo operate daily and are frequent enough to make it unnecessary to book (unless you're taking a car), although bear in mind that there is a reduced service between October and May. For schedules and prices from Milazzo, see p.156.

The **shipping agencies** listed below are all by Milazzo's port and open usual working hours as well as before all departures – Siremar for ferries and hydrofoils, Ústica Lines for hydrofoils only, and NGI for ferries only. You can pick up useful ferry/hydrofoil **timetables** from any of them. There are also daily **excursions** in summer on cruises, usually sailing from Milazzo at 8.30am or 9am, stopping at two or three of the islands, and returning at around 6pm (tickets €35–60).

If you need to leave a car in Milazzo, you can do so at one of several **garages**, the most convenient of which are also listed below; expect to pay around €12 per day. Some offer a shuttle service to the port.

Shipping agencies
Navigazione Generale Italiana (NGI) Via dei Mille 26 ℡090.928.3415 or 800.250.000, Ⓦwww.ngi-spa.it.
Siremar Alliatour, Via dei Mille 19 ℡090.928.3242 or 892.123, Ⓦwww.siremar.it.
Ústica Lines Catalano, Via dei Mille 33 ℡090.928.7821 or 0923.873.813, Ⓦwww.usticalines.it.

Cruise lines
Tar.Nav Via dei Mille 40 ℡090.922.3617 or 340.070.7285.
Navisal Via Nino Bixio 54 ℡334.747.8008 or 340.414.6311, Ⓦwww.navisal.com.

Garages
Central Garage Via Cumbo Borgia 60 ℡090.928.2472. By the Duomo Nuovo, 5min from the port.
Mil Nautica Via Acquaviole 49 ℡090.928.1912. South of the port, on the road to the train station.
Ullo Via Nino 40 ℡090.928.3309. Signposted up Via Minniti from the port.

Accommodation

There are plenty of reasonable **hotels** handy for the port; if you have a car and the inclination to get out of town, you can stay by the sea. The two nearest **campsites** lie on the cape, 3–4km north of town, and are accessible by bus from Piazza Repubblica: the huge *Cirucco* (℡090.928.4746, ⓦwww.cirucco.it) and the cheaper *Riva Smeralda* (℡090.928.2980, ⓦwww.rivasmeralda.it; April–Oct). Both also have bungalows for rent (❸–❻), available by the week only in high summer and considerably cheaper in low season – the *Cirucco* also has caravans, apartments and B&B rooms (❹).

California Via del Sole 9 ℡090.922.1389. Plain en-suite rooms (singles share bathrooms), some a bit dark and dreary but all clean and quiet. No credit cards. ❷

Cassisi Via Cassisi 5 ℡090.922.9099, ⓦwww.cassisihotel.com. Upmarket hotel with a sober, minimalist style. Its up-to-date facilities include Internet connections (also Wi-Fi), but there's no restaurant. ❼

Central Via del Sole 8 ℡090.928.1043. This cheery little place has relatively spacious rooms with shared bathrooms. No credit cards. ❸

Cosenz Via E. Cosenz ℡090.928.2996. Though not one of the nearest hotels to the port, this is probably Milazzo's best budget choice, on account of its clean, quiet rooms, each equipped with a fridge, a/c and fan, and private bathroom. ❸

🏃 **Petit** Via dei Mille 37 ℡090.928.6784, ⓦwww.petithotel.it. Right opposite the port, this "ecological" hotel has ceramic tiles on the walls and floors, a great roof terrace and nourishing breakfasts. A garage and left-luggage service are available for extra charge. Rates drop outside the peak season. ❼

Piazza Roma Via Pistorio 1 ℡320.726.0946, ⓦwww.bbpiazzaroma.it. Smart, modern B&B with spacious, well-equipped rooms, including top-notch mattresses, though there is some traffic noise. Two of the six rooms share a bathroom, and breakfast is taken in a nearby bar. No credit cards. ❹

Riviera Lido Strada Panoramica ℡090.928.3456, ⓦwww.hotelrivieralido.it. Above a pebbly beach on the promontory a couple of kilometres north of town, this family-oriented three-star offers all the comforts for a leisurely stay – though there is no pool. Make sure of a sea-facing room. ❻

Eating and drinking

There's a small but worthy range of **restaurants and trattorias** in Milazzo's centre; those furthest from the port tend to do the best food. The town's *passeggiata* is one of the liveliest in Sicily, with baby buggies, scooters and cars clogging up Lungomare Garibaldi, and a swarm of couples and families dropping in for ice cream at the **bars** along the way, most of which stay open late in summer.

Restaurants

La Baia Via Sant'Antonio ℡090.928.8314. Out of town, on the cape, a reliable pizzeria/ristorante with outdoor seating overlooking the sea. Among the first courses, *spaghetti al cartoccio*, with a sauce of fish and pine nuts, is recommended. Closed Mon Oct–June. Inexpensive–moderate.

🏃 **La Casalinga** Via R. D'Amico 13 ℡090.922.2697. Local favourite for fish, where the speciality is *spaghetti polpa di granchi* (with crab sauce). First courses are around €7, mains €8–13. Worth booking. Closed Sun evening Oct–June. Moderate.

Il Covo del Pirata Lungomare Garibaldi 47–48 ℡090.928.4437. With wooden ceilings and stone walls, this has more atmosphere than most local eateries, and the food is occasionally superb, but inconsistent. Among the first courses, *linguine tuttomare*, a seafood extravaganza, is recommended (€13). Other pasta dishes are around €10, and cheaper pizzas are also available. Closed Wed. Moderate.

Al Gámbero Via Rizzo 5. Right by the port, this *pizzeria-ristorante* is not particularly distinguished, but it's useful and popular, with fast service and outdoor seating. Pizzas are €6–8; the wine is comparatively pricey. Moderate.

Bars

Caffè Antico Via Duomo Antico. Pleasant spot for a drink, just downhill from the castle, with an outdoor terrace for distant views of the coast.
Bar Dama Piazza Mazzini. Excellent little café for a daytime snack, with a few outdoor tables. The fruit granitas are terrific. Closed Mon Oct–June.
Picnic Bistrot Via Manzoni 24. Snacks as well as beers (including Guinness) are served in this lively backstreet bar, with a mainly youthful clientele. Closed Wed.

Festivals

February/March
Carnevale celebrated in **Cefalù** with three days of events, including a costumed children's procession on the last day.

Easter
Holy Week On the Thursday and Friday, bizarre happenings at **San Fratello**, the Festa dei Giudei, with processions and devils' costumes. Processions, too, in **Barcellona**.

May
Festival in **Milazzo** dedicated to San Francesco di Paola.
Start of the theatrical season at **Tyndaris** with events in the ancient theatre; runs through to Aug.

June
Start of the theatrical performances and concerts at the castle in **Milazzo**; runs through to Aug.

July
In the mountain village of **Castroreale**, Castroreale Jazz attracts international musicians in a series of open-air concerts in late July and early Aug.

August
15 Procession of boats along the coast in honour of Madonna di Porto Salvo at **Capo d'Orlando**.

September
A medieval procession, La Castellana, in **Cáccamo**, composed of five hundred characters representing all the notables in the town's history from the eleventh to the nineteenth centuries. Check with tourist office in Palermo for dates (sometimes held in Aug).
7–8 Procession with Madonna delle Luci and her guardians at **Mistretta**.
8 Informal pilgrimage to the sanctuary of the Black Madonna at **Tyndaris**. Pilgrimage, too, at **Gibilmanna**, south of Cefalù.

October
Horse fair in **San Fratello**.

November
Historical fair held in **Sant'Agata di Militello**.

Travel details

Trains

Cefalù to: Messina (12 daily; 2hr 15min–3hr); Milazzo (12 daily; 1hr 40min–2hr); Palermo (1–2 hourly; 1hr).
Milazzo to: Cefalù (12 daily; 1hr 35min–2hr 25min); Messina (1–2 hourly; 30–45min); Palermo (hourly; 2hr 30min–3hr).
Sant'Agata di Militello to: Barcellona (1–2 hourly; 50min–1hr 10min); Capo d'Orlando (1–2 hourly; 15min); Messina (1–2 hourly; 1hr 30min–2hr); Milazzo (1–2 hourly; 55min–1hr 20min); Oliveri–Tíndari (9 daily; 50min); Patti (1–2 hourly; 30–50min).
Términi Imerese to: Cefalù (1–2 hourly; 25min); Messina (hourly; 2hr 30min–3hr); Palermo (every 15–30min; 35min); Sant'Agata di Militello (1–2 hourly; 1hr–1hr 30min); Santo Stéfano di Camastra (hourly; 45min–1hr).

Buses

Barcellona to: Castroreale (4 daily Mon–Sat; 30min).
Cáccamo to: Cefalù (2 daily; 45min); Palermo
(4 daily Mon–Sat; 1hr 15min); Términi Imerese
(8 daily Mon–Sat; 15min).
Castelbuono to: Cefalù (7 daily Mon–Sat, 1–2 daily
Sun; 40min); Collesano (6 daily Mon–Sat; 45min);
Gangi (1 daily; 1hr–1hr 20min); Geraci (2 daily
Mon–Sat, 1 daily Sun; 45min); Isnello (1 daily
Mon–Sat; 25min); Palermo (3 daily Mon–Sat;
1hr 15min); Términi Imerese (2 daily Mon–Sat;
1hr 30min).
Cefalù to: Cáccamo (2 daily; 45min); Castelbuono
(7 daily Mon–Sat, 2 daily Sun; 40min); Gangi
(1 daily; 1hr 45min–2hr); Geraci (2 daily Mon–Sat,
1 daily Sun; 1hr 25min); Gibilmanna (3 daily;
30min); Palermo (3 daily Mon–Sat, 1 daily Sun;
1hr); Petralia (1 daily Mon–Sat; 2hr).
Milazzo to: Messina (1–2 hourly Mon–Sat, 5 daily
Sun; 50min–1hr).
Patti to: Tíndari (2–3 daily; 20min).
Sant'Agata di Militello to: Cesarò (1 daily
Mon–Sat; 1hr 30min); San Fratello (6 daily; 20min);
San Marco d'Alunzio (4 daily; 20min).
Santo Stéfano di Camastra to: Mistretta (6 daily
Mon–Sat, 3 daily Sun; 35min); Nicosia (1 daily
Mon–Sat; 1hr 30min).
Términi Imerese to: Cáccamo (9–10 daily
Mon–Sat; 15min); Castelbuono (2 daily Mon–Sat;
1hr 30min); Collesano (2 daily Mon–Sat; 45min).

Ferries

Ferry timetables change seasonally, so if time is of
the essence, it's always worth checking with the
tourist office or ferry company for the most up-to-
date schedules.
Milazzo *June–Sept* to: Alicudi (6 weekly; 6hr);
Filicudi (6 weekly; 5hr); Ginostra (5 weekly; 5hr
10min–6hr); Lípari (5–10 daily; 2hr–2hr 30min);
Naples (2 weekly; 17hr); Panarea (5 weekly;
4–5hr); Rinella (8 weekly; 3hr 45min–4hr);
Santa Marina (4 daily; 3hr–3hr 40min);

Strómboli (5 weekly; 5hr 50min–6hr 40min);
Vulcano (5–8 daily; 1hr 30min–2hr).
Milazzo *Oct–May* to: Alicudi (5 weekly; 6hr);
Filicudi (5 weekly; 5hr); Ginostra (3 weekly; 5hr
10min–6hr); Lípari (4–5 daily; 2hr–2hr 30min);
Naples (2 weekly; 22hr); Panarea (5 weekly;
4–5hr); Rinella (6 weekly; 3hr 45min–6hr); Santa
Marina (3–5 daily; 3hr–3hr 40min); Strómboli
(5 weekly; 2hr 40min–6hr 40min); Vulcano (4–5
daily; 1hr 30min–2hr).

Hydrofoils

Hydrofoil timetables change seasonally so, if time
is of the essence, it's always worthwhile checking
with the tourist office or hydrofoil company for the
most up-to-date schedules.
Cefalù *June to mid-Sept* to: Alicudi (1 daily; 1hr
15min); Filicudi (1 daily; 1hr 50min); Lípari (1 daily;
3hr 15min); Palermo (1 daily; 55min); Panarea
(1 daily; 3hr 45min); Rinella (1 daily; 2hr 30min);
Santa Marina (1 daily; 2hr 45min); Strómboli
(1 daily; 4hr 25min); Vulcano (1 daily; 3hr 35min).
Cefalù *Mid-Sept to May* to: Alicudi (3 weekly; 1hr
15min); Filicudi (3 weekly; 1hr 55min); Lípari
(3 weekly; 3hr 20min); Milazzo (3 weekly; 4hr
40min); Palermo (3 weekly; 1hr 10min); Rinella
(3 weekly; 2hr 35min); Santa Marina (3 weekly;
2hr 50min); Vulcano (3 weekly; 3hr 40min).
Milazzo *June to mid-Sept* to: Alicudi (3 daily; 2hr
55hr–3hr 15min); Filicudi (3 daily; 2hr 20min–2hr
35min); Ginostra (4 daily; 1hr 20min–2hr 30min);
Lípari (17 daily; 1hr); Naples (1 daily; 9hr); Panarea
(7 daily; 1hr 15min–3hr); Rinella (6 daily; 1hr
35min–2hr); Santa Marina (15 daily; 1hr 40min);
Strómboli (8 daily; 3hr); Vulcano (16 daily; 45min).
Milazzo *Oct–May* to: Alicudi (1–2 daily; 2hr
35min–3hr 10min); Cefalù (3 weekly; 4hr 30min);
Filicudi (1–2 daily; 2hr–2hr 30min); Ginostra
(1 daily; 2hr 15min); Lípari (13–14 daily;
40min–1hr); Panarea (1 daily; 1hr 50min); Rinella
(8 daily; 1hr 40min); Santa Marina (11–12 daily;
1hr 25min); Strómboli (2 daily; 1hr–2hr 30min);
Vulcano (13–14 daily; 40min–1hr).

The Aeolian Islands

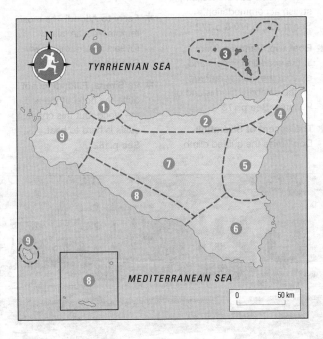

CHAPTER 3 # Highlights

✳ **Upper town, Lípari** The ancient citadel, high above two harbours, shelters the island's magnificent archeological museum. See p.160

✳ **Boutique accommodation, Salina** The up-and-coming island – not so well known as others – has some excellent, stylish accommodation. See p.168, p.170 & p.172

✳ **Boat trip, Panarea** Swim in the sparkling waters and explore the craggy outcrops off the celebrity-filled island of Panarea. See p.173

✳ **The ascent of Strómboli** Don't miss the guided climb up one of the world's most active volcanoes. See p.178

✳ **Abandoned villages, Filicudi** Villages abandoned to emigration, like that of Zucco Grande, make a great target for a hike on Filicudi. See p.181

✳ **Ferry to Alicudi** The most remote Aeolian island reveals its charms slowly See p.182

✳ **La Sirena, Filicudi** Its not quite the hotel at the end of the world, but this charming oasis is hard to beat. See p.182

▲ The waterfront at Lípari

The Aeolian Islands

The **Aeolian Islands**, or Isole Eolie, are a mysterious apparition when glimpsed from Sicily's northern coast. Sometimes it's clear enough to pick out the individual white houses on their rocky shores; at other times they're murky, misty and only half-visible. D.H. Lawrence, on his way to Palermo by train in bad weather, thought they resembled "… heaps of shadow deposited like rubbish heaps in the universal greyness". The sleepy calm that seems to envelop this archipelago masks a more dramatic existence: two of the islands are still volcanically active, and all are buffeted alternately by ferocious storms in winter and waves of tourists in summer. But their unique charm has survived more or less intact, fuelled by the myths associated with their elemental and unpredictable power.

Closest island to the mainland is the tourist magnet of **Vulcano**, with its mud baths, hot springs, black sand beaches and smoking main crater. Across the channel lies the main island, **Lípari**, which is the hub of the ferry and hydrofoil system and so makes the best base for island-hopping. It also has the widest choice of accommodation and restaurants, and is the only island with any kind of life outside the main summer season. Of the central group of islands, **Panarea** is the smallest and most elite, attracting a well-heeled crowd every July and August, while **Salina** springs perhaps the best surprise – second in size only to Lípari, it's increasingly fashionable and atypically fertile, source of the archipelago's most notable wine. A trip up to **Strómboli**'s seething crater is an unforgettable experience, but for a taste of what it was like twenty – or a hundred – years ago make the effort to get out to the two remotest of the Aeolian Islands. **Filicudi** has something of a boutique feel, and is increasingly popular with walkers, while distant **Alicudi** is by far the most obscure of the group and, some would say, the hardest to like.

Individual identity aside, each Aeolian island is embraced by water of a limpid quality rarely found along the coast of Sicily. Sandy beaches are sparse, and tend to be ash-black, but **boat tours** (available at every Aeolian harbour) provide access to any number of secluded coves, hidden caves and quiet snorkelling and scuba-diving waters. Lípari and Salina are the only two islands you might consider taking a car across to, but that's hardly necessary (best leave it in a garage on the mainland). Both islands have a good bus network, while you can rent bicycles, mopeds and scooters on all the main islands, or simply walk around the smaller ones. **Aeolian food** is among the most distinctive in Italy, fish of course providing the mainstay but with the traditional crops of capers, olives and mountain herbs flavouring most dishes, while the *malvasia* grapes provide one of Sicily's more ancient wines. Other foods (as well as much of the water on some islands) have to be imported, so restaurants tend towards the expensive, as does

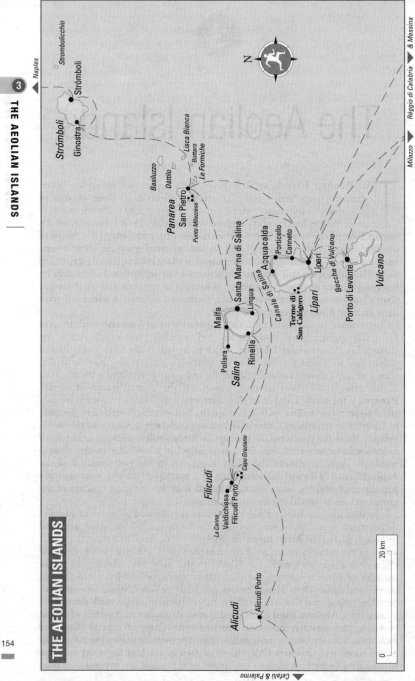

THE AEOLIAN ISLANDS

0   20 km

◄ Cefalù & Palermo

Milazzo ▶   Réggio di Calábria ▶   & Messina

◄ Naples

Alicudi
Alicudi Porto

Filicudi
La Canna
Valdichiesa
Filicudi Porto
Capo Graziano

Salina
Pollara
Malfa
Rinella
Lingua
Santa Marina di Salina
Canale di Salina

Panarea
San Pietro
Punta Milazzese
Basiluzzo
Dáttilo
Lisca Bianca
Bottaro
Le Formiche

Strómboli
Ginostra
Strómboli
Strombolicchio

Lipari
Acquacalda
Porticello
Canneto
Lipari
Terme di
San Calógero

Vulcano
Bocche di Vulcano
Porto di Levante
Bocche di Levante

N

accommodation. Places offering simple rooms vie with boutique and resort hotels throughout the islands, but high prices and limited availability in high season is common to them all (Easter, July & Aug), when many also insist on half-board (*mezza-pensione*, ie dinner, bed and breakfast) and multi-night stays.

Ferries and hydrofoils ply between the islands year-round – their arrival is often the high point of the day in a place like Alicudi. Services are reduced **out of season** (basically Oct to May), but you should still be able to reach most islands daily. Indeed, visiting outside peak season is highly recommended, since there's a refreshing absence of other tourists, and accommodation rates plummet accordingly. However, be warned that many hotels and restaurants close their doors for the entire winter while if the weather turns, you're in danger of being stuck for days – the archipelago is frequently lashed by storms between October and March, and heavy seas can mean the cancellation of ferry and hydrofoil services to both the mainland and the other islands. If this happens, there's no alternative to sitting and waiting the storm out.

Legends and history

Volcanoes have always been identified with the mouths of hell, and it was in the Aeolians that Jupiter's son, **Vulcan**, had his workshop. Vulcano is named after this god of fire and metalworking, while another island takes its name from Liparus, whose daughter Ciane married **Aeolus**, ruler of the winds and master of navigation; Aeolus, in turn, lent his name to the whole archipelago. These winds were kept in one of the Aeolians' many caves, and were presented to Odysseus in a bag to take on his travels. His curious crew opened the bag and, as a result, blew his ship straight back to port.

The first historic settlers exploited the volcanic resources, above all the abundance of **obsidian**, a hard glass-like rock that can be worked to produce a fine cutting edge and was traded far and wide, accruing enormous wealth to the archipelago. The islands were drawn more closely into the Greek ambit by the arrival, at about 580 BC, of refugees from the wars between Segesta and Selinus (Selinunte). Those Greeks based at the fortified citadel of Lípari later allied themselves with Carthage, which made Lípari its base during the First Punic War. For its pains, Greek Lípari was destroyed by the Romans in 251 BC and the islands became part of the Roman province of Sicily, paying hefty taxes on exports of obsidian. The islands subsequently changed hands several times before being abandoned to the frequent attacks of wide-ranging North African **pirates**, culminating in the terrible slaughter that took place in 1544 at the hands of Khair ed-Din, or Barbarossa, who consigned all the survivors of the massacre to slavery – a figure estimated to have been as high as 10,000. Italian unification saw the islands used as a prison for political exiles, a role that continued right up to World War II, with the Fascists exiling their political opponents to Lípari. The last political detainee to be held here was, ironically, Mussolini's own daughter, Edda Ciano, in 1946.

Emigration, especially to Australia, had reduced the Aeolian population to a mere handful of families by the late 1950s, when the arrival of the first hydrofoil signalled salvation by a nascent tourist industry. Today's economy is based largely on **tourism** (though Lípari's pumice industry still flourishes), with hotels sprouting on previously barren ground, and running water and electricity installed (almost) everywhere. Nonetheless, enough primitive splendour has remained for the islands to attract a procession of film crews, the movies ranging from Rossellini's *Stròmboli: Terra di Dio* (1949) to Michael Radford's *Il Postino* (1994), filmed on Salina. Since 2000, the Aeolians have been listed as a UNESCO World Heritage Site.

Getting there

Ferries (*navi* or *traghetti*) and **hydrofoils** (*aliscafi*) depart year-round (weather permitting) from Milazzo, Messina, Palermo and Cefalù. Services are with three main companies, namely **Siremar** (ⓦ www.siremar.it), **Ústica Lines** (ⓦ www.usticalines.it) and **NGI** (ⓦ www.ngi-spa.it), with fares roughly pegged to each other. The most frequent services to all islands are in high season, June to September inclusive. The car-carrying ferries take roughly twice as long to most destinations as the hydrofoils, but are around sixty percent cheaper. The hydrofoils are also more prone to cancellation in bad weather, particularly out to the more distant islands.

The traditional embarkation point is **Milazzo**, an hour from Messina by bus or train, with daily, year-round sailings with Siremar (ferries and hydrofoils), Ústica Lines (hydrofoils) and NGI (ferries). In summer, services depart almost hourly from here to the main islands, and most services from Milazzo call first at either Vulcano or Lípari.

Departures from **Messina** are more convenient if you're coming directly from Catania airport. Ústica Lines runs hydrofoils out to the islands from here all year (at least once daily, even in winter), and also operates summer connections from mainland Italy, from either Réggio di Calabria (some via Messina) or Naples (these calling first at Strómboli). Coming from the west of Sicily (or arriving at Palermo airport), it makes far more sense to use the Ústica Lines hydrofoil services from either **Palermo** or **Cefalù**, which run daily in summer, three times a week the rest of the year. However, note that these services are routed first via Alicudi and Filicudi, which makes for a long and expensive trip if you're heading directly for Strómboli, for example.

Tickets are sold at the companies' harbourside offices before departure, and timetables are posted at every office – or up-to-date schedules are available online on the company websites. Only in August might you need to buy tickets in advance; otherwise, services are rarely full. Sample one-way high-season **fares** from Milazzo are around €15 by hydrofoil, €10 by ferry, to Lípari; €20/14 to Strómboli; and €25/16 to Alicudi. Hydrofoils from Messina to Lípari cost around €18, while from Palermo you'll pay around €20 to Alicudi, €32 to Lípari and €43 to Strómboli. Transporting a car on the car-ferry starts at around €30 (Milazzo to Lípari), while on all services children under four go free and under-12s go half-price. All fares cost a couple of euros less between October and May.

Lípari

LÍPARI is the busiest and most diverse island in the Aeolian archipelago, with a long history of settlement and trade. The main town – also called Lípari – is a thriving little port, dominated by impressive castle walls that surround an upper citadel housing the bulk of the archeological remains and a terrific museum. The road that circles the island from town takes in several much smaller villages, some good beaches and excellent views out to the neighbouring islands. Historically, it has always been Lípari that has guided the development of the Aeolians. In classical times, after obsidian had been superseded by metals, the island's prosperity was based on its sulphur baths and thermal waters, while its alum, too, was much prized, and was found more abundantly here than anywhere else in Italy. Today, with a population of over 10,000, the economy is bolstered by a thriving pumice industry in the north of the island, though the main money-spinner is inevitably Lípari's natural beauty, which brings in

▲ Fishermen on Lípari

tourists by the boatload. But it's certainly not spoiled and, in Lípari town, the island holds the one Aeolian settlement with enough diversions and facilities to warrant spending several days or more.

Arrival, information and transport

Hydrofoils and ferries dock at Lípari town's **Marina Lunga** (sometimes called Porto Sottomonastero). The quickest services from Milazzo take between forty-five minutes and an hour, or it's roughly ninety minutes from Messina. Dockside offices sell tickets and post timetables; Siremar and Ústica Lines are in the same building, just up from the gangways. A fifteen-minute walk south of Marina Lunga, down the main Corso Vittorio Emanuele, is **Marina Corta**, a smaller harbour used by excursion boats. Virtually everything of note lies between these two marinas.

157

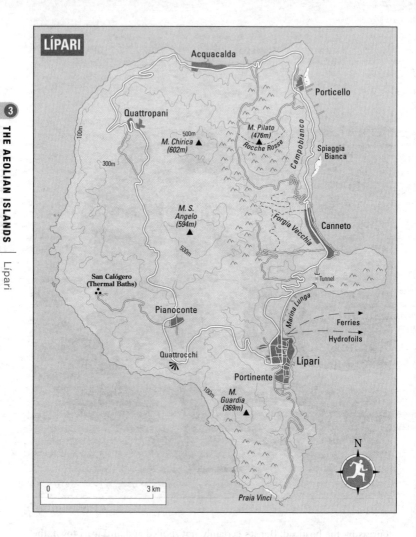

The **tourist office**, Corso Vittorio Emanuele 202 (Mon–Fri 8.30am–1.30pm & 4.30–7.30pm; July & Aug also open later in the evening, plus Sat & Sun 8.30am–1.30pm; ☎090.988.0095, ⓦ www.aasteolie.info), is the most reliable place for information on all the islands, and hands out the very useful *Ospitalità in blu* accommodation and listings booklet; there's also lots of information in English on the website.

Buses leave Lípari town approximately every hour for the rest of the island (every 15–30min in summer for Canneto, fewer on all routes on Sun and outside July and Aug). They depart from an obvious stop at Marina Lunga, opposite the petrol station, close to the quayside ticket agency, and current timetables are posted at the kiosk window; buy tickets on board. Nowhere is more than thirty minutes' ride away.

Accommodation

Although there's more accommodation in Lípari town than anywhere else, you can still find yourself stuck for a room in July and August, so if you don't have a reservation it makes sense to listen to the offers of **rooms** as you step off the boat. Many of the owners of places reviewed below meet arrivals at the quayside. Prices vary so much (often doubling in Aug) that the codes below show the possible range over much of the year; for the cheapest rooms, as a rule, expect to pay €50 per person in August, around €25–30 at other times of the year. There's often a minimum stay (usually three or four nights) in high summer, while hotels will probably require you to take half-board terms. The island's only **campsite**, and the archipelago's only **youth hostel**, are both out at the beach strip of Canneto, 3km north of town, which is easily reached by bus but not a patch on Lípari town as a base.

B&Bs and hotels

Carasco Porto delle Genti ☎090.981.1605, Ⓦwww.carasco.it. Superbly located three-star hotel, with its own terraces, rocky cove, good pool and sparkling views. There's a wide range of rooms (up to suites with lounge and jacuzzi), though not all standard rooms have sea views. It's out of the centre, though not too far from Portinente beach and the Marina Corta. Closed Nov to March. ❻, Aug ❽

Casajanca Marina Garibaldi 109, Canneto ☎090.988.0222, Ⓦwww.casajanca.it. If you don't mind being out at Canneto, you might prefer the boutique style of Casajanca to the resort hotels of town. It's a charming townhouse hotel, three-star standard, 20m back from the beachfront promenade, with ten stylish rooms and personal service. You can also ask about their simpler B&B in Canneto. ❺, Aug ❼

Diana Brown Vico Himera 3 ☎090.981.2584 or 338.640.7572, Ⓦwww.dianabrown.it. Run by a jovial South African and her Sicilian husband, this is a really friendly and well-organized B&B, located in a tiny lane parallel to Corso Vittorio Emanuele. Seven smart rooms have air conditioning/heating, fridges and kettles, while another five also have small kitchenettes, and there's a great roof terrace where you eat breakfast. There's a book exchange and laundry service available, while Diana and her family know lots about the island, and can advise about walks and boat tours. Breakfast is €5, though included in Aug. ❷–❹, Aug ❺

Enza Marturano Via Maurolico 35 ☎368.322.4997, Ⓦwww.enzamarturano.it. Four bright, modern rooms with views, ranged around a communal lounge/kitchen, with a terrace overlooking the corso. No credit cards. ❷–❹, Aug ❺

Enzo Il Negro Via Garibaldi 29 ☎090.981.3163, Ⓦwww.enzoilnegro.altervista.org. "Enzo the black" takes its name from the bronzed owner's local nickname. It's just up from the Marina Corta, where eight rooms, all with a/c and fridge, share one of the best private roof terraces in town. ❸, Aug ❺

Neri Via G. Marconi 43 ☎090.981.1413, Ⓦwww.pensioneneri.it. Breakfast is served on a lovely terrace at this fine old Liberty (ie Art Deco) villa, which has retained its wrought-iron balconies and other original features. They also have a couple of simple apartments out by the beach at Canneto. Closed Nov to Feb. ❹–❺, Aug ❻

Tritone Via Mendolita ☎090.981.1595, Ⓦwww.bernardigroup.it. This superior four-star on the southern edge of the town centre is the best of the resort-style hotels, set away from the town bustle amid quiet gardens. There's a good pool, and rooms all have balcony or terrace. At the associated *Residence Mendolita*, a collection of self-contained villas and apartments set in mature gardens just down the road, accommodation is slightly cheaper throughout the year. ❺–❻, Aug ❼

Villa Meligunis Via Marte 7 ☎090.981.2426, Ⓦwww.villameligunis.it. A converted *palazzo*, this elegant central four-star has excellent views of the citadel and sea from its rooftop restaurant, which sports a pool alongside. Rooms are tastefully turned out, many with sea views and balconies; there is also a beautifully restored eighteenth-century annexe with apartments. ❼, Aug ❾

Hostel and campsite

Baia Unci Canneto ☎090.981.1540, Ⓦwww.liparicasevacanze.it. The hostel (closed Nov–March), a townhouse at the southern end of the seafront, overlooking the beach, is more like mini-apartments, with two five-bedded dorm rooms sharing a kitchen and terrace area. Advance reservations are essential; their bus picks up guests from Lípari harbour. The hostel is virtually next door to the island's only campsite, also called the *Baia Unci* (☎ 090.981.1909, ⊛ www.baiaunci.com;

closed Oct–March), with its own bar and restaurant, or there's the *Ristorante del Pescatore* in between the two. The bus from Lípari stops outside hostel and campsite. No credit cards. Hostel dorm beds €20, though cheaper out of season; cabins available at the campsite.

Lípari Town

LÍPARI TOWN is split into upper and lower sections. Virtually everything of historic interest lies in the upper town, or citadel, protected by the sturdy walls of the castle, while all the shops and services are in the lower town, mostly along and off the main Corso Vittorio Emanuele, with the town's two harbours at either end. The most impressive approach from lower to upper town is from Via Garibaldi, from which long steps cut right up through the thick defensive walls, emerging right outside the Duomo, or cathedral.

The upper town

Most of what remains of Lípari's formidable citadel is sixteenth-century Spanish in style, though it incorporates fragments of earlier medieval and even Greek buildings. Until the eighteenth century, this upper zone was the site of Lípari town itself, which explains the presence of the island's most important church, the **Duomo**, along with the dilapidated ruins of several other Baroque churches. Scattered in between are the excavations of superimposed layers of occupation, from the Neolithic to the Roman age, a continuous record covering almost two thousand years and a unique sequence that has allowed archeologists to date other Mediterranean cultures. The wide excavated trenches don't tell you much, though spare a glance at least at the **Parco Archeológico** at the southern end of the citadel walls (Mon–Sat 9am–dusk; free), which has some Greek and Roman tombs on display, a (modern) amphitheatre and nice views over the rooftops and Marina Corta.

All the archeological finds are displayed in Lípari's superb **Museo Eoliano** (daily 9am–1.30pm & 3–7pm; €6), which is housed in various buildings sited on either side of the Duomo. Though this ranks among Europe's most important prehistoric and classical collections, despite the official opening hours most of the sections are usually only accessible in the mornings – only the **Sezione Classica** tends to keep its full daily hours. This holds classical and Hellenic material retrieved from various necropoli, and includes re-creations of both a Bronze Age burial ground and of the Lípari necropolis (eleventh century BC), where bodies were either buried in a crouching position in large, plump jars or their cremated remains placed in bucket-shaped jars (*situlae*). Most eye-catching of all are the towering banks of amphorae, each 1m or so high, dredged from the ocean under Capo Graziano (Filicudi), many still encrusted with barnacles. There are also shelves of decorated vases – showing sacrifices, bathing scenes, mythical encounters and ceremonies – with many identified as those of an individual known as the Lípari Painter (300–270 BC) and his pupils and rough contemporaries. Other poignant funerary goods include toy vases and statuettes from the grave of a young girl, and delicate clay figurines of working women using mortar and pestle or washing children in a little bath.

The museum, though, is best known for what comes last in the Sezione Classica, namely the oldest and most complete range of Greek **theatrical masks** in existence. Many are models, found in fourth-century BC graves, and covering the gamut of Greek theatrical life from the tragedies of Sophocles and Euripides to satyr plays and comedies. One room has a collection of small

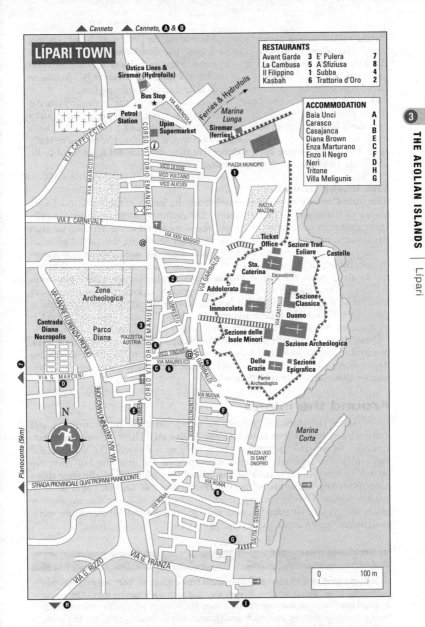

LÍPARI TOWN

Úastica Lines &
Siremar (Hydrofoils)

Bus Stop

Petrol
Station

Upim
Supermarket

Siremar
(ferries)

Marina
Lunga

Ferries & Hydrofoils

PIAZZA MUNICIPIO

VIA AMENDOLA

VICO ULISSE
VICO VULCANO
VICO ALICUDI

PIAZZA
MAZZINI

VIA E. CARNEVALE

VIA XXIV MAGGIO

Ticket
Office

Sezione Trad.
Eoliare

Castello

Sta.
Caterina

Excavations

Addolorata

Immacolata

Sezione
Classica

Duomo

Sezione delle
Isole Minori

Sezione Archeólogica

Delle
Grazie

Sezione
Epigrafica

Parco
Archeologico

VIA NUOVA

Zona
Archeologica

Contrada
Diana
Necropolis

Parco
Diana

PIAZZETTA
AUSTRIA

VIA MADRE FLORENZIA PROFILIO

VIA G. MARCONI

VIA MAUROLICO

VICO TINCARI

VICO TIMPONE

VIA G. RIZZO

VIA ANT. ANTONINO MAGGIORE

STRADA PROVINCIALE QUATTROPANI PIANOCONTE

VIA ROMA

PIAZZA UGO
DI SANT'
ONOFRIO

Marina
Corta

VIA G. FRANZA

SALITA S. GIUSEPPE

Pianoconte (5km)

N

0   100 m

CORSO VITTORIO EMANUELE

VIA CAPPUCCINI

VIA MANCUSO

VIA GARIBALDI

VIA UMBERTO

VIA CASTELLO

VICO S. EUNIMIE

Canneto   Canneto, A & B

RESTAURANTS

Avant Garde	3	E' Pulera	7
La Cambusa	5	A Sfiziusa	8
Il Filippino	1	Subba	4
Kasbah	6	Trattoria d'Oro	2

ACCOMMODATION

Baia Unci	A
Carasco	I
Casajanca	B
Diana Brown	E
Enza Marturano	C
Enzo Il Negro	F
Neri	D
Tritone	H
Villa Meligunis	G

terracottas grouped in theatrical scenes, while there are also statuettes representing actual dancers and actors – nothing less than early Greek pin-ups of the period's top stars.

The seventeenth-century bishop's palace contains the **Sezione Archeólogica**, where you can trace the early exploitation of obsidian, made into blades and exported all over the western Mediterranean – glass cases contain mounds of shards, worked flints, adzes and knives. Meanwhile, the pottery finds from ancient burial sites allowed archeologists to follow the development of the various Aeolian cultures, as burial techniques became gradually more sophisticated and grave goods more elaborate – as in the lid of a mid-sixth-century BC *bothros*, or sacred repository of votive articles, embellished with a reclining lion.

Other museum sections cover subjects as diverse as the prehistory of the minor islands or Aeolian traditions and customs, while the **Sezione Epigrafica** contains a little garden of tombs and engraved stones, and a room packed with more inscribed Greek and Roman tombstones and stelae. Unless you're really keen, though, and come back another day, there are diminishing returns to be had from soldiering on to the bitter end.

The lower town
The main **Corso Vittorio Emanuele** runs the length of the lower town – it's closed to traffic and is packed during the evening *passeggiata*, when its cafés come into their own. Most of the gift shops are found along here, but tourism has never completely dominated life in Lípari so among the carved obsidian trinkets, coral jewellery and Etna postcards there are still shops selling screwdrivers, fishing tackle, goldfish, sets of steak knives and embroidered towels. Just off the main corso, the **Parco Diana Zona Archeológica** (daily 9am–noon & 2.30–6.30pm, though sometimes unaccountably locked; free) preserves more remains of ancient buildings and houses, though the more interesting sight is the nearby **Contrada Diana necropolis**, closed for access but visible off Via G. Marconi, where Greco-Roman tombs stud a sunken field.

Other than this, the best place to explore is down around the **Marina Corta**, overlooked by parasol-shaded cafés. It's where most of the boat excursions depart from, while behind the chapel and up the steps you can get lost in the narrow alleys of the old fishing quarter.

Around the island
Buses run in two directions around the island, clockwise to Quattropani, and anticlockwise to Canneto, Porticello and Acquacalda. There are enough departures (up to ten daily in summer) to be able to get around the whole island easily in a day, although if you're really pushed for time the bus company operates a ninety-minute **tour of the island** (*giro dell'isola*), usually three times a day from July to the end of September (around €4). Or you could drive or scooter around Lípari's winding roads in a couple of hours flat, stopping at places like Monte Guardia, Quattrocchi, Quattropani and Monterosa for some amazing views out across the archipelago.

Boat excursions
Tour operators all over town offer year-round boat excursions, both around Lípari and to all the other islands, which is an easy way to do some sightseeing without bothering about bus timetables and hydrofoil schedules. The boats mostly run from Marina Corta, where several agencies post information boards with times and prices, or visit friendly Da Massimo, Via Maurolico 2 (℡090.981.3086, ⩗www.damassimo.it) to talk over the options. Prices are pitched roughly the same everywhere, from €15 for a Lípari and Vulcano tour, and from €30 to Panarea or Salina, though you can also book "Strómboli by night" trips (from €35) or Strómboli crater climbs (from €80). On day tours, you'll get plenty of time for swimming and lunch. Most operators also run **beach shuttles** in summer to good beaches that are otherwise tricky to reach, like Lípari's Praia Vinci.

Canneto and Campobianco

It's around 3km north from Lípari town to the nearest village, **Canneto**, set on a wide bay on the other side of the headland. A long stony beach fronts the village, which has a rather abandoned feel outside summer when most businesses are closed. For more secluded swimming, stay on the bus until it reaches a stop at the far northern end of the lungomare, at a steep rise. From here, a stepped path runs up, around and down to the **Spiaggia Bianca**, an expansive sand-and-pebble beach that is worth the effort to reach. Refreshments and parasols are available here in summer.

Buses continue north of Canneto, through the Cave di Pomice at **Campobianco**, where pumice workings have left huge white scars on the hillside. For 2 or 3km all around, the ground looks as if it's had a dusting of talcum powder, while years of accumulation of pumice sediment on the sea bed have turned the water a piercing aquamarine colour – very enticing and instantly accessible by sliding the 30m or so down the brilliant white mountains of dust formed by the quarrying. This is nothing new to the islanders, who've been doing it for years; indeed the pumice-chute was used for one of the closing scenes in the Taviani Brothers' epic film *Kaos*.

Above Campobianco, a path leads up the slopes of **Monte Pilato** (476m), thrown up in the eruption from which all the pumice originally came. The last explosion occurred in around 700 AD, leading to the virtual abandonment of Lípari town and creating the obsidian flows of Rocche Rosse and Forgia Vecchia, both of which can be climbed. Although it's overgrown with vegetation, you can still make out the outline of the crater at the top, and you may come across the blue-black veins of obsidian. It's the presence of obsidian on Lípari that makes the island's beaches sparkle.

Porticello and Acquacalda

From the bus stop above the stony beach at **Porticello**, a road (and a quicker, more direct path) winds down to a small bay, which sunbathers share with the Heath Robinson-style pumice-work machinery that connects the white hillside with the pier. Somewhere, you feel, should be someone cranking a

▲ Campobianco

handle on a very large wheel to set it all in motion. There's no shade here, and the pebble beach soon reaches scalding temperatures. A couple of summer vans sell cool drinks and snacks.

Buses all terminate a couple of kilometres further on at **Acquacalda**; you could walk between the two villages in about half an hour, if you wanted some aerial views of the azure waters and pumice quarries, and pick up the return Lípari bus in either place. Acquacalda itself is just a one-street village – not a very attractive one – with more pumice machinery, a long, usually deserted stone beach and a couple of waterfront bars.

Quattrocchi to Quattropani

Heading west from Lípari town, a three-kilometre climb through lush and fertile country leads to **Quattrocchi**, a noted viewpoint over Vulcano and the spiky *faraglioni* rocks, which puncture the sea between the two islands. The curious name ("Four Eyes") is said to derive from the fact that newly wedded couples traditionally come here to be photographed, so gracing every shot with two pairs of eyes.

Just before the fragmented village of Pianoconte, a side road slinks off down to the old Roman thermal baths at **San Calógero**. It's a particularly pleasant route to follow on foot, across a valley and skirting some impressive cliffs, with the baths sited right at the end of the road. The bus from Lípari meanwhile (through Quattrocchi and Pianoconte) ends its run at **Quattropani**, a dispersed settlement with more fine views. If it isn't too hot you could always walk the 5km or so, further along the winding road, to complete the island circle at Acquacalda, and catch the bus back from there.

Eating, drinking and entertainment

There's a fair choice of **restaurants** in Lípari town, though note that many close between October or November and March. Prices are on the high side, but a couple of the restaurants are among the best in the whole archipelago. For self-catering, there's a **supermarket** on the main corso, near the tourist office, and several other *alimentari* and bakeries.

Bars along the corso fill up from early in the evening onwards, as the *passegiata* swings into action, like the *Avant-Garde* at no. 135, where you get a huge plate of nibbles with your drink, or *Bar La Precchia*, no. 191, which occasionally has a DJ spinning lounge music out front. Otherwise, head down to the **Marina Corta** where a line of late-opening bars spills tables out across the harbourfront.

Every summer (June to Sept) Lípari town puts on **dramas and concerts**, including some spectacularly sited events at the Teatro del Castello, the modern Greek-style theatre up at the citadel. There are annual **processions** in town at Carnevale (Feb/March) and at Easter, but Lípari's main **festival**, dedicated to the island's patron, St Bartholomew, takes place over three days around August 24.

Restaurants

La Cambusa Via Garibaldi 72. About the cheapest trattoria in town (dishes €6–10), and a reliable place for a straightforward meal of Sicilian dishes, stuffed sardines to swordfish. Closed Nov–Easter. Moderate.

Il Filippino Piazza Municipio ☏090.981.1002, ⊛www.filippino.it. This stupendous fish restaurant – Lípari's best, in business since 1910 – really knows its stuff. It's in the upper town and has a shaded outdoor terrace where you can eat classy Aeolian specialities like borlotti bean, sardine and fennel soup, *risotto nero* (coloured with squid ink), grouper-stuffed *ravioloni* and local fish in a *ghiotta* sauce (tomatoes, onions, capers and olives). It's going to be €60 a head, more if you give any serious thought to the massive wine list. Closed Mon in Oct/Nov & Jan to March, & closed mid-Nov to Dec. Very expensive.

Kasbah Via Maurolico 25 ☎090.981.1075. Chic restaurant with a long garden, where fish is prepared in original ways – try the *tagliata di tonno*, tuna breaded and cooked with almonds and tomatoes. Closed Mon & Oct–March. Expensive.

E'Pulera Via Diana ☎090.981.1158. A romantic courtyard-garden restaurant specializing in classic Aeolian food: swordfish *involtini*, caper salads, home-made pasta with wild fennel and prawns, almond biscuits and *malvasia* wine. The super cuisine is well worth the highish prices, and it stays open till late (kitchen closes at midnight). It's 2min behind the *Neri pensione*; turn left at the end of Via G. Marconi. Dinner only; closed Oct–Mar. Expensive.

A Sfiziusa Via Roma 29 ☎090.981.1216. Few-frills trattoria back from Marina Corta that's good for simple Aeolian pasta and fresh fish of the day. Though it's a cheap(ish) and cheerful sort of place, three courses and wine will still cost close on €30 a head. Closed Sun Oct–April. Moderate.

Subba Corso Vittorio Emanuele 92 ☎090.981.1352. The island's best and most traditional café, since 1930, has a nice shaded terrace at the rear in the square, where you'll also find Subba's restaurant, *La Piazzetta* (Piazzetta Austria ☎090.981.2522), which serves Lípari's best *forno a legna* pizzas (57 varieties no less!). Café inexpensive, pizzas moderate.

Trattoria d'Oro Via Umberto I 32 ☎090.981.1304. A cut above the town's cheaper trattorias, this shady, rustic place is a cool haven on a hot day, and it's very welcoming to families. *Pasta con le sarde* (with sardines and wild fennel) and stuffed squid are typical dishes, with pasta from €8 and fish mains €10–16. Closed Sun Oct–April. Moderate.

Listings

Banks and exchange There are plenty of ATMs down the main corso, and you can exchange cash at the post office and some travel agencies. All the other islands, except Alicudi, have ATMs, but it's best to make sure you have enough cash before you set off island-hopping, as other island ATMs do occasionally run out of money at inconvenient times.

Bike, scooter and car rental Rental agencies line the dockside at Marina Lunga (the ferry and hydrofoil port); you'll have to leave your passport, credit card or a hefty deposit as security. Bikes from €15/day, scooters from €30, small cars from €60.

Books and newspapers La Stampa, Corso Vittorio Emanuele 170, sells English-language newspapers, books, local maps and guides.

Buses The bus company, Urso Guglielmo, has its office at Via Cappuccini 29, by the Marina Lunga ☎090.981.1262.

Diving Many of the larger hotels can put you in touch with a diving school, or contact Diving Centre La Gorgonia, Salita S. Giuseppe, Marina Corta or ☎090.981.2616 or 335.571.7567, ⓦwww.lagorgoniadiving.it. Three dives from €90, PADI courses from €300.

Hospital Ospedale Civile, Via Sant'Anna ☎090.98.851. The hospital also has a walk-in first aid service ☎090.988.5267.

Ferry and hydrofoil companies Ticket offices are all at the Marina Lunga dockside. NGI ☎090.981.1955; Siremar, hydrofoils ☎090.981.2200, ferries ☎090.981.1312; Ústica Lines ☎090.981.2448.

Left luggage The Siremar/Ústica Lines office at Marina Lunga has a small left-luggage facility (daily from 8.30am; €4 for 12 hrs).

Internet Internet Point, Corso Vittorio Emanuele 185 (daily 9am–1pm & 5.30pm–midnight, reduced winter hours); Net Café, Via Garibaldi 61 (daily 9am–1pm & 4–10pm).

Pharmacies Cincotta, Via Garibaldi 60 ☎090.981.1472; Internazionale, Corso Vittorio Emanuele 28 ☎090.981.1583; Sparacino, Corso Vittorio Emanuele 95 ☎090.981.1392. Pharmacies open late according to a rota system, detailed on the doors of the shops.

Police Carabinieri, Via Madre Florenzia Profilio, near Via G. Marconi ☎090.981.1333.

Post office Corso Vittorio Emanuele 207 (Mon–Fri 8.30am–6.30pm, Sat 8.30am–1.20pm).

Vulcano

Closest of the Aeolians to the Sicilian mainland, and just across the narrow channel from Lípari, **VULCANO** is the usual first port of call for ferry and hydrofoil services from Milazzo. As on more distant Strómboli, volcanic

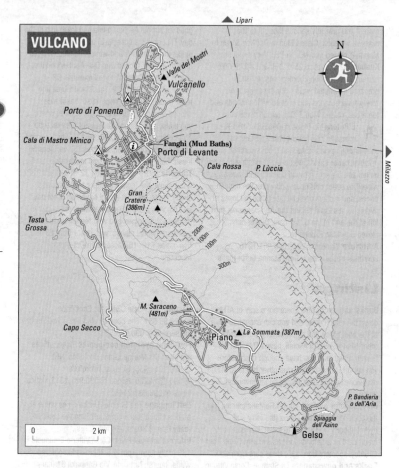

action defines the island, with the main crater hanging menacingly over its northern tip and constant vapour trails issuing from its flanks. It's a very old volcano, in the last, smoking, phase of its life, and although it's highly unlikely to erupt again you often don't even have to disembark to experience its other apparent trait – the disconcerting sulphurous, rotten-egg smell that pervades the island's entire inhabited area when the wind is in the right direction. The volcano was threatening enough to dissuade anyone from living here before the eighteenth century, since when there have been some hasty evacuations – subterranean activity is still monitored round the clock, just in case. In the nineteenth century a Scot called Stevenson bought the island to exploit the sulphur and alum reserves, but all his work was engulfed by the next major eruption. Although the volcano's last gasp of activity occurred between 1886 and 1890, its presence gives Vulcano an almost primeval essence. Everything here is an assault on the senses, the outlandish saffron of the earth searing the eyes, as violent as the intense red and orange of the iron and aluminium sulphates that leak out of the ground in the summer, to be washed away with the first autumn rains.

However, none of those summer incomers bronzing themselves on Vulcano's black sand beaches are discouraged, while many others come to dip themselves in the sulphurous mud baths, under the impression that it's somehow fashionable to do so. Numerous private villas and a few luxury hotels only add to the carefully cultivated impression that Vulcano is among the most exclusive of the Aeolian Islands. That said, it's difficult to recommend a night's stay, even if the lingering smell doesn't put you off. Accommodation is mostly overpriced, while restaurants tend to combine exorbitant prices with only moderate quality. Luckily, you can climb the crater, and cycle or bus across the island and back, all on a day-trip, and stay instead in much nicer Lípari, just a ten-minute hydrofoil ride away.

Around the island

Ferries and hydrofoils dock at **Porto di Levante**, the main harbour, backed by just a couple of streets of restaurants, villas and shops. Walk to the right, towards the multicoloured rock pinnacles, to find the famed **fanghi**, or mud baths (Easter–Oct daily 7am–9pm; €2), more exactly one pool containing a thick yellow soup of foul-smelling sulphurous mud, in which people flop belly-up, caking every inch of their bodies with the stuff. The smell is indescribable, and the degree of radioactivity makes it inadvisable to immerse yourself for any length of time, and unsuitable for young children or pregnant women. Avoid contact with the eyes (it stings like hell) and remove contact lenses as well as any silver or leather jewellery, which will be ruined just by coming into contact with the sand hereabouts. When you've had enough, hobble over to rinse yourself off in the nearby sea, where natural hot water springs bubble up.

A narrow neck of land separates Porto di Levante from **Porto di Ponente**, a fifteen-minute walk past the *fanghi*. Here, a perfect arc of fine black sand lines a bay looking onto the towering pillars of rock that rise out of the channel between Vulcano and Lípari. There are a couple of seafront cafés here, and some fairly elite hotels set back from the sands. From the beach, the only road heads north through the trees to **Vulcanello**, thrown up out of the sea in a famous eruption in 183 BC, and joined to the main island by another flurry of activity a few centuries later. The walk takes less than an hour. On the north side of Vulcanello, the **Valle dei Mostri** – literally the "Valley of the Monsters" – is an area of lavic rock formations, blackened and sculpted by the elements.

In the other direction from Porto di Levante, a road (and bus service) runs south across the island, past **Monte Saraceno** (481m) and the settlement of

Climbing Vulcano's volcano

Vulcano's main crater, the **Gran Cratere**, is just to the south of Porto di Levante – follow the road immediately to the left of the dock and walk up it for 500m or so until you're directed off the road to the left and up the slope (€3 fee charged to climb). It takes an hour to reach the crater, and it's a tough climb, totally exposed to the sun, so do it early or late in the day, and do it in strong shoes. The only vegetation consists of a few hardy gorse bushes on the lower slopes, nibbled at by goats whose bells echo across the scree. The first part of the path ascends a virtually black sand dune before reaching the harder volcanic crust, where it runs above the rivulets caused by previous eruptions. Reaching a ledge with views over all the other Aeolian islands, you look down into the vast crater itself, where vapour emissions – acrid and yellow – billow from the surrounding surfaces. Nerves are not exactly steadied by the admonitory notices at the start of the climb that plead "Do not sit down, Do not lie down".

Piano, as far as the coastal hamlet of **Gelso** – *gelso* is Italian for "mulberry" and they're cultivated here, along with capers. There's a tiny patch of black sand here (and a seasonal trattoria, *Da Pina*), and a better beach at **Spiaggia dell'Asino**, a larger cove accessible from a steep path which you'll have passed on your way into Gelso (there's a bus stop). This is a great spot for a swim, with a summer café and umbrellas and deck chairs available.

Practicalities

The **ferry and hydrofoil** dock is in front of the white *Hotel Faraglione*. Walk to the right for the *fanghi* and Porto di Ponente; Porto di Levante village is straight ahead, up past the traffic circle and the *Cantine Stevenson* bar. The ticket offices are in various buildings near the dock, all signposted, while a summer **tourist office** (June–Sept Mon–Sat 8am–2pm; ☎090.985.2028) is housed in a geodesic dome in the village. There's also a **bank** with an ATM, 100m or so up the crater road, while Da Paolo (☎090.985.2112) and Sprint (☎090.985.2208), also on this road, opposite each other, rent out **mountain bikes and scooters** (from around €20 a day).

Buses run from the dockside, year-round to Piano (Mon–Sat 7–8 daily; 10min), and summer only to Gelso (mid-June to mid-Sept, Mon–Sat 3 daily; 20min). Otherwise, it's a fifteen-kilometer drive out to Gelso, though most **boat tours** (around €15 per person) offered at the port in summer come out this way to visit the caves and bays on the island's west side.

Accommodation

Eden Park Porto di Ponente ☎090.985.2120; ⓦwww.isolavulcano.it. This agreeable holiday site, set in its own peaceful grounds on the south side of the bay and slightly inland, is by far the island's best budget option. Campers can pitch tents on real grass, or even bivouac on the lawn, while there are also single-room apartments (with terrace, shower and kitchen) and "economic" double rooms (two bunk beds, shared bathroom) available. Breakfast available for a charge, and campers pay extra for showers. No credit cards. Closed Dec to Feb. Camping from €10, Aug €20; rooms ❷, Aug ❹; apartments ❹, Aug ❻

Lanterna Bleu Porto di Ponente ☎090.985.2178. A series of one- and two-bedroom apartments with kitchen and small terrace. Prices are pretty reasonable for this end of the island, and drop by up to fifty percent outside July and August. Closed mid-Jan to mid-Dec. ❹

Orsa Maggiore Porto di Ponente ☎090.985.2018, ⓦwww.orsamaggiorehotel.com. It's a few hundred metres from the black sand beach, but this small hotel does have a rather nice pool, terrace and gardens. Closed Nov to March. ❺, Aug ❼

Les Sables Noirs Porto di Ponente ☎090.9850 or 068.339.6880, ⓦwww.fivesenseshotels.com. The finest resort hotel on the island (four-star) fronts the black sand beach, with stylish rooms almost all opening to big private terraces with views. Gardens and terrace-restaurant also make the most of the panoramic bay, and you get your own private bit of beach as well as a small, shaded outdoor pool. Aug rates soar to over €300. Closed Nov to March. ❽

Salina

The ancient name of **SALINA** was *Didyme*, or "twin", referring to the two volcanic cones that give the island its distinctive shape. Both volcanoes are long extinct, but their past eruptions, combined with plenty of ground water – unique in the Aeolians – have endowed Salina with the most fertile soil of all the islands. The slopes are verdant, the island's tree cover contrasts strongly with the denuded crags of its neighbours, and both capers and *malvasia* grapevines – classic Aeolian staples – are vigorously cultivated. The island's central position in the archipelago makes it a good alternative base to Lípari for exploring the others, while Salina itself holds a network of hiking trails, some good beaches and several distinct villages, if no actual sights as such. Tourism here is fairly sophisticated, with some charming boutique-style accommodation and excellent restaurants, especially in the main port, **Santa Marina di Salina**, and in the main town of **Malfa**, but the island certainly isn't a summer fleshpot like Vulcano or Panarea. It's quieter, more relaxed, still very much part of the ebb and flow of traditional Aeolian life, which makes it many people's favourite island.

It's worth noting that there are two ports on Salina, Santa Marina di Salina in the east and smaller Rinella on the south coast. Not all services call at both ports, so it's essential to check timetables carefully if time is tight and connections crucial. There is, however, a regular bus service between both ports, timed to connect with arrivals.

Santa Marina di Salina and around

The main island port, **Santa Marina di Salina**, on the east coast, isn't particularly attractive, but it is where most of the services are located. A long lungomare reaches north from the harbour, fronting a stony beach from which people splash about in the sea. Along a narrow main street, Via Risorgimento, which runs parallel to the water, one block back, lie shops that sell more than just the bare necessities of life – boutiques, even. A couple of the gift shops sell a decent map of the islands.

Three kilometres south, **Lingua** is the prettier spot, connected to Santa Marina by bus, though the undulating road makes a fine forty-minute stroll, weaving around the coves in between the two settlements. Lingua itself is not much more than a seafront promenade and a narrow beach, backed by a tiny cluster of hotels and trattorias facing the shore of Lípari. At the end of the road is the salt lagoon from which Salina takes its name, facing which a small **ethnographic museum** (May–Oct daily 9am–1pm; free) holds examples of rustic art and island culture – mainly kitchen utensils and mill equipment, much of it fashioned from lavic rock.

Walking on Salina

There are well-maintained, waymarked hiking trails right across Salina, in particular to the heights of Monte Fossa delle Felci and the sanctuary of Madonna del Terzito. It's great walking country, since most of the island has been zealously protected: wild flowers are much in evidence, and hunting and shooting are banned, which helps keep the bird numbers high.

For a good day out on the tops, first take the bus to the sanctuary – any between Santa Marina or Malfa and Rinella passes right by. **Madonna del Terzito** is set in the saddle between the two peaks of Salina, with fine views over the sea. A signposted track then leads up to the summit of **Monte Fossa delle Felci** (962m), the archipelago's highest peak. It's a steady climb through forest and mountain parkland, which takes the best part of two hours – only in the latter stages does it become tougher, with a final 100m clamber over rocks to reach the stone cairn and simple wooden cross at the top, from where the views are magnificent.

You can come back the same way to the sanctuary and catch the return bus, but signposts point out alternative approaches and **descents**, particularly to Malfa, Lingua or Santa Marina. However, while the tracks are never anything less than clear, they can be very steep, and soil erosion and the crumbling volcanic underlay can make getting a grip a tricky business. Count on another two hours back down, whichever descent you follow.

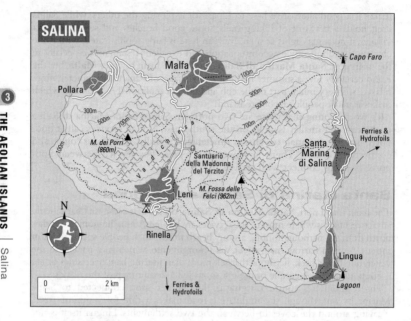

Practicalities

Santa Marina is around 25 minutes by hydrofoil from Lípari. The Siremar (☎090.984.3004) and Ústica Lines/NGI (☎090.984.3003) **ticket offices** stand just back from the dockside, on either side of the church, and usually open thirty minutes before sailings. **Buses** to all points on the island stop on the harbour road (7–8 daily, roughly every 90min; pay on board), bound either for Malfa and Rinella, Malfa and Pollara, or Lingua. You may occasionally have a short wait in Malfa, the island hub, for an onward connection. All the usual bike rental and boat tour options are available in summer, mostly from booths by the harbour. **Services** along Via Risorgimento include a first-aid post, pharmacy, post office, Internet place, and bank with ATM, and another ATM on the seafront just beyond the Ústica Lines office.

Salina holds little in the way of out-and-out budget **accommodation**, though you might have some luck with private rooms and B&Bs, either touted at the harbour in summer or advertised in shops and bars. Hotels tend to demand half-board stays in August, while properties down at Lingua send shuttle-buses to pick up guests. **Restaurants** are largely seasonal, though there's always something open at any time of the year.

Accommodation

A Cannata Lingua ☎090.984.3161, ⓦwww .acannata.it. Set a few metres back from the sea near the church. Not all rooms are en suite, but the best have terraces with wonderful views of Lípari. There's a good restaurant (pizzas available too), while they also have houses to let all over Lingua. *A Cannata* is one of three similar

pension-restaurants with rooms along the lungomare, the others being *Il Delfino* and *Il Gambero*, all of which ferry guests between Santa Marina and Lingua. ➎, Aug ➏

🏃 **Mamma Santina** Via Sanità ☎090.984.3054, ⓦwww.mammasantina.it. The affable Mario presides over a highly personal, boutique-style restaurant-with-rooms, set on wide terraces above the town. The sixteen rooms are in bright seaside colours, with gorgeous Mediterranean tile floors and big bathrooms with walk-in showers, while guests can lounge in hammocks or around the pool. Call to be picked up from the port, or find the hotel signposted to the left off Via Risorgimento (after no. 66). The restaurant is reviewed below; guests pay an extra €30 for half-board. Closed mid-Dec to mid-March. ⑥, July ⑦, Aug ⑧

Mercanti di Mare Piazza Santa Marina 7 ☎090.984.3536, ⓦwww.hotelmercantidimare.it. Harbourfront three-star hotel with nine, white, airy rooms and an attractive terrace that overlooks the water. ⑥, July & Aug ⑦

Da Sabina Via Risorgimento 5c ☎090.984.3134 or 332.272.6025, ⓦwww.bbsalina.it. Classy B&B at the far end of the village from the port (10min walk). Three smart en-suite rooms open onto a big sea-view terrace, where breakfast is served. No credit cards. ⑤, mid-July to mid-Sept ⑥

La Salina Borgo di Mare Lingua ☎090.984.3441, ⓦwww.lasalinahotel.com. This impressive four-star hotel is set in the restored buildings of the old salt-works, by Lingua's lagoon. The rooms are lovely, individually furnished, most with sea views and private terraces, while traditional tile- and stonework enhances public areas. There's no restaurant, but you can eat at nearby *Il Gambero* on a half-board basis. ⑦, Aug ⑧

Cafés and restaurants

Da Alfredo Lingua. Right on the seafront piazza, this little café is famous throughout Italy for its fresh fruit granita – the summer yachties queue up for a taste. The other speciality is *pane cunzato*, a huge round of grilled bread piled with various combinations of home-cured tuna, capers, tomatoes, baked ricotta and olives. Inexpensive.

Mamma Santina Via Sanità ☎090.984.3054. The restaurant at the lovely Mamma Santina is marvellous, and open to non-guests, with outdoor service for most of the year. The emphasis is on island specialities, like a grilled antipasto platter of vegetables and seafood, spaghetti with a pesto of fourteen herbs or grilled seabass (pasta from €10, fish from €13). Closed mid-Dec to mid-March. Moderate.

Nni Lausta Via Risorgimento 188 ☎090.984.3486. Cool bar-restaurant whose New York-trained owner-chef gives an adventurous twist to local dishes – like raw tuna dressed with wild fennel and capers, or crispy fish cakes made from the day's catch. A full meal costs around €35, though you can just have a drink at the bar (until 2am) and an appetizer. Closed Nov to March. Expensive.

Porto Bello Above the harbour ☎090.984.3125. Serves excellent local antipasti, pasta with capers and tomatoes, slabs of swordfish, and good wine. A good meal might cost €30, and from the outdoor terrace you can watch the necklace of lights come on across the water on Lípari. Closed Nov & Wed in winter. Moderate.

Malfa and Pollara

Salina's only road climbs from the harbour at Santa Marina and traces the coast north, turning west at Capo Faro, before winding in through the outlying districts of **MALFA**, easily the island's biggest town and with its grandest accommodation. The town spills down from the wide terrace outside its peach-coloured church to a tiny *mole* at the bottom. The bus stops up by the church, and again a few hundred metres below, above the harbour. The two are connected by a devilishly twisting road, across which cuts a more direct series of paths. There's a good beach at the bottom, stony but picturesquely backed by fishermen's houses.

Just out of Malfa, a minor road (served by several buses a day) snakes off west to secluded **POLLARA**, raised on a cliff above the sea and occupying a crescent-shaped crater from which Salina's last eruption took place some 13,000 years ago. Scenes from Michael Radford's 1994 film, *Il Postino*, were shot down on the narrow beach at the base of cliffs below the village, but the popularity of the beach with boat tours and film pilgrims has caused severe erosion over the years. Boats are no longer supposed to anchor close to the shore, and the beach is closed to land visitors (many of whom had stooped to picking up souvenir sand and rocks).

Accommodation and food

Capo Faro 3km east of Malfa ℡090.984.4330, ⓦwww.capofaro.it. At the five-star Tasca d'Almerita *malvasia* wine estate, a series of stunning, contemporary rooms occupy seven Aeolian-style "cottages" that look down across the vineyards. Facilities are top-notch, from magnificent pool to classy bar and restaurant, and you can tour the vineyards on request or go out on the resort's private boat. Prices start at €200, though for the suites, or an Aug stay, you're looking at double that. ❾

Signum Via Scalo 15 ℡090.984.4222, ⓦwww .hotelsignum.it. The island's finest four-star accommodation, mixing antique furniture and modern styling to produce a highly individual experience. Thirty comfortable rooms (some classed as superior and deluxe) have either terraces or balconies, sea or garden views, and there are more sea and Strómboli views from the splendid infinity pool. There's also a very good terrace-restaurant (reservations recommended for non-guests) serving Aeolian specialities like a mouth-watering *maccheroncini ricotta*. ❻–❼, Aug ❾

Rinella

The smaller port of **Rinella**, on the island's south coast, is 15km from Santa Marina, at the very bottom of a remarkably winding, steep road. It has clear water, a popular beach and the island's only campsite, so it gets a fair number of visitors in summer, though it's otherwise rather remote in feel. Buses meet the boat arrivals on the quayside (and call here several times a day otherwise), and you might be offered a room for rent. Or there's a very nice little hotel and restaurant, *L'Ariana* (℡090.980.9075, ⓦwww.hotelariana.it; ❺, Aug ❼), above the port to the left, occupying an old villa with a frill of terracotta busts around its roof. *Tre Pini* campsite (℡090.980.9155, ⓦwww.trepini.com; closed Oct–April; bungalows ❹) is 200m up the road from the port, with its tent pitches, bar-restaurant and tiny bungalows ranged across pine-shaded terraces. There are two or three local bars with views by the port, and an excellent pizzeria, *Da Marco* (℡090.980.9120; open weekends only in winter), just up the road from *L'Ariana*.

Panarea

Halfway point between the central island group and Strómboli is **PANAREA**, at just 3km by 1.5km the smallest island in the archipelago, and indisputably the prettiest. It's almost Greek in aspect, with freshly painted white houses, their terraces decked with bougainvillea and oleander, and swept narrow lanes shaded by fruit trees. Panarea also holds one of the region's most important archeological sites, located on the dramatic Punta Milazzese, while the entire island is surrounded by clusters of islets set in dazzlingly clear water. It's hardly surprising then that Panarea's cosy intimacy has put it on the radar of the rich, famous and aspirational, and August in particular sees the island resemble the set of "I'm a Celebrity . . ." as Hollywood stars, fashionistas and wealthy Italians descend for a month of diving off blinding white yachts and wading knee-deep in the crystalline water.

Around the island

Panarea's population divides itself between three hamlets on the eastern side of the island – Ditella, San Pietro and Drauto – though, as they meld into one another, it's a distinction that hardly matters. No cars can squeeze onto the island's narrow lanes to disturb the tranquillity, though heavily laden three-wheelers are common, zipping down to the port and back.

Boats arrive at **San Pietro**, tucked onto gentle terraces and backed by gnarled outcrops of rock. It's here that you'll find most of the accommodation, restaurants and facilities, while just to the north, passing through **Ditella**, you'll see evidence of volcanic activity in the steaming gas emissions (*fumarole*) on the gradual ascent to Calcara. The stone beach near here, the **Spiaggia Fumarole**, is an attractively isolated spot.

South of San Pietro through the tangle of lanes, a gentle thirty-minute stroll above the coast leads to the mainly stone beach below **Drauto**. Just beyond here, the path descends to a better, more popular, sandy beach – the only one on the island – overlooked by a seasonal bar-trattoria. Steps at the far end of the beach climb up and across to the headland of **Punta Milazzese**, ten minutes further on, where a Bronze Age village of 23 huts was discovered in 1948; the oval outlines of the foundation walls are easily visible. This beautiful site, occupying a hammerhead of land overlooking two rocky inlets, is thought to have been inhabited since the fourteenth century BC, and pottery found here (displayed in Lípari's museum) shows a distinct Minoan influence – fascinating evidence of a historical link between the Aeolians and Crete that goes some way towards corroborating the legends of contact between the two in ancient times.

Steps descend from Punta Milazzese to **Cala Junco**, a delightful stony cove whose aquamarine water, scattered stone outcrops and surrounding coves and caves make it a popular spot for snorkelling. Beyond the point, a waymarked path (look for the signposts) wends into Panarea's interior, passing below the island's highest peak, the craggy **Punta del Corvo** (421m), before descending back to San Pietro – a hike of two to three hours.

Out to the islands: boat tours, snorkelling and diving

The islets and rocks off Panarea make for a great day out. You can either go on a tour (from around €15 per person) – there'll be plenty of time for swimming – or rent your own boat (from around €60). Check out the seafront kiosks at San Pietro or look for the signs advertising "*Noleggio barche*" (boat rental) in nearly every bar, shop and restaurant. Or, for snorkelling and scuba-diving (including introductory and PADI courses), contact the island's dive centre, Amphibia, in San Pietro (☏335.613.8529, ⊛www.amphibia.it), which also offers day tours and childrens' activities.

The nearest of the islets to Panarea, **Dáttilo**, points a jagged, pyramidal finger skyward and has a minuscule beach. There's better swimming at **Lisca Bianca**, the stark setting of Antonioni's 1960 film *L'Avventura*, where the tranquil water is sheltered by **Bottaro** opposite. Nearby Lisca Nera and Le Formiche (The Ants) are mere wrinkles on the sea surface, albeit a constant hazard to shipping. The largest islet is **Basiluzzo**, formerly inhabited but now only used for caper cultivation.

Practicalities

The quickest services take around an hour from Lípari, 25 minutes from Salina. **Ferries and hydrofoils** all dock at San Pietro's harbourside, where the Siremar (☎090.983.007) and Ústica Lines (☎090.983.344) ticket offices are almost next door to each other. Don't expect to see any celebs in here, buying tickets. They are more likely to use Air Panarea's **helicopter** service (☎090.983.4428 or 340.366.7214, ⓦwww.airpanarea.com), which runs a summer scheduled service from Reggio di Calabria airport (from €200 one-way) plus panoramic fly-overs of Strómboli and the other islands.

Although there's no tourist office, you can get **information** on ⓦwww .panarea.com (in Italian), which has links to a few hotels and rooms places. San Pietro has a pharmacy, an ATM and a summer-only police post, while in the warren of alleys behind the harbour is a little supermarket, two or three *alimentari* and a bakery. The little motorized buggies down at the harbour act as taxis and you should find someone who can take you where you want to go for a few euros. However, all the hotels provide a free pick-up service.

Accommodation is insanely expensive in July and August (over €300 a night in many places) and, although there are cheaper rented rooms (still well over €100 double), the supply simply can't meet the demand in high summer. Prices do drop considerably come September, while many places close between October and Easter (you will always find somewhere to stay, however). **Nightlife** in summer revolves around the bars in the coolest hotels, though the *Bar del Porto* is always good for a harbourside drink and snack. Otherwise, the terrace of the *Raya* is all the rage, where a sophisticated dance party lasts for hours on summer nights.

Accommodation

Lisca Bianca Via Lani ☎090.983.004, ⓦwww .liscabianca.it. This typical Aeolian building – covered wide terraces, blue shutters, white walls – has some gorgeous views, with stylish rooms overlooking either the sea or the bougainvillea-clad gardens and port. You can see Strómboli from the breakfast terrace, and the bar is one of the best on the island. The *Casa Nonna* annexe has a few cheaper rooms in the village on Via Iditella, and if you can avoid August prices aren't too bad at all at either place (website has promotions). Closed Nov to March. ⑥, Aug ⑨; annexe ❷, Aug ❼

Quartara Via San Pietro ☎090.983.027, ⓦwww .quartarahotel.com. Very classy four-star boutique hotel run by a cheerful family, whose thirteen fashionable rooms have elegant wood furniture and stone floors. A terrace jacuzzi out the back overlooks the port and there's a well-regarded restaurant. Closed Nov to March. ❼, Aug ⑨

Raya Via San Pietro ☎090.983.013, ⓦwww .hotelraya.it. Its official two-star rating tells you nothing about the *Raya*'s understated style or popularity with the beautiful people who hang out here every year. From the dramatic tumbling terraces and island-chic rooms to the accomplished lamp-lit terrace restaurant, it exudes such a quiet, laid-back, well-to-do air that many return for summer after summer (at least, those that have €400 or more a night to spare). ⑧, Aug ⑨

Rodà Via San Pietro ☎090.983.006. About the cheapest on the island, a straightforward pension with a garden-restaurant serving pizzas in the evening. Closed Nov to March. ❸, Aug ⑥

Restaurants

Da Francesco ☎090.983.023. Overlooking the harbour, and pretty good value for meals of pasta and fish. It also has rooms to rent in summer. Closed Dec to Feb. Moderate.

O Palmo ☎090.983.155. Just up from the port, a garden restaurant serving decent food and evening pizzas. Moderate.

Da Paolino ☎090.983.008. Walking north towards Ditella, after ten minutes or so you'll reach this family-run restaurant whose terrace has fine views of Strómboli. You can have a very unpretentious meal of pasta and salad here for around €20 – try the rich *mille baci* pasta with greens – and the fish is whatever the family has caught that day. Closed Nov to March. Moderate.

Strómboli

The most spectacular of all the Aeolians, **STRÓMBOLI** is little more than a volcanic cone thrust out of the sea. It's very much alive and kicking, throwing up showers of sparks and flaring rock from the craters at regular intervals, while a handful of more serious eruptions over the last century have caused major lava flows. That of 1930 led to serious damage to many homes and sparked a spate of emigration from the island, while threatening eruptions in 2002 and 2003 spewed volcanic rock into the sea, spawning tsunami waves, and ejected rocks onto rooftops. In 2007, two new craters opened on the summit, creating new lava streams into the sea.

Amazingly, perhaps, people have chosen to live here for centuries, reassured that, historically, the main lava flows have been confined to the channel of the Sciara del Fuoco, down the western side of the island. This leaves the straggling eastern parishes of San Vincenzo, San Bártolo and Piscità (often grouped together simply as Strómboli), and the solitary southern community of Ginostra, to lead something of a charmed life, their white terraced houses adorned with bougainvillea and wisteria, remote from the fury of the craters above. The island's permanent population numbers perhaps five hundred, plumbing is often rudimentary, and access sometimes restricted because of winter storms, but despite this, Strómboli has become something of a chic resort. Its black-sand beaches are overlooked by attractive terraced hotels, while thrill-seekers come from all over the world to climb one of the planet's most accessible volcanoes.

Around the island

The main settlement of **Strómboli** spreads for a distance of around 2km between the lower slopes of the volcano and the island's beaches. It's an utterly straightforward layout of two largely parallel roads and steep, interconnecting alleys, though the profusion of local place names keeps visitors on their toes. From the quayside known as **Scari**, the lower coastal road (Via Marina and Via Regina Elena) runs around to the main beach of **Ficograndе**, a long black stretch overlooked by several hotels. Further on is **Piscità**, the island's best ashy beach, around 25 minutes' walk from the port. There's also a sand-and-stone stretch south of Scari, past the fishing boats, and if you clamber over the rocks at the end of this beach, there's a further sweep of lava-stone beach that attracts a fair bit of nude sunbathing.

Strómboli boat tours

The main daytime boat tour offered is the **round-island excursion** (around €20; 3hr) calling at Ginostra and Strómboli's extraordinary basalt offspring, Strombolicchio. You usually get half an hour to scramble around Ginostra, which is plenty of time to see it, while at Strombolicchio there's swimming and a 200-step climb up the battlemented rock to the lighthouse on its top.

At night, the stock-in-trade is the cruise to see the **Sciara del Fuoco** (around €20; 2hr 30min), the lava channel rising sheer out of incredible deep-blue sea water. No one is allowed to dock on the shoreline, since it's too unpredictably dangerous, but from the boat, through the gloom, you'll see orange and red flashes from the crater above.

You can book tours at any of the stands by the harbour (prices are broadly similar), where you can also charter a boat for longer tours or rent your own.

▲ Strómboli

The other road from the quayside cuts up into what could loosely be described as "the village", where, as Via Roma, it runs as far as the church of **San Vincenzo**, whose square offers glorious views of the Strombolicchio basalt stack. Beyond the square, it's another fifteen minutes' or so walk to the second church of **San Bártolo**, above Piscità, just beyond which starts the path to the crater. Once you've got this far, you've seen all that Strómboli village has to offer. The only "sight", apart from the churches, is the house in which **Ingrid Bergman** lived with Roberto Rossellini in the spring of 1949, while making the film *Strómboli: Terra di Dio*. A plaque records these bare facts on the pink building, just after San Vincenzo church, on the right.

Without seeing its name on timetables, you might not even be aware of the existence of **Ginostra**, the hamlet on the southwest side of the island. From the minuscule harbour, zigzag steps climb into a cluster of typical white Aeolian houses on terraces. It's a refreshingly simple place: donkeys are tethered to posts outside homes; ancient exterior stone ovens lie idle; and cultivated hedges and volcanic stone walls snake up the hillside. Weather permitting, a couple of hydrofoils run to and from Strómboli town per day in summer (once daily in winter), though a boat tour is a more realistic way to see Ginostra (unless you fancy actually staying here at the one small hotel). A century ago, there was also a maintained path that skirted the shore back to Strómboli, but assault by the elements has done for most it. However, you don't need to go very far, following the coast anticlockwise, to find spots where you can swim off the rocks.

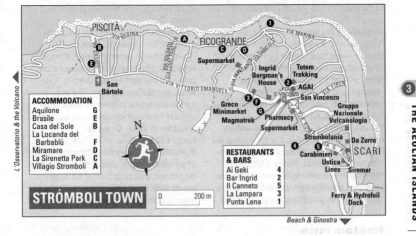

STRÓMBOLI TOWN

ACCOMMODATION
Aquilone	G
Brasile	E
Casa del Sole	B
La Locanda del Barbablù	F
Miramare	D
La Sirenetta Park	C
Villagio Stromboli	A

RESTAURANTS & BARS
Ai Geki	4
Bar Ingrid	2
Il Canneto	5
La Lampara	3
Punta Lena	1

0   200 m

Beach & Ginostra ▼

Practicalities

Most **ferry and hydrofoil** services from Lípari call first at Ginostra, though the main port is Strómboli. It's a good hour and three-quarters by hydrofoil, and up to four hours by ferry. There are also direct summer hydrofoils to Strómboli from Naples (4hr) and Reggio di Calabria (up to 3hr 30min). The Siremar (℡090.986.016) and Ústica Lines (℡090.986.003) **ticket offices** are both by Strómboli harbour, which is a hive of activity in summer, especially with tour agencies and accommodation touts. If you've come without a reservation, accepting a **room** (from €50, cheaper out of season) from one of the touts is as good an idea as any – there's no obligation to stay, if you don't like what you see.

Most other **facilities** are up in the village, including two small supermarkets, pharmacy, police station, post office and ATM. A couple of places have Internet access, while some of the shops sell a good map of Strómboli showing local hiking trails. The **bars** down at the harbour see a lot of action during the day, while at night there's no better spot than *Bar Ingrid* (℡090.986.385; open until midnight, up to 3am in high summer) in the square by San Vincenzo church.

Accommodation

Aquilone Via Vittorio Emanuele 29 ℡090.986.080. Up an alley opposite the Greco minimarket, this is a friendly place, ranged around a rose garden and lemon grove, albeit with plain, rather monastic rooms. There's also a cosy mini-apartment round the back with cooking facilities. Closed Nov to March. ❺

Brasile Via Soldato Cincotta, Piscità ℡090.986.008, ⓦwww.strombolialbergobrasile.it. Tranquil spot at the far end of town, with friendly management and simple rooms with plain tiled floors. Two nicer suites have their own private terraces, or there's a large roof terrace that everyone can use. Half-board at their restaurant is obligatory from mid-June to Aug (€70–80 per person per night). Closed Nov to March. ❹

Casa del Sole Via Soldato Cincotta, Piscità ℡090.986.017. A cheapie in an old building within metres of the sea. Simple four- to six-bed apartments are available all year, and accommodation is pretty flexible, whether you want an off-season single (from €25) or multi-bedded room in summer. Kitchen facilities are available, and there's a sun terrace. No credit cards. ❸

Locanda del Barbablù Via Vittorio Emanuele 17 ℡090.986.118, ⓦwww .barbablu.it. An old Aeolian house, with cosy antique rooms with four-poster beds and original tile floors, provides the most relaxed accommodation on Strómboli. It's combined with an excellent restaurant (dinner only; expensive; reservations essential) – acknowledged as the best on the island – where you can dine under the stars. Closed Nov to Feb. ⑥, Aug ⑦

Miramare Via Vito Nunziate 3, Ficogrande ℡090.986.047, ⊛www.miramarestromboli.it. Small three-star hotel, overlooking Ficogrande beach, with panoramic terraces and restaurant. Rooms are a bit old-fashioned, but rates are reasonable and there's a slightly cheaper associated B&B, *Casa Limone*, not far away. Closed Nov to March. ⑤, July ⑥, Aug ⑦

Petrusa Ginostra ℡090.981.2305. Ginostra's only official accommodation (though you may find rooms if you ask around) has three large rooms with their own terraces, sharing a bathroom. Half-board is obligatory in July and Aug; you can eat at their bar-restaurant, *L'Incontro*, which has fairly high prices (everything has to be shipped

in) but is pretty good. No credit cards. Closed Oct to April. ④

La Sirenetta Park Via Marina 33, Ficogrande ℡090.986.025, ⊛www.lasirenettahotel.it. Four-star hotel set opposite the black sands of Ficogrande. It's also got a decent-sized outdoor pool, a summer nightclub and access to watersports facilities. The room rates drop considerably outside summer and at the beginning or end of the season you can stay for around €120. Closed Nov to March. ⑦, Aug ⑨

Vilaggio Strómboli Via Regina Elena ℡090.986.018, ⊛www.villaggiostromboli.it. With simple rooms jutting up against the breaking waves, this pleasant, quiet place is one of the nicest seaside stays; it also has a good terrace restaurant where you can gaze out over the water. ⑥, Aug ⑦

Restaurants

Il Canneto Via Roma ℡090.986.014. A rustic trattoria where the waiters reel off a list of daily specials, such as spaghetti with clams, or coloured with squid ink, followed by fresh fish. With salad, wine and coffee the bill will run over €30 a head, though you could eat for less. Closed Nov to March. Expensive.

Ai Geki Via Roma ℡090.986.213. Just down a lane off the main street, this popular place has veranda seating and a reasonably varied menu,

with most dishes around €10–15. Dinner only. Expensive.

La Lampara Via Vittorio Emanuele ℡090.986.009. Dine on the large raised terrace on pizza, pasta and grills. Closed Nov to March. Moderate.

Punta Lena Via Marina, Ficogrande ℡090.986.204. Enjoys a marvellous position at the water's edge, and is great for fish – the choice basically depends on the day's catch. Closed Nov to March. Expensive.

Climbing the volcano

Climbing the volcano is big business, and for safety reasons it's no longer the free-for-all it used to be. Public access was only reopened in 2005 (after the eruptions of preceding years), and while you can freely walk along the trails below 400m, to go any higher you have to be accompanied by a licensed guide. Numbers at the crater are also limited, so it's essential to reserve a place on an **organized excursion** (from €22; see below for contact details and other information) as soon as you can. On the day is usually fine for most of the year, but advanced booking is advised in high summer – and be prepared for the trip to be postponed because of poor weather or other climatic or geological reasons. You need to be in decent health, have proper hiking boots and clothes (you can rent these in the village), and carry plenty of water and sun protection. Guides usually supply helmets and dust masks.

Most excursions leave in the late afternoon, taking around five or six hours – this lets you catch the amazing sunsets and gives you around an hour or so at the top, watching the fireworks. The explosions occur roughly every twenty minutes and vary in intensity, but it's always nothing less than impressive, the noise alone something like an express train thundering directly below you. Ignore the warning signs at your peril.

The **route** starts a few minutes' walk beyond San Bártolo church, climbing to the first orientation point, *L'Osservatorio*, a bar-pizzeria (closed in winter) which has a wide terrace and a view of the volcano. You can come this far without a guide. Beyond, you'll see the frighteningly sheer volcanic trail that channels all the lava outflows, known as the **Sciara del Fuoco**, plunging directly into the sea. This is a huge blistered sheet down which thousands of years' worth of volcanic detritus has poured, scarring and pock-marking the hillside. Menacing little puffs of steam dance up from folds in the bare slope, where absolutely nothing grows. If ever a place warranted a "Here Be Dragons" sign, this is it.

Guides, equipment and information

AGAI (Associazione Guide Alpine Italiane) Piazza San Vincenzo ⓣ 090.986.211 or 986.263. One of the main guided operations.

Gruppo Nazionale Vulcanologia Near the harbour ⓣ 090.986.708, ⓦ http://gnv.invg.it. The national vulcanology organization has an office with useful background information on the volcano. It's open most days and shows a video about Strómboli, while the national website has photos, technical information and some very scary seismograph readings from previous eruptions.

Magmatrek Via Vittorio Emanuele, just off the piazza ⓣ 090.986.5768, ⓦ www .magmatrek.it. Local climbing guru, Zazà, and his colleagues have daily volcano treks throughout the year. There's plenty of information offered, and they screen films about the history of the volcano.

Totem Trekking Piazza San Vincenzo 4, opposite the church ⓣ 090.986.5752. Sells and rents out hiking equipment and accessories.

Filicudi

FILICUDI is the larger of the two minor, westerly islands, and closest to the main pack. The small harbour consists of a few colour-trimmed cubes of buildings, and promises little at first sight, but Filicudi turns on its charm the longer you stay. Climb away from the port, and the rest of the pretty island is easily accessible on well-kept paths that crisscross the slopes, lined with volcanic boulders interspersed with great flowering cacti whose pustular blooms erupt upon elephant-ear leaves. You can clamber down to pebble beaches and swim in deserted coves, or make your way around the terraced headlands to deserted villages and phenomenal viewpoints. Filicudi's sheer slopes are all painstakingly lined with stone terracing, a reminder that before mass emigration in the 1950s and 1960s there was a great deal of agricultural activity here. Many terraces were subsequently abandoned, and cultivation is now down to a few vines and olives, but they do serve to reduce soil erosion. Today, there are only 250 or so permanent island residents, and while this number swells perhaps tenfold in August with visitors and returned *emigranti*, Filicudi is still a long way from being overdeveloped.

Around the island

The only real settlement is **Filicudi Porto**, where almost all accommodation and services are found. There's only one road, too, which runs southeast, up away from the harbour and stone beach – where it makes a sharp turn to the right you'll find the start of a steep stone path up to the renowned archeological site, the **Villagio Preistorico** at Capo Graziano. This occupies a grassy plateau, high above the harbour, a twenty-minute walk all told from the dockside. Here, the remains of a dozen or so oval huts mark the place that gave its name to the local Bronze Age culture that immediately preceded Panarea's Punta Milazzese, from the eighteenth to thirteenth century BC. The site is always open and though there's not much to see, it's a fine place from which to watch the comings and goings at the harbour below.

The island road winds around and up to the **Rocche Ciauli** district, where the road forks (at the *Villa La Rosa* hotel and restaurant). You can get to this

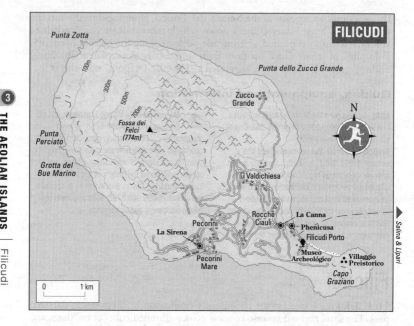

point more directly on a heart-bursting stepped path from the harbour, a fifteen-minute climb. Turn left at the junction and the road swings around to **Pecorini**, no more than a few houses grouped around a church, below which, down the switchbacks, is the little harbour of **Pecorini Mare**. This is 7km by road from Filicudi Porto, though a short cut, by vertiginous donkey track, starts to the side of the church in Pecorini and takes just fifteen minutes down to the harbour (or an hour's total walk from Filicudi Porto). Pecorini Mare is a mere scrap of a fishing hamlet with a small dockside, a Carabinieri post, a "Saloon", which sells drinks and *gelati*, and a couple of trattorias. It's a gorgeous, end-of-the-line place, with a long pebble beach backed by fishermen's houses and holiday homes, and perfectly clear water that's surprisingly warm for swimming.

Turning right instead at the Rocche Ciauli junction, a twenty-minute walk up the switchback road brings you to the dispersed central village of **Valdichiesa**, where the church (*chiesa*) itself is set back on a terrace with splendid views. This is the way to come for the fantastic walk to Zucco Grande (see box), while above church and village lie the heights of **Fossa dei Felci** (774m), reached by vague paths that climb through the terraces.

To explore the island's uninhabited northern and western coasts you'll need to **rent a boat** (about €15–20 a head, depending on numbers). In summer, there's usually someone at Filicudi Porto or Pecorini Mare touting for custom, and any hotel, shop or restaurant can point you in the right direction too. The main sights include the fine natural arch of **Punta Perciato** and the nearby **Grotta del Bue Marino** ("Seal Grotto" – there aren't any), a wide rocky cavity 37m long by 30m wide, its walls of reddish lava barely visible in the pitch black of the interior. Near the island's northwest coast, the startling **Canna**, a rugged obelisk 85m tall, is the most impressive of all the *faraglioni* of the Aeolian Islands.

The walk to Zucco Grande

Many footpaths on Filicudi have been restored in recent years, notably the excellent route to the derelict village of **Zucco Grande** on the island's eastern flank. The path starts from just below Valdichiesa church, at a bend in the road (20min walk from Rocche Ciauli), where a signpost says "*Sentiero, Zucco Grande, m1900*" – there are subsequent fingerposts all the way, so you can't go wrong. It's a good path, beautifully cut, that follows the contours around the cliffs through gorse and prickly pear, until finally reaching the village after another thirty minutes. Finally abandoned forty years ago – the inhabitants mostly left for Australia – the houses are in a parlous state, clinging to the cliffside, with sweeping views out to sea. The current population is three (one man, one goat, one donkey), but a cultivated terrace or two and some recent reconstruction work suggests that life perhaps is slowly returning. In the meantime, you can sit amid the ruins and dwell on the isolation and hardship that forced the original inhabitants to flee to the other side of the world. Either return the way you came, or continue on the path through the village, which eventually climbs up and over the top, back towards Valdichiesa.

Practicalities

Filicudi Porto is an hour by hydrofoil from Lípari, and three hours from Palermo. The Siremar (☎090.988.9960) and Ústica Lines (☎090.988.9949) **ticket offices** are on the dockside, both open before departures. The one-street port has a pharmacy (limited opening), general store, ATM and two or three bar-restaurants, with terraces overlooking the water and Salina in the distance. One of them, *Da Nino sul Mare* (☎090.988.9984), also sells ice cream, postcards and island maps showing some of the footpaths.

There's usually a red **minibus taxi** waiting on the harbour (*bus navetta*), which will take you where you want to go on the island. It costs €12 to Pecorini Mare, less per head if there's a group of you. If it's not there, call D&G Servizio Navetta (☎347.757.5916 or 517.1825). There's also summer **scooter rental** at the port, and a seasonal **scuba-diving** outfit, Apogon (☎090.988.9955, 🌐www.apogon.it, or ask at any of the hotels).

Outside the summer months, it's usually no problem just turning up and finding **accommodation**, though as options are limited a call is still recommended to be on the safe side. Advance reservations are essential in summer, though you can always try asking around for private rooms – a few are available, or contact the house agent Vincenzo Anastasi (☎336.926.560, 🌐www.eolie-filicudi.com), who rents out two- to six-bed houses across the island (from around €500 per week, double that in summer). In July and August, you'll be obliged to have dinner at your hotel, though this is no hardship as the quality is uniformly excellent. Otherwise, a full meal in any of the **restaurants** (all open to non-guests) costs about €30 a head.

Accommodation

La Canna Via Rosa 43 ☎090.988.9956, 🌐www.lacannahotel.it. The best choice near the port, though it's a stiff climb up the steps to Rocche Ciauli; call ahead and they'll pick you up from the dock. Ten lovely bright rooms with tiled bathrooms open onto a spacious terrace with a magnificent view over the bay below. There's a small pool (summer only), and the food here is excellent –

home-made pasta, fresh fish, local caper salads and plenty of home-produced wine and fruit. Half-board in Aug is up to €100 a head, though more reasonable at other times. ❺, July ❻, Aug ❼

Phenicusa Filicudi Porto ☎090.988.9946, 🌐www.hotelphenicusa.com. The only hotel right by the harbour opens for just four months a year – it's a traditional three-star place, with reasonable rooms, though not all have sea views (and you pay a supplement for those that do). Breakfast is served on the sun-soaked terrace, and the decent restaurant has the same sea and harbour views. Half-board from €75. Closed Oct to May. ⑤

🏃 **La Sirena** Pecorini Mare ☎ 090.988.9997, ⓦ www.pensionelasirena.it. An oasis you won't want to leave, this cosy inn sits right on the Pecorini Mare seafront, with the fishing boats drawn up alongside. A varied selection of rooms is available, some with antique furniture and little

waterfront balconies, others in self-contained houses not far away. Out on the shaded terrace is the island's most relaxed restaurant (open lunch and dinner, non-guests welcome). It gets very busy in Aug, but at most times of the year all you can hear is the sound of lapping water as you tuck into things like spaghetti with almond sauce and slabs of grilled tuna. Half-board is a really good deal for most of the year at €65 per person, though it's €80–90 in summer. ④

Restaurant

A Tana Filicudi Porto ☎ 090.988.9089. The best independent restaurant is just a minute or two's walk along the seafront from the port, where you

can dine on *pasta con cozze e vóngole* and other seafood specials on a lovely terrace overlooking the stone beach. Closed Oct–May. Expensive.

Alicudi

Ends of the line in Europe don't come much more remote than **ALICUDI**. Two and a half hours from Milazzo by hydrofoil, or five by ferry, the island forms a perfect cone, a mere Mediterranean pimple, and its precipitous shores are pierced by numerous caves. Up the sheer slope behind the only settlement, terraced smallholdings and white houses cling on for dear life, decorated with tumbling banks of flowers. Indeed, Alicudi's ancient name of Ericusa was the word for the heather that still stains its slopes purple in spring. Its rocky isolation was formerly exploited by the Italian government, who used the island as a prison for convicted Mafiosi, but now it's virtually abandoned by all but a few farmers and fishermen.

It's this quietude, of course, that attracts tourists; not many, it's true, but enough for there to be some semblance of facilities in the village to cater for visitors. You'll be asked by locals if you're a foreigner, meaning *from Italy* – which is about as far-flung as can be imagined here. Life is simple, though not

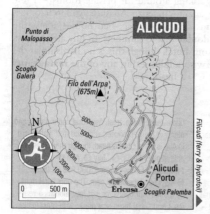

lived entirely in isolation. Electricity arrived at the start of the 1990s, so now there's TV, too. There are two general stores, plenty of fancy boat hardware, even a car or two parked at the dock (though, since there are no navigable roads, it's not clear whether this is bravado or forward planning on behalf of the owners). You have to walk to reach anywhere and the network of volcanic stone-built paths behind the village is extremely steep and tough – all the heavy fetching and carrying is still done by donkey or mule, whose indignant brays echo across the port all day.

▲ Boats along the Alicudi waterfront

The island

Once you disembark at **Alicudi Porto**, things to do are simply enumerated. The most exhausting option is the hike up past the castle ruins to the island peak of **Filo dell'Arpa** (675m). The path runs up through the village houses from the port and there's a proper stone-built track most of the way. Unfortunately, the track looks as though it was created by a malevolent giant emptying a bag of boulders from the top and letting them fall where they will. There's absolutely no shade, and it will take at least two hours to get up, though the magnificent views make it worthwhile.

Otherwise, you'll probably get all the exercise you need clambering over the rocky **shore** to the south of the port. The path soon peters out beyond the island's only hotel and the power station, but the rocks offer a sure foothold as they get larger the further you venture. The water is crystal clear and, once you've found a flat rock big enough to lie on, you're set for more peace and quiet than you'd bargained for. The only sounds are the echoed mutter of offshore fishermen, the scrabbling of little black crabs in the rock pools and the lap of the waves.

Practicalities

From the dock, walk to the left past the beached fishing-boats and in the almost cave-like dwellings in front of you are the Siremar **agency** (open before departures; ℡090.988.9795), Ústica Lines (℡340.301.5047) and – in the arched terrace above – one of the island's **general stores** (the other one is along the path to the hotel).

The modern, twelve-roomed *Ericusa* **hotel** is a fiveminute walk south along the shore (℡090.988.9902, ⓦwww.alicudihotel.it; closed Oct to May; ❼), with sea views, terrace and restaurant. Meals are included in the rate, either on a half- or full-board basis. **Apartment or room rental** is usually quite straightforward too, and available all year round: ask around at the port, or contact *Casa Mulino* (℡090.988.9681, ⓦwww.alicudicasamulino.it; ❹, Aug ❻), which has small apartment rooms with terraces sleeping two, four or six people.

Unless you **eat** at the *Ericusa*, you may have to fend for yourself. Both stores sell bread, cheese, cured meats, olives, beer, ice cream, and whatever fruit and vegetables arrived on the boats. Alternatively, call in on Signore Silvio during the day, who lives up the hill behind the Siremar office (anyone can point you in the right direction). He cooks dinner on request – spaghetti, fresh fish, salad, fruit and wine – for around €25 a head, served on his bougainvillea-covered terrace in the company of whoever else happens to turn up.

Festivals

Easter
Holy Week Procession of the saints in **Lípari**.

June
29 Festival of San Pietro on **Panarea**.

July
17 Festival of Santa Marina in **Santa Marina di Salina**, Salina.

23 Festival of St Mary of Terzito at the **sanctuary of Madonna del Terzito** on Salina.

August
10 Festival of San Lorenzo in **Malfa**, Salina.
24 Procession of San Bartolomeo's statue and relics in **Lípari town** accompanied by fireworks. Celebrations, too, on **Alicudi**.

Travel details

Ferries and hydrofoils year round connect the Aeolians with Milazzo, Messina, Palermo and Cefalù; additional summer (June to Sept) services operate from Naples and Reggio di Calabria on the Italian mainland. Main services are with Siremar (ⓦwww.siremar.it), Ústica Lines (ⓦwww.usticalines.it) and NGI (ⓦwww.ngi-spa.it), whose websites are the best places to consult up-to-date timetables and ticket prices.

Ferries

Lipari to: Alicudi (at least 3 weekly, 1 daily in summer; 3hr 45min); Filicudi (at least 3 weekly, 1 daily in summer; 2hr–2hr 40min); Ginostra (at least 4 weekly, 1 daily in summer; 3–4hr); Milazzo (4–5 daily; 2hr); Panarea (at least 4 weekly, 1–2 daily in summer; 2hr); Salina (2 daily; 50min); Strómboli (at least 4 weekly, 1 daily in summer; 3–4hr); Vulcano (2–3 daily; 25min).

Hydrofoils

Lipari to: Alicudi (1–3 daily; 2hr); Cefalù (at least 3 weekly, 1 daily in summer; 3hr 30min); Filicudi (1–3 daily; 1hr 15min); Ginostra (1–2 daily; 1hr 30min); Messina (1–5 daily; 1hr 30min–2hr 10min); Milazzo (hourly; 45min–1hr); Palermo (at least 3 weekly, 2 daily in summer; 3–4hr); Panarea (3–5 daily; 1hr); Salina (hourly; 25min); Strómboli (3–5 daily; 1hr 45min); Vulcano (hourly; 10min).

Food and wine in Sicily

There are few more compelling reasons to visit Sicily than to enjoy its food and wine. Sicilian cuisine has been described as "the field on which all other cuisines give battle to each other", and dining on the island is like a journey back through history, from the wine and olives that came with the Greeks to the rice, saffron and cinnamon of the Arabs and the meat dishes inherited from Norman and Hohenstaufen invaders. Far from conflicting, these elements coalesce and harmonize, to the point where a good dinner becomes a multicultural experience.

▶▶ There is a full menu reader on p.464

Capers ▲

Fish market in Catania ▲
Fish market in Palermo ▼

Sicilian cuisine

While Italian food and wine are prized the world over, visitors soon learn that there's no such thing as Italian cuisine. Each region has its own specialities, and while Sicilian cooking may lack some of the sophistication of northern Italy, it's often simpler, healthier and cheaper. Even within Sicily, dishes have their own specific provenance. "Locally-sourced ingredients" – an increasingly common boast in countries where food is an industry rather than a life-affirming experience – are taken for granted, and the island's diverse culinary traditions and ingredients are always best sampled on their home turf. So look out for dishes that make the most of pistachios when travelling in the foothills of Etna, walnuts when you're around Agrigento, capers when you're in the offshore islands, and seafood everywhere there's a fishing harbour.

Markets of plenty

"In Baghdad, Valencia or Palermo, a market is more than a market … it's a vision, a dream, a mirage."
Leonardo Sciascia

All year round, something is always being harvested, fermented or cured somewhere on the fertile island of Sicily. The best place to find what's in season is the local **food market**, the repository of bounty and accumulated goodness. Every town, village and neighbourhood has one, either as a constant fixture or a once-a-week affair. In the most famous, the teeming *suqs* of Palermo and Catania, tables groan under precarious mountains of olives, wedges of glistening fish, slabs of raw meat, lavish boxes of fruit and vegetables of every shape and hue. But the Sicilian market is about much more than food: it's a stage of operatic ardour, sometimes raucous, congested and exhausting, but forever riveting as spectacle and performance.

On the menu

Starters

Any restaurant worth its salt will offer an abundant table of antipasti. Half the pleasure is in the presentation, so let your eyes linger over the offerings. Typical elements include cold meats and salamis, anchovies, artichokes, aubergines, peppers and olives.

More than any other dish, pasta – eaten instead of or in addition to antipasti – is an emblem of local pride. One type you'll encounter frequently around Palermo is pasta *con le sarde*, with a rich sauce of sardines, fennel, raisins and nuts, while *alla Norma*, with aubergines, is a speciality of Catania.

Main courses

In a land where vegetarianism is still a distant rumour, meat and fish are the solid heart of any Sicilian meal. In inland areas, such dishes as rabbit and sausage spiced with fennel seeds are common, though seafood is always the main event on the coast. *Pesce spada* (swordfish) is ubiquitous between May and September, best sampled around Messina, where the long-masted *felucche* still ply the Straits, while tuna is the staple in Trápani province.

Desserts and festival food

From the Byzantine Greeks and the Arabs, Sicily has absorbed a taste for sugar-rich cakes and pastries. Once again, the visual impact is as important as the flavour. Even if you can't stomach them, *Frutti di Martorana*, fashioned in the shapes of fruits, are an artistic triumph in the Palermo region. Ice cream, too, is a Sicilian triumph of taste and texture, with myriad concoctions available, even in the most humble gelateria.

▲ Pasta con le sarde

▼ Frutti di Martorana

The wines of Sicily

Home to more vineyards than any other region in Italy, Sicily is these days respected for the quality as well as the quantity of its wines. Scientific growing techniques and quality control have enabled local producers to make the most of the hot sun, relatively high altitudes and low rainfall. While native grape varieties such as the red Frappato and the white Grillo, Inzolia and Cataratto are still used for blending with other wines to provide body and strength, others, such as Nero d'Ávola are increasingly appreciated in their own right. In addition, with the introduction of international varieties such as Cabernet Sauvignon and Chardonnay, more Sicilian wines are being shipped all over the world.

Vineyards near Prizzi ▲
Marsala wine ▼

Favourite Sicilian wines

Álcamo This highly rated, robust, dry white from Trápani province is best served with antipasti and seafood.

Cerasuolo di Vittoria A ruby red and cherry-flavoured wine from southeastern Sicily, often with a high alcoholic content.

Etna Nourished on volcanic soil, and either rosso or bianco, this can be drunk as an aperitif or used to accompany seafood.

Grecánico A crisp white from the centre and west of the island that's often blended with Chardonnay.

Malvasia The variety responsible for these smooth aperitifs or dessert wines is grown all over Italy, and in Sicily in the Aeolian Islands.

Marsala Sicily's best known export, this fortified wine from the west coast can be either sweet or dry. The quality varies – the best are left to mature in the cask for up to ten years.

Moscato A sweet, full-bodied, amber-coloured wine from Pantelleria.

The northern Ionian coast

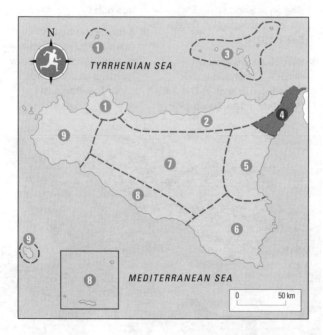

TYRRHENIAN SEA

MEDITERRANEAN SEA

0   50 km

CHAPTER 4

Highlights

* **Ferragosto in Messina** Giant puppets and dazzling fireworks over the Straits are the highlights of this spectacular mid-August party, which takes over the entire city. See p.195

* **Fish supper in Ganzirri** A few kilometres north of Messina, dine on seafood alongside the lakes or facing the Straits. See p.197

* **Sávoca** An unmissable hill-village – mummified bodies and a location seen in *The Godfather* movie. See p.199

* **Teatro Greco, Taormina** The island's most dramatically sited classical theatre makes a superb summer venue for concerts, films and dramas. See p.205

* **The Gola di Alcántara** Wade through the water in the deep gorge of the Alcántara River. See p.211

* **A day at the beach, Giardini-Naxos** The down-to-earth beach resort below Taormina sits on a wide sandy bay. See p.211

▲ Strolling in Taormina

The northern Ionian coast

H emmed in by the mountains, the **northern Ionian coast** is Sicily's most visually exotic strip, crammed with some of the most brilliant displays of colourful vegetation you'll see anywhere on this flower-filled island. Perhaps not surprisingly, it's crowded by an almost unbroken ribbon of development, and is one of Sicily's most popular resort areas, with both Italian and foreign tourists lured by the stunning views down to a turquoise sea. Still at heart the hill-village it once was, **Taormina** is the most illustrious resort – on the entire island, never mind this coast – and its famous ancient theatre, grand hotels and engaging small-town charm disappoint no one who visits. The local beaches are all a short ride below town, including the extensive sands that line the curving bay at **Giardini-Naxos**.

It's **Messina**, just across the busy Straits from mainland Italy, that's the region's major city, though an unfortunate history has left only scant attractions. It does have some enticing spots nearby, from busy summer beaches to unspoiled hill-villages, two or three of the latter distinguished by impressive Norman churches built by Count Roger during the eleventh century to consolidate his grip on the island. At **Sávoca**, mummified bodies on display in the Cappuccini monastery are the big attraction, while further south, beyond Taormina, the only road that penetrates any distance inland takes in the **Alcántara valley** and its spectacular gorge, before heading up to the gnarled old towns of **Francavilla** and **Castiglione di Sicilia**.

Along the coast, it's best to take the train, which traces the shoreline pretty much all the way: on a clear day there are sparkling views across to Calabria, while the ragged cliffs rearing above the tracks are covered with acres of prickly pears. By road, the toll autostrada (the A18) makes a fast alternative, plunging through some fairly dramatic scenery as it cruises above the sea. Some slower local buses, on the other hand, stick to the backstreets of the successive towns and villages between Messina and Taormina – a largely unedifying ride, and an excruciatingly slow one.

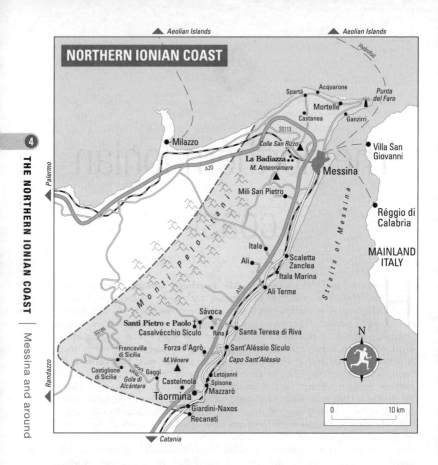

◄ *Palermo*

◄ *Randazzo*

Messina and around

MESSINA may well be your first sight of Sicily, and from the ferry it's a fine one, stretching out along the seaboard, north of the distinctive hooked harbour from which the city took its Greek name – Zancle (Sickle). The natural beauty of its location, looking out over the Straits to the forested hills of Calabria, is Messina's best point; Shakespeare (who almost certainly never laid eyes on the city) used it as the setting for his *Much Ado About Nothing*. Yet the city itself holds only a few buildings of any historical or architectural interest, dotted along traffic-choked streets that are used as a racetrack by drivers who rank among the most reckless in Sicily. The unedifying appearance is not entirely Messina's own fault: the congestion is largely the result of the surrounding mountains, which squeeze the traffic along the one or two roads that link the elongated centre with the northern suburbs. Messina's modern aspect is more a tribute to its powers of survival in the face of a record of devastation that's high even by Sicily's disaster-prone standards.

The greatest damage has been caused by the unstable geological belt on which Messina stands, responsible for a series of catastrophic **earthquakes**. The most notable of these occurred in 1783 and 1908; on the latter occasion

Crossing the Straits

Crossing the Straits of Messina is one of the most evocative entries into Sicily. Two ferry services (*traghetti*) operate from **Villa San Giovanni**, 12km north of Réggio di Calabria: the state-railway-run FS (T 892.021) and a private firm, Caronte (T 800.627.414, W www.carontetourist.it).

If you're **driving**, Caronte, with more frequent crossings, makes better sense: follow signs from the Villa San Giovanni autostrada exit, a straightforward run through town, stopping at the first ticket kiosk (well-marked) where you can park at leisure and sort out your ticket (from €23 for a car one way; returns valid for sixty days cost from €40, three-day returns from €25). If you miss this kiosk there's a second after you pass under the railway, but it can be a bit of a scramble here, with nowhere to park. The queue for boarding begins soon after: the average wait is ten minutes, and even in the peak times of August and rush hour, it won't be much more than 25.

Travelling **by train**, you might want to stay on it if you're crossing at night (though you'll probably be woken by the clanking din as the train is loaded onto the FS ferry), but by day it's quicker to leave the train at Villa San Giovanni station and skip the shuttling operation. Following the signs for the ferries, descend directly from the platform to sea level, where there is an FS ticket office (one way tickets about €1). Overhead signs tell you which bay leads to the first departure, or follow everyone else. There are enough FS ferries (1–2 an hour) to make it unnecessary to walk the 500m to the Caronte ferries. **Journey time** for crossings is 30 minutes on FS and 20 minutes on Caronte ferries. A bar on board serves snacks (including some good *arancini*), coffee and refreshments. Drivers might as well leave their vehicles, though look sharp as the ferry approaches Messina, as disembarkation is a rushed affair (and a suitable introduction to driving in Messina).

From Réggio di Calabria to Messina, there are two to three daily Ústica Lines hydrofoil services (T 0923.873.813, W www.usticalines.it), as well as FS fast-ferry (*nave veloce*) crossings (roughly 6.50am–8.15pm; Mon–Fri hourly, seven only on Sat & Sun), taking about 15 and 25 minutes respectively. In addition, Meridiano Lines runs a night-time service every couple of hours, taking 45 minutes. All services leave from the port, a couple of hundred metres back from Réggio Lido station, and tickets, from the kiosk at the terminal, cost €3.30. For information on hydrofoil and ferry tickets for the **return journey**, see "Listings", p.196.

the shore sank by half a metre overnight and around 80,000 Sicilians lost their lives (plus around 15,000 across the Straits in Calabria). The few surviving buildings, along with everything that had been painstakingly reconstructed in the wake of the earthquake, were subsequently the target of Allied bombardments, when Messina achieved the dubious distinction of being the most intensely bombed Italian city during World War II. Consequently, the attractions of Messina itself are limited, and can be seen quickly. However, if you're here in summer, you'll notice the passage of the tall-masted *felucche*, or **swordfish boats**, patrolling the narrow channel, attracted to these rich waters from miles up and down the Italian coast. You can enjoy their catch the same day in a good choice of restaurants, especially a little way north at **Ganzirri**, where lakeside fish restaurants provide some welcome relief from the city. Beyond, and around the corner of **Punta del Faro**, lidos line the coast at **Mortelle**, whose beaches, bars and pizzerias are where the city comes to relax. There's also no shortage of beaches on the suburban coastal strip south of Messina, while you can break up the journey south with inland detours to interesting old churches in places like **Mili San Pietro** and **Itala**.

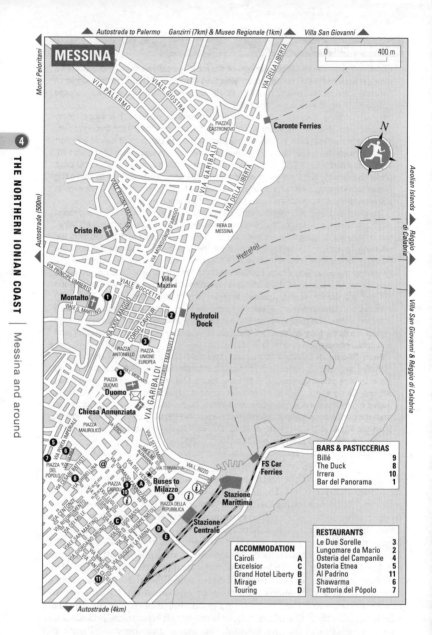

MESSINA

▲ Autostrada to Palermo   Ganzirri (7km) & Museo Regionale (1km) ▲   Villa San Giovanni ▲

Monti Peloritani ◄

Autostrade (500m) ◄

0   400 m

N

Aeolian Islands ►

Reggio di Calabria ►

Villa San Giovanni & Reggio di Calabria ►

VIA PALERMO

VIALE GIOSTRA

VIA DELLA LIBERTÀ

PIAZZA CASTRONOVO

Caronte Ferries

VIA GARIBALDI

VIA DELLA LIBERTÀ

FIERA DI MESSINA

VIALE TERESA MEZZO

VIA MONSIGNOR D'ARRIGO

Cristo Re

Hydrofoil

VIA PRINCIPE UMBERTO

VIALE BOCCETTA

Villa Mazzini

Montalto

VIA XXIV MAGGIO

VIALE G. MARTINO

1

CORSO CAVOUR

2   Hydrofoil Dock

PIAZZA ANTONELLO

PIAZZA UNIONE EUROPEA

PIAZZA DUOMO

4

Duomo

VIA DEI MERCANTI

VIA VITTORIO EMANUELE

VIA GARIBALDI

Chiesa Annunziata

PIAZZA MAUROLICO

VIA PORTA IMPERIALE

5

6

7

PIAZZA DEL PÓPOLO

@

VIA TOMMASO CANNIZZARO

VIA SETTEMBRINI

VIA GHIBELLINA

8

PIAZZA CAIROLI

VIA S. DEL VESPRO

VIA L. RIZZO

VIA TERRANOVA

Buses to Milazzo

i

9

10

i

PIAZZA DELLA REPUBBLICA

FS Car Ferries

Stazione Maríttima

VIA CENTONZE

VIALE SAN MARTINO

VIA DEL MILLE

VIA GIORDANO BRUNO

C

VIA NINO BIXIO

B

D

E

VIA GIUSEPPE LA FARINA

VIA GIUSEPPE NATOLI

Stazione Centrale

11

BARS & PASTICCERIAS
Billé	9
The Duck	8
Irrera	10
Bar del Panorama	1

ACCOMMODATION
Cairoli	A
Excelsior	C
Grand Hotel Liberty	B
Mirage	E
Touring	D

RESTAURANTS
Le Due Sorelle	3
Lungomare da Mario	2
Osteria del Campanile	4
Osteria Etnea	5
Al Padrino	11
Shawarma	6
Trattoria del Pópolo	7

▼ Autostrade (4km)

Arrival, information and city transport

Driving into Messina, leave the autostrada at the Boccetta exit for the centre and ferries. Given that it takes a good hour to reassemble trains from the mainland at Messina's **Stazione Maríttima**, if you're changing trains or stopping here you might as well disembark and walk 100m on to the **Stazione**

Centrale, at Piazza della Repubblica, where most of the local and long-distance buses also arrive and depart. **Buses to Milazzo for the Aeolian Islands** leave from the nearby Giuntabus office, Via Terranova 8, at the junction with Viale San Martino, and also stop in Piazza del Duomo.

Ferries from Villa San Giovanni or Réggio di Calabria also dock at the Stazione Maríttima, though Caronte ferries pull in further up, on Via della Libertà, ten minutes' walk north along the harbour. This is slightly more convenient for the slip road to the Palermo (A20) and Catania (A18) autostradas: drivers arriving off the FS ferries should head up Viale San Martino (well signposted). **Hydrofoils** (from the Aeolian Islands or Réggio di Calabria) dock at the terminal (signposted "*aliscafi*") in the port area.

Each of Messina's three different tourist offices should be able to provide a town map, accommodation listings and information about getting to the Aeolians. Two offices are close together outside the train station, on the right: the city **Ufficio Informazioni Turistiche**, on Piazza della Repubblica (Mon–Thurs 9am–1.30pm & 3–5pm, Fri 9am–1.30pm; ☎090.672.944) is more clued-up than the **provincial tourist office** just beyond, at Via Calabria 301 (Mon–Sat 8.30am–6.30pm; ☎090.674.236, ⓦ www.aptmessina.it). Most of Messina's hotels are scattered around this area, and it's just a short walk to Piazza Cairoli, which holds banks, shops and a third, **local tourist office** upstairs at no. 45 (Mon–Wed 8am–2pm & 3.30–8pm, Thurs & Fri 9am–2pm; ☎090.293.5292, ⓦ www.azienturismomessina.it). The independent **website** ⓦ www.messinacitymap.com is out of date but has useful contact numbers and includes a detailed street map.

You can walk easily from the station or harbour to the Duomo, but to venture anywhere further, take the city's single **tram line** (#28). It runs between Annunziata in the north (for the museum) to Gazzi in the south, with departures from Piazza della Repubblica, Piazza Cairoli and Piazza Municipio every ten minutes (30min on Sun). The tram also stops at Autosilo Cavallotti, the terminal for most of the ATM **city buses** (☎090.228.5263, ⓦ www.atmmessina.it), including #79 and #79/ (barrato) to Ganzirri, and buses #80 and #81/ to Ganzirri and Mortelle. Tickets (valid 3hr) are available at most *tabacchi*; an all-day ticket is available too.

Accommodation

Messina's cheaper **hotels** are near the station, though they're not very scintillating choices. This is one Sicilian city where business travellers take precedence over tourists, and the best reasonably priced accommodation is actually outside the centre, in Ganzirri. There's a **campsite** north of the centre on the very tip of Sicily at Via Circuito, Torre Faro, beyond Ganzirri (bus #79): *Nuovo Camping dello Stretto* (☎090.322.3051, ⓦ www.campingstretto.it).

Cairoli Viale San Martino 63 ☎& ⓕ 090.673.755. Large, old-fashioned, central hotel right next to Piazza Cairoli. All rooms have a/c and en-suite bathrooms. ❹
Excelsior Via Maddalena 32 ☎090.293.1431, ⓔ excelsiorme@virgilio.it. Central, modern three-star hotel, primarily for business travellers but useful if everywhere else is full, and good value. Breakfast (€4) available. ❹

Grand Hotel Liberty Via I Settembre 15 ☎090.640.9436, ⓦ nhliberty.hotelsinsicily.it. Very swish, Art Nouveau-style hotel right opposite the train station, popular with business travellers. Closed mid-July to Aug. ❼
Mirage Via N. Scotto 3 ☎090.293.8844. Down an alley off Piazza della Repubblica, this is a rather shabby lodging, with small but adequate rooms (air-conditioning extra). ❷, en-suite ❸

Touring Via N. Scotto 17 ☎ 090.293.8851, ⓦ www.hoteltouring-me.it. Just up from the *Mirage* and a cut above it, it has bare but spacious rooms, each with bathroom and telephone. Try and avoid rooms on the ground floor, where the desk clerk's TV and the hot-drinks machine can be noisy. No credit cards. ❷, rooms with a/c ❹

The City

Messina's wide remodelled streets and low reinforced buildings guard against future disasters of a natural kind, but make for a pretty uninspiring spectacle. It only takes a couple of hours to see the few monuments that remain – chiefly, the Duomo and the nearby Chiesa Annunziata dei Catalani – though the treasure-trove of art contained in the Museo Regionale makes up for what the rest of the city lacks. Otherwise, Messina's pleasures are to be found in kicking around its portside promenade and absorbing the views across the Straits. Messina by night can be particularly beautiful, especially from the high Via Panoramica (which changes its name along its route west of the centre from Viale Gaetano Martino to Via Príncipe Umberto and Viale Regina Margherita) – from here, with the city at your feet, there's a long, sparkling view across to mainland Italy. From the centre, the closest sections of this route are the Viale Príncipe Umberto and Viale Regina Margherita stretch, where there are bars and pizzerias around two floodlit sanctuaries (Cristo Re and Montalto) and plenty of scope for pleasant evening strolling.

The Duomo and around

Messina's most important monument, the **Duomo** (Mon–Sat 7am–7pm, Sun 7.30am–1pm & 4–7.30pm), epitomizes the city's phoenix-like ability to re-create itself from the ashes of its last disaster. It's the reconstruction of a twelfth-century cathedral erected by Roger II, one of a series of great Norman churches that included the sumptuous cathedrals of Palermo and Cefalù. Formerly, the building dominated medieval Messina, and was the venue for Archbishop Palmer's marriage of Richard the Lionheart's sister Joan to the Norman-Sicilian, William II. Devastated by the earthquake in 1908, it was rebuilt in the years following World War I, only to fall victim to a firebomb in

▲ Fishing boats, Messina

Messina's roaring clocktower

The Duomo's detached **campanile**, or belltower, claims to be the largest astronomical clock in the world, and puts on its best show at noon every day, when a lion (Messina's ancient emblem) unleashes a mighty roar over the city – quite alarming if you're not expecting it. On the side facing the cathedral two dials show the phases of the planets and the seasons, while above them a globe shows the phases of the moon. The elaborate panoply of moving gilt figures facing the piazza, activated on the hour, half-hour and quarter-hour, ranges from representations of the days of the week and the four Ages of Man to Dina and Clarenza, the two women who saved the city from a night attack by the Angevins during the Wars of the Vespers.

1943 that reduced it once more to rubble. What you see today is mostly a faithful copy, which took years to complete, with few elements remaining of the original fabric.

The Romanesque facade is its best aspect, the lower part mostly authentic and dominated by a richly decorated, late-Gothic **central portal**, extravagantly pointed, with good detail, and flanked by two smaller contemporary doors. Almost everything in the undeniably grand **interior** is a reproduction, from the marble floor to the elaborately painted wooden ceiling. Two rows of sturdy columns line the nave, topped by cement capitals faithfully copied from originals, some of which survive in the Museo Regionale. The **mosaicwork** in the three grand apses holds most interest, though it pales into insignificance beside the island's other examples of the genre, and only the mosaic on the left – of the Virgin Mary with St Lucy – is original. All the same, try to find someone to switch on the lights, as the mosaics then take on a majesty that's entirely lost in the gloom that normally shrouds the cathedral's interior. Little else here predates the twentieth century, apart from some salvaged tombs, most handsome of which is that of Archbishop de Tabiatis from 1333, on the right of the altar and heavily graffitied. The **tesoro** (mid-April to mid-Sept Mon–Fri 9am–1pm & 4.30–6.30pm, Sat 9am–1pm; mid-Sept to mid-April Mon–Sat 9am–1pm; €3, or €5 including campanile) holds precious reliquaries, the bejewelled *Manta d'Oro* – a holy adornment for sacred images, of a kind more commonly used in Orthodox rites – and a collection of skilfully crafted silverware. You can also climb to the top of the detached **campanile** to enjoy a great view of the piazza and city (mid-April to mid-Sept Mon–Sat 9am–1pm & 4.30–6.30pm, Sun 10am–1pm & 4.30–6.30pm; mid-Sept to Oct Mon–Sat 9am–1pm, Sun 10am–1pm; Nov to mid-April Sun 10am–1pm; €3.50, or €5 including *tesoro*).

In front of the cathedral and its belltower, the graceful **Fontana di Orione** was daintily carved in the mid-sixteenth century by Montorsoli, a Florentine pupil of Michelangelo. The fountain depicts Orion, the city's mythical founder, surmounting a collection of cherubs, nymphs and giants, and surrounded by four figures (representing the rivers Nile, Ebro, Camaro and Tiber) reclining along the balustrade. The upper part was carefully restored after earthquake damage in 1908.

Just back from the Duomo, the truncated section of the twelfth-century **Chiesa Annunziata dei Catalani** (Mon–Sat 9.30–11.30am; for access at other times call ℡090.675.175) squats below pavement level, Messina's only surviving example of Arab/Norman church-building. The blind arcading around the apses and the Byzantine-style cupola are the perfect antidote to the ugly cement facade surrounding its three portals, and the interior is suitably simple, with the transept and apse true to their original construction. In front, a martial statue by the sculptor Andrea Calamecca (Calamech) stands half-hidden under the trees, depicting a proud Don Giovanni of Austria, victor of the Battle of Lépanto (the victorious Christian fleet sailed from Messina in 1535).

From here, it's a short stroll to the **harbourside**, with its combination of constant activity and compelling vistas over the Straits. Sicily's deepest natural harbour is a port of call for freighters and cruisers of all descriptions, as well as for frequent NATO warships. But the greatest traffic consists of ferries, endlessly plying back and forth, which are Sicily's chief link with the mainland.

The Museo Regionale

Messina's **Museo Regionale**, at Via della Libertà 465 (Mon & Fri 9am–1.30pm, Tues, Thurs & Sat 9am–1.30pm & 4–6.30pm or 3–5.30pm in winter, Sun 9am–12.30pm, closed Wed; last entry 30min before closing; €2.50), is a repository for some of the city's greatest works of art, many of them carefully rescued from earthquake rubble, and includes what is perhaps Sicily's finest collection of fifteenth- to seventeenth-century art. A much larger museum building is being built next door, where the collection is due to be transferred (for an update call ☎090.361.292): until then, the layout of the museum is as described below. Take tram #28 to the last stop, Annunziata; the museum lies on the left, immediately after the Regina Margherita hospital. The collection starts with some lovely Byzantine work, larded with a good helping of Gothic, well evident in a fourteenth-century triptych of the *Madonna with Child between SS Agatha and Bartholomew*, and a remarkably modern-looking wooden crucifix from the fifteenth century, with a sinuous, tragic Christ. The highlight is **room 4**, which holds marvellous examples of fifteenth-century art, notably an ethereal statue of the *Madonna and Child*, attributed to Francesco Laurana, and the museum's most famous exhibit, the *St Gregory* polyptych, by Sicily's greatest native artist, **Antonello da Messina** – a masterful synthesis of Flemish and Italian Renaissance styles that's a good example of the various influences that reached the port of Messina in the fifteenth century. The statue of *Scilla*, the classical Scylla who terrorized sailors from the Calabrian coast (as described in Homer's *Odyssey*), is on display in **room 6**; it's an alarming spectacle, with contorted face and eyes awash with expression. Sculpted by Montorsoli in 1557, it was once adjoined to an imperious figure of Neptune in the act of calming the seas, a copy of which stands on the seafront just up from the hydrofoil terminal. Of the museum's remaining works, the most noteworthy, in **room 10**, are a couple of large shadowy canvases by **Caravaggio**, commissioned by the city in 1609, the better of which is the atmospheric *Raising of Lazarus*. The last room on the ground floor has a monstrous ceremonial carriage from 1742, hauled out for viceregal and other high-ranking visits. Though faded and tarnished, its gilt bodywork is still awesomely grandiose, showing an impressive array of detail. Upstairs is a collection of mainly ecclesiastical silverware, an art at which Messina once excelled.

Eating, drinking and entertainment

Messina has a good range of inexpensive **restaurants**, though you should head away from the port and Piazza Cairoli for a more relaxed atmosphere. If you're here in early summer, make a point of sampling the local **swordfish**; May and June are the best months for this, before the water gets too warm. The streets around Piazza Lo Sardo (also known as Piazza del Pópolo) hold a good mix of rough-and-ready trattorias and more serious eating places, while the area

Ferragosto

If you're in Messina in midsummer, you might catch the festivals around the Feast of the Assumption, or **ferragosto**. Although all the villages on both sides of the Straits hold festivals around this time, with some pretty spectacular fireworks lighting up the sky on any one night, Messina's festivities are grander, beginning around August 12, when two plaster giants (*giganti*) are wheeled around town, and finally stationed near the port opposite the Municipio. These are said to be Messina's two founders, Mata and Grifone, one a white female, the other a burly Moor, and both mounted on huge steeds. On ferragosto itself, August 15, another towering carriage, the Vara, is hauled through the city centre. It's an elaborate column supporting dozens of papier-mâché cherubs and angels, culminating in the figure of Christ stretching out his right arm to launch Mary on her way to Heaven. This unwieldy construction is towed on long ropes, pulled by hundreds of penitents – semi-naked if they're men, all in white if they're women – and cheered on by thousands of people along the way. The whole thing is a sweaty and frenetic performance, finishing up at Piazza del Duomo, where flowers are thrown out to the crowds, many of whom risk being crushed in the mad scramble to gather these luck-bearing charms. Late at night, one of Sicily's best **firework displays** is held on the seafront near Via della Libertà.

around Piazza Cairoli is best for **bar life**, though some of the bars close in August when everyone's at Ganzirri or Mortelle. Exhibitions and classical concerts take place near the port at the church of Santa Maria Alemanna (Via I Settembre), while free **concerts** of classical, jazz, rock and world music are staged in Piazza del Duomo in July and August. This is also the period when **free films** are shown (usually at 8.30pm), generally in the Villa Mazzini public gardens near the hydrofoil dock or nearby next to the church of San Giuliano off Via della Libertà, around the Fiera di Messina – though the venue may change. Watch out for posters giving details of all of these, or ask at the tourist office – and arrive early, as these events tend to get crowded.

Cafés, bars and birrerias

Billé Piazza Cairoli 7. Superb and rather refined *pasticceria* where the piazza joins Via T. Cannizzaro, with ice cream, granitas, pastries and chocolates, as well as salads and *arancini*. There are tables inside and out.

The Duck Via Pellegrino 109. English-style pub, popular with US sailors from the nearby base. Stones bitter on tap and a range of German bottled beers. Rolls and chips also on the menu. Closed Mon & Aug.

Irrera Piazza Cairoli 12. In business since 1910, serving cakes, *frutta di martorana* (marzipan fruits), ices and pastries of renowned quality.

Bar del Panorama Viale Principe Umberto (next to the Santuario Cristo Re). Known as the *Bar del Pappagallo* – a fixture here for 38 years – this serves the best ice cream and granitas in town, along with traditional snacks like *arancini*. A great view to boot.

Restaurants

Le Due Sorelle Piazza Municipio 4 ☎090.44.720. With only nine tables, this is a small and select trattoria, but also innovative and memorable. Specialities such as *paella marinara* and *couscous con pesce* cost about €12, with main courses up to €18. Booking advised. Closed Sat lunch & Sun. Moderate.

Osteria del Campanile Via Loggia dei Mercanti 7 ☎090.711.418. Reliable little trattoria with

outdoor tables to the rear of the Duomo. Try the filling, fresh *maccheroni alla Norma* (€6) or the *linguine inferno* with spicy seafood sauce (€9), and there are pizzas too. Service can be slow. Closed Sun except July & Aug. Moderate.

Osteria Etnea Via Martino 38. Abundant portions and low prices (firsts €4–5, mains €5–7) make this tidy little place near Piazza Lo Sardo popular

195

with locals. The menu's long and service is brisk. Closed Sun. Inexpensive.

Lungomare da Mario Via Vittorio Emanuele 108, with an entrance also on Via Garibaldi. A fine choice for a fish lunch, opposite the hydrofoil dock, though it can be noisy if you sit outside. Pastas and (in the evening) pizzas are around €7, fish courses cost €9–12, and there are three-course fixed-price menus for €16. Closed Wed Sept–July. Moderate.

🎿 **Al Padrino** Via S. Cecilia 54–6. This bare, frills-free neighbourhood trattoria specializes in traditional Sicilian fare, such as *maccu* (mashed fava beans), and the house speciality, *melenzane al Padrino* (aubergines stuffed with fresh pasta and ricotta, €8). A three-course meal will cost around €20. Closed Sat eve and Sun. Moderate.

Trattoria del Pópolo Piazza Lo Sardo ☎090.671.148. You can eat outside at this friendly trattoria, making the most of the rare calm of this corner of the city. Dishes include *sarde allinguate* (fried sardines dressed with vinegar) and *franceschini* (baby squid fried in breadcrumbs); pasta dishes cost €4–6, mains €5–7.50. Closed Sun & mid-Aug. Moderate.

🎿 **Shawarma** Via M. Giurba 8 ☎090.712.213. Tagines, couscous and a range of potato dishes share menu space with pizzas (€5–8) at this popular trattoria off Piazza Lo Sardo, with some outdoor seating. Closed Mon.Inexpensive–moderate.

Listings

Airport Nearest at Réggio di Calabria, for internal services and summer charters only. Info on ☎0965.640.517, ⓦwww.sogas.it.

Bus companies AST, from Piazza della Repubblica or Autosilo Cavallotti ☎090.662.244, ⓦwww .aziendasicilianatrasporti.it (for Barcellona, Forza d'Agrò, Itala, and Patti); Autolinee Federico ☎0965.644.747, ⓦwww.autolineefederico.it, with ten departures daily from Autosilo Cavallotti, near the train station (for Réggio di Calabria airport); Giuntabus, from Via Terranova 8 ☎090.673.782, ⓦwww.giuntabus.com (for Milazzo and the Aeolian Islands); Interbus, from Piazza della Repubblica 6 ☎090.661.754 (for the coast south to Letojanni, Taormina and Catania, also twice-weekly connections to Umbria and Tuscany); Jonica, from Autosilo Cavallotti ☎090.771.400 (for the coast south as far as Santa Teresa di Riva); SAIS Autolinee, from Piazza della Repubblica ☎090.771.914, ⓦwww.saisautolinee.it (for Palermo, Catania and Catania airport); SAIS Trasporti, from Piazza della Repubblica ☎091.617.1141, ⓦwww.saistrasporti.it (for Rome); TAI, from outside the Banco d'Italia near the train station ☎090.675.184 (for Capo d'Orlando, Patti and Tíndari).

Car rental Avis, Via Garibaldi 109 ☎090.679.150; Maggiore, Via Vittorio Emanuele II 75 ☎090.675.476; Sicilcar, Via Garibaldi 187 ☎090.46.942.

Ferry tickets All tickets across the Straits are on sale at the respective terminals; for Villa San Giovanni, contact ☎892.021 (FS) or ☎800.627.414, ⓦwww.carontetourist.it (Caronte).

Hospital Ospedale Piemonte, Viale Europa ☎090.2221. For emergencies call ☎090.222.4347.

Hydrofoil tickets To Réggio di Calabria and the Aeolians, on sale at the hydrofoil terminal; call Ústica Lines on ☎090.364.044, ⓦwww.usticalines.it.

Internet Paritel, Via Centonze 74, three streets up from Piazza Cairoli (daily 8am–8pm). You can also telephone from here.

Left luggage Office at the train station open 8am–1pm (though hours may be extended); €3 per bag for 12hr, then €2 for every subsequent 12hr.

Pharmacy There's an all-night service on a rotating basis: consult any pharmacy window to find out current *farmacie notturne*, or call ☎090.717.589.

Police Carabinieri, Via Monsignor d'Arrigo ☎112; Police, Via XXIV Maggio 155, off Piazza Duomo ☎113 or 090.366.200.

Post office Main office at Largo S. Giacomo, off Piazza Duomo (Mon–Fri 8am–6.30pm, Sat 8am–12.30pm).

Shopping Messina is renowned for its pastries and biscuits. There's a cluster of classy *pasticcerie* around Piazza Cairoli: one of the most famous is Pisani, at Via T. Cannizzaro 45, renowned for its *pignolata* – a sugary confection covered with brown or white icing with a doughy filling. Oviesse is a supermarket for food, clothes and other items on Piazza Cairoli (daily 9am–1pm & 4–8pm), while the lanes running off the square hold smart boutiques and leather shops.

Taxis Ranks at Piazza Cairoli (☎090.293.4880), Piazza della Repubblica, outside Stazione Centrale (☎090.673.703), and at the Caronte terminal (☎090.44.492); there's also a 24-hour radio taxi (☎090.6505).

Ticket agency Theatre tickets, including tickets for some performances at Taormina's Teatro Greco and Tíndari's teatro, are sold at Lisciotto Viaggi: see Travel agents, below.

Travel agents Albertours, Piazza della Repubblica 25 ☎090.712.035; Lisciotto Viaggi, Piazza Cairoli 13 ☎090.719.001. For all air, rail and sea tickets.

Around Messina

Several mountain or coastal destinations, all well worth a visit, are less than thirty minutes from the centre of Messina by bus or car. If you're driving, you might wish to follow the high-level Via Panoramica north rather than the congested coastal road, which is the route the bus takes; but make a point of taking this lower road – an extension of Via della Libertà – at least once, passing fishermen's houses that back onto short sandy strips, in areas that must once have justified their idyllic names of Paradiso, Contemplazione and Pace. In Pace, look out for the British cannons lining the esplanade, pulled out of the Straits where they were sunk during the Napoleonic Wars.

Ganzirri and Punta del Faro

Buses #79, #80 and #81 make a stop in **GANZIRRI**, 10km north of the centre of Messina. In summer especially, this is the hub of crowds milling around the frothy bars and attending Italian **pop concerts** held nightly throughout August. There's mussel-farming on Ganzirri's lake, and you can eat plenty of fresh shellfish, swordfish or whatever else has been hauled in that day by the many boats operating around here. Most of the **trattorias** are squeezed into the wedge of land between lake and sea, and you can eat outside at nearly all of them. Prices tend to be high and the quality variable, but for very reasonably priced, exquisitely cooked seafood dishes, seek out *Lilla Currò*, signposted up a lane on the right side of the lake at Via Lido di Ganzirri 10 (℡090.395.064; no credit cards; closed Mon), where you can enjoy a feast for under €20 – booking is essential for evening meals. Keep going along this road (keeping right, towards Faro) for the cosy *Mínico Il Pescatore* (signposted *Il Pescatore*, just before the church; closed Thurs lunchtime in summer, all day Thurs in winter), which offers a good-value fixed-price menu (€25) of dishes from Sferracavallo, west of Palermo. Bus #79 stops right outside. A decent **pensione**, the airy *Donato*, at Via Caratozzolo 8 (℡090.393.150, 🌐www.hoteldonato.com; no credit cards; ❺), offers excellent value, its smartly restored rooms – all with bath – undisturbed by the scream of Vespas, and just 50m from the sea. It's signposted off the lake, just beyond *Lilla Currò*.

Punta del Faro (also called Capo Peloro) is the very tip of Sicily, the nearest point to Italy. The lighthouse here (the *faro*) is dwarfed by the towering pylon supporting the massive cables that tether the island to the mainland. Here, too, was where the legendary **Charybdis** once posed a threat to sailors – along with Scylla on the opposite shore – still remembered in the locality's name of Cariddi.

A bridge too far

Plans to build the **world's longest suspension bridge**, over the Messina Straits, have been in the air for years. Spearheaded by Berlusconi, fiercely opposed by the environmental lobby and seismologists, and indefinitely shelved by the Prodi administration in 2007, the bridge would have to span the two-mile Straits suspended from pylons as high as the Eiffel Tower, in order to support a twelve-lane motorway and a two-track railway. Seismologists fear that any bridge would be unable to resist a severe earthquake, while environmentalists claim that its pylons would affect the delicate water table that feeds the lakes of Faro and Ganzirri. However, with both the Calabrian and the Sicilian Mafia potentially set to make a killing on construction contracts, the battle lines are drawn.

Mortelle and Acquarone

A couple of kilometres further up the road, on the Tyrrhenian coast, **MORTELLE** is the focus in summer for Messina's bronzed youth, who throng the orderly lidos and sleek bars and pizzerias, filling the air with the screech of motorbikes. The fine sandy **beaches** extend west from here, most easily accessed from such villages as **ACQUARONE** (also called Acqualadrone), 7km from Mortelle, reachable on bus #80 (not Sun) from there or Messina's Autosilo Cavallotti.

Inland

Inland from Messina, the ridge-top of the **Monti Peloritani** offers the best vantage-point of the Tyrrhenian and Ionian coasts and also has some good walking in the woods. To reach the ridge, take the old Palermo road from Via Garibaldi in the city (bus #70 or #71 from Autosilo Cavallotti). On the way, you can stop off at the monastery of Santa Maria della Valle, better known as **La Badiazza** (always open). Secluded in a deep gully, this old Benedictine monastery lies at the end of a twenty-minute walk along a dirt road that leads off to the right just before Via Palermo passes under the autostrada. The monastery dates from the twelfth century, but was reconstructed after a fire in the fourteenth century and later abandoned. Today, recently restored, it has regained its fortress-like appearance and looks quite capable of withstanding a corsair raid.

While you can wander through the pinewoods around here, they are thicker further up the SS113 (Via Palermo); take a left turn at the crossroads at **Colle San Rizzo** (where bus #71 stops), then it's another 10km south to reach the panoramic **Monte Antennamare** sanctuary, a shabby building in a sublime spot (1124m high). Back at Colle San Rizzo, you could make a round trip by descending north to Castanea, another wooded area favoured by hunters, and down to the Tyrrhenian coast at Spartà, on the Messina road.

South down the coast

Messina's ungraceful suburbs extend south almost as far as the autostrada turn-off at Tremestieri. Shortly beyond, a minor road leads off inland from Mili Marina to **MILI SAN PIETRO**, a nondescript little place 2km up the road. As the village swings into view, the grey cupolas of the monastery-church of **Santa Maria** are just visible below the road on the right. The Basilian monastery of which this was a part was founded by Count Roger in 1082, but is now abandoned – irreverently occupied by assorted farmyard animals and permeated by their pungent rural smells. The church survives – just – its exterior displaying some nice interlaced blind arcading on one wall, and a semicircular apse. But the inside is derelict and not particularly interesting, although it's said to contain the burial place of Roger's son, Jordan; ask at the church in the centre of the village for the key. You can get here from Messina on bus #8 from Piazza Dante (every 90min Mon–Sat), for which there are frequent connections from Autosilo Cavallotti.

Further down the coast by 7 or 8km, **SCALETTA ZANCLEA** is a popular resort with an impressive eleventh-century **castle** at its highest point, containing some heraldic knick-knacks. The key is kept at the *Comune*. The next village down, Itala Marina, has an inland parent, **ITALA**, 2.5km up the road from the coast, just beyond which – over the bridge on the road to Croce – is the church of **San Pietro**. Built by Count Roger in 1093, in thanksgiving for a victory over the Arabs, the building has features in common with Santa Maria in Mili

San Pietro, and provided the model for the church near Casalvécchio Sículo built eighty years later. This domed, red-brick construction has been restored and is still in use; indeed the best time to see it is before the 11am service on Sunday morning. Failing that, contact the priest for the key; find him on Itala's main street, at no. 26.

Sávoca

Around 30km south of Messina, the small resort of Santa Teresa di Riva is the jumping-off point for the foothills of the Monti Peloritani and, in particular, the evocatively sited village of **SÁVOCA**. That sits at the end of a winding four-kilometre run up from the coast, its houses and three churches perched on the cliffsides in clumps, with a tattered castle (originally Saracen) topping the pile. Two pincer-like streets, Via San Michele and Via Chiesa Madre, reach around to their respective churches, the grandest being the square-towered thirteenth-century **Chiesa Madre**. Seated on a tiny ridge between two opposing hills, it's a fine vantage-point from which to look down the valley to the sea and across the surrounding hills. Spare a glance, too, at the house next door, lovingly restored and displaying a fifteenth-century stone-arched double window; the house is one of many in the village that have had a face-lift as outsiders move in to snap up run-down cottages as second homes. These days, Sávoca lies within the Taormina commuter belt and most of the people who live here work elsewhere. That's to its advantage: during the day the streets and hillside alleys are refreshingly empty, and the medieval atmosphere still intact.

Signs in the village point you to the **Cappuccini monastery**, whose catacombs (April–Sept Tues–Sat 9am–1pm & 4–7pm, Sun 11am–1pm & 4–7pm; Oct–March Tues–Sat 9am–noon & 4–7pm, Sun 11am–noon & 4–7pm; donations requested) contain a selection of gruesome mummified bodies. These are the remains of local lawyers, doctors and the clergy: two hundred to three hundred years old, they stand in niches dressed in their eighteenth-century finery, the skulls of less-complete colleagues lining the walls above. An added grotesque touch is the green paint with which the bodies have been daubed, the work of vandals and hard to remove without damaging the cadavers. Ask the custodian and you'll probably be shown the church **treasury** as well, which holds a small collection of liturgical books and seventeenth- and eighteenth-century bibles.

More offbeat delight is at hand in the village's ✻ *Bar Vitelli*. An appealing wood-panelled, eighteenth-century stone-flagged building, it (and the village) were used as the scene of Michael Corleone's betrothal to Apollonia in Coppola's film *The Godfather*. A few words of Italian might nudge the woman behind the bar into recounting her memories of the shoot – she's something of an expert on all the *Godfather* films. There are numerous mementoes of other episodes in the bar's past inside, and tables under the pergola outside. In summer, the signora at the *Bar Vitelli* will probably persuade you to sample her delicious lemon granita, which she makes daily. Sávoca also has a *paninoteca* for snacks below the Capuchin monastery and a popular **trattoria**, *La Pineta* (closed Wed in winter), with a panoramic terrace, near the bar.

There's nowhere to stay – a shame really – but you could easily see the village on a day-trip from either Messina or Taormina. AST and Jonica **buses** connect Messina with Santa Teresa di Riva – ask the driver to put you off on the seafront

(Lungomare Santa Teresa), and Sávoca is signposted to the left, with the bus stop for the village one block back from the sea on the corner of a crossroads. Jonica line buses leave three times daily (not Sun) from here for Sávoca and Casalvécchio Sículo. From Taormina, take an Interbus service to Santa Teresa and change there for Sávoca and Casalvécchio. For taxi transport locally, call ☎ 0942.751.566.

Casalvécchio Sículo

The only road beyond Sávoca (and served by the same bus from Santa Teresa di Riva) careers another 2km along the ridge to **CASALVÉCCHIO SÍCULO**, which, if anything, has even better views of the valley from its terraces. There's not much to detain you here, except the quiet village atmosphere, but walk through Casalvécchio and, after about 500m, a rough road drops away to the left (signposted), snaking down into a lush, citrus-planted valley. It's about a twenty-minute hike to the Norman monastery of **Santi Pietro e Paolo**, gloriously situated on a high bank above the river. Built in the twelfth century, its battlemented facade and double domes are visible from a distance through the lemon groves. Though considered Sicily's best example of Basilian (Greek) architecture, the church betrays a strong Arabic influence, particularly in the polychromatic patterns of the exterior. If it's locked, there should be someone around in one of the adjacent buildings with a key.

Either head back up to the main road and wait for the return bus to pass, or continue downhill for a longer **walk**, beyond the monastery to the River Agrò. It's about another hour's tramp, alongside the wide (and mostly dry) river bed to Rina, back towards the sea. The main (SS114) coastal road is signposted from Rina, and in another twenty minutes, through a small tunnel, you're back in Santa Teresa di Riva, on the Messina–Catania bus route.

Forza d'Agrò

The only other worthy diversion into the hills is just a few kilometres south, where the turn-off at **Capo Sant'Aléssio** gives the first views of Taormina. The cliffs here support a sturdy castle, which has been for sale for years; you can climb up to it, but you can't get in.

Four kilometres inland of here, atop a corkscrew road – and most easily reached by four daily Interbus buses from Taormina and Letojanni – is **FORZA D'AGRÒ**. Like so many Sicilian villages, it's a breezy place defiantly crumbling all around its mostly elderly inhabitants and with little left of the Norman **castello** that crowns it. A memorable clamber will take you up to the top: the streets become ever more perilous, and the stone cottages increasingly neglected and held together by rotting spars of wood. One push, it seems, would bring the whole lot down. The lower parts of the village are better maintained, but not much – hi-fi stores and clothes shops are tucked into tiny cottage interiors, and a couple of churches are locked and decrepit.

Still, this is close enough to Taormina to attract the tour buses, which deposit their passengers in the village square, where there are a couple of bars to help idle the time away. And there's a fine, moderately priced **restaurant** too, known to both tourists and locals: 🍴 *L'Abbazia* (☎ 0942.721.226; closed Mon

Nov–May; moderate–expensive). Specialities here include mixed vegetable grill made with local mushrooms, aubergine, peppers and radicchio, which you can eat on a terrace with great views; fixed-price three-course menus cost €25 and €28. There's even **somewhere to stay** if you are so inclined, the small and simple *Souvenir* on Via Belvedere (℡0942.721.078; no credit cards; ❸), where half-board is compulsory in August (€60 per person).

Taormina and around

TAORMINA, dominating two grand, sweeping bays from high on Monte Tauro, is Sicily's best-known and classiest resort. Although it has no beach of its own – they are all sited quite a way below town – the outstanding remains of the classical theatre and the sheer beauty of the town's site, framed by a distant Etna, amply compensate. Beloved of writers, artists and celebrities across the decades, it's an expensive place to stay (perhaps the most expensive in Sicily), but the air of exclusivity at least is only skin-deep – at heart, what was once a small hill-village still can't seem to believe its good luck. Much of its late medieval character is still intact, with the one main traffic-free street presenting an unbroken line of aged *palazzi*, flower-decked alleys and intimate piazzas. The downside is that at New Year and Easter, and between June and September, Taormina simply seethes as the narrow alleys and the beaches below town are filled shoulder-to-shoulder with tourists. Come between October and March instead, and the views of Etna are incomparably clearer, while the spring brings flamboyant hillside displays of flowering plants and shrubs. The town is overlooked by the mountain village of **Castelmola**, visited for the superb views in all directions, while down on the coast the local **beaches** soak up the day trade all summer. The nearby resort of **Giardini-Naxos** is actually a separate town in its own right – cheaper and less pretentious than Taormina in every way.

Arrival, information and transport

Taormina-Giardini **train station** is way below town, on the water's edge – it's actually one of Italy's most attractive stations, in Sicilian-Gothic style with Art Nouveau decoration, and there's a small tourist office here. To get up to town, you either need to take a taxi (around €15) or catch one of the local Interbus buses (every 30min, fewer on Sun; buy your ticket from the driver) from outside the station. These stop in Taormina at the **bus terminal** on Via Luigi Pirandello, where all other bus services stop, including direct services from Catania airport.

If you're driving, unless there's parking at your hotel you'll have to use one of the long-stay **car parks** signposted on the approaches to town, notably outside Porta Catania or at the Lumbi car park. It costs at least €8 to park for two hours (up to €17 for 24hr, and €30 for 48hr). Lumbi car park is further from the centre, and is a lengthy walk up steps to Via Cappuccini, though a free minibus service saves you the ten-minute climb.

The main street, Corso Umberto I, runs right through town, from Porta Messina to Porta Catania at the other end. The useful English-speaking **tourist office** is in the crenellated Palazzo Corvaja, off Piazza Vittorio Emanuele (Mon–Sat 8.30am–2pm & 4–7pm; ℡0942.23.243, ⓦwww.gate2taormina .com). You can pick up a map and various leaflets and tour brochures, while the office also posts comprehensive local bus and train timetables.

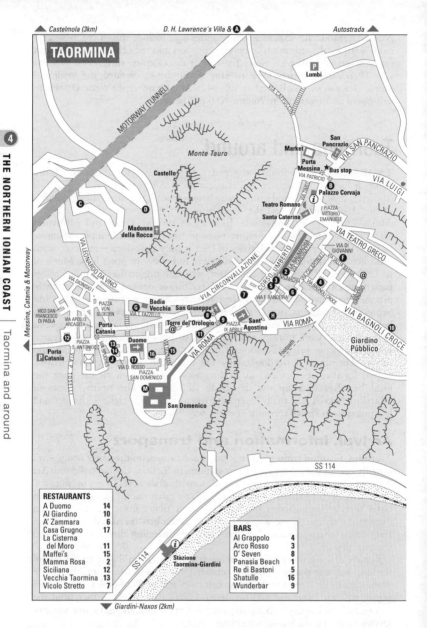

TAORMINA

▲ Castelmola (3km)   D. H. Lawrence's Villa & **A** ▲   Autostrada ▲

Monte Tauro

Castello

Madonna
della Rocca

San
Pancrazio

Market

Porta
Messina

Bus stop

Palazzo Corvaja

Teatro Romano

Santa Caterina

PIAZZA
VITTORIO
EMANUELE

Badia
Vecchia

San Giuseppe

Torre dell'Orologio

Sant'
Agostino

Duomo

San Domenico

Giardino
Púbblico

SS 114

SS 114

Stazione
Taormina-Giardini

Porta
Catania

Porta
Catania

PIAZZA
S. ANTONIO

PIAZZA
SAN DOMENICO

PIAZZA
IX APRILE

PIAZZA
VON
GLOEDEN

VIA SAN PANCRAZIO

VIA LUIGI

VIA TEATRO GRECO

VIA BAGNOLI CROCE

VIA DI
GIOVANNI

CORSO UMBERTO

VIA CIRCONVALLAZIONE

VIA ROMA

VIA F BANDEIRA

VIA LEONARDO DA VINCI

VICO SAN
FRANCESCO
DI PAOLA

VIA APOLLO
ARCAGETA

VIA DIONISIO

VIA T. FAZZELLO

VIA D. ROSSO

VIA L. PIRANDELLO

VIA PATRICIO

Footpath

Footpath

MOTORWAY (TUNNEL)

RESTAURANTS	
A Duomo	14
Al Giardino	10
A' Zammara	6
Casa Grugno	17
La Cisterna del Moro	11
Maffei's	15
Mamma Rosa	2
Siciliana	12
Vecchia Taormina	13
Vicolo Stretto	7

BARS	
Al Grappolo	4
Arco Rosso	3
O' Seven	8
Panasia Beach	1
Re di Bastoni	5
Shatulle	16
Wunderbar	9

▼ Giardini-Naxos (2km)

A free **minibus service** (*bus navetta*) shuttles from Piazza San Pancrazio (just below Porta Messina) to and from the Lumbi car park. Other local bus services depart hourly from Piazza San Pancrazio up to Madonna della Rocca (for the castle) and Castelmola, and down to the beach at Spisone/Letojanni, while buses to Giardini-Naxos leave from the bus terminal. For

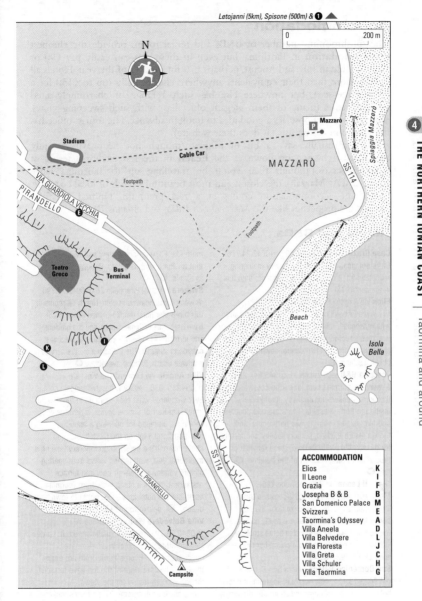

0   200 m

Stadium

Cable Car

Mazzarò

P Mazzarò

MAZZARÒ

Spiaggia Mazzarò

SS 114

VIA GUARDIOLA VECCHIA

PIRANDELLO

E

Footpath

Footpath

Teatro Greco

Bus Terminal

Beach

Isola Bella

K

I

L

VIA L. PIRANDELLO

SS 114

Campsite

ACCOMMODATION	
Elios	K
Il Leone	I
Grazia	F
Josepha B & B	B
San Domenico Palace	M
Svizzera	E
Taormina's Odyssey	A
Villa Aneela	D
Villa Belvedere	L
Villa Floresta	J
Villa Greta	C
Villa Schuler	H
Villa Taormina	G

the other main beach below town at Mazzarò, there's a **cable–car** (*funivia*) service from Taormina (daily 8am–8pm, until 1am in summer; €2, €3.50 return); the station is on Via Luigi Pirandello, between Porta Messina and the bus terminal.

Accommodation

The mushrooming number of B&Bs and rental rooms provide the cheapest **accommodation** in Taormina, but even in these you can easily pay €90 or €100 double in July and August, perhaps €70 for the rest of the year. Hotels all charge more than their equivalents anywhere else in Sicily (up to €150 for a mere three-star), but nowhere else has such a range of charmingly sited establishments (many of them elegant old villas) with such sweeping views. Wherever you choose, it's a good idea to book in advance. The tourist office has full accommodation lists (as does their website).

You can usually save a bit of money (though not necessarily in July and August) by staying down at the **beach** in the less exclusive resort of Giardini-Naxos, though then you'll be travelling up to Taormina fairly frequently. At Mazzarò, the closest and most beautiful stretch of local coastline, beachfront accommodation comes at a real premium, typified by five-star-deluxe properties like the *Mazzarò Sea Palace* and *Atlantis Bay*.

Hotels and B&Bs

Casa Grazia Via Iallia Bassia 20 ☏0942.24.776. Basic but clean rooms, and positively mothering management. It doesn't get any cheaper than this in the centre. No credit cards. ❸

Elios Via Bagnoli Croce 98 ☏0942.23.431, Ⓦwww.elioshotel.com. A smartish two-star hotel with reasonable rooms, most with a sight of the sea, plus a roof terrace with terrific views. It's a short walk from the town centre, down by the public gardens. ❻

Josepha B&B Vico Zecca 31 ☏348.844.2971, Ⓦwww.bbtaormina.com. In a little courtyard, through a hacked-out archway, immediately inside the Porta Messina. There are two doubles and two singles, sharing two bathrooms, and there's also a kitchen, laundry facility and terrace for guests. It's pretty flexible, since families or groups can rent all or part of the building. ❹, Aug ❺

Il Leone Via Bagnoli Croce 126 ☏0942.23.878. The balconies in this longstanding "rooms" place overlook the bay below. It's nothing fancy but is a pretty good deal for the price, and there are also some small, plain, kitchenless apartments and a cheap bar at street level. No credit cards. ❸

San Domenico Palace Piazza San Domenico 5 ☏0942.613.111, Ⓦwww.thi.it. Taormina's finest hotel, a five-star of immense charm, is stunningly situated in a fifteenth-century convent whose grandly proportioned cloisters, rooms and corridors have been retained. Views and facilities are unsurpassed – whether it's the bougainvillea-clad terraces leading down to the heated outdoor pool (summer only), the baronial lounge bar or stylish dining in one of four restaurants. Prices start at around €300, though more like €370 for a sea view and twice that for the luxurious suites. Parking available. ❾

Svizzera Via Luigi Pirandello 26 ☏0942.23.790, Ⓦwww.pensionesvizzera.com. Nearly all rooms in this three-star hotel (family-owned since 1925) have balconies with sea views, and the gardens and terracing are lovely – you can eat breakfast outside in summer. There's also a shuttle service to a private beach. Parking available. ❻

Villa Angela Via Leonardo da Vinci s/n ☏0942.27.038, Ⓦwww.hotelvillaangela.com. Ever wondered what rock stars do in their spare time? Jim Kerr of Simple Minds, a devotee of Taormina, plumped for opening a boutique four-star hotel, high on the Castelmola road above town. It's a swish, contemporary take on a traditional villa, with terrific views from soaring picture windows, open-air pool and terrace restaurant. You're a steep walk from Taormina itself, but the hotel lays on a shuttle to town and beach. ❽, deluxe rooms ❾

Villa Belvedere Via Bagnoli Croce 79 ☏0942.23.791, Ⓦwww.villabelvedere.it. Large cliff-side three-star hotel in an attractive building of 1902. Rooms at the front are easily the best (the ones right at the top have terraces), though you pay dearly for the views, especially in high summer when prices rocket. But there's also a great pool in a lush garden of bougainvillea and citrus trees, and rates fall considerably out of season. Parking. Closed mid-Nov to mid-Feb. ❻, Aug ❽

Villa Floresta Via Damiano Rosso 1 ☏0942.620.184, Ⓦwww.villafloresta.it. Pleasant B&B in a nineteenth-century *palazzo* tucked into a courtyard behind Piazza del Duomo. Breakfast is served at the bar in the square (not Sun or Feb), and guests can get a discount on parking at nearby Porta Catania. **④**, Aug **⑤**

🏃 **Villa Greta** Via Leonardo da Vinci 46 ☎0942.28.286, ⓦwww.villagreta.it. Long a Rough Guide favourite, the friendly, family-run Villa Greta is real value for money, with most rooms having either a terrace or balcony offering the most amazing views over town, bay and volcano. It's a relaxing base, away from the central hubbub, and there's a good restaurant (open to non-guests), with al fresco seating in summer, where fresh fish and typical Sicilian dishes are on the menu alongside speciality vegetarian dishes and couscous. The hotel is a steep 15min walk above Taormina on the Castelmola road, but the bus passes right outside. Closed Jan. **⑥**

🏃 **Villa Schuler** Piazzetta Bastione ☎0942.23.481, ⓦwww.villaschuler.com.

This fine old hotel has been in the same family for over a century, and retains something of an elegant yesteryear feel though rooms have all been updated. There are scintillating bay views from the tranquil, palm-shaded terrace, and an extensive jasmine-draped garden at the back. Borrow a mountain bike, or there's a shuttle service to the beach. Limited parking available. Closed mid-Nov to late-Feb. **⑦**

Villa Taormina Via T. Fazzello 39 ☎0942.620.072, ⓦwww.hotelvillataormina.com. A superior four-star townhouse that oozes old-fashioned charm – and with only eight antique-filled rooms the feel is more private house party than hotel. It's also blessedly quiet, off the main drag, and with a breakfast terrace that has excellent views. Parking and beach shuttle available. Closed Nov to Feb. **⑧**

Youth hostel

Taormina's Odyssey Via G. Martino 2, off Via Fontana Vecchia ☎0942.24.533, ⓦwww .taorminaodyssey.com. Taormina's only hostel is around a 10min walk (signposted) from the bus terminal, in a residential neighbourhood. It's not a huge place, but five nice dorm rooms cater to an international crowd, and you can have breakfast on the outdoor terrace. There are also laundry facilities and a tiny kitchen, and parking nearby. Dorm beds from €18.

The Town

There's no missing Taormina's Greek theatre – just follow the crowds and the signposts – but nor should you. Sited by connoisseurs, the **Teatro Greco** (summer daily 9am–7pm; winter daily 9am–4/5pm; €6) is carved out of the hillside, giving a complete panorama of southern Calabria, the Sicilian coastline and snow-capped Etna – a glorious natural backdrop for the audience. Despite its name, and though founded by Greeks in the third century BC, the existing remains are almost entirely Roman, dating from the end of the first century AD, a period when Taormina enjoyed great prosperity under Imperial Roman rule. As it happened, the reconstruction completely changed the character of the theatre. The arched apertures, niches and columns of the impressive Roman scene-building, for example, must have obscured the views of Etna that were presumably a major reason for the theatre's original siting. Likewise, Imperial Roman drama was strictly gladiatorial, so the stage and lower seats were cut back to provide more room, and a deep trench was dug in the orchestra to accommodate the animals and fighters. To give yourself a fighting chance of avoiding the high-season crowds, come in the early morning or near closing time.

Down at the bottom of Via Teatro Greco, on the main corso, the fourteenth-century **Palazzo Corvaja** – home to Taormina's tourist office – has a courtyard from which a staircase rises to the main hall, where the Sicilian "parliament" met in 1410 to choose a successor to the Aragonese line. This now houses the entertaining **Museo Siciliano d'Arte e Tradizioni Popolari** (Tues–Sun 9am–1pm & 4–8pm; €2.60), a collection of quirky folklore items – ranging

4

D.H. Lawrence in Taormina

If you've got twenty minutes to spare you can turn literary sleuth, though there's nothing to see except the back of a house. From Porta Messina, follow Via Cappuccini and then Via Fontana Vecchia, before dropping down to Piazza Franz Pagano. Follow the road around and a steep left fork – Via David Herbert Lawrence – puts you on the right track for the villa in which **D.H. Lawrence** lived for three years in the 1920s. It's up the hill and just around the corner, on the right-hand side of the road, a pink-and-cream-coloured building, now a private house, and marked by a simple plaque reading: "D.H. Lawrence, English author, lived here 1920–1923".

from painted Sicilian carts to cork-and-wax nativity scenes – that reaches sublimity in the 25 panel paintings of the 1860s showing people being saved by miraculous intervention from such terrible fates as falling onto a stove or being attacked by cats. Opposite Palazzo Corvaja, the church of **Santa Caterina** was built almost on top of a small, brick-built odeon, known as the **Teatro Romano** (originally used for musical recitations): peer down at it through the railings from outside (around the back) and then enter the church to take a closer look at bits of the theatre exposed in the floor of the nave.

Further up the corso, a side alley to the left (Via Naumachia) brings you to the 122m-long niched wall of **La Naumachia**, a Roman water cistern and gymnasium, while if you continue downhill, along Via Bagnoli Croce, you reach the shady **Giardino Púbblico** (open dawn–dusk; free), from where there are some outstanding views. The gardens were endowed by a Scot, Florence Trevelyan, who settled in Taormina in 1899 having been "invited" to leave England in the wake of a romantic liaison with the Prince of Wales, the future Edward VII. She also contributed the curious *apiari* ("beehives") – pavilions, variously resembling rustic log cabins and stone- or brick-built pagodas, and now holding caged birds, plants and a children's play area.

▲ Looking towards Etna from Taormina

Tourists and locals all collide bang in the middle of Corso Umberto I, at **Piazza IX Aprile**, Taormina's "balcony". The restored twelfth-century Torre dell'Orologio (clocktower) straddles the corso here, while sweeping views from the terrace overlook Etna and the bay. It's hard to resist the lure of a café seat here – just be warned that you'll be presented with a big bill, even for just an *espresso*. The two small churches in the square, incidentally, give an indication of how small-scale Taormina was until fairly recently. Squat fifteenth-century **Sant'Agostino** is now a library, while **San Giuseppe**'s seventeenth-century facade is adorned with plaques depicting skulls and crossbones.

Through the clocktower, the next small square – fronted by a pretty seventeenth-century fountain – contains the battlemented **Duomo**, originally built in the thirteenth century, though much restored since. Stepped alleys climb up from here towards the Via Circonvallazione, where the **Badia Vecchia** (Tues–Sun 9am–1pm & 3–7pm; free) survives as one of the old town's most graceful buildings. It's the sole remnant of a fifteenth-century abbey, with the swallow-tailed battlements and twin Gothic windows characteristic of Taormina. Inside are displayed a few relics of the Roman town, including a marvellous carved sarcophagus, with views out through the windows over the rooftops to the sea.

Eating, drinking and entertainment

As with accommodation, so with **restaurants**: Taormina is the most expensive town in Sicily in which to eat, with even moderate places charging €10 or more for a plate of pasta. And while there are lots of restaurants, menus are pretty standard across the board, although a few at the top end stand out as pretty special. On any kind of tight budget you'll probably be eating a lot of pizza – because of the demand, pizzas are widely available here at lunchtime too (unlike most other places in Sicily). **Cafés** and **bars** are similarly pricey, though at least the buzzing evening *passeggiata* along the corso is free. As it happens, despite the high-end clientele, the nightlife scene isn't particularly exclusive, with people milling around the streets all night in summer, hopping from bar to bar until the small hours. Taormina also has a fairly discreet **gay** scene, mostly centred on the style bars around Piazza Paladini. Alternatively, you could always take the bus down to the resort-strip of Giardini-Naxos for a waterfront stroll and a cheaper bite to eat – by no means the worst way to spend an evening. Festivals and parades are staged at Christmas and Carnevale, but the main cultural events are sponsored by **Taormina Arte** (June, July & Aug), featuring a varied theatrical and music programme held at the spectacular Teatro Greco and other venues around town. The **Taormina FilmFest** (Ⓦ www.taorminafilmfest.it) also runs for a week every June, previewing new movies on a big screen at the Teatro Greco.

Restaurants

Casa Grugno Via Santa Maria dei Greci Ⓣ 0942.21.208, Ⓦ www.casagrugno.it. Everyone agrees – the top place in town, if not the region. Chef Andreas Zagerl takes traditional Sicilian cuisine as his starting-point but presents a very modern Mediterranean menu that changes with the seasons – thus, a lasagne of grilled vegetables and marinated fish, or suckling pig roast with wild fennel seeds and beer. Tasting menus start from around €80, and

reservations are essential, especially for the summer courtyard dining. Dinner only; Nov to April closed Sun eve & Mon, also closed Jan & Feb. Very expensive.
La Cisterna del Moro Via Bonnifacio 1 Ⓣ 0942.23.001. This is basically a pizza joint – they are good and crisp – though with the low lights and shady bougainvillea-draped terrace it's a romantic spot for local couples on a night out. Closed Mon. Inexpensive.

Shopping in Taormina

Corso Umberto I is probably the flashiest shopping street in southern Italy, and you'll have no trouble buying a Gucci bag, a €10,000 necklace or a genuine Baroque candelabra. Of course, you can also track down a mass-produced ceramic dish, a Sicilian puppet, a model Etna or an AC Milan football shirt. The bulk of the out-and-out tourist gift shops are up Via Teatro Greco on the way to the theatre, but for quirkier boutiques and souvenirs delve into the side alleys and stepped streets off the corso.

Iosi (Via dei Fabi 6; Ⓦwww.iosi.eu) has original pieces of hand-painted **glassware**, from crystal glasses to mirrors, while at Kerameion (Salita Santippo 16, off the corso, opposite no. 72) the **ceramic workshop** turns out unique espresso cups and platters, among other things. Signor Pancrazio's grandmother first opened the Arte Antica Cacopardo **antiques** store (Corso Umberto I 27, corner Via F. Ingegnere) in 1902 (he's got postcards showing her sitting outside it), and he continues to set out the furniture, porcelain and *objets* on the pavement every day, rain or shine.

There's a daily indoor morning **market** (Mon–Sat) off Via Cappuccini, for fruit and veg, and a weekly **Wednesday market** at Parcheggio von Gloeden, below town, for household items. Meanwhile, La Botiga del Tonno Rosso (Via Bagnoli Croce 6, Ⓦwww.iltonno.com) is the shop you never knew you needed, devoted entirely to tuna fish from the Égadi Islands, including smoked slices, hideously expensive tins of *ventresca* (belly tuna) and not forgetting *lattume di tonno* ("the male seminal liquid") – no, we don't know what you do with it either.

Al Duomo Vico Ebrei 11 ℡0942.625.656, Ⓦwww .ristorantealduomo.it. Fine restaurant with a serious commitment to local ingredients and local dishes such as *maccu* (broad bean soup), pasta with sardines and wild fennel, and lamb stew. Mains cost €18–22. There's a lovely terrace above the Duomo square and a simple, pretty interior. Nov to March closed Wed. Expensive.

Al Giardino Via Bagnoli Croce 84 ℡0942.23.453, Ⓦwww.algiardino.net. With pasta at around €7 and standard meat and fish dishes from €9 (ie normal prices elsewhere in Sicily), this is what passes for inexpensive in Taormina. It's usually busy, and service is amiable and enthusiastic. Closed Tues. Moderate.

Maffei's Via San Domenico de Guzman 1 ℡0942.24.055. If you want one really good fish meal, this formal but not overpowering restaurant is the place. The day's specials (around €20) are written on the board – seabass to lobsters – while oysters, sea urchins, pastas and carpaccios are offered as appetizers. English-speaking staff guide you through the menu, and all you can hear is the gentle clatter of cutlery and contented murmurs. It's only small, so it's an idea to book ahead if you don't want to miss out. Very expensive.

Mamma Rosa Via Naumachia 10 ℡0942.24.361. This does a roaring trade in *forno a legna* pizzas, served at tables spilling down the stepped alley. There's also a full menu, though you'll easily pay €30 a head for a couple of courses and wine. Closed Tues in winter. Moderate.

Siciliana Salita Ospedale 9 ℡0942.24.780. Just outside the Porta Catania, and raised above the square on a cheery terrace, this trattoria is pretty good value (pasta from €8, mains around €13), especially as the menu rings the changes a bit. There's smoked swordfish as an appetizer, lamb as well as fish, and crispy roast potatoes with parsley instead of chips. Closed Wed. Moderate.

Vecchia Taormina Vico Ebrei 3 ℡0942.625.589, Ⓦwww.vecchiataormina .com. Taormina's best pizzeria has a stack of olive wood outside the door for the fire, and tables outside in a sheltered courtyard. Pizzas are light, crispy and blisteringly hot. Closed Wed, also lunchtime July–Aug. Inexpensive.

Vicolo Stretto Vicolo Stretto 6 ℡0942.24.995. Reached up the slimmest of alleys off the corso, by Piazza IX Aprile, this is a wonderfully chic place to try "real Sicilian cuisine" – from pasta made with shrimps and Pachino cherry tomatoes to beef in a Nero d'Avola wine sauce (dishes range €12–21, though fresh fish is sold by weight). Closed Sun in winter. Expensive.

A' Zammara Via Fratelli Bandiera 15 ℡0942.24.408, Ⓦwww.zammara.it. A lovely secluded garden of orange trees entices you in, but this is also one of the best places in town to try authentic Sicilian dishes, such as *tagliolini* with shrimps and Bronte pistachios or spaghetti with anchovies and breadcrumbs. Most dishes are €12–18. Expensive.

Cafés, bars and clubs

Arco Rosso Via Naumachia 7. Quite a rarity is this proper little old-fashioned bar, tucked down steps just off the corso, which sells wine by the glass or bottle and doesn't charge the earth for it. Closed Wed.

Al Grappolo d'Uva Via Bagnoli Croce 6–8. A tourist-friendly *osteria* (wine bar) with a dozen Sicilian wines available by the glass (try before you buy) and antipasti-type snacks. You get a decent-sized glass and it's not too expensive.

O'Seven Largo La Farina 6, off the corso behind the clocktower. An Irish pub in genteel Taormina? Don't worry, there are pretty candles on the tables and they don't usually show the football.

Panasia Beach Via Nazionale, Contrada Spisone ⓦwww.panasiabeach.it. The summer's most happening club – lido by day and a cool club at night – where you can dance the dawn in on the sand.

Re di Bastoni Corso Umberto I 120. The corso's most popular "pub" has a bohemian, folksy feel, and there's regular live music. The house special is a strawberry caipirinha. Closed Mon in winter.

Shatulle Piazza Paladini 4. Currently the main focus of Taormina's gay and lesbian scene, with a chill-out feel, cosy seats and soft lights in the pretty piazza. There are several other cool bars around here too.

Wunderbar Caffé Piazza IX Aprile. Once the haunt of Garbo and Fassbinder, this remains the most favoured spot in town for the see-and-be-seen brigade, with outdoor seats beneath the clocktower and a determinedly elitest pricing policy. The piano is wheeled out every night for ivory-tinkling beneath the stars.

Concerts and events

Taormina Arte Palazzo dei Congressi, Piazza V. Emanuele ☎0924.628.730, ⓦwww .taormina-arte.com. The website has the most up-to-date details of the summer's events at the Teatro Greco and elsewhere, but you can expect music from marching bands to WOMAD world music gigs, symphony orchestras and divas, classical dramas and film premieres. Buy tickets at the Palazzo dei Congressi box office, or buy online via the website.

Listings

Bus information Interbus ☎0942.625.301, ⓦwww.interbus.it, runs regular services to Messina and Catania, and points in between, from the bus terminal. There's a full timetable posted there, plus one outside the train station and more inside the tourist office

Car and scooter rental Avis, Via S. Pancrazio 7 ☎0942.625.549; California, Via Bagnoli Croce 86 ☎0942.23.769; City, Piazza Sant'Antonio 5 ☎0942.23.161; Italia, Via Luigi Pirandello 29 ☎0942.23.973; Sicily By Car, Via Apollo Arcageta 4 ☎0942.21.252.

Emergencies There's first aid at Piazza San Francesco di Paola, outside Porta Catania (☎0942.625.419; summer only); otherwise Ospedale San Vincenzo°, in nearby Piazza San Vincenzo (☎0942.53.745).

Internet Las Vegas, Salita Alexander Humbolt, opposite Corso Umberto I 186 (daily 10am–1pm & 2.30pm–midnight); Internet Point, Via Iallia Bassia (daily 9am–10pm).

Pharmacy British Pharmacy, Corso Umberto I 152 ☎0942.620.101. Late-night openings operate according to a rota system, indicated on pharmacy doors.

Police Carabinieri, Piazza Badia 4 ☎0942.611.111 or 113.

Post office Piazza Medaglia d'Oro, outside Porta Catania (Mon–Sat 8.30am–6.30pm).

Supermarket Upim/Punto SMA supermarket outside Porta Catania (and to the right) on Via Apollo Arcageta.

Taxis There are ranks in Piazza San Pancrazio and Piazza Vittorio Emanuele, or call ☎0942.23.000.

Tours Lots of tours are offered to Etna, the Alcántara gorge and Siracusa, or further afield to places like Palermo and Piazza Armerina, from around €40 for a day in Siracusa or the Etna foothills to €70 for an Etna summit jeep tour. The tourist office has fliers and brochures, or contact an agency directly, like SAT, Corso Umberto I 73 ☎0942.24.653, ⓦwww.sat-group.it.

The castello, Madonna della Rocca and Castelmola

Buses run every hour from town the few minutes' up the winding road to the cliff-top cross and chapel of **Madonna della Rocca**, just above which stand the remains of Taormina's tumbledown medieval **castello**. It's well worth coming up for the glorious views, down to theatre, town and coastline, and there's a couple of restaurants and cafés here too. You can also **walk up** – there's a steep processional path to the chapel (signposted "Castel Taormina/Via Crucis") from Via Circonvallazione, starting just past the Q8 petrol station. It takes around twenty minutes, and an obvious signposted concrete path then continues all the way up the mountain to Castelmola, around an hour in total from town. It's *much* easier of course, and the views are better, to **walk down** from Castelmola – an easy fifteen minutes to Madonna della Rocca, thirty minutes to town.

CASTELMOLA itself is 5km by road above Taormina; the hourly buses from town take about fifteen minutes. The tiny hill-village seems to sprout out of the severe crag beneath it, with just a jumble of precipitous alleys to explore and the remnants of a long-demolished castle. Buses stop 200m below the main square, disgorging visitors for a quick potter around and a gawp at the stupendous views. Hardly surprisingly, Castelmola is entirely given over to tourism, with souvenir shops and up to a dozen bars and restaurants flanking the cobbles. *Bar San Giorgio* in the square is the doyen, smartened up over the years, but purveying drinks and views for decades, as the old newspaper cuttings in the corner attest. Try a glass of *vino alla mándorla* (almond wine), the sweet local brew.

Billboards around Castelmola usually advertise **falconry displays** (April–Oct, 2–3 performances a day, always at noon; €6.50) up at the castle, where an hour's show includes close-up fly-bys of falcons, hawks and owls, set against the backdrop of Monte Vénere (885m).

Local beaches

The **coastline below Taormina**, north and south, is immensely appealing – a mixture of grottoes, rocky coves and good sand beaches – although much of it is either sectioned off as private lidos (which you have to pay to use; prices vary from around €6 to €15 a day) or simply gets very packed in summer. Easiest to reach, by bus or cable car, are the small, stony stretches around Mazzarò. For decent expanses of sand you'll have to travel to Giardini-Naxos, around a five-kilometer, fifteen-minute, bus ride south of Taormina, and very much a separate town, with its own holiday trade and nightlife.

Mazzarò, Spisone and Letojanni

The closest beaches to town are the scintillating pebbled coves at **MAZZARÒ**, protected as a marine-life sanctuary, which you can reach by cable car (*funivia*) from Via Luigi Pirandello in Taormina. There's also a steep path, which starts just below the cable-car station. Of the two beaches, the southernmost is usually the most packed, fronting its much-photographed islet, the **Isola Bella**. The waters are remarkably clear, and you can rent boats, snorkelling and scuba gear down here.

A little further north are the beach bars and restaurants at **SPISONE**, which you can either walk to from Mazzarò (10min) or directly down from Taormina (path from below the cemetery, off Via Guardiola Vecchia, around 30min), though hourly buses from Taormina's Piazza San Pancrazio also run here, passing Isola Bella and Mazzarò on the way. **Letojanni**, 5km north of Taormina, is a little resort in its own right, with a few fishing-boats on a sandy beach and several modest seafront hotels and restaurants. Regular buses head back to Taormina, passing Spisone and the Isola Bella, while local trains link the village with Taormina-Giardini station.

Giardini-Naxos

The best sand beaches close to Taormina are those at **GIARDINI-NAXOS**, south of town, where a long strip of sand curves around the wide bay, backed by a busy promenade of bars, cafés, restaurants and hotels. It's much more of a resort in the Italian style than Taormina – packed and noisy until late September each year, and then largely drawing up the shutters until the following spring. But it's a nice place for a stroll by the sea at any time of year. Half of the beach is free ("*spiaggia libera*"), although the better sands further around the bay towards the cape are partitioned off as private lidos, complete with sun-loungers, shades, watersports gear, bars and restaurants.

Significantly, the bay was the site of the first Greek colony in Sicily. As an obvious stop for ships sailing between Greece and southern Italy, there was a settlement here by 734 BC, named **Naxos** after the Greek island from which the colonists came, though it was never very important. The **excavations** on the site of the ancient settlement (daily 9am–1hr before sunset; €2) lie right on the cape, Capo Schisò, with the entrance right by *La Sirena* restaurant, overlooking the harbour. The remains are disappointingly sketchy, though they stretch across a large area of the cape and it's pleasant to stroll through the olive and lemon groves. There's scarcely any interpretation of what you're seeing – scant foundations of a large, gridded town and a long stretch of ancient, lava-built city wall – and the small museum on site that houses some of the finds doesn't really help either.

Buses run every thirty minutes to Giardini from Taormina's bus terminal (until midnight in summer), passing the train station en route. Or you can walk from the train station itself (turn left) in about fifteen minutes. The seafront promenade road is Via Tysandros, with the **tourist office** at no. 54 (Mon–Fri 9am–1pm & 4–7pm, Sat 9am–1pm, closed Sat in winter; ℡0942.51.010, ⓦwww.aastgiardininaxos.it), next to *La Riva* hotel. The road curves round as far as the fishing harbour and excavations (changing its name from Via Tysandros to Via Schisò), while Via Naxos runs parallel inland. The tourist office is the best first stop for accommodation in summer (it posts a list outside), or just take a walk along the seafront and look for vacancies.

Giardini's **restaurants** are consistently better value than those in Taormina, and a longstanding Rough Guide favourite down here is the moderately priced ✻ *Fratelli Marano*, Via Naxos 181 (closed Tues), with fresh pasta and fish and fine pizzas. Or, at the end of Via Schisò, by the harbour and excavations, you can eat *forno a legna* pizzas, pasta and seafood on the terrace at *La Sirena* (℡0942.51.853, ⓦwww.lasirena-giardininaxos.com; there are rooms here too), where the views stretch right across the bay to Taormina.

The Gola di Alcántara

Etna aside, the main local tour touted in Taormina is to the gorge of the **Alcántara River**, located around 20km west of town. You can also do the trip yourself easily enough, as five buses a day (not Sunday) run out this way from Taormina's bus terminal, through gentle hills covered with citrus groves, olive

▲ The Gola di Alcántara

trees and wild flowers. The road runs over and alongside the river, and the various bridges are a reminder that the name, Alcántara, is a corruption of the Arabic word for bridge.

The river itself has its source up in the Monte Nébrodi and flows for 50km towards the Ionian sea. Interrupted thousands of years ago by a flow of lava from Etna, the Alcántara eventually wore its way through the rock, forming a spectacular gorge. It's an hour's ride all told to the entrance to the **Gola di Alcántara** (open daily; Ⓦ www.parcoalcantara.it), where there's a car park, bar and restaurant. Since the gorge has been protected as the Parco Fluviale dell'Alcántara, access is controlled by the park office, where you pay €5 to descend in a lift to the bottom. There is also a free public entrance, 200m beyond the main entrance (Francavilla direction), though it's two hundred steps down and back. Down at the bottom, in summer you can hire salopettes and wetsuits in order to slosh along the river (it's very cold) through pools and into the main gorge. Note that the last bus back to Taormina currently leaves at 2.35pm.

Francavilla di Sicilia

Walk 4km further from the Alcántara gorge, or pick up the next bus onwards, to reach **FRANCAVILLA DI SICILIA**, alongside the river and overlooked by the few surviving walls of its hillside castle. This was the site of one of the bloodiest battles fought in Sicily, when the Austrian army (given logistical support by the British) engaged with the Spanish in 1719, to no obvious result apart from the loss of some 8000 lives. There's a path up to the ruins, and although much of the town is newly built there's a fair amount of interest in the couple of old central streets, and in walking up to the **Convento dei Cappuccini** that peers over town and river (take the signposted right turn as you approach the village). A modest little museum here shows how the monks – now reduced to fewer than five – passed their time in baking, brewing and crafting. You can also buy some of their honey or grappa-like concoctions to take away. A good **hotel** in Francavilla offers a quiet alternative to staying in Taormina; in fact, in high summer, it's often easier to get a room here than at the beach. ♣ *Hotel d'Orange d'Alcántara* (℡0942.981.374, ⊛www.hoteldorange.it; ❹) is on Via dei Mulini, on the way in from the Gola di Alcántara, and is a friendly, family-run three-star place that serves as a useful base. Walkers can ask about local hikes here, while the hotel can also rent you a car, or book you onto the same local tours available in Taormina; there's also a small pool and restaurant-pizzeria.

Castiglione di Sicilia

Five kilometres above Francavilla, and across the border in Catania province, the numerous church spires and the lofty, ruined rock-built castle of **CASTIGLIONE DI SICILIA** make an inviting target as you approach up the switchback road. It's easy to spend a couple of hours just wandering the quiet streets of this old mountain settlement, which meander up as far as a small piazza at the top of town, where there's little more than a barber with a sign in English offering "individual hair styling", and a flight of steps leading up to the shattered castle, or **Fortezza Greca** (always open), which offers grand panoramic views.

A short walk beyond the piazza, and well signposted all over town, you'll find an excellent pizzeria and restaurant, the *Belvedere d'Alcántara*, whose rooftop terrace takes full advantage of the soaring views. If you're heading back to Taormina, you can either hang around for the return bus to Giardini (it leaves from outside the bar at Via Regina Margherita 174, back down the hill from the piazza), or walk down the hill to Francavilla, an easy hike, and pick up a bus from there. The walk takes around an hour, and at the bottom of the crag, on the way into Francavilla, you cross a sturdy medieval bridge. Just beyond here, at the back of the factory at the side of the road, is the sad ruin of a **Byzantine church**, one of several in the area left to rot.

Festivals

January
1–6 New Year celebrations in **Taormina**. Puppet shows, folk-singing and concerts, ending on Twelfth Night.

February/March
Carnevale Carnival celebrations in **Taormina** and **Giardini-Naxos**: processional floats, fireworks and music for three days.

June
1st week onwards, until August Dance, drama, film and music; all performances held in the Teatro Greco in **Taormina**; runs until early August.
2nd/3rd week International Film Festival in **Taormina**, with screenings in the Teatro Greco.

August
12–14 Procession of the *giganti* in **Messina**.
15 Ferragosto procession and fireworks in **Messina**.

December
20 onwards Christmas and New Year celebrations in **Taormina**. Puppet shows, folk-singing, parades and concerts.

Travel details

Trains

Messina to: Catania (1–2 hourly; 1hr 30min–2hr); Cefalù (12 daily; 2–3hr); Milan (10 daily, most with change at Villa S. Giovanni and Rome; 13hr 30min–17hr 45min); Milazzo (1–2 hourly; 25–45min); Naples (10 daily, most with change at Villa S. Giovanni; 5hr–6hr 30min); Rome (12 daily, most with change at Villa S. Giovanni; 7–10hr); Palermo (12 daily; 3hr 15min–4hr 30min); Taormina (1–2 hourly; 40min–1hr 10min).
Taormina to: Catania (1–2 hourly; 45min–1hr); Messina (1–2 hourly; 40min–1hr); Siracusa (up to 10 daily; 2hr).

Buses

Messina to: Barcelona (hourly Mon–Sat; 1hr); Capo d'Orlando (9 daily Mon–Sat; 1hr 15min–1hr 50min); Catania (1–2 hourly Mon–Sat, 10 daily Sun; 1hr 35min); Catania airport (16 daily Mon–Sat, 7 daily Sun; 1hr 45min); Forza d'Agrò (1 daily Mon–Sat; 1hr 35min); Giardini-Naxos (7 daily Mon–Sat; 1–2hr); Itala (8 daily Mon–Sat; 50min); Letojanni (9 daily Mon–Sat, 3 daily Sun; 1hr 30min); Milazzo (fast service 1–2 hourly Mon–Sat, 4 daily Sun; 55min); Palermo (4–6 daily Mon–Sat, 4 daily Sun; 2hr 40min); Patti (8 daily Mon–Sat; 1hr 20min); Rome (2 daily; 9hr–12hr 30min); Sant'Aléssio (11 daily Mon–Sat, 3 daily Sun; 1hr 20min); Santa Teresa di Riva (1–2 hourly Mon–Sat, 3 daily Sun; 45min–1hr 10min); Scaletta (1–2 hourly Mon–Sat, 3 daily Sun; 30min–1hr); Taormina (9 daily Mon–Sat, 3 daily Sun; 1hr–1hr 50min); Tíndari (3 daily Mon–Sat; 1–2hr).
Taormina to: Castiglione di Sicilia (2 daily Mon–Sat; 1hr 15min); Catania (7 daily Mon–Sat, 5 daily Sun; 1hr 5min); Catania airport (7 daily Mon–Sat, 5 daily Sun; 1hr 25min); Forza d'Agrò (2–3 daily Mon–Sat; 30min); Francavilla di Sicilia (5 daily Mon–Sat; 1hr); Gola di Alcántara (5 daily Mon–Sat; 55min); Messina (14 daily Mon–Sat, 3 Sun; 55min–1hr 40min).
Taormina–Giardini train station to: Castiglione di Sicilia (3 daily Mon–Sat; 1hr 5min); Francavilla di Sicilia (6 daily Mon–Sat; 50min); Gola di Alcántara (6 daily Mon–Sat; 40min); Randazzo (2 daily Mon–Sat; 1hr 10min).

Ferries

Messina to: Villa San Giovanni (FS 1–2 hourly, Caronte every 20min, every 40–60min at night; 20–30min).

Hydrofoils and fast ferries

Messina to: Lípari (5 daily June to mid-Sept, 1 daily mid-Sept to May; 1hr 20min–3hr 25min); Panarea (2 daily June to mid-Sept; 2hr 5min–3hr 20min); Réggio di Calabria (approx hourly Mon–Sat, 9 daily Sun; 15–25min); Santa Marina di Salina (3 daily June to mid-Sept, 1 daily mid-Sept to May; 2hr 10min–3hr 30min); Strómboli (2 daily June to mid-Sept; 1hr 25min); Vulcano (4 daily June to mid-Sept, 1 daily mid-Sept to May; 1hr 40min–3hr).

Catania, Etna and around

CHAPTER 5 # Highlights

* **Pescheria, Catania** Eat a sea urchin, buy some swordfish, have spaghetti and clams for lunch – Catania's raucous fish market is the best of its kind on the island. See p.224

* **Teatro Mássimo Bellini, Catania** Enjoy a night at the opera with the music of Catania's most famous native son. See p.229

* **The ascent of Etna** The smoking cone of Etna dominates much of eastern Sicily, and invites an ascent of its blackened upper slopes, not least for the awesome views. See p.235

* **Nicolosi** The best base on Etna's south side, ideal for winter skiing or summer walking. See p.235

* **Ferrovia Circumetnea** A day-trip by public transport that takes some beating – riding the volcano-train for over 100km around the base of Mount Etna. See p.237

* **Castello Maniace, Bronte** An English country house with a fascinating history, deep in the Sicilian countryside. See p.239

▲ The Pescheria (fish market) at Catania

Catania, Etna and around

C atania is Sicily's second largest city, sited on the eastern (Ionian) coast, its airport the point of arrival for many of the island's foreign visitors. Few stay long – it's by no means a prime tourist destination – yet Catania is actually an intensely vibrant city with a uniformly grand appearance bestowed upon it after the 1693 earthquake that wrecked the whole region. The jagged volcanic coast to the north sustains a series of small resort-villages around the Baroque town of **Acireale**, while to the south the main driving routes to Siracusa, Ragusa and Enna cross the fertile plain of the **Piana di Catania**. This rich agricultural region was known to the Greeks as the Laestrygonian Fields after the Laestrygonians, a race of cannibals who devoured several of Odysseus's crew. It's a pretty enough ride through the windmill-dotted flat fields, but the only detour of interest is to the archeological site of **Lentini**, one of the earliest Greek colonies to be founded in Sicily.

There's absolutely no mistaking the single biggest draw in the province, namely **Mount Etna**, Europe's highest volcano, whose foothills start a few kilometres north of Catania. It's still highly active and its massive presence dominates the whole of this part of the coast, with every town and village in the neighbourhood built at least partly from the lava that it periodically ejects. A road and a small single-track railway, the **Circumetnea**, circumnavigate the lower slopes, passing through a series of hardy towns, such as **Randazzo**, almost foolishly situated in the shadow of the volcano and surrounded by swirls of black volcanic rock. Meanwhile, higher villages and ski stations like **Nicolosi** and the **Rifugio Sapienza** are the base for escorted tours and ascents to the **summit craters**. Depending on the weather and volcanic conditions, you should be able to experience the heights of Etna at first hand between April or May and September or October.

Catania

First impressions don't say much at all for **CATANIA** – there's heavy industry here, a large port and some depressing suburbs, while the traffic-choked city centre is largely constructed from suffocating, black-grey volcanic stone. Indeed,

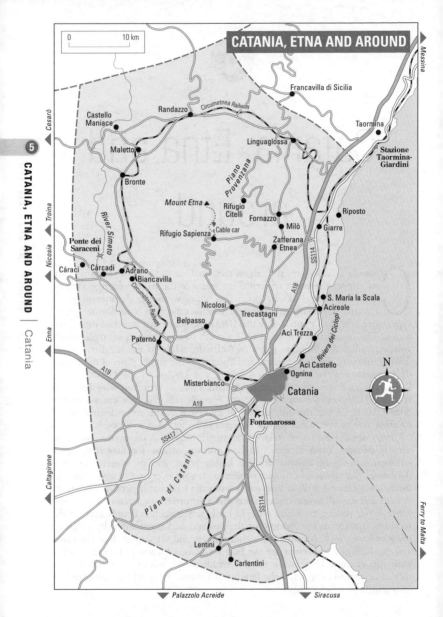

the influence of Etna is pervasive, with the city's main thoroughfare named after the volcano, which looms threateningly just to the north. Still, Catania is Sicily's only large urban centre outside the capital, and while overshadowed in terms of historical monuments by Palermo, it has a more lively, international, radical outlook, and is well worth a day or two's visit. It is first and foremost a commercial place, boasting arguably the island's best two markets, while if you look beyond the darkened shadows of the buildings you'll detect some of the finest Baroque architecture in Sicily, dating from the eighteenth-century rebuilding. A large student population enlivens the city centre – this is another area where Catania outdoes Palermo, and the thronged piazzas and bars make for one of the island's most exuberant evening promenades. The city is also a major transport terminus, for buses and trains south to Siracusa and west to Enna, Agrigento and Palermo, and if you're Etna-bound by public transport you'll have to leave from Catania itself – drivers usually choose to see the volcano from the prettier towns and villages to the north.

Some of the island's first **Greek colonists**, probably Chalcidinians from Naxos, settled the site as early as 729 BC, becoming so influential that their laws were eventually adopted by all the Ionian colonies of Magna Graecia. Later, the city was among the first to fall to the **Romans**, under whom it prospered greatly. Unusually for Sicily, Catania's surviving ancient relics are all Roman (albeit lava-encrusted, after successive historic eruptions). In the early Christian period Catania witnessed the martyrdom of **Agatha**, who, having rejected the improper advances of the praetor, Quintianus, was put to death in 252. She was later canonized (becoming the patron saint of Catania), and it was her miraculous intervention that reputedly saved the city from complete volcanic destruction in the seventeenth century. Even with the saint's protection, Catania has had its fair share of disasters: Etna erupted in 1669, engulfing the city in lava, while the **great earthquake** of 1693 devastated the whole of southeastern Sicily. But making full use of the lava as building material, the eighteenth-century architect **Giovanni Battista Vaccarini** gave central Catania a lofty, noble air that endures today.

Arrival, information and city transport

From Fontanarossa **airport**, 5km south of the city, the cheapest way into the centre is to take the Alibus #457 (every 20min, daily 5am–midnight) from right outside, which runs to the central Piazza Stesícoro (on Via Etnea) and to Stazione Centrale in around twenty minutes; buy tickets from the AST booth as you leave the Arrivals hall. Most regional express buses (to Siracusa, Taormina, Ragusa, Agrigento, Enna and Palermo) also stop at the airport, and you can get a direct bus from the airport to Messina or Milazzo (for the Aeolian Islands). The **taxi** ride from the airport to the centre is among the most outrageously priced on the island, at around €25 (ie around thirty times the bus ticket price).

Trains pull in at **Stazione Centrale** in Piazza Giovanni XXIII, just east of the centre. It's easy to jump on a city bus outside to reach Piazza del Duomo or Via Etnea (see "City transport"), or to take a taxi (around €6–8). Otherwise, the walk to the Duomo takes twenty minutes. **Regional buses** stop in the swirling piazza across from Stazione Centrale. This whole area isn't fantastically salubrious, and at night it's a bit off-putting – if you're going to take a taxi, ignore the touts and use the official rank by the train station. The other city station, the **Stazione Catania Borgo** (Via Caronda, right at the northern end of Via Etnea) is for trains on the Ferrovia Circumetnea (the round-Etna line) – a metro connection from here (see below) delivers you to Stazione Centrale.

Driving into Catania isn't too difficult (just follow signs for "centro" for Via Etnea), but driving around the city once there is a different matter, because of the chaotic traffic, the fiendish one-way system and the utter impossibility of **parking**. Some hotels have their own parking or arrangements with nearby garages, but as you really don't need a car in Catania, the best advice if you're picking up a rental car is to do so on the day you leave the city.

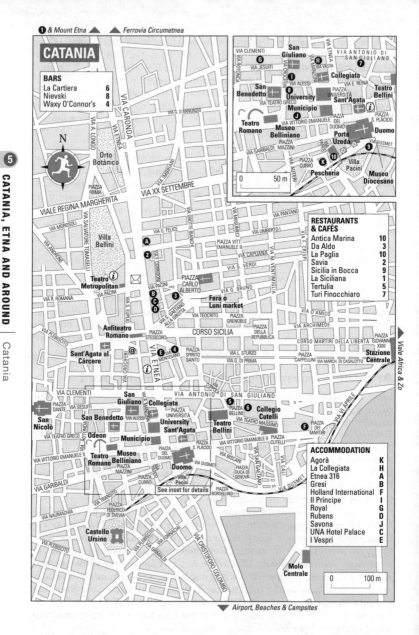

CATANIA

BARS
La Cartiera	6
Nievski	8
Waxy O'Connor's	4

N

RESTAURANTS & CAFÉS
Antica Marina	10
Da Aldo	3
La Paglia	10
Savia	2
Sicilia in Bocca	9
La Siciliana	1
Tertulia	5
Turi Finocchiaro	7

ACCOMMODATION
Agorà	K
La Collegiata	H
Etnea 316	A
Gresi	B
Holland International	F
Il Principe	I
Royal	G
Rubens	D
Savona	J
UNA Hotel Palace	C
I Vespri	E

Information

There are small tourist offices at the airport, Stazione Centrale, the port and at Via Etnea 63 (all varied hours), but the **main office** is at Via Domenico Cimarosa 10 (Mon–Sat 8am–8pm; ☎095.730.621, ⓦwww.apt.catania.it), signposted off Via Etnea, up Via Pacini and on the right. You should find someone who speaks English here, and you'll be able to pick up a B&B booklet, a good city map and information about the province. There's also a useful central **Bureau Turismo** run by the *Comune*, just up from the Duomo at Via Vittorio Emanuele 172 (Mon–Sat 8.15am–1.15pm, plus Tues, Thurs & Fri 1.45–7.15pm; ☎800.841.242, ⊛www.comune.catania.it), which is specifically for city information. Neither website is particularly useful for foreign visitors, but ⊛www.cataniacittametropolitana.it has a good English-language version with plenty of information about the city and its services.

The main tourist office can advise about **tours and transport to Etna**, or contact Geo Etna Explorer (☎349.610.9957, ⊛www.geoetnaexplorer.it), based in Catania, which offers daily tours from the city.

City transport

AMT city buses have a terminal immediately **outside Stazione Centrale**, where a staffed booth sells tickets (valid for 90min, or all-day ticket for €2; punch it inside the bus on the first ride). You can also buy bus tickets at any *tabacchi*. Information boards at the bus ranks detail the routes but, among others, circular bus #1–4 runs along Via VI Aprile and Via Vittorio Emanuele to Piazza del Duomo, while #448 runs along Corso Sicilia to Piazza Stesícoro. The other central bus terminal is **Piazza Borsellino** (below Piazza del Duomo by the Villa Pacini gardens), where there's a stop for the airport bus and for buses out to the local beaches and coast.

The city's **Metropolitana** underground system runs on a limited route from Stazione Centrale, south to Catania Porto and north to Catania Borgo (the terminal for the Ferrovia Circumetnea). There are future plans to run the metro out to the airport and to provide new city-centre stations, but for now it's an under-used facility. Services operate Monday to Saturday every fifteen minutes between 7am and 8.45pm, and tickets are valid for ninety minutes.

Accommodation

Catania's **hotels** have raised their game over recent years, and many of the grubby old pensions have disappeared, replaced by renovated three- and four-star hotels and a few stylish boutique places. Consequently, hotel rooms aren't particularly cheap, and it's always as well to reserve in advance, especially in July and August. There's also a burgeoning number of city-centre **B&Bs** – you'll see several signposted just by walking up Via Etnea – and an excellent central **youth hostel**, but local coastal **campsites** are all a bus ride out of the city and not very convenient for sightseeing.

Hotels and B&Bs

La Collegiata Via Vasta 10 ☎095.315.256, ⊛www.lacollegiata.com. A rather elegant choice in a restored building, just off the main street, with a dozen rooms (most with street views) reflecting its nineteenth-century style. **⑤**

Etnea 316 Via Etnea 316 ☎095.250.3076, ⓦwww.hoteletnea316.it. Real care has gone into the maintenance of this charming old B&B, where ten spruced-up rooms retain their original tile floors and lofty proportions. There's a pretty lounge and breakfast room, and a calm air envelopes all. ❹, Aug ❺

Gresi 3rd floor, Via Pacini 28 ☎095.322.709, ⓦwww.gresihotel.com. A bit of an old-fashioned three-star, this big old building is redeemed by its rather splendid frescoed ceilings and original proportions. The location is good, and some rooms overlook the main street. Breakfast is available but not included in the price. No credit cards. ❺

Holland International Via Vittorio Emanuele 8 ☎095.533.605, ⓦwww.hollandintrooms.it. On the first floor of an ageing *palazzo*, on the edge of the centre, near the station. It's a budget place with few frills, other than retaining some of the old frescoed ceilings, but it's run by a Dutchman who speaks good English and the rooms have tea- and coffee-making facilities (no breakfast served). There are four en-suite doubles, while one cheaper double and a single share a bathroom. There's also parking in the courtyard. ❸

Il Principe Via Alessi 24 ☎095.250.0345, ⓦwww.ilprincipehotel.com. This boutique designer four-star, in an old palace at the foot of the Alessi steps, holds up-to-the-minute rooms with woodblock floors and handsome beds. Bathrooms can be a bit of a squeeze, though deluxe rooms (ie suites) have jacuzzi tubs, and everything throughout is sleek and smart. Book online for the best deals. ❼, deluxe ❽

Royal Via Antonio di San Giuliano 337 ☎095.250.3347, ⓦwww.hotelroyalcatania .it. Four-star hotel occupying a Baroque *palazzo*. Although refurbished in 2004, they resisted the urge to go contemporary and it's all the better for it, presenting twenty rooms in rich colours with traditional period furniture but all mod cons. It has a comfortable, hideaway feel, despite the central location, and a big outdoor terrace lets you breakfast above the Catania rooftops. Also a restaurant, sauna and Turkish bath, and parking. ❻

Rubens Via Etnea 196 ☎095.317.073, ⓦwww.rubenshotel.it. A good-value choice if you want to stay on the main Via Etnea, with seven spacious rooms mostly facing the side and back, double-glazed against the noise. The friendly owners speak English and make more of an effort than most with breakfast (ham, cheese, boiled eggs, croissants), served in a dining room overlooking Via Etnea. ❹

Savona Via Vittorio Emanuele 210 ☎095.326.982, ⓦwww.hotelsavona.it. The location is excellent, close to Duomo and market, and amazingly the noise melts away inside – even more so if you ask for a room at the back overlooking the inner courtyard. It's a family-owned three-star with thirty cool, calm rooms with tile floors and sober furniture – hardly cutting-edge style, but fine for the price. ❺

UNA Hotel Palace Via Etnea 218 ☎095.250.5111, ⓦwww.unahotels.it This contemporary four-star applies Catania's dominant colours – lava-black and Etna snow-white – to its designer rooms, from the marble floors and crisp linen to the signature beds with black headboards and inset medallions. There's plenty of space, a very good buffet breakfast, Turkish bath and fitness centre, but above all there's a fantastic roof-terrace bar and fine-dining restaurant with the best views in town – reserve for dinner (most dishes €10–20). ❼

I Vespri Via Montesano 5 ☎095.310.036, ⓦwww.ivesprihotel.it. A budget "rooms" place, right in the centre, with helpful owners. Not all rooms are en suite but shared facilities are well-kept, and breakfast is available (not included), served in your room. There's a laundry service too. ❷, en suite ❸, Aug ❹

Hostel

Agorà Piazza Currò 6 ☎095.723.3010, ⓦwww.agorahostel.com. The location is fantastic, very near the Pescheria fish market (follow the signs), and lots of people come here to eat in the excellent bistro-style restaurant, catch a DJ or gig, sit out at the funky outdoor terrace or drink in the unique cellar wine bar (housed in a natural lava-cave with one of Catania's underground streams running through it). Hostel rooms (six to ten beds) have bunks and lockers, with separate bathrooms for men and women, and there are some simple private double rooms too. Internet access and washing facilities are also available, and there's 24hr access to the hostel. Dorms from €18, Aug €21, rooms ❷

The City

You could see the whole of central Catania in a busy day's strolling, but the city really deserves more time if you can spare it. Most of the sights are confined within a small area, centred on Piazza del Duomo and the cathedral, from where the wide main avenue, Via Etnea, steams off to the north up to the city's Bellini gardens. Fish market and castle lie to the south, and the landmark Teatro Bellini to the east. Much of this entire area, sections of Via Etnea included, is closed to traffic, so walking around is quite enjoyable, especially at night when certain areas become bar and café zones.

Piazza del Duomo and around

Piazza del Duomo is one of Sicily's most elegant Baroque piazzas, rebuilt completely in the first half of the eighteenth century by the Palermitan, Giovanni Battista Vaccarini, who was made Catania's municipal architect in 1730. With the majestic cathedral as his starting-point, he produced a dramatic open space – kept traffic-free today – softened by the addition of a central fountain, no less than a **lava elephant** supporting an Egyptian obelisk on its back. The elephant has been the city's symbol since at least the thirteenth century, a talismanic protection against Etna eruptions, and this one also features an inscription, *Agatina MSSHDEPL* – an acronym for "The mind of St Agatha is sane and spontaneous, honouring God and liberating the city".

Agatha herself is both Catania's patron saint and the dedicatee of Vaccarini's grandest project, the **Duomo** (daily 7.30am–noon & 4–7pm), which flanks the eastern side of the piazza. The original cathedral here was founded in the eleventh century, and built on the site of earlier Roman baths, but of this medieval church only the beautifully crafted apses survived the 1693 earthquake; you can see them through the gate at Via Vittorio Emanuele 159. Vaccarini added an imposing Baroque facade, on which he tagged granite columns filched from Catania's Roman amphitheatre, while the interior is adorned by a rich series of chapels. The Cappella di Sant'Agata is to the right of the choir, and houses the relics that are paraded through the city on the saint's festival days. Next to it, entered through a fine sixteenth-century doorway,

▲ The Duomo in Catania

The Festa di Sant'Agata

Catania's biggest annual festival, the **Festa di Sant'Agata**, takes place each year between February 3 and 5. It's a 500-year-old celebration of the life and death of the virtuous Agatha, born in the city around 230 AD and destined for dreadful tortures once she had spurned the unwelcome advances of the Roman praetor, Quintianus, in 252 AD; prison, whipping, mutilation and burning followed. The three days of the festival see hundreds of thousands processing through the streets following a silver, bejewelled reliquary that holds the relics of the saint. There's also a procession of decorated candlesticks, up to 6m high, carried for hours at a time by groups representing different trades. On the morning of February 5, the saint's relics are carried back into the Duomo, where they remain until the following year. Meanwhile, there are fireworks, food stalls, special services and concerts throughout the *festa*.

the Cappella della Madonna holds a Roman sarcophagus that contains the ashes of the Aragonese kings – Frederick II, Louis and Frederick III. The tomb of the composer **Bellini**, a native of the city, is set in the floor before the second column on the right as you enter, inscribed with a phrase from his opera, *La Sonnámbula* (The Sleepwalker).

To the right of the Duomo, the **Museo Diocesano** (Tues–Sun 9am–12.30pm & 4–7.30pm; €4.20) houses the cathedral's collection of religious art and silverware, with items dating back to the fourteenth century, including pieces recovered from the pre-1693 cathedral. Below here, the piazza ends in the late seventeenth-century **Porta Uzeda**, a towering gateway under which sit two or three souvenir shops, with the **Villa Pacini** gardens just beyond.

On the other side of the Duomo, across Via Vittorio Emanuele II, the church of **Sant'Agata** is another of Vaccarini's works, though the lighter, pale grey Rococo interior post-dates his death. A little further up the street at Via Vittorio Emanuele 140, there's the minor curiosity that was the home of Catanese erotic poet and philosopher **Domenico Tempio** (1750–1821). It's now desperately neglected, though you can still make out the raunchy figures of men and women playing with themselves, which support the balcony above the blackened doorway.

The Pescheria

Catania's best-known food and fish market, the **Pescheria** (Mon–Sat from dawn), is reached from the back of Piazza del Duomo by nipping down the steps behind a gushing marble fountain. This takes you right into the main part of the fish market, where vendors shout across slabs and buckets full of twitching fish, eels, crabs and shellfish. Brandishing wicked-looking knives, they slice off swordfish steaks to order, while others shuck oysters, mussels and sea urchins for browsing customers. The side alleys off the fish market are dense with fruit, vegetable and dried goods and herb stalls, as well as bloody butchers' tables and cheese counters. There are also two or three excellent trattorias down here, great for lunch, or follow the "hostel" signs through the market to **Piazza Currò** where the *Agorà* hostel has an open-air terrace-café just a stone's throw from all the action. Just opposite the hostel you can also see the remains of the **Terme dell'Indirizzo**, more old Roman baths.

Castello Ursino

Beyond the market and Piazza Currò, the roads wind through a dilapidated neighbourhood to an open space (Piazza Federico di Svevia) punctured by the **Castello Ursino**, once the proud fortress of Frederick II. Originally the castle stood on a rocky cliff, but following the 1669 eruption that reclaimed this entire area from the sea, all that remains is the blackened keep, now the **Museo Cívico** (Mon–Sat 9am–1pm & 3–7pm; free). Wooden walkways run the breadth of the castle, looking down into the foundations and basement rooms, while the walls of the central chambers are hung with retrieved mosaic fragments, stone inscriptions and tombstones. The ground floor is usually taken up with temporary exhibitions, while the permanent exhibits include items as varied as a Greek terracotta statuette of two goddesses being pulled in a sea carriage by mythical beasts, and a seventeenth-century French pistol, inlaid in silver and depicting rabbits, fish and cherubs.

Along Via Crocíferi

The best place to appreciate the eighteenth-century rebuilding of Catania is along its most handsome street, **Via Crocíferi**, where the wealthy religious authorities and private citizens competed with each other to construct dazzling houses, palaces and churches. They were building on the very bones of the Roman and medieval city: the arcaded **Piazza Mazzini** (straddling Via Garibaldi) was constructed from 32 columns that originally formed part of a Roman basilica, while just to the west, at Via Vittorio Emanuele 260, is the entrance to the **Teatro Romano** (Mon–Sat 9am–1.30pm & 3–7pm; €3) of the second century AD, which preserves much of the Roman seating and underground passageway. The smaller **Odeon**, adjacent, was used for music and recitations.

At the bottom of Via Crocíferi, opposite San Francesco church, the house where the composer Vincenzo Bellini was born in 1801 is now open as the **Museo Belliniano** (Mon, Wed, Fri & Sat 9am–1pm, Tues & Thurs 9am–1pm & 3–6pm; free), displaying photographs, original scores, his death mask and other memorabilia. Born into a musical family, Bellini supposedly composed his first work at the age of six, and later studied in Naples, where he produced his first opera in 1825. Ten more operas followed during the next decade – his first big success was *Il Pirata* (1827) – with Bellini living largely in Milan until his early death in Paris, aged only 33. His body was transported back to his native Sicily to be buried, and Catania subsequently did her favourite son proud, with the airport, a piazza, the city's main theatre and a park all named after him, as well as the ultimate accolade – a pasta dish, *spaghetti alla Norma*, named after Bellini's famous 1831 opera *Norma* (see p.228 for the recipe).

North of Piazza San Francesco, narrow Via Crocíferi runs under an imposing Baroque arch, announcing the start of a series of arresting religious and secular buildings, little changed since the eighteenth century. Amble up and you can peer in the courtyards of the *palazzi* (one holds a plantation of banana trees) and poke around the churches. The finest of them, **San Giuliano**, about halfway up on the right, has a facade by Vaccarini and an echoing elliptical interior.

San Nicolò

To see Sicily's biggest church, strike west off Via Crocíferi up to the crescent of Piazza Dante, opposite which looms the unfinished facade of **San Nicolò** (daily 9am–1pm; free), studded by six enormous, lopped columns. It was conceived on a ridiculously grand scale, and the work was ultimately curtailed by earthquake damage and soaring costs. What's left is a stark 105-metre long interior, virtually undecorated save for the sculpted choir stalls and a meridian line etched in marble across the floor of the transept, embellished with zodiacal signs. The famous organ, admired by earlier visitors, was destroyed in the nineteenth century, and the dome is under scaffolding – probably for ever – but some English-language notice boards tell you something of the church's history.

The church is part of an adjoining Benedictine convent, with equally impressive dimensions – it's the second largest convent in Europe after Mafra in Portugal. Through a gate to the left of the church lie the remains of some Roman walls, and, behind, the massive conventual buildings. These are now used by the university's language and literature faculties, so no one minds if you stroll in for a look around, though the once grand cloistered courtyards are closed off and scaffolded.

Along Via Etnea

The main city thoroughfare, **Via Etnea**, runs north from Piazza del Duomo and out of the city. Following its full length would eventually lead you right to the foothills of Mount Etna – and from the street's northern end there are much-trumpeted views of the peak in the distance. The first square off the street, Piazza dell'Università, holds some outdoor cafés and the main building of the **University**, founded by the Aragonese kings in the fifteenth century. The earthquake postponed its completion until the 1750s. The tangled streets off to the east form the heart of the student nightlife zone, converging eventually on the restored Piazza Bellini, overlooked by the flagship **Teatro Mássimo Bellini** (1890).

Halfway up Via Etnea, **Piazza Stesícoro** marks the modern centre of Catania, with its western side almost entirely occupied by the sunken, black remains of the **Anfiteatro Romano** (daily 9am–1.30pm & 3–7pm; free), built from lava blocks in the second or third century AD. Much is still concealed under the surrounding buildings, but a diagram shows the original dimensions of the theatre, which could hold sixteen thousand spectators – it's quite evident that the section you can walk through represents only one tiny excavated corner.

At the back of the amphitheatre, you can wind around to find the twelfth-century church of **Sant'Agata al Cárcere** (closed at the time of writing), built on the site of the prison where St Agatha was confined before her martyrdom at the hands of the Romans. If it's open, a custodian will let you into the third-century crypt and show you the chapel's medieval stone doorway, topped by evil, grinning, sculpted heads and ape-like creatures.

Off the east side of Via Etnea, at Piazza Stesícoro, the stalls are out from early in the morning ranged up Via San Gaetano alle Grotte, heralding the city's other great market. Centred on the broad Piazza Carlo Alberto, the rumbustious **Fera o Luni** market (Mon–Sat from 7am) is not just for food but also for all kinds of clothes, shoes, accessories and household goods. It's all here, from tat piled high on a wooden cart to knock-off designer labels, accompanied by the constant patter ("*buongiorno bella!*") of cheery traders. It's a great spot for souvenir-hunting, even more so on Sundays when an antiques fair takes over the space.

For tourists Via Etnea finishes at the **Villa Bellini**, just beyond the post office, a large, ornamental public garden that provides a welcome touch of greenery. The stand-up drinks bar here is where the local police hang out, whiling away time between meal breaks – on the bar are pinned rather touching photos of the regulars, posing stiffly in uniform on horseback or motorbikes.

Zo centre for contemporary culture

Across in the east of the city, up Viale Africa near Stazione Centrale, Catania's former sulphur works, Le Ciminiere, has been transformed into a cultural centre known as **Zo** (Ⓦ www.zoculture.it). The original red-brick chimneys and lava-block walls have been wrapped in a contemporary glass-and-steel frame, while inside are theatre and performance spaces and a café-restaurant. It's quite an interesting place to visit, even if you don't come for an exhibition or event, and it holds two museums as well, both self-explanatory: the **Museo del Cinema**

(Tues–Fri & Sun 9am–12.30pm, also Tues & Thurs until 5.30pm; €4), and the **Museo Storico dello Sbarco in Sicilia 1943** (Tues–Sun 9am–12.30pm, plus Tues & Thurs 3–5pm; €4), or the Museum of the Allied Invasion of Sicily.

Eating, drinking and nightlife

Unusually for Sicily, Catania's streets teem until late, especially in summer, as seemingly half the population heads out for a stroll, a drink and a meal. **Restaurants** are pretty good value, thanks to the presence of so many students, who also go a long way to ensuring the island's best city nightlife. The whole ambience is helped by the fact that the *Comune* closes old-town streets and squares to traffic (the so-called *café concerto*) and bars spill tables outside until the small hours. For outdoor **cafés**, those in Piazza del Duomo and Piazza dell'Università have the best views in the most touristy locale, while the cooler **bars** are found around Piazza Bellini (particularly down Via Teatro Másimo, in Via Rapisardi and in adjacent piazzas Ogninella and Scammacca). The sole exception is the very funky, most un-Sicilian café, bar and restaurant at the *Agorà* youth hostel, near the Pescheria market.

While the Bellini theatre is the traditional centre of opera, music and ballet, Catania's new focus for **culture and the arts** is out by the train station, at the renovated sulphur works. You can check what's on in the comprehensive, free fortnightly arts and entertainment leaflet, *Lapis* (ⓦ www.lapisnet.it), available at the tourist offices and elsewhere, or get hold of a copy of Catania's daily newspaper, *La Sicilia*, which has city **entertainment listings**. Summer is the best time for **concerts and events**, from open-air jazz in the Villa Bellini gardens to classical concerts in churches and theatres across the city.

Cafés and restaurants

Da Aldo Piazza G. Sciuti 2 ☎095.311.158. The best choice near the Fera o Luni market is this amiable first-floor lunchtime grill-house, where bustling waiters reel off the daily specials (*pasta alla Norma*, stuffed squid or a simple grilled seabass or steak). It's very good value, around €20 for a full meal; you'll find it by taking the first left off Via Pacini, down Via al Carmine, coming from Piazza Carlo Alberto. No credit cards. Lunch only; closed Sun. Moderate.

Antica Marina Via Pardo 29 ☎095.348.197. The fancier of the two Pescheria market trattorias serves excellent seafood pastas and fresh fish, with most dishes around €10–15. Closed Wed. Expensive.

La Paglia Via Pardo 23 ☎095.346.838. Simple trattoria (wipe-clean tablecloths, panel-board walls) that's the best place for a reasonably priced fish-market lunch – when the *signora* runs out of something she just bellows through the kitchen window for more. Dishes cost €6–9, starting say with spaghetti and clams, followed by a piece of grilled tuna, and the house wine is the kind that you can run your car on. Closed Sun. Moderate.

Street food

The Catanese do a lot of eating on the hoof, from grazing in the Pescheria on raw mussels and sea urchins to munching ice cream as they parade up Via Etnea in the evening. February's Festa di Sant'Agata sees food stalls selling traditional nougat and sweets, while during summer kiosks offer that thirst-quenching Catania speciality, soda water and crushed lemon, served with or without salt (*seltz e limone con/senza sale*). In autumn the roast-chestnut vendors are out in force, and around San Martino's Day (November 11) it's the time for *crispelle* – fritters of flour, water, yeast and ricotta or anchovies. A great place to try these and other traditional fried snacks is *Friggitoria Stella* (Via Monsignor Ventimiglia 66; closed Sun), a backstreet establishment that's been going for years.

Savia Via Etnea 302 ☎ 095.322.335. Opposite the main entrance to the Villa Bellini, this is the city's most notable *pasticceria*, open since 1897 and always busy with folk digging into savoury *arancini*, ricotta-stuffed *cannoli*, real *cassata* and the like. Closed Mon. Inexpensive.

Sicilia in Bocca Via Dusmet 35 ☎ 095.250.0208. One of the nicest places to sit outside, this is pizzeria one side, restaurant the other (though in practice you can mix and match menus), sharing a shaded terrace. It's set in the old arched sea wall (through Porta Uzeda from Piazza del Duomo and turn left), and service is friendly and English-speaking. Closed Mon. Pizzas moderate, restaurant expensive.

La Siciliana Viale Marco Polo 52a ☎ 095.376.400. Renowned as one of eastern Sicily's best restaurants, with a thoroughly traditional menu, strong on fish and local specialities like rice with squid ink and fresh ricotta. They also make their own sensational pastries and desserts. In summer there's outdoor garden-terrace seating. However, you'll need to take a taxi as it's way up in the north of the city. Closed Sun evening & Mon. Very expensive.

Turi Finocchiaro Via E. Reina 13 ☎ 095.715.3573. A cavernous pizzeria-steak house in the bar zone, where the atmosphere varies from vacuum to vivacious depending on the time of night. The food's reliable, with pizzas around €7–9 or a mixed grill at €13. It's just off Piazza dell'Università, set back in a courtyard, with a second entrance on Via Cestai. Dinner only; closed Wed. Moderate.

Bars

La Cartiera Pub Via Casa del Mutilato 8. Young, studenty Catanese bar where there's often live music.

Nievski Via Alessi 15–17. They love Che in this "*pub-trattoria alternativo*", where you can come for a plate of organic food at lunchtime, a Fair Trade coffee or a beer at night. There's Internet access too, all kinds of concerts and events, and more goatees than you can shake a stick at. It's at the foot of the Alessi steps up to Via Crociferi. Closed Mon.

Tertulia Via Rapisardo 1. Catania's most laid-back bookshop has a café-bar that opens nightly at 7pm (until 1.30am; sometimes closed in Aug). Belgian beers, organic drinks and snacky food are served at outdoor tables in the pedestrianized street just up from the Teatro Bellini.

Waxy O'Connor's Piazza Spírito Santo. Hugely popular Irish pub that spills onto the square on summer evenings. And if you don't like Waxy's, there's always Joyce opposite.

Spaghetti alla Norma

Catania's tribute to the composer Bellini, *Spaghetti alla Norma* – cooked with tomato and aubergine (*melanzane* in Italian) – is served in most local restaurants. Here's how to prepare it:

Ingredients (serves 4)
Two aubergines, cut into 1/2 inch (1cm) slices (or cubed if you prefer)
Two tablespoons (30ml) olive oil
Two cloves of garlic, peeled and crushed
One tablespoon tomato purée
1lb (454g) fresh plum tomatoes, chopped roughly (use tinned if unavailable)
10oz (300g) spaghetti
Grated hard ricotta salata cheese (or use parmesan or an aged pecorino)
Two tablespoons chopped basil leaves
Salt, black pepper

Fry the aubergine until golden brown (use a low heat). Put to one side. Gently fry the garlic in two tablespoons of olive oil for two minutes, then add chopped (or tinned) tomatoes, one tablespoon tomato purée, and a pinch of salt and pepper, and sauté for thirty minutes, or until the sauce reduces slightly. Add half the chopped basil leaves to the sauce and stir.

Cook the spaghetti in boiling water until *al dente*. Spoon the tomato sauce on top of the spaghetti, add slices of fried aubergine and top with cheese and the remainder of the basil leaves. Eat with a robust red wine, and sing lustily.

Culture and the arts

Teatro Mássimo Bellini Via Perrotta 12, facing Piazza Bellini ☎ 095.730.6111, infoline ☎ 095.715.0921, ⓦ www.teatromassimobellini.it. Catania's impressive opera house has a concert season that runs from Oct until May, and it's not just opera that's offered but also classical music and ballet.

Zo Viale Africa ☎ 095.746.3122, ⓦ www.zoculture .it. The centre for contemporary arts is the place for cutting-edge theatre, electronic and world music, experimental art shows, off-the-wall installations and offbeat festivals. It's a 2min walk from Stazione Centrale.

Listings

⑤

Airport Fontanarossa, flight information on ☎ 095.340.505, ⓦ www.aeroporto.catania.it. Take the Alibus #457 from Stazione Centrale or Via Etnea (every 20min, 5am–midnight).

Beaches The closest sand beaches to Catania are those on the wide Golfo di Catania (Viale Kennedy), reached by taking bus #427 from Stazione Centrale or summer bus #D from Piazza Borsellino. This is also where all the big campsites are.

Books and newspapers Libreria Cavallotto, Corso Sicilia 89, has a good selection of English-language books. Some foreign newspapers are sold at kiosks around Piazza del Duomo, but the most reliable source is the newsagents inside Stazione Centrale.

Buses AMT city buses (☎ 095.751.7111, ⓦ www .amt.ct.it) have terminals at Stazione Centrale and Piazza Borsellino. Other companies have terminals around Stazione Centrale, including: AST (Via L. Sturzo 220 ☎ 095.746.1096, ⓦ www .aziendasicilianatrasporti.it), for Catania provincial services, including Etna, plus Piazza Armerina and Siracusa; Interbus/Etna (Via d'Amico 187 ☎ 095.532.716, ⓦ www.interbus.it), for Acireale, Caltagirone, Enna, Giardini-Naxos, Nicosia, Noto, Piazza Armerina, Ragusa, Siracusa and Taormina; SAIS (Via d'Amico 181 ☎ 095.536.168, ⓦ www .saistrasporti.it) to Palermo, Messina, Agrigento, Enna, Caltanissetta and mainland destinations.

Car rental Most agencies have outlets at the airport and in the city: Avis ☎ 095.340.500, ⓦ www.avis .co.uk; Easycar ☎ 800.939.293, ⓦ www .easycaritalia.it; Europcar ☎ 199.307.030, ⓦ www.europcar.it; Hertz ☎ 095.341.595, ⓦ www .hertz.it; Holiday Car Rental ☎ 095.346.769; Maggiore ☎ 095.340.594, ⓦ www.maggiore.it; Sixt ☎ 095.340.252, ⓦ www.sixt.co.uk.

Ferries and hydrofoils Catania's main ferry and hydrofoil services are to Naples and Malta, but you can also reach Livorno, Ravenna, Genoa and Tunis. Contact Virtu Ferries (☎ 095.535.711, ⓦ www .virtuferries.com) for catamaran services to Malta; TT Lines (☎ 095.734.0211, ⓦ www.ttlines.it) for ferries to Naples; or any travel agent.

Hospital Ospedale Garibaldi, Piazza S. Maria di Gesù 7 ☎ 095.759.4368.

Internet Internetteria, Via Penninello 44 (summer Mon–Sat 10am–10pm, Sun 5–10pm; winter daily 5–10pm).

Shopping in Catania

Via Etnea is the central spine of the city and its major shopping street, with department and chain stores, designer labels, boutiques and brands. Off here, just before the Villa Bellini, **Via Pacini** is devoted to cheap clothes, shoes, underwear and accessories, while at the far end it melds into the unmissable **Fera o Luni market** (Piazza Carlo Alberto). There's fruit, veg and fish in the square outside the church, and the surrounding streets are a hawkers' bazaar, ideal if you're hankering after a picture of the pope or a three-euro handbag. The nearest big **supermarket** is Punto SMA (Corso Sicilia 50). The other daily market, the **Pescheria**, mainly trades in food (not just fish; it's also great for buying things like salted capers, sun-dried tomatoes, hunks of pecorino cheese or bags of wild oregano), though on the fringes you'll find clothes and jewellery too – **Via Vittorio Emanuele II** has a few "ethnic" shops with carvings, beads and fabrics. Across Piazza del Duomo, in the arches under the Porta Uzeda gateway, there are two or three well-stocked Sicilian souvenir stores, for puppets, postcards, ceramics, painted carts and almond wine. And around the back of the Duomo, look for **Nonna Vincenza** in the old Palazzo Biscari (Piazza San Placido 7), the most traditional place in the city to buy artisan sweets in gorgeous packaging.

Left luggage At Stazione Centrale, Piazza Giovanni XXIII (daily 7am–10pm).
Pharmacies Caltabiano, Piazza Stesícoro 36 ☎095.327.647; Croce Rossa, Via Etnea 274 ☎095.317.053; Europa, Corso Italia 111 ☎095.383.536; Cutelli, Via Vittorio Emanuele II 54 ☎095.531.400.
Police In emergencies call ☎112. Otherwise, Carabinieri, Piazza Giovanni Verga 8; Polizia Municipale, Via Veniero 7; and Questura, Piazza S. Nicolella 8.
Post office Main post office, Via Etnea 215, close to the Villa Bellini (Mon–Sat 8.15am–6.30pm).

Trains Mainline services (principally to Messina and Siracusa, but also to Palermo, Enna and Caltanissetta) from Stazione Centrale in Piazza Giovanni XXIII (information and timetables on ☎892.021, ⓦwww.trenitalia.com). Round-Etna services are on the Ferrovia Circumetnea, Stazione Catania Borgo, Via Caronda ☎095.541.250, ⓦwww.circumetnea.it
Taxis Ranks at Stazione Centrale, Piazza del Duomo and Via Etnea (Piazza Stesícoro); call CST ☎095.330.966 for 24-hr service.

The coastal route north to Acireale

The main sandy beaches lie south of Catania, but it's actually the coast north of the city that's the most popular resort area. The lava streams from Etna have reached the sea many times over the centuries, turning the coastline into an attractive mix of contorted black rocks and sheer coves, excellent for swimming. Consequently, what was once a series of small fishing villages is now a fair-sized strip of hotels, lidos and restaurants, idle in the winter but swarming in summer with day-trippers. You can get here easily on city AMT bus #534 from Catania's Piazza Borsellino, or the AST service from Stazione Centrale to Acireale. Incidentally, the prefix "Aci", given to a number of settlements here, derives from the local River Aci, said to have appeared following the death of the herdsman Acis at the hands of the giant, one-eyed Polyphemus.

Ognina, Aci Castello and Aci Trezza

OGNINA, the first stop, is a small suburb on the northern outskirts of Catania, built on lava cliffs formed in the fifteenth century. It holds a few restaurants, overlooking the little harbour, as well as a campsite. Buses run on to **ACI CASTELLO**, 9km from the city, whose castle rises above the sea in splinters from a volcanic rock crag. The base of the rebel Roger di Lauria in 1297, it's remarkably well preserved, despite many threatening eruptions and the destruction wrought by Frederick II of Aragon, who took the castle from Roger by erecting a wooden siege-engine adjacent. The ragged coastline to the north is popular for sunbathing and swimming and, in summer, a wooden boardwalk is built over the lava rocks (you pay a small fee to use the changing rooms and showers).

Aci Castello marks the beginning of the so-called Riviera dei Ciclopi, named after the jagged points of the **Scogli dei Ciclopi** that rise from the sea just beyond town. Homer wrote that the blinded Polyphemus slung these rocks (broken from Etna) at Ulysses as he and his men escaped from the Cyclops in their ships. The largest of the three main sharp-edged islets – also known as *faraglioni* – sticks some 60m into the sky. You could always walk the couple of kilometres north along the rough coast from Aci Castello to **ACI TREZZA**, the fishing village at the heart of nineteenth-century Sicilian novelist Giovanni Verga's masterpiece *I Malavoglia*. Bars, *gelaterie* and seafood restaurants are ranged along the lungomare here.

Acireale

ACIREALE, 16km north of Catania, has the best site of all, high above the rocky shore and the surrounding lemon groves. It's location best appreciated from the public gardens at the northern end of town, from where you can look right back along the Riviera dei Ciclopi. Known since Roman times as a spa centre (the thermal baths are still heavily used), Acireale is also another striking example of Sicilian Baroque town-planning. This is the fourth successive town on the site, rebuilt directly over the old lava streams after the 1693 earthquake and, as in Catania, it relies on grand buildings, a handsome central square and Duomo and some long thoroughfares for its effect.

The town is well known for its celebrations during **Carnevale** (Feb/March), when it hosts one of Sicily's best festivals, with extraordinarily elaborate flower-decked floats and fancy-dress parades clogging the streets for five noisy days. Acireale also has a long tradition of Sicilian **puppet theatre**, with regular shows performed in summer by its surviving theatre companies, like that of Emanuele Macri (Ⓦwww.teatropupimacri.it) or Turi Grasso (Ⓦwww.operadeipupi.com) – the latter also has a small museum at the theatre, at Via Nazionale 195.

It's easiest to get the bus to Acireale, which stops outside the public gardens or near the Duomo; the train station is well to the south of town, near the thermal baths, and a long walk into the centre along Via Vittorio Emanuele. Best target for lunch is actually out of town, an easy two-kilometer downhill stroll or drive to the tiny hamlet of **Santa Maria La Scala**, huddled around a miniscule harbour full of painted fishing-boats, where three or four trattorias overlook the bay. To get here on foot, go down Via Romeo (to the side of the Municipio), across the busy main road and then down the steep rural path to the water.

Lentini and around

Half an hour or so south of Catania, **LENTINI** has a long pedigree that puts it among the earliest of the Greek settlements in Sicily, and the first of all the inland colonies. Established in 729 BC as a daughter city of Naxos, Lentini (Leontinoi) flourished as a commercial centre for two hundred years, before falling foul of Hippocrates of Gela. Later, the city was absorbed by Syracuse, sharing its disasters but never its prosperity. It was Leontinoi's struggle to assert its independence, by allying itself with Athens, that provided the pretext for the great Athenian expedition against Syracuse in 415 BC. Another attempt – this time an alliance with the Carthaginians during the Second Punic War – resulted in the Romans beheading two thousand of its citizens, a measure that horrified the whole island, as no doubt it was intended to do. By the time Cicero got round to describing the city, Lentini was "wretched and empty", though it continued as a small-scale agricultural centre for some time, until the great earthquake of 1693 completely demolished it.

Noisy, sprawling, modern Lentini has little to recommend it, though the ancient city survives as an extensive archeological site, a few kilometres out of town. Some of the finds are on display in the town's **Museo Archeológico** in Piazza del Liceo (Tues–Sun 9am–6pm, Sun 9am–noon; free), though the best artefacts have been appropriated by the museums at Catania and Siracusa, and the museum itself defies directions. The Zona Archeológica is a twenty-minute walk south of the nearby upper town of **Carlentini**, which you can reach directly by bus from Catania with AST. It has a fairly pleasant central square with bars, though most buses also stop in Piazza San Francesco on the outskirts of Carlentini, closer to the zone, as do local buses from Lentini's train station.

The **Zona Archeológica** (Mon–Fri 8.30am–1.30pm; free) is then a five-minute signposted walk away, spread over the two hills of San Mauro and

Metapíccola. The first of these is the more interesting, holding the ancient town's acropolis and substantial remains of a vast necropolis nearby. You'll see the pincer-style south gate immediately, part of a well-conserved system of fortifications that surrounded the town. Together, the hills make a good couple of hours' rambling, while a dirt road to the side of the main entrance climbs around the perimeter fence to allow views over the whole site and down to Lentini in the valley below.

⑤ Mount Etna

One of the world's largest volcanoes, **Mount Etna** (3323m) dominates much of Sicily's eastern landscape, its smoking summit an omnipresent feature when travelling in this area. The main crater is gradually becoming more explosive and more dangerous, with spectacular eruptions in 2001 and 2002 far eclipsing those of the preceding decade (see box on Etna's eruptions, p.236). Despite the risk, the volcano remains a remarkable draw for travellers, though the unpredictability of eruptions – they may be expected, but cannot be pinpointed to a precise time – means that it's often impossible to get close to the main crater.

Etna was just one of the places that the Greeks thought to be the forge of Vulcan, a fitting description of the blustering and sparking from the main crater. The philosopher Empedocles studied the volcano closely, living in an observatory near the summit. This terrifying existence was dramatized by Matthew Arnold in his *Empedocles on Etna*:

Alone! –
On this charr'd, blacken'd melancholy waste,
Crown'd by the awful peak, Etna's great mouth.

Certainly, it all proved too much for Empedocles, who in 433 BC jumped into the main crater in an attempt to prove that the gases emitted would support his body weight. They didn't.

A ring of villages circles the lower slopes of Etna, including the ski-centres of Linguaglossa (on the Circumetnea rail route) and **Nicolosi**, which hold the bulk of the accommodation, restaurants and tour facilities. The two main approaches to the summit are from north and south. Some of the best scenery is on the north side (signposted "Etna Nord"), though the road beyond **Piano Provenzana** is strictly controlled, and even with a four-wheel drive you will be strongly encouraged to leave your vehicle and take an organized jeep trip. From the south side ("Etna Sud"), beyond Nicolosi, the chief departure point is the mountain refuge-hotel of **Rifugio Sapienza**, connected by daily bus from Catania.

What level you actually reach is dictated by current volcanic activity and weather conditions. Access to the **summit** itself is by 10km of rough track, a

Snow, ice and the bishop

Even in winter, the snow on Etna's southern side tends to lie only in patches, partly melted by the heat of the rocks. On the northern side, however, hollows in the ground are filled year-round with snow. From here, the ice used to be cut, covered with ash and then transported to the rest of the island, the mainland and even Malta, for refrigeration purposes – a peculiar export that constituted the main source of revenue for the Bishop of Catania, who owned the land until comparatively recently.

▲ Climbing Mount Etna

large part of it covered by lava, or by means of cable car and 4WD minibus. The higher reaches resemble a lunar landscape, the ground underfoot alternately black, grey or red depending on the age of the lava. The most recent stuff lies in great folds; below, the red roofs and green fields of the lower hills stretch away to the sea. You'll not be in any danger, provided you stay within the limit that is currently deemed safe to reach. Note that ascending the volcano is only possible between about May and October; the rest of the time, it's swathed in snow.

Finally, if you're pushed for time or unable to ascend higher due to adverse weather conditions, you'll have to make do with the glimpses of Etna's peak and hinterland from the Circumetnea railway (see p.237), a circular route from Catania to Riposto that provides one of Sicily's most fascinating rides. Drivers can follow exactly the same route around the volcano foothills as the railway – a minor but perfectly adequate road sticks close to the line.

Etna Nord: the ascent from Piano Provenzana

From Linguaglossa, a tortuous fifteen-kilometre road corkscrews up past the skiing pistes of **Piano Provenzana** and the tourist village of Mareneve. If you don't have your own vehicle, you'll need to take a taxi from Linguaglossa to the Piano, from where 4WD minibuses operated by STAR (daily May–Oct, weather permitting; ☎347.495.7091) shuttle up and down the upper slopes. There are two options: a two-hour excursion that brings you to Pizzi Deneri (at a height of 2800m), from which you must walk about twenty minutes for the best views, costing €44, and one lasting about three hours, costing €60, that takes you to the main crater (3200m) – though this involves a walk of about an hour and a quarter to reach the best vantage point. The early morning and early evening tours are the best – Etna at dawn or sunset is a spectacular sight – but need booking. The minibuses don't run to a fixed timetable – they simply take off when full, and the operation is a lower-key affair than on the southern side. The extent to which you'll be allowed out to explore independently depends on weather

Etna tours and excursions

If you're short on time, the easiest way to see the volcano and climb its slopes is by **organized tour**. Four-wheel-drive minibuses and guided hikes operate out of the ski stations of Piano Provenzana and Rifugio Sapienza, though many tourists simply book an all-day tour from agents and tourist offices in places like Taormina, Giardini-Naxos, Catania or Siracusa. Prices vary, according to how high you go, and whether or not you take the cable car, but for a full day with an ascent to the main crater you can expect to pay around €70. Departures depend on weather conditions and tours don't generally run between September and April.

The do-it-yourself option is to take the daily **AST bus** (8.15am all year) from Catania's Piazza Giovanni XXIII, outside Stazione Centrale, to the *Rifugio Sapienza* (2hr; tickets cost around €5). You'll have enough time to reach the top by tour or even on foot, and get back for the return bus, which leaves at 4.30pm from the refuge.

conditions – even in August the wind-chill can make winter clothing advisable, and wind speeds can be strong enough to blow children off their feet.

Two mountain **refuges**, *rifugi*, stand 100m apart in the pinewoods, 5km below Piano Provenzana (follow the road): *Casa Brunek* (℡095.643.015; €26 per person for a dorm bed, €39 including dinner) and the more comfortable *Ragabo* (℡095.647.841, ✉www.ragabo.it; ❸, or €45 half-board), which has private rooms with en-suite bathrooms. The only place to **eat** in Piano is the moderately priced *Ristorante Monte Conca* (℡095.647.968).

Zafferana Etnea and around

Most pleasant of the villages on Etna's southeastern side is **ZAFFERANA ETNEA**, an hour from Catania by bus. Surrounded by vineyards and citrus groves, it's renowned for its honey, the smell of which lingers in the air. Parts of the outskirts were damaged by lava in 1992, when the village became the operational centre of the effort to halt the flow from the volcano. The centre, however, was untouched, and it retains an eighteenth-century air in its buildings and churches, making it a pleasant stop, say for a coffee in the bar on the corner of the elegant central piazza. The previous eruption to threaten Zafferana occurred in 1792, halted on that occasion – according to local tradition – by the intervention of Our Lady of Divine Providence, whose name was again invoked by God-fearing locals during the last volcanic ructions.

Zafferana has acquired a reputation as a low-key hill-resort, and the population of around seven thousand practically doubles at weekends and holidays as the trippers arrive. Certainly, there's some good walking to be done in the green hills behind the village, and if you fancy a longer stay there's a choice of **hotels**, all sited north of the centre. Try the large, fully equipped *Primavera dell'Etna*, Via Cassone 86 (℡095.708.2348, ✉www.hotel-primavera.it; ❺), set in its own grounds and with superb views from its rooms and terraces, or the smaller *Villa Pina*, Via dei Gerani 19 (℡095.708.1024; no credit cards; ❸), which is popular with German holiday-makers.

Five kilometres or so north of Zafferana, **Milò** offers impressive views of the Valle del Bove above. Maps show a road from Milò that climbs northwest, up the volcano to the *Rifugio Citelli*, and back towards Linguaglossa, but frequent landslides often make this route impossible. You should be able to get some of the way up though, for more striking views of the summit and the coastline below. A lower, more direct road leads 15km north past various old lava flows – of 1852, 1950 and, near Fornazzo, of 1979 – to Linguaglossa.

Nicolosi and around

The tidy little resort of **NICOLOSI** (698m), which had a narrow escape in the 2002 eruption, is a popular winter ski-centre and the most useful base in the foothills on the south side of the volcano. With several hotels and some good places to eat, it is also well-served by frequent AST buses from Catania. It gets pretty busy around here, even in summer, with some good walking possibilities in the area. Best of these, certainly if you're going no further, is the hike up to the **Monti Rossi** craters, around an hour each way. Formed in the eruption of 1669, they're the most important of the secondary craters that litter the slopes of the volcano.

Five kilometres or so east of Nicolosi, **Trecastagni** is worth a look for its main church, the Chiesa Madre, a fine Renaissance building probably designed by Antonello Gagini, and the marvellous views over the coast from its elevated position. Frankly, though, you're hardly likely to come here for just these; better, if you're driving, to look upon Trecastagni as a coffee-stop.

Practicalities

Nicolosi is the last main stop before the steeper slopes begin. There's a helpful **tourist office** on Piazza Vittorio Emanuele (Mon, Wed & Fri 9am–2pm & 4–6pm, Tues & Thurs 9am–2pm; ℡095.914.488, ⓦwww.aast-nicolosi.it), just off the main road that runs through town.

Accommodation in Nicolosi is fairly expensive, but there are some exceptions. The best bet is one of the numerous B&Bs, of which the tourist office can provide a full list. A good, central choice is *Al Centro Stórico*, Via Garibaldi 26 (℡095.910.735 or 348.266.4310, ⓦwww.alcentrostorico.it; ❹), just off Piazza Vittorio Emanuele. In the centre of town, the *Etna Garden*, Via della Quercia 7 (℡095.791.4686 or 347.877.9969, ⓔinfo@etnagardenpark.com; ❸), has a courtyard garden, a small vulcanological museum and en-suite rooms, and IYHF members get a ten percent discount. Otherwise, try the large, group-friendly *Hotel Gemmellaro*, 2km north of town at Via Etnea 160 (℡095.911.060, ⓦwww.hotelgemmellaro.it; ❺), with bright, modern but bland rooms. *Camping Etna* (℡095.914.309), in a shady pinewood with a pool, is on Via Goethe, signposted from town just past the hotels.

Restaurants and pizzerias are ten-a-penny in the centre of Nicolosi. For something a bit different and more contemporary, try ⚒ *Nero di Cenere*, a **wine bar and restaurant** at Via Garibaldi 64; apart from the wines, it serves samplings of cheese and salami (€12), pastas (€7) and various vegetarian dishes (€8), which you can enjoy *al fresco* on the terrace.

Etna Sud: the ascent from Rifugio Sapienza

One bus a day from Catania (at 8.15am) continues past Nicolosi to the mountain refuge/hotel that marks the end of the negotiable road up the south side of Etna. Between mid-June and early January, there's also a departure from Nicolosi at 11.30am (not Sun) to the refuge, an hour-long trip. It's a bizarre ride: the green foothills give way to wooded slopes, then to bare, black-and-grey seas of volcanic debris, spotted with the hardy endemic plants, the yellow-green Spino Santo and Etna violets, that are the only things to grow on the heights of the volcano. The most recent lava streams lie to the right of the road, where you'll also see earlier spent craters, grass-covered on the lower reaches and no more than black pimples further up.

⚒ **Rifugio Sapienza** (℡095.915.321, ⓦwww.rifugiosapienza.com; €69 per person half-board), 1400m below the summit, was the scene of frenetic activity

The eruptions of Etna

Of the scores of recorded **eruptions** of Etna since the 475 BC one described by Pindar, some have been disastrously spectacular: in 1169, 1329 and 1381 the lava reached the sea, while in **1669**, the worst year, parts of Catania were wrecked and its castle was surrounded by molten rock.

During the twentieth century, the Circumetnea railway line was repeatedly ruptured by lava flows, the towns of the foothills were threatened, and roads and farms destroyed. The **1971** eruption destroyed the observatory supposed to give warning of such an event, while in **1979** nine tourists were killed by an explosion on the edge of the main crater. During the **1992** eruption, which engulfed the outskirts of Zafferana Etnea, the American navy joined Italian forces in an attempt to stem the lava flow by dropping reinforced concrete blocks (so-called "Beirut-busters", used to defend military camps) from helicopters into the fissures.

In **2001**, the military helicopters were out again in force, this time water-bombing the forest fires and blazing orchards. Regarded as the most complex in the last three hundred years, the 2001 eruption spewed forth from six vents on Etna's northern and southeastern sides and sent vast, fiery fountains of lava to the skies. Drivers found the roads blocked and air passengers were forced to divert to other island airports, while Catania suffered a rain of black ash day and night. Luckily there were no fatalities; the cluster of buildings around *Rifugio Sapienza* narrowly escaped and the lava flow petered out 4km short of Nicolosi, though the upper cable-car station was destroyed and the hut that held the monitoring live-cam was incinerated (somehow the equipment was saved).

Triggered by an earthquake, the eruption of **2002** saw lava streams pouring down both north and south flanks, destroying restaurants, hotels and a cable car in the ski resort of Piano Provenzana, and threatening the villages of Nicolosi and Linguaglossa below. Emergency teams, however, succeeded in diverting the flow, and a major catastrophe was averted. Some local villagers, on the other hand, preferred to place their faith in parading statues of the Virgin Mary before the volcano, although the devout were far outnumbered by the flocks of sightseers who made excursions as close as they dared, until curtailed by the authorities.

in July and August 2001, when large dams and channels were constructed to contain the molten lava and prevent it from engulfing the tourist complex. As a result, only the lower cable-car station and the car park were damaged, when the lava eventually spilled down and crossed the road in a broad 500m band. It had another narrow escape at the end of 2002, when lava covered a nearby building, causing it to explode. Thirty-two people were injured, but the refuge was untouched – graphic photographs inside illustrate its near escapes.

The refuge is the cheapest place to spend the night, so it's always wise to ring ahead and book. Its modern rooms have clean lines and en-suite bathrooms, and there's a restaurant. Alternative **accommodation** is available at the *Hotel Corsaro* (℡095.914.122, ⊛www.hotelcorsaro.it; ❺), a ski-lodge-type place popular with tour groups, set a little apart from the rest of the site and advertising itself as Etna's highest lodging.

The ascent

The ascent of the volcano from the south side involves a combination of cable car from *Rifugio Sapienza*, a minibus ride and a guided walk. The **Funivia dell'Etna** cable car (daily 9am–3.30/5pm; €25.50; ⊛www.funiviaetna.com) reaches an altitude of 2500m at Monte Montagnola, from where SITAS **minibuses** leave for the crater (April–Oct daily 9am–5.30pm, weather permitting; ℡095.914.141). The total journey (cable car plus minibus) takes around two and a half hours and costs €48. When the wind is up, or conditions are otherwise difficult, the entire journey is undertaken from *Rifugio Sapienza* by minibus. It's also possible (conditions permitting) to **walk to Etna's summit**, which takes around four hours from the *Sapienza*, and much less to return. However you go, take warm clothes, a hat, good shoes or boots and – especially if you wear contact lenses – glasses to keep the flying grit out of your eyes. Weather conditions higher up are often different to those at the *Rifugio Sapienza*, so you might want to take advantage of the padded jackets and boots that are available for rent from the minibus guides.

Depending on conditions, you should be able to reach the so-called **Torre del Filósofo**, a tower that's said to have been the home of Empedocles, but is more likely to be a memorial built by the Romans to celebrate the emperor Hadrian's climb to the summit. Beyond, from the turnaround point for the minibus, you look up to the summit, smoke puffing from the **southeast crater** immediately above. It would be foolish to venture any further – gaseous explosions and molten rock are common this far up. Higher still is the **main crater**: you might see smoke from here too, and, if you're lucky, spitting explosions. Disappointingly, there's often haze or cloud, which can mar the unsurpassed panorama to the sea; for the clearest view, come at sunrise. On the way down, the minibus makes short photo-stops, including the **Valle del Bove**, an enormous chasm almost 20km in circumference, its walls 900m high and streaked with recent lava flows. A massive rent in the side of the volcano, its sunken flank comprises a sixth of the entire surface area of Etna.

The Circumetnea railway

Although there's nothing to beat an ascent of Etna, you can experience something of the awe and majesty of the volcano along the route of the **Ferrovia Circumetnea**, or Circumetnea railway. This is a private line, 110km long, starting in Catania and circling the base of Etna as far as Riposto on the Ionian coast, 30km north of Catania. It's a marvellous ride, running through fertile vegetation – citrus plantations, vines and nut trees – and past (often through) the strewn lava of recent eruptions, with endless views of the summit en route. You can easily do the whole round-trip in a day from Catania; the only places interesting enough to halt the journey overnight are the medieval town of Randazzo or the northern tourist centre of Linguaglossa. The Circumetnea ends its run 20km southeast of Linguaglossa at Riposto, where you switch to the mainline station Giarre-Riposto for frequent trains south to Catania (or north to Giardini-Naxos).

Regular Ferrovia Circumetnea trains (℡095.541.250, ⓦwww.circumetnea.it) depart from Stazione Catania Borgo (Via Caronda; metro from Stazione Centrale) in Catania. They take two hours to Randazzo, three to Linguaglossa and three and a half to Riposto (no Sunday service in winter; seasonal time-tables available on the website), and **tickets** currently cost €5.65 one way.

Paternò

The first part of the Circumetnea route runs out through Catania's grim suburbs, with Misterbianco the first stop. Soon, though, the first of the citrus and olive groves are visible and, by the time you reach **PATERNÒ**, you're well within sight of Etna's southern slopes. A busy town in the valley of the River Simeto, Paternò clusters around its main street, Via Vittorio Emanuele, with the train station at one end and a medieval **castello** at the other. Founded by Count Roger in 1073, the castle dates largely from the thirteenth century (though it's much restored) and is worth a look for the view from the terrace at the top – the reason the Germans used it as an observation post during World War II. They proved hard to dislodge, and four thousand people died here during the subsequent aerial bombardment. If you're lucky, you'll find the doors open, in which case don't hesitate to poke your nose inside, and, if at all possible, have a wander.

Paternò's one **hotel**, the echoing *Sicilia*, is near the station at Via Vittorio Emanuele 391 (℡095.853.604; ❷), about a twenty-minute walk to the old centre, at the other end of Via Vittorio Emanuele. Rooms with air conditioning cost extra. The hotel is pretty rundown, however, and is best regarded as a fallback if you're stuck.

Biancavilla and Adrano

Ten kilometres further on, Biancavilla was founded by Albanian refugees in 1480. The area around is devoted to growing oranges, and small side roads from here run up through the orchards and onto the higher, southwestern slopes of Etna – a nice little diversion if you're coming this way by car.

ADRANO, close by, is one of the more interesting stops hereabouts, built over the site of ancient Adranon, a town founded by Dionysius the Elder. Parts of the Greek lava-built **walls** are still visible in town, though they're barely distinguishable from later fortifications. Much more impressive is the **castello** in Piazza Umberto I, another of Count Roger's creations and, like that at Paternò, squat, solid and battlemented. Inside a small museum holds finds from local sites, including early Bronze Age pottery, but little information (Mon–Fri 9am–1pm & 4–7pm, or 3–6pm in winter; €2). Take a look, too, in the **Chiesa Madre**, next to the castle, which has some good artwork inside, including sixteenth-century panels by Girolamo Alibrandi in the transepts, though the exterior is disfigured by an unfinished modern campanile.

The old centre of Adrano makes a fairly pleasant stroll, with its shady gardens and faded churches; sit-down bars offering snacks face the gardens. For **lunch**, wander 250m down Via Roma alongside the gardens to Piazza Duca degli Abruzzi, where the cosy and rustic *Hostaria Bellini* is tucked away next to the Teatro Bellini (closed Mon); the emphasis here is on local ingredients. Alternatively, the *Caffè Ottocento* opposite has snacks and ice creams, and tables outside.

If you're driving and fancy a side-trip, you can head 8km west of Adrano, near Cárcaci, to the **Ponte dei Saraceni**, a fourteenth-century bridge that arches over the River Simeto (it's at the end of the first road on the right after Cárcaci; keep to the right).

Bronte and around

Some of the best views of Etna are revealed between Adrano and Bronte, as the railway line and road climb ever closer to the lava flows that have marked the landscape further north. **BRONTE** lies about halfway along the Circumetnea route, its rather shabby, amorphous aspect belying a noble past. The town was founded by Charles V in 1535, and many echoes of its original layout survive, particularly in the numerous battlemented and pointed campanili that top its ageing churches. The town gave its name to the dukedom bestowed upon Nelson, the English admiral, in 1799, and his ducal seat (the Castello Maniace – see below) is a few kilometres north of town. Otherwise, Bronte's sole claim to fame these days is as the centre of Italy's pistachio-nut production: the plantations around town account for 85 percent of the country's output, but are only harvested in the early autumn of odd-numbered years. In town, you'll find some great pistachio granitas and ice cream among other sweet goodies at *Bar Il Tartufo*,Via Cavalieri di Vittorio Veneto 28, and the *Caffetteria Luca*,Via Messina 273, while *Bar Conti*, Corso Umberto 275, is famed for its *latte di mándorla* (almond milk). Bronte also makes a handy jumping-off point for an extended trip into the interior of Sicily, with buses heading to Cesarò, from where a fine route, covered in Chapter Seven, cuts west into the Nébrodi hills.

Back on the Circumetnea, the pistachios give way beyond Bronte to walnuts and chestnuts, and the train passes the huge lava flow of 1823 that came close to destroying the town. A little further on, **Maletto** is the highest point on the Circumetnea line. From here, a very minor road leads west to the **Castello Maniace**, founded as a convent in 1174 on the site of a victory over the Arabs by George Maniakes, when he was attempting to regain the island for Byzantium. The 1693 earthquake destroyed much of the building, but the estate was given to Lord Nelson as part of his dukedom, granted by King Ferdinand in gratitude for British help in repressing the Neapolitan revolution of 1799, which had forced the Bourbon court to flee to Palermo. Though Nelson never got round to visiting his Sicilian estate, his family, the Bridports, only relinquished control of the property in 1978. Surrounded by a wooded estate, it's now owned by the *Comune*, but it's still known (and signposted) as "Castello Nelson".

As you pass through the walls, you'll see the restored thirteenth-century **chapel**, displaying chunky lava columns and, over the altar, a fourteenth-century polyptych above a Byzantinesque icon, the so-called *Madonna di Maniace*. As for the **house** (daily 9am–1pm & 2.30–7pm; €3), were it not for the beautiful tiled floors, restored to match the original pattern in yellow, rose and blue, it could easily be mistaken for an English country residence. Its style and furnishings – wallpaper, maritime paintings – were defined by Alexander Hood, one of the Bridports, who lived here for sixty years until the 1930s. The same Englishness is evident in the well-tended garden, planted with box hedges, magnolias and palm trees. On the other side of the river lies the only part of the estate still owned by Nelson's descendants, the English cemetery. Its most celebrated occupant is the Scottish author William Sharp (1855–1905), who wrote under the name of Fiona Macleod and was a regular visitor here. The other literary connection is the origin of the surname of the literary sisters, Anne, Charlotte and Emily; their father, the Rev Patrick Prunty, harboured such an obsession for Nelson that he changed his name to Bronte (and added an umlaut).

The garden, or the grounds outside the gates, would make a pleasant **picnic** spot, with a bar and tables and chairs under the trees. Right opposite the estate's entrance, there's the excellent 🍴 *Nelson* **agriturismo** (☎095.690.806, ⓦ www .nelsonagriturismo.it; ❹), where six air-conditioned chalets arranged on a neat lawn provide comfortable, modern accommodation, and a restaurant/pizzeria offers good-value meals: main dishes, all meat, cost €7–12.

Randazzo

Great rivers of volcanic rubble clutter the slopes on all sides of **RANDAZZO**, the closest town to the summit of the volcano, just 15km away as the crow flies. Occasionally, all that survives of a former orchard or vineyard is a wall, visible through the wreckage. Despite its dangerous proximity, the town has never been engulfed, though an eruption in 1981 came perilously close. Randazzo has not escaped entirely unscathed, however: as one of the main forward positions of the German forces during their defence of Sicily in 1943, the town was heavily bombed, and most of the lava-built churches and palaces you'll see here, originally dating from the wealthy thirteenth- to sixteenth-century era, are the result of meticulous restoration.

Arrival and information

Arriving in Randazzo on the **Circumetnea train**, walk straight up Via Vittorio Véneto to reach the central Piazza Loreto; the medieval town is down Via Umberto I and away to the left. The **bus station** is a couple of blocks back from Piazza Loreto off Via Vittorio Véneto. You'll find a limited amount of information on Etna and the surrounding area at the Parco dei Nébrodi **tourist office** at Via Umberto I 197 (daily 9am–1pm & 3–7.30pm; ☎095.799.1611, Ⓦ www.parcodeinebrodi.it).

Accommodation

Randazzo may not be exactly abounding in **accommodation** possibilities, but if you do fancy breaking your journey here, you should be able to find something that suits you.

Parco Statella Via Montelaguardia ☎095.924.036 or 347.409.7281, Ⓦ www .parcostatella.com. Two kilometres east of town along the SS120 to Linguaglossa, this *agriturismo* has rooms and mini-apartments in the various buildings of an old baronial villa. There's a superb restaurant here (see below), as well as extensive gardens and even a five-a-side football pitch. ❹

Scrivano Via Bonaventura ☎095.921.126, Ⓦ www.hotelscrivano.com. Behind the Agip petrol station, off Piazza Loreto, this plain lodging lacks much character but is adequate for a night, and there's a decent restaurant. ❺

Ai Tre Parchi Bed and Bike Via Tagliamento 49 ☎095.799.1631 or 329.897.0901, Ⓦ www.aitreparchibb.it. Excellent bike-friendly place in the centre of town, offering B&B and self-catering apartments. Walking and bike tours are organized, and bike hire is available. To reach Via Tagliamento, turn left off Via Vittorio Véneto from the station. ❹

The Town

In medieval times, three churches took it in turns to act as Randazzo's cathedral, a sop to the three parishes in town whose inhabitants were of Greek, Latin and Lombard origin and had little in common. The largest, **Santa Maria**, on the main Via Umberto I, is the modern-day holder of the title, a severe Catalan-Gothic structure incorporating chunks of volcanic rock and a fine carved portal with vine decoration. Its interior reveals impressive black lava columns, the capital of one serving as an altar. Further up the road, on the northern edge of town, lies the church of **San Martino**, notable for its restored fourteenth-century campanile, distinctively fashioned in black and white stone. Across the square, the blackened tower that forms part of the old city walls is all that survives of Randazzo's castle, which did duty as a prison from around 1500 until 1973. Nowadays, it serves as the **Museo Vagliasindi** (daily 9am–1pm & 4–8pm, or 3–7pm in winter; €2.60), which holds a good collection of objects, mainly from a nearby fifth- to second-century BC Greek necropolis. Best of all are the *oinochoe*, a jug portraying a little-known mythological scene, more wine jugs in the form of women's heads, and a vessel in the shape of a spunky little rat. Downstairs you'll find serried ranks of dangling Sicilian puppets, variously sporting armour, a velvet cloak or a deer-stalker cap – typically for eastern Sicily, they are taller than the puppets you may have seen in Palermo. The museum's other rooms, including the bare, minuscule cells where inmates once rotted, display agricultural tools and other rustic items. You can buy a combined ticket (€4) for this and another nearby collection, the **Museo delle Scienze Naturali** at Via Beccaria 2, off Via Umberto (same times), which displays a miscellany of birds, butterflies, minerals and fossils.

Eating and drinking

Restaurants in Randazzo are few and far between. In the evening, a lively *passeggiata* parades up and down Via Umberto I, where you'll also find some nice, old-fashioned **bars**, such as the intricately decorated *Arturo* at no. 75.

Parco Statella (see opposite). Run by the same management as the Veneziano and located in a former wine store, the restaurant of this out-of-town *agriturismo* offers great rustic fare, with an emphasis on wild mushrooms. The €23 fixed-price menu includes a choice of antipasti, two first courses, a second course, fruit and wine. Booking advised. Closed Wed in summer, open weekends only Oct–May. Moderate.
San Giorgio e Il Drago Piazza San Giorgio 28 ℡095.923.972. Two hundred metres from

Santa Maria, next to a ruined convent, this upmarket, reconstructed rustic spot has a good range of antipasti, fresh pasta and such meaty dishes as rabbit and *ossobuco* (shin of veal). Most main courses cost around €10. Closed Tues. Moderate.
Trattoria Veneziano Via dei Romano 8a ℡095.799.1353. A good find off Piazza Loreto, offering excellent local dishes and specializing in mushrooms. Main courses from €8–12. Closed Sun eve and Mon. Moderate.

Linguaglossa

Road and rail stick close together around the northernmost stretch of the route, passing the station at Castiglione di Sicilia (a good 5km from the town itself;) and, shortly after, running into **LINGUAGLOSSA**. The main tourist centre on Etna's north slopes, it had a narrow escape from the lava flow during the 2002 eruption, when hotels, restaurants and a ski lift were destroyed at the ski-resort of Piano Provenzana, 15km above. During the summer Linguaglossa is a quiet town with locals' bars lining the cobbled streets, and extensive pine forests out of the centre which are good for a ramble. In winter, however, especially at weekends, it fills with skiers. A very helpful **tourist office**, in Piazza Annunziata (Mon–Sat 9am–1pm & 4–8pm in summer, 3–7pm winter, Sun 9.30am–noon; ℡095.643.094, ⓦwww.prolocolinguaglossa.it), can book taxis up to Piano Provenzana if you don't have your own transport. Behind and above it, a small **museum** displays diverse objects ranging from doorknobs to mushrooms, pickled snakes and lava (same hours as office; free).

If you're going **to stay** in town, it's always worth booking ahead; try the *Happy Day*, 300m to the right of the station at Via Mareneve 9 (℡095.643.484; ❹), a decent hotel with a bar and restaurant. There are also several bed and breakfasts, among them the tidy *Villa Refe*, Via Mareneve 42 (℡095.643.926; no credit cards; ❷), offering private bathrooms, cooking facilities and parking, and *Magmar*, Via Garibaldi 56 (℡095.643.645; ❺), which has two en-suite rooms and a self-catering apartment for four.

Festivals

January
15 Festa di San Mauro in **Aci Castello**.
17 Festa di Sant'Antonio in **Nicolosi**.

February
3–5 Festa di Sant'Agata in **Catania**: boisterous street events, fireworks and food stalls, and the procession of the saint's relics.

February/March
Carnevale Five days of floats, flowers and traditional music in **Acireale** – one of Sicily's best annual events. Smaller-scale affair at **Paternò**.

March/April
Easter Good Friday procession in **Acireale** in traditional costume. Easter Sunday ceremony in **Adrano**, the Diavolata – a symbolic display showing the Archangel Michael defeating the Devil.

May
9–10 Traditional high jinks at **Trecastagni**: a pilgrimage by athletic souls who, barefoot and shirtless, run the main road linking Catania to the sanctuary at Trecastagni, and also assorted costumes, painted carts, etc.

July
19–26 Festival commemorating St Vénera in **Acireale**.
24 Pesce a Mare festival at **Aci Trezza**.

August
15 Procession of the *vara* in **Randazzo**: an 18m-high column with decorative figures representing the Assumption.

November
11 San Martino's Day celebrations in **Catania**.

December
Christmas week Display of eighteenth-century cribs in **Acireale**.

Travel details

Trains

Catania to: Acireale (1–2 hourly; 10min); Caltagirone (6 daily Mon–Sat, 3 daily Sun; 2hr); Caltanissetta (7 daily; 1hr 50min–2hr 10min); Enna (7 daily Mon–Sat; 1hr 20min); Gela (6 daily Mon–Sat, 3 daily Sun; 2hr 40min); Giarre-Riposto (1–2 hourly; 30min); Lentini (hourly; 30min); Messina (1–2 hourly; 1hr 30min); Palermo (3 daily; 3hr 45min); Siracusa (hourly; 1hr 30min); Taormina (1–2 hourly; 50min).

Circumetnea trains

Catania to: Paternò, Adrano, Bronte, Maletto, Randazzo (up to 11 daily Mon–Sat; up to 2hr). **Randazzo** to: Catania (up to 11 daily Mon–Sat; 2hr); Linguaglossa (6 daily Mon–Sat; 30min); Riposto (6 daily Mon–Sat; 1hr 10min).

Buses

Catania to: Acireale (1–2 hourly; 40min–1hr 15min); Agrigento (12 daily Mon–Sat, 7 daily Sun; 2hr 50min); Caltagirone (19 daily Mon–Sat; 1hr 30min); Enna (12 daily Mon–Sat, 3 daily Sun; 1hr 30min–2hr 25min); Gela (13 daily Mon–Fri, 8 daily Sat, 5 daily Sun; 1hr 45min); Giardini-Naxos (1–2 hourly Mon–Sat, 6 daily Sun; 20–40min); Messina (1–2 hourly Mon–Sat; 1hr 35min); Nicolosi (hourly; 40min); Nicosia (8 daily Mon–Sat, 2 daily Sun; 2hr–2hr 30min); Noto (7 daily Mon–Sat, 5 daily Sun; 1hr 25min–2hr 15min); Palermo (hourly; 2hr 40min); Piazza Armerina (3–6 daily Mon–Sat, 2 daily Sun; 1hr 50min); Ragusa (12 daily Mon–Sat, 6 daily Sun; 2hr); Rifugio Sapienza (1 daily; 2hr); Siracusa (1–2 hourly Mon–Sat, 11 daily Sun; 1hr 20min); Rome (2–3 daily; 11hr); Taormina (16 daily Mon–Sat, 6 daily Sun; 1hr 40min); Trecastagni (every 30min Mon–Sat, 2 daily Sun; 40min); Zafferana Etnea (12 daily Mon–Sat, 2 daily Sun; 1hr 15min).
Catania airport to: Agrigento (11 daily Mon–Sat, 7 daily Sun; 2hr 40min); Enna (6 daily Mon–Sat, 3 daily Sun; 1hr 10min); Messina (7–9 daily Mon–Sat, 7 daily Sun; 1hr 50min); Milazzo (1 daily June–Sept; 2hr); Siracusa (11 daily Mon–Sat, 9 daily Sun; 1hr 5min); Taormina (2 hourly Mon–Sat, 16 daily Sun; 1hr 20min).
Randazzo to: Bronte (3–4 daily Mon–Sat; 20–30min); Catania (4 daily Mon–Sat; 1hr 30min); Cesarò (2 daily Mon–Sat; 45min–1hr); Giardini-Naxos (2 daily Mon–Sat; 1hr); Linguaglossa (4 daily Mon–Sat; 30min); Maletto (2 daily Mon–Sat; 20min); Messina (2 daily Mon–Sat; 1hr 50min).

6

Siracusa and the southeast

CHAPTER 6

Highlights

✻ **Piazza del Duomo, Siracusa**
Sicily's most graceful piazza
has been beautifully restored.
See p.252

✻ **Siracusa's Teatro Greco**
Classical dramas and modern
productions are still staged in
the theatre where Aeschylus
attended performances of his
own plays. See p.259

✻ **Pantálica** Walk the gorge
to explore the thousands
of prehistoric tombs that
honeycomb this high ravine.
See p.266

✻ **Ragusa Ibla** Spend the night
in a classy B&B in Ragusa's
chic Baroque old town.
See p.271

✻ **Chocolate-tasting, Módica**
The little Baroque town with
the big crunch – sample
the goods at Sicily's oldest
chocolate manufacturer.
See p.276

✻ **Noto** The apotheosis of
Baroque town planning, Noto
offers glorious vistas at every
turn, from extravagantly
balconied *palazzi* to soaring
church facades.
See p.278

✻ **Cava Grande del Fiume
Cassibile** Eagles soar high
above the Cassibile River
canyon, while a track leads
down to secluded swimming
spots. See p.283

▲ The Teatro Greco at Neapolis, Siracusa

Siracusa and the
southeast

S icily's southeast has always ranked among the island's wealthiest regions, and in **Siracusa** it boasts a city whose long and glorious history outshines all others on the island. Indeed, Siracusa was once the most important city in the western world, though, with most business activity located elsewhere and all political power centred on Palermo, its status today is as a provincial capital. Yet it remains the most interesting destination in this part of the island, charged with historical resonance, and a useful base for visiting many other regional highlights, few more than 45 minutes' drive from the city.

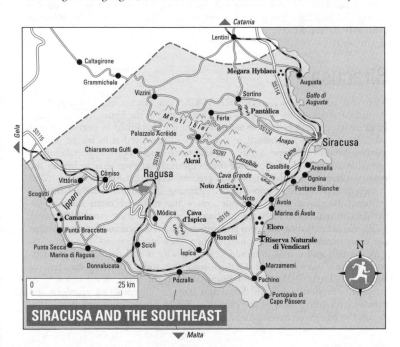

SIRACUSA AND THE SOUTHEAST

Inland, the southeast is characterized by the rough and wild **Monti Iblei**, riven by spectacular ravines, or *cave*, which are riddled with rock-cut tombs that prove occupation of the area as far back as the thirteenth century BC. The most famous is **Pantálica**, west of Siracusa, Sicily's greatest necropolis, while at the **Cava Grande del Fiume Cassibile**, near Ávola, you can peer into the distant depths of Sicily's own "Grand Canyon". Greek colonists later appropriated many early Neolithic sites, founding towns at **Megara Hyblaea**, on the coast north of Siracusa near **Augusta**, and inland at **Akrai**, just outside the attractive small town of **Palazzolo Acréide**. Several other much smaller archeological sites lie strung along the coast, often set beside otherwise unsung sand beaches.

However dramatic the natural scenery, it's the built environment that most defines the southeast. Damaging earthquakes have repeatedly afflicted the area, none so destructive as that of January 11, 1693, which affected the entire region as far north as Catania. This catastrophe did, however, have one lasting effect: where there were ruins, a confident new generation of architects raised planned towns, displaying a noble but vivacious Baroque style that endures today. The gorgeous small town of **Noto** is the pre-eminent example, though **Ragusa** – capital of its own province – and nearby **Módica**, **Scicli** and **Íspica** all hold Baroque centres of varying refinement, as local authorities have slowly awoken to their tourist potential. There are probably more B&Bs in this area than in any other region of Sicily, many housed in restored Baroque mansions, while tours and activities are increasingly available, from mountain-biking to gorge-walking.

The **coast** is a mixed bag, virtually off-limits north of Siracusa thanks to the petrochemical industry that disfigures the **Golfo di Augusta**, and otherwise largely devoted to small-scale beach dormitory towns aimed squarely at a local clientele. The only real exception is the coastline south of Noto, from **Ávola** to Sicily's southern cape, **Capo delle Correnti**, in between which lie assorted pristine beaches, old tuna-fishing villages and market-garden towns, with the undisputed highlight being the lagoons, paths and bird hides of the **Riserva Naturale di Vendicari**.

Siracusa

More than any other Sicilian city, **SIRACUSA** (ancient Syracuse) has a past that is central not just to the island's history, but to that of the entire Mediterranean. Its greatest splendour belongs to antiquity. Syracuse established its ascendancy over other Sicilian cities for more than five hundred years, and at its height was the supreme power in Europe, home to at least three times its present population. Its central position on the major trade routes ensured that even after its heyday the port continued to wield influence and preserve its prestige. All this is reflected in a staggering diversity of monuments, spanning the Hellenic, early Christian, medieval, Renaissance and Baroque eras – the styles are often shoulder-to-shoulder, sometimes in the same building. It's one of the most enjoyable cities in Sicily, with a fascinating old town and outlying archeological and leisure areas that can easily occupy three or four days, if not a week of your time.

As for two and a half thousand years, the city is still divided between its ancient hub, the island of Ortigia, and the four mainland quarters of Achradina, Tyche, Neapolis and Epipolae. **Ortigia** is the heart and soul of Siracusa, a predominantly medieval and Baroque ensemble of mansions and palaces, containing most of the city's best B&Bs, hotels, cafés and restaurants. Across the bridge on the mainland, the modern city is centred on **Achradina**, now, as in Greek times, the busy commercial centre, traversed by the main street of Corso Gelone. North of Achradina, the old residential quarter of **Tyche** holds Siracusa's celebrated **Museo Archeológico** and the extraordinary Santa Lucia and San Giovanni **catacombs** – after those in Rome, Siracusa's catacombs constitute the largest system of subterranean tombs in Italy, and are the oldest in Sicily. **Neapolis** is the site of the **Parco Archeológico**, containing remains of the Greek city's theatres and some extensive quarries, while spread over the ridge to the west of town, **Epipolae** holds the old defensive walls and the remnants of the **Euryalus fort**. Other obvious trips out of the city are to the local beaches, particularly that at **Fontane Bianche**, or a cruise along the **Fiume Ciane** (Ciane River).

A brief history

The **ancient city** grew around Ortigia, an easily defensible offshore island with two natural harbours on either side, fresh springs, and access to extensive trade routes. Though Corinthian colonists arrived here in 733 BC, apparently at the behest of the Delphic oracle, it wasn't until the start of the fifth century BC that the city's political position was boosted by an alliance with Greeks at Akragas (Agrigento) and Gela. With the crushing victory of their combined forces over the Carthaginians at Himera in 480 BC, and the transfer of Gela's tyrant, **Gelon**, to Syracuse, the stage was set for the beginning of the city's long supremacy. The grandest extant monuments are from this period, and more often than not were built by slaves provided from the many battles won by Syracuse's bellicose dictators.

Inevitably, the city's ambitions provoked the intervention of Athens, which dispatched one of the greatest fleets ever seen in the ancient world. This **Great Expedition** was scuppered in 413 BC by a mixture of poor leadership and astute defence: "to the victors the most brilliant of successes, to the vanquished the most calamitous of defeats", commented the historian Thucydides. But Syracuse earned the condemnation of the Hellenic world for its seven-year incarceration of the vanquished Athenians – in appalling conditions – in the city's notorious quarries.

Throughout this period Syracuse was in a state of constant tension between a few overweening but extremely capable rulers, and sporadic convulsions of democracy. Occasionally the tyrants displayed a yearning for cultural respectability that sat uncomfortably beside their shrewd power-seeking. **Hieron I** (478–466 BC), for instance, described by the historian Diodorus as "an utter stranger to sincerity and nobility of character", invited many of the luminaries of the age to his court, including **Pindar**, and **Aeschylus** – who possibly witnessed the production of his last plays, *Prometheus Bound* and *Prometheus Released*, in the city's theatre. **Dionysius the Elder** (405–367 BC) – "cruel, vindictive and a profane plunderer of temples" and responsible for the first of the **Euryalus** forts – comically harboured literary ambitions to the extent of regularly entering his poems in the annual Olympic Games. His works were consistently rejected, until the Athenians judged it politic to give him the prize, whereupon his delirious celebrations were enough to provoke the seizure that killed him. His son **Dionysius II** (367–343 BC) dallied with the "philosopher-king" theories of his tutor **Plato** until megalomania turned his head and Plato fled in dismay. Dionysius himself, recorded Plutarch, spent the end of his life in exile "loitering about the fish market, or sitting in a perfumer's shop drinking the diluted wine of the taverns, or squabbling in the streets with common women".

Rarely, the rulers themselves initiated democratic reforms – men such as **Timoleon** (343–337 BC), who arrived from Corinth to inject new life into all

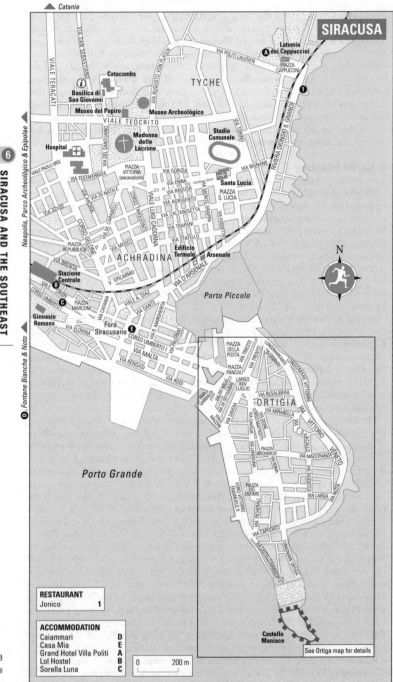

SIRACUSA

- Catania
- VIA SAN SEBASTIANO
- VIALE TERACATI
- VIA POLITI LAUDIEN
- Latomia dei Cappuccini **A**
- PIAZZA CAPPUCCINI
- Catacombs
- Basilica di San Giovanni **i**
- Museo del Papiro
- Museo Archeológico
- VIA AUGUSTO VON PLATEN
- TYCHE
- VIALE TEOCRITO
- **1**
- RIVIERA DIONISIO IL GRANDE
- Madonna delle Lácrime
- Stadio Comunale
- Hospital
- VIALE PAOLO ORSI
- VIA DEL SANTUARIO
- PIAZZA VITTORIA (excavations)
- VIA GORIZIA
- VIA TORINO
- VIA TESTAFERRATA
- VIA ENNA
- VIA RAGUSA
- VIA BIGNAMI
- Santa Lucia
- PIAZZA S. LUCIA
- VIA ADIGE
- CORSO GELONE
- VIA ANCONA
- VIA M. GARIBALDI
- VIALE LUIGI CADORNA
- CORSO TIMOLEONTE
- VIA AGRIGENTO
- VIA CALTANISETTA
- VIA MONTE GRAPPA
- VIA RUGGIETO
- VIA DI NATALE
- VIA TRAPANI
- VIA MOSCO
- VIA STATELLO
- PIAZZA REPUBBLICA
- VIA BRENTA
- ACHRADINA
- Edificio Termale
- Arsenale
- VIA D'ARSENALE
- Stazione Centrale **B**
- VIA F. CRISPI
- CORSO UMBERTO
- **C** PIAZZA MARCONI
- V. EPICARMO
- VIALE A. DIAZ
- VIA CATANIA
- Porto Píccolo
- N
- Ginnasio Romano
- VIA ELORINA
- Foro Siracusano
- VIA R. MARGHERITA
- VIALE DANTE
- CORSO UMBERTO I
- **E**
- VIA PALERMO
- VIA MALTA
- VIA BENGASI
- VIA RODI
- PIAZZA DELLA POSTA
- VIA TRIESTE
- LUNGOMARE
- LUNGOMARE VITTORINI
- PIAZZA PANCALI
- LARGO XXV LUGLIO
- VIA DEL MILLE
- VIA XX SETTEMBRE
- VIA SAVOIA
- VIA MAZZINI
- VIA RESALIBERA
- ORTIGIA
- VIA MIRABELLA
- VIA LOGOTETA
- VIA GARGALLO
- VITTORIO VENETO
- VIA GARIBALDI
- VIA MATTEOTTI
- VIA CAVOUR
- PIAZZA ARCHIMEDE
- VIA LANDOLINA
- VIA MAESTRANZA
- VIA GIUDECCA
- VIA LARGA
- VIA NIZZA
- PIAZZA DEL DUOMO
- VIA PICHERALI
- FORO VITTORIO EMANUELE II
- VIA CAPODIECI
- LUNGOMARE ORTIGIA
- VIA CASTELLO MANIACE
- Porto Grande
- Neapolis, Parco Archeológico & Epipolae
- D Fontane Bianche & Noto
- Castello Maniace
- See Ortiga map for details

RESTAURANT

| Jonico | **1** |

ACCOMMODATION

Caiammari	**D**
Casa Mia	**E**
Grand Hotel Villa Politi	**A**
Lol Hostel	**B**
Sorella Luna	**C**

0   200 m

the Sicilian cities, and **Hieron II**, who preserved Syracuse's independence from the assertions of Rome by a novel policy of conciliation, abandoning expansion in favour of preserving the status quo. His long reign (265–215 BC) saw the construction of such monuments as the **Ara di Ierone II**, and the enlargement of the **Teatro Greco** to more or less its existing proportions.

Following the death of Hieron, Syracuse, along with practically every other Sicilian city, sided with Carthage against Rome in the Second Punic War. For two years the city was besieged by the Romans, who had to contend with all the ingenious contrivances devised for its defence by **Archimedes**, though Syracuse eventually fell in 211 BC, an event that sent shock waves rippling around the classical world. The city was ransacked, and Archimedes himself – the last of the great Hellenic thinkers – was hacked to death, despite the injunctions of the Roman general Marcellus.

Syracuse languished under Roman rule, though its trading role still made it the most prominent Sicilian city, and it became a notable centre of early Christianity, as attested by its extensive **catacombs**. The city briefly became the capital of the Byzantine empire when Constans moved his court here in 663 AD, but otherwise Syracuse was eclipsed by events outside its control and played no active part against all the successive waves of Arab, Norman and other medieval conquerors. The 1693 earthquake laid low much of the city, but provided the impetus for some of its Baroque masterpieces, notably the creations of the great Siculo-Spanish architect Giovanni Verméxio, who contributed an imposing facade to the **Duomo**, itself adapted from the bones of an early Greek temple and later Norman cathedral – and thus a building that encapsulates perfectly the polyglot character of modern Siracusa.

Arrival, information and transport

The **train station** is on the mainland at the end of Via Francesco Crispi, while AST and Interbus regional **buses** stop just around the corner on the parallel Corso Umberto. You can walk from here to Ortigia in around twenty minutes, or there's a taxi rank outside the train station. Many of the orange AST **city buses** also make a stop at the bus terminal, while on Ortigia the main stop is at Riva della Posta (outside the main post office, close to the bridge). Routes are sometimes impaired by road closures, but most main routes run up Corso Umberto, stop at the bus terminal and then head up Corso Gelone. Tickets (valid for 2hr) must be bought in advance; they're available from booths at the bus terminal and in Piazza della Posta, or from any *tabacchi*.

Drivers will find the city a breeze after Palermo and Catania, though driving onto the island of Ortigia is restricted and street parking there is almost impossible for non-residents. However, there is a monumental parking garage called **Talete**, to which all visitors are directed, at the end of Via Trieste (look for the sign) on the lungomare. It's free up until 9pm and you pay just €1 to leave your car there overnight – buy a ticket from the machine. The garage is an easy walk from the centre of Ortigia, though a free **shuttle-bus** (*navetta*) leaves from outside every fifteen minutes, dropping passengers in Piazza Pancali and Piazza Archimede.

There's a useful **tourist office** on Ortigia, at Via Maestranza 33 (summer Mon–Sat 8.30am–1.45pm & 4.30–7pm; winter Mon–Thurs 8.30am–1.45pm & 3–5.30pm, Fri 8.30am–1.45pm; ℡0931.464.255), which posts current opening hours and bus routes for all city attractions. The main office, covering the whole province, is on the mainland opposite the Basilica de San Giovanni at Via San Sebastiano 43 (Mon–Fri 8.30am–1.30pm & 3–6pm, Sat 8.30am–1pm; ℡0931.67.710, ⓦwww.apt-siracusa.it).

Accommodation

Siracusa holds a lot of **accommodation**, much of it in the old town on Ortigia, which is by far the best place to stay. Development here has been rapid in the last few years, with scores of **B&Bs** opening and at least two new water-front four-star hotels due by 2009. Unless your chosen establishment has private parking, it's best to leave the car overnight in the Talete garage. The very cheapest beds are at the **youth hostel** by the train station; **camping** is not so convenient, with the best local site actually 20km to the south at Fontane Bianche beach. For **longer stays** contact Lynette Chaplin (T0931.464.362 or 339.685.8461, Wwww.casa-giulietta.it), who has two self-contained studios beneath her home on Ortigia, one double with sitting area (from €245–385 per week), and one small single (€175–245).

Hotels and B&Bs

L'Acanto Via Roma 15 T0931.461.129, Wwww .bebsicilia.it. Central Ortigia B&B with small but neat en-suite rooms; the one at the front can be noisy, others are grouped around a courtyard. ❹

🏃 **Alla Giudecca** Via Alagona 52 T0931.22.255, Wwww.allagiudecca.it. A stunning renovation in the old Jewish quarter has brought an interconnected series of medieval houses back to life as an exquisite little boutique hotel. There's exposed stone, soaring arches, colourful tapestries and dried flowers everywhere, while the 23 rooms feature eye-catching wrought-iron beds, flagged floors and antique furniture. ❻

L'Approdo delle Sirene Riva Garibaldi 15 T0931.24.857, Wwww.apprododellesirene.com. B&B in a tastefully renovated Ortigia waterfront building. The rooms are mostly nice and bright, though you pay a premium for balconies and views, while great home-made breakfasts are served on a terrace overlooking the sea. There's also a boat available for excursions, canoes for hire and bikes for free use around town. ❻

🏃 **Ares** Via Mirabella 49 T0931.461.145 or 338.788.5687, Wwww .aresbedandbreakfast.it. The owner, Enzo, has restored this Ortigia townhouse with great flair, searching Sicily for antique furniture to set off the spacious, modern rooms, which have pattern tile floors, wooden beams, pristine stonework and street balconies. There's a terrific roof garden with colourful Caltanissetta floor tiles and rooftop views; breakfast is by voucher in the Piazza del Duomo café, a few minutes' walk away. ❺

Casa Mia Corso Umberto 112 T0931.463.349, Wwww.bbcasamia.it. Not on Ortigia, but not far away either, there's attentive service at this friendly B&B. The quiet rooms are furnished with grand old antique beds, and are separate from the family's living quarters, though there's a shared terrace where breakfast is served in summer. ❹

Diana Piazza Archimede 2 T0931.722.232. The location's great, in an old mansion on the piazza, and two of the three B&B rooms have a balcony overlooking the fountain. Breakfast is served at a café below. Closed Jan & Feb. No credit cards. ❹

Domus Mariae Via Vittorio Veneto 76 T0931.24.858, Wwww.sistemia.it/domusmariae. Most of the rooms here have views to the sea, and they are all efficiently maintained if a little plain – all becomes clear when you know that the building was originally a religious school, and it's still owned and run by an order of nuns. It's three-star standard, with roof terrace, parking and, of course, its own chapel. ❼

Grand Viale Mazzini 12 T0931.464.600, Wwww .grandhotelsr.it. This veteran four-star establish-ment enjoys a prime position in Ortigia, overlooking the Porto Grande. The overall style is fin-de-siècle luxury, though rooms are contemporary updates, and for the considerable bill (sea-view rooms from €250) you also get a terrific panoramic restaurant and access to a private beach. ❾

Grand Hotel Villa Politi Via M. Politi 2 T0931.412.121, Wwww.villapoliti.com. Really the only quality choice on the mainland worth considering, the four-star Villa Politi was once a rich-and-famous port of call, though it's been rather superseded in recent years by more contemporary, more convenient places. Still, it's a comfortable, if idiosyncratic hotel, built right on top of the Cappuccini quarries, which are effectively the hotel gardens, and it has a large outdoor pool. ❽

🏃 **Gutkowski** Lungomare Vittorini 26 T0931.465.861, Wwww.guthotel.it. There's a real seaside feel to this lovely townhouse hotel on Ortigia's east side, whose chic bare-bones rooms have tile floors, stylish furnishings and good bathrooms. Only four have face-on sea views, and you can't usually guarantee one of these without a long advance reservation. Breakfast includes fresh juice from organic oranges, locally made preserves and, in summer, almond granita. There's parking in front of the hotel, or at nearby Talete garage. ❻

🏃 **Roma** Via Roma 66 ☎ 0931.465.626, Ⓦ www.hotelroma.sr.it. A serene four-star oasis in the old centre, the chic Roma presents spacious, contemporary rooms with wood-block floors and excellent bathrooms. Staff are charming, breakfast is an extensive buffet spread, and there's also a fine-dining restaurant, fitness area and sauna. There's more of a resort feel at the sister

hotel, *Caiammari* (Ⓦ www.caiammari.sr.it), a restored country villa across the bay, with lovely gardens and two pools – this is not central, but there's a shuttle service to and from Siracusa and nearby Arenella beach. ❼

Sorella Luna Via Francesco Crispi 23 ☎ 0931.21.178, Ⓦ www.sorellalunasrl.it. A step up in quality from the cheap hotels near the train station, this classy three-star, housed in a renovated conventual building, has tasteful modern rooms in bold colours, and offers breakfast on a sunny terrace under a gazebo. There's free street parking right outside. ❺

Youth hostel

Lol Hostel Via Francesco Crispi 92 ☎ 0931.465.088, Ⓦ www.lolhostel.com. The city's hostel is just a few steps down from the train station, in a converted old hotel, with either four-bed dorms or private singles and doubles, all

air-conditioned and with en-suite bathrooms. Reception is 24-hr, no membership is required, and there's Internet access and the cheapest bike rental in town, plus use of a kitchen. Dorms €20, rooms ❷, June–Sept & hols ❸

Campsite

Fontane Bianche Fontane Bianche, 20km south of Siracusa ☎ 0931.790.333. This big summer campsite, just a short walk from the beach, is the best-equipped site for campers,

though you'll need to be more geared towards beach and bar than city sightseeing. Take bus #21 or #22 from Riva della Posta on Ortigia. Open May–Oct.

Ortigia

The ancient nucleus of Siracusa, **Ortigia** best conserves the city's essential spirit. Here the artistic vestiges of over 2500 years of history are concentrated in a space barely 500m across, 1km in length and all within an easy stroll through quiet streets and alleys. Although parts of Ortigia were badly neglected in the past, there's been a lot of sensitive restoration and development in recent years, which has helped to restore the old town's lustre.

The Tempio di Apollo and Piazza Archimede

Siracusa announces its long history immediately across the narrow ribbon of water that severs the island from the mainland. The **Tempio di Apollo**, on Largo XXV Luglio, is thought to have been the first of the great Doric temples built in Sicily (seventh-century or early sixth-century BC) and, though not much survives apart from a couple of columns and part of the south wall of its cella, it's a dignified old ruin. A scale model in Siracusa's archeological museum shows you what it looked like in its heyday – the arched window in the wall dates from a Norman church that incorporated part of the temple into its structure.

Ortigia's **market** (Mon–Sat mornings) spreads along nearby Via Trento, with fish and shellfish sold down the parallel Via de Benedictis. The other way, up the shopping street of Corso Matteotti, leads to **Piazza Archimede**, its centrepiece a twentieth-century fountain depicting the nymph Arethusa (the symbol of Ortigia) at the moment of her transformation into a spring. The square is surrounded by restored medieval *palazzi*, while down the skinny Via Montalto you can admire the facade of the **Palazzo Montalto**, graced by immaculate

▲ Fountain in Piazza Archimede, Ortigia

double- and triple-arched windows, and with an inscription dating the building's construction to 1397. This is one of the few surviving examples of the style favoured by the powerful Chiaramonte dynasty.

Piazza del Duomo

Ortigia's most impressive architecture belongs to its Baroque period, and nowhere does this reach such heights as in the city's (some would say Sicily's) loveliest square, the **Piazza del Duomo**. It's been gloriously restored, and the traffic kept out, so that the encircling seventeenth- and eighteenth-century buildings are now seen at their best from the pavement cafés, notably the **Municipio** (corner of Via Minerva) and the **Palazzo Beneventano** opposite. The southern end of the piazza is marked by the late seventeenth-century church of **Santa Lucia alla Badia**, dedicated to the city's patron saint. Her festival day (December 13) sees thousands thronging in the piazza, as the saint's statue is carried through town.

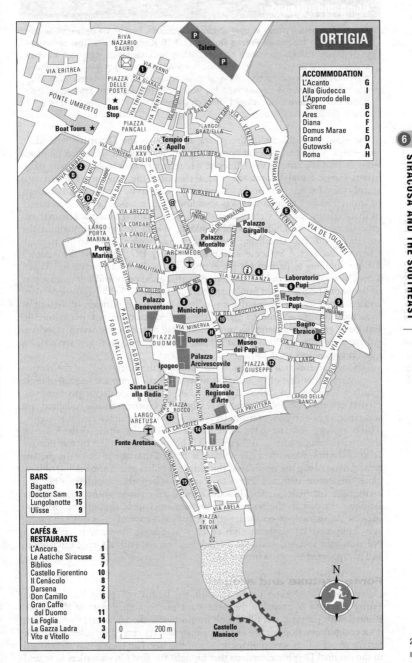

ORTIGIA

RIVA NAZARIO SAURO

VIA PERNO

P Talete

P

VIA ERITREA

VIA GIARACA

PIAZZA DELLE POSTE

VIA TRIESTE

VIA TRENTO

VIA RESALIBERA

VIA BAG NARA

VIA V. VENETO

PONTE UMBERTO

★ Bus Stop

PIAZZA PANCALI

LARGO GRAZIELLA

Boat Tours ★

LARGO XXV LUGLIO

Tempio di Apollo ∴

C SO G. MATTEOTTI

VIA RESALIBERA

A

LUNGOMARE ELIO VITTORINI

RIVA GARIBALDI

2

VIALE DEL MILLE

VIA XX SETTEMBRE

VIA SAVOIA

VIA MIRABELLA

C

VIA V. VENETO

VIA DE TOLOMEI

B

D

VIA AREZZO

@ VIA TINTORI

E

LARGO PORTA MARINA

VIA CORDARI

VIA CANDELAI

VIA GEMMELLARO

PIAZZA ARCHIMEDE

VIA DEL MONGIBELLESI

Palazzo Montalto

Palazzo Gargallo

VIA S. CORONATI

Porta Marina

VIA RUGGERO SETTIMO

VIA AMALFITANIA

3 F

VIA CHIUSI

i 4

VIA MAESTRANZA

Laboratorio Pupi 6

VIA DELLA GIUDECCA

VIA VIGLIENA

9

PASSEGGIO ADORNO

FORO ITALICO

VIA COLLEGIO

VIA CONS. REG.

7 5 6

Teatro Pupi

VIA DELLA MALTA

Palazzo Beneventano

8 Municipio

VIA DEL CROCIFISSO

Bagno Ebraico

VIA MINERVA

10

VIA ROMA

VIA LOGOTETA

H

11 PIAZZA DUOMO

✝ Duomo

Museo dei Pupi

VIA M. MINNITI

VIA NIZZA

VIA FELO

Ipogeo

Palazzo Arcivescovile

PIAZZA S GIUSEPPE 12

VIA LARGA

LARGO DELLA GANCIA

Santa Lucia alla Badia

VIA CONCILIAZIONE

Museo Regionale d'Arte

PIAZZA S. ROCCO

VIA PICHERALI

13

LARGO ARETUSA

VIA CAPODIECI

14 San Martino

VIA PRIVITERA

Fonte Aretusa

VIA S. TERESA

LUNGOMARE ALFEO

VIA SALOMONE

VIA MANIACE

15

VIA ABELA

PIAZZA F. DI SVEVIA

⊠

Castello Maniace

N

0   200 m

ACCOMMODATION

L'Acanto	G
Alla Giudecca	I
L'Approdo delle Sirene	B
Ares	C
Diana	F
Domus Marae	E
Grand	D
Gutowski	A
Roma	H

BARS

Bagatto	12
Doctor Sam	13
Lungolanotte	15
Ulisse	9

CAFÉS & RESTAURANTS

L'Ancora	1
Le Aatiche Siracuse	5
Biblios	7
Castello Fiorentino	10
Il Cenácolo	8
Darsena	2
Don Camillo	6
Gran Caffe del Duomo	11
La Foglia	14
La Gazza Ladra	3
Vite e Vitello	4

Going underground

An entrance on the piazza in the Palazzo Arcivescovile, next to the cathedral, leads down into the **Ipogeo di Piazza Duomo** (daily 9.30am–1pm; €2). This series of underground tunnels and water cisterns, dating back centuries, was used by the *siracusani* as an air-raid shelter during the heavy Allied bombing of 1943, and a small exhibition tells you something of the inhabitants' day-to-day experience. Then you can follow one of the tunnels right the way under the piazza, to emerge by the harbour on the Foro Italico, close to the Fonte Aretusa.

The absolute highlight of the piazza, however, is the **Duomo** itself (daily 8am–noon & 4–7pm, closes at 6pm in winter), whose great age is first glimpsed from around the side in Via Minerva, where stout Doric columns (part of an earlier Greek temple) form the very skeleton of the structure. The site was already sacred when the Greeks started work on an Ionic temple to Athena here in about 530 BC, though this was abandoned when a new temple was begun in thanksgiving for the victory over the Carthaginians at Himera. The extravagant decoration that adorned this building spread its fame throughout the ancient world, and tantalizing details of it have come down to us through Cicero, who visited Syracuse in the first century BC and listed the temple's former contents as part of his prosecution of the Roman praetor and villain Verres, who appeared to have walked off with a good proportion of them – part of the booty he plundered from many Sicilian temples. The doors were of ivory and gold, and its walls painted with military scenes and portraits of various of Syracuse's tyrants – claimed to be the earliest examples of portraiture in European art. On the temple's roof stood a tall statue of the warrior-goddess Athena carrying a golden shield which, catching the sun's rays, served as a beacon for sailors out at sea.

Although all this rich decoration has vanished, the main body of the temple was saved further despoliation thanks to its conversion into a Christian church, which was elevated to cathedral status in 640 AD. A more drastic overhaul was carried out after the 1693 earthquake, when the Norman facade collapsed and was replaced by the present formidable Baroque front, with statues by Marabitti. This is in sharp contrast to the more muted **interior**, in which it's the frame of the ancient temple that is still prevalent. The aisles are formed by the massive Doric columns, while the cella walls were hacked through to make the present arched nave. Along the north aisle, the distorted pillars give some inkling of how close the entire structure came to toppling when the seventeenth-century earthquake hit Siracusa. The Duomo's south aisle shows more characteristic Baroque effusion in the series of richly ornate chapels, though the first one (nearest the main door, on the right) – actually the baptistry – is from an earlier age. Enlivened by some twelfth-century arabesque mosaics, it contains a Norman font that was cut from a block still marked with a Greek inscription, and is supported by seven bronze lions.

Fonte Aretusa and around

Down from the Duomo to the seafront, the freshwater spring known as the **Fonte Aretusa** is probably the next most photographed part of the island. Planted with papyrus, and filled with bream below the water and ducks above, it's a compulsory stop on the evening *passeggiata*. It's ringed by cafés, while the terrace above offers sweeping views across the bay. The spring was mentioned in the original Delphic directions that brought the first Greek settlers here, and

the number of myths with which it's associated underlines the strong senti-
mental links that continued to bind the colonists to their motherland. This was
where the nymph Arethusa rose after swimming across from the Peloponnese,
having been metamorphosed into a spring by the goddess Artemis to escape the
attentions of the predatory river-god Alpheus; all in vain, though, for the determined Alpheus pursued her here to mingle with her in a watery form. Other
legends declared that the spring's water would stain red at the time of the annual
sacrifices at the sanctuary of Olympia, and that a cup thrown into the river there
would rise here in Ortigia.

The promenade runs both ways from the Fonte Aretusa, south towards the
castle and north along the tree-lined Foro Italico to the **Porta Marina**, a
fifteenth-century gateway surmounted by a curlicued Spanish heraldic device.
The vast, still pool of the **Porto Grande** spreads out beyond, dotted with
fishing-boats, liners and tankers, and the odd millionaire's yacht.

Head inland instead, along Via Capodieci, and Siracusa's tradition of architectural hybridism is again apparent in the **Palazzo Bellomo** (Via Capodieci 14),
with a courtyard that features thirteenth-century arcading and a Spanish-style
stairway leading up to the loggia. The palace is the home of the city's **Museo
Regionale d'Arte Medioevale e Moderna**, which is currently closed for
long-term restoration, though one of its former treasures, Caravaggio's *Burial of
St Lucy*, has in the meantime been returned to the Basilica Santa Lucia, up in
the modern city. Just around the corner in Via San Martino, the church of **San
Martino** is among Siracusa's oldest. Originally a sixth-century basilica, it was
rebuilt in the fourteenth century and smartened up with a good-looking rose
window and Gothic doorway. It's usually closed except for ceremonies and
concerts, but the dusky interior is a treat – plain stone columns leading to a tiny
mosaic half-apse with a fifteenth-century triptych to the right of the choir.

Castello Maniace

The dangling southern limb of Ortigia is entirely taken up by the parade
grounds and buildings of the stout **Castello Maniace** (Mon–Sat
8.30am–1.30pm, last entry 1pm; €2), a defensive bulwark erected around 1239
by Frederick II, but named after George Maniakes, the Byzantine admiral who
briefly reconquered Syracuse from the Arabs in 1038. Now that the military has
moved out, the barracks buildings are used by the university's archeological
department, while visitors are allowed to enter through the imposing main gate
and wander the echoing halls, chambers and defensive ramparts. Restoration
work continues to shore up the neglected castle interior – one of the rooms
displays a copy of the famous bronze ram statue, known as *L'Ariete*, a pair of
which once guarded the castle gates. The original is now in Palermo's archeological museum.

The Giudecca

Via della Giudecca, off Via Maestranza, recalls Siracusa's old **Jewish quarter**,
which existed in the skinny alleys here until the mass expulsion of 1492. The
site of the ritual baths has been uncovered on Via Alagona, underneath the *Alla
Giudecca* hotel (no. 52), and there are short tours on the hour of what's now
known as the **Bagno Ebraico** (Mon–Sat 11am–7pm, Sun at 11am & noon;
€5). On Via della Giudecca itself, the city's most famous **puppet theatre**
company survives – the theatre is at nos. 17–19 (see "Eating, nightlife and entertainment"), but don't miss the tiny **Laboratorio** (Mon–Sat 9.30am–1pm &
4–8pm; free), or workshop, down the street at no. 5, where craftsmen create little
suits of armour for knights and Saracens, as well as devils and monsters and all

the other stage-show paraphernalia. Meanwhile, the **Museo Aretuso dei Pupi**, on nearby Piazza San Giuseppe (Tues–Sat 10.30am–1pm & 3–7pm; winter 11am–1pm & 4–8pm; Sun all year 10.30am–1pm; €2; ⓦwww.pupari.com) delves further into the history of puppet theatre in Sicily.

Mainland Siracusa

Modern development in the mainland quarters of Siracusa makes it difficult to picture the ancient city that Plutarch wept over when he heard of its fall to the Romans. Much of the new building dates from World War II, when Siracusa was bombed twice over – once by the Allies, then, after its capture, by the Luftwaffe in 1943. But even so, some extraordinary relics survive, both in **Achradina**, the nearest mainland quarter to Ortigia, but far more impressively in the northern district of **Neapolis**, where the main archeological park is sited. There's plenty more to see too in **Tyche**, the location of the city's unsurpassed **archeological museum**, while that district in particular is riddled with underground **catacombs** (two are open to the public). Regular city buses run to all these places, departing from Riva della Posta on Ortigia, or you can walk to the museum, catacombs or archeological park in under half an hour from Ortigia.

Achradina

Over the bridges from Ortigia, the main drag of Corso Umberto runs up to the park area known as the **Foro Siracusano**, once site of the old town's *agora*. There's not much to see, though the gardens and main street approaches are slowly being restored and improved, so it might become a more pleasant place for a stroll in years to come. On Via Elorina, to the west, the little-visited **Ginnasio Romano** (Mon–Sat 9am–1pm; free) was never actually a gymnasium at all but a small Roman theatre, probably built in the first century AD when the ancient city's much grander Greek theatre was requisitioned for blood sports.

Over on the eastern edge of Achradina, close by the crowded huddle of boats in the Porto Píccolo, you'll find a much less recognizable ruin, the **Arsenale**, by the railway line, which is fenced off to the public. This was a provisions centre, where ships were refurbished, hoisted up from the port by devices that clamped into the ground – and the slots that engaged them are about the only thing to look at here. Adjacent is the **Edificio Termale**, a Byzantine bathhouse claimed to be the very same one in which, in 668 AD, the Emperor Constans was assassinated, knocked on the head by a servant wielding a soap dish. It lies under a modern block of flats, and only a few piles of stones are visible.

Basilica Santa Lucia

At the northern end of the huge Piazza Santa Lucia sits the church of **Santa Lucia** (daily 9.30am–12.30pm & 3–6pm; €5, joint ticket with San Giovanni catacombs €8), built in 1629 and supposedly marking the spot where St Lucy, Siracusa's patron saint, was martyred in 304 AD. The church retains its fine wooden ceiling and Norman tower, while outside in the piazza stands Giovanni Verméxio's octagonal chapel of **San Sepolcro** – the mortal remains of the saint were originally preserved below the chapel, before being carried off to Constantinople by the Byzantine admiral Maniakes in 1038, and later shipped to Venice as part of the spoils plundered by the Venetian "crusaders" in 1204. The point of a visit, however, is to view Caravaggio's *Burial of St Lucy*, returned to prominence in the church after a long restoration and, even more excitingly, to explore part of the extensive network of **catacombs** lying beneath this site. Tours take off at intervals during the opening hours; buses #2 or #5 run close by.

Santuario della Madonna delle Lácrime and Museo del Papiro

The gargantuan **Santuario della Madonna delle Lácrime** (daily 8am–noon & 4–7pm; bus #1 or #4), fronting Viale Teócrito, dominates the skyline on most approaches to Siracusa. It was completed in 1994 to house a statue of the Madonna that allegedly wept for five days in 1953 (*delle Lácrime* means "of the tears"), and the church was apparently designed to resemble a giant teardrop (or possibly one of Tracy Island's missing Thunderbirds). As you can't sink a spade into the ground in Siracusa without turning up a relic or two, it came as no surprise during the building work to discover the extensive remains of **Greek and Roman houses** and streets, which are fenced-off but visible just to the south in Piazza della Vittória.

Across the main Viale Teócrito from the church, next to the archeological museum grounds, the small **Museo del Papiro** (Tues–Sun 9am–1.30pm; free) is worth a visit to see papyrus art, ancient and modern, including models of boats and even sandals made of the stuff. Ever since papyrus was introduced to Siracusa in the reign of Hieron II, there's been a thriving papyrus industry here, and gift shops on Ortigia are awash with the stuff.

Museo Archeológico

If you have any interest at all in the archeological finds made in this extraordinary city, then all roads lead to Siracusa's **Museo Archeológico**, on Viale Teócrito (Tues–Sat 9am–7pm, Sun 9am–2pm; last entry 1hr before closing; €6, joint ticket with Parco Archeológico €10; bus #1 or #4). It was purpose-built for Sicily's most wide-ranging collection of antiquities, and it's certainly worth seeing, though there are caveats. It's often extremely confusing to find your way around, with notes in English either non-existent or mind-numbingly detailed and academic, and to cap it all sections are sometimes closed as continuing renovations attempt to address its organizational shortcomings. The museum is basically split into four sections: prehistoric (section A); items from Syracuse, Megara Hyblaea and the Chalcidinian colonies (B); finds from Gela, Agrigento, Syracuse's subcolonies and the indigenous Sikel centres (C); and Greek and Roman Siracusa (D).

It's section D that's the easiest to understand; no coincidence that it's the most recently opened. Here, Siracusa in the **Greek and Roman age** is laid bare in an extraordinary series of tomb finds and public statues, none more celebrated than the statue of **Venus Anadiomene**, also known as *Landolina*, after the archeologist who discovered her in 1804. *Anadiomene* means "rising from the sea", which describes her coy pose: with her left hand she holds a robe, while studs show where her broken-off right arm came across to hide her breasts. Probably Roman-made in the first century AD, from a Greek model, the headless statue has always evoked extreme responses, alternately exalting the delicacy and naturalism of the carving, and condemning her knowing sensual attitude that symbolized the decline of the vigorous classical age and the birth of a new decadence. By the statue's feet, the dolphin, Aphrodite's emblem, is the only sign that this was a goddess. Of the tomb finds, pride of place is given to the superb **Sarcófago di Adelfia**: a finely worked fourth-century marble tomb found in the catacombs below San Giovanni. It held the wife of a Roman official, the couple prominently depicted and surrounded by reliefs of scenes from the Old and New Testaments.

Elsewhere, eyes will possibly glaze over eventually at the thousands of pottery shards, burial urns, amphorae, statues, figures and temple fragments. However, **section B** does at least put many of the finds into context, showing where excavations occurred in the city, and even reconstructing useful models of the fallen temples. Among the earlier Hellenic pieces, the museum has some excellent **kouroi** – toned, muscular youths, one of which, from Lentini, is one of the most outstanding fragments still extant from the Archaic age of Greek art – around 500 BC. A striking image from the colony of Megara Hyblaea dates from the same period: a **mother/goddess suckling twins**, its absorbed roundness expressing a tender harmony as close to earth and fertility rites as the *Venus Landolina* is to the cult of sensuality.

The catacombs at Basilica di San Giovanni

Close to the museum lies the most extensive series of catacombs in the city, their presence explained by the Roman prohibition on Christian burial within the city limits (Siracusa having by then shrunk back to its original core of Ortigia). They lie below the ruined **Basilica di San Giovanni** (daily 9.30am–12.30pm & 2.30–5.30pm; €5, joint ticket with Basilica Santa Lucia €8), just opposite the tourist office on Via San Sebastiano. Fronted by a triple arch, most of the church was toppled in the 1693 earthquake and the nave is now open to the sky, but you can still admire the seventh-century apse and a medieval rose window. This was once the city's cathedral, built over the crypt of St Marcian, first bishop of Siracusa, flogged to death in 254.

The tours (departing regularly) take you down into the crypt to see Marcian's tomb, the remnants of some Byzantine frescoes and an altar that marks the spot where St Paul is supposed to have preached, when he stopped in the city as a prisoner on his way to Rome. Then, you're led into the catacombs themselves, labyrinthine warrens hewn out of the rock, though often following the course of underground aqueducts, disused since Greek times. Numerous side-passages

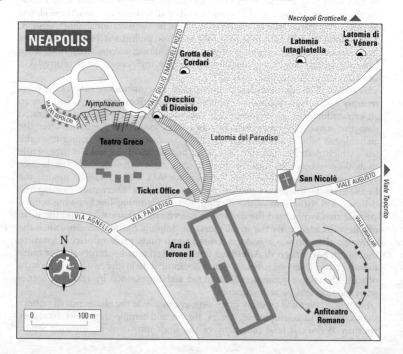

lead off from the main gallery (*decumanus maximus*), often culminating in *rotonde*, or round caverns used for prayer; other passages are forbiddingly dark and closed off to the public. Entire families were interred in the thousands of niches hollowed out of these walls and floors, anxious for burial close to the tomb of St Marcian. Most of the treasures buried with the bodies have been pillaged, though the robbers overlooked one – an ornate Roman-era sarcophagus unearthed from just below the floor in 1872 and now on show in the archeological museum.

Parco Archeológico della Neapolis

Siracusa's **Parco Archeológico** (Tues–Sun 9am–7pm; €6, joint ticket with archeological museum €10) encompasses the classical city district that was Neapolis. This contained most of the ancient city's social and religious amenities – theatres, altars and sanctuaries – and was thus never inhabited, though these days it's in danger of disappearing under the sheer weight of visitors. The ticket office is hidden beyond a street market of souvenir stalls and ice-cream stands, catering to the busloads of tourists that arrive every few minutes in the summer. Many buses run right past the approach road to the site, including #1, #3, #6, #8, #10, #11, #12 and #13, but basically you can catch anything that goes up Corso Gelone and Viale Tercati/Viale Teócrito.

From the ticket office, you ascend to the **Teatro Greco**, Siracusa's most spectacular monument. One of the largest and best-preserved Greek auditoriums anywhere, its site has been home to a theatre since at least the fifth century BC, though it was frequently added to at different periods. Hieron II expanded it to accommodate 15,000 people, in nine sections of 59 rows (of which 42 remain). The inscriptions around the top of the middle gangway on the west side of the theatre – faint but still visible – date from the third century BC, giving the names of the ruler and his family, with Zeus Olympios in the middle. Most of the alterations carried out by the Romans were made to adapt the arena for gladiatorial combat, and they also installed some marble-faced seats for privileged spectators, while the seventeenth row was removed, possibly to segregate the classes. The high terrace above the theatre contains the **Nymphaeum**, a large artificial grotto (fed by water from an ancient aqueduct) where a number of statues were found. To the left of here, the overgrown **Via dei Sepolcri** (Street of the Tombs) is deeply rutted by the carts that plied to and fro, and is flanked by more votive niches.

At the ticket office, another path descends to the largest of Siracusa's huge *latomie* (pits or quarries), from which the rock for the city's multifarious monuments was excavated. Now planted with citrus, oleander and bay trees, the so-called **Latomia del Paradiso** is more garden than quarry, and a steady stream of tour parties troops down mainly to see the remarkable ear-shaped cavern known as the **Orecchio di Dionisio** (Ear of Dionysius), which is over

▲ Latomia del Paradiso, Neapolis

60m long and 20m high. A second cave, the **Grotta dei Cordari**, was used by the ancient city's ropemakers, who found that its damp air prevented rope strands from breaking under stress. However, this and the other two neighbouring quarries remain closed indefinitely to visitors, and most of the garden paths are blocked off, which makes the overrun Latomia del Paradiso a bit of a disappointment – the Cappuccini quarries are far more exciting to visit.

On your way to the ticket office, you'll have passed the ruined base of the **Ara di Ierone II** (no public access), a 200-metre-long altar erected by Hieron II in the second half of the third century BC. It commemorated the achievements of Timoleon, who liberated the city from tyranny and decline, and was the biggest construction of its kind in all Magna Graecia. It was also the venue for some serious sacrificing: Diodorus records that 450 bulls were led up the ramps at either end of the altar to be slaughtered in the annual feast. Nearby, there's also a separate entrance to the **Anfiteatro Romano** (show your park ticket), a large elliptical arena built in the third century AD to satisfy the growing lust for circus games. The rectangular tank in the centre of the arena is too small to have been used for aquatic displays, and is more likely to have been for draining the blood and gore spilled in the course of the combats. But not before the spectators had had their fill: at the end of the contests the infirm, ill and disabled would attempt to suck warm blood from the bodies and take the livers from the animals, in the belief that this would speed their recovery.

Latomie dei Cappuccini

If you were disappointed by the quarries at the archeological park, you'll be charmed by the **Latomie dei Cappuccini** (Mon–Fri 9am–1pm, last entry at 12.15pm; €2), gouged out of the hillside below the Cappuccini monastery and *Grand Hotel Villa Politi* in the north of the city. Buses #2 and #4 run right to the gates (Largo Latomia), and it's a nice idea to combine a visit with lunch at the excellent *Jonico* restaurant. Known since at least the sixth century BC, the wide, vertically walled quarries provided a harsh but effective prison for the 7000 Athenian prisoners of war following the fiasco of the Great Expedition. The quarries were later acquired by Capuchin monks in the sixteenth century, who turned them into both market garden and contemplative retreat, which is why the cavern floors are so lush. Sinuous paths wind through the overgrown quarries, past natural rock pillars, huge caverns and early Christian tombs – there's even a cavern-theatre down here, sometimes used for performances – and as you delve further and further in, the city noise and traffic slowly dissipates.

Epipolae and the Castello Eurialo

The outlying area of **Epipolae**, 7km west of the city, was the site of ancient Siracusa's military and defensive works. It's a twenty-minute ride on bus #11 or #25 to the village of Belvedere, and you can also pick up the bus from Corso Gelone outside the Parco Archeológico.

These heights were first fortified by Dionysius the Elder in about 400 BC, and subsequently modified and extended over a couple of centuries. What remains today consists of a great wall, which marked the city's western limit, and the **Castello Eurialo** (daily 9am–1hr before sunset; €2), just before the village on the right. This is the major extant Greek fortification in the Mediterranean, most of it dating from Hieron II's time, when Archimedes, as his General of Ordnance, must have been actively involved in its renovation. Despite the effort and ingenuity that went into making this site impregnable, the castle has no very glorious history: ignored altogether by the attacking Carthaginians, it surrendered without a fight to the Roman forces of Marcellus in 212 BC.

Assailants had to cope with three defensive trenches, designed to keep the new artillery of the time at bay, as well as siege-engines and battering rams. The first of the trenches (approached from the west, where you come in) lay just within range of catapults mounted on the five towers of the castle's keep, while in the trench below the keep you can see the high piers supporting the drawbridge

Just southwest of the city, the source of the **Fiume Ciane** (Ciane River) forms a pool said to have been created by the tears of the nymph Cyane when her mistress Perse-phone was abducted into the underworld by Hades. The pool and the river banks are overgrown by thickets of papyrus, apparently the gift of Ptolemy Philadelphus of Egypt to Hieron II, making this the only place outside North Africa where the plant grows wild. **Boat cruises** operate between early March and mid-November from the bridge over the Ciane, about a five-kilometre signposted drive from Siracusa on the SS115, or take bus #21, #22 or #23 from Riva della Posta. There are daily departures between 9.30am and 4.30pm, with tickets costing around €10 per person. As well as the river, you'll also see the scant but evocative remains of the **Olympieion**, or Tempio di Giove Olimpico, a Doric temple built in the first half of the sixth century BC. The hillock the ruin stands on, a vital strategic point in classical times, was often occupied by Siracusa's enemies when the city was under attack. The pestilential air of the Lysimelia marshes below saved the day on more than one occasion, infecting the hostile armies with malaria.

that once crossed it. Long galleries burrow beneath the walls into the keep, serving as supply and escape routes, and also enabling the defenders to clear out by night the material thrown in by attackers during the day.

Behind the keep is a long, wedge-shaped fortification, to the north of which is the main gateway to the western quarter of the city. This, the **Epipolae gate**, was built indented from the walls, allowing the defenders to shower attackers with missiles, and is reminiscent of the main gate at Tyndaris, a city that shared the same architects. The longest of the underground passages surfaces here, stretching 180m from the defensive trenches. From the gate, you can stroll along Dionysius' extensive walls, looking down over the oil refineries and tankers off the coast north of the city, and back over Siracusa itself, with Ortigia clearly visible pointing out into the sea.

Local beaches

Since the coast north of Siracusa has become an evil depository for noxious chemicals, all the city's main **beaches** lie to the south. They all get very crowded in summer, and while you're likely to be on your own out of season, there also won't be any facilities open then. The closest, **Arenella**, is the only sandy beach in the immediate area (bus #23 from Riva della Posta), though most of it consists of private lidos, at which you have to pay to use the beach. There are rocky stretches further south, where the inlets create clear pools that are good for snorkelling. You can walk to these easily enough from Arenella, or else take bus #21 to **Ognina**, where there's a small fishing port and marina, and walk back a little way. However, it's **Fontane Bianche**, 20km south of Siracusa (buses #21 or #22; 30min journey), that the locals love best, with a wide arc of sand that provides some of the best swimming hereabouts. It's also the one that's most like a resort, with a campsite, hotel and various bars and restaurants. There is one free public beach (signposted *spiaggia libera*, near the car park), but all the others are private lidos.

Eating, drinking and entertainment

Ortigia holds the best array of **cafés and restaurants**, most within a short walk of each other. Prices are on the high side for Sicily, though there are few nicer places to sit outside in a medieval street or courtyard and while the evening away. Ortigia also has excellent **bars** – from Italian-style pubs to cocktail joints – and most of the late-night action is concentrated on the streets and alleys near the Fonte Aretusa, particularly around Piazzetta San Rocco and along Lungomare Alfeo. Siracusa is one of the easiest places to catch a traditional Sicilian **puppet theatre** performance, while the annual **Ortigia Festival** in September (ⓦ www.ortigiafestial.it) focuses on contemporary music and performance art. However the best-known cultural entertainments on offer are the open-air classical **Greek dramas**, performed every May and June in the Teatro Greco.

Cafés

Le Antiche Siracuse Via della Maestranza 2 ⓣ 0931.465.706. Corsino's of Palazzolo Acreide has been making sweets and pastries since 1889, and their outlet in Siracusa – an old-school "gran caffe" of mirrors and gleaming counters – stocks a fine range, along with famous ice cream, and has an associated deli-gift shop and a restaurant-pizzeria.

Biblios Via del Consiglio Regionale 11 ⓣ 0931.21.491. Locals drop into this bookshop café more to drink coffee than buy books. Closed all Wed & Sun morning.
Gran Caffe del Duomo Piazza del Duomo 18 ⓣ 0931.21.544. The best view in the finest square in Sicily – and, most amazingly of all, prices for drinks and snacks that are entirely reasonable.

Restaurants

L'Ancora di Giancarlo Russo Via Perno 7 ⓣ 0931.462.369. The best of the restaurants near the market has a breezy outdoor terrace, so it's a good place for an al fresco lunch. There's a long list of pasta dishes with seafood (mussels, clams, sea urchins, anchovies and breadcrumbs etc), while mains are the day's catch, with most dishes priced at around €10–12. Closed Mon. Moderate.

Castello Fiorentino Via del Crocifisso 6 ⓣ 0931.21.097. The finest pizzas in the city centre – people queue out of the door waiting for tables. It's really good value, and the in-your-face waiters and general mayhem at peak times are all part of the charm. Closed Mon. Inexpensive.
Il Cenácolo Via del Consiglio Regionale 10 ⓣ 0931.65.099. Sit outside in a little square under the palm trees – very pretty at night – and eat from a wide-ranging menu that also includes

pizzas (dishes up to €12) and house speciality couscous (from €15). Closed Wed. Moderate.
Darsena Riva Garibaldi 6 ⓣ 0931.61.522, ⓦ www .ristorantedarsena.it. Overlooking the fishing boats near the bridge, this long-established fish restaurant is a popular Sunday-lunch spot, with a large, conservatory-like dining room. It's among the top places for a traditional seafood blow-out, with the day's fish and shellfish on display at the front of the restaurant. Closed Wed. Expensive.
Don Camillo Via della Maestranza 96 ⓣ 0931.67.133, ⓦ www .ristorantedoncamillosiracusa.it. If locals want to impress visitors, they bring them to this refined restaurant in the fifteenth-century vaults of a former convent. The fish is fantastically fresh, and the restaurant emphasizes its more unusual Sicilian specialities, like pasta with tuna, mint and tomatoes or a whole fish baked inside a crust of golden bread.

Meal prices

The restaurants listed are graded according to the following price categories:
Inexpensive: under €15
Moderate: €15–30
Expensive: €30–50
Very expensive: over €50
These prices reflect the per person cost of a full meal including wine and cover charge.

It also has Siracusa's finest wine cellar. Prices are high, up to €15 for pasta and fish dishes from around €18. Closed one week in July. Very expensive.

🏃 **La Foglia** Via Capodieci 29 ☏ 340.66.235, ⓦ www.lafoglia.it The city's most idiosyncratic eatery, from the antique shop-art gallery furnishings to the hippy-chic tableware and place settings. It's actually quite romantic, and a very laid-back place to sample their Mediterranean and vegetarian cooking (dishes €10–15), from rustic soups and homemade ravioli to veggie platters or fish *matalotta* (with tomatoes, onions, capers and olives). Expensive.

🏃 **La Gazza Ladra** Via Cavour 8 ☏ 340.060.2428. Most of the restaurants around Via Cavour are very similar, but the "thieving magpie" tries to do things a little differently. The friendly family-run *osteria* has just eight tables and concentrates on authentic Sicilian cuisine with a homestyle touch, using staple ingredients like courgettes, aubergines, tuna, capers, olives, mint and oregano to great effect in their antipasto platters and pasta dishes. Mains of the day (mostly fish) are chalked on the board, or

you can just drop in for a salad, panino and a drink, and with most dishes around €6–9 it's a great deal. Closed Mon. Moderate.

🏃 **Jonico** Riviera Dionisio Il Grande 194 ☏ 0931.65.540. A fixture since the 1970s, the rustic Jonico is perched on crags above the sea near the Cappuccini quarries, in the north of the city. Though the menu is written entirely in Sicilian, the owner speaks enough English to guide you through the specialities – say gnocchi with swordfish, wild fennel, pink peppercorns and cherry tomatoes, or spaghetti with dried bread-crumbs, olive oil and parsley, followed by swordfish *involtini* or the grilled fish of the day. It's a bit of a slog from town, but very worthwhile, and a full meal should cost €35–40. Take bus #2 or #3 from Ortigia to Largo Latomia, from where it's a 2min walk, or take a taxi. Closed Tues. Expensive.

Vite e Vitello Piazza F. Corpaci 1, at Via della Maestranza ☏ 0931.449.877. A Sicilian steakhouse that's the place for grilled meat (steak, pork, sausages, lamb), plus the best home-made fries in the city. There's shaded outdoor seating opposite San Francesco church. Closed Sun. Moderate.

Bars

🏃 **Il Bagatto** Piazza San Giuseppe 1. A cracking little pub, with beat-up wooden tables inside and out, and Belgian and German beers on draught.

Doctor Sam Piazzetta San Rocco 4. The little square is at the hub of Ortigia's night-scene and this funky bar is a popular hang-out.

Lungolanotte Lungomare Alfeo. Modish wine bar and restaurant, magnificently sited overlooking the harbour.

Ulisse Lungomare di Levante. Ortigia's Irish bar has sea views from the best terrace in town, and hosts regular gigs and DJ nights.

Puppet theatre

Piccolo Teatro dei Pupi Via della Giudecca 17 ☏ 0931.465.540, ⓦ www.pupari.com. Traditional puppet shows by the Vaccaro-Mauceri family, Siracusa's puppeteers, are held at least twice

Shopping in Siracusa

Siracusa's daily **market** (Via Trento, not Sun) offers the usual fruit, veg, meat and fish alongside vendors flogging bead jewellery, sunglasses, big pants and cheap clothes. The biggest concentration of **souvenir stands** in the city is outside the gates of the archeological park, where you can buy typical Sicilian gifts like puppets, ceramics, cowboy hats and Manchester United football shirts. For better, more authentic stuff you can look in the **gift and craft shops** down Via Cavour and around the Fonte Aretusa, where there are some rather good places among the tourist dross. Fish House (Via Cavour 29) is a funky craft gallery offering ceramic fish and driftwood sculpture, while at Sete d'Incanto (Via Roma 27) the owner-artist is inspired by Ortigia's architectural forms and natural elements to produce her hand-painted silk scarves and wall-hangings. At Galleria Bellomo (Via Capodieci 15) you can learn something about the traditional **papyrus** industry in Siracusa – prices here range from a few euros to a few hundred. For designer and high-street **clothes**, most of the best shops and boutiques are down Corso Matteotti.

weekly (and daily except Mon in Aug) in their thriving puppet theatre. You can check up-to-date schedules on the website; behind-the-scenes tours and special shows take place throughout the year. Tickets from €7.

Greek dramas

Istituto Nazionale del Dramma Antico (INDA) Palazzo Greco, Corso Matteotti 29 ☎0931.487.248, ⓦwww.indafondazione.org. Classical Greek drama is performed each year (May and June, usually Tues–Sun from around 6.30pm) at the Teatro Greco in the Parco Archeológico. It's a real spectacle, though performances are in Italian only. Tickets range from €25 to €60, with cheaper last-minute tickets available for some performances. Get details on the INDA website or from Siracusa's tourist offices; tickets are available at the INDA box office or online.

Listings

Boat trips Ortigia Tours ☎368.317.0711, ⓦwww.ortigiatour.com, offers daily cruises around the city's harbours and local coastline. Boats leave from near the bridge on Ortigia (from 9am in summer, 10am, weather permitting, in winter), and trips last an hour or so; tickets €10 per person. In summer, a kiosk on the quayside provides tickets and information.
Buses All buses depart from Corso Umberto, near the train station. AST ☎0931.462.711, ⓦwww.aziendasicilianatrasporti.it (for Augusta, Lentini, Catania, Cómiso, Íspica, Módica, Noto, Palazzolo Acréide, Ragusa, Sortino and Vittória); Interbus ☎0931.66.710, ⓦwww.interbus.it (for Catania, Noto, Pachino, Palermo and Taormina).
Hospital 24-hr accident and emergency service at Ospedale Umberto I, Via Testaferrata, near Madonna delle Lacrime church ☎0931.68.555.

Internet Libreria Gabo, Corso Matteotti 38 (daily 9.30/10am–1pm & 4.30/5–8pm).
Pharmacies Farmacia Centrale, Via Maestranza 42; and Gibiino, Via Roma 79.
Police There's a Carabinieri post in Piazza San Giuseppe, Ortigia. Call ☎112 in an emergency.
Post office Main post office, Piazza delle Poste 15, Ortigia (Mon–Fri 8am–6.30pm, Sat 8am–1pm).
Taxis Ranks in Piazza Pancali ☎0931.60.980 and at the train station ☎0931.69.722.
Tours Allakatalla, Via Roma 10 ☎0931.67.452, ⓦwww.allakatalla.it, is a Noto-based agency with a Siracusa office that offers regional tours, cultural events, outdoor activities, and bike and scooter rental.
Trains The main routes are to Catania and Messina, with a change for Palermo. Other services are to Modica, Noto and Ragusa. Timetables are available on ⓦwww.trenitalia.com.

Augusta and Megara Hyblaea

The coast north of Siracusa, the **Golfo di Augusta**, sports one of the largest concentrations of chemical plants in Europe. This mammoth industrial zone employs one-tenth of the local population, and fills the air with acrid fumes and the sea with chemicals. Hardly surprisingly, it figures on no holiday itineraries, though the industrial port of **AUGUSTA** – half an hour by train or bus from Siracusa – does at least offer the compensation of a handsome, if crumbling, Baroque centre. Despite the town's superficial resemblance to Siracusa – its old centre detached from the mainland on its own islet, surrounded by two harbours – the port has never attained the same importance and didn't even exist until 1232. Frederick II, who founded Augusta, characteristically stamped his own personality on it in the form of a castle (no public access), though everything else of the medieval town was entirely destroyed by the 1693 earthquake. The Villa Comunale below the castle is a shady public garden, on both sides of which are views out to sea, on one side over the port and tankers, on the other to the headland. A few blocks down the main Via Príncipe Umberto, a piazza holds the eighteenth-century Duomo and a solemn Palazzo Comunale, its facade crowned by Frederick II's imperial eagle.

There are a couple of small resorts to the north of Augusta, at **Monte Tauro** and **Brúcoli**, though quite how tempted you'll be to swim anywhere around here is debatable. Far better for drivers is the short trip out to see the extensive remains of **MEGARA HYBLAEA** (signposted; daily 9am–1hr before sunset; €2), considered to be the most complete model of an Archaic city still surviving. It prospered as a Greek colony after the Sikel king of Hybla had granted land alongside his own to Greeks from Megara (near Athens). By the middle of the seventh century BC, the population had done so well out of trade and their high-quality pottery that they were able to found some minor colonies of their own, including Selinus in the west, though their city was eventually submerged by Syracusan ambitions and destroyed by Gelon in 482 BC. The town flourished again later in the fourth century BC, but was finally levelled by the Romans in the same avenging campaign that ended Syracuse's independence in 214 BC. Most of the ruins belong to the fourth-century revival, but the fortifications were erected a century later, interrupted by the Romans' arrival. Various buildings lie confusingly scattered over a wide area, though all the finds are in Siracusa's Museo Archeológico.

Pantálica

PANTÁLICA, Sicily's greatest **necropolis**, lies in the folds of the Monti Iblei, around 40km northwest of Siracusa. Here, in the deep gorge of the Ánapo River, you can follow tracks past several thousand tombs hollowed out of the valley sides at five separate locations. Several skeletons were found in each tomb, suggesting that a few thousand people once lived in what is now largely a craggy wilderness. This extraordinary location, now a UNESCO World Heritage Site, is hard to see by public transport. Drivers, however, will find it an easy and well-signposted diversion en route to either Ragusa or Catania. The approaches are from the small towns of Sortino or Ferla, at either end of the gorge, with parking at various points near both places. The northern necropolis, approaching via Sortino, makes the most dramatic introduction to the area.

The site (always open; free) was first used between the thirteenth and tenth century BC by Sikel refugees from the coast. After the eighth century BC, it is thought to have been the location of the city of **Hybla**, whose king invited Megarian Greeks to colonize Megara Hyblaea; remains from this era are visible, but all pale into insignificance in contrast with the five thousand or so tombs hewn out of the gorge below. In some were found the traces of several separate skeletons, probably of the same family, while others show evidence of habitation – though much later, when the Syracusans themselves were forced to flee inland from barbarian incursions. The atmosphere is primeval and almost sinister – for Vincent Cronin, even something terrifying: "Here is Sicily of the stone age, intent on nothing higher than the taking of food and the burial of its dead." For Cronin, the free play of nature in this ravine embodied Sicily's own particular contribution to the man-made wonders bestowed later by the island's conquerors, and as such – symbolized by a honeycomb he came across in one of the caves – the object of the quest described in his book, *The Golden Honeycomb*.

The road ends at a parking area at the entrance to the **northern necropolis**, 6km from Sortino (follow the signs). An obvious but rocky path leads around a plateau, then down to the river and up the other side (where there's another parking area, but this time accessed from Ferla – the road was originally planned to span the gorge, but never completed). You'll soon see the **tombs**, first just dotting the walls of the valley in clusters and finally puncturing the whole vertical cliff face – this last view is about 1km, or a thirty-minute walk, from the parking area. There are superb views from the higher reaches and the path and rock-cut steps remain good all the way.

You can continue down across the river and up the other side of the gorge, where the road begins again and runs west to Ferla, another 9km beyond. This is the upper road to Ferla, with a parking area allowing access to the foundations of the **Anaktoron**, or prince's palace, a building from ancient Hybla, and to the **southern necropolis**, where more rock tombs are visible. There's also the basic *Ristorante Pantálica* along the road, which sells a map of the area. A lower road from Ferla has another parking area, from where you can stroll easily along the bottom of the gorge for a while.

Sortino and Ferla

Both Sortino (1hr 15min) and Ferla (1hr 30min) are linked to Siracusa by bus, though neither is really close enough to the gorge to make a day-trip feasible. **SORTINO** is a busy, rather sprawling little town, but other than stopping for a quick coffee there's no reason to linger. **FERLA** is much prettier, with a stately church or two and a pleasingly restored square on the long, sloping main street. It has a good trattoria, *Del Carmine*, at the bottom of the street, and there are also a couple of local B&Bs, one, the *Ginestra* (T 0931.870.396; ❸), right by the trattoria. Or there's rural *agriturismo* accommodation at *Il Giardino di Pantalica* (T 095.712.2680, W www.pantalica.it), where one- and two-bedroomed apartments (from €50 per person) and a summer swimming pool sit on an estate within the Pantálica natural reserve.

Palazzolo Acréide

Set on a hill some 40km west of Siracusa, **PALAZZOLO ACRÉIDE** is a mainly Baroque town with one of the most interesting of the province's classical sites lying just outside the modern settlement. It's a good excursion, or would make a rather quiet overnight stop, somewhat stranded from the main road and rail links across the province.

AST buses from Siracusa pull up in Palazzolo's main square, **Piazza del Pópolo**. This is the heart of the Baroque town, two sides dominated by the handsome church of San Sebastiano and the gleaming town hall. From here lanes radiate down past opulent facades, hidden courtyards and gargoyled balconies, eventually leading to a trio of fine Baroque churches, the Chiesa Madre, San Paolo and the Annunziata. But the main focus of interest – at least for anyone curious about the roots of Sicilian culture – is the **Casa-Museo di Antonino Uccello** (daily 9am–1pm & 2.30–7pm; free), tucked away in an old house at Via Machiavelli 19. The fruit of one man's thirty-year obsession to preserve the traditions of rural Sicily, this constitutes an important documentation of folk art, showing trousseaux, ceramics, olive presses, puppets, reconstructions of houses and stables, and anything else judged by Uccello to be in danger of extinction.

Accommodation

Fattoria Giannavi Contrada Giannavi ☏0931.881.776, ⊛www.fattoriagiannavi.it. A farm with rooms, pool and a restaurant serving home-grown, home-cooked food (meals from €20). It's set high on a bluff with extensive views, 8km from Palazzolo on the Giarratana/Ragusa road (10min drive). ④

Santoro Via San Sebastiano 21 ☏0931.883.855, ⊛www.hotelsantoro.com. The town centre's main hotel is a simple place, just below Piazza del Pópolo. ③

Restaurants

Barocco Via Duca d'Aosta 27 ☏0931.883.266. Straightforward lunches (*pranzo turistico* is €12) and evening pizzas. Closed Mon. Inexpensive.

Il Portico Via Orologio 6 ☏0931.881.532. Dining at the *Portico* is more of an occasion, with dishes like homemade ravioli and grilled meats (dishes €6–12) as well as pizzas. Closed Tues. Moderate.

Akrai: the ancient city

The **Zona Archeológica** (daily: summer 9am–1hr before sunset; winter 9am–2pm; €2) is a twenty-minute walk up from the town centre, or you can park close to the entrance. The first inland colony of Siracusa, **Akrai** thrived during the peace and security that characterized Hieron II's reign during the third century BC. It declined under the Romans, but later re-emerged as an important early Christian centre (as shown by the number of rock-cut tombs in the area), only to be eventually destroyed by the Arabs.

Of the visible remains, the most complete is the small **Teatro Greco**, built towards the end of Hieron's reign. A perfect semicircle, the theatre held six hundred people and retains traces of its scene-building. Behind the theatre to the right is a small **senate-house**, or *bouleuterion*, a rectangular construction that was originally covered. Beyond lies a 200-metre stretch of *decumanus* that once connected the two gates of the city. Crossed at regular intervals by junctions and paved in lavic rock, it's in better condition than many of the more recent roads in the area.

Other remains give little impression of their former grandeur. You'll have a job identifying the excavated Roman **Tempio di Persefone**, above the theatre, an unusually round chamber that was formerly covered by a cupola. Equally fragmentary is the much older **Tempio di Afrodite**, sixth- or fifth-century BC, lying at the head of what was the *agora*. From here you can look straight down into one of the two quarries from which the stone to build the city was taken. Later they were converted into Christian burial chambers, and in the first of them, the **Intagliata**, you can plainly see the recesses in the walls: some of them catacombs, others areas of worship, the rest simply rude dwellings cut in the Byzantine era. The narrower, deeper quarry below it, the **Intagliatella**, holds more votive niches and a relief cut from the rock-face, over 2m long, that combines a typically Greek scene – heroes banqueting – with a Roman one of heroes offering sacrifice. It's thought to date from the first century BC.

There are more niches and chambers in a lower quarry, the **Templi Ferali**, though you'll have to ask the custodian to let you see this, along with the much more interesting **Santoni** further down (a 15min walk from the site). If it's a slack day and he can't be bothered to make the trip, you may well be told that they are "closed", which would be a shame, since these twelve rock-cut sculptures (carved no later than the third century BC) are of a fertility goddess, Cybele, a predominantly eastern deity whose origins are steeped in mystery. Certainly there's no other example of so rich a complex relating to her worship, and the local name tagged to these sculptures – *santoni*, or "great saints" – suggests that the awe attached to them survived until relatively recently.

Ragusa and around

The 1693 earthquake destroyed many towns and cities that were then rebuilt in a different form, but the unique effect on Ragusa was to split the city in two. The old town of **Ragusa Ibla**, on a jut of land above its valley, was comprehensively flattened, and within a few years a new planned town emerged on the higher ridge to the west, known simply as **RAGUSA**. However, Ibla was stubbornly rebuilt by its inhabitants and rivalry between the two was commonplace, until 1926 when both towns were nominally reunited. For decades Ibla suffered, as all the business and industry relocated to the prosperous upper town – even oil was discovered here, and derricks are scattered around modern Ragusa's higher reaches. But there's been a complete transformation over the last ten years as Ibla has benefited from European funding to tidy up its once dilapidated streets, giving its central core a gleaming veneer. Boutique tourism has taken off here in a big way, with old houses and *palazzi* now given over to classy B&Bs, designer cafés and trendy trattorias. Even so, it's not recklessly touristy – more gourmet deli than gift shop – and Ragusa Ibla makes for a very agreeable night or two's stay.

To the south and west of Ragusa, the largely unsung Baroque towns of **Cómiso** and **Vittória**, the views from **Chiaramonte Gulfi** or the low-key resorts and beaches along the local **coast**, can fill another day's touring, but these are all mere sideshows compared with Ragusa itself.

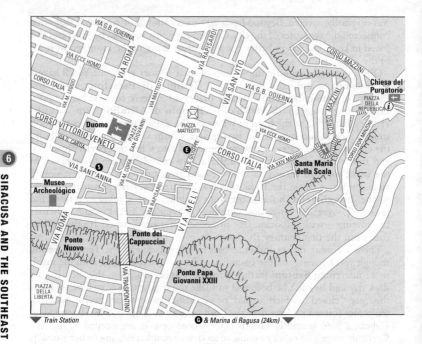

▼ Train Station　　　　　　　　　　　Ⓖ & Marina di Ragusa (24km) ▼

Arrival and information

Drivers can follow the signs into Ragusa Ibla, where you should eventually find somewhere to park. **Buses** and **trains**, however, all arrive in the upper town, the adjacent stations near Piazza del Popolo being a five-minute walk from the Ponte Nuovo and Via Roma.

The **bus navetta** (#1 or #3; every 30–60min) plies between the upper and lower towns, and runs down Via Roma and Corso Italia, stopping outside both Santa Maria and Purgatorio churches, ending its run in Ibla outside the Giardino Ibleo. To go up to Ragusa, you can either catch it here or in Largo Camerina – you'll need a ticket in advance from any *tabacchi*.

There's a small **tourist office**, marked "*Punto Incontro*", outside the Chiesa del Purgatorio (Mon–Sat 9.30am–12.30pm & 3.30–7.30pm), and another in Ragusa Ibla at Via Capitano Bocchieri 33 (Tues–Sun 9am–2pm & 4–6pm; ☎0932.221.511, Ⓦwww.ragusaturismo.it). You can pick up a map and an accommodation booklet from either; there's also useful information (though mostly in Italian) on the websites Ⓦwww.ragusa.net and Ⓦwww.ibla.net.

Hybla Bike (☎0932.667.419, Ⓦwww.hyblabike.com), based in Ragusa, offers bike rental and **mountain-bike tours** in the region, aimed at all levels of experience.

Accommodation

It's infinitely preferable to stay the night in Ragusa Ibla, where you can stroll the traffic-free streets in the evening and hop from bar to trattoria. It holds more than two dozen **B&Bs** alone, as well as a handful of small, stylish **hotels** – all signposted – and most can find you a parking space outside or nearby. There's a

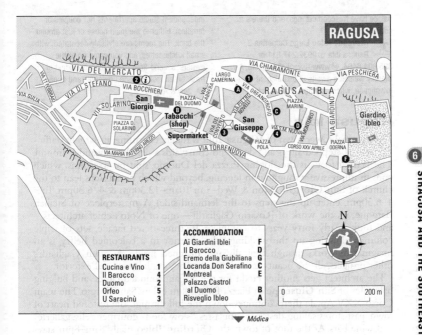

RAGUSA

VIA CHIARAMONTE
VIA PESCHIERA
VIA DEL MERCATO
LARGO CAMERINA
VIA DI STEFANO
VIA BOCCHIERI
VIA SOLARINO
San Giorgio
PIAZZA DEL DUOMO
San Giuseppe
RAGUSA IBLA
PIAZZA MARINI
Tabacchi (shop)
Supermarket
VIA TORRENUOVA
PIAZZA POLA
CORSO XXV APRILE
Giardino Ibleo
PIAZZA ODERNA

N

RESTAURANTS

Cucina e Vino	1
Il Barocco	4
Duomo	2
Orfeo	5
U Saracinù	3

ACCOMMODATION

Ai Giardini Iblei	F
Il Barocco	D
Eremo della Giubiliana	G
Locanda Don Serafino	C
Montreal	E
Palazzo Castrol al Duomo	B
Risveglio Ibleo	A

0   200 m

▼ Módica

similar number of B&Bs in the upper town, as well as a few largely colourless business-type hotels.

Il Barocco Via Santa Maria la Nuova 1, Ragusa Ibla ☎0932.663.105, ⓦwww.ilbarocco.it. A very charming old-town hotel set around a bright courtyard – the rooms are in traditional style, with tile floors and oak furniture, but it's a modern place, all very tasteful and understated. Their excellent restaurant is just a short walk up the street. ⑥

Eremo della Giubiliana Contrada Giubiliana, 7.5km south of Ragusa on the Marina di Ragusa road ☎0932.669.119, ⓦwww.eremodellagiubiliana.it. This glorious five-star country property is housed in the restored buildings of a feudal estate and hermitage dating back to the twelfth century. Rooms (converted from monks' cells), suites and self-contained estate cottages all feature traditional Sicilian furnishings, the grounds are ravishing, and you can dine on their own organically grown food. It's no surprise to find it also has its own airstrip and private beach, plus pool, nature trails and all sorts of tours and activities available. ⑨

Ai Giardini Iblei Via Normanni 4, Ragusa Ibla ☎0932.246.844 or 338.640.1238, ⓦwww.aigiardini.it. Sunny rooms right next to the town

gardens, simply but tastefully furnished, some a little larger than others. Kitchen facilities also available. ④

Locanda Don Serafino Via XI Febbraio 15, Ragusa Ibla ☎0932.222.0065, ⓦwww.locandadonserafino.it. Beautifully set within the hefty stone walls of a nineteenth-century mansion, this four-star boutique hotel has only ten rooms, all rather gorgeously appointed. The stylish restaurant (most pastas and mains €17–25) is among the best places to eat in town, offering a modern take on traditional dishes – things like grilled vegetable pie, beef fillet flavoured with tobacco, or rabbit with bacon and pistachios. They also have a lido and restaurant down on the coast at Marina di Ragusa, open April to mid-Oct. ⑦

Montreal Via San Giuseppe 8, Ragusa ☎0932.621.133, ⓔmontreal@sicily-hotels.net. A three-star hotel in the upper town that offers decent prices for reasonable rooms; it also has garage parking. ⑤

Palazzo Castro al Duomo Piazza del Duomo 2, Ragusa Ibla ☎0932.621.887 or 349.266.0528, ⓦwww.palazzocastro.it. Right on Ibla's majestic cathedral square, rooms in this old palace have frescoed ceilings, and there's a courtyard garden. ❹

🏃 **Risveglio Ibleo** Largo Camerina 3, Ragusa Ibla ☏ 0932.247.811 or 335.804.6494, ⓦ www.risveglioibleo.com. A very friendly welcome awaits at this elegant townhouse, where accommodation is in

independent studio apartments (for couples or families), either in the main house or just around the back. The rooms are stylishly decorated, with small kitchenettes, and you come up to the owners' second-floor rooms for a breakfast of fresh bread, home-made preserves and honey. ❹, July & Aug ❺

Ragusa Ibla

The original lower town of **Ragusa Ibla** is totally charming, its largely traffic-free streets, stepped alleys and dead-end courtyards a delight to wander around. The central focus is the sloping Piazza del Duomo, split by six palms, which ends in impressive wrought-iron fencing, beyond which broad steps lead to the church of **San Giorgio** (Mon & Wed–Sun 10am–12.30pm & 4–6.30pm, Tues 4–6.30pm; enter up the steps to the lefthand side). A masterpiece of Sicilian Baroque, it's the work of Rosario Gagliardi – one of Noto's chief architects – and took nearly forty years to complete. Its three-tiered facade, sets of triple columns climbing up the wedding-cake exterior to a balconied belfry, is an imaginative work, though typically not matched inside. As with Gagliardi's other projects, all the beauty is in the immediacy of the powerful exterior.

The architect gets another credit for the elegant rounded facade and bulging balconies of **San Giuseppe** in Piazza Pola, 200m below San Giorgio. The main Corso XXV Aprile then continues down the hill through the restored heart of town, past stores selling designer sunglasses, "slow food" gourmet delis, galleries and wine bars. At the foot of town, the **Giardino Ibleo** (daily 8am–8pm, stays open later in summer) is where everyone comes for an evening stroll and a drink in the nearby cafés. You can enjoy dramatic views from the very edge of the spur on which the town is built, while the violet-strewn flowerbeds set off the remains of three small churches, abandoned in the grounds. To the right of the garden's entrance stands the **Portale San Giorgio**, a surviving Gothic church portal whose badly worn stone centrepiece depicts a skeletal St George killing the dragon.

Ragusa: the upper town

If you're driving – in which case you can head straight to Ibla – you might not visit the **upper town of Ragusa** at all, though that's where most of the city's shops and services are located. It's built on a grid plan, slipping off to right and left on either side of the sloping Corso Italia, just off which stands the sombre Duomo, completed in 1774. Although Baroque Ragusa received its share of good-looking buildings (like the few grand *palazzi* down Corso Italia), most of the architects' efforts seem to have been devoted to keeping the streets as straight as possible, and the town's most striking vistas are where this right-angled order is interrupted by a deep gorge, exposing the bare rock on which the city was built. Three bridges span the gorge: at the Ponte Nuovo, just below Via Roma, the city's **Museo Archeológico** (daily 9.30am–1.30pm & 3.30–6.30pm; €3) deals mainly with finds from the Greek site of Kamarina (sixth-century BC), on the coast to the southwest. However, there are plans to relocate the museum to Ragusa Ibla in future.

Actually, the best part of Ragusa is leaving it. Thanks to the shuttle bus (*bus navetta*) that connects the upper and lower towns, you can jump on a bus up from Ibla, get off at the Duomo in the upper town and then walk back down. That takes about half an hour, heading down Corso Italia and the narrow Via

XXIV Maggio, with an initial stop on the terrace by the restored fifteenth-century church of **Santa Maria della Scala** (which features the remains of an unusual exterior pulpit). A mighty view lies beyond, of the weatherbeaten roofs of Ragusa Ibla straddling the outcrop of rock, rising to the prominent dome of San Giorgio. From the church terrace, steps descend beneath the winding road to another church, the **Chiesa del Purgatorio**, from where winding alleys climb back into the heart of Ragusa Ibla.

Eating and drinking

Good **restaurants** are easy to find in Ibla, while a few cafés put out tables in the Piazza del Duomo – as night falls, and the lights come on, it's not too much of an exaggeration to suggest that this is the prettiest square in Sicily. **Ibla in festa** is a summer (Aug & Sept) series of folk music concerts, recitals and entertainments held in piazzas Duomo and Pola.

Il Barocco Via Orfanotrofio 27–29, Ragusa Ibla ☎0932.652.397. The most reliable place for a good-value meal – there's a rustic interior or streetside tables, but you should get there in good time for the latter. Most mains cost €6–10, though splash out €24 on a two-person mixed grill and you get a mountainous platter of grilled meat, stuffed veg and antipasti that you'll struggle to finish. Moderate.

Cucina e Vino Via Orfanotrofio 91, Ragusa Ibla ☎0932.686.447. Typical of the more modish operations in Ibla, this old *palazzo* with a street terrace has separate menus of regional meat (€7–10) and fish (€11–14) dishes, things like lamb with artichokes, ravioli with pork stuffing or mackerel fillet with black olives. Moderate.

Duomo Via Capitano Bocchieri 31, Ragusa Ibla ☎0932.651.265, ⊛www.ristoranteduomo.it. Chef Ciccio Sultano deconstructs his Ragusa roots to produce the glorious concoctions –

they're scarcely mere dishes – that have gained his restaurant a name across Sicily. It's highly refined, highly individual and, of course, highly expensive, with main courses around €30 and the *menu degustazione* a cool €110. Still, you're unlikely to eat as well or as interestingly anywhere else. Very expensive.

Orfeo Via Sant'Anna 117, Ragusa ☎0932.621.035. If you're in the upper town it's worth seeking out this place for traditional dishes like broad bean soup, stuffed sardines or the local pasta, *cavati ragusana* (fresh pasta with a pork *ragù*). Closed Sun. Moderate.

U Saracinu Via del Convento 9, Ragusa Ibla ☎0932.246.976. It's been here donkey's years, even before the fancy old-town restoration, and sticks with a traditional Sicilian menu of pasta and meat grills (most dishes €5–9), though pricier couscous and fish specials are also on offer. Closed Sun. Moderate.

Around Ragusa

Módica apart, there's not much else that need delay you in **Ragusa province**, though if you're driving north into the interior or west to Agrigento you can plot an enjoyable half day's route. By public transport, to be frank, it's barely worth the trouble to visit any of the places covered below.

Chiaramonte Gulfi

Twenty kilometres north of Ragusa, **CHIARAMONTE GULFI** merits a visit largely for its far-reaching views. This is one of several places dubbed the "balcony of Sicily" and, though hazy in summer, the panorama (west towards Gela and north to Etna) embraces dun-coloured farmland interspersed with solitary villages – a still, silent scene, but for the occasional dog's bark or the whine of a Vespa. An excellent **restaurant** here, *Majore*, Via Mártiri Ungheresi 12, off Piazza Duomo (☎0932.928.019; closed Mon & July), specializes in pig meats – the area is famous for its salamis and cured hams, which you can buy to take away at the restaurant shop.

Cómiso and Vittória

Heading west, both Cómiso (17km) and neighbouring Vittória (24km) are on the main train line from Ragusa to Gela, though the road provides the best approach, crossing a barren 600-metre-high plateau that looks away to the distant sea. A Baroque spirit infuses **CÓMISO**, most prominent in its two major churches, the Chiesa Matrice and the nearby Santíssima Annunziata, which overwhelm everything within reach of their ponderous shadows. Not much of medieval Cómiso survived the 1693 earthquake, save the thirteenth-century church of San Francesco, to which a rich Renaissance chapel was added in 1517 to house the tombs of the powerful Naselli family. **VITTÓRIA**, meanwhile, holds more Baroque buildings and a rather splendid main square, Piazza del Pópolo, though the town is better known as the source of the well-regarded Cerasuolo di Vittória wines.

Marina di Ragusa and Kamarina

Southwest of Ragusa, it's a straight 24-kiolmetre run down to **the coast**, and the start of the so-called "riviera", which extends as far as Gela. The small resort of **MARINA DI RAGUSA** is easy to reach (buses every hour in summer from Ragusa, fewer out of season), though it's a typical Sicilian mix of private lidos and apartments, and bars and restaurants that really only do business for four or five months of the year.

A coastal road westwards (though no public transport) offers access to more beaches near Punta Secca and Punta Braccetto, and if you're driving this way you might as well follow the signs to find the desolate remains of ancient **Kamarina** (also spelt Camerina), a Syracusan colony founded in 599 BC. It lies on a headland overlooking beaches on either side, where a **Museo Archeologico** (daily 9am–2pm & 3–7.30pm; €2.60) contains everything that wasn't appropriated by Ragusa's museum. Behind the antiquarium is all that's left of a fifth-century BC Tempio di Atena, surrounded by the rubble of city walls and the various ruins of the Hellenistic-Roman city.

Módica

The small but busy town of **MÓDICA**, 18km south of Ragusa, is another in the region that is enjoying a new lease of life as a select tourist destination, based again on its remarkable late-Baroque heritage. A powerful medieval base of the Chiaramonte family, and later the Cabreras, it was once far more important than Ragusa itself, though ironically, following the reconstruction after 1693 (which has now earned it UNESCO World Heritage status) it never regained its erstwhile prestige.

Arrival and information

Make the journey from Ragusa to Módica by road if you can – the train route isn't half as spectacular. Regional **buses** drop you right in the centre on Corso Umberto I; the **train station** is a good ten-minute walk away at the other end of town – walk up to the ornamental fountain at Piazza Rizone and bear left for the corso. Drivers can **park** on the street, but in most central areas you need to buy a parking voucher (from *tabacchi*) to put in your window (it's free for a couple of hours at lunchtime and again overnight). Note also that if you're going to the Cava d'Íspica, you can drive directly to the northern section closest to Módica (there's a brown sign at the ornamental fountain) – you don't need to take the main road to Íspica itself.

A **tourist office** at Corso Umberto I 149 (daily: summer 9am–1pm & 4–8pm; winter 9am–1pm & 3.30–7.30pm; ℡0932.753.324, ⓦwww.comune .modica.rg.it), can supply a map and other local information.

Accommodation

Módica holds plenty of quality **B&Bs**, many in fine *palazzi* and old buildings in the upper town, though it can be a real slog chasing up and down the stepped alleys to check them out. You can always consult the tourist office, which has stacks of B&B cards and brochures.

Il Cavaliere Corso Umberto I 259 ℡0932.947.219, ⓦwww .bbilcavalieremodica.it. A friendly young couple makes you feel right at home in this classy B&B in a restored *palazzo* – the entrance is through a baronial courtyard, and the chic rooms feature exposed stone walls, slabs of colour and stylish furnishings, with a/c and Internet access throughout. Breakfast is served in an upper salon with original painted ceiling and fine views over the San Giorgio facade. ❹

Palazzo Failla Via Blandini 5 ℡0932.941.059, ⓦwww.palazzofailla.it. A handsome upper-town palace, by the Santa Teresa church, reborn as a comfortable four-star hotel. The cheaper rooms are modern attic rooms on the second floor, but you may well prefer the more elegant traditional rooms, with tiled floors, high frescoed ceilings and antique beds. *La Gazza Ladra* restaurant at the same address is reviewed below. ❻, superior rooms ❼

I Tetti di Siciliando Via Cannata 24 ℡0932.942.843, ⓦwww.siciliando.it. Atmospheric rooms here have balconies with great town views, there's a small garden, while breakfast is eaten under a vaulted frescoed ceiling. It's also an art and activity place, with craftwork courses held, and bike tours and rental bikes available. Look for the sign opposite the Agip petrol station towards the top of the corso (where you'll have to park), and follow the steps up around the passageway for the signposted "bed, bike and breakfast". ❸

The upper and lower towns

Módica is split into upper and lower towns, the two being divided by the long main drag of **Corso Umberto I** – which was originally a river until a flood of 1902 prompted the authorities to cover it over. The corso is flanked by a run of handsome *palazzi*, whose balconies are buttressed by gargoyles, twisted heads and beasts, while its churches make grandiose Baroque statements of intent. That of **San Pietro**, for example, has a wide flight of steps framing the life-sized statues of the Twelve Apostles. However, it's the warren-like upper town of **Módica Alta** where true genius lies, in the shape of the magnificent eighteenth-century facade of **San Giorgio**, a worthy rival to the church of the same name in Ragusa Ibla. It's thought that architect Rosario Gagliardi was responsible for this, too: the elliptical facade is topped by his trademark, a belfry, while the approach is characteristically daring – twin flights of stairs zigzag up across the upper town's hairpins, ending in a terrace before the church. From here, and from the tight streets above San Giorgio, you can look back over the grey-tiled roofs and balconies of the town, built up two sides of a narrow valley. There are more views from the remains of the **castle** and its clocktower, which perches on a rocky spur above the main part of town.

There's really not much more to Módica – a night would do it full justice – but it is an enjoyable place to visit. The local civic collections, archeology to art, are in the **Museo Civico** on the corso by the tourist office (Tues–Sun 10am–1pm & 5–8.30pm; €2), or you can simply stroll the corso and window-shop in the boutiques, fancy shoe shops, *enotecas* and gourmet delis.

Eating and drinking

In addition to its fine crop of **restaurants**, Módica has more cafés and *pasticcerie* than is seemly for a place its size; above all, there is **chocolate** in abundance, for which the town is famous throughout Italy. Sicily's oldest chocolate manufacturer, the **Antica Dolceria Bonajuto**, up the alley at Corso Umberto I 159 (ⓦ www.bonajuto.it), has been making the stuff since 1880, a grainy, crunchy confection that is flavoured with orange, cinnamon and vanilla, or even salt or peppercorns. The shop's a beauty, filled with old display cabinets, and you can sample from dainty little tasting dishes on the counter before you buy.

La Contea Via Grimaldi 15, opposite San Domenico church ☎ 0932.944.812. No-frills family-run place, serving a range of pizzas and pastas. Inexpensive.
Fattoria delle Torri Vico Napolitano 14, off the corso across from Piazza Matteotti ☎ 0932.751.286. This is the one everyone talks about in town – a highly regarded restaurant for choice local dishes and an extensive Sicilian wine list. While not exactly economical, it's a memorable gastronomic experience for which booking is advised. Closed Sun eve & Mon. Very expensive.
Gargantua Corso Umberto I 261 ☎ 0932.752.927. The dishes on offer here make a real change, more bistro in style, starting with say a ricotta and *funghi porcini* soufflé followed by herb-stuffed rabbit in a light curry sauce. And with *primi* at €10 and *secondi*

at €15, it's not too badly priced. Closed Sun eve & Mon. Expensive.
La Gazza Ladra Via Blandini 5 ☎ 0932.755.655, ⓦ www.ristorantelagazzaladra.it. Top-class restaurant at the same address as the *Palazzo Failla* hotel, offering creative Sicilian cuisine (couscous with squid ink and seafood broth, tuna with a tomato crust, rabbit in sweet-sour sauce) at around €50 a head plus drinks. Very expensive.
Osteria Pozzo dei Pruni Vico Napolitano 18 ☎ 0932.943.579. Regional cuisine at very reasonable prices – things like ricotta-stuffed ravioli in a pork *ragù* and steak in Nero d'Avola wine sauce, with most dishes priced at €5–10. The stone-arched dining room has old Módica photos, or there's alley seating outside. Closed Wed. Moderate.

Scicli

SCICLI, just 10km south of Módica, is dramatically pitched against the bottom of a knobbly bluff. It too has seen a fair amount of restoration in recent years, especially around the main Piazza Italia where pale-yellow eighteenth-century churches and balconied *palazzi* exude an air of faded grandeur. Just off the main piazza, the fantastic **Palazzo Beneventano** features some spectacularly ugly eighteenth-century exterior decoration: manic grinning faces with lolling tongues and bald heads tucked under the balconies and clinging to the walls. From the *palazzo*, climb up the stepped path, past abandoned houses, to the terrace by the empty church of San

Matteo to enjoy grand views over Scicli below. Just below the church, a further stepped path (signposted "Chiesa S. Lucia") leads to the remains of another church; at the top of the ridge here, you're standing right above a series of abandoned **cave-dwellings** that litter the hills around, used from Neolithic times until fairly recently. From the vantage point you can make out bricked-up entrances, caves and doorways in the tree-dotted cliffs below.

The handsome centre is certainly worth an hour or two, and if you're touring by car Scicli is an easy stop en route to or from Módica or Ragusa. Whether you'd particularly bother by public transport is a moot point, though there are buses and trains from either place. Cafés ring the main piazza, a few restaurants are signposted here and there, and there's even a **B&B** or two, notably the *Conte Ruggero* in a restored palace on the square at Piazza Italia 24 (℡0932.931.840, Ⓦwww.conteruggero.it; ⑤).

Íspica and the Cava d'Íspica

At **ÍSPICA**, 18km southeast of Módica, human settlement can be traced back 4000 years, to the cave dwellings and tombs carved out of the wide gorge of the **Cava d'Íspica**. These were later used by generations of Sikels, Greeks and early Christians to bury their dead, while during medieval times a strong fortified castle, town and churches were built on the rocky bluff above the southern section of the gorge. Then, in 1693, disaster struck, as the great quake levelled thousands of years of habitation in one swift blow. A new town was rebuilt on the neighbouring hill, which is where modern Íspica thrives today – a rather sprawling place set around a central kernel of restored squares and Baroque churches. The major interest, however, remains in the nearby gorge, signposted "Parco Forza" on the way into town from either Módica or Siracusa. There's parking at the gates to the **Parco Archeologico della Forza** (daily 9am–1.45pm & 3–7pm; free) – or you can walk there easily enough from the town centre – where a path leads up to a viewing point over the gorge. More paths wind steeply down, past the broken remains of palaces and churches, and into the southern section of the gorge itself where caves were used as houses, storerooms, stables, workshops and cemeteries, right up until 1693. A separate path from the parking area leads to the church of Santa Maria La Cava, cut into the rock and dating back to the very earliest days of Christianity in Sicily – some medieval frescoes can be seen inside.

While there's no great reason to dally in Íspica itself – nearby Módica or Noto make much more pleasant overnight stops – you can get lunch in the central Piazza Regina Margherita (where it's also usually easy to park). The *Barone Francesco* (℡0932.951.054; closed Mon) serves an inexpensive menu of antipasto platters, pasta and grills, plus pizza in the evenings.

Cava d'Íspica Nord

The Íspica gorge actually runs for 13km northwest (towards Módica), with rock-cut dwellings and tombs lining the entire route. It's possible to walk through the gorge, starting either at Íspica or at the northern section, the **Cava d'Íspica Nord** (Mon–Sat 9am–7pm, winter may close earlier, Sun 9am–1.45pm; €2), which is around 7km east of Módica (no public transport). There's a direct road route from Módica, or a sign on the main SS115, roughly halfway between Módica and Íspica, points you 6km up a minor

From the port of **Pozzallo**, 19km south of Módica, Virtu Ferries (🖰www
.virtuferries.com) runs a year-round high-speed passenger ferry service to Malta.
There's a scheduled day-return service (90min each way; from €65, Aug €75), but
every Thursday (April–Oct) and Monday (mid-July to mid-Sept), they offer an
excursion fare of €90 that includes lunch and a tour of Malta. The return to
Pozzallo on regular and excursion services is in the evening, but there are several
B&Bs and hotels in the town.

road to the site. From the entrance (where there's a café), a landscaped path
descends into the gorge, where towering fronds of bamboo and wild fennel
grow amid the fig, pomegranate and walnut trees. There are catacombs
immediately below the site entrance, while the path meanders back through
the site past tombs and dwellings cut into the cliff face. The walking path
through the gorge starts on the other side of the road from the entrance,
running under the road bridge.

Noto

The captivating town of **NOTO** represents the apogee of the wholesale
renovation that took place following the cataclysm of 1693, a monument to
the achievement of a few architects and planners whose vision coincided with
the golden age of Baroque architecture. Although a town called Noto, or
Netum, has existed in this area for centuries, what you see today is in effect a
"New Town", conceived as a triumphant symbol of renewal. The fragile
Iblean stone used in its construction was grievously damaged by modern
pollution, but years of restoration work have gradually shaken off the grime
and most of the harmonious buildings have regained their original honey-
coloured facades. Some characterful B&B accommodation, and traffic-free
old-town streets that are at their most charming as the lights come on at dusk,
make this one of the island's essential stopovers.

Some history

Noto was flattened on January 11, 1693, and a week later its rebuilding was
entrusted to a Sicilian-Spanish aristocrat, **Giuseppe Lanza, Duke of
Camastra**, on the strength of his work at the town of Santo Stéfano di
Camastra, on the Tyrrhenian coast. Lanza visited the ruins, saw nothing but "un
montón de piedras abandonadas" (a mountain of forsaken rocks), and quickly
decided to start afresh, on a new site 16km to the south. In fact, the ruins
weren't abandoned; the city's battered population was already improvising a
shantytown, and even held a referendum when Lanza's intentions became
known, rejecting the call to relocate their city. But partly motivated by the
prestige of the undertaking, partly by the need to refurbish the area's defences,
Lanza ignored the local feeling, even pulling down their new constructions and
the old town's remaining church.

With the help of the Flemish military engineer Carlos de Grunemburg,
Lanza devised a revolutionary new **plan**, based on two gridded sections that
were to be almost completely separated from each other – a lower area for
the political and religious establishment, the upper town for the people. The
best **architects** were to be used: Vincenzo Sinatra, Paolo Labisi and the

master craftsman Rosario Gagliardi – not innovators, but men whose enthusiasm and experience enabled them to concoct a graceful synthesis of the latest architectural skills and forms. Their collaboration was so complete that it's still difficult to ascribe some buildings to any one person. Within an astonishingly short time the work was completed: a new city, planned with the accent on symmetry and visual harmony, from its simple street plan to the lissom figures adorning its buildings. It's easily the most successful post-earthquake creation and, for a time, in the mid-nineteenth century, the new Noto replaced Siracusa as the region's provincial capital.

Arrival and information

Noto is 32km southwest of Siracusa, 53km east of Ragusa. **Buses** stop at the Giardino Púbblico at the eastern end of town, close to the Porta Reale; the **train station** is a good ten minutes' walk away down Via Príncipe di Piemonte. Traffic through town is all one-way and while it's easy enough to drive in (follow "centro" signs) or out (destinations are all well signposted), finding a particular spot in a car can be difficult. The best advice is to park first (there's a free waste-ground car park behind the stadium, among others) and get your bearings. Many hotels and B&Bs are signposted through town as well.

There's a **tourist office** in Piazza XVI Maggio, behind the Hercules fountain (Mon–Fri 8am–2pm & 3.30–6.30pm, Sat 9am–noon & 3.30–6.30pm, closed Sat in winter; ℡0931.573.779, ⓦwww.comune.noto.sr.it), while for **tours and excursions**, and rental bikes and scooters, contact Allakatalla, Corso Vittorio Emanuele 47 (℡0931.574.080, ⓦwww.allakatalla.it).

Accommodation

While **accommodation** is plentiful in Noto, it's worth booking ahead in July and August, when you can expect prices to be at their highest. Even B&Bs charge up to €80 double in the high summer, though prices drop to €60 or so outside peak season.

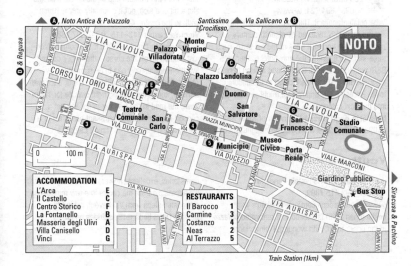

ACCOMMODATION
L'Arca — E
Il Castello — C
Centro Storico — F
La Fontanello — B
Masseria degli Ulivi — A
Villa Caniselo — D
Vinci — G

RESTAURANTS
Il Barocco — 1
Carmine — 3
Costanzo — 4
Neas — 2
Al Terrazzo — 5

Among the ruins of Noto Antica

Until finally abandoned in 1693, the original town of Noto had several times been a significant historical stronghold: one of the few Sicilian towns to resist the looting of the Roman praetor Verres, it was also the last bastion of Arab Sicily before the Normans arrived. Only sparse remnants of the old town survive, but **Noto Antica** make a fascinating side-trip nonetheless. It's 16km northwest of Noto, signposted from the western end of the corso in town (there's no bus) – the turn-off to the site is also that for the convent of Santa Maria delle Scale, with Noto Antica another 5km past the convent. You park outside the surviving castle gate (occupied from the eleventh to the seventeenth century), where renovation work has rebuilt some of the circular tower – early Christian catacombs honeycomb the rock beneath the tumbled walls that line the valley cliff. An unsurfaced country lane pushes on through the castle gate past the now-puzzling, completely overgrown remains of an abandoned city – square-cut stone blocks, shattered arches, bramble-covered courtyards and crumbling walls. If you come out here, you might as well plan the day to take in the Cava Grande canyon too, which is only another twenty minutes' drive away (back past the convent to the main road, turn left and look for the signposted right turn).

Hotels and B&Bs

L'Arca Via Rocco Pirri 14 ℡0931.838.656 or 333.140.4324, ⊛www.notobarocca.com /arcarooms. Convenient, friendly B&B that offers three cheerfully furnished rooms and a panoramic terrace. Closed Oct to March. No credit cards. ❹

Centro Storico Corso Vittorio Emanuele 64 ℡0931.573.967, ⊛www.centro-storico.com. The name says it all – it's right on the main drag in the historic centre, with a couple of en-suite rooms available. Closed Feb & Nov. No credit cards. ❸

La Fontanella Via Rosolino Pilo 3 ℡0931.894.724, ⊛www .albergolafontanella.it. Thirteen charming rooms in a sympathetically restored nineteenth-century *palazzo* on the northern edge of the old town. It's a three-star place, and is the only hotel (rather than B&B) actually in the centre. Parking around here is easy, and it's a 10min walk down to the middle of town. Prices in July and August might just creep into the next category up. ❹

Masseria degli Ulivi 12km north of Noto, SS287 ℡0931.813.019, ⊛www.masseriadegliulivi.com.

If you prefer country living, this rural estate deep in the countryside fits the bill. It's been beautifully restored using traditional materials, and there's a good restaurant, plus outdoor pool under the olive trees. ❼

Villa Canisello Via Cesare Pavese 1 ℡0931.835.793, ⊛www.villacanisello.it. An old farmhouse on the western outskirts of town in a quiet residential suburb; rooms open to a patio or terrace, and there's parking. Signs lead you right there from the western end of the corso; it seems like a bit of a slog, but it's actually only a 10min walk to the centre. ❺

Vinci Via Cavour 113–115 ℡347.807.2385, ⊛www.bedandbreakfastvinci.it. A "rooms" place just a block up off the corso – the owner doesn't live there and usually has to be summoned by phone. Four large air-conditioned rooms, each with a fridge, and street parking right outside (or 100m down the road in the free car park). You get a coupon for a coffee-and-croissant breakfast at a bar down on the corso. No credit cards. ❹

Youth hostel

Il Castello Via Fratelli Bandiera 2 ℡392.415.7899, ⊛www.notobarocca.com/ostello. Noto's youth hostel (open 24hr) is housed in a renovated *palazzo* in the upper town, with wonderful views, large

dormitories, excellent showers and laundry service. It's accessible from the centre in a few minutes up signposted steps from Via Cavour, behind the Duomo. Dorm beds €15, includes breakfast.

The Town

From the public gardens on the eastern side of town, the centre of Noto is approached through the monumental **Porta Reale**, built in 1838 and topped by the three symbols of the town's allegiance to the Bourbon monarchy: a dog, a tower and a pelican (respectively, loyalty, strength and sacrifice). The main **Corso Vittorio Emanuele**, running from here through the heart of the lower, patricians' quarter, is lined with some of Sicily's most glorious buildings – now the traffic's kept out you can stand back and admire them at will, while floodlights, many set into the pavement, show them off to glorious effect at night.

Halfway along, **Piazza del Municipio** forms the dramatic centrepiece of the design, with the imposing twin-towered **Duomo** now magnificently restored. Following the collapse of its dome in 1996, it was closed and swathed in scaffolding for years, but it was reopened before assembled dignitaries and expectant crowds in June 2007. First completed in 1776, it's said to have been inspired by models of Borromini's churches in Rome – the story of its reconstruction, and some of the Duomo's treasures, are on display around the back of the cathedral (entrance on Via Cavour; daily 9.30am–1pm & 3.30–8pm; €1.50). The church piazza is bordered by gleaming, restored buildings that look now as they must have done when first built, including the **Palazzo Ducezio** (or Municipio, the Town Hall) opposite, presenting a lovely, convex front of columns and long stone balconies.

The next street west of the Duomo, the steep Via C. Nicolaci, culminates in the elliptical **Monte Vergine** church. It's a perfectly framed view that's enhanced during the annual **Infiorata** flower festival (third weekend of May), when flower petals are laid up the entire street in a swirl of intricate designs. **Palazzo Villadorata**, the palace that flanks the west side of the street, also makes rather an unusual, not to say eccentric, sight. Onto a strictly classical front six extravagant balconies were grafted, supported by the last word in sculpted buttresses – griffins, galloping horses and bald and bearded figures with fat-cheeked cherubs at their bellies. The *palazzo* is currently closed to the public, though it has been open in the past for guided visits. Back on the corso, at the bottom of Via Nicolaci, there are panoramic views from the top of the belltower of the church of **San Carlo** (daily 9am–1pm & 3.30–7.30pm; €1.50).

The corso sweeps on to Piazza XVI Maggio, with the tourist office on one side and Noto's **Teatro Comunale** on the other (concert season is Octto May). A €3 combination ticket lets you into the richly decorated theatre auditorium, as well as the so-called "Hall of Mirrors" in the Municipio with its splendid *trompe l'oeil* ceiling, and the **Museo Civico** (closed Mon) of contemporary art on the corso – the town's archeological and historical collections are still locked away pending renovation. Opening hours for all vary, and the theatre and Town Hall are sometimes closed for rehearsals and events, but the tourist office can tell you the latest.

Finally, it's well worth leaving the corso to explore the upper part of town, where few tourists tread. It's filled with massive monastic houses and the dwellings of Noto's poorer eighteenth-century citizens, who had their own church, Gagliardi's **Santíssimo Crocifisso**, in Piazza Mazzini. The elegant former monastery of **San Tommaso**, which flanks the square, is now a prison, of all things, its cell bars screened by opaque glass windows.

▲ The Duomo at Noto

Eating, drinking and entertainment

Although there are surprisingly few **restaurants** in the centre of Noto, you'll be able to ring the changes over a couple of days, and prices are reasonable. The cafés along the corso come into their own during the evening *passeggiata*, while the local authorities put on a full range of **concerts and events** throughout the year, from religious processions at Easter to summer music festivals.

Il Barocco Via Cavour 8 ☎0931.835.999. Housed in the former stables of a *palazzo*, the best thing here is the courtyard dining. The menu is fairly standard – pasta and grilled meat and fish for €6–10, plus pizzas in the evening – though the house special spaghetti springs a surprise as you open the foil to reveal a *frutti di mare* sauce. Moderate.

Costanzo Via Silvio Spaventa 7–11 ☎0931.835.243. A well-known *pasticceria* and *gelateria*, known for its locally made sweets and pastries, including dreamy *cassata*. Inexpensive.

Neas Via Rocco Pirri 30 ☎0931.573.538. Dine under a jasmine canopy in the courtyard of the Palazzo Battaglia. There's a good-value menu of pasta and fish (€7–12), including dishes like swordfish dressed with mountain herbs or stuffed sardines. Closed Tues in winter. Moderate.

Al Terrazzo Via A. Baccarini 4–6 ☎0931.839.710. The place for pizza in the centre, just behind the Municipio, with sheltered outdoor picnic-style tables raked down the sloping street. Inexpensive.

Trattoria del Cármine Via Ducezio 1 ☎0931.838.705. Locals recommend this for a good meal at low cost and it's certainly pretty remarkable value, with rustic antipasto and pasta dishes running €4–6 and most grilled fish around €9. The downside? It's very brightly lit, the house wine is challenging to say the least and the interconnected rooms get very busy, but it defines perfectly the phrase "cheap and cheerful". Closed Mon. Inexpensive.

Ávola and the Cava Grande

Around 15km northeast of Noto, on the Siracusa road, the agricultural town of **ÁVOLA** also has an old Baroque centre, though in this instance partly reconstructed on a hexagonal design after earthquake damage. An idea of its erstwhile proportions can be gleaned in the huge central Piazza Umberto, which together with the long main Corso Vittorio Emanuele is lined with gracious *palazzi*. Regular buses and trains come here from Noto (the bus drops you closer to the main piazza), but it hardly warrants a special trip, and you're more likely to call in if you're driving. Glinting in the distance is the seaside settlement of **Ávola Marina**, 2km to the east, where even out of season you'll be able to find somewhere open for lunch. However, the best trip is up into the hills above Ávola to the Cava Grande.

Cava Grande del Fiume Cassìbile

A spectacular winding route northeast of Ávola climbs past the Convento di Ávola Vecchia to the magnificent gorge and nature reserve of the **Cava Grande**. That's about a 15km drive, or you can also approach from Noto up the SS287, past the turn-off for Noto Antica, in which case you can return *down* the switchbacks instead towards Ávola. There's parking by a sensational viewpoint over the Cassibíle River gorge, which really is quite Grand Canyon-esque, with sheer rock walls visible across the divide, birds of prey circling, and the river glistening far below. The very steep path that leads down to the valley bottom is closed at times of high fire risk, and an information booth posts dire warnings of the dangers of the descent. You certainly need to be properly shod, fit enough to climb back out, and to carry plenty of water. The round trip requires a good three hours, plus any time you spend splashing in the natural swimming pools or following the footpath alongside the river, which runs for most of the gorge's 11km length. At the top, at the parking area, you can get a drink or a meal from a rustic tavern, the *Trattoria Cava Grande*.

The coastal route to the cape

South of Noto and Ávola lies the most undeveloped stretch of coast on the east side of the island, sheltering some excellent sand beaches and an extensive nature reserve. Minor roads run all the way south to the **Capo delle Correnti**, the southernmost point of Sicily, while in between a couple of old restored fishing villages serve as small-scale summer resorts. Just inland, the country town of **Pachino** stands in the middle of a thriving market-garden region, the fields given over to greenhouses and polytunnels sheltering tomatoes, strawberries and artichokes – the small Pachino cherry tomatoes, particularly, are a staple on local restaurant menus. With a car, you can see the whole of the coast from Noto in a day, as far as the cape and back, though there are also several good rural **accommodation** options. Local **buses** (summer only) run from Noto to the nearest bit of coast at Lido di Noto, and there's also a regular year-round service from Siracusa/Noto to Pachino.

Lido di Noto, Eloro and the Riserva Naturale di Vendicari

Noto's local beach, 5km southeast at **LIDO DI NOTO**, is fine for a swim and a bite to eat (in summer at least). You can walk from here (though it's easier to drive) just south to the seaside ruins of Helorus, or **Eloro** (daily 9am–1pm; free), a Syracusan colony founded in the seventh century BC at the mouth of the Tellaro River. It's all a bit ramshackle, and the few remains are quite difficult to make head or tail of, but its position right above the shore is very attractive. The broad expanse of sand below offers good swimming, but direct access is tricky from the site: a road to the south, across the river, leads directly to the beach.

A few kilometres further south down the main Pachino road (SP 19), a signposted turn leads to the excellent **Riserva Naturale di Vendicari** (always open; free), which protects the local marshes, lagoons, dunes and disused saltpans from future development. There's parking at the entrance (€3 if someone's there), but no other facilities; you can get the Pachino bus to drop you on the main road and walk the short distance to the reserve. Loads of waterbirds can be seen from the hides (though the more than three hundred flamingos can be elusive at times), while sandy tracks and boardwalks fan out north and south through the marshland, leading to some splendid sand crescents. The reserve takes its name from the brick tower, the Torre Vendícari, which looms over a part-restored *tonnara* (tuna-fishing village) by one of the beaches. Its internal courtyards and sandstone pillars gleam brightly against a turquoise sea. Another good beach, signposted **San Lorenzo**, lies just a short drive further south of the reserve, down the main Pachino road, which has very clear water and a small summer lido.

Accommodation and food

Dancing Flamingo Contrada Calcicera, near Villa Bimmisca, 5km west of Riserva Naturale ☎339.818.1742, ⓦwww.dancingflamingo.com. Billed as a summer country resort, the *Dancing Flamingo* offers a wide array of rooms, from wooden bungalows with shared bathrooms to a rustic garden suite with a private courtyard, and you can even camp here too. Prices vary considerably, depending on type of accommodation, but are roughly €25–35 per person for most of the summer, breakfast included (not campers), but higher from mid-July to Aug. Lunch and dinner are available – the food has an international flavour, and is inexpensive – while you can book a Thai massage and other stress-busting treatments. A shuttle bus runs to Noto or the local beaches. Closed Oct–May. ❷–❺

Il Roveto Contrada Roveto-Vendicari ☎0931.66.024, ⓦwww.roveto.it. This beautifully restored old farmhouse is signposted at the Riserva Naturale turn-off on the SP19 Pachino road. Self-contained apartments with kitchen sleep either two, four or six people, and you're only a few hundred metres from the pristine Torre Vendícari beach. Three-night minimum stay. ❹, July & Aug ❺

Pachino, Marzamemi and the cape

All roads locally zero in on the area's main town, **PACHINO**, which while pleasant enough isn't really the point of a visit to the cape region. A minor road (and local buses) runs 4km out to the coast at **MARZAMEMI**, prettily set around a crescent harbour, backed by the port's old *tonnara*, which is currently being given a holiday face-lift. Behind the shell of a church and *palazzo*, the restored *tonnara* square shelters a few bars and restaurants that come into their own in high summer, when tourists descend on Marzamemi in their cars and yachts.

Eight kilometres south of Marzamemi, down the rugged coastal road, **PORTOPALO DI CAPO PÁSSERO** is another low-key summer resort, again with a ruined *tonnara*, and also with several bars along the main street, a local campsite and three or four reasonable hotels, though none that stands out. You might be able to persuade someone to row you over to the little islet that lies just offshore, complete with a seventeenth-century castle. Otherwise, follow the minor cape road out to the southeastern point of **Isola delle Correnti**, where another campsite sits in happy isolation behind its own unspoiled sandy bay. You're on the southernmost tip of Sicily here, with nothing between you and Africa.

Festivals

April
Last Sunday St George's Day celebrations in **Ragusa Ibla**: statues paraded through the streets and a costumed procession.

May
1 Procession in **Siracusa**, with the statue of St Lucy carried around town.

May/June
Classical drama festival at **Siracusa**, events taking place in the Greek theatre.

August
First Sunday Boat race (*palio*) round Ortygia island in **Siracusa**, in which the five traditional quarters of the city compete with raucous enthusiasm.

27–29 Festivities in **Ragusa** to mark the city's patron St John the Baptist; more processions and statues.
29 Start of Madonna delle Lácrime festival (devoted to the "weeping" Madonna) in **Siracusa**; runs until September 3.
Last Sunday Festival of St Corrado in **Noto**.

December
13 Festival of St Lucy in **Siracusa**: a procession to the church of Santa Lucia.

Travel details

Trains

Ragusa to: Cómiso (5 daily; 30min); Gela (5 daily; 1hr 20min); Íspica (5 daily; 1hr 10min); Módica (Mon–Sat 8 daily, Sun 6 daily; 20min); Noto (5–6 daily; 1hr 30min); Scicli (5–6 daily; 35min); Siracusa (5–6 daily; 2hr); Vittória (5–6 daily; 40min).
Siracusa to: Augusta (10–11 daily; 30min); Catania (10 daily; 1hr 25min); Lentini (10 daily; 55min); Messina (9 daily; 3hr); Módica (Mon–Sat 9 daily, Sun 6 daily; 1hr 50min); Noto (Mon–Sat 9 daily, Sun 6 daily; 30min); Ragusa (4 daily; 2hr 10min); Taormina (10 daily; 2hr).

Buses

Módica to: Catania (Mon–Sat 10 daily, Sun 6 daily; 2hr); Catania airport (Mon–Sat 10 daily, Sun 6 daily; 1hr 45min); Íspica (Mon–Sat 13 daily, Sun 3 daily; 20min–1hr); Pachino (Mon–Sat 2 daily; 1hr 20min); Ragusa (Mon–Sat hourly, Sun 2 daily; 25min); Scicli (Mon–Sat 14 daily, Sun 2 daily; 30–40min); Siracusa (Mon–Sat 8 daily, Sun 3 daily; 2hr–2hr 30min).
Noto to: Ávola (19 daily Mon–Sat, 5 daily Sun; 15min); Eloro (Mon–Sat 4 daily; 20min); Íspica (12 daily Mon–Sat, 8 daily Sun; 50min); Siracusa (Mon–Sat 7 daily, Sun 3 daily; 55min).
Pachino to: Marzamemi (Mon–Sat 11 daily; 10min); Portopalo di Capo Pássero (Mon–Sat 11 daily; 15min); Siracusa (8 daily Mon–Sat, 3 daily Sun; 1hr 30min).
Ragusa to: Kamarina (Mon–Sat 9 daily; 1hr); Catania airport/Catania (Mon–Fri 12 daily, Sat & Sun 5–6 daily; 1hr 45min–2hr); Chiaramonte Gulfi (Mon–Sat 7 daily; 55min); Gela (Mon–Sat 2 daily; 1hr 40min); Íspica (Mon–Sat 7 daily; 1hr); Módica (Mon–Sat 12 daily, Sun 3 daily; 30min); Noto (Mon–Sat 10 daily, Sun 1 daily; 1hr 50min); Palermo (Mon–Sat 4 daily, Sun 2 daily; 4hr);

Scicli (Mon–Sat 9 daily, Sun 2 daily; 40min); Siracusa (Mon–Sat 9 daily; 2hr 15min).

Siracusa to: Augusta (Mon–Sat 9 daily; 40min); Ávola (9 daily Mon–Sat, 3 daily Sun; 40min); Catania (16 daily Mon–Sat, 4 daily Sun; 1hr 20min); Catania airport (6–7 daily; 1hr); Ferla (Mon–Sat 1 daily; 1hr 30min); Lentini (Mon–Sat 12 daily; 55min); Módica (8 daily Mon–Sat, 3 daily Sun; 2hr); Naples (1 daily; 10hr); Noto (12 daily Mon–Sat, 4 daily Sun; 40min); Pachino (8 daily Mon–Sat, 3 daily Sun; 1hr 30min); Palazzolo Acréide (16 daily Mon–Sat, 8 daily Sun; 1hr); Palermo (6 daily Mon–Sat, 3 daily Sun; 3hr 15min); Piazza Armerina (Mon–Sat 1 daily; 2hr 30min); Ragusa (Mon–Sat 5 daily; 2hr 15min); Sortino (Mon–Sat 9 daily; 1hr 15min).

The interior

CHAPTER 7

Highlights

✳ **Enna** Spend a day exploring the old town and museums of this ancient hill-town, and take in the view from Castello di Lombardia that extends to Etna. See p.291

✳ **Driving the SS120** Wending its way through some gorgeous landscape, this picturesque road makes a wonderful jumping-off point for a leisurely drive, cycle or hike through the heart of Sicily. See p.297

✳ **Petralia Sottana** A beautifully preserved and sited small town, high in the Madonie National Park, that's a great base for walkers. See p.301

✳ **Villa Romana del Casale, Piazza Armerina** One of the foremost sights of the island, thanks to their scale, diversity and vitality, the Roman mosaics near Piazza Armerina should not be missed. See p.311

✳ **La Scala, Caltagirone** In a town famed for its ceramics, these 142 steps are adorned with beautiful patterned tiles. See p.319

▲ Roman mosaic at Villa Romana del Casale, near Piazza Armerina

The interior

... for the last five hours all they had set eyes on were bare hillsides flaming
yellow under the sun ... They had passed through crazed-looking villages washed
in palest blue; crossed dry beds of torrents over fantastic bridges; skirted sheer
precipices which no sage and broom could temper. Never a tree, never a drop of
water; just sun and dust.

Giuseppe di Lampedusa, *The Leopard*

Though Sicily's slow cross-country trains and the limited-exit autostrada
(the A19) do little to encourage stops in the island's vast and mountainous
interior, only here can you truly begin to get off the tourist trail. It's an
intensely rural region that holds just two or three decent-sized towns,
bunched together almost in the dead centre of the island. Outside these, much
of the land is burnt dry during the long summer months, the cracked fields
and shrivelled plantations affording a meagre living to the sparse population.
Unlike elsewhere in Italy, those who cultivated the land here (if it was
cultivable) preferred to travel to work from their towns and villages rather than
living on site. Now thoroughly depleted by mass emigration, the countryside
is empty and you're unlikely to see much sign of life outside the small hill-top
towns. Even so, these settlements, though often moribund, occasionally possess
an exuberance and vitality that's in startling contrast to the stillness of the
interior's rolling hills.

Travelling in the interior can get monotonous, as much of the land is given
over to extensive cornfields – a feature of the Sicilian landscape since Greek
times – but there are compensations for coming this far off the beaten track.
Certain minor inland routes provide fascinating glimpses of a life that's all but
disappeared in the rest of Sicily, indeed Italy, and offer some of the finest
itineraries and views on the island, as well as some of its most curious towns.

A blustery mountain settlement dominating the dry hills below, **Enna** is as
central as you can get, and makes a good starting point for trips to the
untouched towns and villages of the **northeastern interior**, of which **Nicosia**
is the main attraction. The largest town in the region, **Caltanissetta**, is also the
most disappointing, largely modern and devoid of charm. With your own
transport, however, the region beyond – the little-visited **western interior** –
makes an absorbing journey, stretching to **Corleone**: an agricultural centre that,
like so many in the neighbourhood, is tainted by its Mafia associations.

Although the Arabs settled the centre of the island, leaving their mark in a
number of place names and warren-like towns, the Greeks and Romans tended
to leave Sicily's interior alone. Nevertheless, the **southern interior** boasts some
unexpected ancient gems, not least the pictorial mosaics of **Villa Romana del
Casale**, built and decorated on a sumptuous scale in the rolling countryside

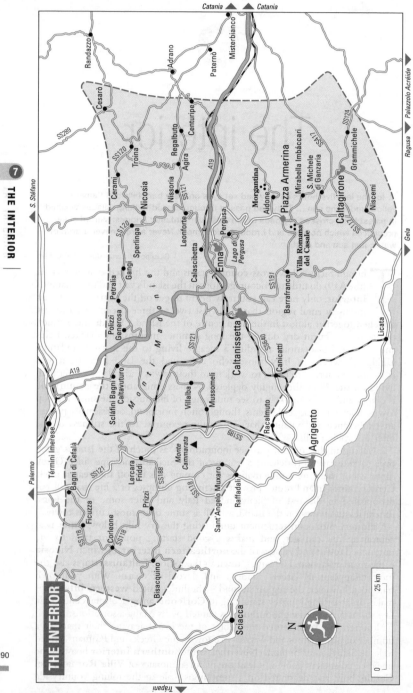

THE INTERIOR

25 km

0

N

Catania   Catania

Randazzo

Cesarò

SS289

S. Stéfano

SS120

Troìna

Cerami

Nicosia

SS120

Gangi

Sperlinga

Petralia

Polizzi
Generosa

M o n t i   M a d o n i e

A19

Sclàfini Bagni
Caltavuturo

Bagni di Cefalà

Términi Imerese

Palermo

Trápani

SS118

Ficuzza

SS118

Corleone

SS118

Bisacquino

Lercara
Friddi

Prizzi

SS121

SS188

SS118

Sant'Angelo Muxaro

Monte
Cammarata

Raffadali

SS681

Racalmuto

Agrigento

Sciacca

Adrano

Paternò

Misterbianco

Centuripe

Regalbuto

Agira

A19

SS121

Nissoria

Leonforte

Calascibetta

Calascibetta

Enna

Pergusa
Lago di
Pergusa

SS121

Villalba

Mussomeli

Caltanissetta

SS640

Canicattì

Licata

SS191

Barrafranca

Morgantina
Aidone

Piazza Armerina

Mirabella Imbáccari

S. Michele
di Ganzaria

Villa Romana
del Casale

SS417

Grammichele

Caltagirone

Niscemi

SS117bis

SS124

Palazzolo Acréide

Ragusa

Gela

Licata

outside **Piazza Armerina**. There's interest, too, in the excavations at **Morgantina**, while ceramic-studded **Caltagirone** makes a handy departure point for the Baroque towns of the southeast.

As you might imagine, public transport is patchy at best, though you can easily reach all the important centres – Enna, Caltanissetta, Piazza Armerina and Caltagirone – by bus or train. It's more difficult to travel away from the large towns, into the mountains: most accessible are the hill-top towns of the northeast, with **buses** running out of Enna and along the two major routes, the SS120 and SS121. The towns and villages west of Caltanissetta are far more difficult to reach without your **own transport**, and a car would make visiting the rest of the region a lot easier, too. If you are dependent on public transport, and only have limited time, then it's hard to look beyond Enna and Pizza Armerina as the two most impoatant destinations.

Enna and the northeastern interior

Despite its stranded mountain-top position and frontier feel, it takes no great effort to reach **Enna** these days: there are regular buses and trains from Catania and Palermo. Without your own transport, however, you'll usually have to be prepared to spend the night, certainly if you intend to move further into the **northeastern interior** to some of the least-developed parts of the island. Fairly frequent **buses** leave Enna for towns along the eastbound **SS121**, which eventually runs to Catania. From **Leonforte**, first stop on this route, buses head north to **Nicosia**, which sits in the middle of a second route, the **SS120**. Eastward, this runs to **Cesarò** and on into the foothills of Etna, though it's fairly hard to travel this section by public transport; heading west to **Polizzi Generosa** is an easier choice, as all the towns are connected by bus. A few places along the SS120 (east and west) can also be reached from towns on the Tyrrhenian coast, cutting across dramatic tracts of the Nébrodi and Madonie mountains.

Enna

From a bulging V-shaped ridge almost 1000m up, **ENNA** lords it over the surrounding hills of central Sicily. One of the most ancient towns on the island, Enna has only ever had one function: Livy described it as "inexpugnabilis", and, for obvious strategic reasons, the town was a magnet for successive hostile armies, who in turn besieged and fortified it. The Arabs, for example, spent twenty years trying to gain entrance to Enna before eventually, in 859, resorting to crawling in through the sewers. The approach to this mountain stronghold is still formidable, the road climbing slowly out of the valley and looping across

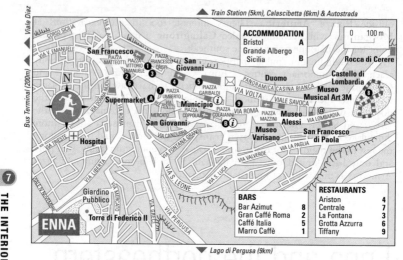

ACCOMMODATION
Bristol A
Grande Albergo
Sicilia B

Rocca di Cerere

0   100 m

Duomo
Castello di Lombardia
Museo Musical Art 3M
Museo Alessi
San Francesco di Paola
Museo Varisano
Municipio
San Giovanni
Supermarket
San Francesco
San Giovanni
Hospital
Giardino Pubblico
Torre di Federico II

ENNA

BARS
Bar Azimut   8
Gran Caffè Roma   2
Caffè Italia   5
Marro Caffè   1

RESTAURANTS
Ariston   4
Centrale   7
La Fontana   3
Grotta Azzurra   6
Tiffany   9

Lago di Pergusa (9km)

the solid crag to the summit and the town. Enna remains medieval at heart, as any foray into its densely packed streets shows, and even the modern development echoes the town's defensive past, its office buildings and apartment blocks rising like so many watchtowers from a distance.

The very distinct hill-town atmosphere here makes it worth staying overnight. Summer evenings in Enna are among the most enjoyable in Sicily, watching the sun set from some of the finest vantage points imaginable. Come in winter and you should expect snow, the wind blowing hard through the streets, and white slopes blending with the anaemic stone buildings.

Arrival and information

Most long-distance and local buses use the **bus terminal** on Viale Diaz in the new town – to reach Piazza Vittorio Emanuele from the terminal, turn right, right again down Corso Sicilia, and it's around a ten-minute walk. The **train station**, however, is 5km north of town: a local bus runs roughly hourly to the town centre (less frequently on Sun), for which tickets cost €1.35; a taxi into town will cost around €10. For train information, call ☎0935.500.910 or 848.888.088.

Everywhere in Enna itself can be reached very easily on foot. Hourly **buses to Pergusa** (until 10.15pm) depart from Piazza Matteotti, outside San Francesco church; you'll need a ticket (€1) before you get on, bought from *tabacchi* and valid for one hour. **Taxi** ranks can be found along Viale Diaz, near the bus terminal, on Via Pergusa and at Piazza Vittorio Emanuele; alternatively, call ☎0935.500.905.

Information on both Enna and Piazza Armerina is available from the **tourist office** at Via Roma 413 (Mon, Tues & Thurs–Sat 8.30am–1.30pm, Wed 8.30am–7pm; ☎0935.528.288, ⓦwww.apt-enna.com), which can also supply a good free **map** of Enna. There's a smaller office in Piazza Colaianni (Mon, Tues, Thurs & Fri 8am–2pm, Wed 8am–6.15pm; ☎0935.500.875), next to the *Grande Albergo Sicilia*.

Accommodation

Enna itself holds only two **hotels**, both dead-central. If these are full, or too expensive for your budget, the best alternative is in the neighbouring village of Calascibetta. Otherwise, try the selection at nearby Pergusa.

Affittacamere Da Pietro Contrada Longobardi, Calascibetta ☏ 0935.33.647 or 340.276.5763. Surrounded by a garden, this pleasant B&B, well signposted on the lower edge of the village of Calascibetta, 6km north of Enna, has a wide terrace where breakfast is served. No credit cards. ❷

Bristol Piazza Grisleri ☏ 0935.24.415, ⓦ www .hotelbristolenna.it. Though it's much more up-to-date than the *Grande Albergo*, the fully-equipped

rooms at the more secluded *Bristol* are fairly bland. Rates include breakfast. ❺

Grande Albergo Sicilia Piazza Colaianni ☏ 0935.500.850, ⓦ www.hotelsiciliaenna.it. Behind its brutalist exterior, the Grande Albergo hides an Art Deco lobby and nicely refurbished rooms kitted out with hand-painted furniture and fine art; you might even swing a discount if they're not full. Rates include breakfast. ❺

The Town

Despite the numerous wars that have touched the town over the years, most of Enna's remains are medieval and in good condition. The prize exhibit, the thirteenth-century **Castello di Lombardia** (daily: summer 8am–8pm; winter 9am–5pm; free), dominates the easternmost spur of town. Built by Frederick II, it's a mighty construction with its strong walls complete, guarding the steep slopes on either side of town. Six surviving towers (out of an original twenty) provide lookouts; the tallest, the Torre Pisana, is worth climbing for great views of Enna itself, the rugged countryside in all directions, and across to Mount Etna. Back down, it's a good spot to lounge about with a picnic.

A road to the side of the castle climbs a little way further to the **Rocca di Cerere**, an exposed outcrop where some scattered foundations are presumed to be the remnants of a temple erected by Gelon in 480 BC. Enna was the centre of the Greek cult of Demeter, the fertility goddess (her Roman counterpart was Ceres, hence the rock's name), and the most famous of the myths associated with the goddess – the carrying off of her daughter, Persephone, to the underworld – is supposed to have taken place just a few kilometres away, at Lago di Pergusa.

Attractive chunks of the **old town** survive intact too, albeit much worn by the brisk winds that scurry across the squares and streets, even in summer. Tightly packed houses hug the two ridges that divide Enna, occasional gaps revealing swirling drops down into the valleys. Though it's fun to wander through the crumbly southern and eastern sections of Enna, virtually all the accredited sights lie stretched out along and around the narrow, better-preserved **Via Roma**, a continuation of Via Lombardia that descends from the castle. First stop down is the **Museo Musical Art 3M** at Via Roma 533 (Tues–Sun 9am–1pm & 3–7pm; €2), a mishmash of an exhibition that features projections of the work of artists who have a (sometimes remote) connection with Sicily – for example Caravaggio, Lo Zoppo di Gangi and Antonello di Messina – all to the rather hammy accompaniment of originally composed orchestral music. A few photographs and costumes are also on show, as well as a reconstruction of a sulphur mine, a reminder of an industry that once dominated this part of Sicily. If you're in a tolerant mood, it'll do to pass twenty minutes or less.

The street carries on, interrupted by small piazzas, one of which fronts the hemmed-in **Duomo** (daily 9am–noon & 4–7pm), dating in part from 1307. Rebuilt several times since, its long medieval wall, which has Gothic touches, is hardly complemented by the Duomo's thin Baroque facade, while the spacious sixteenth-century interior, whose every surface is ornamented, features huge supporting dark-grey columns, the bases of which are carved with grotesques – manic heads with human hands and snake bodies, snarling mouths and dome-like pates.

Outside the Duomo, the **Museo Alessi** normally holds the impressive contents of the cathedral's own treasury, but is currently closed indefinitely for bureaucratic reasons. If you do find it open, however, it's worth looking into for some remarkable examples of handiwork, including a tall eighteenth-century wooden cabinet that opens to reveal a silver throne, and a seventeenth-century gold and crystal crown decorated with minute scenes from the life of Christ, picked out with studded jewels. It holds a rich collection of local church art too, downstairs, and cases of old coins on the floor above. A second archeological museum, equally good, lies at the back of the Piazza Mazzini, opposite the cathedral – the **Museo Varisano** (Tues–Fri 8am–7pm; €2), which covers Neolithic to Roman times. All the exhibits, which include a fine series of painted Greek vases, were dug up in the locality.

Via Roma continues down past the Catalan-Gothic **Palazzo Pollicarini**, opposite the *Grande Albergo Sicilia*. The *palazzo* has now been turned into apartments, but you can peek into the courtyard to see the typical medieval Catalan exterior staircase that climbs up to the first floor. Immediately west, in Piazza Coppola, the fourteenth-century church of **San Giovanni** has a Catalan-Gothic facade and a tower crowned by a little cupola.

The western extremity of Via Roma is marked by the sloping, rectangular **Piazza Vittorio Emanuele**, focal point of the evening *passeggiata*. Off here, a long cliff-edge promenade looks out to the little rust-coloured village of Calascibetta over the valley. The plain, high wall of the church of **San Francesco**, which flanks the piazza, has a massive sixteenth-century tower, previously part of the old town's system of watchtowers that linked the castle with all Enna's churches.

One watchtower still stands in isolation in the **Giardino Púbblico**, in the largely modern south of the town. An octagonal tower, 24m high, the **Torre di Federico II** (Mon–Sat 8am–6pm, Sun 8am–1pm; free) is a survivor of the alterations to the city made by Frederick of Aragon, who added a (now hidden) underground passage connecting the tower to the castle. You can climb to the top for more great views.

Calascibetta

Close to Enna, on a lower hill to the north across the valley, the small town of **CALASCIBETTA** hints at what Enna would be like without the tower blocks. Once a Saracen town, it was fortified by Count Roger in his successful attempt to take Enna in 1087, and the brooding atmosphere in its tangled streets seems straight from that age. Tightly packed red-stone buildings are perched above a sheer drop on the eastern side, rising to the restored Chiesa Madre at the very top. There are frequent buses to Calascibetta from Enna's bus terminal (or every couple of hours from Enna's train station), but only two on Sunday.

Eating and drinking

When it comes to eating and drinking, Enna offers considerable choice. Try one of the reasonably priced **restaurants** listed below, or, for a drink or a snack, drop into one of the many appealing *pasticcerie* and **bars** in town, most stretched along Via Roma. You can buy your own food from stalls in the traffic-free **Mercato Sant'Antonio**, off Piazza Coppola, or the Upim **supermarket** on Via Roma.

Restaurants

Ariston Via Roma 353 ☎ 0935.26.038. Formal place specializing in fresh pasta and good Sicilian dishes; expect to pay €25–30 a head for a full meal with wine. Closed Sun. Moderate.

Centrale Piazza VI Dicembre 9 ☎ 0935.500.963. Off Via Roma, this place attracts a local crowd with its bright interior and large table of antipasti. You'll spend €15–20 for two courses, or go for one of the fixed-price menus. Closed Sat. Moderate.

La Fontana Via Vulturo 6 ☎ 0935.25.465. Friendly place offering good meat specialities, with some outdoor tables near a spouting fountain. A full meal costs around €18. Closed Fri off-season. Moderate.

Grotta Azzurra Via Colaianni ☎ 0935.24.328. Run for 45 years by the charming Giuseppe and Maria, this tiny place serves the cheapest meals in town: €3 for *primi* and €4.50 for *secondi*. Snug and lively, it's just down the hill between Piazza Matteotti and Piazza Vittorio Emanuele: follow the signs up the alley. Closed Sat off-season. No credit cards. Inexpensive.

Tiffany Via Roma 487. Handily placed, just down from the cathedral, this offers pizzas and regular Italian dishes from €6–10. Closed Thurs. Moderate.

Bars

Bar Azimut Castello di Lombardia. A good place for a shady drink, just inside the castle grounds.

Gran Caffè Roma Via Roma 312. Off Piazza Vittorio Emanuele, this place serves wine by the glass and has tables at the back. Closed Tues.

Caffé Italia Piazza Garibaldi. Tasty snacks, drinks and light meals.

Marro Caffè Piazza Vittorio Emanuele. With outdoor seating, a lively central spot for a drink and nibbles. Closed Thurs.

Listings

Bank Several banks with ATMs are located along Via Roma.

Bus companies All are at the bus terminal: SAIS ☎ 0935.500.902, ⓦ www.saisautolinee.it (for Calascibetta, Caltanissetta, Catania, Catania airport, Messina, Palermo and Piazza Armerina); Interbus ☎ 0935.565.111, ⓦ www.interbus.it (for Agira, Catania, Leonforte and Nicosia); ISEA ☎ 095.464.101, ⓦ www.iseaviaggi.it (for Cerami, Cesarò, Nicosia and Troina).

Cinema Cinema Arena Pergusa, on the road just out of Pergusa towards Enna, puts on outdoor screenings between July and mid-Sept: pick up a programme from the tourist office or call ☎ 0935.542.319 or 335.772.9664.

Emergencies Ambulance ☎ 118; police ☎ 113.

Hospital Ospedale Umberto I, Contrada Ferrante in Enna Bassa, on the road to Pergusa ☎ 0935.516.111.

Internet Ciemme, Via Lombardia 31 (Mon–Sat 9am–9pm).

Pharmacies Librizzi, Piazza Vittorio Emanuele 20 ☎ 0935.500.908; Farmacia del Centro, Via Roma 315 ☎ 0935.500.650.

Police Questura at Via San Giuseppe 4 ☎ 0935.522.111.

Post office Via A. Volta, off Piazza Garibaldi (Mon–Fri 8am–6.30pm, Sat 8am–12.30pm).

Lago di Pergusa

Nine kilometres south of Enna (and served by regular buses), the **Lago di Pergusa** is the legendary site of Hades' abduction of Persephone to the underworld. The story has it that Persephone, surrounded by nymphs, was gathering flowers on the lush banks of the lake when Hades emerged from a chasm beneath the water and spirited her away. Demeter searched in vain for her daughter, and her grief at the loss of Persephone prevented the corn from growing. To settle the matter, Zeus ruled that Persephone should spend half the year as queen of the Underworld, and live for the other six months in Sicily with her mother as one of the island's goddesses. In her gratitude, Demeter, as goddess of grain and agriculture, made the corn grow again – a powerful symbol in a traditionally fertile land.

These days, the lake is encircled by a motor-racing track. Though things are peaceful enough when there are no race meetings, it's hard now, despite the pleasant wooded banks beyond the water, to imagine a less romantic spot. Mary Taylor Simeti's journal, *On Persephone's Island*, labels the Lago di Pergusa "a brilliant example of the Sicilians' best efforts to ruin their landscape". There's really no point coming to the lake for any glimpse of the truth behind the legend, though it does make a possible base near Enna.

Practicalities

Several modern **hotels** are located alongside the lake. The best value option on the Enna road is the *Garden* (℡0935.541.694, Ⓦ www.hotelgardenenna.it; ❸), nestled in greenery and with modern, fully equipped rooms. Overlooking the lake on Via Autodromo Pergusa, the *Riviera* (℡0935.541.267, Ⓦ www .hotelrivieraenna.it; ❻) has stylish rooms with wooden floors, as well as a swimming pool. If you don't want to go back into Enna, there are plenty of **places to eat** at reasonable prices, including the modern *Al Carretino* restaurant, on the main road next to the Q8 petrol station, whose pasta speciality (*Cavatelle al Carretino*) is both excellent and cheap (€5.50). Opposite, *Da Carlo*, serves good *gelati* and granitas as well as pizzas, and *La Paglia* has snacks and pastries.

The SS121: Enna to Centúripe

To the east of Enna, the minor SS121 weaves through countryside punctuated by a succession of sleepy little towns and villages. **Leonforte** makes an interesting stop, with its fine old fountain, but the pick of the crop is the dramatic hill-town of **Agira**, which holds considerably more facilities for overnight visitors.

Leonforte

Around forty minutes by bus east of Enna, beyond Calascibetta, **LEONFORTE** is typical of the region, with its roots firmly in the seventeenth century and an attractive central square that sprouts bars in profusion. Besides the impressive Duomo, there's great interest in the domineering Palazzo Baronale, whose bulky facade is recognizable from way outside town. However, Leonforte's most noteworthy sight is **La Granfonte**, about 300m on foot down from the Chiesa Madre overlooking the hills on the edge of town. Built in 1651, it's not so much a fountain as a row of 24 waterspouts set in a sculpted facade of carvings and inscriptions. If you're driving, you'll see the sign for it as you enter the town, but it involves a hefty doubling back on yourself along the one-way system. The fountain is a good place to fill water bottles, and a little bar opposite offers drinks with a view. A couple of reasonable trattorias up in the town centre make it possible to stay the night.

Agira

The bus from Enna steers a course further east from Leonforte through attractive **Nissoria**, whose central leafy street is lined with bars occupied by old men shooting the breeze across the moving traffic. It's another 7km on to **AGIRA**, once more in a fine location on the brow of a hill. From a distance, its buildings form a perfect cone, with the ruins of a long-neglected medieval castle prominent atop the peak.

Practicalities

Agira is the best place along the SS121 for an **overnight stop**, either at the tidy if worn *Albergo Aurora*, Via Annunziata 6 (✆0935.691.416; no credit cards; ❷), with its entrance on Via Bellopadre, 25m up the road, or at the more uplifting *Casa Albergo*, a B&B on the road up to the castle at Via Palazzo 16 (✆0935.691.457 or 333.972.7511; no credit cards; ❸), which offers en-suite rooms, a garden and lofty views from its panoramic terrace.

Agira also boasts a decent selection of places to **eat** and **drink**, including a trio on Via Vittorio Emanuele, the main road through town: *Ristorante al Capriccio*, at no. 423, has great views and inexpensive prices; *Al Muretto* at no. 343, is good for a quick pizza and drink (closed Mon); and steps away at no. 336, the pub-like *De Paris* makes a nice stop for a drink and a snack of roast pork. Just down from the castle at Via Rametta 27, the *Belvedere* (✆0935.696.091) serves good pasta dishes (from €6) and has a terrace with superb panoramas of the lake and hills.

A **Pro Loco** at Piazza Crispi, just off Via Vittorio Emanuele, can provide further information (Mon–Sat 9am–1pm & 3–7pm; ✆0935.961.239). Two or three daily **buses** run north from here to Troina – useful if you want to get to the SS120.

Regalbuto and beyond

The SS121 continues beyond Agira through tiny **REGALBUTO** and eventually to Catania, a journey that strikes through land fiercely contested during the short Sicilian campaign of World War II. The hills between Agira and the western slopes of Etna saw most of the heaviest fighting. Just out of Agira, close to the **Lago di Pozzillo**, there's a poignant **war cemetery** sited on a gentle hillside, the resting place of 490 Canadian soldiers killed in July 1943.

Centúripe

Some 15km on from Regalbuto, a minor road leads south for 8km through orange and olive groves to the isolated outpost of **CENTÚRIPE**, which faces Etna across the Simeto River valley, giving it a strategic importance that accounts for its various power struggles over the centuries. Several medieval campaigns destroyed the town, while the last great battle in August 1943 dislodged German forces. Modern Centúripe is an uneasy mix of new building and an untouched central piazza, near which a terrace provides the outstanding views that earned Centúripe the tag "balcony of Sicily". After gazing at the views, you'll exhaust the town's possibilities in around two minutes flat – perhaps ten, if you stop for a drink at one of the bars in the central square.

The towns beyond Centúripe, on and off the SS121, are covered in the section on the Circumetnea railway; see p.237.

Across the mountains: the SS120

Before the Palermo–Messina coastal road was constructed, traffic between the two cities passed inland, on a long mountainous route that took in some of the island's most impressive scenery. Today, free from the traffic that clogs the coast,

▲ Mountain landscape near Enna

the **SS120** makes an attractive trans-island alternative, across some of the remoter stretches of the Madonie and Nébrodi mountains. Make sure you reserve whatever **accommodation** you may need in advance, though, as the few hotels tend to fill up quickly.

Nicosia

The biggest town on the SS120, and the best base for excursions east and west, is **NICOSIA**, a convoluted, basically medieval mass of cracked *palazzi* topped by the remains of a Norman castle. In the cramped town centre, the chatter-filled Piazza Garibaldi is the site of Nicosia's lovely old cathedral, **San Nicola**, a stately construction with a fourteenth-century facade and belltower, and a sculpted Gothic portal.

Behind the cathedral, Via Salomone rises steeply to the former Saracen district of the town, a jumble of streets occupying one of the four hills on which Nicosia is built. At the top, **Santa Maria Maggiore**, founded in 1267 but rebuilt after an eighteenth-century landslide, has the bells from its campanile piled up outside – they fell down after another earthquake and the sound of them is now electrically reproduced. Inside, amid "No Spitting" notices, you'll find an impressive marble polyptych by Antonello Gagini and a throne used by Charles V when he passed through here in 1535, on the way back from his Tunisian crusade. The views from outside encompass the town's other three promontories, on the highest of which sits the ruined **castello**.

Practicalities

Buses to and from Catania, Enna, Leonforte, Mistretta Palermo, Santo Stéfano di Camastra and Términi Imerese leave Nicosia from Piazza Marconi or Piazza San Francesco di Paola, at the bottom of Via Vittorio Emanuele. You can **stay** centrally at *Umberto I* (☎0935.640.771 or 347.153.53.82; no credit cards; ❸), a tiny B&B at Via Umberto I 34, with all rooms en suite, or for a more comfortable sojourn head for ✦ *Baglio San Pietro*, a kilometre west of town in Contrada San Pietro (signposted from Via Panotto, off the Sperlinga road), a restored farm dating from the seventeenth century; mountain bikes, a pool and a good restaurant with outdoor seating in summer are all on hand (℡0935.640.529 or 328.068.8663, Ⓦwww.bagliosanpietro.com; ❺). Alternatively, if you're driving, you could seek out the comfortable *Vigneta* (℡0935.646.074, Ⓦwww.lavigneta .com; ❷), in Contrada San Basile, about 7km north of town, though it's a somewhat characterless, modern hotel; to find it, follow signs to Mistretta.

Having your own transport will also enable you to seek out *La Cirata* **restaurant**, about 5km towards Enna on the SS117 (℡0935.640.680; closed Mon & Nov), for dishes based on local produce; it's a vast place, catering mainly to passing coach groups, but makes a good alternative to the few basic places in the centre; the four-course tourist menu costs €20.

For a nightcap or ice cream at any time, the **bars** in Piazza Garibaldi are worth a visit: the *Diana*, next to the cathedral, serves *Sapori di Sicilia*, a delicious creamy home-made *gelato* with cinnamon, pistachios and almonds.

East to Cesarò

The towns **east of Nicosia** are set in a bare landscape astride the Monti Nébrodi, dominated ever more dramatically by the giant silhouette of Etna. ISEA buses from Enna and Nicosia run to the first stop, **CERAMI**, 21km away, which lies at the foot of a massive rock topped by the remains of a castle, and to the next town east, **TROINA**, a tortuous thirty-kilometre ride to what, from a distance, appears like a thimble perched on a hill, 1120m high. Troina played a prominent role in the reconquest of Sicily from the Arabs, when it became one of the first cities to be taken by the Normans. Count Roger withstood a siege here for four months in 1064 that nearly put paid to his Sicilian adventures, a victory he commemorated by founding the convent of **San Basilio**, now in ruins near the present Capuchin convent. For modern-day sustenance, *La Tavernetta* at Via Arcirù 30 (℡0935.656.979; closed Mon off-season) offers standard pizzeria fare for around €5, and has some tables outside.

CESARÒ, 20km further east, stands at the crossroads with the SS289, which runs north to the coast. Well within the lee of Etna, it's endowed with remarkable views over to the volcano on a clear day. For the best panorama, climb up to the mammoth bronze statue of Jesus, the **Cristo Signore della Montagna**, in the cemetery above town. As Cesarò is also within the Parco dei Nébrodi (see p.139), it holds a **visitor centre** for the park at Via Bellini 79 (℡095.773.2061, Ⓦwww.parcodeinebrodi.it; Mon, Tues, Thurs & Fri 7.30am–2pm, Wed 7.30am–7pm, also open weekends in summer), where maps and itineraries are dispensed. It's not possible to reach Cesarò from the west by public transport, though there is one very early **bus** (not Sun) from Sant'Agata di Militello on the Tyrrhenian coast and one leaving in the early afternoon from Catania on the Ionian, the latter route taking you through the foothills of Etna.

Of Cesarò's brace of **hotels**, the most central is the *Nébrodi*, Via Margherita 30 (℡095.696.107; no credit cards; ❷), where some rooms have balconies over the street, but the best choices are at the back of the building from where you can enjoy sweeping views over the valley. At the bottom of the village on Via Conceria, the *Mazzurco* (℡095.773.2100; ❸) has five small but clean rooms, none has a view, though other rooms with vistas may open in future. Further up the street from the *Nébrodi* hotel, and across Piazza San Calógero, the *Saint Carlos*, a **B&B** at Via Cavour 6 (℡095.697.063 or 320.621.6487, Ⓦwww .saintcarlosbb.it; no credit cards; ❸), offers an attractive alternative, with good-size en-suite rooms. The *Nébrodi* has a decent **restaurant**, but the *Mazzurco* offers the best food in town, specializing in mushrooms, pork and pistachios, and it has a pleasant garden for dining al fresco (restaurant closed Thurs except Aug). There's a Banca di Sicilia with an ATM on the main road going up, on the right-hand side.

West to Polizzi Generosa

The towns and villages on the western stretch of the SS120 – of which **Sperlinga**, **Petralia Sottana** and **Polizzi Generosa** are among the most interesting – are easier to reach by bus, being linked by several services from Nicosia.

Sperlinga

Just fifteen minutes by bus from Nicosia, **SPERLINGA** owes its name to the Latin *spelunca* (cave), a reference to the numerous cave-dwellings, some hundreds of years old, that pit the sandstone slopes on which the town stands. Sprouting above is a formidable battlemented **castello** (daily 9.30am–1pm & 3–7pm, or 2.30–6.30pm in winter; €2), its storerooms, cellars, stables and steps hewn out of the rock. The lookouts above give onto a ruckled brown landscape that's typical of this part of Sicily, described by Giuseppe di Lampedusa as "a sea suddenly petrified at the instant when a change of wind had flung the waves into a frenzy". On a wall in the castle, you can make out an old Latin inscription, "Quod Siculis placuit sola Sperlinga negavit", referring to the time when Sperlinga was the only town in Sicily to open its doors to the Angevins, bloodily expelled from other Sicilian towns during the thirteenth-century Wars of the Vespers: barricading themselves inside the castle, the French held out for a year before surrendering. Just below the castle, a small archeological and ethnographical **museum** contains a motley collection of historical items from the area, alongside agricultural and domestic artefacts (same ticket and times as castle).

Gangi

Half an hour on, just inside Palermo's provincial boundary, **GANGI** forms a symmetrical mound on its hill-top, the shape of a tortoise's shell. Although today it consists mostly of unattractive concrete buildings, in its seventeenth-century heyday the town produced two artists, each known as Zoppo di Gangi ("Cripple of Gangi"), one of whom has an excellent *Last Judgement* in the church of **San Nicola** – identifiable by its incomplete fourteenth-century campanile.

Gangi's only **hotel** is the once-modern *Miramonti*, Via Nazionale 19 (☎0921.644.424; ❸), on the main road below town, but you're much better off heading 5km south of town (follow the signs from the centre) to the 🏠 *Tenuta Gangivecchio* (☎0921.689.191, ⓦwww.tenutagangivecchio.com; closed July; no credit cards; ❺), a small inn and restaurant in lush wooded grounds. The air here in the valley is kinder and breezier than in town, and the lodging consists of a few nicely furnished, stone-tiled rooms with terrace, as well as a pool (reservations essential). The **restaurant** next door (☎0921.644.804; lunch only; booking required) is run by Wanda and Giovanna Torabene, a mother-daughter team that has published several award-winning cookbooks in both Italian and English; you can enjoy some serious Italian cooking here, for a fixed-price menu (including drinks and coffee) of €25.

One daily **bus** from Gangi runs along the minor SS286 north to Castelbuono and down to the coast at Cefalù, finishing up in Palermo (6am Mon–Sat, 7.25am Sun in summer, 2.55pm Sun in winter).

Petralia Sottana and Petralia Soprana

Fourteen kilometres beyond Gangi, on the southern edge of the Madonie range of mountains, the two towns of Petralia lie on opposite sides of a hill. It's the lower town, **PETRALIA SOTTANA**, that holds most of the interest, and the only accommodation. Of the several weathered medieval churches strung along its lively main street, Corso Agliata, the most evocative is the **Chiesa Madre**, whose pretty belltower looks down upon an elegant piazza. The sacristy holds a tenth- or eleventh-century Islamic bronze candelabra – unique in Sicily – which is kept locked away: short of bribing the sacristan, your only chance to see it will be at a religious ceremony. There's further distraction in a pair of museums housed in the same building at Corso Agliata 102: the **Geopark Madonie**, a well-presented collection of rocks and fossils from the Madonie mountains, and **Museo Collisani**, showcasing the archeological heritage of the region (both daily 8.30am–2pm & 3–8pm; €2 combined ticket).

The museums also share space with the local **tourist office** (☎0921.641.811, ⓌWww.petraliasottana.net; daily 8.30am–2pm & 3–8pm). Petralia Sottana is something of a centre for hikers and skiers in the Monti Madonie, running south from here; for information on the region, including **hikes**, contact the Parco delle Madonie office at Corso Agliata 16 (daily 8am–2pm, also Tues 4–6pm; ☎0921.684.011, Ⓦwww.parcodellemadonie.it). The Club Alpino Italiano, Corso Agliata 154 (☎329.805.7940), can also supply details about escorted excursions.

The pick of several good **accommodation** options in the village are the *Madonie*, Corso Agliata 81 (☎0921.641.106; ❺), which has rooms decorated with contemporary paintings, and a great third-floor restaurant with views over the hills, and the old-world-style *Il Castello*, just steps from the Chiesa Madre at Via Generale Di Maria 27 (☎0921.680.105, Ⓦwww.il-castello.net; ❸), which along with its stone walls, tiled floors and beams, offers a restaurant with some outdoor seating. There are also a few decent **B&Bs**, including *Al Casale*, Via Rocca 25 (☎0921.641.973 or 348.749.6860, Ⓦwww.alcasalebedandbreakfast.it; no credit cards; ❸), which has four boldly painted rooms with en-suite bathrooms and views of the village from the windows.

If you don't want to **eat** in either of the hotels, good, reasonably priced **trattorias** around town include *Petra Leium*, at Corso Agliata 113 (☎0921.641.947; closed Fri evening except Aug), which features local mountain dishes such as grilled meats and wild mushrooms, and offers a generous tourist menu for €20, and the *ristorante*-pub *Saxum*, just up from the war memorial at Via Gangi 3 (open evenings only until late; closed Wed), with *panini* and pizzas on the menu and outdoor seating. For a drink or ice cream with a view, head to *La Terrazza* (closed Mon), just by the church.

It's 3km across to the upper town, **PETRALIA SOPRANA**, quieter and older than its neighbour, at an altitude of nearly 1150m. This was the birthplace of the craftsman Fra Ùmile da Petralia (1580–1639), whose wooden crosses are to be found in churches all over southern Italy. From the edge of the village you get a long view over the Madonie and Nébrodi mountains, as well, if you're westward bound, as a last dim sight of Etna.

Polizzi Generosa, Caltavuturo and around

Minor roads connect the Petralias with the lovely Madonie mountain region to the north, centred on Piano Battaglia, but there's no bus this way. The service along the SS120 branches off for **POLIZZI GENEROSA**, half an hour west and right in the heart of the Monti Madonie. Stop here to see the grand old **Chiesa Matrice**, containing the area's greatest work of art: a triptych of the *Madonna and Child* flanked by saints. Attributed to a mysterious fifteenth-century Fleming known only as the "Maître au Feuillage brodé", it's reckoned to be his best work. A decent **restaurant** just up from here in Piazza Castello: *U Bagghiu* (☎0921.649.546; closed Tues) serves dishes for €6–8, including a great seasonal speciality, *Penne al Bagghiu* (cheesy penne with tomato and garlic); alternatively, *L'Orto dei Cappuccini* (☎0921.688.535; closed Mon), Via Cappuccini 3, on a side street off the road up to town, is highly recommended, with its nice cloistered garden and creative fish and meat dishes; a full meal should cost €15–20. If you just want an ice cream or home-made pastries, the *Pasticceria Al Castello* in Piazza Castello will serve.

For **accommodation** in the area, head 7km north of town (towards the Scillato autostrada junction) to **Contrada Santa Venera**, where the same family that runs *U Bagghiu* also operates a comfortable **agriturismo**, *Santa Venera*, with seven en-suite rooms and a pool (☎0921.649.421, ⊛www .santavenera.com; ❹).

From Polizzi, between one and three buses per day cross the autostrada and head to **CALTAVUTURO**, a predominantly Baroque town despite its Saracen castle and Arabic name. Nearby, smaller **SCLÁFANI BAGNI** also attests to its former importance as a fief of the Scláfani family by notching up two fourteenth-century castles and a cathedral. These, though, are minor diversions, and you might as well sit tight in Polizzi Generosa and await the onward bus to the Tyrrhenian coast, or to Palermo, an hour and a quarter away. If you're driving from Polizzi Generosa to the A19 autostrada, take the access road that heads north; it's much more scenic than the southern route, and better surfaced.

Caltanissetta and the western interior

With twice as many inhabitants as Enna, **Caltanissetta** is easily the largest town in the interior, though little else about it is remarkable. It does, however, hold some of the area's few accommodation possibilities. Beyond lie the rolling expanses of Sicily's **western interior**, the rural heart of the island. The towns and villages you'll pass through are mostly poor and raddled; at times, positively ghost-like. Many, like **Corleone**, have names that have become familiar through their Mafia associations, but few are worth even a coffee-stop. The only place that merits more than a cursory glance is the village of **Sant'Ángelo Muxaro**, whose 3000-year-old tombs dot the hill below.

Access **by public transport** is very awkward: you can get to Caltanissetta easily enough, but otherwise you're unlikely to be able to see much more of the region than what you can glean from a bus window on the fast route between Agrigento and Palermo. From Caltanissetta, the railway line meanders northwest (ultimately to Palermo), past a series of empty upland plains occasionally pocked by unexpected crags and gullies, one of the most desert-like of Sicilian journeys.

Caltanissetta and around

Despite the modern sheen that marks out **CALTANISSETTA** from other inland towns, this provincial capital is immersed in the same listless torpor that you find throughout Sicily's interior. Consequently, it's not exactly the most exciting place to end up, though it has some good eating and sleeping possibilities for anyone travelling through.

With time to kill, you could take a spin round the sagging walls of the seventeenth-century **Palazzo Moncada**, off Corso Umberto I, an aristocratic mansion belonging to one of Sicily's great feudal dynasties and sporting an impressive row of waterspouts, or strike out to one of the island's stranger castle sites, the **Castello di Pietrarossa**, at the town's eastern extremity, though within easy walking distance from Caltanissetta's centre. Improbably balanced on an outcrop of rock, the castle – of Arab or Norman origin – looks like it should have fallen down years ago, and you get the feeling that no one would notice if it did. For views and fresh air in this traffic-drowned town, stroll down Viale Regina Margherita (a continuation of Corso Umberto I), where there's a park and belvedere.

A pair of more compelling attractions, however, lie on the outskirts of town, about 3km north (signposted "Contrada Santo Spírito", off SS122bis), which drivers en route to Enna might find worth a stop. Oddly relocated here from the centre of Caltanissetta, the **Museo Archeológico** contains

Badia di Santo Spírito & Museo Archeologico

RESTAURANTS
L'Archetto 3
Delfino Bianco 6
Fuori Orario 4

Sant' Agata

VIA ROSSO DI SAN SECONDO

VIA LINCOLN

VIA FERRANOVA

VIA PALMERI

VIA BENINTENDI

VIALE TESTASECCA

VIA KENNEDY

ACCOMMODATION
Coccolátevi D
Giulia B
Plaza C
San Michele A

VIA GATTUSO

VIA GAETANI

CORSO UMBERTO I

VIA RE D'ITALIA

Palazzo Moncada

Municipio

CORSO V. EMANUELE II

CORSO V. EMANUELE II

VIA PALERMO

VIA ALAIMO

PIAZZA MARCONI

VIA AJALA

San Sebastiano

PIAZZA GARIBALDI

Duomo

VIA EMILIANO GIUDICI

VIA SAN DOMENICO

SS120 & Enna

Castello Pietrarossa (500m)

VIA ELENA

VIA CAVOUR

VIA CRISPI

Train Station

PIAZZA ROMA

Bus Station

VIA MAZZINI

VIA LANZIROTTI

VIA GIOBERTI

CORSO UMBERTO I

VIA ROMA

VIALE AMEDEO

VIA XX SETTEMBRE

BARS
Gran Caffè Romano 7
La Luna Storta 5
Matahari 1
Medina 2

VIA COLAJANNI

VIA SETTIMO

VIALE REGINA MARGHERITA

San Giuseppe

N

0 100 m

CALTANISSETTA

SS640, Canicatti & Agrigento

a modest collection of some of Sicily's earliest finds, including vases and Bronze Age sculpted figures (daily 9am–1pm & 3.30–7pm; closed last Sun of month; €2).

Nearby lies a restored twelfth-century abbey, the **Badia di Santo Spírito**, founded by Count Roger and – a rare thing in Sicily – purely Norman in form. On the outside, the plain structure is only enlivened by three tiny apses at the back, though the interior holds more distraction in the form of a fifteenth-century fresco over the central apse and a twelfth-century font. If the church is locked, ring at the door on the right (home of the parish priest).

Practicalities

Caltanissetta's **bus and train stations** are centrally located at Piazza Roma, about a ten-minute walk from Corso Vittorio Emanuele. For all bus services, call SAIS at ☎0934.564.072. (Note that train travellers **heading to Enna** are advised to take a bus instead from Caltanissetta, as Enna's train station is a long way out of town: see p.292.)

The **tourist office** is at Corso Vittorio Emanuele 109 (Mon–Fri 9am–2pm, also Wed 3–6pm; ☎0934.530.440, Ⓦwww.aapit.cl.it).

Accommodation

Coccolátevi Piazza Garibaldi ☎0934.26.436 or 340.379.5803, Ⓦwww.piazza-garibaldi.it. A first-class B&B, very central, in an old building with colourful bedrooms sporting idiosyncratic murals. All three rooms are en suite with a/c, and two have balconies. ❹

Giulia Corso Umberto 85 ☎0934.542.927, Ⓦwww.hotelgiulia.it. The least expensive of Caltanissetta's hotels, the *Giulia* has characterless but clean and modern rooms with fridges and Internet connections. ❸

Plaza Via Gaetani 5 ☎0934.583.877, Ⓦwww .hotelplazacaltanissetta.it. Off Corso Vittorio Emanuele, this smart hotel is decorated in restful dark blue colours. ❹

San Michele Via Fasci Siciliani ☎0934.553.750, Ⓦwww.hotelsanmichelesicilia.it. West of the centre off Via della Libertà, near the Campo Sportivo, this swanky four-star boasts a pool. ❻

Eating and drinking

Restaurants

L'Archetto Via Palmieri 10. Informal *pizzeria-ristorante* serving mussel soup, a couscous paella and pasta dishes including *fettuccine allo scoglio* (with seafood). Fixed-price menus cost €10 and €15. Closed Tues. Moderate.

Delfino Bianco Via Scovazzo 19. This long, modern, white-walled trattoria offers fresh pasta (€3–4) and a good selection of meat and fish dishes (€5–7). Closed Sun. Moderate.

Fuori Orario Via Gattuso 29. Tasty pastas, pizzas and steaks are served in an upmarket, rustic interior. Closed Sun lunch. Moderate.

Bars

Gran Caffè Romano Corso Umberto I 147. This traditional bar has great almond biscuits (the local speciality), *cannoli* and other ricotta delights, as well as *arancini* and pizza slices.

La Luna Storta Via Arco Calafato 13. Friendly pub and tapas bar that occasionally hosts live music and exhibitions. Open weekends only.

Matahari Via Tamburini. You'll find a congenial atmosphere in the evening here, plus occasional live jazz and blues music.

Medina Via Tamburini. Opposite the *Matahari*, this Arab-themed bar has a mellow feel.

San Cataldo

Seven kilometres west of Caltanissetta, the village of **SAN CATALDO** is especially good to visit during its Easter celebrations, when the trial and crucifixion of Christ are re-enacted (Caltanissetta's tourist office has details).

U'Anzalone, on Piazza Crispi (☎0934.586.624), is an inexpensive and very traditional *osteria* specializing in such local delicacies as snails, tripe and calves' hooves (mains cost around €5).

Into the western interior

Unless you're driving, the only part of the **western interior** you'll see much of lies on the train or bus route between Agrigento and Palermo. The quickest route between the two places – and the path that the direct Agrigento–Palermo bus takes – is along the **SS189**. If you have the time, however, you might consider driving along the less-used **SS118**, which passes through some of the remoter inland towns and villages. Either way, several short detours are worth taking. Both the routes below are described heading north from Agrigento.

The SS189

Around 40km north of Agrigento, a side road off the main **SS189** turns east up to **MUSSOMELI**. On the other side of the town stands the extraordinary, crag-perched castle of **Castello Manfredónico**, erected in the fourteenth century by the powerful Chiaramonte family. It makes a vivid impression on the unsuspecting traveller, tilting over its tall rocky base as if lashed by a strong wind.

About 10km west of the SS189, **Monte Cammarata** (1578m) was a key point of the Axis defences in World War II, an impregnable redoubt that was expected to cause serious delays to the American advance on Palermo in 1943. In the event it was taken without a shot being fired, apparently due to pressure exerted on the Italian soldiers by Calógero Vizzini (Don Calò), head of the island's Mafia.

The main claim to fame of **LERCARA FRIDDI**, back on the main road halfway between Agrigento and Palermo, is as the birthplace in 1897 of the Sicilian-American gangster **Lucky Luciano**, whose family emigrated to the US in 1907. While serving a thirty- to fifty-year prison sentence in the US, following his conviction on 62 counts of "compulsory prostitution", Luciano was like Don Calò enlisted by the Americans to aid their Sicilian campaign, which was fully backed by the Mafia in its desire to end the Fascist rule. His reward when the war was over was to be freed, on the condition that he returned to Sicily. The town's main piazza was packed to welcome him home in 1946, and he repaid the adulation by opening Lercara Friddi's first cinema – apparently with a screening of the gangster movie, *Little Caesar*.

A few kilometres north of Lercara, you pick up the SS121, which winds across the entire length of Sicily from Catania and finishes its run in Palermo. Twenty-five kilometres north of the junction at **BAGNI DI CEFALÀ** – signposted just off the SS121 – are some eleventh-century Arab baths, flowing with thermal waters, which the locals use for washing clothes, though you can swim here too. Few other examples of Arab architecture in Sicily are in such good condition.

Sant'Ángelo Muxaro

Taking the alternative **SS118**, a minor road that wriggles all the way to Palermo, turn off 30km north of Agrigento at Raffadali for **SANT'ÁNGELO MUXARO**, another 15km along. This small agricultural centre in the

▲ Vineyard at Ficuzza

middle of the steeply sloping Plátani River valley boasts a number of local *tholos* (tombs) hollowed out of the rock in dome-shaped caves. The earliest date from the eleventh century BC, but most are from around the eighth to the fifth century BC, and recall Minoan and Mycenaean examples in design. You'll spot them as you approach the bare hillside on which the village stands: the road leads up past a ramshackle brick wall, beyond which a path heads along the sheer rock to the "beehive" caves. At the bottom, the largest is known locally as the **tomba del Príncipe**: later converted into a Byzantine chapel, it's half-hidden by overhanging trees and you may have to backtrack to get inside. Like all the others, it's empty now, the finds scattered in various museums around Europe.

Practicalities

You can get to Sant'Ángelo by **bus** from Agrigento with the Lattuca line, leaving from Agrigento's Piazza Vittorio Emanuele (Mon–Sat at 9am, 2.10pm & 5.30pm, Sun at 8.15am; the last bus back leaves at 4pm, but 7am on Sun). A great **accommodation** option, 🏕 *Val di Kam*, based in the centre of town at Piazza Umberto I 39 (☏0922.919.670 or 339.530.5989, ⓦ www.valdikam.it; ❸), offers en-suite rooms in different parts of the village at various prices. Breakfast is usually a grand affair, with local delicacies, served in your room. *Val di Kam* also organizes hiking, caving and archeological trips around Sant'Ángelo, and is a mine of useful information on the area.

Corleone

Back on the SS118, the best countryside begins past the village of **Alessandria della Rocca**, the road climbing up to 1000m at **Prizzi**, before skirting the eponymous lake and fetching up after 20km at **CORLEONE**. A fairly large town for these parts, squeezed between a couple of rocks with a craggy column at its centre, it attracts a trickle of tourists, most of them on the scent of the Mafia. Especially in the immediate postwar years, statistics showed the town to have one of the highest murder rates in the world, with 153 violent deaths (out of a population of 18,000) in the four years between 1944 and 1948. The town's notoriety has been fuelled since it lent Mario Puzo's fictional Godfather, Don Corleone, his adopted family name, though it is also the real-life name of Sicily's most notorious Mafia clan.

Corleone holds little to see besides the **Museo Anti-Mafia** (also called CIDMA) at Via Orfanotrofio 7, off the central Piazza Garibaldi (Mon–Sat 8.30am–1pm & 3.30–7.30pm, Sun 8.30am–1pm; free), in which two rooms display a chilling collection of blown-up photographs illustrating the violent history of the Mafia, including pictures of a manacled Luciano Leggio on his way to trial in 1978, and of the bosses Salvatore Riina and Bernardo Provenzano.

Practicalities

A couple of old-fashioned bars clustered around Piazza Garibaldi offer refreshments at outdoor tables, while one of the area's few **hotels** sits on the southern approach road to town, the modern and clean *Belvedere* (☎091.846.4000, ⓦ www.hotelbelvederecorleone.it; ❹), with a pool and views over Corleone

---

Corleone and the Mafia

Mario Puzo chose the name **Corleone** for his central character in *The Godfather* with good reason: for over fifty years the town has been the stamping ground of some of the most feared – and respected – Mafia leaders. Many of the so-called *capo di tutti capi* (literally "boss of all the bosses"), who have held sway over an international network of crime and corruption, came originally from the town, including Luciano Leggio and his effective successors Salvatore Riina and Bernardo Provenzano.

Luciano Leggio (also known as Liggio) was hailed as the "Scarlet Pimpernel" for his long-running evasion of the forces ranged against him. He was far from the dashing figure that the nickname suggests, however, having been responsible for one of the most notorious political killings of the twentieth century, that of the trade union leader **Plácido Rizzotto**, who took advantage of the Mafia's internal preoccupations to do the unthinkable and manoeuvre a left-wing town council into power in Corleone. Two years after his disappearance in 1948, the fire brigade hauled out his dismembered corpse from a ninety-foot crevice near Corleone (along with sackfuls of other bodies of Mafia victims). His killers were eventually acquitted for lack of evidence, the most common end to murder charges brought against *mafiosi*. Leggio was finally imprisoned in 1974 and died in jail 1993.

At the time of his arrest in 1993, Leggio's trusted deputy, **Salvatore Riina**, was the most wanted man in Italy, allegedly responsible for ordering at least 150 murders, 40 of which he's said to have committed himself. His capture came as a complete surprise – he was informed on by his driver, a native of San Giuseppe Iato, northwest of Corleone – and triggered a wave of accusations, since it became clear that for over twenty years Riina had lived with his family openly in Corleone, registering his children at local schools and hospitals, and coming and going pretty much as he pleased. This, it's said with some justification, could only have been the case if he had enjoyed a degree of high-level protection.

The most notable among several further members of the Corleonese clan who have been put away since Riina's arrest is **Bernardo Provenzano** (known as "the Tractor" on account of his brutal methods). He was finally captured in 2006, having been convicted in absentia of a string of murders, including the 1992 killings of the two anti-Mafia investigators Giovanni Falcone and Paolo Borsellino. Such arrests may yet end the hegemony of this sleepy inland town.

For more on the Mafia, see Contexts, "The Mafia in Sicily" (p.437).

from some rooms. Further up the hill, there's a **restaurant** under the same management, *A'Giarra*, a popular place for pizzas and local dishes, with outdoor tables. You'll find a more central trattoria, *Al Capriccio*, at Via Sant'Agostino 19 (signposted from Piazza Garibaldi), adorned with old black-and-white photos of the town and offering a €10 tourist menu (☏091.846.7938; closed Tues).

Ficuzza

From Corleone, regular buses run through the hills to Palermo, 60km away. If you're driving, though, you could stop at **FICUZZA**, around 25km north, backed by the wooded heights of Rocca Busambra (1613m), which is crisscrossed by a network of mountain paths. Once a hunting centre, the tiny hamlet is still dominated by Ferdinand III's hunting lodge, the stately **Palazzina Reale**. That's currently closed for renovation work, but in any case there's not a great deal of interest inside. Although Mussolini's troops burnt most of the palace, the Sala da Pranzo survives, decorated with hunting scenes, as does the queen's bidet. You could have **lunch** in one of the trattorias in the piazza, before heading into the hills along the waymarked paths radiating out from here. Twenty kilometres north, the road leads to Piana degli Albanesi, 25km from Palermo.

The southern interior

Sicily's **southern interior** has a tamer feel than any of the other inland areas. Journeys here are easy on the eye, through intensely cultivated slopes to a succession of busy country towns, for example **Piazza Armerina**, a good base for visiting the region's major draw, the lavish Roman mosaics at the **Villa Romana del Casale**. Also featuring high on any list of Sicily's top attractions, **Caltagirone** is plastered with assertive Baroque buildings but is most renowned for its eye-catching ceramics. Other brief diversions might take in the extensive Greek ruins of **Morgantina** and the planned eighteenth-century settlement of **Grammichele**.

The southern interior is well served by **public transport**. Regular buses run to Piazza Armerina from Enna and Caltanissetta, and Caltagirone and Grammichele are accessible by train and bus from Gela or Catania.

Piazza Armerina

Less than an hour's drive from Enna, **PIAZZA ARMERINA** lies amid thickly forested hills. A quiet, unassuming place, it's mainly seventeenth- and eighteenth-century in appearance, with a skyline pierced by towers and houses huddled together under the joint protection of castle and cathedral. Despite the dense traffic that fills its lanes and thoroughfares, idling around can be thoroughly pleasant, though most travellers in the area by-pass it altogether, given the enticement of the nearby Villa Romana del Casale (see p.311).

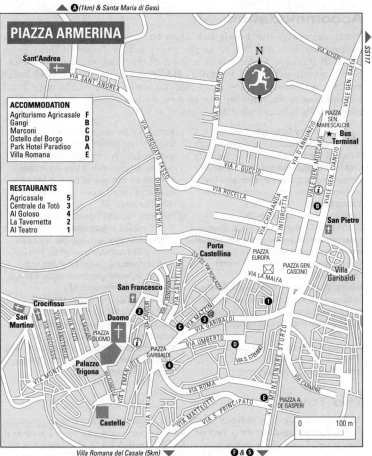

PIAZZA ARMERINA

Sant'Andrea

ACCOMMODATION

Agriturismo Agricasale	F
Gangi	B
Marconi	C
Ostello del Borgo	D
Park Hotel Paradiso	A
Villa Romana	E

RESTAURANTS

Agricasale	5
Centrale da Totò	3
Al Goloso	4
La Tavernetta	2
Al Teatro	1

N

PIAZZA SEN. MARESCALCHI
★ Bus Terminal

San Pietro

Porta Castellina

PIAZZA EUROPA

PIAZZA GEN. CASCINO

Villa Garibaldi

San Francesco

Crocifisso

San Martino

Duomo

PIAZZA DUOMO

Palazzo Trigona

PIAZZA GARIBALDI

PIAZZA A. DE GASPERI

Castello

0   100 m

Villa Romana del Casale (5km) ▼   Ⓕ & Ⓖ ▼

Arrival and information

Most **buses** will drop you off at Piazza Senatore Marescalchi, on the main road, Viale Generale Muscara, in the lower, modern town. For **bus information** and **tickets** to Aidone, Caltagirone and Dittaino (the nearest train station to Piazza Armerina, 35km north), ask in the *Bar della Stazione* in Piazza Marescalchi, or the AST office next door. The city **tourist office** is in the old town further up the hill, tucked away behind Piazza Garibaldi on Piazza Santa Rosalia (Mon–Fri 8.30am–1.30pm & 2.30–7pm; ☏0935.683.049, ⓦwww.piazza-armerina.it), while a separate office at Viale Muscara 13 covers the whole province (Mon–Fri 9am–2pm, also Wed 3–6.30pm; ☏0935.684.814).

Free **parking** can be found at Piazza Garibaldi and Piazza Duomo, though drivers have to get there early in the morning to find a space. There's a **taxi** rank in Piazza Generale Cascino. **Banks** are found along Via Generale Ciancio, which runs between piazzas Cascino and Marescalchi, and in Piazza Garibaldi in the old town. Sabinet, Via Mazzini 35, offers **Internet** connections (Mon–Fri 9.30am–1pm & 4.30–8pm).

Accommodation

Piazza Armerina's few **hotels** lack character, being mainly geared towards business travellers, and they're on the pricey side. A cluster of them lie in Contrada Ramaldo, a kilometre or so north of the centre, but you'll find more central accommodation in the town's **B&Bs** and an excellent **hostel**. Some peaceful **agriturismo** places are located just out of town; one of them, listed below, has space for **camping**. For all these, it's best to book ahead. For places near the Villa Romana, see p.312.

Agriturismo Agricasale ☎0935.686.034, ⓦwww.agricasale.it. Five kilometres south of Piazza Armerina, and signposted everywhere by a red fox, this great-value place is worth the effort to track down for its peaceful rooms, great food and huge swimming pool. Camping pitches are also available. ❸

Gangi Via Generale Ciancio 68–70 ☎0935.682.737, ⓦwww.hotelgangi.it. Housed in a sympathetically restored old *palazzo* with exposed stone walls and a cobbled courtyard, this smart hotel has well-equipped rooms with Internet connections. ❺

Marconi Via Marconi 12 ☎0935.682.989, ⓦwww.bbmarconi.com. Above the central *Bar Marconi*, this B&B holds clean en-suite rooms in warm colours grouped around a quiet courtyard. No credit cards. ❸

Ostello del Borgo Largo San Giovanni 6 ☎0935.687.019, ⓦwww.ostellodelborgo.it. Fourteenth-century monastery at the eastern end of Via Umberto which has been refurbished to hold hostel accommodation in dorm-style rooms (€16.50 per bed), as well as en-suite private rooms upstairs. All rooms are fairly spartan but quiet and clean. Inexpensive Internet access and bike hire is also offered for guests. ❸

Park Hotel Paradiso Contrada Ramaldo ☎0935.680.841, ⓦwww.parkhotelparadiso.it. One of Piazza Armerina's top hotels, 1km beyond the church of Sant'Andrea, and signposted from just about everywhere in town. It has stylish, well-equipped bedrooms, glitzy public rooms, a gym, a pool and a formal restaurant. ❻

Villa Romana Via A. de Gasperi 18 ☎&ℱ0935.682.911. Noisily situated on a major road on the southern edge of town, on the signposted route to the mosaics, this is geared towards business travellers and consequently lacks much atmosphere. It's a good fall-back, though, with functional rooms. ❻

The Town

Although seeing the mosaics of the Villa Romana will be your priority, Piazza Armerina deserves a detour and even an overnight stop. Its central core is small enough to cover in a morning's stroll. A score of dilapidated but graceful churches and *palazzi* line the narrow streets and squares of the hill-top old-town area, which centres around sloping **Piazza Garibaldi**. From here, Via Cavour winds up to **Piazza del Duomo** and the elegant seventeenth-century **Duomo** itself (daily 8am–noon & 4–7pm), built at the town's highest point and boasting a cool blue-and-white interior; you enter through the small green door on the northern side. The earlier (fifteenth-century) campanile sports blind Catalan-Gothic windows, a nice contrast to the Baroque antics of the rest of the church. What really sets off this handsome, view-laden square is the simple facade of the eighteenth-century **Palazzo Trigona** adjacent, its spruced exterior crowned by a spread-eagle plaque.

Narrow alleys lead down from the terrace of Piazza del Duomo into the older parts of town: an endearing jumble of cobbled flights of steps and faded grandeur. Just behind the cathedral, on a spur off Via Cavour, the seventeenth-century church and former convent of **San Francesco** is now in use as a hospital. At the bottom of a steep street nearby, Via Castellina, the surviving medieval town wall has had a rough arch hacked through it for traffic access, and the adjacent watchtower is now a home. The other way, down Via Floresta (to the side of Palazzo Trigona), leads to the closed and tumbledown **castello**, built at the end of the fourteenth century and surrounded by once-rich *palazzi* in a similar state of decay. Best of all, though, is the route down the steep **Via Monte**, formerly the medieval town's main street. Just east of the Duomo, the adjacent **Piazza Europa** and **Piazza Generale Cascino** are lively, grassy pedestrian walks teeming with activity, and great spots for people-watching.

The town is compact enough for you to get out fairly easily into the fields and slopes beyond. It's only a kilometre's walk to the twelfth-century Norman church of **Sant'Andrea**, north of town and still impressive despite its simple proportions. Another kilometre or so down the same road, through orchards and gardens, stands the sixteenth-century church and convent of **Santa Maria di Gesù**, a low building set amid gentle green hills.

Eating and drinking

Piazza Armerina's **nightlife** is based around the cafés and bars that line piazzas Europa and Cascino: *Break Coffee*, just in front of the Villa Garibaldi, is one of the most popular. The next-door *Mirus* has good ice cream, cakes and outdoor tables.

Agriturismo Agricasale 5km south of Piazza Armerina ℡0935.686.034. Out of town (see opposite), this place serves plentiful portions of great home-grown organic food and is open to non-residents. The multi-course fixed-price menu costs €20, and the almond wine is recommended. Moderate.

Centrale da Totò Via Mazzini 29 ℡0935.680.153. This local institution has decent prices and a friendly atmosphere. The house speciality *bocca di lupo* is a delicious steak dish with prosciutto, aubergine and mozzarella (€8), and there's also a good range of pizzas. Closed Mon in winter. Moderate.

Al Goloso Via Garao 4 ℡0935.685.693. Good-value trattoria, with a nice terrace in front; the *antipasto rustico* is superb, as are the *pasta della casa* with grilled aubergine and the *coniglio* (rabbit) in mushroom sauce (€8). Closed Wed in winter. Moderate.

La Tavernetta Via Cavour 14 ℡0935.685.883. Reasonable value for money, with fish specialities at €9–13. There's a small selection of meat dishes. Closed Sun in winter. Moderate.

Al Teatro Via del Teatro. Small, friendly trattoria, where the outside tables have nice views of the upper town. Try the homemade *pappardelle alla nonna*, or one of the thirty-odd different types of pizza (€5–8). Closed Wed in winter. Moderate.

Villa Romana del Casale

Built on terraces in the sparsely inhabited neighbourhood of **CASALE**, 5km southwest of Piazza Armerina, the **Villa Romana** was hidden under mud for seven hundred years until excavations began in 1950, revealing multicoloured mosaic floors that are unique in the entire Roman world for their quality and extent. Today the site is visited by a continuous stream of coach parties, which makes for a congested – but still rewarding – experience. If you're here in summer, try to come early or late in the day in order to avoid the heat and crowds, as it's rather like being in a greenhouse.

Getting there

From Piazza Armerina, a **bus** (Line B; May–Sept) leaves Piazza Marescalchi for the Villa Romana on the hour between 9am and noon, and between 3pm and 6pm, with a stop at Piazza Cascino; the return service is on the half-hour, starting at 9.30am. You might also consider **walking**: head down Via

Matteotti or Via Principato and follow the signs – it takes around an hour on foot and is an attractive and enjoyable stroll, though one to avoid in the heat of the sun. If you're pushed for time, a **taxi** from Piazza Generale Cascino in Piazza Armerina costs around €10 one way. Stalls at the entrance sell good illustrated guidebooks in English.

Daily Astra buses leave **Caltanissetta** at 6am, 8.15am, 12.15pm, 2.30pm and 6.05pm (Sun 8.15am & 2.30pm only), and arrive at Piazza Armerina an hour later, with return trips at 1.15pm, 3.15pm and 6pm (Sun 1.15pm & 6pm). These buses stop in **Enna** roughly thirty minutes after departure from Caltanissetta; call ☎0934.573.315 to confirm departure times, as schedules sometimes change slightly. Bear in mind that you'll still have to get from Piazza Armerina itself to the site.

Accommodation

If you want to **stay the night** in the vicinity of the villa, there's no necessity to travel the 5km to Piazza Armerina, though you'll find things fairly quiet around here after dark.

Mosaici da Battiato Contrada Paratore ☎0935.685.453, Ⓦwww.hotelmosaici.com. A kilometre towards Piazza Armerina, at the turn-off to the Villa Romana, this place has smart rooms at reasonable prices and an outdoor terrace. The bus to the mosaics passes right by. Closed Nov–Dec. ❷

La Ruota ☎0935.680.542. A little way up the road from the Villa Romana, this well-regarded restaurant has only one room for B&B, so worth booking well ahead. It's small, quiet and comfortable, with en-suite facilities. There's also space in the garden for camping, though it's not an official campsite. ❷

The site

The **site** itself (daily from 8am until an hour before sunset; €6; Ⓦwww .villaromanadelcasale.it) is a confusing swatch of rooms and passages. Dating from the early fourth century AD (though constructed over an earlier structure), it remained in use right up until it was largely covered by a mudslide in the twelfth century. Comprehensive excavations began in the 1950s, but it's been covered again, more recently, to protect the mosaics. A new roof and walls were added to indicate the original size and shape, as were walkways to lead visitors through the rooms.

Though conflicting theories surround the **function** of the villa, the most convincing explanation of its location in the middle of deserted slopes and woods is that it was an occasional retreat and hunting lodge. That theory is supported by the many mosaics of animals and birds, including two specific hunting scenes. It's immediately clear from the extent of the uncovered remains that the complex belonged to an important owner, possibly Maximianus Herculeus, co-emperor with Diocletian between 286 and 305 AD. It consists of four separate groups of buildings, built on different levels of the hillside and connected by passageways, doors and courtyards. Nearly all of what you see would have been occupied by the family for which it was built, though the slaves' housing, presumably also fairly extensive, and other outbuildings, are still to be excavated properly. Yet it's not the building that's the main attraction – although few enough examples survive of such splendid Imperial Roman wealth – so much as the unrivalled interior decoration. The floors of almost the entire building are covered with bright **mosaics** of excellent quality, stylistically belonging to an early fourth-century Roman-African school, which explains many of the more exotic scenes and animals portrayed. Their design also

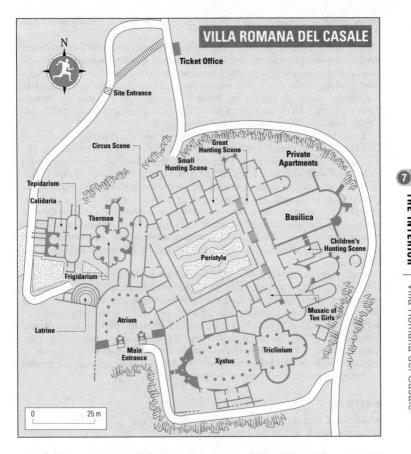

contains several hints as to their period and patron, though given their extent they're likely to have taken fifty or sixty years to complete.

What's left of the villa's **main entrance** gives one of the best impressions of its former grandeur, the approach leading through the remains of a columned arch into a wide courtyard. Today's site entrance, though, is through the adjacent **thermae** (or baths): a typical arrangement of dressing/massage rooms and plunge-baths around an octagonal **frigidarium**, its central mosaic a marine scene of sea nymphs, tritons, and little cherubs rowing boats and spearing fish. A walkway leads out of the baths and into the villa proper, to the massive central courtyard or **peristyle**. This is where guests would have been received, and the vestibule displays a badly fragmented mosaic depicting a formal welcome by an attendant holding an olive branch. The corridor around the four sides of the courtyard is covered with a series of animal-head medallions: snarling tigers, yapping dogs and unicorns. Just off here, a balcony looks down upon one of the most vivid pictures, a boisterous circus scene showing a chariot race. Starting in the top right-hand corner, the variously coloured chariots rush off, overtaking and crashing at the turns, until finally there's victory for the green faction. The next room's mosaic shows a family attended by slaves on their way to the baths.

Period detail – footwear, hairstyles and clothes – helped archeologists to date the rest of the mosaics.

Small rooms beyond, on either side of the peristyle, reveal only fragmentary geometric patterns, although one displays a **small hunting scene**, an episodic adventure that ends with a peaceful picnic in the centre. Another room contains what is probably the villa's most famous image, a two-tiered scene of **ten girls**, realistically muscular figures in Roman "bikinis", taking part in various gymnastic and athletic activities. One of the girls, sporting a laurel wreath and a palm frond, is clearly the winner of the competition.

The peristyle is separated from the private apartments and public halls beyond by a long, covered corridor, which contains the best of the villa's mosaic works. The **great hunting scene** sets armed and shield-bearing hunters against a panoply of wild animals, on sea and land. Along the entire sixty-metre length of the mosaic, tigers, ostriches, elephants and even a rhino, destined for the games back in Rome, are pictured being trapped, bundled up and down gangplanks and into cages. The caped figure overseeing the operation is probably Maximianus himself. Much of the scene is set in Africa, Maximianus's main responsibility in the Imperial Tetrarchy, while an ivy-leaf symbol on the costume of the attendant to his right is that of his personal legion, the Herculiani.

Family apartments and public halls beyond are nearly all on a grand scale. A large courtyard, the **xystus**, gives onto the **triclinium**, a dining room with three apses, whose mosaics feature the labours of Hercules. One bloody scene portrays his fight against the giants, all stuck by arrows, who writhe and wail with contorted faces. A path leads around the back to the **private apartments**, based around a large basilica, with mosaics echoing the spectacular scenes of the main building: a **children's circus**, where the small chariots are drawn by colourful birds, and a **children's hunt**, the tiny tots being chased and pecked by the hares and peacocks they're supposed to snare.

Eating

As for **food** near the villa, you can either head for the adequate bar-restaurant at the site, or eat well at the hotels listed below.

Mosaici da Battiato Contrada Paratore ☎ 0935.685.453. Specializing in grills, this hotel dining room is subject to an influx of tour groups at lunch times. Moderate.
La Ruota ☎ 0935.680.542. In an attractive rustic setting, this hotel offers shaded outdoor seating

and serves excellent homemade pasta (€7–8), as well as hearty meat dishes including local sausage (€6) and rabbit (€9). There's also a €12 tourist menu. Moderate.

Aidone and the site of Morgantina

The extensive remains of the Greek city of **Morgantina**, which was at its height in the fourth century BC, lie 15km northeast of Piazza Armerina. It's not easy to reach without your own transport: several **buses** make the fifteen-minute trip each day from Piazza Armerina (from Piazza Senatore Marescalchi) to **Aidone**, but the site itself is a long, hot walk further on, another 5km beyond the village, along the minor SS288. If you're driving, turn off the SS117 for Aidone at the crossroads known as Madonna della Noce, where there's a large **restaurant-pizzeria**; it's then a gorgeous seven-kilometre ride through the trees to the village.

Aidone

With its quiet central square and thoroughly laid-back air, **AIDONE** itself is a charming little spot. It holds a couple of agreeable bars, a crumbling church, and – signposted in the upper part of the village – the **Museo Archeológico** (Tues–Sun 9am–6.30pm; €3, includes site of Morgantina). Housed in a former Capuchin monastery, the museum makes an indispensable preliminary to seeing the archeological remains at Morgantina. As well as gathering together all the removable bits and pieces from the ancient city – ceramics, statuettes and third-century BC busts, as well as some domestic artefacts – it displays aerial photos, plans and a model of the excavations that provide a useful idea of the layout of the site.

Aidone has a useful **hotel** with a reasonably priced rustic-style restaurant, the *Morgantina*, Via Adelasia 42 (☎0935.88.088, ⓦwww.hotelmorgantina.it; ❹), steps away from the main Piazza Cordova.

Morgantina

Two kilometres northeast of Aidone, at the end of a long cobbled lane that's signposted left off the main road, the **site of Morgantina** (daily 9am–1hr before sunset; €3, includes Museo Archeológico at Aidone) occupies two quiet, dusty hillsides. A car park is located just beyond the main entrance under the east hill. No buses come this way.

After its demise, the city became buried and forgotten for almost two thousand years, and even after the site's discovery it wasn't identified as Morgantina until 1957. To date, only a fifth of the city has been excavated, but the finds have shed much light on the island's pre-Hellenic Sikel population, who inhabited central Sicily from the ninth century BC. In the sixth century BC, Chalcidian Greeks settled here and lived in harmony alongside the Sikels until the city became the centre of a revolt led by the Sikel leader Ducetius, who destroyed it in the mid-fifth century BC. Swiftly rebuilt on a grid-plan with walled and towered defences, Morgantina reached its apogee in the fourth and third centuries BC under the protection of Syracuse, and many of the surviving buildings date from this period. A couple of hundred years later the city was in decline and soon after was abandoned altogether.

A path from the main entrance leads directly to Morgantina's most distinctive ruin, the **agora**, bounded by three stepped sides that served as seats for public meetings. The small **teatro** to its right was built in the third century BC, but reconstructed in Roman times. Performances of Greek plays and modern drama are held here in the summer: check with the site office (☎0935.87.955) or the tourist offices in Enna or Piazza Armerina; tickets cost €12. Immediately in front is a Roman building, behind which (next to the *agora*) is a fourth-century BC **santuario** of Demeter and Kore. On the level ground behind the *agora* is a granary and square slaughterhouse, beyond which stretches the 100-metre-long **east stoa**. Further up the hillside stand the ruins of some Hellenic **houses**, with two mosaic floors. One, the "House of Ganymede", has an illustration of the youth Ganymede being carried away to Olympus by Zeus's eagle to become the cupbearer of the gods.

Excavations on the **west hill**, a twenty-minute walk across the site, are less revealing, but you'll come across the fairly substantial remains of houses, some with mosaics, roads and walls, in what was once a residential area of the ancient city. In recent years, the remains of a second temple and a spring and aqueduct have been unearthed, but these aren't open for public viewing yet.

South to Caltagirone

Around 16km south of Piazza Armerina, the minor SS124 breaks east off the Gela road and heads for Caltagirone, passing through fine farming country, at its best around the village of **SAN MICHELE DI GANZARIA**. There's no particular reason to break your journey here, though you might be tempted by *Pomara*, at Via Vittorio Véneto 84 (℡0933.976.976, ⓦwww .hotelpomara.com; ❻), a surprisingly fine **hotel** for the sticks with a large pool and excellent views, or by the village's couple of pizzerias. The bus from Piazza Armerina also comes this way, though diverting first to the even tinier **Mirabella Imbáccari**, just to the north. All told, it's just under an hour from Piazza Armerina to the heights of Caltagirone.

Caltagirone

Though the presence of settlers in **CALTAGIRONE** well before the Greeks makes this one of the most ancient of Sicilian towns, its present name derives from the Arabic (*kalat*, "castle" and *gerun*, "caves"). Nothing from these periods survives, and the dominant impression of the town is Baroque. Its central swathe of monumental buildings dates from rebuilding after the 1693 earthquake that flattened the area. Well before that, though, Caltagirone had acquired a reputation for the excellence of its **ceramics**, an industry given an added dimension by the arrival of the Arabs. They introduced local craftsmen to the glazed polychromatic colours – in particular, blues and yellows – that have subsequently become typically Sicilian in execution. Until the great earthquake, the town supported a population of around 20,000, of whom perhaps five percent were actively engaged in the tiled decoration of churches and public buildings. The Baroque rebuilding saw a further burst of creative construction; later, during the nineteenth century, came the principal period of ceramic figurative work, excellent examples of which are on display in the town museum. Today, Caltagirone's traditional industry is flourishing once more, with around eighty accredited ceramicists – and many more unaccredited – displaying work at galleries across the town.

Arrival and information

Buses all stop at the bus station in the lower town, next to the **train station** in Piazza della Repubblica, a couple of kilometres below the old centre, and connected to it by half-hourly local bus #1. The main **tourist office** (Mon–Fri 8am–2.30pm & 3–6.30pm; ℡0933.53.809) is in the upper town, down an alley (Via Volta Libertini) just off Piazza Umberto, and there's a useful city tourist office in Galleria Luigi Sturzo, Piazza Municipio (Mon–Sat 9am–7pm, Sun 9am–1pm & 3–7pm; ℡0933.41.365, ⓦwww.comune.caltagirone.ct.it). Link di Cusumano Desirée, Via A. Manzoni 46, near the station in the new town, provides **Internet** access (Mon–Sat 9am–1pm & 5–9pm). The Art Nouveau **post office** is in the old centre at Via Vittorio Emanuele 37 (Mon–Fri 8am–1.30pm, Sat 8am–12.30pm).

Accommodation

Caltagirone's upper town offers a good selection of **B&Bs** and *affittacamere* (at which breakfast is not available), all conveniently located for the sights, so there's no need to head for the pricier and blander hotels in the new centre.

S. FRANCESCO DI PAOLA

PREGATE PER NOI!...

100 giorni di indulgenza concessi da S.E.Mons.Pietro Capizzi - 15 APRILE 1965

▲ Painted tilework at Caltagirone

Carneade Via Vittorio Emanuele 96 ℡0933.352.394, Ⓔcarneade .rooms@tiscali.it. Pleasant, quiet and comfortable *affittacamere* with friendly management and spacious en-suite rooms, simply but stylishly furnished. ❸

Il Piccolo Attico Via Infermeria 82 ℡0933.21.588 or 320.077.3315, Ⓔilpiccoloattico@hotmail.com.

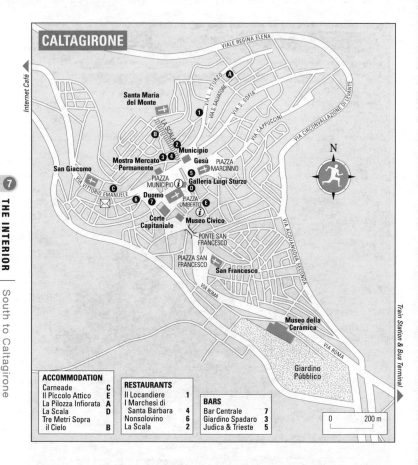

CALTAGIRONE

Internet Café

Train Station & Bus Terminal

N

Santa Maria
del Monte

Municipio

Mostra Mercato
Permanente

Gesù

PIAZZA
MARCINNO

San Giacomo

PIAZZA
MUNICIPIO

Galleria Luigi Sturzo

Duomo

PIAZZA
UMBERTO

Corte
Capitaniale

Museo Civico

PONTE SAN
FRANCESCO

PIAZZA SAN
FRANCESCO

San Francesco

Museo della
Cerámica

Giardino
Púbblico

VIALE REGINA ELENA
VIA L. STURZO
VIA S. SALVATORE
VIA S. SOFIA
VIA CAPPUCCINI
VIA CIRCONVALLAZIONE DI LEVANTE
LA SCALA
VIA VITTORIO EMANUELE
VIA ACQUANUOVA SECONDA
VIA ROMA
VIA ROMA

0   200 m

ACCOMMODATION	
Carneade	C
Il Píccolo Attico	E
La Pilozza Infiorata	A
La Scala	D
Tre Metri Sopra il Cielo	B

RESTAURANTS	
Il Locandiere	1
I Marchesi di Santa Barbara	4
Nonsolovino	6
La Scala	2

BARS	
Bar Centrale	7
Giardino Spadaro	3
Judica & Trieste	5

One large double room with a bathroom, and one attic apartment composed of two double rooms, with great views on all sides, taking in Etna. Book in advance in summer. **④**

La Pilozza Infiorata Via San Salvatore 97 ☏0933.22.162 or 339.735.2861, ⓦwww .lapilozzainfiorata.com. Rather fancy B&B in a restored "Liberty"-style *palazzo* with five individually – somewhat idiosyncratically – styled en-suite rooms. There's no view to speak of but the rooms are spacious and comfortable, and there's a small terrace. **⑤**.

La Scala Piazza Umberto I 1 ☏0933.52.609, ⓦwww.affittacamerelascala.it. Plain but spacious

and clean rooms right in the main square, two of the six with private bathrooms. Expect a degree of noise in the rooms that face the piazza. No credit cards. **②**

Tre Metri Sopra il Cielo Via Bongiovanni 72 ☏0933.193.5106 or 392.568.6121, ⓦwww.bbtremetrisoprailcielo.it. Just two air-conditioned rooms in this perfectly sited B&B right next to La Scala: one small double with an external bathroom, one larger en-suite room. Breakfast is taken on the terrace with a stupendous view over the town and surrounding hills. **④**

The Town

The old **upper town** has great public edifices, decorative churches and public gardens spread across three hills, the effect lightened by the tiled decoration found in nooks and crannies everywhere. Boosted by recent renovations, plus a good selection of shops and the general air of activity, it has an upbeat feel.

The most effective decorations are the ceramic flowers and emblems that flank both sides of the **Ponte San Francesco** on the way into the centre from the train station. The grandest statement, though, is undoubtedly made by the 142 steps of **La Scala**, which cut right up one of Caltagirone's hills to the sorely neglected church of Santa Maria del Monte at the top. The risers in between each step are covered with a hand-painted ceramic pattern, no two the same. It's a long climb, but the views from the top are magnificent, across town to the distinctive spire of the Sicilian Baroque church of San Francesco all'Immacolata, with the plain stretching away into the distance beyond. The staircase was originally conceived at the turn of the seventeenth century as a road between the Santa Maria del Monte church, then the town cathedral, and the Senatorial Palace below; the steps were added once it was clear that the incline was too steep, but the majolica-tile risers are a much more recent addition, in place only since 1954. On July 24 and 25 every year, the steps are lit by thousands of coloured paper lamps as part of the celebrations for the feast of St James (San Giácomo).

On either side of the staircase, all the way up, are some of the **workshops** and galleries of today's ceramicists, all worth venturing inside even if you're not planning to buy. Below the large public garden, the **Museo della Cerámica**, with its entrance on Via Roma (daily 9am–6.30pm; €3), is stuffed full of original ceramic ware, while the **Mostra Mercato Permanente** (daily 9am–8pm), with venues on both Via Vittorio Emanuele, just to the right at the bottom of La Scala, and Piazza Umberto, is the best place to see and buy modern ceramics made by local artists. If you visit the Museo della Cerámica, take the time to whirl round the adjacent **Giardino Púbblico**, where there's a quiet bar and shady picnic spots. The centrepiece is the Art Nouveau bandstand, one of several elegant examples in Caltagirone of the **"Liberty" style** – you'll pass the Art Nouveau theatre outside the main entrance to the gardens.

At the top of La Scala, the church of **Santa Maria del Monte** itself shows touches of the Liberty style in its ceiling, but otherwise it holds little of interest beyond a venerated image from the thirteenth century, the *Madonna dei Conadomini*, and a belltower which, when open, affords excellent views over the town. Several more striking buildings can be admired in the upper town, however, including (beyond Piazza Umberto and the restyled **Duomo**), the seventeenth-century **Corte Capitaniale**, a sturdy, long and low edifice decorated by the Gagini family and used today for temporary exhibitions. In Piazza Municipio, exhibitions are also held in the grand, modern **Galleria Luigi Sturzo**, named after the locally born Luigi Sturzo (1871–1959), mayor, reformer and anti-Fascist. This handsome public hall also holds a bar and a helpful information desk.

Back below Piazza Umberto, a solid square-built block with grilled windows and spike-studded metal doors that was a Bourbon prison in the eighteenth century now houses the **Museo Cívico** (Mon, Wed & Thurs 9.30am–1.30pm, Tues, Fri & Sat 9.30am–1.30pm & 4–7pm, Sun 9.30am–12.30pm & 4–7pm; €2.85). While there's nothing all that spectacular inside, it's well worth a leisurely look for its intriguing collection of local curios, including architectural fragments, paintings by the Vaccaro family who renovated the cathedral in the nineteenth century, and a gilded, sixteenth-century processional cart.

Eating and drinking

There's not a great deal of choice when it comes to **eating** in Caltagirone, though the following, all located in the old centre, should satisfy most appetites. The town's **bars** are good for a snack or a sit-down.

Restaurants

Il Locandiere Via Luigi Sturzo 55 ☎0933.58.292. Only fish is served in this smart restaurant in a tastefully restored old building with arches. The antipasti are terrific, while menu choices depend on what's in (though fish coucous is usually available); first cousrses and mains are each €9–11. Closed Mon. Moderate.

I Marchesi di Santa Barbara Via San Bonaventura 22 ☎0933.22.406. The nicest restaurant in the upper town, located within a cavernous former residence of the aristocracy. There's an upmarket menu at good prices, and it's usually packed in the summer, especially on the terrace. First courses are €6–8 (try the *Marchese pasta*), mains €10–16, and pizzas are also available. Closed Mon. Moderate.

Nonsolovino Via Vittorio Emanuele at Piazza Municipio. Somewhat touristy, this nonetheless represents good value, with first courses at €5–7 and mains at €6–10. Closed Mon. Moderate.

La Scala Scala Santa Maria del Monte 8 ☎0933.57.781. While this may be touristy and pricey, you can't fault the location, right on La Scala. Firsts are €6–9, second courses €8–13, pizzas are €5–8, and a tourist menu costs €22. Closed Wed. Moderate.

Bars

Bar Centrale Via Vittorio Emanuele 23. With indoor and outdoor seating, this place serves sandwiches and great ice cream.

Giardino Spadaro Via San Giuseppe 5. Garden bar close to La Scala, cool and shady by day, often thronged in the evening. Panini and other snacks available. Closed Tues.

Judica & Trieste Discesa Collegio. A peaceful bar and *távola calda*, with an outdoor terrace in front of the Gesù church.

Around Caltagirone: Grammichele and Monte San Mauro

Just ten minutes **east** of Caltagirone by train, **GRAMMICHELE** ranks among the most ambitious of the new towns built after the 1693 earthquake. The best place to appreciate its hexagonal design would be from the air – failing that, position yourself at the dead centre of the town's imposing central piazza to see the six radial streets reaching out, each bisected by secondary piazzas. The shape's no longer entirely perfect, due to a surfeit of new streets around the station at the southern edges of town, but it makes for an intriguing couple of hours' stroll, with all the streets in each segment corresponding exactly to their neighbours in dimension and appearance.

Despite the grand design, Grammichele is a rather tatty, predominantly rural-looking town – be prepared to meet a donkey in the road, or see chickens cooped up in a back yard, and farms near the train station. **Piazza Carafa**, the main square, has a handful of old-fashioned **bars** where most of the town's over-60s gather. A few streets back from Piazza Carafa, off Corso Vittorio Emanuele heading northwest, the small *Il Rústico* trattoria at Piazza G. Attaguile 12 (☎0933.942.365; closed Mon) serves *piadine*, pizzas, and pasta with *sugo ai noci* (walnut sauce), among other local dishes – worth booking. In the piazza, the modern *Bar Royal* is the place for snacks. You'll also find a couple of banks with cash machines across the piazza.

If you're driving or travelling by train **south** of Caltagirone, look out for the hill of **Monte San Mauro**, halfway to Niscemi, which was the scene of the one battle that could be called a separatist uprising in Sicily. At the end of 1945, Concetto Gallo, lawyer, landowner and commander-in-chief of the Separatist army (EVIS), led 58 men in a last stand against a force of five thousand Italian troops commanded by three generals. Gallo's inevitable defeat signalled the effective end of the Separatist movement in Sicily.

Festivals

March/April

Easter Holy Week celebrations in **Enna**; including processions, special Masses and the parade of saintly relics. Though it runs all week from Palm Sunday to Easter Sunday, the best day is Good Friday, when thousands march in silent procession dressed in the white-hooded costumes of the medieval fraternities. Other costumed processions can be seen at **Caltagirone**, **Troina** and at **Caltanissetta** (best days Maundy Thursday and Good Friday), featuring processional carts (the *misteri*) and monks. **Prizzi**, in the western interior, is a good place to be on Easter Sunday, when giant statues of Christ and the Virgin Mary are taunted by masked figures representing Death and the Devil, to whom onlookers are forced to give money. The **motor racing** season starts at the Autodromo di Pergusa, around the **Lago di Pergusa**, running until Sept.

May

Sagra del Lago Throughout the month at **Lago di Pergusa**, with folk events and fireworks, singing competitions and games.
Penultimate Sunday Festa dei Rami at **Troina**, in which laurel branches are carried to the tomb of St Silvester.

July

Estate Ennese Start of a series of concerts and opera in the open-air theatre at the castle in **Enna**. Runs until end of Aug.
24–25 Festival of San Giácomo in **Caltagirone**, during which the La Scala steps are illuminated.

August

12–14 Il Palio dei Normanni in **Piazza Armerina**, a medieval pageant commemorating Count Roger's taking of the town in the eleventh century. Processional entry into town on the twelfth, ceremonial joust on the fourteenth, along with costumed parades and other festive events. Similar events take place around the same time in a number of surrounding towns, but Piazza's is by far the largest.

September

Festival of Madonna dell'Alto in **Petralia Sottana**, with a nocturnal procession on horseback and a maypole dance known as the Ballo della Cordella.

December

Annual exhibition of terracotta sculpted cribs in **Caltagirone**.

Travel details

Trains

Caltagirone to: Catania (7–8 daily Mon–Sat; 1hr 40min); Gela (8–9 daily Mon–Sat; 40min); Grammichele (7–9 daily Mon–Sat; 15min).
Caltanissetta to: Agrigento (5–6 daily Mon–Sat, 2 daily Sun; 1hr 25min); Canicattì (10 daily Mon–Sat, 6 daily Sun; 30min); Enna (7 daily Mon–Sat, 5 daily Sun; 35min); Gela (3–4 daily; 2hr); Licata (3–4 daily; 1hr 20min); Palermo (4 daily; 2hr).
Enna to: Caltanissetta (7 daily Mon–Sat, 5 daily Sun; 35min); Catania (6 daily; 1hr 20min); Palermo (2 daily Mon–Sat, 1 daily Sun; 2hr 20min).

Buses

Agira to: Troina (3 daily Mon–Sat, 2 daily Sun; 50min).
Caltagirone to: Catania (1–2 hourly Mon–Sat, 4 daily Sun; 1hr 30min); Enna (2 daily Mon–Fri, 1 daily Sun; 1hr 25min); Gela (2 daily Mon–Sat; 1hr–1hr 10min); Grammichele (2 daily Mon–Sat; 30–40min); Piazza Armerina (5 daily Mon–Sat; 1hr–1hr 20min); Ragusa (2 daily Mon–Sat; 2hr).
Caltanissetta to: Agrigento (3–4 daily Mon–Sat, 1 daily Sun; 1hr 35min); Catania (13 daily Mon–Sat, 8 daily Sun; 1hr 35min); Enna (4–5 daily Mon–Sat; 50min); Palermo (7–10 daily Mon–Sat, 4 daily Sun; 1hr 40min); Piazza Armerina (5–8 daily; 30min).

Cesarò to: Catania (3 daily Mon–Sat; 2hr 15min); Randazzo (1 daily Mon–Sat; 1hr); Sant'Agata Militello (1 daily Mon–Sat; 1hr 45min).

Enna to: Agira (7 daily Mon–Sat, 2 daily Sun; 1hr); Calascibetta (8–12 daily Mon–Sat, 2 daily Sun; 30min); Caltagirone (2 daily Mon–Fri, 1 daily Sun; 1hr 25min), Caltanissetta (4–5 daily Mon–Sat; 55min); Catania (8–10 daily Mon–Sat, 5 daily Sun; 1hr 15min); Gela (3–4 daily; 1hr 15min); Leonforte (8 daily Mon–Sat, 2 daily Sun; 35–45min); Nicosia (3 daily Mon–Sat; 1hr 30min); Palermo (3–5 daily; 1hr 35min); Pergusa (4–9 daily Mon–Sat, 4 daily Sun; 20min); Piazza Armerina (4–6 daily; 30min).

Gangi to: Palermo (4 daily Mon–Sat, 2 daily Sun; 3hr).

Leonforte to: Catania (8–9 daily Mon–Sat, 3 daily Sun; 1hr 20min–1hr 50min); Enna (8 daily Mon–Sat, 2 daily Sun; 35–45min); Nicosia (4–5 daily Mon–Sat, 1 daily Sun; 40min).

Nicosia to: Agira (1 daily Mon–Sat; 1hr 20min); Catania (5 daily Mon–Sat, 1 daily Sun; 2hr); Enna (3 daily Mon–Sat; 1hr 30min); Gangi (4–7 daily Mon–Sat, 2 daily Sun; 40min); Leonforte (4–5 daily Mon–Sat, 1 daily Sun; 40min); Palermo (4 daily Mon–Sat, 2 daily Sun; 3hr 10min); Petralia Soprana (4–5 daily Mon–Sat, 2 daily Sun; 1hr 10min); Petralia Sottana (4–5 daily Mon–Sat, 2 daily Sun; 1hr 20min); Polizzi Generosa (2 daily; 2hr); Sperlinga (4–7 daily Mon–Sat, 2 daily Sun; 15min).

Piazza Armerina to: Aidone (6–13 daily Mon–Sat, 2 daily Sun; 15min); Caltagirone (5 daily Mon–Sat; 1hr–1hr 30min); Catania (3–6 daily Mon–Sat, 2 daily Sun; 1hr 40min); Enna (3–6 daily; 30min); Gela (3–4 daily; 40min); Palermo (3–5 daily; 2hr 15min).

Polizzi Generosa to: Caltavuturo (1–3 daily Mon–Sat, also 1 daily Sun in July & Aug; 35min); Palermo (2 daily; 1hr 20min); Términi Imerese (1–2 daily Mon–Sat; 1hr 45min).

Troina to: Agira (3 daily Mon–Sat, 2 daily Sun; 50min); Nicosia (4 daily Mon–Sat, 1 daily Sun; 1hr).

The south coast

N

TYRRHENIAN SEA

MEDITERRANEAN SEA

0   50 km

CHAPTER 8 Highlights

* **Museo Archeológico, Gela**
Stunning painted vases were
a speciality of Greek Gela,
and the town's museum holds
scores of fine examples.
See p.327

* **Tempio della Concordia,
Agrigento** This simple,
elegant temple provides the
backdrop for an atmospheric
walk in the past. See p.334

* **Eraclea Minoa** A superb
sandy beach overlooked by

the impressive remains of a
Greek city. See p.340

* **Sciacca** Medieval buildings
and quirky stone heads at
Castello Incantato make
underrated Sciacca a
worthwhile stop.
See p.341

* **Lampedusa** The rocky
shore, cliffs and grottoes of
Lampedusa are best seen on
a boat tour of the island.
See p.348

▲ Greek amphora at Eraclea Minoa

8

The south coast

The long south coast, from Gela to Sciacca, should be one of the most attractive parts of Sicily. Sparsely developed, it holds good beaches and some low-key Mediterranean ports and resorts that are barely known to Italians, let alone other tourists. Nevertheless, sporadic but spectacularly ugly coastal industrial development conspires to put off many people. The sea is heavily polluted in some areas, particularly around **Gela**, a large port and petrochemical town. To miss this coast altogether, however, would be to ignore some of the most important sights on the island. Gela itself retains its extensive Greek fortifications, while further west the hill-top town of **Agrigento** overlooks a series of splendid ancient temples, unrivalled in extent and preservation outside Greece.

To either side of Agrigento, isolated sandy **beaches** – packed with locals on summer weekends – warrant the occasional trip off the busy main road, the SS115. One of the best lies just below another Hellenic site, **Eraclea Minoa**, while the port of **Licata** offers a few old-town diversions to go with its beach. Of the other coastal towns, **Sciacca** is perhaps the most enjoyable, a fishing port and summer resort with amazing cliff-top views, and from here you can make a couple of detours into the tall and craggy mountains that back this part of the coast. Or you might consider heading out to the **Pelágie Islands**: these barren spots in the Mediterranean are closer to Africa than Europe, but are connected by regular ferry and hydrofoil with **Porto Empédocle**, near Agrigento.

Regular **train** and **bus** services link the coastal towns and villages, while less frequent services access the inland towns. **Hotel** accommodation is limited outside the major settlements, but there are plenty of opportunities to **camp** at sites along the coast.

Gela

GELA couldn't present a worse aspect on first sight: drivers have to negotiate a tangle of untidy backstreets, while the train line weaves through a mess of futuristic steel bubbles and pipes. Despite a few fine dune-backed beaches in the vicinity, it's no place to bathe; serious doubts surround the cleanliness of the water, and there's occasionally a chemical tang to the air. It was not always so. Gela was one of the most important of Sicily's Greek cities, founded in 688 BC, and under Hippocrates in the fifth century BC it rivalled even ancient Syracuse as the island's political hub. Its artistic eminence attracted literary stars, most notably the dramatist Aeschylus, who left his mark on the city (literally) when

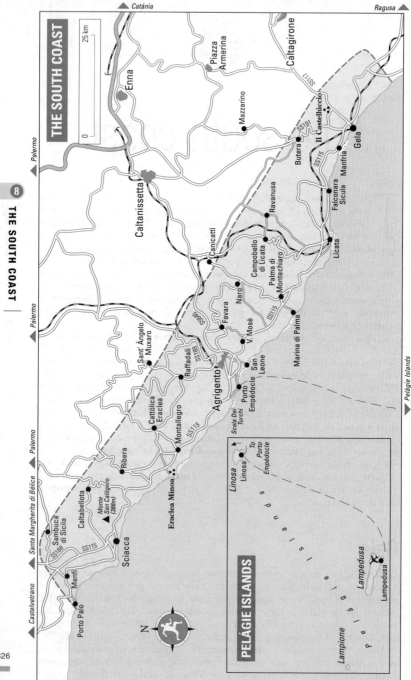

THE SOUTH COAST

0   25 km

▲ Catánia   Ragusa ▲

▲ Palermo

Enna

Piazza
Armerina

Mazzarino

Caltagirone

SS117

▲ Palermo

Caltanissetta

Canicatti

Ravanusa

Butera

SS191

Il Castellúccio

Gela

SS115

Falconara
Sícula

Manfria

Campobello
di Licata

Palma di
Montechiaro

Licata

▲ Palermo

SS640

Naro

Favara

SS115

Sant'Ángelo
Muxaro

SS189

Raffadali

V. Mosè

Marina di Palma

Cattólica
Eraclea

Montallegro

Agrigento

San
Leone

Porto
Empédocle

SS115

Scala Dei
Turchi

▲ Santa Margherita di Bélice

Ribera

▲ Palermo

▲ Castelvetrano

Sambuca
di Sicila

SS188

Caltabellota

SS115

Menfi

Porto Palo

Sciacca

Monte
San Calógero
(388m) ▲

Eraclea Minoa

Pelágie Islands ▶

N

PELÁGIE ISLANDS

Linosa

Linosa

To
Porto
Empédocle

P e l á g i e   I s l a n d s

Lampione

Lampedusa

Lampedusa

Lampedusa

felled by a tortoise dropped by an eagle, which – the tale relates – mistook his bald head for a stone on which to dash its prey. However, Gela's heyday was short-lived. Hippocrates' successor, Gelon, transferred his power and half the city's population east to Syracuse in 485 BC, the deep-water harbour there being more to the tyrant's liking. Gela was subsequently smashed by the Carthaginians and the Mamertines, its walls razed in the third century BC and abandoned to the encroaching sands. Modern Gela was the first Sicilian town to be liberated by the Allies in 1943, but otherwise – beyond an excellent archeological museum and a fine set of Greek defensive walls – is almost entirely without interest.

Gela's Greek remains

There's really no need to stay longer than half a day in Gela. That gives you enough time to see the only two sights, which lie at either end of the town's main Corso Vittorio Emanuele. At its eastern end, a twenty-minute walk from the centre, the **Museo Archeológico** (daily 9am–6pm; €3, includes entry to Greek fortifications) is notable largely for its important collection of painted vases upstairs. Mainly seventh- to fifth-century BC, the black and red jugs and beakers were Greek Gela's speciality: most major world museums tend to feature one or two, but the bulk are here. Other impressive finds include an animated sculpture of a horse's head (sixth century BC), and objects unearthed from necropolises belonging to Geloan dependencies. Outside the museum, a small **acropolis** has been uncovered, consisting of a few walls and a single temple column from the fifth century BC, though the small site is drained of all romance by the brooding, dirty industrial plant that dominates the beach below.

More archeological remains can be seen at **Capo Soprano**, at the western end of town. Head along the corso and take a left fork (Via Manzoni), which runs parallel to the sea as far as the red gates of the site, a three- to four-kilometre walk. The **Greek fortifications** here (daily 9am–1hr before sunset; €3, includes entry to Museo Archeológico) date from the fourth century BC. Preserved by the sand dunes under which they were discovered, the walls stand nearly 8m high in parts, made up of perfectly fitted stone blocks topped by a layer of brick and now covered in protective glass panels. It's a beautiful site, and you're free to wander around the line of the walls: in some places you can make out the remains of watchtowers and gateways, while waves crash onto a duned stretch of beach below. If you've come this far out of town, you may as well nip around the corner (back towards the centre and left, by the hospital), to Via Europa, to see the remains of Gela's fourth-century BC **public baths**, the only ones from Greek times discovered in Sicily and still equipped with their original seats.

Practicalities

Driving into town, simply follow the signs for museum and fortifications – it's slow going on the SS115, which cuts right through the centre. **Buses** leave from directly outside the **train station** (tickets and information from the Autolinee office, across the square: ☎0933.923.248); regular departures serve nearby towns, including Licata and Agrigento, Vittória, Caltanissetta and Siracusa. From the station, turn right down the main road and, at the junction, bear right for the town centre and Corso Vittorio Emanuele.

Information can be obtained at the **tourist office** at Via Pisa 65, off Via Bresmes, which cuts across Corso Vittorio Emanuele (Mon, Tues, Thurs & Fri

8am–2.15pm, Wed 8am–2.15pm & 3.30–6.15pm; ☎0933.913.788, ⓦwww
.aastgela.it).You're unlikely to want to **stay** in Gela, but if you get stuck, the *Sole*
on Via Mare 32 (☎0933.925.292, ⓔg.vitale_hotelsole@alice.it; ❹) isn't bad,
with air-conditioned, en-suite rooms. A long row of bars, pizzerias and trattorias
lines the endless lungomare.

Around Gela

With your own transport, you can pay a quick visit to Gela then strike off
inland to the medieval hill-town of **Butera** or west along the coast to find a
beach. Gela's surroundings don't improve until you're a good few kilometres out
of town in any direction. Best for scenery are the two **inland** routes north:
either up the SS191 to Butera, or northeast along the scenic SS117, which
swoops towards Caltagirone and Piazza Armerina, following the line of the
fertile Gela Valley. By car, you can be in either of the latter within the hour, the
road taking you through rolling cornfields and vineyards. For the coast **west of
Gela**, stick to the main SS115, which runs through town.

Inland to Butera

Around 8km out of Gela on the SS117, at a small road junction, a forlorn
Norman keep – **Il Castellúccio** – sticks out on a hillock, in the middle of land
keenly contested at the start of the Allied landings in Sicily in 1943. Defensive
concrete pillboxes still stud the dirt-brown hillsides on either side of the keep.

From Il Castellúccio, a minor road runs 7km west to join the rather more
direct SS191 from Gela, which runs to **BUTERA** in twenty winding kilometres. Important during the sixteenth century, under the control of the Barresi
princes, Butera today idles along in its lofty, remote way, pulling in the
occasional stray driver to Caltanissetta, another 50km north. It's a pretty little
place, with the drive up alone revealing why Butera was once coveted by
medieval overlords – the town sits on an impregnable crag, overseeing a
patchwork of walled fields, burnt hillsides, bare peaks, regimented rows of vines
and tomato plantations.

All traffic (including buses from Gela and Caltanissetta) pulls into Piazza
Dante, the main square. From there, Via Aldo Moro leads up in five minutes to
the **Castello dei Normanni**, a yellowing pile of which one battlemented wall
and the central keep survive, incongruously tucked between modern apartment
blocks. The terrace beyond enjoys tremendous views, to Gela and the coast.

Back in Piazza Dante, you can get a drink while contemplating the next move.
La Lanterna has outdoor seats, and doubles as an inexpensive pizzeria-restaurant,
while *Big Ben* and the adjacent *Britannia* bars are as oddly named a pairing as
you'll come across in Sicily.

West along the coast to Falconara Sicula

The long, empty coastline **west of Gela** is dotted by more pillboxes left
behind after the war. Following the SS115 from Gela, you come to a decent
sand **beach** at **MANFRIA**, just off the main road. You won't get to stop here

if you're travelling by train, however, as the tracks loop inland soon after Gela, and the next stop is at **FALCONARA SICULA**, a few kilometres beyond. Though neither place holds much apart from its respective beach, Falconara does boast a fourteenth-century castle, the private property of Palermitan aristocrats. It also has a **hotel**, the *Lido degli Angeli* (℡0934.349.054, ⓦwww .hotellidodegliangeli.it; no credit cards; ❹), with a ristorante/pizzeria, sports facilities and a **campsite** attached (℡0934.349.033), all right by the beach off the main SS115.

Licata and around

Ten kilometres further along the coast, the port of **LICATA** is the only other worthwhile coastal stop before Agrigento, though everything here can be seen in an hour or so. There's certainly nothing left of ancient Phintias, the settlement founded here in 280 BC by Greeks from Gela whose own city had been destroyed in successive attacks. Instead, the centre of Licata is largely Baroque in character, with a lower town split into two distinct halves: pavement cafés line the two wide corsos that form an L-shape at the heart of town, meeting at Piazza Progresso. Behind here, the narrow crisscrossed alleys of the old town reach back to the harbour. There's a lido and **beach** just up from the harbour, though as Licata is still a working port, full of maritime hardware, it's not exactly enticing. For a view over the harbour, climb to the top of the town from the main Corso Roma and then work your way around the hill to reach an imposing sixteenth-century **castello**. Other strolls can take in the lively old-town **market** (over by 2pm), held in the cobbled square in front of the church, and some of Licata's good *palazzi*, the most prominent being the gargoyle-studded **Palazzo Canarelli** on Corso Roma. Housed in a sixteenth-century convent on Piazza Sant'Angelo, and reached by walking down Via Dante off Corso Umberto, the **Museo Archeológico** (Mon–Sat 9am–6.30pm, Sun 9am–12.30pm; free) displays a good deal of local prehistoric and Greek material, as well as medieval art.

Practicalities
Buses pull up on Corso Roma, right in the centre; the bar at no. 36 posts timetables and sells tickets for departures to Agrigento, Gela, Catania and Palermo. The **train station** is five minutes' walk away: go back down the corso to the church, turn right down Via Giovanni Améndola, left at the bottom and then take the fifth right, down a little street called Via Stazione.

Neither of the town's two **hotels** is terribly alluring. To reach the simple *Roma*, Corso Serrovira 54 (℡0922.774.075; no credit cards; ❷), walk down Corso Roma to Piazza Progresso, turn left down Corso Umberto, and after 200m take a left again onto Corso Serrovira. Alternatively, *Al Faro*, Via Dogana 6 (℡0922.775.503; ❺), by the port and near the lido, has its own decent restaurant, though the surroundings are nothing special.

Licata's **dining** choices are also limited, but there's one exceptional place, *L'Oste e il Sacrestano*, a small, smart but unpretentious *hostaria* with moderate prices at Via Sant'Andrea 19 (℡0922.774.736; closed Mon), near the Duomo and Corso Vittorio Emanuele. Otherwise, a few pizza joints are located by the lido – for example *Le Fiabe* at Piazza Regole 37, just around the corner from *Al Faro*, which has outdoor seating – or try any of the bars on and around Piazza Progresso.

Around Licata: Palma di Montechiaro and Naro

If you're heading straight for Agrigento, it's quicker to pick up a direct bus at Licata than to stick with the train, which swoops inland to Canicattì before doubling back to the coast. If you're driving, though, you could make a couple of stops along the way.

From Licata, it's 20km to shabby **PALMA DI MONTECHIARO**, which lies just off the SS115; the Agrigento–Licata bus passes this way too. This was once the seat of the Lampedusa family, the last of whom – **Giuseppe Tomasi di Lampedusa** – wrote the acclaimed novel, *The Leopard*. He died in 1957 (*The Leopard* was published a year later), but the palace in Palma had lain derelict for a long time before that. Indeed, far more resonant for *Leopard* fans are the ruins in the western Sicilian town of Santa Margherita di Belice (see p.410). Today, the only echoes of the great feudal family recorded in the novel are to be found in Palma's imposing seventeenth-century **Chiesa Matrice**, built by one of Lampedusa's ancestors and approached by a wide flight of crumbling steps, and the ruined site of the **Castello di Palma**, a few kilometres west of town at the end of a small track. Four kilometres south of town, on the coast, **MARINA DI PALMA** has a strip of beach, mobbed by locals during summer weekends.

North of Palma, the road climbs 17km up to medieval **NARO**, whose thirteenth- and fourteenth-century buildings merit a look if you have time on your hands. SAIS **bus** services run here from Agrigento (Mon–Sat 4 daily, last one returning at 3.15pm; call ☏0922.595.933 for up-to-date schedules). The finest of the buildings are the Chiaramonte **castello** at Naro's highest point, and the nearby ruins of the old cathedral; other churches in this walled and battlemented town are emphatically Baroque. Architecturally harmonious though Naro is, the real attraction is not so much the end destination as the drive itself, from Palma and Agrigento, which is rewarded by extensive sweeping views down to the coast.

Agrigento

No one comes to **AGRIGENTO** for the town, though its worn medieval streets and buildings soak up thousands of tourists every year. The interest instead focuses on the substantial remains of **Akragas**, Pindar's "most beautiful city of mortals", a couple of kilometres below. Strung along a ridge facing the sea, its series of Doric temples are the most captivating of Sicilian Greek remains and are unique outside Greece.

In 581 BC, colonists from nearby Gela and Rhodes founded the city of Akragas between the rivers of Hypsas and Akragas. This was the concluding act of expansion that had seen Geloans spread west along the high points of their trade routes, subduing and Hellenizing the indigenous populations as they went. They surrounded the new city with a mighty wall, formed in part by a higher ridge where they placed the acropolis (and where, today, the modern town stands). The southern limit of the ancient city was a second, lower ridge, and it was here, in the so-called **Valle dei Templi** (Valley of the Temples), that the city architects erected their sacred buildings during the fifth century BC. They were – and are – stunning in their effect, reflecting the wealth and luxury of ancient Agrigento: "Athens with improvements", as Henry Adams had it in 1899.

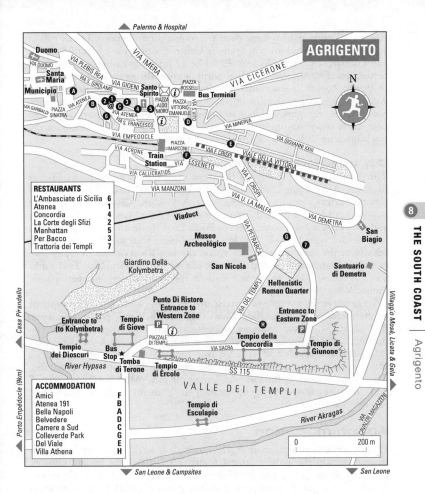

As so often, however, Agrigento's Hellenic pre-eminence was no buffer against the cruel tide of Sicilian history. Conquered and sacked by successive waves of Carthaginians, Romans (twice), Saracens and Normans, the ancient city lost its status and many of its finest treasures. In a way, Agrigento never really recovered, and despite the undoubted modern pulling power of the temples, which fills the town with tourists throughout much of the year, it has little sense of purpose these days. Ugly modern suburban building and road viaducts on the coast below town lack all sense of proportion and are creeping ever closer to the temples themselves. Meanwhile, government statistics show Agrigento to be one of Italy's poorest towns. Consequently it comes as no surprise to learn that the Mafia has an undue local influence, not least in the sphere of speculative building projects.

Arrival, city transport and information

Public transport arrives in the centre of town. While you could easily jump straight on a bus to the Valle dei Templi archeological site, the town itself is worth exploring, and has some decent accommodation options. **Trains** pull in at the edge of the old town at Stazione Centrale, which has a beautiful garden and a number of luggage lockers (€2.50 for 12 hr) – don't make the mistake of getting out at Agrigento Bassa, 3km north of town. **Buses** arrive at the terminal in Piazza Rosselli, a few minutes' walk to the north. If you're **driving** into Agrigento, be warned that the one-way system in the old town is a nightmare. Some hotels are signposted, but you may well not be able to **park** anywhere near where you're staying (ask about *parcheggio* when you book). You can usually bag a space on Viale della Vittória or Via F. Crispi.

City transport and information

The old town stretches west of the three main interlocking squares, piazzas Marconi, Aldo Moro and Vittorio Emanuele. Via Atenea is Agrigento's principal artery, running west from Piazza Aldo Moro. **City buses** (€0.90 for 90min) head from outside the train station on Piazza Marconi to the temples and the beach at San Leone; buses to Porto Empédocle for the Pelágie Islands leave from Piazza Rosselli. Buy bus tickets before your journey from kiosks, *tabacchi* or the station bar, or pay €1 on the bus. Kiosks stand to either side of Piazza Marconi, though they're not always open on Sundays. **Taxi** ranks are at Piazzale Aldo Moro and outside the train station; for taxi phone numbers, see "Listings", p.338.

Agrigento holds a couple of **tourist offices**, with one focusing on the town in the middle of Piazzale Aldo Moro (Mon–Fri 8.30am–1pm & 4–7.30pm; ☎0922.20.454, ⓦwww.comune.agrigento.it), and one covering the whole province located inside the Prefettura building at the back of the piazza (Mon–Fri 8am–2pm & 2.30–7pm, Sat 8am–1pm; ☎800.236.837 or 800.315.555, ⓦwww.provincia.agrigento.it); both can supply useful maps and brochures. There's also a kiosk at the Valle dei Templi car park (Mon–Sat 9am–1.30pm). The **website** ⓦwww.agrigentonatura.it is a useful resource for events, accommodation and transport.

Accommodation

Finding **accommodation** in Agrigento itself is rarely a problem, although in peak season the nearby coastal resorts fill fast. All the budget choices, primarily small family-run establishments, are in the old town above the temples. Tour groups tend to stay in the grander hotels a few kilometres east of town at **Villaggio Mosé**, on the coast road into Agrigento. That's an unattractive traffic-choked suburb, lined with stores, garages, furniture shops and apartment blocks, but the hotels themselves – glossy, three- and four-star holiday palaces – are fine. The nearest **campsites** lie 6km south of town at the coastal resort of San Leone (see p.340), also the site of a good B&B.

Amici Via Acrone 5 ☎0922.402.831, ⓦwww
.hotelamici.com. Handy for the train station, the bright, air-conditioned rooms here have TVs, tiled floors and gleaming bathrooms. Some larger rooms sleep three and four; those on the ground level are smaller but have great coastal and valley views (especially room 101) and balconies. Breakfast can be poor. Parking available. ❹

🏃 **Atenea 191** Via Atenea 191
☎0922.595.594, ⓦwww.atenea191.com.

A real find, this B&B on the main drag has huge, tastefully designed en-suite rooms, most with balconies offering distant views of the sea. One room has painted walls and ceiling. Breakfast is served on the roof terrace in summer. No credit cards. ❺

Bella Napoli Piazza Lena 6 ☎0922.20.435, ⓦwww.hotelbellanapoli.com. A reasonable budget choice at the far western end of the old town, with a cheery owner. Rooms facing the square have balconies but can be noisy. Paying slightly more, you can stay in the nearby sister hotel, *Antica Foresteria Catalana*, for more comfort and antique touches. Parking available. ❸

Belvedere Via San Vito 20 ☏ 0922.20.051, ⓦ www.hotelbelvedereagrigento.com. Above and behind the main squares of the old town – climb the vast flight of steps opposite Banco di Sicilia or by road follow the sign at the back of Piazza Vittorio Emanuele – this faded hotel represents good value. Room 30 has an enormous balcony (though not much of a view); others are trim and clean without being exciting, though rooms 40, 42 and 44 open onto a shady garden. Rooms are fan-cooled. Private bathrooms cost extra, breakfast is €3 extra, and a garage is available for €10 a day. You can claim a five percent discount with this Guide. No credit cards. ❷

Camere a Sud Via Ficani 6 ☏ 349.638.4424, ⓦ www.camereasud.it. This bijou B&B in an alley off Via Atenea has charming hosts, three modish, en-suite rooms and a roof terrace for breakfasts. Internet access. No credit cards. ❹

Colleverde Park Via Panorámica dei Templi ☏ 0922.29.555, ⓦ www.colleverde-hotel.it.

Large, modern hotel, halfway to the archeological zone, with English-speaking staff, Wi-Fi, parking and beautiful gardens. It's quite pricey, even given the location and facilities, but you'll find good rates online, and it's worth bargaining; valley-facing rooms cost most, the two fourth-floor rooms have wide roofterraces, and there are cheaper town-facing rooms. ❼

Del Viale Via del Piave 12 ☏ 0922.20.063, ⓦ www.hoteldelviale.it. A good mid-range choice with clean, comfortable, air-conditioned rooms with private bathrooms and TVs. It's signposted off Piazza Cavour, behind an apartment block. Free parking is always available. ❹

Villa Athena Località Templi ☏ 0922.596.288, ⓕ 0922.402.180. The only reason to stay in this hotel is for its unrivalled location, just a brief stroll from the Valle dei Templi. It has landscaped grounds and a small pool, but most rooms are drab, the food is mediocre and the whole place could do with an overhaul. It may all be worth it if you can get one of the terraced rooms overlooking the Concordia temple. ❼

The Town

It would be a mistake not to scout around the modern **town of Agrigento**. Modern only in comparison with the temples, it's thoroughly medieval at its heart. Unlike the mean streets of many less commercialized Sicilian towns, **Via Atenea**, the long, main drag, flaunts a run of quality jewellers, trendy boutiques, bookshops and *pasticcerie*. Window-shopping here is a positive pleasure, especially in the late afternoon, when it's closed to traffic.

The streets off both sides revert to type, however, harbouring ramshackle *palazzi* and minuscule *cortili* (courtyards), among which a couple of specific buildings are worth seeking out. North of Via Atenea, the **Santo Spírito** church, at the end of Via Foderà, was built for Cistercian nuns in 1290. You can usually find someone to show you round, in return for a small tip. Inside, florid early eighteenth-century monochrome stuccoes by Serpotta sprawl across the walls and trompe l'oeil domed ceiling. Upstairs, just before the entrance of the small **folk museum** (Mon–Fri 9am–1pm & 3–6.30pm; €2.50), you'll find some decorative nineteenth-century pictures of angels and saints inlaid with mother-of-pearl; the museum itself contains local artefacts, including Toby jugs. It also enjoys marvellous views of the temples across the fields. Back downstairs, if you ring the bell marked "*monastero*" and ask for "*dolci di mándorla*", a nun will bring you a tray of almond cakes, which are expensive, chewy, and worth the experience.

Via Atenea cuts right through the oldest part of town, at its most grand at the western end, around the **Municipio**, in Piazza Sinatra, housed inside a seventeenth-century convent. The narrowest and steepest of the streets spread up the hill from here, passing the church of **Santa Maria dei Greci**, built over a Greek temple of the fifth century BC. The flattened columns can be seen in the nave, while outside, visible from an underground tunnel in the flower-filled courtyard, the stylobate and column stumps are incorporated into the church's foundations. Inside are the remains of Byzantine frescoes; if the church is closed, you can get a key from the guardian at Via Santa Maria dei Greci 15, opposite. Just up from here, Via Duomo leads past a line of decrepit *palazzi* to the massive **Duomo**, set on a terrace at the top of the hill and fronting a spacious piazza below. It's currently under restoration due to land subsidence, but when it's open you can visit (9am–12.30pm & 4–6.30pm), except when there's a service.

The Valle dei Templi

A road winds down from Agrigento to the **Valle dei Templi**. Buses #1, #2 and #3 from outside the train station will drop you at a car park between the two separate sections of archeological remains, the eastern and western zones; a taxi will cost around €10. You'll pass Agrigento's Museo Archeológico on the way; if you're intent upon doing the ancient site and museum in one go, you'll need a full day here. Take a picnic, or use the bar-*távola calda* at the car park. Entrance to both the eastern and western temple sites costs €6, or €10 including the museum (July–Sept 8.30am–9.30pm; Oct–June 8.30am–7.30pm). There's a useful audioguide (€5), and **guided tours** are sometimes offered in English – ask at the information kiosk in the car park for details. On August and September evenings, open-air **concerts** take place on the edge of the archeological zone at Piana San Gregorio, with tickets from €10: phone ☎0922.401.129 for details of the programme, or look up Ⓦwww.agrigentonatura.it.

The eastern zone

The **eastern zone** is the more popular, and is at its least crowded in the early morning or late at night when floodlit in striking amber light. A path climbs up to the oldest of Akragas's temples, the **Tempio di Èrcole** (Herakles). Probably begun in the last decades of the sixth century BC, it's a long structure, nine of the original 38 columns re-erected, everything else scattered around like a half-finished jigsaw puzzle.

Retrace your steps, back across what remains of a deep, wheel-rutted Greek street, and the main path continues up past the site of the city's ancient necropolis to the **Tempio della Concordia** (Concord), dating from around 430 BC. Perfectly preserved and beautifully situated, with fine views to the city and the sea, the tawny stone lends the structure warmth and strength. It's the most complete of the temples, and has required less renovation than the others, mainly thanks to its conversion in the sixth century AD to a Christian church. Restored in the eighteenth century to its (more or less) original layout, the temple has kept its simple lines and slightly tapering columns, although sadly it's fenced off from the public. Circle the temple at least once to get a decent view, and stand well back to admire its elegant proportions.

The path continues, following the line of the ancient city walls that hug the ridge, to the **Tempio di Giunone** (Juno, or Hera), an engaging structure, half in ruins, standing at the very edge of the spur on which the temples were built. A long altar has been reconstructed at the far end of the temple; the patches of red visible here and there on the masonry denote fire damage, probably from the sack of Akragas by the Carthaginians in 406 BC.

The western zone

The **western zone**, back along the path and beyond the car park, is less impressive, though still archeologically engaging – a vast tangle of stone and fallen masonry from an assortment of temples. Most notable is the mammoth pile of rubble that was the **Tempio di Giove** (Jupiter, or Zeus). The largest

▲ The Tempio della Concordia at Agrigento

Doric temple ever known, it was never completed, left in ruins by the Carthaginians and further damaged by earthquakes and the removal of stone to build the port of Porto Empédocle to the south. Still, the stereobate remains, unnaturally huge in scale, while on the ground, face to the sky, lies an eight-metre-high telamone: a supporting column sculpted as a male figure, arms raised and bent to bear the weight of the temple. As excavations continue, **other**

scattered remains litter the area, not least piles of great column drums marked with a U-shaped groove, which enabled them to be lifted with ropes.

Beyond, behind the excavated gates and walls of the Greek city, is the earliest sacred site, the Sanctuary of the Chthonic Deities, marked by two altars (one square and fire-reddened, the other round), dating from the seventh century BC, before the official foundation of the colony. This is also the site of the so-called **Tempio dei Dioscuri** (also known as Tempio di Castore e Polluce, or Castor and Pollux), rebuilt in 1832, its columns and corner-work actually made up of unrelated pieces from the confused debris on the ground.

Near here is the entrance to the **Giardino della Kolymbetra**, for which you need a separate ticket (daily: May–Oct 10am–6.30pm; Nov–Dec & Feb–April 10am–5.30pm; €2). Part of the city's irrigation system in the fifth century BC, it's now an extensive sunken garden, lush and green amid the aridity of the rest of the archeological zone. There is nothing monumental here, but it makes a pleasant relief from temple-touring, the olive, almond and citrus groves overlooked by honey-toned calcareous cliff walls draped with cactus and pitted with caves. It also holds banana, pistachio and pomegranate trees, all meticulously labelled and explained, and a reedy stream.

The Museo Nazionale Archeológico

The road that leads back to town from the car park, Via dei Templi, runs past the excellent **Museo Nazionale Archeológico** (Tues–Sat 9am–7pm, Mon & Sun 9am–1pm; €6), outside which buses will stop on request. It holds an extraordinarily varied collection, devoted to finds from the temples, the ancient city and the surrounding area. There are brief notes in English throughout, and an informative audioguide (€5). Count on spending two or three hours here, more if you combine it with seeing the remains of the residential area of the old city, just over the road.

Unusually for an archeological museum, much of what's here holds artistic merit as well as historical interest. You could skip most of the initial local prehistoric and Bronze Age finds, though in **room 1** look out for the gold signet rings, engraved with animals. **Rooms 3 and 4** feature an outstanding vase collection, beguiling sixth- to third-century BC pieces, one of which depicts the burial of a warrior. The highlight is a stunningly detailed white-ground *krater* from 440 BC portraying a valiant Perseus freeing Andromeda. But it's the finds from the temples themselves that make this collection come alive: leaving **room 4**, you'll pass a series of sculpted lion's-head water-spouts, a common device for draining the water from the roofs of the city's temples, while **room 6** is given over to exhibits relating to the Tempio di Giove, with three enormous stone heads from the temples sitting in the recessed wall. Some useful wooden model reconstructions help to make sense of the disjointed wreckage on the ground, although the prime exhibit is a reassembled telamon stacked against one wall: all the weather damage can't hide the strength implicit in this huge sculpture. The finest statue in the museum is in **room 10**, where the Ephebus, a naked Greek youth, displays a nerveless strength and power that suggests that the model was probably a soldier. Rooms beyond hold coins, inscriptions and finds from local necropolises; typical is an alabaster child's sarcophagus in **room 11** showing poignant scenes from his life, which was cut short by illness. The last couple of rooms contain finds from the rest of the province, one of which, in **room 15**, is the equal of anything that's gone before, amply demonstrating the famed Geloan skill as masters of vase-ware: a fifth-century BC *krater* displays a graphic scene from Homer in which Achilles slays the queen of the Amazons at the moment when he falls in love with her.

In the grounds of the museum, look out for the Gothic doorway of the adjacent church of **San Nicola**. From the terrace outside, you get an invigorating view over the temple valley, while just beyond is a small odeon (third-century BC) used for public meetings, during which the participants stood rather than sat in the narrow rows. Nip over the road on the way out of the museum, too: the **Hellenistic-Roman quarter** opposite (daily 9am–1hr before sunset; free) contains rows of houses, inhabited (on and off) until the fifth century AD, many with mosaic designs still discernible.

Other archeological remains

While you could see everything thus far described in four or five hours, without your own transport the archeological park's remaining sights mean a lot of extra walking. The quickest way to reach the most distant is to climb over the wall to the side of the Tempio di Concordia and scramble down through the field to the road. Here, at the end of a dusty track, stands the undersized **Tempio di Esculapio** (Asclepius), with solid walls instead of a colonnade. Nearby, back along the main road and close to the crossroads, is a large two-storeyed Roman tomb (75 BC), the **Tomba di Terone**, mistakenly named by historians after the Greek tyrant Theron. The road then heads up, past the car park and museum, where a right fork followed by another right turn (Via Demetra) leads to the tiny church of **San Biagio**, a 3km walk. A Norman chapel, this was built over the visible remains of a temple, contemporaneous with the ones below on the ridge. It's currently closed for restoration, but hang around and a custodian will lead you down the cliff behind the chapel to the eerie **Santuario di Demetra** (be prepared to tip). A stone-built chambered shrine hides two dingy caves that stretch 20m into the hillside. The thin corridor between building and caves was a sort of vestibule with niches for water so that worshippers could wash themselves. The most ancient of Agrigento's sacred sites, it was once devoted to the cult of Demeter and Persephone, and in use even before Akragas was founded. A mysterious and evocative place, it's at its best as the sun sets, when shadows flit across the dark and silent caves.

Eating and drinking

Agrigento has a fairly good choice of **restaurants**, many clustered around Via Atenea and offering some kind of *menu turístico*. They tend to be a bit touristy, though prices are usually low. Only two or three places in town offer pizzas – most **pizzerias** are at Villaggio Mosé, east of town, below the temples, or at the coastal resort of San Leone (see p.340).

There are two distinct areas for **cafés and bars**. The town-centre *passeggiata* focuses on Via Atenea, and once the shops re-open in the late afternoon the whole street is packed. To watch the action, choose a seat at one of the little bars in Piazzale Aldo Moro, a nice place to sit in the early evening, despite the occasional burst of organ music from a local crooner. For sunsets and views, stroll along Viale della Vittoria to the park: four or five cafés along here cater more to a local family crowd. For example, *Caffeteria Nobel*, Viale della Vittoria 11, is a good place for an ice cream or a beer under the shady trees of the avenue, open until late.

L'Ambasciate di Sicilia Via Giambertoni 2 ℡0922.20.526. Fairly standard food in folksy surroundings, though tables on the outdoor terrace provide one of the few good views in town. The *antipasto rústico*, house pasta and

involtini are good choices. Closed Mon except Aug. Moderate.

Atenea Via Ficani 12 ℡0922.20.247. Family-run budget restaurant, set in a quiet courtyard with outdoor tables in summer. Expect simple, no-frills pasta, meat (around €6) and fish (€8) dishes of variable quality, or try the €14.50 tourist menu with wine. No credit cards. Closed Sun. Inexpensive.

Concordia Via Porcello 8, opposite Via Atenea 61 ☎0922.22.668. Tourist prices and clientele, with decent food, a chatty *padrone*, and an air-conditioned dining room with a bit of exposed ancient wall – in summer, you can eat outside in a private courtyard across the way. Spaghetti (*alla sarde*, pesto, or with prawns) or grilled fish are the best choices; first courses cost €7–9, mains €8–14, and meat and fish tourist menus cost €15 and €20 respectively (wine extra). Closed Sun off-season. Moderate.

La Corte degli Sfizi Cortile Contarini, opposite Via Atenea 169. Little trattoria with a summer walled courtyard where you can eat tasty pasta (like *cavatelli* with aubergines), or dishes such as grilled sausage or swordfish. Also pizza in the evenings. Nice staff and very reasonable food for the price. Fixed-price menus including wine cost €18 (meat) and €20 (fish). Closed Tues. Moderate.

Manhattan Salita Madonna degli Angeli 9. Popular alleyway trattoria that serves a host of fresh pastas, nearly all €7, and a good fish soup. The menu is pretty standard, but the food is nicely prepared. Usually busy at lunchtime. Closed Sun. Moderate.

Per Bacco Vícolo Lo Presti ☎0922.553.369. Fish dominates the menu in this small, smart trattoria favoured by locals. There's a good selection of salads (€5) and risottos (€7). Expect to pay around €30 for a full meal including drinks. Evenings only. Closed Mon. Moderate–expensive.

Trattoria dei Templi Via Panoramica dei Templi 15 ☎0922.403.110. Fresh seafood in a traditional restaurant halfway between town and the Valle dei Templi. Among their ample pasta dishes, opt for *ravioli sapore di Sicilia*, filled with fish and with a lemon and cream sauce (€7), or splash out on the *fettuccine all'aragosta*, served with a chunk of lobster (€14). Closed Sun in summer, Fri rest of the year. Moderate.

Listings

Banks and exchange ATMs at banks along Via Atenea (nos. 2, 15 and 145); on Piazza Vittorio Emanuele, and on Piazzale Aldo Moro 1. There's an exchange office at the post office.

Buses Services operating from the bus terminal at Piazza Rosselli include: Camilleri (☎0922.596.490) to Palermo and Raffadali; Cuffaro (☎091.616.1510, @www.cuffaro.info) to Palermo and Sant'Ángelo Muxaro; Lattuca (☎0922.36.398) to Sant'Ángelo Muxaro; SAL (☎0922.401.360, @www .autolineesal.it) to Licata, Gela, Palma di Montechiaro and Porto Empédocle; SAIS Trasporti (☎0922.595.933, @www.saistrasporti.it) to Caltanissetta, Canicattì, Catania and Naro; Salvatore Lumia (☎0922.20.414, @www .autolineelumia.it) to Castelvetrano, Marsala, Mazara, Montallegro, Ribera, Sciacca and Trápani. There's a SAIS bus ticket/information office in the corner of the piazza. Otherwise, buy tickets on the bus. Timetables are posted in front of the various companies' stops.

Car rental Avis, Piazzetta San Calógero 11 (near train station) ☎0922.26.353; Hertz, Via Imera 209 ☎0922.403.091.

Car repairs ACI, Via Matteo Cimara 38 ☎0922.604.284 or ☎116.

Cinema Cine Astor, Piazza Vittorio Emanuele.

Hospital Ospedale Civile San Giovanni, Contrada Consolida, just outside town ☎0922.442.111.

Internet Internet Train, Cortile Contarini, opposite *La Corte degli Sfizi* (Mon–Sat 9.30am–1.15pm & 3.30–9pm); you can also log on at the provincial tourist office in the Prefettura (first 15min free).

Pharmacies Averna, Via Atenea 325 ☎0922.26.093; Maria Teresa Indelicato, Piazza Vittorio Emanuele 13 ☎0922.23.889; Minacori, Via Atenea 91 ☎0922.25.089.

Police Call ☎112 or 113, or contact the Questura on Piazza Vittorio Emanuele ☎0922.483.111, or the Carabinieri at Piazzale Aldo Moro 2 ☎0922.499.000.

Post office The circular building in Piazza Vittorio Emanuele (Mon–Sat 8.30am–6.30pm).

Taxis You'll find ranks at Piazzale Aldo Moro (☎0922.21.899) and outside the train station (☎0922.26.670), otherwise call ☎340.252.1471.

Travel agents For ferry tickets to the Pelágie Islands and other services: Edrega Viaggi, Via Atenea 21 ☎0922.594.155; Trasportaereo, Via Imera 23 ☎0922.596.333.

Around Agrigento: Caos and Casa Pirandello

Just **out of Agrigento** (at the end of the flyover leading out towards Porto Empédocle; SAL buses once or twice hourly from the bus or train station), the suburb of **Caos** was the birthplace of **Luigi Pirandello**, and the inspiration for the Taviani Brothers' film, *Kaos*, based on four of his short stories. One of the greats of twentieth-century Italian literature, Pirandello is best known for his dramatic works, such as *Six Characters in Search of an Author* and *Henry IV*, though his 1934 Nobel Prize was awarded as much for his novels and short stories. He had a tragic life: his wife was committed to an asylum having lapsed into insanity following the ruin of her family and the birth of their third son, and for much of his life Pirandello was forced to write to supplement his frugal living as a teacher. His drama combines elements of tragedy and comedy with keenly observed dialogue, and the nature of identity and personality, reality, illusion and the absurd are all recurring themes. Pirandello's ideas – and innovations – formed the blueprint for much subsequent twentieth-century drama.

Although he left Agrigento while still young, Pirandello spent time here every summer at the **Casa Natale di Luigi Pirandello**, Contrada Caos just off the SS115, past the Valle dei Templi (daily 9am–1pm & 2–7pm; €2), and you can see the study where he wrote, crammed with foreign editions of his works. As well as a couple of murals he painted, it holds stacks of photos, including one sent by George Bernard Shaw, and a fifth-century vase, depicting a bearded man attacking a young woman, that was formerly used as an urn for Pirandello's ashes. After seeing the house, with its bamboo and daub interior, you can wander down through the grounds to where the writer's ashes are interred, though the views he once enjoyed over the sea are now ruined by a patch of industrial horror.

Porto Empédocle and around

Six kilometres southwest of Agrigento, **PORTO EMPÉDOCLE** is of main interest as the departure-point for ferries to the Pelágie Islands. Though it's an unprepossessing, functional port, much of it dominated by an enormous cement works, its lack of pretension also makes it a welcome antidote to tourist-ridden Agrigento. If you're waiting for a ferry, you can enjoy a pleasant enough stroll along the central pedestrian walkway in town, or dine at good, inexpensive fish **restaurants** such as *La Lámpara*, in what looks like a long wooden shed a few minutes' walk along the seafront at Via F. Crispi 3, where an abundant three-course meal plus good local wine will cost around €25. SAL **buses** leave for the port once or twice hourly from Agrigento's bus and train stations (a 25min journey), dropping you in Piazza Italia, one block from the waterfront; the last bus from Agrigento leaves at 8.30pm (6.30pm on Sun). A **taxi** from Agrigento will cost about €25.

About 7km west of Porto Empédocle, following signs for Realmonte, you'll find a stunning sandy **beach** at the bottom of furrowed and gleaming-white cliffs at **Scala dei Turchi**. A hideous abandoned construction has defaced the magnificent landscape on the left, less-visited side of the beach, but the water is crystalline (beware the shoals of biting fish!). At the top of the steps leading down to the beach, the *Lido Scala dei Turchi* provides welcome sustenance in the form of delicious seafood **meals** for less than €20.

San Leone

A far less spectacular but still decent beach lies east down the coast, 6km south of Agrigento, at the resort of **SAN LEONE**. With a handful of accommodation options, including the two campsites nearest to Agrigento (both open all year), this would make a good alternative to staying in Agrigento itself, to which it's connected by bus #2 from outside the train station (every 30min until 9pm); taxis from Agrigento charge around €25. Most of the many **places to eat** that are open in summer are pizzerias and fast-food joints. For something more substantial, head for *Trattoria Caico*, Via Nettuno 35 (☎0922.412.788; closed Tues and Nov), in business for half a century, where you can dig into such dishes as *cavatelli alla Siciliana* (pasta with tomato and aubergine), *spaghetti vóngole* or grilled meats and fish on the vine-shaded patio; main courses cost around €15, and pizzas from the wood-fired oven are available in the evening.

Hotels and B&Bs

Arcadias Via Carrà 4 ☎0922.413.579, ⓦwww.arcadias.it. Close to the beach, the front-facing rooms of this smart, modern B&B have balconies, and there are bikes to rent and ping-pong for guests. ❺
Hotel Costazzurra Via delle Viole 2 ☎0922.411.222, ⓦwww.hotelcostazzurra.it. A

five-minute walk from the beach, this family-run hotel offers quiet, modern and spacious rooms, air-conditioned and fully-equipped with TV and Wi-Fi. There's a good restaurant, spa whirlpool and free bikes. The bus stops right outside. ❻

Campsites

Nettuno Via Lacco Ameno 3 ☎0922.416.268, ⓦwww.geocities.com/campingnettuno. Right by a sandy beach at the southern end of San Leone, with pinewoods that provide shade for camping. There's a restaurant, pizzeria and store, and apartments sleeping two–four are available for weekly rent.

Valle dei Templi Viale Emporium 192 ☎0922.411.115, ⓦwww.campingvalledeitempli .com. A kilometre or so from the temples and 700m from the sea (with a bus stop close by), this has a bar, restaurant and pizzeria, and ten bungalows that are usually booked up in high summer.

Eraclea Minoa

Thirty-five kilometres along the coast northwest of Agrigento is the third important Greek site in this stretch of seafront, **ERACLEA MINOA**. According to the historian Diodorus, this was originally named Minoa after the Cretan king Minos, who chased Daedalus from Crete to Sicily and founded a city where he landed. The Greeks settled here in the sixth century BC, later adding the tag Heraklea. A buffer between the two great cities of Akragas, 40km to the east, and Selinus (Selinunte), 60km west, Eraclea was dragged into endless border disputes, but flourished nonetheless. Most of what's left dates from the fourth century BC, the city's most important period, three hundred years or so before it fell into decline.

It can be a challenge to **reach the site** without your own transport. In summer it's slightly simpler: regular Lumia buses from Agrigento go to Montallegro, from which, between June and September, three Raffadali buses run daily to Eraclea (8.30am, 11am & 2pm). In other periods, however, you'll have to catch any bus between Agrigento and Sciacca and ask the driver to put you off at the turning, 5km west of Montallegro, on the SS115. The site is 3.5km distant from there, with the beach another 1km below. **Heading on** west from the site turn-off, you should be able to flag down a bus en route to Sciacca.

The site

The **site** (daily 9am–1hr before sunset; €2) sits on a ridge high above a beautiful arc of sand, with the mouth of the River Plátani on the other side. Among the most attractive of all Greek sites in Sicily, it occupies a headland of which only around a third has so far been excavated. What there is to see is the fruit of successive excavations by foreign universities, who, together with the local *Comune*, have landscaped the remains to good effect. Don't stray too far off the paths, though, as snakes lurk in the undergrowth.

Apart from the city **walls**, once 6km long and with a good part still standing, the most impressive remains are of the sandstone **theatre**. Now restored to its former glory, after years of deterioration of the seats, which are made of very soft stone, the theatre is protected from the worst of the elements by a plastic roof. Concerts and classical **drama productions** are staged here every evening in July and August, with tickets costing €12: call ☎0922.846.005 for information and bookings.

Above the theatre, excavations have also revealed tombs and traces of a Greco-Roman temple, while below stand the ruins of a grand house, with fragments of Roman mosaics, though these are currently covered and inaccessible. Many of the finds are displayed in a small on-site **museum** (same ticket).

The beach

While you're here, you'll be hard put to resist a trip down to the **beach**, one of the finest on Sicily's southern coast, backed by pine trees, chalky cliffs and a strip of holiday homes. It's hideously busy in July and August; unless you get here early, you'll never find a space to park. You can rent loungers and parasols on the beach, which also holds a couple of good **bar-restaurants**: the *Sabbia d'Oro*, which stays open all year and offers a four-course set menu for €20, including drinks, and *Lido Garibaldi*, which has pizzas, pastas and good breakfasts. Next to the *Sabbia d'Oro*, the beach bar *Rotta Su Itaka* also has food and DJ sounds until late.

You'll find a few **rooms** advertised in the houses and villas here, though in high season these are usually booked up. Alternatively, you can **camp** just steps from the sea at the pine-shaded *Eraclea Minoa Village* (☎0922.846.023, ⓦwww .eracleaminoavillage.it), which also has one- and two-bedroom bungalows (⑤) and a bar, pizzeria, restaurant and disco. There's a **supermarket** on the road running eastwards on the one-way system.

Sciacca

Just over 30km further up the coast from Eraclea Minoa, **SCIACCA** comes as a welcome surprise after the ugly industry around the southern coast's other towns. Although not immediately attractive – it is, after all, a working fishing port, and run-down in parts – it does have a good-looking upper town that's virtually untouched by tourism. A spa town for nearby Selinus in ancient times, it enjoyed great prosperity under the Arabs, from whom its modern name is thought to derive (the Arabic *xacca* meaning "from the water"). The town was at the centre of a feud between Catalan and Norman

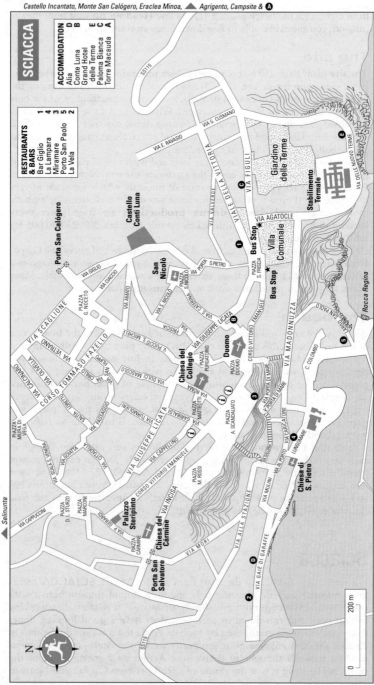

SCIACCA

ACCOMMODATION
Alia   D
Conte Luna   B
Grand Hotel
delle Terme   E
Paloma Bianca   C
Torre Macauda   A

RESTAURANTS
& BARS
Bar Giglio   1
La Lampara   4
Miramare   3
Porto San Paolo   5
La Vela   2

THE SOUTH COAST

8

342

▲ Selinunte

▲ Castelvetrano & Selinunte

families that simmered on for a century, resulting in the deaths of a good half of the local population. Several notable buildings are scattered about, which infuse Sciacca's agreeable Mediterranean air with more than a passing historical interest and make for some pleasant strolling through the weaving streets. The town is the main centre of **ceramic** production on Sicily's south coast, and you'll see colourful plates, vases and ornaments on sale everywhere.

Arrival and information

Buses pull up on Via Figuli and Via Agatone, by the Villa Comunale (the town gardens) at the eastern end of Sciacca. Bus tickets to Agrigento and Trápani are sold at the *Bar Giglio* on Viale della Vittória. All of Sciacca's three **tourist offices** are on Corso Vittorio Emanuele: at no. 84 (Mon–Sat 8am–2pm; ☎0925.21.182, ⓦwww.aziendaturismosciacca.it); no. 94 (Mon–Fri 8am–2pm & 3–6pm, mid-June to mid-Sept also 7pm–late; ☎0925.20.478); and no. 127 (Mon–Fri 8am–1.30pm & 3–7pm; ☎0925.87.012). All can supply maps, public transport timetables, hotel lists and information in English, though not everything is always up to date.

Accommodation

While Sciacca itself offers a small selection of **hotels and B&Bs**, other resort-style hotels and campsites can be found out of town by the local beaches, for example at nearby Contrada Sovareto. Nine kilometres east of town in Contrada San Giorgio, the *Makauda Beach Residence* (☎0925.997.001, ⓦwww.makaudabeach.it) is a good **campsite** right on the beach, with apartments also available.

Alia Via Gaie de Garaffe 60 ☎0925.905.388, ⓦwww.aliai.com. First-rate B&B in the lower town, where the smartly renovated rooms boast antique touches. Always call ahead. ❹

Conte Luna Vícolo Gino 1 ☎0925.993.396 at mealtimes, otherwise ☎348.120.3647, ⓦwww.contelunasciacca.com. A welcoming B&B in the heart of the upper town (off Via Licata), where four of the seven en-suite rooms have cooking facilities. There's a spacious lounge and a panoramic terrace. No credit cards. ❹

Grand Hotel delle Terme Viale Nuove Terme 1 ☎0925.23.133, ⓦwww.grandhoteldelleterme.com. The top place in town, set in its own park and with great views out to sea. Various packages are available to include thermal spa treatments, and there are good rates for singles. ❼

Paloma Bianca Via Figuli 5 ☎0925.25.130. Some of the rooms at this hotel close to the bus stop have little balconies and a view over the Villa Comunale. Adequate for a night or two. ❸

Torre Macauda Contrada Macauda ☎0925.968.500, Ⓕ0925.997.007. Nine kilometres east of town, this large, family-friendly hotel and apartment complex has two pools and full sports and beach facilities. Most rooms face the pool area, which can be irritating during evening entertainments. ❺

The Town

Sciacca's still-walled upper town can be entered through any of five grand gates. The westernmost, **Porta San Salvatore**, leads onto the **Chiesa del Cármine**, whose facade is lent a skew-whiff air by an off-centre Gothic rose window. Past the church, up Via P. Gerardi, the fifteenth-century **Palazzo Steripinto** is even more ungainly, its embossed exterior only partially offset by some slender arched windows.

From here, the main **Corso Vittorio Emanuele** runs right the way down to the lovely **Piazza A. Scandaliato**, a large terrace with some good cafés, enhanced by wide views over the port and distant bays. The most enduring Arab

▲ Strolling in Sciacca's Piazza A. Scandaliato

legacy in town is the street layout and, back from the piazza, above the **Duomo**, a Moorish knot of passages and steep alleys leads up to the rather feeble remains of the fourteenth-century **Castello Conti Luna**, which belonged to one of the feuding families that disrupted medieval Sciacca. A little way down from here, the twelfth-century church of **San Nicolò** is a tiny construction with three apses and some elegant blind arcading. Back up beyond the Duomo, at the end of Via Madonnuzza, are Sciacca's *Stabilimento Termale*, or **thermal baths**

(Mon–Fri 8am–noon, Aug 8am–2pm), where you can take a cleansing dip in the therapeutic waters and indulge in a range of massages and treatments from €12.

Steps from Piazza Scandaliato lead down the cliffside to the lower town and **port**, whose most distinctive feature is a steepled modern church. Just north of the church you'll see further steps, each riser decorated with contemporary ceramic tiles, some depicting sea life, some just patterned, and each one different. Fishing vessels lie tied up at the quayside, lorries unload salt by the bucketful for anchovy- and sardine-processing, and repairmen, foundry workers and chandlers go about their business, breaking off work for a drink in some scruffy portside bar.

Just outside town, a couple of kilometres east of Sciacca (follow the yellow signs or take bus #1 or #4), **Castello Incantato** on Via Ghezzi is a garden full of thousands of stone heads (Tues–Sun: April–Sept 10am–noon & 4–8pm; Oct–March 9am–1pm & 3–5pm; free). Carved in naive style over a period of fifty years by Filippo Bentivegna, their faces are serious, beautiful and disturbing. After being rejected by his girlfriend, beaten up and left for dead on the streets of America, Bentivegna returned home to Sciacca and devoted his life to carving these heads, symbols of his imaginary enemies, until his death in 1967. The eccentric artist would walk the streets of Sciacca with a short stick and a sceptre, and liked to be addressed as "Your Excellency".

Eating and drinking

Although there are a couple of decent pizza places in the upper town, along Viale della Vittoria and Corso Vittorio Emanuele, Sciacca's best **places to eat** are the fish restaurants down by the port. As for **bars**, check out *Bar Charlie*, by the fishing port on Via Gaia di Garaffe, where you can sit outside until late sipping beers and nibbling ice creams or pastries; panini are also available.

La Lampara Via Caricatore 33 ☎0925.85.085. Slightly pricier than some other places in the port, and better quality, with a fancy upstairs dining area where you can enjoy your meal overlooking the boats. *Pasta con sarde* and *risotto ai frutti di mare* both go for €8, tourist menus are €17 and €23, and there's a good wine list. Closed Mon. Moderate.

Miramare Piazza Scandaliato. The main attraction in this upper-town restaurant is the terrace with its excellent panoramas; the food itself is rather mediocre. Pizzas from €5.50. Inexpensive–moderate.

Porto San Paolo Largo San Paolo 1 ☎0925.27.982. Come here for the finest view in town, from a fantastic terrace overlooking the harbour. Delicious dishes such as seafood risotto and lobster fettuccine are served, and you can get pizza in the evening. Arrive early for the best tables, and in any case book ahead in summer. Closed Wed. Moderate.

La Vela Via Gaie de Garaffe 60 ☎0925.23.971. This quayside eatery serves a €25 set menu, which includes two firsts and two second courses plus dessert but not drinks – all very abundant and usually exquisite. Booking advisable. Closed Wed except Aug. Moderate.

Around Sciacca

If you have a car, Sciacca makes a good base for a day's circular drive, taking in a few minor **inland towns**, including the superbly sited village of **Caltabellotta**. Local buses also make certain simple excursions into hinterland possible.

Monte San Calógero

The easiest side-trip from Sciacca is to the vaporous caves at **Monte San Calógero** (388m), 8km north of town. Bus #5 runs here in ten minutes, leaving from Sciacca roughly every hour. Excavations and finds have shown that the site has been used as a place of healing since antiquity, though the mountain takes its contemporary name from the saint whose sanctuary is at the summit, near some natural caves.

Caltabellotta

Twenty kilometres northeast of Sciacca, the village of **CALTABELLOTTA** perches magnificently on three jutting fangs of rock at a height of 950m above sea level. Tremendous views stretch out on all sides, apparently taking in 21 villages. On the highest pinnacle, you can pass through the solitary surviving entrance of the Norman **castello** (always open; free) that once stood here, and climb up steep, rock-cut steps to the very top, from which the village below appears as a patchwork of grey roofs. The castle itself, ruined by an earthquake, was where the Angevins and Aragonese signed the peace treaty that ended the Wars of the Vespers in 1302. Immediately below sit the Norman **Chiesa Madre** and the Gothic **Chiesa di San Salvatore**, both wonderfully sited against a rocky backdrop.

Lumia **buses** run direct to Caltabellotta from Sciacca three times daily (not Sun), the last one back leaving at 3pm. It's an impressive ride, past sparkling fresh streams and jagged outcrops of rock. There's a **B&B** close to the castle entrance, for anyone interested in staying right off the beaten track: *Mulè*, Via Venezia 5 (T0925.951.145, Wwww.olioevinosanleonardo.com; no credit cards; ❷), a typical village dwelling where the plain rooms share a bathroom. You can also taste and buy local wine, oil and other rural products, and view a collection of old-fashioned domestic items.

Sambuca di Sicilia

Continue north from Caltabellotta onto the SS386, and turn west at Chiusa Sclafani to reach the little town of **SAMBUCA DI SICILIA**, on a hill west of the Arancio lake. Sambuca's Arab past is just about discernible in its convoluted old-town layout. A sixteenth-century church in Piazza della Vittória, the **Chiesa del Cármine**, is home to a statue that's reputed to be by Antonello Gagini, and you can **eat** at two or three very cheap trattorias. In addition, a ten-kilometre detour north enables you to see the low-key excavations (always open; free) at **Monte Adranone**, a Greek city of the sixth century BC which fell to Carthage in the fourth.

Menfi and Porto Palo

Ten kilometres west of Sambuca you join the main SS188 which sweeps back to Sciacca, though there are a couple of other diversions before that: either head north for 6km to Santa Margherita di Belice, or south for 9km to **MENFI**, planned in the eighteenth century but devastated by an earthquake in 1968. Today Menfi presents a very mean aspect: lacerated churches on derelict central streets, a jumble of untidy prefab housing – still being used – and bland rebuilding on the outskirts.

If this is all a bit depressing, things improve when you drive on 7km to the coast at **PORTO PALO**, a fishing village and summer resort with a nice beach – the waters around here are classified among Sicily's cleanest. Though facilities are few, a first-class **restaurant** stands apart at the eastern end of the village, signposted at the end of a dirt lane: ⚘ *Da Vittorio* (T0925.78.381, Wwww.davittorioristorante .com), a fairly large place that's often completely full. Highly recommended, the food here is very reasonably priced and abundant, with the freshest seasonal ingredients. It's worth booking one of the tables on the broad covered terrace, right next to the beach. You can also **stay** here in pleasant en-suite rooms with sea views for €75 per person half board. If there's no room here, there's the simple *Miramare* hotel, Via Piemonte 34 (℡0925.78.211; ❸), with a beachside restaurant; obligatory half-board in July and August comes to €60 per person.

Back at Menfi, it's just 20km to Sciacca, either along the minor road or the faster SS115.

The Pelágie Islands

The remote **Pelágie Islands** (Isole Pelágie) are little more than dry rocks bang in the middle of the Mediterranean, even further south than Malta. Throughout history they've been neglected, often abandoned or uninhabited, and only occasionally has their strategic importance been recognized. In 1943 the Allies bombed the main island, Lampedusa, prior to springing into Sicily, and Colonel Gaddafi of Libya nearly gave a repeat performance in 1987 when he retaliated against the American bombing of Tripoli by targeting missiles at the US base on Lampedusa. Italian troops were mobilized and Sicily was on a virtual war-footing for three days, though in the event the missiles dropped into the sea short of the island. In recent years, the island has been the site of detention centres for enormous numbers of immigrants from Africa, either dumped here by unscrupulous people-traffickers, or intercepted at sea by naval vessels. Often they stay for months on end until the legal processes for their inevitable repatriation are completed. You'll see absolutely no evidence of their presence on the island, however – the camps are all out of bounds away from the gaze of tourists.

The largest island, **Lampedusa**, attracts Italians in ever-increasing numbers, not least for the scuba-diving and snorkelling possibilities in its wonderfully clear waters, and it's pretty jam-packed in July and August. Smaller, volcanic **Linosa**, is much quieter, generally hotter and less breezy than Lampedusa, while the tiniest islet, **Lampione**, is uninhabited and rarely visited.

Getting there by ferry and hydrofoil

Most visitors get to the islands by sea from **Porto Empédocle**, 6km southwest of Agrigento and connected to it by frequent buses. Daily **ferries** leave Porto Empédocle at midnight daily except Friday, calling at Linosa (5hr 45min) and Lampedusa (8hr 15min). **Tickets** can be bought from the Siremar office (℡0922.636.683 or 636.685), right on the quayside in Porto Empédocle, or from travel agents in Agrigento. A one-way ticket is around €35 to Linosa, or €42 to Lampedusa; returns cost double. It's worth reserving either a couchette (€16) or *poltrona* (reclining chair, €6) if you don't want to sleep on the deck or bend yourself round a couple of seats in the grimy TV lounge. A bar on board sells snacks.

Ústica Lines **hydrofoils** run six times a week (not Tues) from May to October. They leave Porto Empédocle at 3pm (May to mid-Sept) or 2.30pm (mid-Sept to Oct), arriving in Linosa three hours later and at Lampedusa about four hours later. **Tickets** (€33 to Linosa, and €51 to Lampedusa one-way) are sold from the Ústica Lines office right by the dock (℡0922.636.110, ⓦwww.usticalines.it).

There's no point taking a car to the islands: leave yours in the Gieffe di Gamba Corta **garage**, just east of the port on Via Molo (℡333.792.3049; from €7 per day), open until midnight. Alternatively, you might find a parking spot in the roads around the port, though make sure your car is empty. Don't leave your vehicle inside the port itself, as it may be towed away.

Getting there by plane

Direct **flights** connect Lampedusa with Palermo, Catania, Trápani, Milan, Bologna, Verona and Rome, though most are summer-only. AirOne (℡ 199.207.080, Ⓦ www.flyairone.it) flies all year **from Palermo** in less than an hour (2–4 times daily), while Alitalia (℡ 06.2222, Ⓦ www.alitalia.com) serves a range of other routes. Flights from Palermo start at €50 one-way, but good discounts are available on the Internet or with advance booking via a travel agent.

Lampedusa

LAMPEDUSA, 205km from Porto Empédocle, and lying further south than Tunis, was originally a fragment of the African continent. The largest of the Pelágie Islands (23 square kilometres), it's the centre of activity of this scattered archipelago, inhabited by around 5000 people, mostly based in the town of the same name. Many still earn a living from fishing, but the majority depend on the influx of tourists who swell the population to around 20,000 every August, the vast majority of them Italian.

Historically, however, Lampedusa has been as neglected as the other Mediterranean islands off Sicily. In 1667 it passed into the hands of the **Tomasi** family (as in Giuseppe Tomasi di Lampedusa, of *The Leopard* fame), one of whose descendants attempted to sell the island to Queen Victoria in 1839 when it still had only twenty or so inhabitants. The queen lost out on the sale, at a cost of twelve million ducats, to Ferdinand II, the Neapolitan king, who was no doubt aghast at the prospect of losing such a scraggy but strategically important island.

The island is long, thin, flat and dry, the main attraction being the **beaches**, almost all of them on the south coast. For years the pristine water has offered some of the best swimming and diving in the Mediterranean, with abundant fish life; you might also see dolphins, or even, in March, the **sperm whale migration**.

Apart from the simple pleasures of sun, sea and sand, Lampedusa's attractions are fairly low-key: there's a religious sanctuary in the middle of the island, an offshore nature reserve where turtles come to lay their eggs, and some good cliff-walks to divert you from your tan. And, for the views of the cliffs and grottoes alone, it's worth taking a **boat trip** around Lampedusa. Remember that it's a small, exposed island, so evenings are cooler than on the mainland; it's not really somewhere you'd want to holiday in winter, when the wind whips across the barren landscape.

Arrival and information

Lampedusa's **airport** practically sits in the town, and most hotels and campsites arrange courtesy buses for guests. Arriving by ferry at the **harbour** (Porto Vecchio), it's a ten-minute walk up to town, or a twenty-minute walk west to the larger harbour of Porto Nuovo, which is home to the pleasure- and fishing-boats, as well as the main beach and the bulk of the hotels. A minibus meets the ferry in summer, and for a small charge will take you wherever you want to go, or you can jump in a taxi.

If you're lucky, the Pro Loco **tourist office** (℡ 0922.971.390), at Via Vittorio Emanuele 87, will be open; if not, try the friendly environmental agency, Legambiente, Via V. Emanuele 27 (℡ 0922.971.611). Both places keep highly erratic hours and are usually closed completely in winter, but when open, one or the other should be able to provide information in

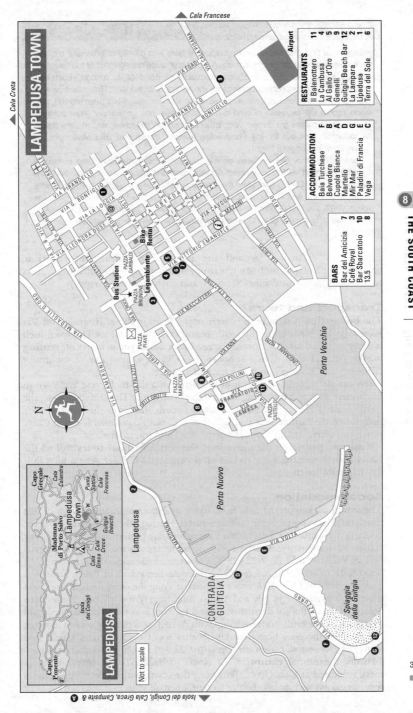

The flora of Lampedusa

Although at first glance Lampedusa appears bare and devoid of greenery, a closer look reveals a wide range of plant life. A myopic attitude during most of the twentieth century meant that the island was practically stripped of its natural vegetation, resulting in soil erosion that accounts for the arid state of the land. Recently, however, a programme of reforestation in a couple of the shallow valleys has been started, thus encouraging the regrowth of pine and mastic trees, and germander (from the mint family). **Date palms** are dotted along otherwise barren stretches, and, at Cala Galera in particular, look out for the **Phoenician juniper**, **carob** and **wild olive** trees, all survivors of the original blight.

Rare plants, too, can be seen on the island, including the *caralluma europa*, a cactus-like plant with star-shaped flowers, and the *centaurea acaulis*, from the centaury family. During mid-May, the **flowers** really come into their own as squills, irises, crocuses, orchids, echinops and thyme make up a vibrant display. Along the roads you'll see more common tall cacti, which rival the telegraph poles in height – poles that only arrived in 1963, when the telephone system was installed.

English on excursions around the island. For **online information**, Ⓦ www.lampedusa.to and Ⓦ www.lampedusa.it provide useful listings, links to accommodation and other services, and current weather reports.

Transport and tours

The **bus station** is right in the centre of the town in Piazza Brignone, off Via Roma; hourly buses go to the south-coast beaches in summer. The town itself is easily explored on foot, but for the rest of the island you're better off **renting** a **bike** (around €6 a day), a **scooter** (€15–20) or a small **car** or minimoke (€30–40): see "Listings" on p.353 for rental outlets.

You can do a complete circuit of the island in a day by bicycle, and even in the hottest months a refreshing breeze blows constantly. The cliff road along the north coast is rough and stony, as are the roads that cross the island – they deteriorate the further west you go – but the south coast road is easier. Carry provisions (there are no shops along the way) and insect repellent.

Numerous people on the quayside at the port offer **boat tours** around the island with swimming stops: reckon on paying about €25 per person for a full-day trip with lunch.

Accommodation

The season on Lampedusa runs from Easter to November, and for most of that time you'll have no problem finding a **hotel**. During July and August, however, booking is essential and there's often a minimum stay of three nights, with full- or half-board compulsory. **Apartments** can be rented by the week from Servizi Mikael, Via Ariosto 53 (Ⓣ0922.628.320, Ⓦ www.servizimikael.com), Licciardi, Via Siracusa 18 (Ⓣ0922.970.768, Ⓦ www.lampedusa-licciardi.it), or Greco Ettore, Via Sanvisente (Ⓣ0922.970.456), either in town or along the coast, though, again, you must book in advance in July and August. Alternatively, you can stay in a modern version of the traditional **dammusi**: these shepherds' huts, found only in Sicily and North Africa, are small, stone buildings with domed roofs that stay cool in summer, and most of the ones here have kitchenettes too. Contact Servizi Mikael (see above) or *Dammusi di Borgo Cala Creta* (Ⓣ0922.970.394, Ⓦ www.calacreta.com).

Finally, the official **campsite**, *La Roccia* (Ⓣ0922.970.055, Ⓦ www.laroccia .net), is located at Cala Greca, 3km from the town, with its own beach and a few bungalows and mobile homes to rent, open all year.

Baia Turchese Via Lido Azzurro ℡0922.970.455, ℗www.guitgia.com. Spacious, comfortable and only 30m from the beach. The seventy pastel-coloured rooms are air-conditioned and have minibars and safes, but if you want a view you'll pay more. Umbrellas and sun loungers are provided. At least half-board only (from €125 per person in Aug). ⑥

Belvedere Piazza Marconi 4 ℡0922.970.188, ℗www.hotelbelvedere-lampedusa.it. Friendly, family-run hotel overlooking the harbour. Rooms are clean and modern, and some have a balcony (rooms with a view cost extra). There's a good restaurant, though room-only rates are also available. It is sometimes block-booked by groups, so call ahead to check availability. Closed Nov-Feb. ⑥

Cupola Bianca Via Madonna ℡0922.971.274, ℗www.hotelcupolabianca.it. A luxury outfit 2km out of town, with a North African feel and plush standard rooms as well as upmarket *dammusi*-style accommodation. At least half-board is required, from €170 per person in peak season. Closed Nov to late May. ⑨

Martello Piazza Medusa ℡0922.970.025, ℗www.hotelmartello.it. A chic modern hotel near the harbour, 80m from the beach, whose restaurant has panoramic sea views. A diving school operates from here, and boat trips can also be arranged. Half-board compulsory in July and Aug (€120 per person). Closed Nov–Feb. ⑦

Mir Mar Contrada Guitgia ℡0922.970.093, ℗www.isoladilampedusa.net. Right above the beach, with panoramic views, this hotel offers half-board rates for €75 in summer. The nine rooms are basic, but all have showers. No credit cards. ⑤

Paladini di Francia Via Alessandro Volta ℡0922.970.550, ℗www.hotelpaladinidifrancia.it. This modern, upmarket hotel above the fishing port resembles an unfinished bunker from the outside, but the interior reveals flair and elegance. Four of the twelve unfussy rooms (costing extra) have views right onto the port, and there's a good restaurant. It's popular with tour groups, so book well in advance. Closed Nov–Feb. ⑥

Vega Via Roma 19 ℡0922.970.099, ℗www.lampedusa-hotelvega.it. Smaller than most, this is one of the few hotels in the town itself. It provides good and friendly service, with clean, functional rooms, some with a view of the port. ⑥

Around the town and island

The gridded system of streets in the upper part of **LAMPEDUSA TOWN** funnels down to the harbour, from where a gentle walk westwards brings you to the busy beach, **Spiaggia della Guitgia**, around which the main cluster of hotels is sited. Activity in town centres on Via Roma, which turns pedestrian in the evenings for the *passeggiata*. Lining the pavements are the usual souvenir shops selling beach paraphernalia and fruits of the sea, especially sponges, as well as hand-crocheted Arab caps that the women make in between serving customers.

You should have no problem finding spots to **swim** away from the port (though in season you'll never be alone on the beaches), and there are plenty of opportunities for diving and snorkelling. You can hire gear fairly easily in town (see "Listings" below for addresses; expect to pay around €35 for a dive, and €24 for full equipment rental), and there's good fish-watching only a few metres away from the beaches. If you don't fancy the small main beach, try **Cala La Croce**, the next bay west of Spiaggia della Guitgia, or the rockier **Cala Francese**, a ten-minute walk east of town. East of here, the cape of **Punta Sottile** on the southeast point of the island is the southernmost point of Europe.

On the island's east coast, **Cala Creta** is home to the World Wildlife Fund's **Centro Recupero Tartarughe Marine** (summer Mon–Fri 6–8pm, also Sat 6–8pm in Aug; call first at ℡338.219.8533, ℗www.isolablu.org), a museum and infirmary where you can visit turtles who have been injured by fishing nets or plastic flotsam. Ask about their *liberazioni tartarughe* (turtle emancipations), held at Calamadonna beach every week in summer, where the healthy turtles are released back into the sea. Just north of here, the rocks at **Cala La Calandra** provide crowd-free swimming spots – but watch out for tar.

Five kilometres west of Lampedusa Town, the popular **Isola dei Conigli** (Rabbit Island) is accessible by hourly bus from town. If you have your own transport, leave it at the top of the cliff and clamber down the jagged path to a stretch of fine, white sand – arguably Lampedusa's best – and gorgeous aquamarine waters. There are no facilities here, so you'll need to bring your own provisions. Just offshore is the little island itself, which you can reach either on foot or by swimming, depending on the tide. A **nature reserve** (open at all times; free), it's the only place in Italy where you can see the turtle *Caretta Caretta* laying its eggs. During summer evenings, the turtles deposit between 100 and 150 eggs in deep holes, from which the babies stagger out after sixty days. The nests are individually fenced off, but that doesn't help protect them from the peregrine falcons which also nest here. The islet is also the only habitat in Italy of the *psammodromus algarus* lizard – a common species in North Africa. **Organized trips** to the island are advertised along Via Roma, back in town, or contact Legambiente (see "Arrival and information"). The Centro Ricerca Delfini, Lungomare Luigi Rizzo 157 at Porto Vecchio (summer Mon–Sat 9.30am–1pm, 4–8pm & 10pm–midnight), also displays information on marine life local to these waters.

You can only swim on the **north side of the island** from a boat – it's mostly sheer cliffs, which tier down like a wedding cake, often pierced by deep grottoes. Neither is there a great deal to see **inland**, apart from a stream of boy racers zapping around on scooters. Off the main road west out of town, the church of the **Madonna di Porto Salvo** can be appreciated for its scenic location, its white steeple set in a little wooded valley, flowers and bougainvillea abounding in the garden in front. A pilgrimage here every September commemorates a sixteenth-century Italian slave, captured by Saracens, who was shipwrecked on the island and made his way to the sanctuary here. Afterwards, he used the image of the Madonna on the sail of his makeshift raft to return safely to Liguria.

Eating and drinking

Lampedusa is well endowed with places to **eat**. Prices tend to be a little higher than on the mainland, but you'll still find less expensive tourist menus. Fish, of course, is a speciality, along with couscous, either as a main dish or an antipasto. At night the whole of the Via Roma becomes one long lively café, with chairs and tables sprawling on the pavements. Some recommended **bars** are listed below. Most places are closed from mid-October to mid-May but open daily in season.

Restaurants

Il Balenottero Via Sbarcatoio 40, Porto Vecchio ☏0922.970.830. A cool, family-style restaurant in the old port with good seafood dishes. Less crowded than the more central places, with a fairly laid-back atmosphere. Closed Dec–Feb. Moderate.

La Cambusa Piazza Municipio ☏0922.970.826. Capacious and popular pizzeria where fish and meat dishes are also served. Pizzas (€6–8) are cooked in a wood oven. Evenings only. Inexpensive–moderate.

Al Gallo d'Oro Via Vittorio Emanuele 45 ☏0922.971.297. You can enjoy fine fish dishes in this smart, cheerful trattoria, including the occasional couscous. A three-course meal plus drinks will cost around €35. Closed Nov–Easter. Expensive.

Gemelli Via Cala Pisana 2 ☏0922.970.699. Right by the airport, this quiet spot is well worth the few minutes' walk for its Arab specialities – notably couscous – as well as *bouillabaisse*, paella and *crespelle di pesce* (fish pancakes). Oil lamps on the tables and Arab decoration add to the ambience. Booking essential in Aug. Open evenings only. Expensive.

Guitgia Beach Bar and Spaghetteria Via Lido Azzurro. If you're on the beach, use this as a pit-stop for good sandwiches (try the unleavened bread). At night, sit under bamboo thatch by candlelight and enjoy the lapping of the waves. Standard food, but excellent location. Inexpensive.

La Lampara Via Madonna ☎0922.971.617. Watch the evening *passeggiata* of mobile phones and Vespas along the harbourside as you sample the local fish, spicy couscous and sweet tomatoes. The antipasti are recommended; first courses cost €10–12, seconds €10–15. Moderate.

Lipadusa Via Bonfiglio 12 ☎0922.970.267. With a smart interior and some tables outside, Lampedusa's classiest restaurant offers a splendid array of seafood inventively prepared and beautifully presented. The risotto is also recommended. Reckon on paying €30–40 for a full meal, excluding drinks. Open evenings only. Closed Oct–April. Expensive.

Terra del Sole Via Vittorio Emanuele 30 ☎0922.970.072. A fine restaurant offering homemade pasta with pistachio- and coconut-flavoured sauces, and such interesting seafood dishes as *crepes frutti di mare* and *ravioli di cernia* (a local fish). The only minus is the muzak, but there's also a quiet garden at the back. Closed Nov to mid-May. Moderate.

Bars

13.5 Via Roma 39–41. Cavernous bar with fabulous ice creams and sorbets, an extensive buffet for food, and cocktails and DJs in the evening.

Bar del Amicizia Via Vittorio Emanuele 34. Deliciously light *latte di mandorla* and granitas are sold here.

Café Royal Via Roma 83. Pause here on your *passeggiata* to sample the lip-smacking ice cream.

Bar Sbarcatoio Via Sbarcatoio 39. Great coffees, for an early-morning stop on the way to catch the ferry, and a cool place to while away an evening.

Listings

Airport Information ☎0922.970.006.

Banks ATMs at Banco di Sicilia, Via Roma 123, and Banco Popolare Sant'Ángelo, Via Roma 50; both open Mon–Fri 8am–3pm and 3–4.30pm. Money exchange also at post office.

Bike & scooter rental Maggiore, Porto Nuovo ☎338.854.7159, rents scooters for €18 per day; Noleggio Ecologico, Via S. Pellico 12 ☎333.324.6668, rents bikes for €6 per day, scooters for €20. Prices drop out of season.

Boat rental Maggiore, listed above; DAG, Via N. Bixo 1 ☎0922.970.755, ⓦwww.autonoleggiodag .com; Licciardi, Via Siracusa 18 ☎0922.970.768. You'll pay around €50 per day, plus petrol costs.

Car rental Maggiore and DAG, both listed above.

Diving centres Blue Dolphins, Via A. Volta 18 ☎339.740.3490, ⓦwww.bluedolphins.it; Lo Verde Diving, Porto Vecchio ☎0922.971.986, ⓦwww .loverdelampedusa.it; Mediterraneo Immersioni Club, Via A. Volta 8 ☎0922.971.526, ⓦwww .mediterraneoimmersionclub.it; Moby Diving Center, Via delle Grotte 6 ☎339.956.4543, ⓦwww .mobydiving.it. Most places are open April–Nov. Many hotels also offer equipment, excursions and boats at reduced rates.

Ferry/hydrofoil tickets Siremar, Porto Vecchio ☎0922.971.964, ⓦwww.siremar.it: ferry to Linosa/Porto Empédocle daily at 10.15am (not Sat; one-way ticket to the mainland around €42, extra for seat or cabin). Ústica Lines, Porto Vecchio ☎348.353.8218, ⓦwww.usticalines.it: hydrofoil to Linosa/Porto Empédocle May–Oct daily except Tues at 7.30am (one-way tickets to the mainland €51), also to Linosa at 9am or 9.30am, and 4.45pm or 5.15pm. You can also buy tickets at Agenzia Maríttima Strazzera, Lungomare Rizzo 1 ☎0922.970.003.

Hospital Via Grecale ☎0922.970.604.

Internet L'Edicola, Via Roma 150 (daily 8am–8pm).

Pharmacy Dottore Inglisa, Via Vittorio Emanuele 35 (Mon–Sat 9am–12.45pm & 5–7.30pm, Sun 10am–noon & 6–7.30pm; ☎0922.970.195).

Police Carabinieri, Via Roma 37 ☎0922.970.001 or ☎112.

Post and telephone office Piazza Piave (Mon–Fri 8am–1.30pm, Sat 8am–12.30pm).

Sailing Courses and excursions are offered between Easter and November at Centro Vela, Porto Vecchio ☎333.540.1360, ⓦwww .centrovelalampedusa.com. Accommodation also arranged.

Supermarket Sisa, Via Mazzini.

Travel agents Agenzia Maríttima Raccomandataria, Lungomare Luigi Rizzo ☎0922.971.964; La Pelágie, Via Roma 155 ☎0922.970.170.

Linosa

Fifty kilometres north of Lampedusa, **LINOSA**, the northernmost of the Pelágie Islands, is the tip of a submerged volcano, with four extinct craters to poke around, some lava beaches, and not much else in the way of sights. With an area of five square kilometres, it's much smaller than Lampedusa. A haven for pirates in the sixteenth century, Linosa wasn't really settled until the mid-nineteenth century, and even now the only village has just a few hundred inhabitants, rather fewer cars and a minimal road system. Until the advent of tourism, the only exciting events to disturb the tranquillity were when the government in Rome regularly sent their latest star Mafia prisoner to be detained on the island pending trial, a practice suspended since the tourist trade picked up. Exuding tranquillity, the scene is enlivened by the bold colours painted onto the square white houses. If you take the tracks that lead away from either side of the port, you can clamber around the cliffs and coves, and reach the couple of black-sand beaches with crystal clear water.

The rocky shores here offer great opportunities for **diving**: contact Linosa Diving Centre, Via Scalo Vecchio 3–5 (☎0922.972.054, ⓦwww .linosadivingcenter.it), or Mare Nostrum, Via Re Umberto 84 (☎0922.972.042 or 328.169.8697, ⓦwww.marenostrumdiving.it; open June–Sept) for scuba excursions and courses.

Getting to Linosa

In summer, you can see Linosa on a **day-trip** from Lampedusa, only an hour away by Ústica Lines **hydrofoil** (May to mid-Sept leaves Lampedusa daily at 7.30am, 9.30am & 5.15pm, returns 10.45am, 6.15pm & 6.35pm; mid-Sept to Oct leaves Lampedusa daily at 7.30am, 9am & 4.35pm, returns 10.15am, 5.35pm & 5.40pm; one-way tickets €20). Alternatively, if you plan to overnight in Linosa, you might opt for the cheaper **ferry**, which leaves from Lampedusa daily throughout the year at 10.15am, and arrives at noon (one-way tickets €13.50); the only hydrofoil from Linosa for Porto Empédocle leaves at 8.45am. See Lampedusa's "Listings" (p.353) for ticket details.

Practicalities

Linosa has a few good **trattorias**. Both the *Ristorante-Bar Errera*, Via Scalo 1 (☎0922.972.041), and the rustic-style *Da Anna*, Via Veneto, at the top of the village with good views (☎0922.972.048, ⓦwww.linosavacanze.it), are worth trying; they serve pizzas in the evenings, and are closed in winter. The best place to **stay** is the pricey *Residence La Posta* (☎393.498.2649, ⓦwww.linosaresidencelaposta.it; closed Nov–March; ❻), which has smartly furnished, air-conditioned accommodation in the heart of the village on Via Alfieri. Both restaurants also offer self-catering **apartments** to rent (there are no hotels) for around €30–35 per person, as does the Mare Nostrum diving centre. There's neither a bank nor an ATM on the island, and credit cards can only be used at the **post office** on Via Alfieri (Mon–Fri 8am–1.30pm, Sat 8am–12.30pm).

Lampione

Lampedusa is also the starting point for trips to the third island, **LAMPIONE**, a mere speck of land to the west. Starkly vegetated and uninhabited, the island offers spectacular diving and wonderful offshore fishing – you should be able to persuade someone to take you in their boat from

Lampedusa Town, or ask the diving centres about diving trips to the reefs around the island.

Festivals

February
First/second week Almond-blossom festival, the Sagra del Mandorlo in Fiore, at **Agrigento**: events take place in the Valle dei Templi – costumes, music and processions.

February/March
Carnevale at **Sciacca**, with participation of the entire town in five days of parades and competitions.

March/April
Easter Holy Week processions at **Agrigento**.

June
27–29 Sagra del Mare at **Sciacca**: a statue of St Peter is paraded on a boat at sea; there's a big fish fry-up and maritime-themed games at the port.

July
First/second Sunday Festival at **Agrigento** in honour of St Calógero.
Pirandello week Plays and concerts held at Pirandello's house at **Caos**, near **Agrigento**.

September
22 Pilgrimage and religious procession at **Lampedusa**, in honour of the Madonna di Porto Salvo.

Travel details

Trains

Agrigento to: Caltanissetta (6 daily Mon–Sat, 3 daily Sun; 1hr 20min); Canicattì (for Gela, 6 daily Mon–Sat, 3 daily Sun; 1hr); Enna (3 daily; 1hr 50min–2hr 25min); Palermo (11 daily Mon–Sat, 8 daily Sun; 2hr).
Gela to: Catania (7 daily Mon–Sat; 2hr 25min–2hr 40min); Caltagirone (7 daily Mon–Sat; 45min–1hr); Canicattì (for Agrigento, 4–5 daily; 1hr 15min); Licata (7 daily Mon–Sat, 4 daily Sun; 30min); Ragusa (5–6 daily; 1hr 15min); Vittória (5–6 daily; 30min).

Buses

Agrigento to: Caltanissetta (12 daily Mon–Sat, 8 daily Sun; 1hr 15min); Canicattì (8–10 daily; 40min); Catania (hourly Mon–Sat, 8 daily Sun; 2hr 50min); Gela (4 daily Mon–Sat; 1hr 40min); Licata (4 daily Mon–Sat; 1hr); Montallegro (for Eraclea Minoa, 9 daily Mon–Sat, 1 daily Sun; 45min); Palermo (14 daily Mon–Sat, 5 daily Sun; 2hr); Palma di Montechiaro (1–2 hourly Mon–Sat; 30min); Porto Empédocle (1–2 hourly; 25min); Ribera (for Eraclea Minoa, 10 daily Mon–Sat, 1 daily Sun; 1hr–1hr 30min); Sant'Ángelo Muxaro (5 daily Mon–Sat, 2 daily Sun; 1hr–1hr 30min);

Sciacca (11 daily Mon–Sat, 1–2 daily Sun; 1hr 30min); Trápani (3 daily Mon–Sat, 1 daily Sun; 3hr 20min–3hr 50min).
Gela to: Agrigento (4 daily; 1hr 40min–2hr); Caltagirone (2 daily Mon–Sat, 1 daily Sun; 1hr 15min); Caltanissetta (7 daily Mon–Sat, 2 daily Sun; 1hr 45min); Catania (9–12 daily; 2hr); Enna (3–4 daily; 1hr 10min); Licata (4 daily Mon–Sat; 45min); Palermo (3–4 daily; 2hr 45min); Piazza Armerina (3–4 daily; 40min); Siracusa (2 daily Mon–Sat; 4hr); Vittória (3 daily Mon–Sat; 40min).
Sciacca to: Agrigento (11 daily Mon–Sat, 2 daily Sun; 1hr 45min); Caltabellotta (4 daily Mon–Sat, 1 daily Sun; 40–50min); Castelvetrano (3 daily Mon–Sat; 1hr 40min); Menfi (7 daily Mon–Sat, 1 daily Sun; 25min); Palermo (12–13 daily Mon–Sat, 5 daily Sun; 1hr 40min–2hr 40min); Trápani (3 daily Mon–Sat, 1 daily Sun; 2hr).

Ferries

Lampedusa to: Linosa (6 weekly; 1hr 45min); Porto Empédocle (6 weekly; 7hr 45min).
Linosa to: Lampedusa (6 weekly; 1hr 45min); Porto Empédocle (6 weekly; 5hr 45min).
Porto Empédocle to: Lampedusa (6 weekly; 8hr 15min); Linosa (6 weekly; 5hr 45min).

Hydrofoils

Lampedusa to: Linosa (May–Oct 1 daily; 1hr); Porto Empédocle (May–Oct 1 daily; 4hr 15min).
Linosa to: Lampedusa (May–Oct 1 daily; 1hr); Porto Empédocle (May–Oct 1 daily; 3hr).

Porto Empédocle to: Lampedusa (May–Oct 1 daily; 4hr 15min); Linosa (May–Oct 1 daily; 3hr).

Planes

Palermo to: Lampedusa (2–4 daily; 1hr).
Lampedusa to: Palermo (2–4 daily; 1hr).

Trápani and the west

CHAPTER 9

Highlights

* **Riserva Naturale dello Zíngaro** Hike the footpaths or swim from isolated pebble coves within Sicily's most beautiful nature reserve. See p.366

* **Segesta** Perhaps the most romantic of all Greek sites on the island, beautifully positioned amid rolling hills. See p.367

* **The procession of the Misteri, Trápani** Trápani's annual Good Friday celebrations see life-sized wooden statues, representing scenes from the Passion, paraded through the old-town streets. See p.372

* **Cable car to Érice** A stunning panorama opens up on this slow ascent from Trápani to the mountain town of Érice. See p.374

* **Lévanzo** Take a tour to see the remarkable Paleolithic drawings in the Grotta del Genovese. See p.389

* **Pantelleria** It takes a five-hour ferry ride to reach it, but up-and-coming Pantelleria is Sicily's most fashionable offshore retreat. See p.410

▲ Rock stacks at the Tonnara di Scopello, in the Riserva Naturale dello Zíngaro

9

Trápani and the west

C loser to North Africa than the Italian mainland, Sicily's western reaches are traditionally poor and remote, the economy dependent on fishing and small-scale farming. Since the opening of the A29 autostrada, the region has become more integrated with the rest of Sicily than ever before, but even today, access by public transport is limited. Indeed, much of the appeal of the area lies in the fact that it's still very different from the rest of the island. Historically, the region has always been distinct, influenced by a strong **Phoenician** and **Arab** culture rather than the Greek and Norman traditions that prevail elsewhere in Sicily. The Arab influence can still be tasted in its food – couscous is a local favourite – and visually too, the flat land, dotted by white cubic houses, is strongly reminiscent of North Africa.

On the northern coast, the **Golfo di Castellammare** is only an hour's train ride from Palermo. Despite patches of industrial development along the gulf, it still manages to offer some empty beaches and a couple of unspoiled villages at its western end. In particular, the coastline between the old tuna-fishing village of **Scopello** and the resort of **San Vito Lo Capo** encompasses Sicily's first and most beautiful nature reserve, the **Zíngaro**. The capital of the province that embraces almost this entire area, **Trápani**, is a congenial port town within sight of the flat saltpans on which its wealth was based. It is also a departure point for the **Égadi Islands**, and makes a good base for visiting the mountain town of **Érice** – originally a centre of Punic influence, though diverging from the region's dominant trend in its uniform Norman and medieval character. The pattern re-establishes itself a little way down the coast at **Mózia**, Sicily's best-preserved Phoenician site, while further south the Moorish imprint is discernible in the secretive alleys and courtyards of **Marsala** and **Mazara del Vallo**.

Although the Greeks never wielded much influence in the area, the Hellenic remains at **Segesta** and **Selinunte** (Selinus) count among the island's most stunning. Between the two, the Valle del Belice delineates the region struck by an earthquake in 1968, which left a trail of destruction still visible in many towns and villages. This is most notable at **Gibellina**, abandoned in its ruined state as a powerful reminder, and at the little town of **Santa Margherita di Belice**, whose once-proud palace and church were immortalized in that quintessential Sicilian novel, *The Leopard*. There could be no greater contrast to this disorder than the peaceful island of **Pantelleria**, a distant outpost, much nearer to Africa than Europe, mountainous and wind-blown, and adopted as a chic resort by a few high-profile glitterati.

You'll find **getting around** the coast a simple matter, as frequent buses and trains cover the short distances between all the towns and villages. There's much

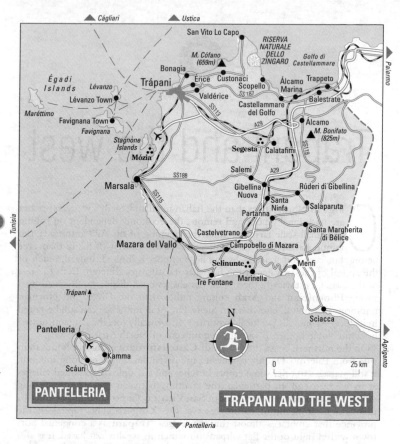

Cágliari   Ustica

San Vito Lo Capo

RISERVA
NATURALE
DELLO
ZINGARO

Golfo di
Castellammare

M. Cófano
(659m)

Palermo

Bonagia   Érice   Custonaci   Scopello

Trápani   Álcamo   Trappeto
Marina

Valdérice   SS187

Égadi
Islands   Lévanzo   Castellammare   Balestrate
del Golfo

Lévanzo Town

A29   Álcamo

Maréttimo   Favignana Town   M. Bonifato
(825m)

Favignana   SS113

Stagnòne   Segesta   Calatafimi   SS119
Islands

Mózia

Salemi   A29

Marsala   SS188   Gibellina   Rúderi di Gibellina
Nuova

Santa   Salaparuta
Ninfa

Tunisia   Partanna

SS115   Castelvetrano   Santa Margherita
di Bélice

Mazara del Vallo   Campobello di Mazara

Menfi

Selinunte

Tre Fontane   Marinella

N

Sciacca

Agrigento

0   25 km

Trápani

Pantelleria

Kamma

Scáuri

PANTELLERIA   **TRÁPANI AND THE WEST**

Pantelleria

less public transport, though, if you strike off **inland**: what interior bus services there are depart from Marsala or Castelvetrano. As for driving, apart from the two arms of the A29 autostrada there are only two other main roads, the SS115 following the coast between Trápani and Castelvetrano and the inland SS188 between Marsala and Salemi.

The Golfo di Castellammare

Backed by a forbidding wall of jagged mountains, the wide bowl of the **Golfo di Castellammare** is almost entirely made up of small holiday towns. Some are uncomfortably close to industrial plants, though these disappear as you progress west. The main train line from Palermo (and the SS187 road) skirts the bay from Trappeto to Castellammare del Golfo, but despite the ease of access and the consequent development the resorts have not entirely shrugged off their original role as fishing villages – though they have completely lost the mean look they had when fishing was the only source of income. If you're after a beach, some of these make a reasonable morning's halt, though be warned that in July and August it's slow going on the roads and the sands are packed.

Otherwise, the train ride is as fair an entertainment, hugging the coast at the base of massive wedges of rock, often of a raw red colour, echoed by smaller, weathered nuggets poking out of the sea.

Trappeto, Balestrate and Álcamo Marina

Today, the two villages of **TRAPPETO** and **BALESTRATE**, just 5km apart (and both on the train line), display a tidy sense of wellbeing that's in sharp contrast to the poverty that Danilo Dolci found when he came to the region in 1952. His *Sicilian Lives* records his first impressions of Trappeto: "Coming from the North, I knew I was totally ignorant. Looking all around me, I saw no streets, just mud and dust. Not a single chemist – or sewer. The dialect didn't have a word for sewer." Nowadays, things have dramatically improved, and the beaches on either side of the villages, backed by orange groves, are regularly visited by Palermitan holiday-makers. Both places hold popular summer pizzerias, and even a couple of hotels, but there's no real reason to stay: in summer it's just too busy and in winter too funereal. There's more of the same 10km further west at **ÁLCAMO MARINA**, where a few more bars and restaurants provide sweeping views of the gulf.

Álcamo

Inland, and just inside the Trápani provincial boundary, **ÁLCAMO** itself is the only large town, founded by Frederick II early in the thirteenth century and spread across a low hill overlooking the sea. Good wine is made from Álcamo grapes, and the town has also become renowned for the atmospheric descriptions in **Mary Taylor Simeti**'s classic memoir *On Persephone's Island*, much of which is set hereabouts. Otherwise, Álcamo will mainly be of interest to fans of medieval castles: adjacent to the broad main Piazza della Repubblica, the beautifully restored fourteenth-century **Castello dei Conti di Módica** in Piazza Castello (daily 9.30am–12.30pm & 4.30–7.30pm; free) holds a small collection of archeological scraps and farming items as well as regular exhibitions; more museums are destined to be housed here. Álcamo also boasts some fine ecclesiastical architecture, its largely Baroque **churches** all found along and around the lengthy main street of the old town, Corso VI Aprile. The Chiesa Madre on the corso is typical, with its bold frescoes and elaborate sculptures by members of the Gagini family.

Practicalities

Álcamo's **tourist office** is in the castle (Mon–Fri 9am–12.30pm & 4–7pm, Sat 9.30am–1pm; ☏0924.22.301). It's not really practical to come here by train, since the **train station** (Álcamo Diramazione) lies 5km below town, off the main SS113. There are regular **bus** connections from Palermo and Trápani.

You're unlikely to want to stay over in Álcamo, but it does hold a trio of **hotels**. The two cheapest lie west of the centre at the end of Corso VI Aprile: the small, plain *Miramare*, Corso Médici 72 (☏0924.21.197; ❸), which has en-suite, air-conditioned rooms, and the modern *La Principessa*, Via Canapè 5 (☏0924.507.789, ❺www.albergolaprincipessa.it; ❺), geared towards business travellers, with fully equipped if rather bland rooms, as well as apartments to rent. A new youth hostel is due to open outside town on Monte Bonifato in 2008: check ❺www.ostellionline.org for details.

Off Corso VI Aprile, the lovely pedestrianized square of Piazza Ciullo holds some pleasant **cafés** for a sit-down and snack, or try the *Moulin Rouge* bar on Piazza Libertà, a five-minute walk from the corso down Via Vittorio Emanuele and Via Buonarroti. Round the corner from here at Via Libertà 1, *Salsapariglia* (℡0924.508.302; closed Mon) is a first-rate, moderately priced **restaurant** with pizzas in the evenings.

Monte Bonifato

Five kilometres south of Álcamo – a well-signposted climb up a corkscrew road – **Monte Bonifato** (825m) is worth the drive for the panoramic views from the top. The other local attraction is the **Stabilimento Termale Gorga** (℡0924.23.842, ⓦwww.termegorga.com; ❸), a thermal spa where you can bathe in the exquisitely hot pool for €6, or take other treatments, such as a mud bath (€12), or a sauna (€10). You can also stay here – all rooms have bath and phone – while non-guests can eat in the *ristorante*-pizzeria. It's just a couple of hundred metres along the right-hand dirt track from the train station (don't go down under the bridge). At a second spa, **Terme Segestane** (℡0924.530.057; no credit cards), five to ten minutes' drive west, mud treatments (June–Oct only) cost €20, and entrance to the pool (closed Dec) is €6.

Castellammare del Golfo

CASTELLAMMARE DEL GOLFO is the last coastal stop on the gulf before the train line winds inland to Trápani. It's the biggest of the local fishing ports, entirely surrounded by high hills and built on and around a hefty rocky promontory that's guarded by a squat castle from which the town takes its name. Castellammare's incredible pedigree of bloodshed once gave it one of the worst reputations in Sicily for Mafia violence. The writer Gavin Maxwell, who lived locally during the 1950s, claimed that in that period eighty percent of the town's adult males had served prison sentences, and one in three had committed murder: coupled with this are the official statistics for the same period that classify one family in six as destitute. Needless to say, all of this is extremely hard to believe today: strolling down the sloping Corso Garibaldi towards the castle and harbour, past handsome *palazzi* interspersed with bars and shops selling beach gear, it seems a most benign place, ideal for a few days' relaxation.

Arrival and information

The local **train station** is 4km east of town; a bus meets arrivals and shuttles you into Castellammare, passing the campsite on the way. It drops you at the **bus station** in the upper part of the town on Via della Repubblica, which runs off Via Segesta. Regular services run from here **to Scopello** (Mon–Sat at 7.10am, 9am, 1.30pm and 4.15pm, Sun from mid-June to mid-Sept at 9.30am, 12.20pm, 4pm and 6.30pm), and (in summer) **to Lo Zíngaro**, as well as to the beach ("*Spiaggia*"), and to San Vito, Palermo, Trápani, Álcamo and Calatafimi/ Segesta. Note that few services run on Sunday.

You'll find the **tourist office** inside the castle (Mon–Fri 9am–1pm & 4–8pm, or 3–7pm in winter; ℡0924.30.217). **Banks** are on the main Corso Garibaldi.

Accommodation

Castellammare holds several good **accommodation** options, while the local **campsite**, *Nausicaa* (℡0924.33.030, ⓦwww.nausicaa-camping.it; closed Oct–March), lies a kilometre or so east, and is handy for the beach.

Belvedere Contrada Belvedere ℡0924.35.808, ⓦwww.hotelbelvedere.net. Above town on the slopes of Monte Inici. All eleven rooms have a terrace and views, and there's a restaurant – handy, as it's too far to walk into town. It's signposted off the main SS187 west of Castellammare. ❹

Cala Marina Via Don Leonardo Zangara 1
℡0924.531.841, ⓦwww.hotelcalamarina.it. In a
prime position right by the marina and beach, this
smart, modern hotel provides a relaxed atmosphere. Ask for one of the three bright rooms with
balconies and sea views. ⑥

  Nonna Giò Via A. Mario ℡334.594.1224,
  ⓦwww.sicilianelgolfo.it. Four good-value,

en-suite and air-conditioned rooms are available in
this friendly place just up from Piazza Petrolo and
the seafront. Though, strictly speaking, it's an
affittacamere rather than a B&B, you can negotiate
a breakfast at a nearby bar included in the price.
No credit cards. ④

The Town

Originally Norman but much remodelled in later centuries, the **castello**
today contains minor collections dedicated to the history, archeology and
maritime culture of the area (Tues–Sat 9am–1pm & 4–8pm, or 3–7pm in
winter, open daily in Aug; free). Beneath the castle walls, on the harbourside,
a row of cafés and restaurants face the fishing-boats, a nice place to kill time
and eat lunch. There's a scrappy sand beach at the harbour, though you may
prefer the fine sands 2km east of the centre, between the town and train
station. Between May and September, you can also take a **boat tour** up the
coast to Zíngaro and San Vito Lo Capo, leaving from the port every morning
at 8.15am or 9.15am, returning at 4.15pm or 6pm (€33 including lunch); call
℡0924.34.222 for details.

   Away from the sea, the pinewood slopes of **Monte Inici**, accessed from the
SS187 2km west of town, are a popular spot for picnics and views. It provides
some relief from the summer heat, and there is a hotel and restaurant here (both
listed below).

Eating and drinking

Most of the **restaurants** around the centre of Castellammare feature *cuscus a
pesce* – try the places listed below, or any of the moderately priced alternatives
down by the harbour. This is also the place for an evening stroll and **drink**, with
a selection of late-opening bars.

La Cambusa ℡0924.30.155 and Salvinius
℡0924.30.185 Cala Marina. The best of the
harbourside eateries, these two restaurants next to
each other offer very similar fare, prices and
ambience, with a selection of the catch of the day
displayed for your order. First and second courses
are each €9–15. Arrive early or book for the best
tables. Moderate–expensive.

  A Muciara du Rais Via Don Sturzo 18
  ℡0924.531.034. Popular backstreet

trattoria just down the steps from the town
gardens, with a vaulted stone interior and a few
tables outside. Dishes have a pronounced North
African influence (first courses €7–8, mains
€9–12). Closed Mon. Moderate.
La Pineta Quetzal Contrada Belvedere
℡0924.35.230. Popular pizzeria-restaurant with
tables under the trees below Monte Inici, on the
main road west of town. Abundant set-price menus
for €20 (meat) and €25 (fish). Moderate.

Scopello and Lo Zíngaro

The coastline northwest of Castellammare is perhaps the most beautiful in the
whole of Sicily, abounding in unspoiled coves and gravel beaches, connected by
paths to the road above. The road passes **Baia di Guidaloca**, a small scrubby
bay with a stony beach with a stream running into it and pleasant swimming.
Some people believe this to be the spot where Nausicaä found the naked,
shipwrecked Odysseus and finally set him on the last leg of his journey home
to Ithaca. Soon after this cove, 10km from Castellammare, a turn-off leads to

Scopello, a tiny hamlet a little way inland that once serviced an old tuna fishery (*tonnara*) on the coast below.

The road stops 3km beyond the Scopello *tonnara*, at a nature reserve, the **Riserva Naturale dello Zíngaro**, where you can proceed on foot through pristine country and past further extremely beautiful coves and beaches. This is not exactly unknown territory, since hundreds of Palermitani descend on Scopello and its surroundings on summer weekends, but at other times – and especially out of season – it's one of the most tranquil places in Sicily. In addition, since the whole area is regulated by building restrictions that actually seem to be enforced, the water quality – and hence the swimming – is excellent.

The Tonnara di Scopello

The road to Scopello from Castellammare forks just before the village, with one strand running the few hundred metres down to the coast and to the **TONNARA DI SCOPELLO**, set in its own tiny cove. This old tuna fishery and its associated outhouses was where the writer Gavin Maxwell lived and worked in the 1950s, basing his *Ten Pains of Death* on his experiences there. It's almost too picturesque to be true – not least the row of abandoned buildings on the quayside, fronted by lines of rusting anchors, and the ruined old watch-towers tottering on knobbly columns of rock above the sea. From the shore, it's still precisely as Maxwell described it forty years ago: "a sea of purple and blue and peacock green, with a jagged cliff coastline and great *faraglioni* [rock towers] thrusting up out of the water as pinnacle islands, pale green with the growth of cactus at their heads".

The *tonnara* remained in intermittent use until the 1980s. Although it's still privately owned, the gate is always open (free) to allow visitors to wander around the quayside – provided, according to the notice, they don't bring with them a whole host of proscribed items (dogs, radios, chairs, umbrellas). An injunction like this is usually as a red rag to a bull to your average Sicilian, and the place is regularly engulfed with all of the above on summer weekends – though more strictly enforced regulations may yet come into effect. Most visitors come to swim in the most crystal clear of waters off the tiny shingle **beach** here. Whether or not you indulge in a dip, it's a thoroughly photogenic spot (and scenes from the film *Ocean's Twelve* were shot here). There are beverage machines inside the building.

Scopello

The road past the *tonnara* runs on to Lo Zíngaro (see below), with a loop heading back to the village of **SCOPELLO DI SOPRA** – or simply Scopello – which perches on a ridge a couple of hundred metres above the coastline.

Getting there

The **bus** from Castellammare drops you in Scopello's square; out of season, four services a day (Mon–Sat) run back to Castellammare, the last at 4.45pm. In summer, there are four additional services, and eight services on Sunday; the last returns to Castellammare at 7pm.

Accommodation

Scopello can be rather an exclusive retreat, given the building restrictions that limit the accommodation choices. Book well in advance if you want to stay here in summer, and be prepared to accept half-board terms in the *pensioni*. Out of season you'll be able to pick and choose, and the prices drop a little too.

All the official **places to stay** are within a thirty-second walk of the square – official street names are a bit pointless, but are given in case you want to write and book. If everything is booked up, you might find some **rooms to rent**; try asking around in the bars and shops. The nearest **campsite** is *Baia di Guidaloca* (T 0924.541.262, W www.campingguidaloca.it; closed Nov–Easter), 3km south of Scopello, a stone's throw from Cala Bianca (see below), a shady spot with a pizzeria-restaurant, shop and sports facilities.

Angelo Via Marco Polo 4 T 338.697.4276, W www.angelobedandbreakfast.it. Small B&B with a terrace overlooking Piazza Fontana. Alternatively, ask here about another place, *Casale Corcella*, 1km north of Scopello and ideal for walkers in Lo Zingaro. No credit cards. Both closed Nov–March and both ❹

La Tavernetta Via A. Diaz 3 T 0924.541.129, W www .albergolatavernetta.it. Pleasant rooms in mellow colours, some small, and some with balconies and sea views. The food is recommended; half-board costs €85 per person. ❺

Torre Bennistra Via Natale di Roma 19 T 0924.541.128, W www.hoteltorrebennistra.it.

Though lacking much warmth or character, this modern hotel on the edge of Scopello has palatial public rooms and fully equipped, mostly spacious bedrooms, some (costing extra) enjoying glorious views over the coast. Worth taking half-board here for the exceptional food (see below). Rates plummet out of season. No credit cards. ❻

La Tranchina Via A. Diaz 7 T 0924.541.099, F 0924.541.232. Comfortable *pensione* run by a friendly family that includes an English and Spanish speaker. It has modern rooms and there's an open fire in winter (when the nights can get chilly). Great dinners are served too. ❻

The village

The village of Scopello consists of little more than **Piazza Fontana** – a paved square and a fountain – and a couple of alleys running off it. On one side of the square sits the gateway and enclosed courtyard of the village's eighteenth-century **baglio**, or manor house, now the focus of local life. In here – centred on a huge eucalyptus tree – the courtyard buildings harbour a ceramicist's workshop, artist's studio, craft shop, a couple of bars and a pizzeria-restaurant. With the lights on and the wind rustling the leaves, it's a magical place at night, though in July and August – when every bar table is full and queues develop – you could be forgiven for wishing for more solitude. Outside high summer, traditional village life is more to the fore: men playing cards at the tables, people gossiping around the fountain and neighbours helping out in each other's fields.

Elsewhere in the village – you won't have to look far to find everything – there's an *alimentari*, a bakery, a butcher's shop, a couple of bars and a post office, and there's an ATM inside the *baglio* courtyard.

Three kilometres south of Scopello, the lovely bay of **Cala Bianca** offers some great swimming; the bus from Castellammare stops here.

Eating

For such a small place, Scopello has a profusion of **restaurants**, many of them tucked away in back lanes. At weekends, when booking is advisable, they can be full to bursting, while most places close out of season.

Il Baglio Baglio Isonzo 4 T 0924.541.200. Extremely popular place for pizzas, pastas and seafood dishes, with attractive outdoor seating in the *baglio* courtyard. Eat early to avoid queues in summer. Open weekends only in winter. Moderate.
Al Cantuccio Via Statale. On the main road, this casual place serves a range of antipasti and

spaghetti dishes, as well as meat, fish and crepes, on a terrace. Moderate.
La Tavernetta Via A. Diaz 3 T 0924.541.129. Reliable pasta and fish dishes using local ingredients, doled out either inside or out on the terrace. A hearty three-course meal with local wine runs to around €35, though you could eat for less. Expensive.

Torre Bennistra Via Natale di Roma 19
☎ 0924.541.128. The best food in the
village, with the accent on home-made pasta and

the freshest fish. Tables by the windows enjoy
wonderful views over the *faraglioni*. Expensive.

The Riserva Naturale dello Zíngaro

The southern entrance to the **Riserva Naturale dello Zíngaro** (daily: April to mid-Sept 7am–8pm; mid-Sept to March 8am–4pm; €3; ☎800.116.616, ⓦ www.riservazingaro.it) is just 3km from Scopello village. It's reached via a road that affords wonderful views of the *tonnara*'s towers and the gulf beyond, passing fairly unobtrusive holiday homes, fields of vines and grazing horses. In summer, Russo buses from Castellammare del Golfo to Scopello carry on to the southern entrance of the reserve.

The first nature reserve established in Sicily, Lo Zíngaro comprises a completely unspoiled seven-kilometre stretch of coastline backed by steep mountains. Its genesis was the proposal to force a coast road through from Scopello to San Vito, an idea that horrified environmentalists, who persuaded six thousand supporters to march in protest in May 1980. The road was scrapped and the reserve established, following which great efforts have been made to attract sympathetic visitors to the site. Most, it's true, come for the isolated cove **beaches**, which provide scintillating swimming, but since there's no vehicle access beyond the entrances it's not hard to escape the crowds by simply walking further into the reserve. Around forty different bird species nest and mate here, including the rare **Bonelli's Eagle**, and there are some six hundred species of plant. Apart from the wide variety of fauna and flora, there's great archeological interest in an area that supported some of Sicily's earliest prehistoric settlements. The waters around this coast are reckoned to be among the best in the region for **diving**, with wrecks and grottoes to explore; if you're interested, contact Cetaria, Via Marco Polo 3, Scopello (☎368.386.4808, ⓦ www.cetaria.it), for dives, excursions and equipment hire.

At the Scopello entrance, **Ingresso Sud**, there's a car park and an **information hut** (daily: summer 7.30am–8pm; winter 8am–5pm), where you can pick up a simple map showing the trails through the reserve. If you're heading off from the coastal path, treat the map with some scepticism and make sure you carry plenty of water – any water you see along the way may not be fit for drinking. There's a water fountain at the information hut and, in summer, a van selling ices and drinks.

The easiest and best-maintained of the network of **paths** through the reserve keep close to the coast. Of the two main routes, the **Sentiero Alto** is best in spring for the vegetation and natural life, while the **Sentiero Basso**, hugging the shore, is best in summer if you want to stop for swims. The mid- and high-mountain routes are favoured by well-prepared walkers and ornithologists; refuges here can be used at night, so long as you book ahead through the park authority.

Following the Sentiero Basso, it takes less than twenty minutes to reach the first beach, **Cala Capreria**, which can as a result be crowded at weekends and in July and August. When it's not, it's perfect: a tiny cove of white pebbles, azure water, shoals of little fish nibbling at the edge and baby squid darting in and out. A small **Museo Naturalístico** and visitor centre stands just above the beach. Three more museums (all open daily, roughly 10am–5pm; free) are located further up the coast, one – above **Cala del Varo**, another twenty minutes or so onward – dedicated to manna and the flowering manna-ash, examples of which grow hereabouts.

Sticking with the coastal path, it's 3km from the southern entrance to the successive coves of **Disa**, **Berretta** and **Marinella**, which should be a little more secluded. The next cove, **Cala dell'Uzzo**, holds a museum of rural life, while the **Cala Tonnarella dell'Uzzo** (7km from the southern entrance) has a museum of fishing and other marine activity. Five hundred metres beyond here, at the **Ingresso Nord** – the northern, San Vito Lo Capo, park entrance – you'll find water and, in summer, refreshments. If you're walking on to San Vito, note that it's another 11km from the entrance, and there's no public transport or facilities of any kind along the way.

Segesta and around

Set amid deserted green countryside, around 15km south of Castellammare del Golfo (and 30km east of Trápani), the remains of the ancient city of **SEGESTA** are among the most inspiring on the island. All that still stands is a Doric temple and a brilliantly sited theatre, relics of a city whose roots – like Érice's – lay back in the twelfth century BC. Unlike Érice, though, ancient Segesta was eventually Hellenized and spent most of the later period disputing its border with Selinus. The temple dates from a time of prosperous alliance with Athens, but it was never finished – work on it was abandoned when a new dispute broke out with Selinus in 416 BC.

If you're driving, it's easiest to see the site en route between Palermo and Trápani, since it lies just off the motorway. By public transport, the best approach is by bus from Trápani. However you arrive, the only possibility of an overnight stop in these lovely surroundings is the small hotel at **Calatafimi**, the nearest town to the ruins.

The site

The site of **Segesta** (daily 9am–1hr before sunset; last entry 1hr before closing; €6.50) is best seen early or late in the day, when visitors are fewer and the light less blanching in its effect. The **temple** itself, started in 424 BC, crowns a low hill beyond the café and car park. From a distance you could be forgiven for thinking that it's complete: the 36 regular stone columns, entablature and pediment are all intact, and all it lacks is a roof. However, get closer (and for once you're allowed to roam right inside) and you see just how unfinished the building really is: stone studs, always removed on completion, still line the stylobate, the tall columns are unfluted, and the cella walls are missing. In a way, this only adds to the natural grandeur of the site, and it's not too fanciful to imagine that the pitted and sun-bleached temple simply grew here – a feeling bolstered by the birds nesting in the unfinished capitals, the lizards scampering over the pale yellow stone, and, in spring, the riot of flowers underfoot.

From the main entrance, a road winds up through slopes of wild fennel to a small **theatre** on a higher hill beyond; if you don't relish the twenty-minute climb you can use the half-hourly **bus service** (€1.50). The view from the top is terrific, across green slopes and the plain to the sea, the deep blue of the bay a lovely contrast to the theatre's white stone – the panorama not much damaged by the motorway snaking away below. Behind the theatre, **excavations** (explained by information boards) have revealed the foundations of a mosque and Arab-style houses. These were pulled down in the thirteenth century when a Norman castle was erected on the high ground – though this itself lasted less than a hundred years, as political forces on the island waxed and waned. There

▲ The temple at Segesta

are also the remains of a late medieval church, built for local shepherds and landholders and used, in one form or another, until the nineteenth century. Thus it is a site of enormous significance and utility, spanning generations.

In odd-numbered years, summer **concerts and plays** are staged at the theatre between late July and early September. Ask at the tourist offices in Palermo and Trápani for details, or consult ⓦ www.calatafimisegesta.it. Special excursion buses leave from both cities to coincide with the performances, and tickets for the various productions cost €10–25.

Practicalities

Coming from Trápani or Palermo by car, the easiest way to Segesta is to take the A29 autostrada. Apart from the small café and shop at the site, the café-restaurant near the signposted turn-off is the only nearby place for refreshments.

To reach the site by **bus**, catch one of the Tarántola services from Piazza Malta in Trápani, which leave Monday to Saturday at 8am, 10am, 2pm and 5pm, returning at 1.10pm, 4.10pm and 6.35pm. The only feasible Sunday departure is at 10am, returning at 1.10pm. Tarántola also operates two daily buses in summer from Castellammare del Golfo. The **train** from Trápani to Álcamo/Palermo stops at Segesta-Tempio; it's a twenty-minute walk uphill to the site from here, with the temple up on the right. Services are infrequent, though, at roughly every two hours, and just three times daily on Sundays.

Calatafimi

The small town of **CALATAFIMI** lies 4km south of its train station, so it's better to come by bus – there are four services daily here from Trápani. Defended by a castle (hence the Arabic *kalat* of its name) whose remnants top a wooded hill, the town gained fame as the site of the first of Garibaldi's victories against the Bourbon forces in 1860, which opened the way to Palermo and hence the rest of Sicily. The battle took place on the Salemi road, around 1km south of Calatafimi and then 3km up a hill, the summit marked by a white obelisk. It's signposted "*Ossario di Pianto Romana*", and named as such because the bones of the fallen from the battle are collected here. They used to be on display in cases for the edification of the local population; now they're hidden behind commemorative tablets underneath an Italian flag. The custodian might attempt an explanation of the history if your Italian is up to it – a tip wouldn't go amiss. The views outside, to Calatafimi itself, Érice and the Castellammare gulf, are magnificent.

The old town isn't much more than a strip of development along a single main street, at the top of which stands the church and, just beyond, the only **hotel**, the modern *Mille Pini*, at Piazza F. Vivona 2 (℡0924.951.260, ⓦwww .hotelmillepini.com; ❷). This has ten simple rooms with balconies and valley views, and a **restaurant** where you can eat well for around €15 – overall, it's a very nice place for a quiet night in the sticks.

Trápani

Although predominantly modern, **TRÁPANI**, the first of three major towns on Sicily's western edge, has an elegant old centre that's squeezed into a narrow arm of land pointing out to sea. Lent an end-of-the-line feel by its port, the town's inconspicuous monuments give no great impression of its long history. Nonetheless, Trápani flourished as a Phoenician trading centre and as the port for Eryx, modern Érice, profiting from its position looking out towards Africa. As an important stopover on the sea routes linking Tunis, Naples, Anjou and Aragon, the town played an enduring role throughout the Middle Ages, when Europe's crowned heads virtually passed each other on the quayside. The Navarrese king Theobald died here of typhoid in 1270; two years later Edward I of England touched down after a Crusade to learn he'd inherited the throne, while Peter of Aragon arrived in 1282 to claim the Sicilian throne, following the expulsion of the Angevin French. The city's growth over the last century has been founded on the development of salt, fishing and wine industries, though severe bombardment during World War II has given rise to miles of dull postwar building around the outskirts.

Still, as a **touring base** for the rest of the west, Trápani can't be beaten. It offers a good few accommodation possibilities, all in the old-town area; regular trains south to nearby Marsala and Mazara del Vallo; buses to Érice, the resort of San Vito Lo Capo and the more distant site of Segesta; and the nearest of the Égadi Islands is only twenty minutes away by hydrofoil.

The best time to visit Trápani itself is at **Easter**, to see the famous procession of the **Misteri** – eighteenth-century wooden images arranged in scenes representing the last days in the life of Christ. If you're aiming to be here then, make sure of a hotel room in advance, though you should have no problem finding space at any other time.

Arrival, orientation and information

The **train station** and main **bus station** (for regional buses) are at the edge of the modern part of town, in Piazza Umberto and the adjacent Piazza Malta (also known as Piazza Montalto) respectively. **Buses from Palermo and Agrigento** drop you either at the bus station or at the **hydrofoil** dock

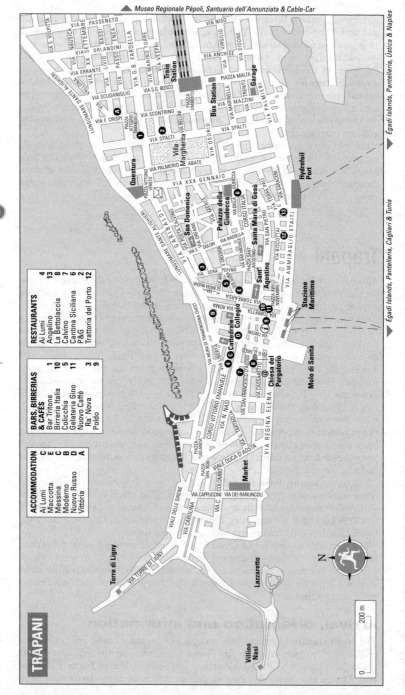

TRÁPANI

▲ Museo Regionale Pépoli, Santuario dell'Annunziata & Cable-Car

► Égadi Islands, Pantelleria, Ústica & Naples

► Égadi Islands, Pantelleria, Cagliari & Tunis

ACCOMMODATION

Ai Lumi	C
Maccotta	E
Messina	C
Moderno	B
Nuovo Russo	D
Vittória	A

BARS, BIRRERIAS & CAFÉS

Bar Tritone	1
Birreria Italia	10
Colicchia	5
Gelateria Gino	11
Nuovo Caffè	3
Poldo	9

RESTAURANTS

Ai Lumi	4
Angelino	13
La Bettolaccia	8
Calvino	7
Cantina Siciliana	6
P&G	2
Trattoria del Porto	12

200 m

N

on Via Ammiraglio Staiti, or the **Stazione Maríttima** at Molo di Sanità, from where there are **ferries** to the Égadi Islands, Pantelleria, Ústica, Naples and Cágliari (Sardinia). Trápani's **airport** has connecting flights to the major Italian cities as well as Pantelleria, and is 15km south of the city at Birgi: hourly AST buses connect with flights and run to the train station and port (45min), with less frequent services on Sunday. There's also a once-daily Segesta service **from Palermo airport** direct to Trápani (Mon–Sat; 1hr 10min). See "Listings" (p.375) for all ticket office addresses and "Travel details" at the end of the chapter for full schedules.

The narrow, irregularly shaped **old town** occupies around a square kilometre at Trápani's western end, centred on the main **Corso Vittorio Emanuele**, which is about a fifteen-minute walk from the train station. Everything in the old town is easily reachable on foot, though you'll need to catch a **city bus** to visit Trápani's museum, in the new part of the city: most routes depart from Piazza Vittorio Emanuele. Tickets are available from *tabacchi*, and are valid for one hour. During the day, **taxis** usually wait outside the train station – just make sure they switch on the meter, or you could be in for a surprise.

Despite the unhelpful staff, the **tourist office**, at Casina delle Palme, in the old town's public garden near the dock (Mon–Sat 8am–2pm; ☎0923.29.000, ⓦwww.apt.trapani.it), has plenty of information, accommodation listings and free maps.

Accommodation

All Trápani's cheaper **accommodation** is in the old town, where driving and parking can be difficult. Outside Easter, finding somewhere to stay is usually no problem. The nearest (summer-only) **campsite** is up the coast from Trápani, near Bonagia (see p.380).

Ai Lumi Corso Vittorio Emanuele 71 ☎0923.872.418, ⓦwww.ailumi.it. Entered through a lovely arcaded courtyard filled with potted plants, this bed and breakfast has five small but elegant rooms and apartments. English, French and German spoken. Guests get a discount at the eponymous restaurant a couple of doors along. Closed Nov. ❺

Maccotta Via degli Argentieri 4 ☎0923.28.418, ⓦwww.albergomaccotta.it. Smart and friendly place behind the Palazzo Senatorio, holding twenty spacious modern rooms with comfortable beds but small bathrooms, a/c and Wi-Fi available. ❹

Messina Corso Vittorio Emanuele 71 ☎0923.21.198. The city's cheapest option occupies the first floor of the eighteenth-century Palazzo Bernardo Ferro, and is entered through the same grand courtyard as *Ai Lumi* (see above). The nine rooms, with shared bathrooms, are less impressive, and the owners can be grumpy. Nonetheless, it's often full. ❶

Moderno Via Ten. Genovese 20 ☎0923.21.247, ⓦwww.hotelmoderno.trapani.it. As you might imagine, the *Moderno* is no such thing, though it

does have more character than some, housed in an old *palazzo* with a courtyard where limited parking is available. Some of the simple rooms have French windows opening onto little balconies over the street. ❷

Nuovo Russo Via Tintori 4 ☎0923.22.166, Ⓔalbergorusso @sicilyhotels.it. The best choice in the old town for comfort at moderate prices. Bright, a/c rooms have tiled floors and coordinated colours, and good bathrooms with decent water pressure. Front rooms face the cathedral and its bells (mercifully, silent at night) and feature tiny terraces for corso views. Breakfast available for small extra charge. ❸

Vittória Via Francesco Crispi 4 ☎0923.873.044, ⓦwww.hotelvittoriatrapani.it. Facing Trápani's only real open space, not far from the bus and train stations, this is the most reasonably priced new-town option. It's fairly business-style, with fully equipped, Wi-Fi-enabled rooms and parking. Good views from the upper floors. ❺

The City

Almost everything of interest in Trápani is found in the **old town**, west of the Villa Margherita gardens. Some churches and palaces have been renovated over the years, but off the main corso and away from the central shopping streets there's a scruffy, tatty air to much of Trápani, with litter blowing down the alleys and *palazzi* crumbling under the onslaught of years of accumulated grime.

You don't see any of this if you stick to the **Corso Vittorio Emanuele**, the old town's pedestrianized main street, dominated at its eastern end by the pinkish marble front of the **Palazzo Senatorio**, the seventeenth-century town hall. With its twin clocks separated by an imperious eagle, it adds a touch of grandeur to the thin promenading strip, otherwise hemmed in by balconied *palazzi*, a couple of Baroque churches, and the **Cattedrale** on the right, with its Baroque portico, cupolas and vast interior. Dedicated to San Lorenzo, there's a *Crucifixion* inside, in the fourth chapel on the right, attributed to Van Dyck.

The corso runs to the very tip of the curving promontory from which the town took its Phoenician name of Drepanon (sickle), ending at the **Torre di Ligny**, a squat Spanish fortification dating from 1671. This holds a collection of prehistoric finds as well as photographs of drawings from the Grotta del Genovese on the island of Lévanzo, but it's privately owned, so it's only sporadically open: ℡0923.547.922 for details. On the way back into town, a walk down the north side of the promontory will show you what's left of the medieval city wall, the *bastione*, breached by the thirteenth-century **Porta Botteghelle**.

Back at the eastern end of the corso, **Via Torrearsa** is one of the old town's main shopping streets. At its southern end, the church of **Sant'Agostino** on Piazzetta Saturno boasts a pretty fourteenth-century rose window of interlocking stone bands; the church is occasionally used as a concert hall (details of performances from the tourist office). Architecturally more appealing is the sixteenth-century church of **Santa Maria di Gesù**, on Via San Pietro to the east, whose two doors display a diversity characteristic of the town, the right-hand one Gothic, the other defiantly Renaissance, and there's a fine relief in the architrave. Step inside, and at the end of the nave, a terracotta *Madonna col Bambino* surrounded by angels, the work of Andrea della Robbia, shelters beneath a graceful marble canopy carved by Antonello Gagini.

Trápani's Misteri

One of Sicily's most evocative religious processions, held since the seventeenth century, takes place in Trápani at Easter, when the **Misteri**, extraordinary life-sized wooden statues depicting scenes from the Passion, are carried shoulder-high through the streets on Good Friday. The procession through the town takes ten hours, starting at 2pm and finishing back at Purgatorio at midnight. Sculpted from cypress wood and cork in the eighteenth century, each of the twenty groups of chocolate-brown figures is associated with one of the town's trades – fishermen, metalworkers, saltworkers, and so on – whose representatives undertake to maintain them and, draped in cowls and purple robes, annually parade them. The rest of the time the statues are kept in the **Chiesa del Purgatorio**, on Via Generale Domenico Giglio, south of the main corso, where in theory they can be viewed (Mon, Wed & Fri 10am–noon & 4–7pm), though in practice the church is often locked. When it's open, there's usually a priest around to explain which of the trades is responsible for each of the sculpted groups, and what the particular figures represent – though most of the scenes are familiar enough. If it's closed, try to arrange admission at the tourist office.

There's little more to see in this part of town apart from a few unusual facades, one of them buried in the wedge of hairline streets and alleys north of Corso Italia, at Via della Giudecca 43, where the sixteenth-century **Palazzo della Giudecca** sports a plaque-studded front and some Spanish-style Plateresque windows. The building lies at the heart of Trápani's old **Jewish quarter**, an area dating from Trápani's medieval heyday at the centre of Mediterranean trade. From here, it's not far to the **Villa Margherita**, the shady town gardens (open dawn to dusk) which hold a small zoo and host summer concerts (information available from the tourist office).

The modern city

While Trápani's **modern city** mainly consists of a dull grid of right-angled streets, a trio of specific attractions are well worth seeking out. For two of these, drivers should follow Via Fardella east, bearing right at Via Pépoli (or take bus #25 or #28 from Piazza Vittorio Emanuele) to **Villa Pépoli**, a park. In front of it stands the lavishly decorated **Santuario dell'Annunziata** (daily 8am–noon & 4–8pm, closes 7pm in winter; free), a fourteenth-century convent and church whose cloisters incorporate the town's main museum. The sanctuary was rebuilt in 1760 and only the facade, with its Gothic portal and magnificent rose window, is original. Inside (entrance on Via Pépoli), you'll find a series of sumptuous **chapels**, two dedicated to Trápani's fishermen and seamen – one echoes the facade's shell motif around the sides of the room – and, best of all, the **Cappella della Madonna**, containing Trápani's sacred idol: the beautiful, smiling *Madonna and Child*, attributed to Nino Pisano in the fourteenth century. Responsible for a host of miracles, the statue is housed beneath a grandiose marble canopy sculpted by Antonello Gagini and surrounded by polychrome marble – as well, generally, as a crowd of hushed worshippers.

Adjacent, and entered through Villa Pépoli, the **Museo Regionale Pépoli** (Mon–Sat 9am–1.30pm, Sun 9am–12.30pm; €4) was designed by one of Italy's foremost architects in the field, though it's equipped with abysmal lighting, as it was intended that the exhibits should be seen in full daylight; come early, preferably in the morning. The wide-ranging collection takes in everything from exemplary Gagini statuary to seventeenth-century coral craftwork. Highlights downstairs include a little bronze horse and rider by Giácomo Serpotta and a sixteenth-century marble doorway by Berrettaro Bartolomeu, taken from the old church of San Giuliano, which, though badly worn in parts, displays a lively series of tableaux. Downstairs, too, bizarrely, is a grim wooden guillotine from 1789 with a basket for the head, and a coffin at the ready. The museum houses a good **medieval art** section – including a powerful *Pietà* by Roberto Oderisio, and a couple of fine fifteenth-century triptychs by the anonymous *Maestro del Políttico di Trápani* (presently under restoration). Other displays include a coin collection, with Greek, Roman, Arab and Italian examples; an eighteenth-century majolica-tiled scene of *La Mattanza* (tuna slaughter), with the fishermen depicted corralling the fish in their boats; a small archeological section with a few finds from Selinunte and Mózia, though nothing outstanding, and some intricate coral work, including crib scenes with alabaster and shell decoration.

Eating and drinking

Eating out in Trápani is a real treat – although that should probably be "eating in", since there are very few places where you can sit outside, Mediterranean-style, other than a couple of pavement cafés along the pedestrianized Via

The Funierice cable car to Érice

Even if it weren't the quickest means to reach Érice – far more convenient than driving or catching a bus – the Funierice **cable-car** (*funivia*) ride from Trápani would be worth the excursion. In fact the ascent, which takes about twelve minutes, constitutes one of the region's most memorable experiences, revealing a gradually expanding panorama that extends over the flat saltpans to the south, the mountainous coast north, and out over the narrow limb that holds the old city to the Égadi Islands and the blue sea beyond. By night, the scene is very different, with Trápani's lights sparkling under a starry sky.

From the Trápani terminal on Via Caserta, departures are continuous (Mon 2–8.30pm, Tues–Fri 7.30am–8.30pm, Sat & Sun 9.45am–midnight; ⓦ www .funiviaerice.it), with tickets costing €2.70 one way, €5 return. The only slight hassle is getting to the cable-car station on Via Caserta, at the extreme eastern end of the modern city. Driving from the old centre, follow Via Fardella east, bear left at Corso Mattarella, keep straight along this and its continuation Via Manzoni (following signs for Érice), and turn left at the end into Via Fratelli Aiuto, from which it's a right turn into Via Caserta and the large car park. By bus, you can take bus #21 or #23 from Piazza Vittorio Emanuele.

Garibaldi. Nonetheless, you can get fresh fish and couscous almost everywhere, while the local pasta speciality, *alla trapanese*, is terrific – either spaghetti or home-made *busiate* served with a pesto of fresh tomato, basil, garlic and almonds, sometimes accompanied by fried potatoes. There are quite a few lively **bars** around, too, good for breakfast and snacks and bustling at night with people stopping off from the rowdy *passeggiata* that fills Via Torrearsa and the bottom end of Corso Vittorio Emanuele.

A good daily morning **market** takes place at the west end of town, on Via Ranúncoli: fish, fruit and vegetables, local tuna products, olives, capers and cheeses are all on sale, and many can be sampled.

Restaurants

🏃 **Angelino** Via A. Staiti 87 ☎0923.26.922. Examine the mouthwatering displays in this fashionable *pasticceria-távola calda*, take a ticket, order at the bar and grab a table in the conservatory. You're spoiled for choice – *involtini* of aubergine rolled around spaghettini, stuffed sardines, rosemary-roast potatoes, lasagne and *foccacia*, with wine by the glass, and coffee and cake to follow if you wish. Closed Mon lunch except Aug. Inexpensive.

La Bettolaccia Via Gen. Enrico Fardella 25 ☎0923.21.695. Popular with locals, this modern *osteria* is known for its excellent risotto and *busiate* dishes (mainly seafood). The oven-baked *bucatini* with sardines are also good. First courses are €6.50–9, mains €12–14. The atmosphere is informal but sophisticated. Closed Sat lunch & Sun. Moderate.

🏃 **Calvino** Via N. Nasi 77 ☎0923.21.464. An excellent backstreet pizzeria, with Moorish-style cubbyhole rooms where superb hot pizza is served on squares of grease-proof paper. Try the *Rianata*, made with fresh oregano, tomato, garlic, anchovies and pecorino cheese – a local speciality – and wash it down with cold beer. No credit cards. Closed Tues. Inexpensive.

Cantina Siciliana Via Giudecca 32 ☎0923.28.673. In the old Jewish quarter, this rated restaurant serves reasonably priced traditional Sicilian dishes as well as fish couscous. Pastas are €7 or €8, meat and fish mains €7–10. The lemon ice cream with limoncello is delicious. With blue-tiled walls, it's nice and cosy for a romantic dinner. Moderate.

Ai Lumi Corso Vittorio Emanuele 71–77 ☎0923.872.418. Well-regarded local taverna with a brick vaulted interior and such regional dishes as *ghiotta di pesce* (seafood soup), home-made pasta, grilled meats and simple grilled fish. First courses are €9–14, mains €12–18. Closed lunchtime, Sun & Nov. Moderate.

P&G Via Spalti 1 ℡ 0923.547.701. Smarter than most of the options listed here, this restaurant lays on a fine selection of antipasti, seafood and grilled meats. Among the pastas (€7–12), try the fresh *busiate casarecce*, with a pesto of anchovy, garlic, pine nuts and tomato. There are a few tables outdoors, and pizzas in the evening. Closed Mon. Moderate–expensive.

Trattoria del Porto Via A. Staiti 45 ℡ 0923.547.822. Friendly, family-run trattoria (also known locally as *Da Felice*) opposite the port with occasionally slow service but good food and outdoor tables under the arches. Top choices are the *spaghetti marinara*, fish couscous, roast squid or, in season, *involtini di spada* (swordfish roulades). Good-value tourist menus are €20 and €30. Closed Mon. Moderate.

Bars, birrerias and cafés

Colicchia at the corner of Via delle Belle Arti and Via Carosio, just off Via Torrearsa. Fine bar-*pasticceria* with a super array of cakes; a good place to sample a granita. No seats.
Gelateria Gino Piazza dalla Chiesa. Make a beeline here for excellent ice cream, from kiwi to coconut. Good *frullati* too. Closed Wed in winter.
Birreria Italia Via Torrearsa 5–7. One of several bars at this end of town, the boisterous *Italia* has bottled beer, snacks and cakes, and streetside tables for *passeggiata*-watching. There's pizza by the slice, too, over the way at *Passa a Taglio*. Closed Sun off-season.

Nuovo Caffè Ra' Nova Via Garibaldi. Busy café with a range of hot snacks, and a large outdoor area on a traffic-free road. There's also a huge array of ice creams and cocktails.
Poldo Piazza dalla Chiesa. A noisy *birreria* and *panineria*, busy at night, serving hot sandwiches and big mugs of beer. Closed Mon.
Bar Tritone Piazza Vittorio Emanuele 38. Not many places in town have any kind of view – here, you can sit among the palm trees, sip a drink or munch on *gelato*, and wonder exactly what kind of bird it is that the statue of King Vittorio Emanuele has on his head.

Listings

Airline tickets from Egatour (see Travel agents).
Airport information For Trápani airport flight info, call ℡ 0923.842.502, ⓦ www .aeroportotrapani.com.
Airport transport Hourly AST buses run from the port and bus station to Trápani's airport at Birgi. There's also a Segesta bus from the port and bus station to Palermo airport Mon–Sat at 9am (1hr 10min).
Banks Banks with cashpoints (ATMs) on Piazza Umberto I, Corso Italia, Via Garibaldi and at the Stazione Maríttima.
Buses AST ℡ 0923.23.222, ⓦ www .aziendasicilianatrasporti.it, from Piazza Malta (for destinations within the province, including Érice, Marsala, Mazara del Vallo, Castelvetrano, Gibellina, San Vito Lo Capo, Salemi, Valderice and the airport); S. Lumia ℡ 0922.20.414, ⓦ www .autolineelumia.it, from Piazza Malta (for Marsala, Mazara del Vallo, Castelvetrano, Sciacca and Agrigento); Autoservizi Segesta ℡ 0923.21.754, ⓦ www.segesta.it, from Piazza Garibaldi (for Palermo and Palermo airport); Tarantola ℡ 0924.31.020, from Piazza Malta (for Segesta).
Car rental Europcar at Stazione Maríttima ℡ 0923.22.874, ⓦ www.europcar.com; Serse, Via Passo Enea 30 ℡ 0923.21.843; Sixt, Via Staiti 85 ℡ 0923.22.874, ⓦ www.sixt.com.

Ferry tickets Siremar ℡ 0923.545.455, ⓦ www .siremar.it (for the Égadi Islands and Pantelleria); Tirrenia ℡ 892.123, ⓦ www.tirrenia.it (for Cágliari); Ústica Lines ℡ 0923.873.813, ⓦ www.usticalines.it (for Tunis and Sousse). All the ferry companies have offices at the Stazione Maríttima, Molo di Sanità, Via A. Staiti.
Garage Bulgarella, a 10min walk from the dock at Via Mazzini 17 ℡ 0923.547.022; €10 per day.
Hospital Ospedale S. Antonio Abate, Via Cosenza ℡ 0923.809.111; 24hr emergency first-aid ℡ 0923.809.450.
Hydrofoil tickets Siremar (for the Égadi Islands); Ústica Lines (for the Égadi Islands, Naples and Pantelleria). Both companies have ticket booths on the dockside, open 15min before departures. See Ferry tickets for contact details.
Internet Viale Regina Elena 26–28 (Mon–Sat 10am–1pm & 4–8pm), with fax, phones and mobile phone charge-cards as well.
Pharmacies Rizzi, Via Fardella 136; Vivona, Corso Vittorio Emanuele 211; and Zichichi, Via N. Nasi 27.
Police Questura at Piazza Vittorio Véneto ℡ 0923.598.111; Carabinieri, Via Orlandini ℡ 0923.27.122.
Post office At Piazza Vittorio Véneto, at the bottom of Via Garibaldi. Mon–Sat 8am–6.30pm.

Supermarket Oviesse, Via Libertà 6–10 for clothes and everyday items; Di Per Di near the port on Via San Pietro for food. Both open daily roughly 9am–1pm & 4.30–8.30pm.

Taxis Ranks at train station and port. Call ☎0923.22.808, 0923.21.088, 368.681.488 or 368.734.0893.

Train information FS information line is ☎89.20.21, ⊛ www.ferroviedellostato.it.

Travel agents CTS Viaggi, Via Marsala 159, ☎0923.542.484; Egatour Viaggi, Via A. Staiti 13 ☎0923.21.754. All agents can provide information and tickets for getting to Pantelleria, plus all other hydrofoil and ferry tickets, and some bus tickets.

Érice

Despite being just a brief hop from Trápani and the coast, **ÉRICE** couldn't be further away in spirit. It's a walled mountain town – around 750m above sea level – thoroughly medieval, with its creeping hillside alleys, grey stone buildings and silent charm, but boasting a truly ancient lineage. Founded by Elymians, who claimed descent from the Trojans, the city was known to the ancient world as Eryx. A magnificent temple, dedicated to Aphrodite Erycina, Mediterranean goddess of fertility, once topped the mountain and was big enough to act as a landmark to sailors. According to legend, it was here that Daedalus landed, unlike his son Icarus who flew too near the sun, after fleeing from Minos; he presented the temple with a honeycomb made of gold as his gift to the goddess. Even though the city was considered impregnable, Carthaginian, Roman, Arab and Norman armies all forced entry over the centuries, but all respected the town's sanctity, the Romans rebuilding the temple and setting two hundred soldiers to serve as guardians of the shrine. Later, the Arabs renamed the town Gebel-Hamed, "Mohammed's mountain", while Count Roger called it Monte

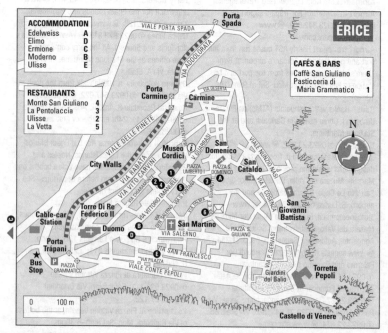

▲ Church facade in Érice

San Giuliano, a name that stuck until Mussolini returned its ancient moniker in 1934. Nowadays it's a centre for scientific conferences, and you're likely to see as many foreigners with labels on their lapels as you are tourists.

The only modern blots in the town's otherwise homogeneous aspect are the pylons that tower above the grey walls, and the tourists, though as people have always come to Érice to sightsee and worship, it seems churlish to resent these.

In any case, there are enough cobbled alleys and quiet spots to enable you to avoid the tour groups, and the views from Érice's terraces are superb, taking in Trápani, the Égadi Islands and even (allegedly) distant Cap Bon in Tunisia.

Érice is only a small town, with a population of a few hundred, though this multiplies considerably in summer – in **August** the streets are busy until late at night as trippers and holiday-home owners negotiate the polished cobblestones. **Easter** is another popular time to visit, when the *Misteri* sculptures representing the Stations of the Cross are paraded through the streets on Good Friday.

Arrival and information

From Trápani, it's a twisty half-hour's **drive**, or a fifty-minute **bus** ride, to Érice; the buses stop outside the Porta Trápani, where there's also a handy **car park** (don't even think of taking your car into the old-town streets). By far the most rewarding way to arrive, however, is by **cable car**, which takes less than fifteen minutes from the base station at Via Caserta (see p.374 for details). The upper terminal is right outside Porta Trápani.

The helpful **tourist office** (Mon–Fri 9am–2pm; ☎0923.869.388, ⓦwww .prolocovalderice.it) is just off Piazza Umberto I on Via Tommaso Guarrasi. The **post office** stands on Via G.F. Guarnotti Mon–Fri 8am–1.30pm, Sat 8am–12.30pm), and there's a **bank** at the top of Via Vittorio Emanuele, by Piazza Umberto I – both have ATMs.

Accommodation

Staying the night in Érice is relatively expensive, and in summer, or at Easter and Christmas, you'd do well to book in advance. If you stay in the old town you'll have to park outside Porta Trápani and carry your luggage up. The other option is to stay in Valderice (see below), about twenty minutes' drive back down the mountain.

Edelweiss Cortile Padre Vincenzo 5 ☎0923.869.420, ⓔedelweiss@libero.it. Tucked up a cobbled alley off Piazza San Domenico, this *pensione* has thirteen plain, smallish rooms, all with shower. The staff are somewhat gloomy, but it'll do for a night. ❺

Elimo Via Vittorio Emanuele 75 ☎0923.869.377, ⓦwww.hotelelimo.it. Beautifully restored building with a little courtyard garden – though somewhat snooty in tone. The luxurious rooms have great views – as does the quality restaurant where you take breakfast. ❼

Ermione Via Pineta Comunale 43 ☎0923.869.138, ⓦwww.ermionehotel.com. Five minutes' walk below the Porta Trápani, this gruff building (think 1970s Soviet Union) improves dramatically inside – an interior brightened by wall paintings and prints, nice staff, reasonably

spacious rooms with huge views (those on the third floor have balconies) and a pool (though rarely in use given the stiff clifftop wind). There's a bar and restaurant. ❺

Moderno Via Vittorio Emanuele 63 ☎0923.869.300, ⓦwww.hotelmodernoerice.it. The best aspect of the *Moderno* is it's panoramic roof terrace, where there's a bar and where breakfast can be taken. The rooms aren't so terrific, at least not for the price, though rates are more reasonable in low season. ❼

🏃 **Ulisse** Via Santa Lucia ☎0923.860.155, ⓦwww.sitodiulisse.it. A great budget choice, this *affittacamere* offers rooms with or without private bathrooms spread over two buildings. Opt for those grouped around a peaceful central courtyard, where rugs and colourful ceramic floors lend a North African ambience. ❹

The Town

The greatest pleasure in Érice is simply to wander around. You'll soon get lost in the winding alleys, but the most convoluted of routes is only going to take a couple of hours, and every aspect is delightful. Square and solid from the outside, the houses hide pretty courtyards, and while most of the churches are locked, there's usually something to admire – a carved door, a cupola or a belltower. The number of tourists means a fair amount of tat in the souvenir shops, from tea towels to puppets, but **traditional industries** still flourish, in particular the making of ceramics, tapestries and *dolci di badia* (almond-paste sweets).

You enter through the Norman **Porta Trápani**, at the southwestern edge of town. Just inside is the battered stone **Chiesa Madre** (daily: March 10am–4pm; April–June & Oct 10am–6pm; July & Aug 10am–8pm; Sept 10am–7pm; Nov–Feb 10am–12.30pm), dating from around 1314, though the massive Gothic entrance was added a century later and much of the structure was rebuilt in the nineteenth century. The neo-Gothic interior preserves some exceptional lace-like carving. To the left of the church, the stout, battlemented campanile owes its name, **Torre di Re Federico Secondo** (same hours; €1), to its original role as a lookout tower for Frederick III of Aragon (Frederick II of Sicily), who made Érice his base during the Wars of the Vespers. Climb to the top for sublime views over village, mountains and sea. From the ticket office, you can acquire a Passe Partout ticket (€5) that allows entry to a handful of Érice's attractions, including this one.

From Porta Trápani, the main Via Vittorio Emanuele climbs steeply past houses, shops and *pasticcerie* to the pretty **Piazza Umberto I**, where café tables are strewn adventurously across the sloping cobbles. The small **Museo Cordici** (Mon–Fri 8am–2pm, Mon & Thurs also 2.30–5pm; free) here boasts a good *Annunciation* by Antonello Gagini and the pick of the local archeological finds. Further north, the medieval **Porta Cármine** marks the other end of town, from where the line of ancient **city walls** leads back to the Chiesa Madre.

Heading east instead from the Porta Trápani, along Viale Conte Pepoli, you get the best of the views across the plains and out to sea. You'll eventually come to the ivy-clad, twelfth-century **Castello di Vénere** (daily 9am–5pm; free), built on the site of the famed ancient temple of Aphrodite, chunks of which are incorporated into the walls. The castle is built on the most precarious of crags, offering grand views in all directions, while stuck in the middle of the public garden below is a restored fifteenth-century tower, the **Torretta Pépoli**. From here, you can wind towards Piazza Umberto I, perhaps passing clifftop **San Giovanni Battista** and its distinctive dome before eventually negotiating the minuscule **Piazza San Domenico**, whose church and palace facade is one of the town's most harmonious sights. The *Antica Pasticceria del Convento* on one corner of the square does a fierce trade in locally produced sweets and pastries.

Eating and drinking

Though **restaurant** prices are a good bit higher in Érice than elsewhere in the region, you can still eat at a reasonable price if you stick to the set-price menus. Bring a picnic and you can sit in the gardens, or there's a *panineria* on Via Vittorio Emanuele.

Restaurants

Monte San Giuliano Vícolo San Rocco 7 ℡0923.869.595. Entering this backstreet restaurant is like visiting a castle, through a stone archway and up steps. There's a sort of courtyard too, where tables are spread out amid plants with seaward views. Try the *ravioli védova allegra*

("happy widow"), with ricotta and squid ink. First courses are €8–9, mains are €10–13. Closed Mon. Moderate.

La Pentolaccia Via G.F. Guarnotti 17 ℡0923.869.099. Housed in an old monastery, this popular restaurant specializes in home-made *busiate* with aubergine, basil, pine nuts and *ricotta salata*. Couscous is good too, or there are simple grills and cheap local wine. Pasta dishes cost €7–10, meat and fish €8–14. Closed Tues and Jan & Feb. Moderate.

Ulisse Via Chiaramonte 45 ☎0923.869.333. Reached down the stepped Vico San Rocco, just off the main square, and with a nice courtyard-garden. The pizzas here are the best in town (and Sun sees a queue form early), while the regular menu is good too, if on the pricey side. Closed Thurs in winter. Moderate for pizza, otherwise expensive.

La Vetta Via G. Fontana ☎0923.869.404. Signposted off Piazza Umberto (and also called *Da Mario*), this place serves standard trattoria meals and evening pizzas, and fish couscous is prepared daily. Eat upstairs or at outdoor tables in the alley in summer. Closed Thurs. Inexpensive–moderate.

Cafés and bars

Pasticceria di Maria Grammatico Via Vittorio Emanuele 14. Famous speciality cake shop/café selling marzipan fruits, *amaretti* and the like. You can admire the view from a minuscule balcony.

Caffè San Giuliano Via G.F. Guarnotti 11. When the wind blows, retreat to this stone-walled bar, sip a marsala and nibble on *arancini*, panini or salads.

North to Custonaci

North of Trápani, the main attraction is the resort town of San Vito Lo Capo (see below), though with a car you could explore the rugged coastline en route. Between Trápani and the cape, 40km away, two wide gulfs – Bonagia and Cófano – are backed by holiday homes and small plantations, overlooked both by the heights of Érice and by its lower neighbour **VALDERICE**, a ribbon development occupying a prominent ridge. The buses from Trápani to Érice come this way. There's no real reason to stop, save for the coastal views from Valderice's belvedere, although there are a couple of **hotels**, both under the same ownership. The *Érice Valle*, Via del Cipresso 1 (☎0923.891.133, ⓦwww.bagliosantacroce.it; ⑤), is a modern place at the southern (Trápani) end of the main road, whose rooms open onto a Mediterranean garden. Five kilometres out of Valderice on the SS187 (and signposted), the *Baglio Santa Croce* (☎0923.891.111, ⓦwww.bagliosantacroce.it; ⑦) is a glorious renovation of an old, seventeenth-century stone-built estate, whose rooms have beamed ceilings, exposed walls, tiled floors and iron bedsteads (some rooms are in the modern annex). There's a lovely pool and superb views to the coast, and the restaurant is locally renowned.

From Valderice, a minor road winds 5km down to the coast at **BONAGIA**, where the old tuna fishery has been transformed into a very stylish and swanky **hotel** with a pool and numerous other luxury facilities, the *Tonnara di Bonagia* (☎0923.431.111, ⓦwww.nh-hotels.it; closed Nov–March; ⑤). Nearby, boats bob in the small harbour, overlooked by a couple of fairly smart restaurants. The swimming, though, isn't much good, thanks to the swathes of kelp which infest the coast – which may be why the only other hotel here, also on the harbour, the smart, modern *Saverino* (☎0923.592.727, ⓦwww.saverino.it; ③), is relatively reasonably priced. Trápani's nearest **campsite**, *Lido Valdérice* (☎0923.573.477, ⓦwww.campinglidovalderice.com; closed Nov–March), is also in the Bonagia locality, by the sea; up to seven buses a day (Sun in summer only) come this way from the Trápani bus terminal, a 25-minute ride. From Bonagia, the coastal road runs the 12km back into Trápani, passing a couple more hotels and some less attractive bits of coastline.

On from Bonagia, the road weaves under some of the gigantic outcrops of rock that characterize Sicily's west. The most spectacular, **Monte Cófano**

(659m), is protected as a nature reserve. The village of **CUSTONACI**, 20km from Trápani and famous as a marble-cutting centre, nestles under here, slightly inland. The road then plunges east and inland – passing through purgatory (well, the settlement of Purgatorio) – to re-emerge beside sparkling clear water and more rocky beaches leading up to the San Vito cape, 40km from Trápani.

San Vito Lo Capo and around

With its dense ranks of trattorias, hotels and bars, **SAN VITO LO CAPO** is certainly geared to holiday consumers, but its comparative remoteness has helped to stave off the worst pressures of the tourist industry, even in high season. All the same, you'll have a lot more elbow-room outside the peak months – the best time to appreciate the presence here of one of Sicily's finest beaches.

Arrival and information

Regular daily **buses** run to San Vito from Trápani's bus terminal and from Palermo's Piazza Marina, stopping on Via P. Matarella, close to the seafront; the central Via Savoia is three blocks to the right. The last bus back to Trápani leaves at 7.40pm (8.30pm Sun); it's a bit too far for a day-trip from Palermo. **Parking** is highly restricted during the summer months: your best bet is to search out one of the car parks on the edge of town, costing €5–6 per day. From the biggest of these, Parcheggio Comunale Sud (Villaggio Azzurro) – for which take an early right turn onto Via La Piana as you enter town – a free shuttle runs to the centre in the summer months. Alternatively, you can park between the blue lines in a few more central areas (€1 per hour, buy a scratch-card from *tabacchi*).

The **tourist office** is at Via Savoia 61 (June & Sept daily 10am–1pm & 5–9pm; July & Aug daily 10am–1pm & 5–11pm; Oct–May Fri–Sun 10am–1pm; ⊤0924.974.300), and there's a Pro Loco at Via Venza 12 (daily 9am–1pm & 5–9pm, reduced hours in winter; ⊤800.135.422, Ⓦwww.comune.sanvitolocapo.tp.it). The **post office** is at Via Savoia 58 (Mon–Fri 8am–1.30pm, Sat 8am–12.30pm), between two **banks** with ATMs.

Accommodation

Accommodation in San Vito is plentiful and mostly central – as with all resorts, the nearer the sea, the more expensive the room. It's worth noting that in July and August and during the Cous Cous Fest of late September, many places virtually double their prices. Furthermore, you'll almost always have to agree to half-board terms, and you're unlikely to find anything suitable without an advance reservation. In winter, you won't find many places open; ask around the bars in the centre if you get stuck. There are several **campsites** in the area (see below). The "No camping" signs on the town beach should be heeded.

Hotels and B&Bs

🏃 **Baglio Luna** Via del Secco 11 ⊤335.836.2856, Ⓦwww.bagliolaluna.com. Seven kilometres out of town, on the Zíngaro road and so ideal for forays into the reserve, this rural B&B boasts lofty views from its terrace, and complete tranquillity. The airy white-washed interior with tiled floor has three simple rooms and a suite. Two nights' minimum stay, or a week in August. Breakfast available July–Sept only. No credit cards. Closed Oct–March. ❺

Bougainville Via Mulino 61 ⊤0923.972.207, Ⓦwww.sanvitoweb.com/bougainville. Quite a walk from the beach – 300m down Via Savoia, past the Municipio, and on the left – this friendly place features climbing plants, five decent rooms and a spiral staircase leading to a roof terrace. Fridge available for guests. Closed Nov–March. **4**

Capo San Vito Via San Vito 1 ℡ 0923.972.122, Ⓦ www.caposanvito.it. Right on the beach, at the end of Via Savoia, this top-of-the-range hotel has air-conditioned rooms. Those at the front (costing extra) have terraces and sea views. Meals are taken in the terrace restaurant, and a small garden gives on to the beach. **7**

Costa Gaia Via Savoia 125–127 ℡ 0923.972.268, Ⓦ www.hotelcostagaia.com. A good, central first choice, though with only seven en-suite rooms this little *pensione* fills quickly. Half- or full-board only in Aug (€80 or €95 per person). **5**

Eden Via Mulino 58 ℡ 0923.972.460. One of the cheapest places in San Vito, a ten-minute walk from town centre and beach, holding a selection of clean, reasonably spacious rooms with bathrooms, simply furnished but perfectly adequate. Parking available. No credit cards. **4**

Egitarso Via Lungomare 54 ℡ 0923.972.111, Ⓦ www.hotelegitarso.it. A low block right on the beach, offering bright air-conditioned rooms with balconies and fine views, and a few apartments. There's a buffet breakfast included, plus 24hr bar

and beachside service. Half-board adds another €20 per person, and good reductions are available off-season. **7**

Pocho Contrada Macari ℡ 0923.972.525, Ⓦ www .pocho.it. Making the most of its coastal location, 4km south of town (near *El Bahira* campsite), this cliffside hotel-restaurant makes a soothing base for anyone with transport, with twelve quiet and elegant rooms and terrific food (see "Restaurants", below). There's access to the small rocky beach below. Closed Nov–March. **6**

Poseidon Via P. Matarella 28 ℡ 0923.972.444, Ⓦ www.poseidonresidence.com. Good for families, these stylish one- and two-room apartments have a/c, kitchenette and shower, plus parking. Ground-floor rooms have garden access but no views; you get more light and a balcony higher up. Prices start at €820 weekly for a two-person apartment in peak season; low-season rates are negotiable. Closed Nov–March. **6**

Sabbia d'Oro Via Cavour 90 ℡ 0923.972.508, Ⓦ www.sabbiadorohotels.com. At the eastern end of town, this family-friendly hotel has functional, air-conditioned rooms with TV and balcony, and there's a private beach. You can spend a little less in the associated *Ocean View* (**6**), nearer the beach on Via Santuario, which has a small internal tropical garden. Closed Dec. **7**

Campsites

El Bahira Contrada Macari ℡ 0923.972.577, Ⓦ www.elbahira.it. The largest and classiest of San Capo's sites, in a dramatic setting 4km south of town, with a range of facilities as well as a private beach. Closed Oct–March.

La Fata, Via P. Matarella ℡ 0923.972.133, in winter 833.369, Ⓦ www.trapaniweb.it/lafata. Most

central and the smallest of San Capo's sites, with minimal facilities – though there's a bar. It's just up from the bus stop.

La Pineta ℡ 0923.972.818, Ⓦ www .campinglapineta.it. A 20min walk from town along the seafront (towards Scopello), with a bar, pizzeria, bungalows to rent and a pool.

The town and beach

Running down to the beach, San Vito's long shop- and restaurant-lined main strip, the partly pedestrianized **Via Savoia**, is the focus of the evening *passeggiata*, with its shops staying open late in summer. It holds a couple of sights: the curious, square and fortified-looking **church** (concerts are held outside in summer; check posters around town), and a little further up, the small **Museo del Mare**, though this is presently closed, and in any case the marine exhibits inside are unlikely to grab your attention.

A pleasant promenade backs the **beach**, which stretches east of town. Framed by the looming cliffs behind and overlooked by jagged slabs of rock, the wide, curving stretch of white sand is ideal for swimming and sunbathing, though it gets pretty congested in August, when getting into the water is an irresistible temptation.

A twenty-minute walk in the other direction, past the harbour, brings you to the point of **Capo San Vito** itself – a rocky and windswept plain adorned with a fenced-off lighthouse. For views you need to climb above the town (bear left on the way out to the lighthouse), up a steep road leading to the top of the high cliffs and looking down over the Golfo di Castellammare. The other local walk is east to the Riserva Naturale dello Zíngaro, a nature reserve, covered in more detail on p.366.

Eating and drinking

Via Savoia and the lungomare are lined with **bars**, ice-cream parlours and pizzerias, and there's no shortage of fish **restaurants** either, most on the pricey side. Things get impossibly busy in August and during the **Cous Cous Fest** (ⓦ www.couscousfest.it), which takes place over six days in late September and includes free samplings of dozens of versions of the dish, as well as nightly concerts in Piazza Santuario and a fireworks extravaganza on the last night at midnight. It's always worth booking during these periods, and restaurant queues are common. Most places stay open throughout the winter too.

Restaurants

Agorà Piazza Marinella 5 ☏ 0923.974.442. Always busy, this smart trattoria near the seafront sells pastas for €8–12, meat dishes for around €7, and fish for €10–16. The house speciality is *cassatelle Agorà*, fresh pasta stuffed with zucchini, pistachio and basil, served with mussels and shrimps. Booking essential. Closed Wed. Moderate–expensive.

Delfino Via Savoia 15 ☏ 0923.972.711. A pizzeria-trattoria on the main street and near the beach, with smoked-fish antipasti, fresh pasta, *couscous di pesce* and a short list of decent pizzas to eat in or take away. One of the cheaper places in town, it offers a €12 tourist menu. Inexpensive–moderate.

Il Giardino Via Mulino 18 ☏ 329.246.3342. While this place may be pricey, the food is generally good and the surroundings are pleasant, in a grassy garden planted with vines, figs and citrus trees. Pasta dishes, the risotto del giorno and *couscous di pesce* cost €14–15, mains are €12–18. Expensive.

Gna' Sara Via Duca degli Abruzzi 6 ☏ 0923.972.100. Great pizzas and seafood pastas at reasonable prices; the couscous is especially good. A popular place, with queues at peak times. Inexpensive–moderate.

Pocho Contrada Macari ☏ 0923.972.525. Small and casually chic, and with an unparalleled location overlooking the rocky coast 4km south of town – you eat on the panoramic terrace in summer – this place serves up inventive and toothsome dishes on a six-course set menu (€35 including drinks). The owner, Marilù, occasionally ends the evening with Sicilian songs. Closed lunchtime except Sun, also all Tues mid-Sept to mid-June. Expensive.

Thaam Via Duca degli Abruzzi 32–36 ☏ 0923.972.836. Elaborately decorated restaurant with a marked Tunisian influence, with *merguez*, kebabs and couscous (all €10) featuring alongside more mainstream Italian dishes. First courses cost €10–15, mains €12–16. The outdoor tables beneath a tent-like canopy fill fast, so book or arrive early. Expensive.

Bars

Caffè Pino Via Savoia. Also known as *Bar Cusenza*. Next to the church, this is the best place for breakfast, with friendly service, good cakes and pastries, and tables in the square – and is liable to get very busy. Try the *torrone* ice cream. Closed Mon in winter.

La Sirenetta Via Savoia, corner of Via Faro. *Gelateria* overlooking the beach, with a choice of twenty ice creams and a summer shaded terrace. Specialities are *gelsomino* (jasmine flower, summer only), *torrone* and *caldofreddo* (with hot chocolate sauce). Closed Nov–March.

Listings

Bike rental Bikes can be hired June–September from a stall behind the beach near the *Egitarso* hotel (☏ 347.308.3021; €2.50 per hour or €10 per day).

Boat excursions Between May and September boats run daily to Zíngaro and Scopello at 9.15am (☎334.251.3450; €20) and 10.15am (☎333.323.7900; €15), returning at 1.30pm. Ask at the tourist office about fishing trips.
Car rental Serse, Via Dogana 3B (☎0923.974.434).
Diving Contact Argonauta, based in the summer at the port (☎0923.621.020, ⊚www .argonauta-divingcenter.com).

Internet You can log on and make long-distance calls at Internet Point, Via di Bella Orazio 17, at the northern end of Via Savoia (summer daily 9am–2pm & 4pm–midnight; winter weekends only and reduced hours).
Scooter rental Auto Vesco, Via di Bella Orazio 20 (April–Oct; ☎338.877.9971; €30–40 per day).

Getting to Lo Zíngaro

The **northern entrance** to the isolated **Riserva Naturale dello Zíngaro** (for full details, see p.366) is 11km southeast of San Vito. Accessible by your own transport or on a boat trip from San Vito Lo Capo, it's also a fine walk, initially following the road along the lungomare from San Vito and across the flat headland, before winding up into the mountains. In the higher reaches, the views are exhilarating, with the surrounding scenery almost alpine in character – fir trees, flowers flanking the road, and the clank of bells from goats roaming the hillsides. Sadly, though, the road through this secluded and dramatic landscape offers few opportunities to descend to the alluringly deserted coves below.

The **access road** to the reserve is signposted just before the ruined Torre dell'Impiso, around a three-hour walk from San Vito. From the sign to the park entrance itself is about another 1km, following a gravel track and then a path, which runs down into the reserve, past the Tonnara dell'Uzzo. At the San Vito **entrance** (Ingresso Nord; daily April to mid-Sept 7am–8pm; mid-Sept to March 8am–4pm; €3; ☎800.116.616, ⊚www.riservazingaro.it), you'll find a car park and hiking information.

The beautiful little cove-beach below the entrance offers translucent water, with glorious peace and quiet all around – at least, whenever the first few little creeks here aren't inundated with bathers. Travel on for less crowded spots, or else take one of the higher paths for greater isolation. You can pick up a map of the various **trails** running through the reserve; Scopello is a ten-kilometre walk south from the San Vito entrance. Hikers should note that there are no shops, bars or restaurants along the road from San Vito, or in the park itself, though there's usually a refreshment stall at the park entrance, and that shade and shelter are only sporadically available. In short, come prepared.

The Égadi Islands

Moored off the western coast, the three **Égadi Islands** (Isole Égadi) are the easiest of Sicily's offshore islands to visit – which accounts for the summer crowds that swarm over **Favignana**, the nearest of the Égadis to the Sicilian mainland. The other islands are much less affected, however, and if you come out of season things are noticeably quieter everywhere.

Before the advent of tourism, the economic success of the islands was largely based on a historical relationship with the northern Italian city of Genova, whose sailors plied the trading routes on which the Égadis stood throughout the Middle Ages. The seal was formalized in the middle of the seventeenth century, when the Bourbon King Philip IV sold all the islands, in lieu of a debt, to Genoan businessmen. Then, as now, the major element in the local economy was the **tuna fish**, which congregate here to breed at the end of spring.

Getting there

Ferries (operated by Siremar ℡0923.545.455, Ⓦwww.siremar.it) and **hydrofoils** (operated by Siremar and Ústica Lines, ℡0923.873.813, Ⓦwww.usticalines.it) depart several times daily **from Trápani**. They're more frequent between June and September, and most frequent in July and August. They generally call at Favignana, Lévanzo and Maréttimo, in that order, though Lévanzo is sometimes the first stop, and some services don't run as far as Maréttimo.

Ferries depart from the Stazione Maríttima in Trápani, and hydrofoils from further east along Via A. Staiti; you can buy **tickets** at booths on the dockside. Ferries are less frequent than hydrofoils and take at least twice as long, but they're cheaper. One-way ferry tickets from Trápani to Favignana and Lévanzo cost around €6, and to Maréttimo around €10, less in low season; one-way hydrofoil tickets are around €7.50 and €16 respectively; all return tickets cost double. In summer, Siremar also runs fast ferries (*navi veloci*) to Favignana and Lévanzo, which may take half the time of a normal ferry, depending on the route.

Ústica Lines also operate a year-round hydrofoil service to the islands **from Marsala** and, in summer, from Ústica and Naples. See "Travel details" (p.419) for frequencies and journey times from Trápani and Marsala.

Channelled through the straits between the two main islands during their migrations around the Sicilian coast, they are systematically slaughtered in an age-old rite known as **La Mattanza**.

Favignana, only 15–30 minutes from Trápani by hydrofoil, is the biggest island and site of the main fishery. The Genovese link is most apparent in the island of **Lévanzo**, across the strait, which is named after a quarter in Genova and shelters the **Grotta del Genovese**, a cave in which a rich bounty of prehistoric cave paintings was discovered. These days, with the annual tourist influx, the greatest hope for peace and quiet lies in the furthest island, **Maréttimo**, whose rugged coasts are indented with a succession of coves, ideal for clean and secluded swimming. The island also offers a choice of **hikes** across its interior and along the rocky coasts.

You could easily see any of the islands as a **day-trip** from Trápani; seeing two on the same day is also feasible. If you want to stay longer, be warned that **accommodation** is extremely limited, and in summer you should phone ahead to reserve a room. It's certainly worth staying over, though you should also bear in mind that, in general, **prices** for rooms and food are higher than on the mainland.

Favignana

The main island, **FAVIGNANA**, has progressed over the years from tuna centre to prison, and now tourist resort. Shaped like a lopsided butterfly, the island is almost split in two, its narrow "waist" holding the port and most of the population. To the east lie Favignana's best swimming spots, the water accessible from a succession of rocks and inlets, while the western half of the island is only reachable along the southern coastal road, which tunnels through Favignana's sole hill, **Monte Santa Caterina** (300m). Its peak is topped by an abandoned Norman **castello**, floodlit at night, and reached by a crazy-paved stairway from the west side of town. The castle, though, is in such a parlous state and so full of rubbish that it's far nicer to follow the lower path over the mountain to a crest with views to Maréttimo. The path down the other side, however, is hard to follow and you may end up scrambling over walls and through fields to reach the road.

La Mattanza

Every May and June, for centuries, Favignana has witnessed the bloody spectacle of **La Mattanza**, the slaughter of the local tuna catch. Usually the killings take place two or three times a week, presided over by a *Rais* – a title handed down from the Arabs. The huge fish are surrounded, netted, impaled, dragged aboard and bludgeoned to death. Most of the meat is sold to the vast Japanese vessels that call in at fishing ports all over the Mediterranean; they transport the cargo back to Japan, where it's put into cans and re-exported back to Europe, although there are still a couple of small canning factories in the Trápani area. There's also a tuna artisan on Favignana itself, Alessandro Sammartano (at Favonia, Via Garibaldi 16, Favignana Town), who prepares *bottarga* (salted and dried tuna roe) and other traditional tuna products by hand.

In recent years the slaughter has become something of a tourist attraction, with local operators offering boat tours to get a glimpse of the action – check with the tourist office in Favignana for the various options.

The port, **FAVIGNANA TOWN**, is the focus of most of the tourist traffic. As the archipelago's only town, it holds the island's main services and best choice of accommodation and restaurants, but otherwise there's no particular reason to hang around. The only distinctive feature is the imposing building near the port, the **Palazzo Florio**. Now part of the town hall, this was built by Ignazio Florio, an entrepreneur who took over the islands in 1874 and revitalized the fisheries; there's a statue of him in nearby Piazza Europa. His tuna fishery, **Stabilimento Florio**, is similarly impressive, its vaulted nineteenth-century buildings a solid counterpoint across the bay. It is currently being restored and may reopen in 2008 as cultural and conference centre. Otherwise, all there is to do is window-shop in the many places selling "*tipici*" products – tinned tuna, of course, as well as *bottarga*, oil, local dried herbs, wine and bloody postcards of *la Mattanza*.

The **rest of the island** is tidily cultivated, pitted with square white houses built from **tufa** quarried from curious pits all over the island – an export that has historically provided Favignana with a second source of cash (after fishing). One of the old quarries, behind the town church by the decrepit chapel of Santa Anna, has been landscaped and turned into a quirky sunken garden.

You can swim at the beach near the town, but the sandy beach at **Lido Burrone**, on the island's south side, is better, featuring a friendly pizzeria-restaurant-bar that rents out parasols and sun-loungers. Otherwise, just follow the coast roads and plunge in off the rocks, or settle down on one of the tiny handkerchiefs of sand. Call in at **Cala Azzurra**, below the lighthouse at the island's eastern end, where there's a beautiful blue bay, but little sand, or, just north, the spectacular **Cala Rossa**, where you can swim off rocks at the base of towering tufa cliffs. Its name – Red Cove – is said to derive from the blood washed ashore after the Roman defeat of the Carthaginians in a fierce sea battle in 241 BC. The road to Cala Rossa in particular is noted for its tufa quarries – just before the cove itself is a huge quarry where stacks of tufa and unexcavated pillars rise high from the gloomy depths. On the other side of the mountain, the best beach is at **Cala Rotonda**, where, local legend would have it, Odysseus washed up before being attacked by the Cyclops.

Arrival, information and transport

From the port, you can see the dome of the church: aim for that and you'll reach the main square, Piazza Madrice, with the **tourist office** at no. 78

(Mon–Sat 9am–1pm & 4–8pm, Sun 9am–1pm; stays open till 10pm in Aug, closes earlier in low season, and usually closed Nov–Feb; ☎0923.921.647). Everything else is contained in the short streets between here and the nearby Piazza Europa.

The best way to **get around** the island is by bike, since the flat terrain and good road surfaces enable you to see the whole of Favignana in an afternoon. **Bike rental** shops are all over town, including down at the port – look for the words "*noleggio bici*". A **bus service** (June–Aug) leaves from down by the port on three routes: #1 to Cala Azzurra, #2 to Punta Sottile, #3 to the turn-off for Cala Rossa. Departures are roughly hourly during the day; tickets on board (€0.70). **Boat tours** of the island's offshore grottoes are offered down at the port, costing €35 per person including lunch for a full day (less for a two- or three-hour excursion) – there's always someone around in summer, but you may have to ask in town at other times.

Accommodation

Favignana's **hotels** are not cheap, but still get packed out in peak season. You can find bargain rates at the few places remaining open in winter. **Campsites** lie out of town, an easy bus ride or walk, and well signposted from the port; both are closed November–March.

Hotels

Approdo di Ulisse Cala Grande ☎0923.925.000, ⓦwww.aurumhotels.it. The pick of the out-of-town accommodation, a luxurious resort-style hotel close to the sea on the western tip of the island. It has cottage-style accommodation, tennis court, pool and disco. Closed Nov–March. ❽

Bouganville Via Cimabue 10 ☎0923.922.033, ⓦwww.albergobouganville.it. One of the cheaper hotel choices on the island, with decent rooms and a restaurant in the garden. It's on the southwestern edge of town: follow Via Diaz and Via Battisti from the centre. Closed Nov–March. ❻

Hotel delle Cave Contrada Torretta ☎0923.925.423, ⓦwww.hoteldellecave.it. Favignana's most striking accommodation is built on the lip of an abandoned quarry, with gardens and a restaurant inside the quarry itself. The structure is severely functional, but the rooms are full of designer features. Closed Nov–March. ❽

Quattro Rose Via Punta Marsala ☎0923.921.223, ⓦwww.hotel4rose.it. A few minutes south of town, and 300m from the beach at Lido Burrone, you'll find clean, air-conditioned rooms in a leafy garden. There's a nice restaurant, and at least half-board (€80 per person) is obligatory in Aug. Closed Nov–March. ❹

Villa Antonella Via Punta Marsala ☎0923.921.073, ⓦwww.egadi.com /villantonella. Next to *Quattro Rose*, this *affittacamere* has plain, good-value rooms, run by a friendly local family who can arrange to pick you up from the port. There's a restaurant, and a good-value self-catering apartment with its own terrace. ❹

Campsites

Camping Egad Contrada Arena ☎0923.921.555, ⓦwww.campingegad.it. A little over 1km east of town, and 500m from the beach at Lido Burrone, this has a range of accommodation, including rooms and igloo-type apartments sleeping four. Facilities include bar, restaurant, store, disco and scooter and bike hire, and there's transport to and from the port.

Miramare Località Costicella ☎0923.921.330, ⓦwww.villaggiomiramare.it. More expensive and much larger than Egad, this site 1km west of town has a grassy garden, playground, kids' club and a decent restaurant. Self-catering bungalows with verandas available, and there's a beach 50m away.

Eating and drinking

Piazza Madrice, Piazza Europa and the surrounding streets are where you'll find Favignana's **bars and restaurants**, but be warned: restaurant prices on the island tend to be high. Excellent slices of pizza, *schiacciata* and the like are sold at the bakery *Costanza* on Via Roma, just up the hill from Piazza Madrice, or you may prefer to **picnic** on the town beach. For picnic provisions, carry on up the hill to the SMA supermarket, where the deli counter has local ricotta and a good range of cheeses and hams. For ice cream and almond goodies try *Bar Albatros*, or join the locals sitting on rows of chairs either side of the street at *Grammático*, on Via Pilota di Garibaldi, just off Piazza Europa.

Restaurants

Amici del Mare Piazza Marina ☎0923.922.596. Good quality pasta and seafood dishes and some great antipasti, all within view of the harbour. Arrive early (or book) for one of the terrace tables. Also good for drinks and snacks. Moderate.

Arte Pizza Via Mazzini 16, off Piazza Madrice. You can pick up excellent pizzas here from the wood-fired oven. Inexpensive.

Pizzeria Da Salvador Via Nicotera. This family-run place serves good pizza as well as local specialities like couscous, and in summer has plenty of seating outside. Inexpensive.

La Tavernetta Piazza Madrice 54 ☎0923.921.639. Just across from the church, this place has good fish dishes, friendly service and decent prices. You can sit outside in summer. Moderate.

Listings

Airport transfer Siciltransfert (☎348.262.0089, ⓦwww.siciltransfert.it) arranges transport direct to Favignana from Palermo (€37 per person) and Trápani (€24) airports, including minibus and hydrofoil crossing.

Banks Banca Nuova, Piazza Europa, and Banco di Sicilia, Piazza Madrice, both have ATMs.

Bike and scooter hire Isidoro, at Via Mazzini 40 ☎347.323.3058, stays open all year; for a bike, expect to pay about €3 a day, or €5 in high season. Scooters are around €20 a day, €35 in Aug.

Ferries and hydrofoils Siremar ☎0923.921.368, ⓦwww.siremar.it; Ústica Lines ☎0923.873.813, ⓦwww.usticalines.it.

Internet Elyos, Piazza Madrice 37 (Mon–Sat 9am–1pm & 3–7pm). You can also log on at the bar-restaurant *Amici del Mare* (see above).

Pharmacy Dottore Abramo, Piazza Europa (English-speaking); Rizza, Piazza Madrice.

Post office Via Marconi 2 (Mon–Fri 8am–1.30pm, Sat 8am–12.30pm).

Taxi ☎347.479.6745.

Lévanzo

LÉVANZO, 4km north of Favignana, is the smallest of the three main islands. Most of it is used to pasture sheep and goats, and, with its turquoise seas and white houses, it has very much the feel of a Greek island. Its population is concentrated in **LÉVANZO TOWN**, little more than a cluster of square houses and holiday homes around a tiny port, where you'll find the island's two hotel-restaurants and a couple of bars.

The coastline is rocky and largely inaccessible, but you can get around on foot by following the dirt paths along the shore and over the hills. Following the only road twenty minutes west of the port, you'll come to a rocky spire sticking out of the sea – the Faraglione – beyond which a rocky path leads north up the coast. On the island's northwest coast, on a slope overlooking the sea, the **Grotta del Genovese** is the main attraction for most visitors, famed for its prehistoric cave paintings.

The walls of the cave display some remarkable Paleolithic **incised drawings**, discovered in 1949, as well as later Neolithic pictures; they're mostly of animals, and are between six and ten thousand years old. Despite their age, the evocative

All visits to the **Grotta del Genovese** (ⓦwww.grottadelgenovese.it) have to be arranged through the official custodian, Signor Natale Castiglione, who lives at Via Calvario 11 (ⓣ0923.924.032 or 339.741.8800), above the quay. Rates are negotiable, depending on how many are in your party, but you shouldn't have to pay more than €15 each either by jeep or by boat. **By boat**, the round trip will take about two hours, usually departing at 10.30am and (if there's enough demand) 3.30pm. Note that the smallest swell may be enough to make it impossible for the boat to pull into the narrow rocky disembarkation point. You can also extend the tour by opting for the round-island trip (€20), taking about three hours including a swimming stop.

  By jeep, the two-hour round trip is roughly 10km, following an inland route through the valley in the centre of the island. The fairly difficult descent on foot to the grotto from where the jeep stops is not recommended for anyone infirm. You might negotiate a discount jeep fare if you feel like walking back. Booking for either route is essential. Winter tours generally take place only on weekends when the conditions are right – again, always telephone ahead.

drawings retain their impact, drawn by prehistoric man in an attempt to harness and influence the power of nature: one lovely picture of a deer near the entrance dates from when the island was still connected to the Sicilian mainland. The later Neolithic sketches are easy to pick out too; less well drawn, more stylized representations of men and even of tuna fish and a dolphin.

Many other grottoes on the island were formerly used by locals to hide from the corsairs who regularly called on raiding missions. To see a few, you might bargain for a **boat rental** at the port.

If you fancy stretching your legs in the island's lovely **interior**, walk west along the road from the port (towards the Faraglione), turning right up the steep tarmacked road. That becomes a stone and dirt track once it reaches the upper part of the valley. If you stick to it, it takes around an hour to reach the lighthouse at **Capo Grosso** at the northeastern point of the island.

On your way to the cape, you can swim at the lovely white **Tramontana bay**: just before you reach an old metal gate, a track leads down the red-earth mountainside, ending in an acute concrete slope, which you can just about slither down, though scrambling back up is hard work.

Tracing the coast eastwards from Lévanzo Town, you can reach **Cala Minnola** in about fifteen minutes – a lovely rocky cove ideal for swimming.

Practicalities

The **port** is just below the island's only road, Via Calvario. In summer both Siremar and Ústica Lines have ticket booths at the port; in winter, they move into the town, out of reach of stormy waves (precise locations vary from year to year). **Boat excursions** round the island are advertised here in summer.

There are just two **hotels** with a total of 25 rooms, so booking ahead is advisable; ask around, though, and you may find someone who'll rent you a **room**. Closest to the port, next to the bar, the *Paradiso* (ⓣ0923.924.080, ⓦwww.albergoparadisolevanzo.it; ⑤) has a terrace-restaurant and marvellous sea views from the en-suite, air-conditioned rooms. Just behind, the *Pensione Dei Fenici* (ⓣ0923.924.083; ⑤) is a little fancier and has the same good views. In summer, both hotels will usually only accept guests on half-board terms (respectively €85 and €90 per person), though as the only other options for food on the island are two bars, an *alimentari* and a bakery, this is no hardship. In any case, the food is good at both places.

Maréttimo

Wildest and furthest out from Trápani, **MARÉTTIMO** was claimed by Samuel Butler, in his *The Authoress of the Odyssey*, as the original Ithaca, home of Odysseus. Even more far-fetched, Butler also thought that Homer himself was the princess Nausicaä of ancient Trápani. These theories aside, there are compelling reasons to come to Maréttimo. Its spectacular fragmented coastline is pitted with rocky coves sheltering hideaway beaches, and numerous walks can take you all over the island. Even in high season, you're likely to have much of Maréttimo to yourself, as few tourists can be bothered to visit a place with limited accommodation and no more than half a dozen trattorias. That said, there are signs of heightened interest these days in the shape of a sprinkling of new holiday homes, while EU money has gone towards paving a couple of sections of track. However, such "improvements" are still fairly low-key and, at least for now, the island retains its air of being far off the beaten track.

Arrival, information and boat tours

There's no **information** office on Maréttimo, but you can gather details of accommodation, food, itineraries and transport from the website Ⓦwww .marettimonline.it. Maréttimo's main street, Via Umberto, is about a minute's walk from the harbour where the ferries and hydrofoils dock. It holds a **bank** with an ATM, a Siremar **ticket agency** and an Ústica Lines agency in a little shop just up from Piazza Umberto. Other services include a pharmacy, an *alimentari*, bakery and fresh fish shop.

Boat trips can be organized from *Rosa dei Venti* (see below). Various options are possible: around the island to Cala Bianca for swimming costs €12 per person, or the same with a picnic, including home-cured fish, and local cheeses and wines is €25 per person. On either, you can be left at a cove to swim and be collected an hour or so later.

Accommodation

Maréttimo offers little choice of **accommodation**, with a couple of B&Bs and a few holiday residences for weekly rents. It also holds a few **rented rooms**, for which you'll have to ask around in the bars and restaurants, as places are rarely advertised. It's always best to book before you come.

I Delfini Via Umberto 34 ℡0923.923.137 or 339.239.9867, Ⓦwww.idelfinimarettimo. it. Central B&B with good sea views on one side. Rooms are simple but comfortable, and there's a roof terrace. No credit cards. ❺

Maréttimo Residence Via Telégrafo 3 ℡0923.923.202, Ⓦwww.marettimoresidence.it. Small resort-cluster of cottages above a stony beach south of the main port. Demand is high and in August you'll have to stay for a week. Closed Nov to mid-March. ❼

Rosa dei Venti Punta Simone 4 ℡0923.923.249 or 368.768.1571, Ⓦwww.isoladimarettimo.it. As well as operating various other tourist activities, this outfit has fourteen self-catering apartments dispersed around the island, also available for short stays. ❷

Exploring the island

As you pull into port and explore its few streets, **MARÉTTIMO TOWN** appears almost North African in character, with its flat-roofed cube houses with blue shutters and painted tiles, and alleys full of tumbling bougainvillea. There's one main street, a little square and church, and a second harbour, the fishing port, just along from the main harbour.

Two of the island's most popular **bathing** spots are conveniently close, one near the main harbour, one near the fishing harbour, but you'll find other places

To the Case Romane

Maréttimo's simplest walk takes you to some old **Roman defensive works**, which are still in pretty good condition. Climb up the road to the side of *Caffè Tramontana* and, at the top, scout around to the left and then right to find the signpost for the start of the walk. The remains are half an hour on, sitting next to a small and dilapidated church that shows marked Arab characteristics but is thought to have been built by Byzantine monks in the twelfth century.

To Cala Sarde and Cala Nera

Follow the road south of Maréttimo port, turning inland after about 1km where the path divides. There's a steep climb, with the town's cemetery below you, rising to about 300m. After about half an hour, you'll pass a pine forest and a small outhouse, looking out on views towards Tunisia; below is the **Cala Sarde**, a small bay reachable along a smaller path to the left in another half an hour.

Instead of descending to the bay, continue for about an hour on the main path along the island's rocky west coast. You'll pass a lighthouse and a route down to **Cala Nera**, where you can swim off the rocks in perfect isolation.

To the castle at Punta Troia

This walk follows the footpath all the way to the northeastern tip of the island, a hike that should take you around three hours; you'll need a head for heights in certain stretches. Go past the fishing harbour with the sea on your right, and keep to the coast along the path for about ten minutes, until the terrace wall on your left stops. When a sign here ("Castello Punta Troia") points to the left, cut up to find the main path on a small spur above you. This stretches along the whole length of the island about 100m above the sea, ending at some concrete steps that descend to a lovely secluded beach and the foot of the **castle**, perched on an impregnable rocky crag. This precipitous fortification was originally built by the Saracens, enlarged by Roger II, and further extended by the Spanish in the seventeenth century, when it became a prison, and acquired a dire reputation for cruelty.

on the way to destinations further afield – at Cala Sarde and Cala Nera on the south coast, or at the Saracen castle at the northeastern point of the island (see box). None of the walks is particularly onerous, though you might have to scramble at times – and you should take water with you in the summer if you're planning to stay away from the village for any length of time (around three litres a day per person minimum).

Alternatively, you could take a three-hour **boat tour** of the island (a "*giro dell'isola*") from the main harbour, which allows you to see Maréttimo's entire rocky coastline and dive into otherwise inaccessible waters that are clean and clear and a joy for snorkellers. You'll doubtless be offered a tour on arrival at the port; expect to pay around €12 per person.

Eating and drinking

Maréttimo offers a reasonable range of **eating** options, though prices are a little higher than on the mainland, given the cost of shipping in ingredients. Not all the places listed below stay open throughout the year, but there's always something open. There's a **supermarket** on Via Garibaldi, off the main drag.

Baia del Sole Piazza Umberto. Next to the Siremar office on the main road, this bar has a few tables and excellent ice cream and granitas.

Il Pirata Via Scalo Vecchio ℡ 0923.923.027. *Couscous di pesce* and *pasta con le sarde* are among the specialities in this pleasant trattoria by the fishing harbour. Moderate.

La Scaletta Via Telegrafo. A good spot for an ice cream, overlooking the main port.

Il Timone Via Garibaldi ℡ 0923.923.142. A smart little trattoria just off the northern end of the main street, with tables outside. Try

the fresh pasta, or fish-stuffed ravioli. Closed Oct–Easter. Moderate.

Caffè Tramontana Via Campi. On the road above the fishing harbour, people gather here for the superb sea views. Snacks available.

Il Veliero Via Umberto ℡ 0923.923.274. This trattoria has good *cucina casalinga* and a summer cane-and-fishing-trap-bedecked terrace by the harbour. Firsts, such as pasta with squid ink or tuna roe, cost around €12, mains aren't much more. Closed Nov. Moderate.

Mózia and around

Fifteen kilometres down the coast from Trápani, the uninhabited **Stagnone Islands** (Isole dello Stagnone) have been mostly given over to salt extraction since the fifteenth century. On the mainland opposite, several windmills still stand near the surviving **saltpans**, which form a crystalline patchwork between Trápani and Marsala. Offshore, the long, thin Ísola Grande shelters the only one of the Stagnone group that you can visit, San Pantaleo, in the middle of a shallow lagoon that is now the year-round scene of **windsurfing, kitesurfing and sailing**. You can hire the equipment from shacks strung along the coast road – for example Kite Loose (℡ 0923.745.755 or 329.876.7111) – for around €60–70 a day, and tuition is offered. Other outlets rent **canoes** for around €6 for half a day, allowing you to weave around the saltpans.

The big cultural attraction hereabouts, however, is on the isle of San Pantaleo, which holds the site of the ancient Phoenician settlement of Motya (or **Mózia** in Italian). Along with Palermo and Solus (Solunto), Motya was one of the three main Phoenician bases in Sicily, settled some time during the eighth century BC and completely razed to the ground by Dionysius I in 397 BC. It's the only one of the three sites that wasn't subsequently built over, though it remained undiscovered until the seventeenth century, and wasn't properly excavated until Joseph "Pip" Whitaker (amateur archeologist and member of one of the marsala wine dynasties) bought the island in the late nineteenth century and started to dig it up.

You reach the island site and its archeological museum by a short **ferry** ride from the mainland. Although the linguistic link between the archipelago's name (Stagnone) and our "stagnant" is not entirely coincidental, that doesn't deter some visitors from wading into the lagoon on the mainland side and crossing to Mózia in beachwear – the island museum, at least, has had enough and won't allow entry to anyone who's not properly clothed.

The island: the remains of Motya

Flat, cultivated and only 2.5km in circumference, **MOTYA** is one of the most manageable of Sicily's ancient sites, with the unique Phoenician ruins spread across the whole island. You could circle the perimeter in an hour or so, but it's more enjoyable to make a day of it and bring a picnic. A little kiosk by the island jetty sells water and cold drinks (summer only).

You buy **entrance tickets** (daily: 9am–12.45pm & 2–7pm, or 3–6pm in winter; €6) on the way up the path to Joseph Whitaker's house – once incongruously furnished in Edwardian style and now converted to use as the

Museo Whitaker. Outside stands an aristocratic bust of its founder, "Giuseppe" Whitaker, with a shaded picnic area under the trees nearby. You might as well call in to the museum first to see the finds from the island. Its cool rooms are packed with a beautiful collection of jewellery, arrowheads, terracotta figurines and domestic artefacts, with the earliest pieces dating from the eighth century BC. Pride of place goes to the magnificent fifth-century BC marble sculpture of a youth, *Il Giovinetto di Mozia*, sensual and self-assured in his pose. The identity of the subject is unknown, but he was likely to have been a high-ranking official, suggested by the subtle indentations round his head, indicating some kind of crown or elaborate headwear.

The remains on the ground start immediately outside the museum. In front and 100m to the left is the **Casa dei Mosaici**, two houses containing some faded black-and-white mosaics made from sea pebbles. One, probably belonging to a patrician, shows animal scenes; the other, thought to be a craftsman's, yielded numerous shards of pottery. Further along the path you come to the **cothon**, a small artificial boat dock built within the ancient town's walls and similar in style to a much larger one at Carthage itself.

The other way, back past the museum, leads along the rough tracks, set amongst flowering cacti and vine plantations, that were once the city's main thoroughfares, most of which end at one of the gates on Motya's formerly well-fortified shore. The once-strong **north gate**, now a ragged collection of steps and ruined walls – up beyond the museum and right – lies at the head of a causeway built by the Phoenicians in the sixth century BC to connect the island with the mainland (and a necropolis) at Birgi, 7km to the north. The road is still there, although these days it's submerged under the water. Left along the shore from the gate is the **Tophet** burial ground. Most of the information about day-to-day life in Motya has come from here, the sanctuary revealing a number of urns containing the ashes of animals sacrificed to the Phoenician gods (chiefly Baal Hammon) and of children, probably stillborn or who died of natural causes. A remarkable series of inscribed votive stele from the Tophet is on display in the museum. Just inland of the gate, the **Cappiddazzu** site shows the foundations of a large building, probably a temple, while between gate and Cappiddazzu is a Punic **industrial zone** that was dedicated to the production of pottery and ceramics. This was where the famous marble sculpture was found, probably hidden by the city's inhabitants as the Greeks stormed the island.

The saltpans and salt museum

Glistening in the shallows between Trápani and Marsala lie a series of **saltpans** that have been worked since Phoenician times. Barechested men toil with shovels, carting full wheelbarrows across from the pans to a rising conveyor belt that dumps two-metre-high mounds of white salt along the banks. At different times of the day, as the light changes, there's a pink tint to the saltpans, while Maréttimo rises in the distance through the haze. On the mainland, just opposite Mózia, one of three windmills has been turned into a showroom, the **Salina Ettore e Infersa** (April–Oct daily 9am–6.30pm; call ☎0923.966.936 for winter visits). It's free to enter if you just want to browse the locally produced foods and crafts, or you can pay €4 for an instructive guided tour of the whole salt-making process.

Practicalities

From Marsala, take the local AST bus from Piazza del Pópolo to the Mózia ferry-landing; in summer a special bus, Linea D, runs far more frequently.

Return buses are on a similar schedule; a much reduced service in either direction operates on a Sunday. **From Trápani**, you'll have to take the bus or the train first to Marsala.

Ferries out to the island are run by Arini & Pugliese (☎347.779.0218). A steady flow of visitors ensures that there's usually a ferry waiting (daily: April–Oct 9am–6.30pm; Nov–March 9.30am–3pm); tickets for the ten-minute crossing cost €3 return. **Parking** is available near the two embarkation points. One of these lies 500m along the shore from the **bar-restaurant** *Mamma Caura*, by the windmill and saltpans, where you can eat well, and they also offer **rooms** (⑥) and canoes to rent.

Marsala

When the island-city of Motya had been put to the sword by the Syracusans, the survivors founded Lilybaeum (modern **MARSALA**), 10km to the south. The main city of the Phoenicians in Sicily, and the only one to resist the Greek push westwards, Lilybaeum finally succumbed to Rome in 241 BC, and not long after was used as a springboard for an attack against the Carthaginian heartland itself. The town's position at Sicily's western tip later made it the main Saracenic base on the island, and it was renamed Marsah Ali, Arabic for the "port of Ali", son-in-law of the Prophet, from which its modern name derives.

The town scored a place in modern Italian history for its role in the saga of the **Risorgimento**, the struggle for Italian unity in the nineteenth century. It

MARSALA

Capo
Boeo

Insula Romana
(Lilybaeum)

Municipal
Gardens

VIA DEI GASPERI

VIA TRÁPANI

Ⓐ & Mózia

Ⓑ & Trápani

Wine
shops

Museo
Archeológico

VIA LUNGOMARE BOEO

VIA VITTÓRIO VENETO

VIALE PIAVE

VIALE C. BATTISTI

VIALE A. DIAZ

PIAZZA G. MARCONI

VIA A. LINCOLN

PIAZZA
DELLA
VITTÓRIA

VIA XIX LUGLIO

VIA FRISELLA

CORSO GRAMSCI

VIA PASCASINO

VIALE N. SAURO

Porta Nuova

San Giovanni

VIALE ISONZO

VIA A. DIAZ

VIA GARRAFFA

PIAZZA
CARMINE

VIA XI MAGGIO

Museo
degli Arazzi

@ Library

Complesso San Pietro

VIA PIPITONE

PIAZZA
CASTELLO

VIA LUNGOMARE BOEO

VIA SIBILLA

VIA TIBRILLA

VIA DELLE SIRENE

PIAZZA DELLA
REPUBBLICA

Pinacoteca

Chiesa Madre

ⓘ

PIAZZA
MATTEOTTI

VIA AMENDOLA

Porta Garibaldi

VIA ABELE DAMIANI

PIAZZA
DEL POPOLO

VIA BOEO

VIA SCIPIONE
L'AFRICANO

VIA DEL MILLE

VIA GARIBALDI

VIA ALAGNA

VIA M. NUCCIO

VIA DELLO SBARCO

VIA ROMA

Mazara del Vallo

VIA CAMBINI

Ⓔ

VIA F. FAZIO

C. CALATAFIMI

PIAZZA
PIEMONTE E
LOMBARDO

BARS
Bar della Vittoria   2
E&N   4

ACCOMMODATION
Baglio Vajarassa   A
Hotel Carmine   D
Centrale   C
Garden   E
Villa Favorita   B

RESTAURANTS
Al Capo   1
Divino Rosso   3
Trattoria Garibaldi   5
Juparana   7
Nashville   6

Hydrofoil
Dock

LUNGOMARE
MEDITERRANEO

VIA MAZZINI

VIA CRISPI

VIALE F. PIZZO

PIAZZA
F. PIZZO

Train
Station

N

0   100 m

▼ *Égadi Islands*   ▼ *Stabilimento Florio*

was here that Garibaldi kicked off his campaign to drive out the Bourbons, in the company of his red-shirted "Thousand". Until a planned Garibaldi museum on Marsala's eastern seafront (on Via Scipione Africano) gets round to opening, memorials to the swashbuckling freedom-fighter are confined to a few statues and street names, and the nearby Porta Garibaldi, at the end of Via Garibaldi, which recalls the hero's entry into the town. Local enthusiasts clad in red shirts parade through the gate each year on May 11, in commemoration of the exploits of the "Thousand".

Arrival and information

Trains to Marsala, from Trápani in particular, are quicker and more frequent than buses. The **train station** is at the southeastern edge of town on Via A. Fazio, a fifteen-minute walk from the centre. **Buses** arrive centrally at Piazza del Pópolo (also known as Piazza Marconi), near Porta Garibaldi. **Hydrofoil** services to and from the Égadi Islands are operated by Ústica Lines (☎348.357.9863) at the harbour, fifteen minutes' walk from the centre – you can buy tickets on the dockside.

There's a **tourist office** at Via XI Maggio 100, off Piazza Repubblica near the Chiesa Madre (Mon–Sat 8am–7.50pm, may open Sun; ☎0923.714.097). You'll find a **post office** on Via Garibaldi, and a **bank** with an ATM, the Banco di Sicilia, at Via XI Maggio 83, plus others along Via Roma. The library on Via XI Maggio has cheap **Internet** access (Mon–Fri 9am–noon, also Tues & Thurs 3.30–5.30pm).

Accommodation

Marsala holds little budget **accommodation**, though it does offer a fine selection of mid- and upper-range hotels, any of which make a nice base for exploring the region.

Baglio Vajarassa Contrada Spagnola ☎0923.968.628, ⓦwww.bagliovajarassa.com. You'll need a car to stay at this old manor house, 6km north of town on the coastal SP21 to Mózia. Just four well-kept rooms with antique furnishings are available, and hearty local meals and home-made produce to take away are on offer too. ④

Hotel Carmine Piazza Cármine 16 ☎0923.711.907, ⓦwww.hotelcarmine.it. Very central, Marsala's most stylish hotel combines modernity with antique trimmings. Spacious rooms have exposed brickwork and wood or tiled floors, some with balconies, some overlooking the internal garden. ⑥

Centrale Via Salinisti 19 ☎0923.951.777, ⓦwww .hotelcentralemarsala.it. Plain but comfortable en-suite rooms with a/c and minibars, arranged around a courtyard. The hotel has a quiet location in the old town, and there's parking. Breakfast is in a nearby bar. ④

Garden Via Gambini 36 ☎0923.982.320, ⓦwww .albergogardenmarsala.it. The cheapest hotel in town, located behind the train station, is not great, but it's modern and clean enough. It only has nine rooms (five with bathroom), so ring ahead. No credit cards. ③

Villa Favorita Via Favorita 27 ☎0923.989.100, ⓦwww.villafavorita.com. This beautiful secluded villa on the outskirts of town is set in its own gardens and has a pool and charming restaurant. Book in advance since the value-for-money prices mean it's often full. It's 2km north of the centre (and signposted). ⑥

The Town

Marsala's town centre is a predominantly Baroque assortment of buildings, though there are hints of the older town's layout in the narrow, largely traffic-free streets around the central **Piazza della Repubblica**. The elegance of the square is due to its two eighteenth-century buildings: the arcaded **Palazzo**

▲ The Florio Winery at Marsala

Comunale, and the **Chiesa Madre** – dedicated to San Tommaso di Canterbury, patron saint of Marsala – from which four statues peer loftily down. The church's large but rather disappointing interior has a few Gagini sculptures.

Behind the Duomo, at Via Garraffa 57, the sole display at the **Museo degli Arazzi** (Tues–Sat 9am–1pm & 4.30–6pm, Sun 9.30am–1pm; €2.50) is a series of eight enormous hand-stitched wool and silk tapestries depicting the capture

The making of marsala wine

The Baglio Anselmi, which houses Marsala's archeological museum, is one of a number of old *bagli*, or warehouses, conspicuous throughout this wine-making region. Many are still used in the making of the famous dessert wine that carries the town's name. It was an Englishman, John Woodhouse, who first exploited the commercial potential of **marsala wine**, when he visited the town in 1770. Woodhouse soon realized that, like port, the local wine could travel for long periods without going off, when fortified with alcohol. Others followed: Ingham, Whitaker, Hopps and many more whose names can still be seen on some of the warehouse doors. Interestingly, it was the English presence in Marsala that persuaded Garibaldi to launch his campaign here rather than Sciacca (his first choice), judging that the Bourbon fleet wouldn't dare to interfere so close to Her Majesty's commercial concerns.

Marsala owes much of its current prosperity to the marketing of its wine, which is still a thriving industry, though no longer in British hands. You can visit some of the *bagli* and sample the stuff for free: try the **Cantina Montalto** (Mon–Sat 9am–noon & 3.30–6pm), on Lungomare Mediterraneo, to the south of town beyond the port. Call to arrange a free guided tour (℡0923.969.667) – though the samplings of five wines accompanied by bruschetta and olives costs €6. Enthusiasts can also visit an **Enomuseum** (same times; free) at Contrada Berbaro (3km along the road to Mazara del Vallo), where you can look over the old apparatus and techniques for wine-making. Otherwise, you'll find marsala or the sweeter *marsala all'uovo* (mixed with egg yolks) in every bar and restaurant in town.

of Jerusalem. Made in Brussels in the sixteenth century, they were the gift of the Spanish ambassador, who doubled as the archbishop of Messina, and are beautifully rich, in burnished red, gold and green. Threading up from Piazza della Repubblica, Via XI Maggio is lined with smart shops and *palazzi* with pretty courtyards, and it also holds the **Complesso San Pietro** (Tues–Sat 9am–1pm & 4–8pm; €2), a fifteenth-century monastery now fully restored as a cultural centre, which contains the town library, a courtyard for open-air performances and a café-bar. Further up, a left turn leads into Piazza del Cármine, where another religious house, originally a fourteenth-century convent, has been stylishly renovated to hold the **Pinacoteca Comunale** (Tues–Sun 10am–1pm & 6–8pm, or 5–7pm in winter; free). Visitors can enjoy a good collection of art and regular exhibitions – mostly contemporary and with local connections.

At the far end of Via XI Maggio, through the eighteenth-century **Porta Nuova**, Piazza della Vittória has a gate into the municipal gardens and a bar where you can sit and admire the austere Art Deco front of the Cine Impero, so out of keeping with the Baroque arch opposite. Beyond the piazza lies **Capo Boeo**, the westernmost point of Sicily that was the first settlement of the survivors of annihilated Motya. All the town's major antiquities are concentrated here, including the old **Insula Romana**, closed to the public at present, but normally accessible from Via Vittorio Véneto. The site contains all that's been excavated so far of the city of Lilybaeum, though most of it is third-century BC Roman, as you might guess from the presence of a *vomitarium*, lodged in the most complete section of the site – the **edificio termale**, or bathhouse. There's some good mosaicwork here: a chained dog at the entrance and, much better, a richly coloured **hunting scene** in the atrium, showing a stag being savaged by a wild beast.

From Piazza della Vittoria, Viale N. Sauro leads to the church of **San Giovanni**, under which is a grotto reputed to have been inhabited by the sibyl

Lilibetana, endowed with paranormal gifts. There's another slice of mosaic here, and a well whose water is meant to impart second sight. A pilgrimage takes place every June 24.

The Museo Archeológico

Beyond the church, one of the stone-vaulted warehouses that line the promenade contains the **Museo Archeológico** (daily 9am–6pm; €3), mostly dedicated to a very skeletal but still surprisingly well-preserved warship from the classical period. Displayed in a heat- and humidity-regulated environment, it ranks as the only extant *liburnian*, a specifically Phoenician or **Punic warship**, probably sunk during the First Punic War in the great sea battle off the Égadi Islands that ended Carthage's rule of the waves. It was discovered in 1971 and brought here after eight years of underwater surveying by a British team working under the archeologist Honor Frost. Originally 35m long, nearly 5m wide and rowed by 68 oarsmen, the vessel has been the source of much detailed information on the period, including what the crew ate and the stimulants they chewed to keep awake. Scattered about lie ranks of amphorae and anchors, and other items found in or around the ship, plus photographs and explanations (in Italian and English) of the ship's retrieval from the sea.

On the right-hand side of the building is displayed a medley of archeological finds from various sites hereabouts, both on land and sea. Prize exhibit is a marble torso dredged up from the sea in 2005, the **Venus of Lilybaeum**: comparable in style to the more famous Venus Landolina in Siracusa, it's probably a Roman copy of a Hellenistic statue of the second century BC. Other items include more mundane ceramics from the Punic tophet on Motya and other ancient necropolises in the neighbourhood, a good Roman mosaic and some colourful examples of Italian and North African pottery.

Eating and drinking

In the centre of Marsala at least, which empties of life after 9pm, **restaurants** can be hard to come by, but you'll eat well and relatively cheaply at the ones listed below. The couple of **bars** in Piazza della Repubblica are good for a *tè freddo alla pesca* (cold peach tea), accompanied by earnest discussion of lottery numbers – otherwise try the places listed below.

For general groceries, there's a lively daily **market** just inside the Porta Garibaldi, spilling over into the adjacent Piazza del Pópolo. To sample some **marsala wine**, visit either the *Enoteca Sombrero*, Via Garibaldi 32, or one of two adjacent *enoteca*-souvenir shops in Via Lungomare Boeo, by the archeological museum.

Restaurants

Al Capo Via Lungomare Boeo 40 ☎0923.956.872. In a restored warehouse near the Museo Archeológico, this makes a handy pre- or post-museum lunch stop. Try the fresh *busiate* with swordfish and aubergine. There are pizzas in the evenings and fish couscous on winter weekends. Closed Tues off-season. Moderate.

Divino Rosso Largo di Girólamo. Excellent pizzeria and wine bar where you can sit outside opposite a seventeenth-century *palazzo*. You can snack on cheeses, cold meats, panini and salads, or go for a range of tasty pizzas (€5–7). There's also a fantastic range of wines. Closed daytime. Inexpensive.

Trattoria Garibaldi Piazza Addolorata 5 ☎0923.953.006. Cosy, upmarket trattoria in the centre. Fish and couscous are the specialities, though you'll spend less if you choose grilled meat. Closed Sat lunch & Sun eve. Moderate.

Juparana Piazza F. Pizzo 12. This sleek bar-restaurant near the station is popular with office-workers at lunchtime, and makes a great stop if you want something fast, filling and nourishing, including salads, *arancini* and pasta. Prices are slightly higher in the evening, when you eat upstairs and a full range of antipasti, pasta dishes (€8–10) and mains (€9–12) are available. Closed Wed eve. Inexpensive–moderate.

Nashville Piazza F. Pizzo 24 ☎ 0923.951.826. Very nice pizzas (€4–6) served on a summer terrace in the square, and a standard Sicilian menu that won't break the bank, with meat and fish dishes for €10–13, and tourist menus for €10.50 (meat) and €13 (fish). Inexpensive–moderate.

Bars

E&N Via XI Maggio 130. This classy *pasticceria* and *gelateria* has a small courtyard and a selection of snacks. Closed Wed.

Bar della Vittoria Piazza della Vittoria. Good spot outside the Porta Nuova for a sightseeing pause by day or a beer or ice cream after dinner.

Mazara del Vallo

The North African element in Sicily's cultural melange is at its strongest in the major fishing port of **MAZARA DEL VALLO**, 22km and a thirty-minute train or bus ride down the coast from Marsala. Under the Muslims, Mazara was one of Sicily's most prosperous towns and capital of the biggest of the three administrative districts, or *walis*, into which the island was divided – hence the "del Vallo" tag. The first Sicilian city to be taken by the Arabs, and the last they surrendered, Mazara's prosperity lasted for 250 years, coinciding with the height of Arab power in the Mediterranean. Count Roger's anxiety to establish a strong Norman presence in this Muslim powerbase ensured that Mazara's importance lasted long after his conquest of the city in 1087, and it didn't give up its rank as provincial capital until Trápani took over in 1817.

The Arab links have revived since the port became the prime Sicilian destination for Tunisian immigrants flocking across the sea to work in the vast

Campsite ▼

fishing fleet – one of Italy's biggest. Indeed, wandering through Mazara's casbah-like backstreets, there are moments when you could imagine yourself to be in North Africa, passing Tunisian shops and a café plastered with pictures of the Tunisian president, and Arab music percolating through small doorways. For the visitor, the attraction of Mazara is its profusion of fine churches in a slowly reviving – though far from genteel – old town. The tree-shaded lungomare and seafront gardens add another facet to its character, and with a row of sea-view restaurants, Mazara is one of the few towns in the west to make the most of its coastal location.

Arrival and information

Buses stop at Via Salemi, either outside the **train station** or 200m up at Piazza Matteotti. Drivers will find **parking** spots on Lungomare Mazzini. Ústica Lines runs **fast ferries** in summer for Pantelleria from the port (see "Travel details", for frequency); tickets are sold at the agency at Via Molo Caito 55 (℡0923.941.116).

The main **tourist office** is in the old part of town in Piazza S. Veneranda (Mon–Sat 7.45am–2.15pm, Wed also 2.45–6.15pm, Sun in summer 9am–noon; ℡0923.941.727), and there's also a Pro Loco in a gift shop at Via XX Settembre 5 (Mon–Sat & first Sun of month 9am–1pm & 4–8pm; ℡0923.944.610). **Banks** with ATMs can be found on Piazza Mokarta and up Corso Umberto I.

Accommodation

Mazara holds a small but varied array of **accommodation**, adequate for a night's stay. The local **campsite**, *Sporting Club* (℡0923.947.230, Ⓦwww .sportingclubvillage.com; closed Oct–March), at Località Bocca Arena, a few kilometres out of town (signposted from the lungomare), is resort-like, with grassy pitches and good facilities.

Foresteria San Michele Arcángelo
℡0923.906.565, Ⓦwww.foresteriasanmichele
.com. Very plain but clean and quiet rooms are available in this old-town convent annexed to San Michele church. You probably won't see any sign of the ten nuns who are resident here. No single rooms. Breakfast €4. Closed Nov to mid-March. ❷
Hopps Hotel Via G. Hopps 29 ℡0923.946.133, Ⓦwww.hoppshotel.it. Large resort-style three-star centred on a palm-fringed pool, five minutes' walk

down the lungomare from the public gardens. Rooms are spacious if a bit dated, and breakfast is by the pool. All in all good value for what you get, though poolside entertainments in summer can be noisy. ❺
🏃 **Nosteon** Via Plebiscito 9 ℡0923.651.619
or 347.571.8904, Ⓦwww.nosteon.it. Great-value B&B off Piazza Plebiscito: an apartment consisting of one double in the loft and a bunk downstairs, with a kitchen and bathroom. Breakfast is taken at a nearby bar. No credit cards. ❷

The Town

Mazara's **old town**, where all the interest lies, is bordered by the Mázaro River and sea on two sides and the main corsos – Umberto I and Vittorio Véneto – on the others. At the southern end of Corso Umberto, Piazza Mokarta holds the scant ruins of Count Roger's **castello**, magnificently floodlit at night, when the square is the focus of promenading crowds. Fronting the garden to one side of the piazza is the **Duomo**, originally Norman but completely remodelled in the late seventeenth century – though the relief over the main door showing a mounted Count Roger trampling a Saracen underfoot was carved in 1584. The light and airy interior reveals an almost indigestible profusion of stuccoed and sculptured ornamentation, including, behind the altar, a group of seven marble statues depicting the *Transfiguration*, carved by Antonello Gagini. To the right, a niche reveals a fragment of Byzantine fresco, dating from the end of the thirteenth century, while, through the marble doorway on the right side of the nave, you'll find some excellently chiselled Roman sarcophagi, with reliefs of a lively hunting scene and a battle, rich with confusion.

Outside the Duomo, **Piazza della Repubblica** heralds a harmonious set of Baroque buildings: the square itself is flanked by the elegant, double-storey porticoed facade of the **Seminario** and the **Palazzo Vescovile**, both eighteenthcentury. In nearby Piazza del Plebiscito, the fifteenth-century church of Sant'Egido now houses the **Museo del Sátiro** (daily 9am–6pm; €6), whose centrepiece is a rather risqué fourth-century BC bronze satyr captured in the ecstatic throes of an orgiastic Dionysian dance. It was, quite literally, caught by a Mazara fishing-boat in the waters between Pantelleria and Cap Bon, Tunisia, in 1998. Sadly, as the fishermen hauled the catch aboard, one of the arms broke off and has yet to be recovered. A 25-minute video with English subtitles relates the story.

Opposite the museum, and entered through a rather fine sculpted doorway, the earlier **Collegio dei Gesuiti** houses the tiny **Museo Cívico** (currently closed for restoration; call ☎0923.671.111 for an update), displaying a smattering of minor, mainly Roman, finds from the area. As a possible substitute, though rather different in tone, the engaging social club-cum-museum that is the **Museo Ornitológico**, opposite the public gardens on Via San Salvatore (daily 9.30am–12.30pm & 3.30–8.30pm; free), displays a roomful of stuffed and rather raggedy owls, ibises and herons, among other birds (nothing is labelled).

Many other Baroque constructions are tucked away in the intricate network of streets and squares that makes up Mazara's old town, including several monumental churches. **Santa Veneranda**, in the square of the same name, is perhaps the most beautiful of these, its twin belltowers styled with a jaunty twist. On the edge of the old town, on a platform overlooking the Mázaro River, the church of **San Nicolò Regale** has a more restrained air. A restored Norman church, it has strong Arab elements, with a honey-toned, battlemented exterior and a simple interior rising to a single cupola.

Most of the churches were built after Mazara's teeming Arab population had dwindled to nothing – but it's here in the old town, especially in the Pilazza neighbourhood, that their descendants have returned, making up a low-key **Tunisian quarter** centred on Via Porta Palermo and nearby Via Bagno. Stroll around the quiet alleys here and you'll pass authentic Tunisian cafés and shops, and the occasional social club resounding to Arab tapes and the clack of backgammon tables.

West of the quarter, the waters of the Mázaro River are hidden by the hulls of the two hundred-odd trawlers that clog Mazara's **port**. Heavy overfishing and the use of illegal explosives (dropped into the sea to stun the fish) have greatly decreased the catch in recent years, but the rich waters above the continental shelf have ensured that there are enough fish left to make it worthwhile for the fishermen to pursue their trade – at least, given the reduced wages that the Tunisians are prepared to accept.

Out of the centre: the beach and Santa Maria della Giummare

Crossing over the bridge further down the river, you can walk past the docks to Mazara's seafront, mostly sandy **beach**, though a good part of it is choked by seaweed. Things improve the further up you go, but bathers might bear in mind that the stretch between Mazara and the Stagnone Islands has suffered from intense pollution in the past. If you're looking for a **swim** you'd be better advised to drive or jump on a bus from Mazara's train station to the lidos a couple of kilometres south, or, further afield, head for the white sands and clear waters of **Tonnarella Lido**, 7km south.

There's one more easy excursion out from the centre of Mazara – walkable this time – a couple of kilometres away on the outskirts of town, though drivers could see it on their way in or out by following Via Circonvallazione, the main SS115 running to Marsala. Signposted "Madonna del Alto", the chapel of **Santa Maria della Giummare** sits on a slight elevation on the right-hand side of the road (looking north). Built as a Basilian convent by a daughter of Count Roger's in 1103, its portal also shows a strong Saracen strain.

Eating and drinking

As you might expect in a Sicilian/Tunisian fishing port, you can eat well in Mazara. There's a line of **restaurants** near the public gardens, each offering variations of fish couscous and all with tables outside.

Restaurants

La Béttola Via Maccagnone 32 ☎0923.946.422. Near the train station, this old-fashioned place is good for regional specialities. First courses cost €9, mains €10–15. Closed Wed. Moderate.

Eyem Zemen Via Porta Palermo 36. Tiny place, with three or four tables outside and authentic and cheap Tunisian snacks – *brik* (fried pastry parcels), oily aubergine salads and couscous. Inexpensive.

Alla Kasbah Via Itria 10 ☎0923.906.126. Don't be fooled by the name: apart from a very acceptable fish couscous, the food here is less North African than modern Sicilian specialities. Fixed-price menus come to €15 and €20. The ambience is relaxed and friendly. Closed Mon. Moderate.

Lo Scoiáttolo Via N. Tortorici 9 and Lungomare Mazzini. "The Squirrel" has a fine antipasto buffet and daily fish specials, though many locals come here at night for the huge choice of pizzas. Tables outside. Inexpensive–moderate.

Bars

Bar Garden Piazza della Repubblica. Facing the town's most harmonious buildings, this is a nice place for a breakfast or sit-down by day, and to soak up the weird green illuminations in the evening.

Villa delle Rose Via Conte Ruggero. With tables under shady trees in the public gardens, this is a good vantage point for a quiet drink at any time.

Zelig Via Tortorici and Lungomare Mazzini. *Birreria* with plenty of outdoor tables, rock videos and occasional live music. Snacks include panini and plates of spaghetti.

Selinunte and around

SELINUNTE, the site of the Greek city of Selinus, lies around 30km east of Mazara del Vallo, stranded on a remote corner of the coast in splendid isolation. It's a crucial sight if you're travelling through the west of Sicily, its series of mighty temples lying in great heaps, where they were felled by earthquakes.

Most westerly of the Hellenic colonies, **Selinus** reached its peak during the fifth century BC. A bitter rival of Segesta, whose lands lay adjacent to the north, the powerful city and its fertile plain attracted enemies hand over fist, and it was only a matter of time before Selinus caught the eye of Segesta's ally, Carthage. Geographically vulnerable, the city was sacked by Carthaginians, any attempts at recovery forestalled by earthquakes, which later razed it altogether. However, people continued to live here until 250 BC, when the population was finally transferred to Marsala before the Roman invasion. The Arabs did occupy the site briefly, but the last recorded settlement at Selinunte was in the thirteenth century, after which time it remained forgotten until rediscovered in the sixteenth century. Despite the destruction, the city ruins have exerted a romantic hold over people ever since.

By **public transport**, it's easiest to approach from Castelvetrano, which is about thirty minutes' ride from Mazara del Vallo by road or rail. Selinunte is another thirty minutes south from there, via buses that run five or six times daily from Piazza Matteotti.

Marinella di Selinunte

The archeological site of Selinunte is situated just west of the modern village of **MARINELLA DI SELINUNTE**, which makes a far better base than Castelvetrano, and is also where the buses stop. Although it can get a bit hectic in summer, Marinella is an atmospheric place to spend a few hours. Its most appealing parts lie on and around the long, narrow road that winds down to the small harbour, where fishing boats are hauled up onto the sands by pulleys.

Arrival and information

Marinella's **bus station** is south of the entrance to the temple site, but most buses continue to the entrance as well. The small but obliging **tourist office** (Mon–Sat 8am–1.50pm & 2.10–7.50pm; ☎0924.46.251), which is often thronged with visitors in summer, is on the roundabout outside the entrance. Just opposite on this road there's an **alimentari**, while beyond it, in the main residential district – home to most of the cheap accommodation – you'll find a bigger **supermarket** behind the *Alceste* hotel. The road then descends to the seafront, where most of the hotels and restaurants are situated, and where you'll also find **telephones**, an **exchange office** and a few shops. There's a **bank** with ATM above the harbour, and another ATM in the entrance lobby of the archeological site.

Accommodation

You may well be offered **rooms** as you get off the bus, which are worth accepting in summer when the hotels and pensions in the village fill rapidly. Two **campsites** stand virtually side by side on the main road, about 1.5km north of the village: the *Athena* (☎0924.46.132, ✉athenaselinunte@tin.it), with a ridiculous temple facade and a good pizzeria, and *Il Maggiolino* (☎0924.46.044, ⊛www.campingmaggiolino.it); the bus to and from Castelvetrano passes right by them.

Garzia Via A. Pigafetta 6 ☎0924.46.660, ⊛www.hotelgarzia.com. The most expensive choice on the seafront road, this large, Arabic-style building has a wide range of rooms; those with sea views cost more. The hotel has its own patch of beach. ❺

Lido Azzurro Via Marco Polo 98 ☎0924.46.256, ✉lazzurro@freemail.it. A charming villa on the seafront road, with laid-back staff, prints on the walls, rugs on the floors and attractive rooms with sea-facing balconies. The owner speaks good English. The only drawback is that it's liable to be noisy in summer thanks to all the activity in the nearby restaurants and bars. Half-board €50 per person in Aug. ❸

Il Pescatore Via Castore e Polluce 31 ☎0924.46.303, ✉il.pescatore@alice.it. With a roof terrace that enjoys good views over to the temples and sea, this place offers eight simple rooms (two sharing a bathroom) with access to a kitchen, and breakfast includes fresh fruit. Alternatively, you can sleep on the roof for €12,

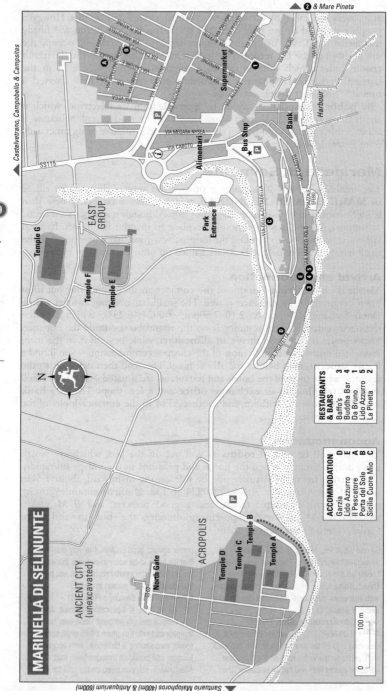

MARINELLA DI SELINUNTE

▲ Castelvetrano, Campobello & Campsites

❷ & Mare Pineta

ANCIENT CITY
(unexcavated)

ACROPOLIS

North Gate

Temple D
Temple C
Temple B
Temple A

P

▼ Santuario Malophoros (400m) & Antiquarium (600m)

EAST GROUP

Temple G
Temple F
Temple E

Park Entrance

N

SS115

VIA CABOTO

VIA MEGARA NYSEA

Alimentari

Bus Stop ★

P

Bank

Supermarket ❶

Harbour

VIA PALINURO

VIA PEL CANTONE

VIA PIGAFETTA

VIA MARCO POLO

VIA DELLA CITTADELLA

PIAZZALE
FEBO

ℹ️

VIA VEGA
VIA SIRIO
VIA PERSEFONE
VIA ARCO
VIA ISOLE EGADI
VIA DELPHINE
VIA PERISTILIO
VIA AGRIGENTO
VIA NAVISTA
VIA CARTAGINE

VIA ALCESTE
VIA ANTENORE

VIA PLATONE
VIA ARISTOTELE
VIA PASSEGGIATA
VIA MIRISIDE
VIA PIRASTRO
VIA PAPINO

A
B

P

C

D

E
3 4 5

RESTAURANTS & BARS
Baffo's	3
Buddha Bar	4
Da Bruno	1
Lido Azzurro	5
La Pineta	2

ACCOMMODATION
Garzia	D
Lido Azzurro	E
Il Pescatore	A
Porta del Sole	B
Sicilia Cuore Mio	C

0   100 m

and there are also four self-catering apartments. No credit cards. ❷

Porta del Sole Via Apollonio Rodio 32 ⓣ0924.46.035. Six basic rooms with private bathrooms. The same family runs the *Holiday House* across the road, where a couple of the larger rooms have balconies (not that there's a view), though furniture and beds are from the visit-grandma school of comfort. No credit cards. ❷

Sicilia Cuore Mio Via della Cittadella ⓣ0924.46.077 or 336.612.769, ⓦwww .siciliacuoremio.it. Right across from the archeological site, and with the sea in front, this friendly modern B&B offers five rooms, three with a sea view and two of them in a separate building next door with a kitchen for guests' use. Closed Dec–March. ❺

The town and its beaches

Marinella is no longer the isolated place it used to be, with new buildings and streets in evidence everywhere, while the seafront has become top-heavy with trattorias, and shops selling Tunisian carpets, souvenirs and beachwear. But it remains an attractive place, of particular appeal if you're planning to use the fine sand **beach** that stretches west from the village to the ruins. The water isn't great to swim in, since it's often clogged with seaweed at the sand's edge, though this doesn't deter the kids. However, the surfing here is particularly good, and you can rent equipment in the summer, as well as pedalos, chairs, shades and all the usual beach paraphernalia. Another beach is located east of the village, the **Mare Pineta**, backed by pine trees stretching into the distance; follow the road beyond the port for ten minutes.

Eating and drinking

All the best **eating** and **drinking** places are located on Via Marco Polo, the road above the west beach. That starts down at the little harbour where a couple of bars put out tables from which you can watch the sun set, while the fishermen chatter and dispute among themselves. At night in summer, visitors emerge from their holiday homes to join locals from the surrounding villages on foot, in cars and on Vespas, and the party chugs along merrily until well after midnight.

Baffo's Via Marco Polo 51. Sea views and a good menu that includes magnificent *forno a legna* pizzas (€4–7), a range of tasty fettuccine dishes and grilled fish. Moderate.

Da Bruno Via Alceste. In the residential district, this cheerful trattoria with bright white walls offers superlative antipasti and locally inspired fish dishes, like pasta with tuna and capers. In the evenings, you can enjoy crispy pizzas cooked in a wood-burning oven. Moderate.

Buddha Bar Via Marco Polo. Lively *birreria* overlooking the sea, open late. Closed weekdays in off-season.

Lido Azzurro Via Marco Polo. Opposite the eponymous hotel, this has a huge open dining-room terrace overlooking the sea, and offers such dishes as couscous with fish soup (€12). Pastas are around €7. Closed weekdays in winter. Moderate.

La Pineta on the east beach, Mare Pineta. This beach-bar has a trattoria at the back (closed in winter) serving fresh fish meals: a real find, it stays open in the evenings during July and Aug, but take a torch if you do go at night, as the road is unlit. Moderate.

Selinus: the site

The **ruins** of Selinus are back behind the main part of the village, split into two parts with temples in each, known only as temples A to G and O. The two parts are enclosed within the same site, with the car park and **entrance** (daily: summer 9am–7pm; winter 9am–5pm; last entry 1hr before closing; €6) lying through the landscaped earthbanks that preclude views of the east group of temples from the road. Selinus is claimed to be the biggest archeological site in Europe, so it can be quite a challenge if you want to see everything; you might make use of the buggy service, or **navetta**, for the remoter sites (tickets €5 for the nearer temples, €15 for the complete circuit). On foot, you could cover everything in two or three hours, but the total lack of shade makes for very hard work in the full heat of summer.

Shrouded in the wild celery that gave the ancient city its name, the **East Group** temples are in various stages of reconstructed ruin. The most complete is the one nearest the sea (Temple E), probably dedicated to Hera (Aphrodite) and re-erected in 1958. A Doric construction, almost 70m by 25m, it remains a gloriously impressive sight, its soaring columns gleaming bright against the sky, its ledges and capitals the resting place for flitting birds. Temple F, behind, is the oldest in this group, from around 550 BC, while the northernmost temple (Temple G) is an immense tangle of columned wreckage, 6m high in places and crisscrossed by rough footpaths. In Sicily, the only temple larger than this is the Tempio di Giove at Agrigento.

The road leads down from here, across the (now buried) site of the old harbour, to the second part of excavated Selinus, the **acropolis**, containing what remains of the other temples (five in all), as well as the well-preserved city streets and massive stepped **walls** that rise above the duned beach below. These huge walls were all constructed after 409 BC – when the city was sacked by the Carthaginians – in an attempt to protect a limited and easily defensible area of the old city.

Temple C stands on the highest point of the acropolis, giving glorious views out over the sparkling sea. Built early in the sixth century BC (and probably dedicated to Apollo), it originally held the finest of the metopes (decorative panels) that are now on show in Palermo's archeological museum (see p.84). Its fourteen standing columns were re-erected in the 1920s: other fallen columns here, and at the surrounding temples, show how they were originally constructed – the drums lying in a line, with slots and protrusions on either side that fitted into each other.

The buildings immediately behind temples C and D were shops, split into two rooms and with a courtyard each. At the end of the main street beyond stands the **north gate** to the city – the high blocks of stone marking a gateway that was 7m high. Behind the north gate stood the rest of the ancient city, still largely unexcavated, though crisscrossed by little paths through the undergrowth. The **agora** was sited just north of here, and a necropolis further up, while to the west, across the Modione river, stood the **Santuario Malophoros**, part of a complex that marked the western boundary of the city. Animal sacrifices were performed at the small well in front of the structure. Beyond it, on the edge of the archeological zone, the **Antiquarium** holds statuettes and terracotta fragments, mostly excavated in the 1980s from a temple dedicated to Hera Matronale, south of the Malophoros.

Campobello and the Cave di Cusa

If you have your own transport, it makes some sense to call in at the quarries where the stone for the building of Selinus was extracted in the fifth century BC. They lie 3.5km south of the scruffy town of **CAMPOBELLO DI MAZARA**, deep in olive country. From Selinunte, a lovely twenty-kilometre drive takes you along country roads lined with olive groves and vines. When you reach Campobello, take the road to Tre Fontane and follow the signs ("Cave di Cusa"), keeping your eyes peeled and fingers crossed.

At the site of the **Cave di Cusa** (9am–1hr before sunset; free), a path leads into a bucolic setting that owes more to English Romanticism than to ancient Greece. In early summer, workers fork hay into piles in between the rock ledges and tended shrubs, while behind them stretch shaded groves of olives. Everywhere, you can see the massive column drums and stumps lying randomly about, quarried and chiselled into shape here before being dragged to the ancient city on wooden carts, where they formed part of the great temple complex. There are examples of all the various stages of the process, with unfinished pieces poignantly abandoned, the work interrupted when Selinus was devastated in 409 BC. The most impressive pieces are those stone drums and column sections that remain in place where they were being excavated. A couple are 6m high and 2m across, with a narrow groove dug all the way around in which the stonemasons had to work – the reflected heat must have been appalling. Other rock sections indicate clearly where drums have already been cut – parts of the site look as though someone has been through with a giant pastry-cutter.

Castelvetrano and around

It's hard to recommend a visit to **CASTELVETRANO**, 15km inland from Campobello, for any reason other than to get the bus straight out again. A depressed town, it's lightened only marginally by an elegant if traffic-choked centre, where the **Teatro Selinus** – looking rather like a copy of a Greek temple – boasts a proud plaque commemorating Goethe's visit in 1787. Just around the corner stands a good-looking **Chiesa Madre** from the sixteenth century. The church's finely engraved doorway leads into an interior warmly illuminated by stained-glass windows – a rare thing in Sicily – and ornamented by a number of stuccoes by Serpotta and Ferraro. Off the adjacent square, Piazza Garibaldi, it's a short walk down to Via Garibaldi 50 and the **Museo Cívico** (Mon–Sat 9am–1pm & 3–6pm, Sun 9am–1pm; €2.50), home of the bronze *Efébo di Selinunte*, a statue of a young man from the fifth century BC.

From behind the church, Via Vittorio Emanuele leads down towards Piazza Matteotti and the train station. Piazza Matteotti marks the end of Via Serafino Mannone, where aficionados of banditry can visit the courtyard in which the body of the island's most notorious outlaw, **Salvatore Giuliano** (see p.108), was found on July 5, 1950. The courtyard is between Via Mannone 92 and 100, though it's a rather less appealing spot than its legend might suggest.

Santíssima Trinità di Delia

Three and a half kilometres **west of Castelvetrano**, a twelfth-century Norman church makes a pleasant rural excursion for anyone not in a blazing hurry. Head down Via R. Séttimo from Piazza Umberto, along a country lane fringed by vineyards, keeping left where the road forks. The domed church, **Santíssima Trinità di Delia**, is signposted before you arrive at the artificial lake of Lago Trinità: ring the bell to the right of the church for the key. The small, square building, its four slender columns and triple apse reminiscent of Saracenic styles, was meticulously restored by two brothers, whose mausoleum the church has become. Their tombs, dominating the small interior, rival those of the Norman kings in Palermo for splendour.

Practicalities

To reach the town centre from the **train station**, in Piazza Améndola, walk up to the main road and turn left: it's just a few minutes to Piazza Matteotti, from where Via Vittorio Emanuele – the main shopping street – leads all the way to the rear of the church. **Buses** from Marsala and Trápani stop outside the *Bar Selinus* on Via Selinunte. There's a basic **tourist office** (Mon–Sat 8am–8pm, Sun 9am–2pm; ☎0924.904.932) in the museum on Via Garibaldi.

To **get to Selinunte** from Castelvetrano, take the bus for Marinella from outside the train station – a timetable is posted inside the station – or from Piazza Regina Margherita in town.

Inland: Salemi, Gibellina and Santa Margherita di Belice

North of Castelvetrano and east of Marsala, the interior of Trápani province is intensely rural, its few small towns little changed by the coming of the A29 autostrada, which cuts across the region. The whole area is green and highly fertile, mainly given over to vine-growing; indeed, the wine around the **Salemi** district is among Sicily's best. But, hard though it is to believe, the entire region still hasn't recovered from the **earthquake** of January 15, 1968, which briefly spotlighted western Sicily, sadly more for the authorities' inadequate response to it than for the actual loss of life. Four hundred died and a thousand were injured, no great number by Sicilian standards, but it was the 50,000 left homeless that had the most lingering impact on this already depressed part of the island, and the effects of the earthquake are still evident everywhere. Ruined buildings and ugly temporary dwellings being used four decades later testify to the chronically dilatory response to the disaster, aggravated by private interests and particularly by the Mafia contractors who capitalized on the catastrophe. Even where rebuilding went ahead, such as in the new town of **Gibellina**, it's still possible to see the dread hand of inertia.

It goes without saying that this is a little-visited area of Sicily, but it's intriguing nonetheless. This is, after all, the part of the world known best to Giuseppe di Lampedusa, whose classic novel, *The Leopard*, is partly set in the little town of **Santa Margherita di Belice** – also badly damaged in 1968 but emerging slowly from the doldrums, and an essential stop for anyone who's read the book. Local buses run to all the towns in the region, but it's impossible to construct any kind of sightseeing itinerary using them – you have to have your own car, not least to avoid the possibility of getting stuck in backwaters with no accommodation.

Salemi

The town of **SALEMI**, 20km north of Castelvetrano and 30km east of Marsala, oddly enjoyed the privilege of being the first capital of a united Italy in 1860, albeit for only three days, as recorded by a plaque in front of its heavily restored thirteenth-century **castello** on Piazza Alicia, at the top of the town. Another plaque marks Garibaldi's declaration of a dictatorship, asserting that "in times of war, it's necessary for the civilian powers to be concentrated in the hands of one man" – namely Garibaldi himself, though King Vittorio Emanuele still gets a mention. On Via d'Aguirre, leading down from the piazza, the former Collegio

Festivals & events

There's nothing to beat arriving in a Sicilian town or village to discover that it's festival time. Many annual feast days have remained unchanged for decades, if not centuries, celebrating the life of a patron saint or some notable event lost in the mists of time. But whatever the reason for the party, you are guaranteed the time-honoured ingredients for a Sicilian knees-up – old songs and dances, a costumed procession, perhaps a traditional puppet show, special food and sweets, and noisy fireworks to finish.

▶▶ You'll find a calendar of local festivals at the end of each chapter.

Carnival time

Carnevale (**Carnival**, or Mardi Gras) is celebrated in the five days immediately before the start of Lent. It's a floating festival, which in practice occurs some time between the end of February and the end of March. Traditionally, its significance is as the last bout of indulgence before the abstinence of Lent, which lasts for forty days and ends with Easter. True, Sicily isn't Rio de Janeiro, but most towns manage to put on a little bit of a show and a costumed parade. The best carnival festivities on the island are generally judged to be at **Acireale** on the Catania coast, where flower-filled floats, parades and concerts keep the townspeople occupied for days.

Easter pomp and circumstance

Easter week is celebrated all over the island, with slow-moving processions and ostentatious displays of penitence and mourning. Particularly dramatic events take place in the west of the island at places like **Érice** and **Marsala**, and at **Taormina** in the east, while at **Enna** in the interior, thousands march in silent procession behind holy statues and processional carts. It's in **Trápani**, however, that the procession of statues is raised to an art form. Just as they have been every year since the seventeenth century the city's "Misteri" figures, portraying life-sized scenes from the Passion, are paraded through the streets on Good Friday. Meanwhile, at the Albanian village of **Piana degli Albanesi**, near Palermo, the villagers retain their ancient Orthodox traditions and costumes. Other, less conventional parades take place at **Prizzi** in the western interior, and at **San Fratello** above the Tyrrhenian coast, where masked and hooded devils taunt the processions.

Holy Friday, Trapani ▲
Good Friday procession, Emna ▼

The weird and wonderful

Sicily can boast some of the Mediterranean's most idiosyncratic festivals. The conquest by the Normans is echoed in August's **Palio dei Normanni** in Piazza Armerina, a medieval-costumed procession with jousting knights, while the similar **La Castellana** throngs the streets of Cáccamo in September. The island's fishermen have their own rituals, from the annual tuna slaughter known as **La Mattanza** to the festive boat parade and fish-fry of **Sagra del Mare** at Sciacca. During May's **Pesce a Mare** festa at Aci Trezza, on the Catania coast, as the local tourist brochure puts it, "a fisherman pretends to be a fish and excitedly the local fishermen catch him". Unmissable, as for different reasons is the pilgrimage every May in the Etna foothills, when the pious run, barefoot and shirtless, up to the sanctuary at **Trecastagni**.

▲ San Paolo feast, Palazzo Acreide

▼ Festa della Vara, Messina

Summer's here

The biggest island-wide celebration, bar none, is high summer's *ferragosto*, the Feast of the Assumption of the Virgin Mary. The day is actually August 15, but anywhere with a celebration of any size makes a meal of it, perhaps starting with services and parties a few days earlier before culminating, like all *ferragosto* celebrations, with spectacular fireworks on the night of the 15th. This is a particularly good time to be in Messina, where the procession of the city's enormous patron giants is followed by a mad scramble when the elaborate carriage known as the *Vara* is pulled through the streets. As the night wears on, flowers are thrown to the crowds before fireworks light up the Straits of Messina late at night.

A night at the theatre

Puppet theatre (*teatro dei pupi*) has been popular in Sicily since the fourteenth century. The shows are always the same, and all Sicilians know the stories, which centre on the clash between **Christianity** and **Islam**. As each strutting, stiff-legged knight, such as Orlando (Roland) and Rinaldo , is introduced, the puppeteer lists his exploits. There may be a love interest, perhaps a jousting tournament to win the hand of Charlemagne's daughter, before the main business of staged battles between the Christians and the Saracen invaders.

Museo della Marionette, Palermo ▲

Classical drama, Siracusa ▼

Sicily's top cultural events

▶ **Teatro Greco, Taormina**. See p.205. A superb summer setting for music, film and drama.

▶ **Parco Archeológico, Siracusa**. See p.259. The classical dramas here are Sicily's most famous annual theatrical productions.

▶ **Tyndaris**. See p.143. The Roman theatre puts on concerts and classical dramas almost nightly in summer.

▶ **Teatro Mássimo, Palermo**. See p.85. The opera season at this spectacular theatre runs from October to June.

▶ **Orestiadi, Gibellina**. See p.409. Classic and contemporary performances deep in the neglected western interior.

▶ **Café Concerto, Catania**. See p.227. Catania's old-town streets are closed to traffic every summer evening.

▶ **Valle dei Templi, Agrigento**. See p.334. The archeological zone is a great summer backdrop for open-air concerts.

▶ **Eraclea Minoa**. See p.341. These fine ruins stage concerts and plays in July and August.

dei Gesuiti holds a trio of museums (all Tues–Sun 9am–2pm & 4–7pm; free). The **Museo del Risorgimento** holds assorted pieces of "Garibaldini" – letters, documents and arms connected with the town's finest hour; the **Museo Archeólogico** contains finds from local excavations including Monte Polizzo; and the **Museo dell'Arte Sacra** gathers together treasures from various local churches, including the cathedral destroyed in the earthquake.

There's a **tourist office** at the bottom of the hill on Piazza Libertà (daily 9am–1pm & 4–8pm; ☏0924.981.426), where buses stop.

Gibellina

Salemi escaped the earthquake lightly, even though a third of the population had to abandon their shattered homes. Other towns, like Gibellina, were completely flattened, and the population moved en masse to a site close to Santa Ninfa. This is **GIBELLINA NUOVA**, a modern town that has become a symbol of progress in the region, with innovative buildings that deliberately diverge from old styles: weird shapes and forms abound, designed by a handful of modern architects with big budgets. A vast stainless-steel star straddles the motorway where you exit for Gibellina, while the town also holds huge white spheres, giant ploughs, snails and much besides – 47 constructions in all, with a few in the Egyptian style still to come. Many buildings are apparently crumbling already, and the designs themselves are embarrassingly frozen in the images of what appeared modern in the 1970s. The town, meanwhile, bakes in the summer sun, since all the modern piazzas are vast concrete spaces with little shade.

You can get a taste of what Gibellina is all about by driving to the main square – Piazza XV Gennaio 1968, in case there was any doubt about whose fault all this was – where the arcaded City Hall is fronted by some particularly abstract examples. Staff at the **tourist office** here (Mon–Sat 8am–2pm; ☏0924.67.877) can supply a map showing where everything is, and supply a list of local B&Bs for anyone wanting to stay over after attending the Orestiadi (see below). There's a local museum with separate archeological and anthropological sections, a modern art gallery, and even a botanical garden, though it's a dedicated visitor who takes in any of these. For a **lunch** stop, look no further than *La Massara*, Viale dei Vespri Siciliani 29 (closed Sun), an inexpensive trattoria ten minutes' walk from the piazza, whose very filling house pasta, *busiate napoleonica* (€8), is made with aubergines, tomato and sausage. Alternatively, pick up provisions from the supermarket on the parallel Viale Sturzo.

Eighteen kilometres east along the SS119 (through Santa Ninfa), overlooked by ranks of wind turbines, the old town of **RÚDERI DI GIBELLINA** complements the new: a mountain of rubble from which smashed and mutilated houses poke out, strewn over a green hillside. On the way into town, you'll pass what is ironically its best-preserved fragment: a shady cemetery stretching down the side of the valley, where the inhabitants of the new town return every year to remember the catastrophe. Further down, modernism has left its mark here too, in the form of a wide, grey-white mantle of concrete, **Il Cretto**, poured over one slope, and carved through by channels that recall the previous layout of streets. It's an arresting spectacle, not least for its sheer scale.

Everything else remains as it was after the earthquake struck: only a church has since been restored. Nearby, a jumble of scaffolding on a hummock cradles a stage that's one of the two venues for the **Orestiadi**, a series of classical and modern dramas, concerts and events performed every year (July–Sep). As well as works by Euripides, Sophocles and others, there are modern interpretations by the likes of Jean Cocteau, Stravinsky and John Cage, and a full programme of exhibitions, cinema and world music. Performances also take place in Gibellina Nuova, at Baglio di Stéfano (signposted outside the centre); more details are available from the tourist office at Gibellina Nuova, or see Ⓦwww .orestiadi.it.

Santa Margherita di Belice

Often ranked among the finest of all historical novels, Giuseppe di Lampedusa's *The Leopard* ("Il Gattopardo" in Italian) is a masterpiece of manners and morals, written by a Sicilian prince who only ever completed this one work. Set in 1860s Sicily, it draws heavily on Lampedusa's own experiences, not least the summers he used to spend in his grandmother's palace in **SANTA MARGHERITA DI BELICE**, a small village 35km east of Castelvetrano. This is the Donnafugata of the book – the fictional prince's summer home, a place cherished for the "sense it gave him of everlasting childhood". The 1968 earthquake, unfortunately, completely wrecked the seventeenth-century palace and church described so intently in the novel, though fragments of the palace have been incorporated in a gleaming new Town Hall (Municipio). This, with its cool internal courtyards and lovely garden to the side, at least echoes the spirit of the original. More poignant is all that's left of the adjacent Chiesa Madre – a two-storey corner open to the elements, displaying its elegant marble tracery and painted medallions to the birds. Having paid your literary dues, it's a quick matter to look around the rest of Santa Margherita, which shows a few signs of revival these days – there's a thoroughly modern church with a space-rocket spire, new extensions grafted onto older, damaged buildings, and a traffic-free stretch of street where you can grab a cold drink in the *Caffè Gattopardo*.

Pantelleria

With an area of 83 square kilometres, **PANTELLERIA** is the largest of Sicily's offshore islands. Forty kilometres closer to Tunisia than to Sicily, it has been occupied since early times by whichever power controlled the central Mediterranean. By the time of the Phoenicians, who colonized it in the seventh century BC, it was called Hiranin, "island of the birds", after the birds who still stop over here on their migratory routes; for the Greeks, it was Kossyra, or "small". Its present name probably derives from the Arabic *bint ar-riah* ("daughter of the winds"), after the restless breezes that blow around the island's rocky shores. Pantelleria has always attracted its fair share of famous visitors, and former aficionados like Truman Capote and Aldous Huxley have been replaced in time by the current celebrity A-list, with Madonna and Sting both enamoured of its charms. Parts of *Il Postino* (*The Postman*) were filmed here, too.

There are no beaches of any kind in Pantelleria, its rough black coastline consisting mainly of jagged rocks, but the swimming is still pretty good in some exceptionally scenic spots. Inland, the largely mountainous country offers plenty of rambling opportunities, all an easy moped or bus ride from the port, which holds most of the accommodation options. If you're spending any length of time on Pantelleria, a novel option is to rent one of the local *dammuso* houses: their strong walls and domed roofs keep the temperature down indoors.

The main drawback to spending time on Pantelleria is the **cost of living**: there are only a few pricey hotels, while food (and water) is mostly imported

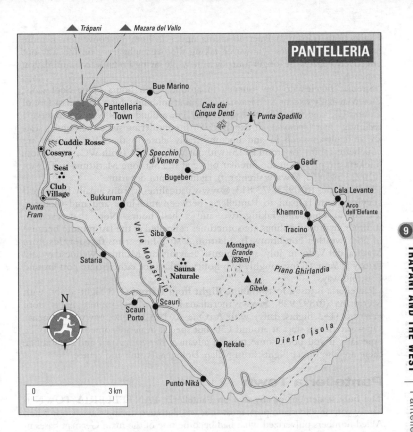

PANTELLERIA

Bue Marino

Pantelleria
Town

Cala dei
Cinque Denti   Punta Spadillo

Cuddie Rosse
Cossyra

Specchio
di Venere   Gadir

Sesi   Bugeber

Club
Village   Bukkuram   Cala Levante

Punta
Fram   Khamma   Arco
dell'Elefante

Siba   Tracino

Valle Monastero   Montagna
Grande
(836m)

Sataria   Sauna
Naturale   Piano Ghirlandia

M.
Gibele

N   Scauri

Scauri
Porto   Dietro Ísola

Rekale

0   3 km   Punto Nikà

and therefore relatively expensive. The island does offer some unique gastronomic experiences, though, including what are touted as the best capers in the Mediterranean. At some point, you ought to sample the locally produced ricotta-type cheese known as *tumma*, which is one of the ingredients of *ravioli con menta e ricotta*, a slightly bitter but fresh-tasting dish for which Pantelleria is famous. Pasta often comes served with *pesto pantesco*, a rough sauce of tomatoes, garlic and basil; while an *insalata pantesca* utilizes tomatoes, onions, cubes of boiled potato, and local capers and herbs. The **wine** is well thought of too, made from the *zibbibo* grapes that grow well in this volcanic soil. The day-to-day drinking stuff – *vino pantesco* – is mostly white, with a nice fruity fragrance, while for something considerably stronger try the fortified *Moscato*, a sweet, amber-coloured dessert wine. Even better is the raisin wine, known generically as *passito*, which has a rich golden colour and a dry and heady flavour – the best-known variety is *Tanit*.

Despite the expense, a few days spent here will probably leave you wanting more. Best times are May/June or September/October, to avoid the summer's ferocious heat; try to book your accommodation before you arrive.

Getting to Pantelleria

You can reach Pantelleria by (year-round) ferry or (summer-only) hydrofoil services from Trápani, and by fast ferries from Mazara del Vallo (July & Aug).

Flights from Trápani or Palermo taking under an hour are convenient if more extravagant alternatives – however, taking the overnight ferry on the way out effectively negates the longer journey time while saving a night's accommodation expense.

Siremar **ferries** do the journey in around seven hours (June–Sept daily; Oct–May daily except Sat), leaving Trápani at midnight, for a deck-class fare of around €32 one way (€28 in low season). For around €5.50 you can reserve a reclining chair (*poltrona*), an expense worth considering since the regular seats are difficult to sleep in and uncomfortably close to the TVs; or there are couchette-cabins for around €15 (without WC) or €21 (with WC) per person. **Tickets** are on sale in the Siremar office at the Stazione Maríttima in Trápani (℡0923.545.455, Ⓦwww.siremar.it), right up until departure.

Ústica Lines (℡0923.873.813, Ⓦwww.usticalines.it) runs a daily **hydrofoil service** from Trápani to Pantelleria between mid-June and mid-October, leaving at 6pm and taking two and a half hours. Note that, even in summer, hydrofoil sailings are sometimes cancelled at the last minute because of poor weather conditions. In addition, Ústica Lines runs **fast ferries** from Mazara del Vallo in July and August, leaving on Monday, Wednesday and Friday at 9am, taking roughly two hours. Tickets for either route cost around €36 one way.

Pantelleria is just a forty-minute **flight** from Trápani (1–3 flights daily) with Meridiana (℡892.928, Ⓦwww.meridiana.it), or a fifty-minute flight from Palermo (1–2 flights daily) with AirOne (℡199.207.080, Ⓦwww.airone.it). One-way tickets start at around €50, but special deals are sometimes on offer, especially if you book some time in advance. Between April and September, there are also direct flights from Milan, Bologna, Rome and Venice.

Pantelleria Town

The only settlement of any size on Pantelleria, **PANTELLERIA TOWN** is hardly your idyllic island port: most of it was flattened during the last war when Allied bombers pulverized what had become one of the main German bases in the Mediterranean, and the scars are still evident. Consequently, much of the town has a homogenous, modern appearance, its buildings mainly consisting of low-rise concrete cubes spread back two or three streets deep from the harbour. The only building here that predates the war is the morose, black **Castello Barabacane** on the far side of the harbour, a legacy of the Spaniards. Its partly restored interior, holding a few Roman busts among other items, is open in summer (July & Aug daily 10am–1pm & 6–8.30pm; €5) and for occasional art exhibitions. In case you'd forgotten you're still in Sicily, a plaque on the harbour-facing wall honours assassinated anti-Mafia judge Paolo Borsellino and his five bodyguards.

Yet to call the town unattractive and devoid of interest, as many do, would be to miss the point. Though small and remote, it's not as unsophisticated as the other offshore islands – it's long been on the African shipping route – and possesses a distinct liveliness, especially in the evening when the traffic starts to circle the harbour and the harbourside café-bars fill with perambulating locals. Arriving here off the ferry at dawn is also rather romantic, as the town lights flick off to reveal a spread of white-painted cubes which – only close up – emerge as modern rather than medieval. Throughout the day delivery vessels and fishing smacks come and go, while the marina sees the manoeuvrings of some uncommonly flash yachts and even the odd schooner or two.

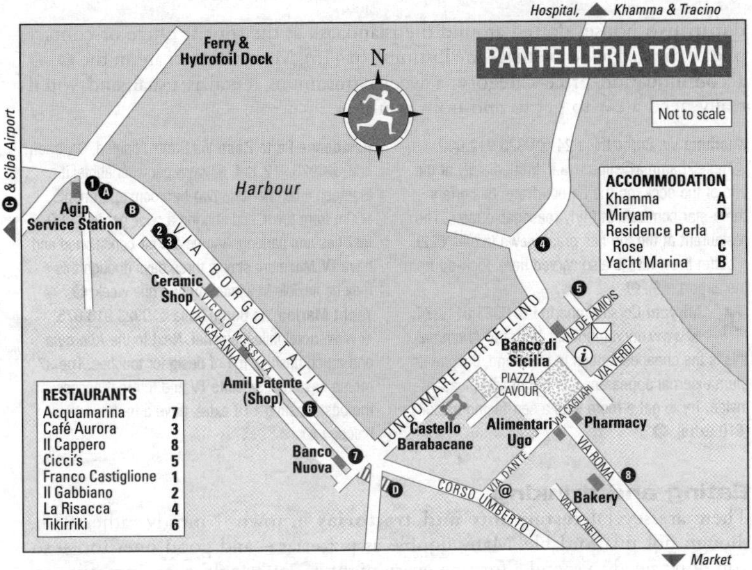
Hospital, Khamma & Tracino
PANTELLERIA TOWN
Not to scale
N
Ferry & Hydrofoil Dock
Harbour
C & Siba Airport
Agip Service Station
Ceramic Shop
VIA BORGO ITALIA
VICOLO MESSINA
VIA CATANIA
Amil Patente (Shop)
Banco Nuova
LUNGOMARE BORSELLINO
Castello Barabacane
Banco di Sicilia
PIAZZA CAVOUR
VIA DE AMICIS
VIA VERDI
VIA CAGLIARI
Alimentari Ugo
Pharmacy
VIA DANTE
VIA ROMA
CORSO UMBERTO I
VIA A. D'AIETTI
Bakery
Market
ACCOMMODATION
Khamma A
Miryam D
Residence Perla Rose C
Yacht Marina B
RESTAURANTS
Acquamarina 7
Café Aurora 3
Il Cappero 8
Cicci's 5
Franco Castiglione 1
Il Gabbiano 2
La Risacca 4
Tikirriki 6

Arrival, information and transport

The **airport** is 5km southeast of town. A bus service runs into town five times daily – a 12min journey – from a stop outside, reached by turning right out of the arrivals hall and walking 250m. Taxis into town charge €5; alternatively, it's a 45-minute downhill walk. **Arriving by sea**, you'll disembark right in the centre of town, close to most of the bars, restaurants and hotels. In bad weather, you may be deposited instead at Scauri, a smaller port on the island's south-western side, from where a bus takes foot passengers into town. Both Siremar and Ústica Lines agencies are along Via Borgo Italia on the harbourfront.

There is a **tourist office** (June & Sept Mon–Sat 9am–1pm; July & Aug Mon–Sat 9am–1pm & 6–8pm, Sun 9–11am; ⓣ0923.911.838, ⓦwww.prolocopantelleria.it) on the main square, Piazza Cavour, and you can usually pick up a booklet (in Italian) packed with local information at La Cossira, a travel and accommodation agency at Via Borgo Italia 77. The **website** ⓦwww.pantelleria.it is also useful.

Little local **buses** make regular departures from Piazza Cavour to all the main villages on the island – there are no services on Sundays. Buy tickets in advance from any *tabacchi* for €0.80, or on the bus for €1. The tourist office has routes and timetables. For more independence, you might consider **renting a scooter or car**: see "Listings" (p.415) for details. Bikes are currently unavailable.

Accommodation

While the town itself offers limited accommodation, other **hotels** – mostly quite pricey – can be found at Cuddie Rosse, Specchio di Vénere, Punta Fram and Bue Marino. Even in town prices are generally high, though low-season bargains are usually available. During July and August, some places impose a minimum stay of three days or even a week – at other times of the year, prices drop considerably. There's no **campsite** on the island, and camping rough is impractical given the terrain and lack of water. To rent one of the idiosyncratic

dammuso houses dotted around the island, ask at the tourist office or contact one of the *dammuso* agencies in "Listings" (p.415). Most *dammusi* are in the ❼–❾ accommodation price category; a week's minimum rental is usual, and you'll really need a car to get to and from them.

Khamma Via Borgo Italia 24 ☎0923.912.680, ⒺⒶhotelkhamma@supereva.it. Immediately at the end of the dock, on the harbourfront, this offers three-star comforts at fairly reasonable rates. The restaurant at the top has great views (meals €22); a buffet breakfast is also served here. Pick-up from the airport (€5). ❻

🏃 **Miryam** Corso Umberto I ☎0923.911.374, ⓦwww.miryamhotel.it. With the *Khamma*, this is the cheapest option in town and, despite its glum external appearance, is bright and pleasant inside. Try to get a room with a sea-facing balcony (€10 extra). ❻

Residence Perla Rosa Via Dante Alighieri, Contrada Itria ☎0923.912.114, ⓦwww.pantelleriahotel.it. Eighteen little one- and two-bedroom apartments, 500m from town, and sharing a pool, garden, BBQ facilities and parking. Rooms are air-conditioned and have TV. Minimum stay is three days (though this may be flexible in winter), in Aug one week. ❻

Yacht Marina Via Borgo Italia ☎0923.913.075, ⓦwww.hotelphilosophy.net. Next to the *Khamma* and much flashier, full of designer touches. The 37 rooms have a/c, satellite TV and Internet access; the best, costing €10 extra, have a harbour-view balcony. ❻

Eating and drinking

There are several **restaurants and trattorias** in town – mostly rather flash, though not unaffordable. Many double as pizzerias – and good ones too – so you don't need to spend a fortune every night. If you're **self-catering**, you can buy your own food from Alimentari Ugo in the main Piazza Cavour, which sells local cheese, among other things, or from the SISA supermarkets on Via Catania and Via Nápoli, and there's a fruit and vegetable shop and a bakery, respectively on and just off Piazza Cavour. Most shops are open 8am–1pm and 5–8.30pm, closed Wednesday afternoon and Sunday.

As for drinking, the **bars** on the harbourfront are where all the action is, starting at 6am (when they open their doors for the arriving ferry passengers) and finishing any time between midnight and 2am depending on season and inclination. All have tables by the water, where prices are higher.

Restaurants

Acquamarina Via Catania 2 ☎0923.911.422. This trendy little joint is the best-placed restaurant in town, with large windows overlooking the harbour. There's a long menu, including *tumma* cheese served with local capers and olive oil, and fish couscous every Thurs. Closed Oct–May. Expensive.

🏃 **Il Cappero** Via Roma 31 ☎0923.912.601. Just off the main piazza, this is probably the best place to eat in town (if not the island), serving the local ravioli stuffed with *tumma*, fresh fish (including large tuna steaks) and popular pizzas (also available to take away, *d'asporto*). There's a good antipasto table too. Sat night is very busy. First courses are €8–12, mains €10–14. Closed Tues in winter. Moderate.

Franco Castiglione Via Borgo Italia 24 ☎0923.911.448. Sleek, air-conditioned restaurant that offers an excellent (mostly veggie) antipasto

table. Follow it with pizza (about €5) and local wine and you'll escape lightly; full meals are pricier (most dishes €10–15). Closed Wed. Moderate.

Il Gabbiano Via Trieste 5 ☎0923.911.909. Just off the seafront, this modest, white-walled and vaulted trattoria offers some of the cheapest food in town, nothing exceptional but the usual range of island specialities and a calm atmosphere. Pastas are around €7, seafood €10–12. Moderate.

La Risacca Via Errera 18 ☎0923.912.975. At the end of the harbour, this busy ristorante-pizzeria with a terrace has an array of grilled seafood and outdoor seating. Try the *ravioli con pomodoro, burro e salvia* (with tomato, butter and sage), or, in the evening, fish couscous (€13). You'll pay around €10 for pastas, €12 for mains. Closed Mon in winter. Moderate.

Bars

Café Aurora Via Borgo Italia. With a fine seating area overlooking the port, this bar serves evening drinks with a dish of olives and other nibbles.

Cicci's Via Cágliari. Just off the main piazza, ths place has a lively evening crowd, musical accompaniment and snacks. Closed Sun.

Tikirriki Via Borgo Italia. Good snacks, pastries and ice cream, which you can eat by the harbour. Closed Sun in winter.

Listings

Airport ☏ 0923.911.172, ⊛ www.pantelleriairport.it.
Banks ATMs at Banco di Sicilia, Piazza Cavour, and Banco Nuova, Via Catania 5.
Boat tours Daily from the port in summer; a *giro dell'isola* (round-island tour) costs around €35 per person for a full day (leaving around 9.30am, returning at 4pm), including a spaghetti lunch. Call ☏ 0923.911.469 or 339.398.4810 for details.
Car and scooter rental Autonoleggio Policardo, Via Messina 31 and airport ☏ 0923.912.844. Expect to pay from €35–50 per day for cars, €15–30 per day for scooters.
Dammuso agencies Call Tour, Via Cágliari 14 ☏ 0923.911.065, ⊛ www.calltour.it; Dammusi di Rukia ☏ 335.120.6226, ⊛ www.pantelleria.com; Pantelleria Travel ☏ 199.44.862, ⊛ www.pantelleriatravel.com.
Ferries and hydrofoils Siremar operates a ferry service to Trápani leaving at noon (June–Sept daily and Oct–May Fri & Sat) or at 10am (Oct–May Mon–Thurs); tickets from Agenzia Rizzo, Via Borgo Italia 65 ☏ 0923.911.120, ⊛ www.siremar.it. Ústica Lines operates hydrofoils to Trápani (mid-June to mid-Oct, leaving daily at 8.30am), and fast ferries to Mazara del Vallo (July & Aug, leaving Tues, Thurs & Sat at 12.25pm) and to Sousse, in Tunisia (July & Aug, leaving Mon, Wed & Fri at 11.15am); tickets from Agenzia Minardi, Via Borgo Italia 15 ☏ 0923.911.502, ⊛ www.usticalines.it.
Hospital For first-aid and medical matters, go to the Ospedale, Via Almanza ☏ 0923.911.844.

Internet Internet Point, Via Dante 7 (daily 8.30am–2pm & 4.30–9pm). Phone, fax and Western Union services also available here.
Market Every Tuesday and Friday morning on Via San Leonardo. Fresh fish is sold at stalls on the road to the hospital and the lighthouse, on the far side of the harbour from the dock.
Pharmacy Farmacia Greco on Piazza Cavour (Mon–Sat 8.30am–1pm & 4.30–8pm; ☏ 0923.911.310).
Police Carabinieri, Via Trieste 13 ☏ 0923.911.109.
Post office The island's main post office is off Piazza Cavour on Via Verdi (Mon–Fri 8am–1.20pm, Sat 8am–12.30pm).
Shopping A couple of good ceramicists work on Pantelleria, and shops at the harbour sell decent stuff. Look out for local Moscato and passito wines and capers. You can find these and much more, including home-made marmalade, olive paste, preserved seaweed and pasta sauces at two places on Via Catania: Amil Patente (also marked "*Prodotti locali*"), and Emporio del Gusto.
Taxi Consolo, Piazza Castello ☏ 0923.912.716 or 339.715.7586.
Tours Excursions by jeep, on foot and on horseback are organized by the Gira l'Ísola agency at Vícolo Messina 21 ☏ 0923.913.254, from about €30 per person. Diving also offered.
Travel agency La Cossira, Via Borgo Italia 77 ☏ 0923.911.078 (for airline tickets).

Around the island

Surprisingly, most of Pantelleria's population of 8500 are farmers rather than fishermen. With a soil nourished by frequent past eruptions (the last in 1831), the islanders traditionally preferred tilling to risking life and limb in a sea swarming with pirates on the prowl. Farming on Pantelleria does have its problems, however, not least the numerous chunks of lava and basalt in the earth that preclude mechanical ploughing, not to mention the incessant wind, scorching sun and almost complete lack of water. The islanders have devised methods of minimizing these disadvantages by some ingenious devices that would bring a gleam to an ecologist's eye. The prolific *zibbibo* vines are individually planted in little ridges designed to capture the precious rainwater;

and the famous *giardini arabi* – high walls of stone built round orange trees and other plants – afford protection from the wind and the salt it carries with it. All over the island, various **co-operatives** (often signposted from the road) sell local produce to visitors and locals – capers, wine, jojoba oil, honey and candles. If you want to buy, look for the words "*azienda agricola*".

Otherwise, it's a blackened landscape, thick with volcanic debris, in which the local **dammuso** houses, when whitewashed, provide some visual relief. Unembellished, these sombre cubic dwellings, unique to the island, blend in perfectly with their environment. These, too, are examples of technological adaptation, the thick walls and shallow-domed roofs designed to maintain a cool internal temperature, while ridges in the roofs catch the rain.

It's easy enough to get around the island by bus or bike, but to visit the isolated coves of the southeastern Dietro Ísola, and other good swimming spots, you'll need to **rent a boat**. There are notices in the agencies along the harbour, in every hotel, and on the boats themselves. If you don't want to navigate yourself, you'll find **boat tours** from the port.

Along the southwest coast

Six daily buses (not Sun) run along the **southwest coast** to both Scauri and Rekale. If you intend to walk any stretch of this, you're advised to take the bus first to Scauri (20min) and then walk back as far as the Sesi (see below); at a couple of hours or so, that's more than enough for most people.

The route south of town is initially very unpromising, through an industrial wasteland of noisome and noisy factories, abandoned farmhouses and past a military barracks. Things pick up after a couple of kilometres at the **Cuddie Rosse**, volcanic red rocks that mark the site of a prehistoric cave settlement. There's nothing much to see, but the rocks are overlooked by the good-value *Cossyra Hotel* (℡0923.911.154, ⓦwww.cossyrahotel.it; ❼), with a pool; half-board is usually obligatory in July and August (€100 per person).

Fifteen minutes' walk further on, a signposted track on the left leads up 300m to the first of the island's strange **Sesi**, massive black Neolithic funeral mounds of piled rock, with low passages leading inside; a second one lies further up the left. They're thought to be products of Pantelleria's first settlers, possibly from Tunisia. The main one here is 6m high, a striking sight, completely at one with its lunar-like environment. Scores of these must once have dotted the island, satisfying some primeval fears and beliefs. That so few survive is not so hard to understand when you take a look around at the regular-shaped stones from which the *dammuso* houses are built – centuries of plunder have taken their toll.

Beyond the Sesi, at **Punta Fram**, the island's poshest resort, the *Club Village Punta Fram* (℡0923.918.075, ⓦwww.aurumhotels.it; June–Sept; ❾), has a tennis court, a fine outdoor swimming pool and steps leading down to its own little rocky cove, where guests can swim happily. There's public access to the coast here, just back down the road a little way towards the Sesi; look for a footpath, marked "*Discesa a mare*", opposite a side road to a little tower.

On foot, it's just over an hour all told from the Sesi to **SATARIA**, where concrete steps lead down to a tiny square-cut sea-pool, ideal for splashing around in. In the cave behind are more pools where warm water bubbles through, reputed to be good for curing rheumatism and skin diseases: a handful of people can usually be found jumping from pools to sea. There's room on the concrete apron around the pool to lay out a towel, and it's the only place for kilometres around with any shade: a nice place to eat your picnic.

From the port at **SCAURI**, 2km (30min on foot) further on, you can see Cape Mustafa in Tunisia on a clear day. There's a nice **bar-restaurant** here,

La Vela (☎0923.916.566), with a terrace right on the portside, where you can eat ravioli with ricotta and mint, grilled fish and sweet, ricotta-filled *baci*. The village itself is a steep twenty-minute walk above its harbour, and consists of no more than a minuscule church perched on a shelf of land, surrounded by a cluster of houses; it does at least hold a bakery and pharmacy, as well as an *alimentari* that does decent panini.

From here, the only other stop (and end of the bus line) is **REKALE**, an even smaller and more remote hamlet, beyond which the extensive southeastern segment of the island, the **Dietro Ísola**, curves round. Further hot springs at **Punto Nikà** are most easily reached by boat, though you can get there on foot.

The northeast coast

Eight or nine daily buses (not Sun) run along the northeast coast to both Khamma and Tracino. The latter village marks the end of the line, a thirty-minute ride from town.

Very early on you'll pass **Bue Marino**, which, though not the most striking part of this coast, has reasonable swimming from the rocks. It also offers accommodation, in the shape of the *Turistico Residenziale* (☎0923.911.054, ⓦ www.fortunatoerrera .it; ❹), and *Bue Marino* (☎0923.912.715; June–Sept; ❻), whose eight self-contained studio apartments have sea-facing balconies, though rental is by the week only – contact the *Miryam Hotel* in town for more information.

The best swimming is actually a little further on, from the flat rocks below the road junction to Bugeber. East of here lie the **Cala dei Cinque Denti**, where fantastic-shaped rocks jut out of the sea like monstrous black teeth. Hence its name, "Bay of the Five Teeth" – though the rocks are really best seen from the sea. Just beyond, a minor road cuts away to the lighthouse at **Punta Spadillo**, where the cliff edges are covered with a carpet of surprising greenery that's somehow taken hold in the volcanic rocks.

At a fork further on in the road, the bus can drop you at the top of the smartly engineered route down into **GADIR**, one of the most perfect spots on Pantelleria. It's a small anchorage, with just a few houses hemmed in by volcanic pricks of rock, which – when the wind is up – can be battered and lashed by violent waves. At other times, people lay about on the flat concrete harbourside, and splash in the small thermal pools hereabouts.

The lower road from Gadir to Tracino is one of the loveliest on the island, following slopes that are terraced and corralled behind a patchwork of stone walls. Vines grow in profusion, with capers and blackberry bushes in the hedgerows. It's an easy, fairly flat hour's stroll to the charming **CALA LEVANTE**, a huddle of houses around another tiny fishing harbour. There's good swimming from the rocks – provided the sea's not too rough – and a **bar-restaurant** above, the *Cala Levante* (☎0923.691.134), with a terrace overlooking the sea. Where the road peters out, bear right along the path at the second anchorage and keep along the coast for another five minutes until the **Arco dell'Elefante**, or "Elephant Arch", hoves into view. It's named after the lovely hooped formation of rock that resembles an elephant stooping to drink. Again there's no beach, but it's a good place to swim anyway.

From the harbour, a stupendously steep road climbs all the way up to **TRACINO** in around twenty minutes, passing old *dammusi*, newer holiday homes, and striking gardens of vines and flowers. The top of the road marks the centre of Tracino, where there's a small square and a bar-restaurant. It's difficult to see where Tracino ends and adjacent **KHAMMA** starts, though this matters little once you're on the bus back to town.

Keen **hikers** make Tracino the start of their route into the pretty **Piano Ghirlandia**. The road runs out the other side of Tracino and soon becomes a track, which continues all the way down to meet the road on the south coast near Rekale.

The Specchio di Vénere and Bugeber

From the first road junction on the northwest coast, it's a ten-minute walk up and around before you get the initial stunning views of the island's small lake, **Specchio di Vénere** (Venus's Mirror), shimmering below in a former crater. Though it glistens aquamarine in the middle, it has a muddy-brown edge, deposits of which you're supposed to apply to your body and allow to bake hard in the sun. Then you dive in and swim, washing all the mud off in the pleasantly warm water. A path skirts the edge of the lake, around which horse races take place every August as part of the ferragosto celebrations.

Beyond the trattoria by the lake shore, *Da Pina*, the road climbs up for another 2km to the hamlet of **BUGEBER**, set amid tumbling fields of vines and craggy boulders. The bus back to town runs past here four times a day (not Sun); alternatively, walk the 3km past the lake back to the main road, where you can pick up any of the buses from Tracino.

Siba and the Montagna Grande

The other inland destination is the highest reaches of Pantelleria's main volcano, the Montagna Grande, whose summit is the island's most distinctive feature when seen from out at sea. Buses (five daily) run from the port, turning sharp left past the airport for the crumbly old village of **SIBA**, perched on a ridge below the volcano, with views over the terraced slopes and cultivated plains to the sea. Few of the ancient *dammusi* here are so much as whitewashed, let alone bristling with mod cons. Outside, large wooden water barrels sit on the mildewed dry-stone volcanic walls, while the hamlet's only services are an *alimentari* and a *tabaccaio*. If time hasn't exactly stood still here, it's in no great hurry to get on with things either.

To climb the peak of **Montagna Grande** (836m), keep left at the telephone sign by the *tabaccaio* here, and strike off the main road. The mountain's slopes afford the best views on the island, and are pitted by numerous volcanic vents, the **Stufe de Khazen**, marked by escaping threads of vapour.

From Siba, another (signposted) path – on the left as you follow the road through the village – brings you in around twenty minutes to a natural sauna, **Sauna Naturale** (or Bagno Asciutto), where you can sweat it out for as long as you can stand. It's little more than a slit in the rock-face, where you can crouch in absolute darkness, breaking out into a heavy sweat as soon as you enter. It's coolest at floor-level; raising yourself up is like putting yourself into a pizza oven, while the ceiling is so hot it's impossible to keep the palm of your hand pressed flat against it. Ten minutes is the most you should attempt the first time – emerging into the midday sun is like being wafted by a cool breeze. Bring a towel.

From the road that descends from Siba to Scauri and the coast, you can take a track off to the left that runs through the so-called **Valle Monastero**. This lovely route leads past the abandoned monastery which gives the valley its name. Make sure you carry enough water if you tackle this hike, which is best accomplished early in the day. The path meets the road midway between Scauri and Rekale.

Festivals

February

3 Festival of St Biagio in **Salemi**, with pasta figures given to children and a slippery-pole competition.

March

19 Festival of St Joseph at **Salemi**, with poetry recitals and sculptures of Jesus, Mary and Joseph made out of bread.

March/April

Good Friday Procession of the Misteri in **Trápani** and **Érice**.

Easter Thursday Enactment of the Passion in **Marsala**, in brightly jewelled processions with gorgeous finery.

Easter Sunday Symbolic meeting of statues of Christ and Mary in **Mazara del Vallo**.

May/June

La Mattanza tuna slaughter in **Favignana**, though check first with the tourist office in Favignana.

June

19–21 Festival of Santa Maria dei Mirácoli at **Álcamo**, with a pilgrimage to Monte Bonifato.

29 Feast of SS Peter and Paul in **Pantelleria**.

July

Music festival in **Trápani** at the Villa Margherita.

10–13 Feast of the Three Maries in **Pantelleria**.

August

Festival of modern Italian art in **Marsala**.

15 Horse race around Specchio di Vénere lake in **Pantelleria**.

September

Last week International couscous festival at **San Vito Lo Capo**.

December

24 Procession of characters from the Nativity story in **Salemi**.

Travel details

Trains

Castelvetrano to: Marsala (14 daily Mon–Sat, 6 daily Sun; 45min); Mazara del Vallo (14 daily Mon–Sat, 6 daily Sun; 20min); Palermo (4 daily Mon–Sat, 1 daily Sun; 2hr 30min); Trápani (14 daily Mon–Sat, 6 daily Sun; 1hr 10min).

Marsala to: Castelvetrano (13 daily Mon–Sat, 6 daily Sun; 45min); Mazara del Vallo (13 daily Mon–Sat, 6 daily Sun; 20min); Trápani (14 daily Mon–Sat, 6 daily Sun; 30min).

Mazara del Vallo to: Campobello di Mazara (13 daily Mon–Sat, 6 daily Sun; 10min); Castelvetrano (13 daily Mon–Sat, 6 daily Sun; 20min); Marsala (14 daily Mon–Sat, 6 daily Sun; 20min); Trápani (14 daily Mon–Sat, 6 daily Sun; 50min).

Trápani to: Álcamo (9 daily Mon–Sat, 5 daily Sun; 40min); Castelvetrano (13 daily Mon–Sat, 6 daily Sun; 1hr 10min); Marsala (13–14 daily Mon–Sat, 6 daily Sun; 30min); Mazara del Vallo (13 daily Mon–Sat, 6 daily Sun; 50min); Palermo (8 daily Mon–Sat, 5 daily Sun; 2hr 15min–3hr 45min); Segesta-Tempio (3–4 daily; 20min).

Buses

Castellammare del Golfo to: Álcamo (12 daily Mon–Sat, 2 daily Sun; 25min); Calatafimi (3 daily Mon–Sat, 1 daily Sun; 30min); Palermo (6–9 daily Mon–Sat, 1–3 daily Sun; 1hr–1hr 30min); San Vito Lo Capo (2–4 daily Mon–Sat, 1–3 daily Sun; 1hr); Scopello (4 daily Mon–Sat, 4 daily Sun in summer; 20min); Segesta (2 daily mid-June to mid-Sept; 30min); Trápani (4 daily Mon–Sat; 1hr).

Castelvetrano to: Agrigento (3 daily Mon–Sat, 1 daily Sun; 1hr 40min–2hr 25min); Campobello (1–2 hourly Mon–Sat, 2–3 daily Sun; 15min); Gibellina (6 daily Mon–Sat; 1hr); Marinella (for Selinunte, 5–6 daily; 30min); Marsala (10 daily Mon–Sat; 35min–1hr 15min); Mazara del Vallo (10 daily Mon–Sat, 1 daily Sun; 25–40min); Palermo (10 daily Mon–Sat, 2–3 daily Sun; 1hr 45min); Salemi (2 daily Mon–Sat; 35–45min); Sciacca (3 daily Mon–Sat, 1 daily Sun; 30–55min); Trápani (11 daily Mon–Sat, 1 daily Sun; 1hr–2hr 10min).

Érice to: Trápani (10 daily Mon–Sat, 4 daily Sun; 50min).

Marinella/Selinunte to: Castelvetrano (5–6 daily; 20min).

Marsala to: Agrigento (3 daily Mon–Sat, 1 daily Sun; 2hr 20min–3hr 30min); Campobello (5 daily Mon–Sat; 1hr); Castelvetrano (6 daily Mon–Sat, 1 Sun; 35min–1hr 25min); Mazara del Vallo (6 daily Mon–Sat, 1 daily Sun; 20–45min); Palermo (11–20 daily Mon–Sat, 6–8 daily Sun; 2hr 25min); Trápani (6 daily Mon–Sat, 1 daily Sun; 35min–1hr).

Mazara del Vallo to: Agrigento (3 daily Mon–Sat, 1 daily Sun; 2–3hr); Campobello (6 daily Mon–Sat; 20min); Castelvetrano (6 daily Mon–Sat, 1 Sun; 25–40min); Marsala (7 daily Mon–Sat, 1 daily Sun; 20–35min); Palermo (8–14 daily Mon–Sat, 4 daily Sun; 2hr); Trápani (6 daily Mon–Sat, 1 daily Sun; 1hr–1hr 30min).

Pantelleria Town to: Bugeber (3–4 daily Mon–Sat; 20min); Khamma (8–9 daily Mon–Sat; 25min); Rekale (6 daily Mon–Sat; 30min); Scauri (6 daily Mon–Sat; 20min); Siba (5 daily Mon–Sat; 30min); Tracino (8–9 daily Mon–Sat; 30min).

San Vito Lo Capo to: Palermo (winter 1–2 daily, summer 3–4 daily; 2–3hr); Trápani (8 Mon–Sat, 4 daily Sun; 1hr 20min).

Scopello to: Castellammare del Golfo (4 daily Mon–Sat, 4 daily Sun in summer; 20min).

Trápani to: Álcamo (4–7 daily Mon–Sat, 2 daily Sun; 1hr–1hr 30min); Agrigento (3 daily Mon–Sat, 1 daily Sun; 3–4hr); Bonagia (5–7 daily Mon–Sat, 2 daily Sun in summer; 25min); Castellammare del Golfo (5 daily; 1hr); Castelvetrano (5 daily Mon–Sat, 1 daily Sun; 1hr 35min–2hr); Érice (10 daily Mon–Sat, 4 daily Sun; 50min); Marsala (5 daily Mon–Sat, 1 daily Sun; 45min); Mazara del Vallo (5 daily Mon–Sat, 1 daily Sun; 1hr 5min–1hr 30min); Palermo (hourly Mon–Sat, 12 daily Sun; 2hr); Palermo airport (1 daily Mon–Sat; 1hr 10min); San Vito Lo Capo (8 daily Mon–Sat, 4 daily Sun;

1hr 20min); Segesta (4 daily Mon–Sat, 2 daily Sun; 40–55min); Trápani airport (hourly Mon–Sat, 7 daily Sun; 45min).

Ferries

Pantelleria to: Trápani (1 daily June–Sept, Mon–Sat Oct–May; 5hr 15min–6hr).

Trápani to: Cágliari (1 weekly; 10–12hr); Favignana (June–Sept 3 daily; Oct–May 1–3 daily; 1hr–1hr 25min); Lévanzo (3 daily June–Sept, 1–2 daily Oct–May; 50min–1hr 40min); Maréttimo (1 daily; 2hr 35min–3hr); Pantelleria (1 daily June–Sept, Sun–Fri Oct–May; 6hr 45min); Tunis (3 weekly; 9hr).

Hydrofoils and fast ferries

Marsala to: Favignana (5 daily June–Sept, 3 daily Oct–May; 30min); Lévanzo (2 daily June–Sept, 1 daily Oct–May; 55min–1hr 20min); Maréttimo (3 daily June–Sept;1hr 15min–2hr).

Mazara del Vallo to: Pantelleria (3 weekly July & Aug; 1hr 45min).

Pantelleria to: Mazara del Vallo (3 weekly July & Aug; 1hr 45min); Trápani (1 daily mid-June to mid-Oct; 2hr 30min).

Trápani to: Favignana (hourly; 15–35min); Lévanzo (hourly; 15–40min); Maréttimo (4–5 daily; 1hr 5min); Naples (3–4 weekly June–Sept; 6hr 45min); Pantelleria (1 daily mid-June to mid-Oct; 2hr 30min); Ústica, via Lévanzo and Favignana (3–4 weekly June–Sept; 2hr 30min).

Planes

Pantelleria to: Palermo (1–2 daily; 50min); Trápani (1–3 daily; 40min).

Trápani to: Pantelleria (1–3 daily; 40min).

Contexts

Contexts

Sicily's history

S icily has a richer and more eventful past than any of the other islands dotted around the Mediterranean. Its strategic importance made it the constant prey of conquerors, many of whom, while contributing a rich artistic heritage, also turned Sicily into one of the most desolate war zones in Europe, their greed utterly transforming its ecology and heaping misery onto the vast majority of its inhabitants.

Early times

Numerous remains survive of the **earliest human settlements** in Sicily, left mainly along the coast by people originally from mainland Europe. The most interesting of these are the cave paintings in Addaura, on the northern face of Monte Pellegrino, and those in the Grotta del Genovese, on Lévanzo in the Égadi Islands, which give a graphic insight into late Ice Age **Paleolithic** culture, from between 20,000 and 10,000 BC.

During the later **Neolithic period**, between 4000 and 3000 BC, a new wave of settlers arrived from the eastern Mediterranean, landing on Sicily's east coast and in the Aeolian Islands. Examples of their relatively advanced Stentinello culture – incised and patterned pottery and simple tools – are displayed in the museum on Lípari in the Aeolians. Agricultural advances, the use of ceramics and the domestication of animals, as well as the new techniques of metal-working imported by later waves of Aegean immigrants in the **Copper Age** (3000–2000 BC), permitted the establishment of fixed farms and villages. In turn, this caused an expansion of trade, and promoted greater contact with far-flung Mediterranean cultures. The presence of Mycenaean ware, from the Greek mainland, became more noticeable during the **Bronze Age** (2000–1000 BC), an era to which the sites of Capo Graziano and Punta Milazzese on the Aeolian Islands belong. In about 1250 BC, further population movements took place, this time originating from the Italian mainland: the Ausonians settled in the Aeolians, and the **Sikels** in eastern Sicily, pushing the indigenous tribes inland. It was the Sikels, from whom Sicily takes its name, who are thought to have first excavated the vast necropolis of Pantálica, near Siracusa. At about the same time, the Sicans, a people believed to have originated in North Africa, occupied the western half of the island. Little more is known about another tribe in western Sicily, the **Elymians**, who claimed descent from Trojan refugees: their chief city, Segesta, was alleged to have been founded by Aeneas' companion, Acestes.

The Carthaginians and the Greeks

After about 900 BC, Mycenaean and Aegean trading contacts began to be replaced by **Carthaginian** ones from North Africa, particularly in the west of the island. The Carthaginians – originally Phoenicians from the eastern

Mediterranean – first settled at Panormus (modern Palermo), Solus (Solunto) and Motya (Mózia), during the eighth and seventh centuries BC. Their arrival coincided with the establishment of **Greek colonies** in the east of Sicily. As was the case in previous migrations, the Aegean Greeks who colonized Sicily's eastern coast were driven by a shortage of cultivable land back home. The first Greek settlements had already been made on the Italian mainland in Tuscany and around the bay of Naples, and the colonization of **Naxos** in 734 BC was undertaken primarily for strategic reasons. The possibilities for expansion soon became apparent, and the Chalcidinians and Naxians who founded this colony were quickly followed by Megarians at **Megara Hyblaea**, north of Siracusa, Corinthians at **Ortigia** in Siracusa itself, and Rhodians, Cnidians and Cretans in **Gela**. While continuing to have close links with their original homes, these cities became independent city-states and founded subcolonies of their own, most important of which were **Selinus** (Selinunte) and **Akragas** (Agrigento). Along with the Greek colonies on the Italian mainland, these scattered communities came to be known as Magna Graecia, "Greater Greece", whose wealth eventually overtook that of Greece itself.

The settlers found themselves with huge resources at their disposal, not least the island's fertility, which they quickly exploited through the widespread cultivation of corn – so much so that Demeter, the Greek goddess of grain and fecundity, became the chief deity on the island (the lake at Pergusa, near Enna, was claimed to be the site of the abduction of her daughter, Persephone). The olive and the vine were introduced from Greece, and commercial activity across the Ionian Sea was intense and profitable. The magnificence of the temples at Syracuse and Akragas often surpassed that of the major shrines in Greece. But the settlers also imported their native rivalries, and the history of Hellenic Sicily is one of almost uninterrupted warfare between the cities, even if they did generally join forces in the face of common foes such as the Carthaginians. It was the alliance against Carthage of Gela, Akragas and Syracuse, and the resulting Greek victory at **Himera** in 480 BC, that determined the ascendancy of **Syracuse** in Sicily for the next 270 years. The defeat, in about 450 BC, of a rebellion led by **Ducetius**, a Hellenized Sikel, extinguished the remnants of any native resistance to Greek hegemony, and the following century has been hailed as the "Golden Age" of Greek Sicily.

The accumulation of power by Syracusan **tyrants** attracted the attention of the mainland Greek states; Athens in particular was worried by the rapid spread of Corinthian influence in Sicily. In 415 BC, Athens dispatched the greatest armada ever to have sailed from its port. Later known as the **Great Expedition**, the effort was in response to a call for help from its ally, Segesta, while at war with Syracuse-supported Selinus. By 413 BC Syracuse itself was under siege, but the disorganization of the attacking forces, who were further hampered by disease, led to their total defeat, the execution of their generals and the imprisonment of 7000 soldiers in Syracuse's limestone quarries, many of whom were destined for slavery. This victory represented the apogee of Syracusan power. Civil wars continued throughout the rest of the island, attracting the attention of the Carthaginian **Hannibal**, who responded to attacks on his territory by sacking in turn Selinus, Himera, Akragas and Gela. A massive counterattack was launched by the Syracusan tyrant **Dionysius I**, or "the Elder" (405–367 BC). That culminated in the complete destruction of the Phoenician base at **Motya**; its survivors founded a new centre at Lilybaeum, modern Marsala, on the western tip of the island.

The general devastation in Sicily caused by these wars was to some extent reversed by **Timoleon** (345–336 BC), who rebuilt many of the cities and re-established democratic institutions with new injections of settlers from Italy and Greece. But the carnage continued under the tyrant **Agathocles** (315–289 BC), who was unrivalled in his sheer brutality. Battles were fought on the Italian mainland and North Africa, and the strife he engendered back in Sicily didn't end until **Hieron II** (265–215 BC) opted for a policy of peacekeeping, and even alliance, with the new power of the day, Rome. The **First Punic War**, which broke out in 264 BC after the mercenary army in control of Messina, the **Mamertines**, appealed to Rome for help against their erstwhile Carthaginian protectors, left Syracuse itself untouched. It did however once again lead to the ruin of much of the island, before the final surrender of the Carthaginian base at Lilybaeum in 241. For Syracuse and its territories, though, this was a period of relative peace, and Hieron used the breathing space to construct some of the city's most impressive monuments.

Roman Sicily

Roman rule in Sicily can be said to have begun with **the fall of Syracuse**. That momentous event became inevitable when the city, whose territory was by now the only part of Sicily still independent of Rome, chose to side with Carthage in the **Second Punic War**, provoking a two-year siege that ended with the sacking of Syracuse in 211 BC. For the next seven hundred years, Sicily was a province of Rome, though in effect a subject colony, since few Sicilians were granted citizenship until the third century AD, when all inhabitants of the empire were classified as Romans. Much of the island's present appearance was determined during this period. Large parts of the remaining forests were cut down to make way for the grain cultivation that was to become Sicily's major function. The island was Rome's granary or, as Cato had it, "the nurse at whose breast the Roman people is fed". The land was apportioned into large units, or *latifondia*, which became the basis for the vast agricultural estates into which Sicily is still to a certain extent divided. Conditions on these estates were so harsh that the second century BC saw two **slave revolts**, in 135–132 BC and 104–101 BC, involving tens of thousands of men, women and children, most of whom had been Greek-speaking citizens from all over Rome's newly won Mediterranean and Asian empire. Far more damaging to the island, however, was the **civil war** between Octavian, the future Emperor Augustus, and Sextus Pompey, who seized Sicily in 44 BC. For eight years the island's crucial grain exports were interrupted, and the final defeat of Sextus – in a sea battle off Mylae, or Milazzo – was followed by harsh retribution.

These were isolated incidents, however, and on the whole Sicily benefited from the relative calm bestowed by the Romans. But little of the heavy tribute exacted by Rome was expended on the island itself and, though a degree of local administration existed, all important decisions were taken by the Roman Senate. That was represented on the island by two tax collectors, or quaestors, stationed in Syracuse and Lilybaeum, and a governor (praetor), who normally spent his year-long term extracting as much personal profit from the island as he could. The praetor **Verres** used his three terms of office, from 73 to 71 BC, to strip the countryside and despoil a large part of the treasure still held in the island's lavish temples. **Cicero**'s prosecution of Verres, though undoubtedly exaggerated, constitutes our main source of information on Sicily under the Roman Republic. It gives some idea of the extent of the ruination wreaked by the unscrupulous praetor: "When I arrived in Sicily after an absence of four years, it seemed to me a land in which there had been fought a prolonged and cruel war. Those fields and hills which I had seen bright and green I now saw devastated and deserted, and it seemed as if the land itself wept for its ancient farmers."

Once Octavian was installed as emperor, in 27 BC, Sicily entered a more peaceful period of Roman rule, with isolated instances of imperial splendour, notably the extravagant villa at Casale, near Piazza Armerina. The island benefited especially from its important role in Mediterranean trade, and Syracuse, which handled much of the passing traffic, became a prominent centre of **early Christianity**, supposedly visited by SS Peter and Paul on their way to Rome. Here, and further inland at Akrai, catacombs were burrowed from the third century AD onwards – and in caves throughout Sicily, Christian sanctuaries took their place alongside the shrines of the dozens of other cults prevalent on the island.

Barbarians, Byzantines and the Arabs

Though Rome fell to the Visigoths in 410 AD, Sicily became prey to another Germanic tribe, the **Vandals**, who launched their invasion from the North African coast. The island was soon reunited with Italy under the Ostrogoth Theodoric, but the barbarian presence in Sicily was only a brief interlude, terminated in 535 AD when the **Byzantine** general Belisarius occupied the island. Although a part of the population had been Latinized, Greek remained the dominant culture and language of the majority, and the island willingly joined the Byzantine fold. In 663, Syracuse even became the centre of the eastern empire for a short time, possibly for political reasons but no doubt partly with an eye to the reconquest of barbarian lands and the ultimate revival of the Roman Empire.

Constantinople was never able to give much attention to Sicily, however. The island was perpetually harried by piratical attacks, particularly from North Africa, where the Moors had become the most dynamic force in the Mediterranean. In around 700, the island of **Pantelleria** was taken, and only discord among the Arabs prevented Sicily itself from being next. In the event, trading agreements were signed, Arab merchants settled in Sicilian ports, and a fully fledged **Arab invasion** did not take place until 827, when a Byzantine admiral rebelled against the emperor and invited in the Aghlabid Emir of Tunisia. Ten thousand Arabs, Berbers and Spanish Muslims (known collectively as **Saracens**) landed at Mazara del Vallo, and Palermo fell four years later, though the invading forces only reached the Straits of Messina in 965. As with the Roman invasion, however, the turning point came with the fall of Syracuse in 878, when its population was massacred and the city plundered of its legendary wealth.

Palermo became the capital of the **Arabs in Sicily**, under whom it grew to become one of the world's greatest cities, wholly cosmopolitan in outlook, furnished with gardens, mosques (more than anywhere the traveller Ibn Hauqal had seen, barring Cordoba) and luxurious palaces. The Arabs brought great benefits to the rest of the island, too, resettling rural areas, renovating and extending the irrigation works, breaking down many of the unwieldy *latifondia* and introducing new crops, including citrus trees, sugar cane, flax, cotton, silk, melons and date palms. Mining was developed, the salt industry greatly expanded and commerce improved, with Sicily once more at the centre of a flourishing trade network. Many Sicilian place names testify to the extent of the Arab settlement of the island. Prefixes such as *calta* (castle) and *gibil* (mountain) are plentiful, while other terms still in use indicate their impact on fishing, such as the name of the swordfish boats prowling the Straits of Messina (*felucca*), or the tuna-fishing terminology of the Égadi Islands. Taxation was rationalized and reduced, and religious tolerance was greater than under the Byzantines, though non-Muslims were subject to a degree of social discrimination – a factor that probably helped to persuade a large number of Christians to adopt the Muslim faith.

The Arabs were prone to divisive feuding, however, and when in the tenth century the Aghlabid dynasty was toppled in Tunisia and their Fatimid successors shifted their capital to Egypt, Sicily lost its central position in the Arab Mediterranean empire and was left vulnerable to external attack. In 1038, the Byzantine general **George Maniakes** attempted to draw the island back under Byzantine sway, but he was unable to extend his occupation much beyond Syracuse. The real threat came from western Europe, particularly from the **Normans**, some of whom had accompanied Maniakes and seen for themselves the rewards to be gained. One of these, William "Bras de Fer" ("Iron Arm"), who had earned his nickname by his slaying of the Emir of Syracuse with one blow, was the eldest of the Hauteville brothers, whose exploits were soon to change the map of southern Europe.

The Normans

The **Hauteville brothers** had long been active in southern Italy by the time the youngest of them, Roger, seized Messina in 1061 in response to a call for help by one of the warring Arab factions. It took another thirty years to take control of the whole island, in a series of bloody and destructive campaigns that often involved the enlistment of Arabs on the Norman side. In 1072 Palermo was captured and adopted as the capital of **Norman Sicily**, and was subsequently adorned with palaces and churches that count among their most brilliant achievements.

The most striking thing about the Norman period in Sicily is its brief span. In little more than a century, five kings bequeathed an enormous legacy of art and architecture that is still one of the most conspicuous features of the island. When compared with the surviving remains of the Byzantines, who reigned for three centuries, or the Arabs, whose occupation lasted roughly two, the Norman contribution stands out, principally due to its absorption of previous styles: the finest examples of Arab art to be seen in Sicily are elements incorporated into the great Norman churches. It was this fusion of talent that accounted for the great success of Norman Sicily, not just in the arts but in administration, justice and religious tolerance.

The policy of acceptance and integration was largely determined by force of circumstances: the Normans could not count on having adequate numbers of their own settlers, or bureaucrats to form a governmental class, and instead were compelled to rely on the existing framework. They did, however, considerably streamline and centralize administration, and gradually introduced a Latinized aristocracy and clerical hierarchy from northern Italy and France, so that the Arabic language was largely superseded by Italian and French by 1200.

The first of the great Sicilian-Norman dynasty, **Count Roger**, or Roger I, sustained his power in accordance with Byzantine notions of absolutism and through his retention of a permanent mercenary army and strong fleet. He was a resolute and successful ruler, marrying his daughters into two of the most powerful European dynasties, one of them to the son of the western emperor Henry IV. Roger's death in 1101, followed soon after by the death of his eldest son, left Sicily governed by his widow Adelaide as regent for his younger son, who in 1130 was crowned **Roger II**. This first Norman king of Sicily was also one of medieval Europe's most gifted and charismatic rulers, who consolidated his father's gains by making the island a great melting pot of the most vigorous and creative elements in the Mediterranean world. He spoke Greek, kept a harem and surrounded himself with a medley of advisers, notably **George of Antioch**, his chief minister, or Emir of Emirs. As well as being a patron of the arts, Roger extended his kingdom to encompass all of southern Italy, Malta and parts of North Africa, and more enduringly drew up the first written code of law in the island.

His son, William I (1154–66) – "**William the Bad**" – dissipated these achievements by his enthusiasm for pleasure-seeking and his failure to control the barons, who exploited racial tensions to undermine the king's authority. During the regency that followed, the Englishman Walter of the Mill had himself elected archbishop of Palermo and dominated the scene for some twenty years, along with two other Englishmen, his brother Bartholomew and Bishop Palmer. This triumvirate preserved a degree of stability, but also encouraged the new king William II (1166–89), "**William the Good**", to establish a second archbishopric and construct a cathedral at **Monreale** to rival that of Palermo, just 10km away. The period saw a general consolidation of Christianity and a shift away from Muslim influence, though Arabs still constituted the bulk of the rural population and William himself resembled an oriental sultan in his style and habits, building a number of Arab-style palaces.

The death of William, aged only 36 and with no obvious successor, signalled a crisis in Norman Sicily. The barons were divided between **Tancred**, William's illegitimate nephew, and **Constance**, Roger II's aunt, who had married the Hohenstaufen (or Swabian) Henry, later to become the emperor Henry VI. Tancred's election by an assembly was the first sign of a serious erosion of the king's authority: others followed, notably a campaign in 1189 against Muslims living on the island, which caused many of them to flee; and a year later the sacking of **Messina** by the English Richard I, on his way to join the Third Crusade. Tancred's death in 1194 and the succession of his young son, **William III**, coincided with the arrival in the Straits of Messina of the Hohenstaufen fleet. Opposition was minimal, and on Christmas Day of the same year Henry crowned himself king of Sicily. William and his mother were imprisoned in the castle at **Caltabellotta**, never to be seen again.

Hohenstaufen and the Angevins

Inevitably, Henry's imperial concerns led him away from Sicily, which represented only a source of revenue for him on the very outer limits of his domain. A revolt broke out against his authoritarian rule, which he repressed with extreme severity, but in the middle of it he went down with dysentery, died, and the throne passed to his three-and-a-half-year-old son, who became the emperor Frederick II, **Frederick I** of Sicily.

At first the running of the kingdom was entrusted to Frederick's mother Constance, but there was little stability, with the barons in revolt and a rash of race riots in 1197. Frederick's assumption of the government in 1220 marked a return to decisive leadership, with an immediate campaign to bring the barons to heel and eliminate a Muslim rebellion in Sicily's interior. The twin aims of his rule in Sicily were to restore the broad framework of the Norman state, and to impose a more authoritarian and imperial stamp on society, indicated by his fondness for classical Roman allusions in his promulgations and coinage. He allowed himself rights and privileges in Sicily that were impossible in his other possessions, emphasizing his own authority at the expense of the independence of the clergy and the autonomy of the cities. As elsewhere in southern Italy, strong **castles** were built, such as those at Milazzo, Catania, Siracusa and Augusta, to keep the municipalities in check. When the most progressive of these, Messina, rebelled in 1232, the port was ruthlessly punished.

A unified legal system was drawn up, embodied in his *Liber Augustales*, while his attempts to homogenize Sicilian society involved the harsh treatment of what had now become minority communities, such as the Muslims. He encouraged the arts, too, championing Sicilian vernacular poetry, whose pre-eminence was admitted by Petrarch and Dante. A multitalented ruler, Frederick acquired the name **"Stupor Mundi"** ("Wonder of the World"), reflecting his promotion of science, law and medicine, and the peace that Sicily enjoyed during the half-century of his rule.

However, Frederick's mounting preoccupation with his other territories was to the detriment of the island. The balance of power he achieved within Sicily laid the foundations for many of the island's future woes – for example, the weakening of the municipalities at a time when most European towns were increasing their autonomy. His centralized government worked so long as there was a powerful hand to guide it, but when Frederick died in 1250, decline set in, despite the efforts of his son **Manfred**, who strove to defend his crown from the encroachments of the barons and the acquisitiveness of foreign monarchs. New claimants to the throne were egged on by Sicily's nominal suzerain, the pope, anxious to deprive the Hohenstaufen of their southern possession, and he eventually auctioned it, selling it to the king of England, who accepted it on behalf of his eight-year-old son, Edmund of Lancaster. For ten years Edmund was styled "King of Sicily".

But a new French pope deposed Edmund, who had never set foot in Sicily, and gave the title instead to **Charles of Anjou**, brother of the French king, "St" Louis IX. In 1266 the Angevin forces defeated the Hohenstaufen army in a battle on the Italian mainland, in which Manfred was slain, and in 1268 another battle resulted in the public beheading of Manfred's 14-year-old nephew, his heir Conradin. Backed by the papacy, and with a degree of popular support, Charles of Anjou embarked on a punitive campaign against the majority of the Sicilian population, who had supported the Hohenstaufen. He plundered land to give to his followers, and imposed a high level of taxation to recoup the cost of the recent war. The nobility, too, were affected by Charles's draconian measures and some began to negotiate with the Ghibelline anti-papal faction in Aragon, where the king, Peter, had become the champion of the Hohenstaufen cause by marrying Manfred's daughter. In the end, however, it was a grassroots revolt that sparked off the **Sicilian Vespers**, an uprising against the French that began on Easter Monday 1282; it is traditionally held to have started after the bell for evening services, or Vespers, had rung at Palermo's church of Santo Spirito. The incident that sparked it all off was an insult to a woman by a French soldier, which led to a general slaughter in Palermo, soon growing into an

CONTEXTS | Sicily's history

island-wide rebellion against the French. This was the one moment in Sicilian history when the people rose up as one against foreign oppression – though in reality it was more an opportunity for horrific butchery and the settlement of old scores than a glorious expression of patriotic fervour.

The movement was given some direction when a group of nobles enlisted the support of Peter of Aragon, who landed at Trápani five months after the initial outbreak of hostilities and was acclaimed king at Palermo a few days later. The ensuing **Wars of the Vespers**, fought between Aragon and the Angevin forces based in Naples, lasted for another 21 years, mainly waged in Spain and at sea, while, in Aragonese Sicily, people settled down to over five centuries of Spanish domination.

The Spanish in Sicily

Sicily's new orientation towards Spain, and its severance from mainland Italy, meant that the island was largely excluded from all the great European developments of the fourteenth and fifteenth centuries. There was no liberation from feudalism, and little impact was made by the Renaissance. Rather, the feudal bonds were reinforced at the expense of social mobility, with the granting of large portions of land to a Spanish aristocracy in return for military service. Intellectual life on the island, meanwhile, was suffocated by the strictures of the Spanish Inquisition.

Although Peter of Aragon insisted that the two kingdoms of Aragon and Sicily should be ruled by separate kings after his death, his successor James ignored this and even reopened negotiations with the Angevins to sell the island back to them. His younger brother Frederick, appointed by James as Lieutenant of Palermo, convened a "parliament", which elected him king of an independent Sicily as **Frederick II** (1296–1337). As a result of the barons' support for him, Frederick was obliged to increase their feudal privileges, to the detriment of his own. Factions arose, growing out of the friction between Angevin and Aragonese supporters and fuelled by Angevin Naples. Open warfare followed until 1372, when the independence of Sicily – or Trinacria ("three-cornered"), as it was known under the terms of the subsequent treaty, an ancient name revived to distinguish the island from the mainland Regnum Siciliae, ruled by the kingdom of Naples – was guaranteed by Naples in return for an annual tribute and the recognition of the suzerainty of the pope.

It was the populace that suffered most from this feuding, since the policy of both sides was to avoid pitched battles and strike instead at the food sources in the country. This, combined with the effects of the Black Death, led to the interior of Sicily becoming depopulated and unproductive. The feudal nobility spent time mainly in the **towns**, and here at least there is some evidence of wealth in the mansions constructed during this period, in the **Chiaramonte** or the later, richly ornate **Catalan-Gothic** styles. A tradition of artistic patronage grew up, though most of the artists operating in Sicily came from elsewhere – for example, Francesco Laurana and the Gagini family were originally from northern Italy. A notable exception was **Antonello da Messina** (1430–79), who soaked up the latest Flemish techniques on his continental travels. Following the closing off of the eastern Mediterranean by the Ottoman Turks in the fifteenth century, Sicily was isolated from everywhere except Spain – from which, after 1410, it was ruled directly. The ports of Palermo and Messina continued to do a certain amount of business, but most of the merchants were from Genova, Pisa and Lucca. Sicily found itself on the very fringes of Europe, an Aragonese outpost in the firing line from Turkish incursions and raids from North Africa. The unification of Castile and Aragon in 1479, followed soon after by the reconquest of the whole Spanish peninsula from the Moors, meant that Sicily's importance to its Spanish monarchs declined even more, and the island soon became of most use as a source of cash, crucial for the financing of the Reconquista and the wars against the Turks.

Although **Alfonso II** (1416–58) made the island the base for his expansion to Naples, the two territories were separated again after his death, and Sicily came under the rule of a succession of **viceroys**, who were to wield power for the next four hundred years. Few of these were Sicilian (none at all after the first fifty years), while the only Spanish king to visit the island during the entire viceregal period was Charles V, on his way back from a Tunisian crusade in 1535.

Little else of note happened in the **sixteenth century**, though the curse of piracy was partially removed by the victory of the combined fleets of Spain, Venice and the Vatican against the Ottomans in 1571, at the Battle of Lépanto. But with the Spanish centres of power removed from the Mediterranean, and mercantile and imperial interest focused instead on the Atlantic, the period saw the utter **stagnation** of Sicily. The island's close bond to Spain meant that its degeneration deepened in tandem with Spain's decline in the **seventeenth and eighteenth centuries**. The aristocracy maintained their power and privileges while they were being eroded everywhere else in Europe, and corruption thrived in the viceroy's court. Offices were bought and sold, and political patronage was the order of the day. Throughout this period, Sicily still had a parliament, though it was largely symbolic. More far-reaching was the influence of **the Church**, one of the main pillars of the State and mainly non-Sicilian at its highest levels, which was bolstered by the wide powers of **the Inquisition**. Both institutions helped to create and enforce a sense of loyalty to, and even a veneration of, the Spanish Crown, though the overall effect was a docile acceptance of the status quo on the part of Sicilians. Certainly few serious attempts at rebellion took place during this period, apart from a couple of isolated and short-lived uprisings in Sicily's two major towns, Palermo and Messina. There were also occasional revolts against the excesses of the zealous Inquisition, but on the whole discontent manifested itself in a resort to **brigandage**, for which the forest and wild maquis of Sicily's interior provided an ideal environment. The mixed fear and respect that the brigand bands generated played a large part in the future formation of an organized criminal class in Sicily.

Already burdened by the ever-increasing taxes demanded by Spain to finance its remote religious conflicts (principally, the 1618–48 Thirty Years' War), the misery of the Sicilians was compounded by sporadic outbreaks of **plague**, and at the end of the seventeenth century by two appalling natural disasters. The **eruption of Etna** in 1669 devastated a large part of the area around Catania, while the **earthquake** of 1693 – also in the east of the island – flattened whole cities, and killed around five percent of the island's population. These disasters did at least provide an opportunity for the Sicilian craftsmen who were called upon to repair the damage to show off the latest **Baroque building** techniques. With the death of Charles II of Spain in 1700 and the subsequent Wars of the Spanish Succession, the island once more took a back seat to mainland European interests. It was bartered in the **Treaty of Utrecht** that negotiated the peace, and given to the northern Italian House of Savoy, only to be swapped for Sardinia and given to Austria seven years later.

The **Austrian government** of the island – as usual administered through viceroys – lasted only four years, cut short by the arrival of another Spaniard, Charles of Bourbon, who claimed the throne of the Two Sicilies (the title of the combined southern Italian possessions of the Spanish and Bourbon kings of Naples) for himself. Though he never visited Sicily again after his first landing, **Charles III** (1734–59) brought a refreshingly constructive air to the island's administration, showing a more benevolent attitude towards his new subjects, to whom he granted significant tax concessions. But, with his succession to the Spanish throne in 1759 and the inheritance of the Neapolitan crown by his son, **Ferdinand IV**, it was back to the bad old days. Any meagre attempts at reform made by his viceroys were opposed at every turn by the reactionary aristocracy, who were closing ranks in response to the progress of the Enlightenment and the ideas unleashed by the French Revolution. When the ensuing **Napoleonic Wars** wracked Europe, Sicily, along with Sardinia, was the only part of Italy not conquered by Napoleon, while the Neapolitan *ancien régime* was further buttressed by the decision of Ferdinand (brother-in-law of Marie Antoinette) to wage war against the revolutionary French. He was supported in this by the British, who sustained the Bourbon state, so that when Ferdinand and his court were forced to flee Naples in 1799, it was **Nelson**'s flagship they sailed in, accompanied by the British ambassador to Naples, Sir William Hamilton, and his wife Lady Emma. Nelson was rewarded for his services by the endowment of a large estate at Bronte, just west of Etna.

Four years later, Ferdinand was able to return to Naples, though he had to escape again in 1806 when Napoleon gave the Neapolitan crown to his brother Joseph. This time he had to stay longer, remaining in Palermo until after the defeat of Napoleon in 1815 – a stay that was accompanied by a larger contingent of British troops and a heavy involvement of British capital and commerce. **Liberalism** became a banner of revolt against the king's continuing tax demands, and Ferdinand's autocratic reaction provoked the British commander William **Bentinck** to intervene. Manoeuvring himself into a position where he was the virtual governor of Sicily, Bentinck persuaded the king to summon a new parliament and adopt a **constitution** whereby the independence of Sicily was guaranteed and feudalism abolished.

Although this represented a drastic break with the past, the reforms had little direct effect on the peasantry, and, following the departure of the British, the constitution was dropped soon after Ferdinand's return to the mainland. He now styled himself "Ferdinand I, King of the Two Sicilies" and repealed all the reforms previously introduced. Renewed talk of independence in Sicily spilled over into action in 1820, when a rebellion was put down with the help of Austrian mercenaries. The **repression** intensified after Ferdinand I's death in 1825, and the island's fortunes reached a new low under Ferdinand II (1830–59), nicknamed Re Bomba for his five-day **bombardment of Messina** following major insurrections there and in Palermo in 1848–49. Another uprising in Palermo in 1860 proved a spur for Garibaldi to pick Sicily as the starting point for his unification of Italy.

Unification and two world wars

On May 11, 1860, five weeks after the Palermo revolt, **Giuseppe Garibaldi** landed at Marsala with a thousand men. A professional soldier and one of the leading lights of **Il Risorgimento**, the movement for Italian unification,

Garibaldi intended to liberate the island from Bourbon rule, in the name of the Piedmont House of Savoy. His skill in guerrilla warfare, backed by an increasingly cooperative peasantry, ensured that the campaign progressed with astonishing speed. Four days after disembarking, he defeated 15,000 Bourbon troops at **Calatafimi**, closely followed by an almost effortless occupation of Palermo. A battle at **Milazzo** in July decided the issue: apart from Messina (which held out for another year), Sicily was free of Spain for the first time since Peter of Aragon acquired the crown in 1282.

A **plebiscite** was held in October, which returned a 99.5 percent majority in favour of union with the new kingdom of **Italy** under Vittorio Emanuele II. The result, greeted by general euphoria, marked the end of Garibaldi's five-month dictatorship, and the official **annexation** of the island to the Kingdom of Savoy. Later, however, many began to question whether anything had been achieved by this change of ruler. The new **parliamentary system**, in which only one percent of the island's population was eligible to vote, made few improvements for the majority of people, and political patronage, as ever, determined voting tendencies. Attempts at opposition – and local uprisings such as that at Palermo in 1866 – were met with ruthless force, sanctioned by a distant and misinformed government convinced that the island's problems were fundamentally those of law and order. Sicilians responded with their traditional defence of *omertà*, or silent non-cooperation, along with a growing **resentment** of the new Turin government (transferred to Rome in 1870) that was even stronger than their distrust of the more familiar Bourbons.

A series of reports made in response to criticism of the Italian government's failure to solve what was becoming known as "**the southern problem**" found that the lot of the Sicilian peasant was, if anything, worse after Unification than it had been under the Bourbons. Power had shifted away from the landed gentry to the *gabellotti*, the middlemen to whom they leased the land. These men became increasingly linked with the **Mafia**, a shadowy, loosely knit criminal association that found it easy to manipulate voting procedures, while simultaneously posing as defenders of the people. Everywhere, liberal programmes of reform were similarly subverted by the deep-rooted power relationships of the rural society onto which they had been grafted. But at the end of the nineteenth century a new, more organized opposition appeared on the scene in the form of **fasci** – embryonic trade-union groups demanding legislation to protect peasants' interests. Violence erupted and, when landowners called for repressive measures, the Italian prime minister, **Francesco Crispi** – a native Sicilian who had been one of the pioneers of the Risorgimento – dispatched a fleet and 30,000 soldiers to put down the "revolt", making use of an armoury of autocratic measures in the process, such as closing newspapers, censoring postal services and detaining suspects without trial. But, just as rashly, he soon followed repression with a radical series of reforms designed to effect a fairer and more efficient distribution of the land. These proposals, and others to grant partial autonomy to the region, were rejected by conservative Sicilians, who complained of interference in their affairs.

Although there were some signs of progress by the **end of the nineteenth century**, in the formation of worker cooperatives and in the enlightened land-reform programmes of individuals such as **Don Sturzo**, mayor of Caltagirone, the overwhelming despair of the peasantry was expressed in **mass emigration**. Despite their intimate attachment to the land and their close-knit family structure, one and a half million Sicilians decided to leave in the years leading up to 1914, most going to North and South America. Many had been left homeless in the wake of the great **Messina earthquake** of 1908, in which upwards of 80,000 lost their lives. Though the high rate of emigration was a crushing indictment of the state of affairs on the island, it had many positive effects for those left behind, who benefited not only from huge remittances sent back from abroad but from the wage increases that resulted from labour shortages.

However, any advantages were offset by Italy's military adventures. The **conquest of Libya** in 1912 was closely followed by **World War I**, and both were heavy blows to the Sicilian economy. In 1922 **Mussolini** gained power in Rome – largely without Sicilian support – and dispatched **Cesare Mori** to solve "the southern problem" by putting an end to the Mafia. Free of constitutional and legal restrictions, Mori was able to imprison thousands of suspected *mafiosi*. The effect was merely to drive the criminal class deeper underground, while the alliance he forged with the landed classes to help bring this about dissolved all the gains that had been made against the ruling elite, setting back the cause of agrarian reform. In the **1930s** Mussolini's African concerns and his drive for economic and agricultural self-sufficiency gave Sicily a new importance for Fascist Italy, the island now vaunted as "the geographic centre of the empire". In the much-publicized "**Battle for Grain**", wheat production increased, though at the cost of the diversity of crops that Sicily required, resulting in soil exhaustion and erosion. Mussolini's popularity on the island is best illustrated by his order, in 1941, that all Sicilian-born officials be transferred to the mainland, on account of their possible disloyalty.

During **World War II**, Sicily became the first part of Europe to be invaded by the Allies, when, in July 1943, Patton's American Seventh Army landed at Gela, and Montgomery's British Eighth Army came ashore between Pachino and Pozzallo further east. This combined army of 160,000 men was the largest ever seen in Sicily, but the campaign was longer and harder than had been anticipated, with the Germans mainly concerned with delaying the advance until they had moved most of their men and equipment across the Straits of Messina. Few Sicilian towns escaped **aerial bombardment**, and Messina itself was the most heavily bombed of all Italian cities before it was taken on August 18.

Modern times

The **aftermath** of the war saw the most radical changes in Sicily since Unification, and a series of intense and convoluted struggles between competing interests. With anarchy and hunger widespread, a wave of banditry and crime was unleashed, while the **Mafia** were reinstated in their behind-the-scenes role as adjudicators and power-brokers, now allied to the landowners in the face of large-scale land occupations by a desperate peasantry. **Separatism** became a potent rallying cry for protesters of all persuasions, who believed that Sicily's ills could best be solved by cutting its links with the mainland. A Separatist army was formed, financed by some of the gentry, but it lacked the organization or resources to make any great impact. It was largely in response to this call for independence that, in 1946, Sicily was granted **regional autonomy**, with its own assembly and president – a status comparable to that of Scotland in the UK. The same year saw the declaration of a republic in Italy, the result of a popular mandate.

Autonomy failed to heal the island's divisions, however, and brute force was used by the Mafia and the old gentry against what they perceived as the major threat to their position – **communism**. The most famous bandit of the time, **Salvatore Giuliano**, who had previously been associated with the Separatists, was enlisted in the anti-communist cause. He organized a campaign of bombings and assassinations, most notoriously at the 1947 May Day celebrations at **Portella della Ginestra**, a mountain pass near Palermo. Giuliano's betrayal and murder in 1950 was widely rumoured to have been carried out to prevent him revealing who his paymasters were, though it all helped to glorify his reputation in the popular imagination.

By the **1950s**, many saw the **Christian Democrat** party, Democrazia Cristiana, as the best hope to defend their interests. Along with the emotional hold it exerted by virtue of its close association with the Church, the DC could draw on many of the Sicilians' deepest fears of change. It became especially important after **Fanfani**'s revitalization of the party after 1954, with Sicily holding about a third of his supporters country-wide. But the party was too closely involved with business and the land-owning classes to have any real enthusiasm for reform. All attempts at enterprise were channelled through the party's offices, and favours were bought or bartered. Cutting across party lines, political patronage, or **clientelismo**, grew to be stronger than ever. It still affects people's lives on every level today, especially in the field of work – from finding a job to landing a contract. The favours system was also evident in the workings of the island's sluggish **bureaucracy**, considered even more contorted than that of the mainland, so that the smallest reforms proved complicated to put into practice, and often took years to effect. A law was passed to improve the functioning of the bureaucracy in 1971, but although progress has been made, the essential problem is unchanged, with the elaborate machinery of the civil service often exploited to accumulate and dispense personal power.

One area that managed to avoid bureaucratic control or planning of any sort was **construction** – one of Sicily's greatest growth industries, the physical evidence of which is among the visitor's most enduring impressions of the island. The building boom was inextricably connected with the Mafia's involvement in land speculation, and boosted by the phenomenal rate of **urban growth** all over Sicily. But in both the towns and rural areas, the minimum safety standards were rarely met, as highlighted by the **1968 earthquake**, in which 50,000 were made homeless along the Valle di Belice in the west of the island, although the quake was seismically quite small. And while large expanses of the countryside have been blighted by rapid and often unsafe development, other areas remain badly neglected, for instance Palermo, where, in some areas, bomb damage remains unrepaired more than sixty years on, even if recent years have seen marked improvements.

Industry, too, has been subject to mismanagement, and, apart from isolated cases, has rarely fulfilled the potential it promised after the discovery of **oil** near Ragusa and Gela in the 1950s, and the development of refineries and petrochemical plants on the Golfo di Augusta. Despite the huge resources allocated to them, other projects have failed miserably. **Agriculture**, on the other hand, has been deprived of both funds and attention, though investment and the better use of land can produce outstanding results, as shown by the success of citrus cultivation in the north and east of the island, and the draining of the Piana di Catania. Substantial subsidies have helped in these programmes, mainly through a financial agency called the Cassa del Mezzogiorno, set up in 1950 but discontinued in 1983, and from the **European Union**, which Italy joined in 1958.

Subsidy and support, meanwhile, have not prevented Sicilians from complaining of being left out of Italy's great "economic miracle". While Italy claims to be in the "top ten" of Western economies, it is the great urban centres in the north that flaunt their prosperity, while the south of Italy, known as Il Mezzogiorno, is left far behind. The other side of the coin is that the huge financial concessions made to the island have provoked resentment from Italy's more self-sufficient regions, by whom the failure of land-reform programmes and industrial development is chiefly attributed to corruption and incompetence in the island itself. Few Sicilians would wholly deny this; a longer view, however, argues that Sicily's disadvantages are derived principally from the past misuse of resources, coupled with a culture and mentality that have never given much credence to collectivist ideals. Even so, **progress** has been made, and the manifold increase of per capita income in the last fifty years is reflected in greater numbers of newer and bigger cars jamming the island's roads every year, while new laws relating to land distribution and reform of the bureaucracy show a greater commitment to change. There is more awareness, too, on the part of the state that the fight against **organized crime** requires more than moralistic speeches. Indeed, in **1992**, following the murders of anti-Mafia investigators Falcone and Borsellino (see p.440), the Chief of Police of Palermo was sacked, while 7000 troops were sent to the island to patrol prisons and search towns with a known Mafia presence. There have been significant breakthroughs, though these are mostly connected with a change in the public attitude towards criminality, resulting in part from a campaign to reform Sicily's dilapidated **education** system, itself often a victim of Mafia corruption. In the 1990s, a campaign of anti-Mafia education began in Sicilian schools, aiming to cut the secondary-school drop-out rate, still reaching over forty percent in some regions, by encouraging children away from the traditional path of corruption, crime and Mafia involvement.

Despite such superficial improvements, the deep problems that have always bedevilled Sicily remain in some form. Unemployment, still high at fifteen to twenty percent, is not helped by the diminishing opportunities for **emigration**, though a million still managed to escape the island between 1951 and 1971, along with the majority of Sicily's most outstanding artists and writers. Ironically, the late 1990s saw the problem of **immigration** hitting the agenda for the first time in several centuries, as economic refugees from North Africa arrive by regular boatloads on the island's southern littoral, particularly the two southernmost islands of Lampedusa and Pantelleria. These *extracomunitari* (literally, "those from non-EU countries") are routinely rounded up and sent to crowded processing centres, where they languish for months, before almost all are eventually returned to their countries of origin. Others slip through and join the already strained jobs market. Despite harsh anti-immigration legislation introduced by **Silvio Berlusconi**'s right-wing Forza Italia! party, illegal immigration continues to be a contentious issue that has affected Italy more than most EU countries under Berlusconi's successor as prime minister, the left-of-centre **Romano Prodi**.

In the long run, perhaps the greatest hope for Sicily lies in **tourism**: the annual deluge of mainly French, Swiss and Germans is growing in numbers and impact, while more and more Italians are discovering the island's holiday potential, especially its outdoor attractions and wildlife. The creation of **regional parks** in Etna and the Nébrodi and Madonie ranges, and the **marine reserves** around Ústica and the Égadi and Pelágie islands, are a reflection of this, and an encouraging pointer for the future.

The Mafia in Sicily

In Sicily, there is "*mafiosità*" and there is "the Mafia". *Mafiosità* refers to a criminal mentality, the Mafia to a specific criminal organization. In Italy's deep south, a man can look *mafioso*, or talk like a *mafioso*, meaning he has the aura, or stench, of criminality about him, even though he has no explicit connection to the crime syndicate. And, while notions of family solidarity and the moral stature of the outlaw mean that *mafiosità* can never be completely extirpated from Sicilian society, the Mafia is an entity whose members can be eliminated and its power emasculated.

What has always prevented this is the shadowy nature of the organization, protected by the long-standing **code of silence**, or *omertà*, that invariably led to accusations being retracted at the last moment, or to crucial witnesses being found dead with a stone, cork or a wad of banknotes stuffed into their mouths, or else simply disappearing off the face of the earth. As a result, many have doubted the very existence of the Mafia, claiming that it's nothing more than the creation of pulp-thriller writers, the invention of a sensationalist press and the fabrication of an Italian government embarrassed by its inability to control an unusually high level of crime in Sicily.

In 1982, however, proof of the innermost workings of the Mafia's organization emerged when a high-ranking member, **Tommaso Buscetta**, was arrested in Brazil, and – after a failed suicide attempt – agreed to prise open the can of worms. His reason for daring this sacrilege, he claimed, was to destroy the Mafia. In its stampede to grab the huge profits to be made from the international heroin industry, the "Honoured Society" (La Società Onorata) had abandoned its original ideals: "It's necessary to destroy this band of criminals", he declared, "who have perverted the principles of Cosa Nostra and dragged them through the mud." He was doubtlessly motivated by revenge: all of those he incriminated – Michele Greco, Pippo Calò, Benedetto Santapaola, Salvatore Riina and many others – were leaders of, or allied to, the powerful Corleone family who had recently embarked on a campaign of terror to monopolize the drugs industry, in the process eliminating seven of Buscetta's closest relatives in the space of four months, including his two sons.

The background

Buscetta's statements to **Giovanni Falcone**, head of Sicily's anti-Mafia "pool" of judges, and later to the Federal Court in Manhattan, were the most important revelations about the **structure** of Cosa Nostra since Jo Valachi – a prominent member of the New York Genovese family – provided the first inside view in 1962. Mafia "families" are centred on areas, he revealed: villages or quarters of cities from which they take their name. The boss (*capo*) of each group is chosen by election, and appoints a lieutenant (*sottocapo*) and one or more *consiglieri*, or counsellors. Larger groups also have officers known as *capodecini*, each in command of ten men. Above the families is the *cupola*, or **Commission**, a governing body that includes representatives from all the major groupings. Democracy and collective interest, Buscetta claimed, had been replaced in the Commission by the greed and self-interest of the individuals who had gained control. Trials of strength alone now decided the leadership, often in the form of bitter feuds between rival factions – or *cosche* (literally, "artichokes", their form symbolizing solidarity).

The existence of the Commission sets the Mafia apart from the normal run of underworld gangs, for without a high level of organization the international trafficking in heroin in which they engage would be inconceivable. The route is circuitous, starting in the Middle and Far East, moving on to the processing plants in Sicily, and ending up in New York, where American Mafia channels are said to control sixty percent of the heroin market. This multimillion-dollar racket – known in the US as the **"Pizza Connection"**, because Sicilian pizza parlours were used as covers for the operation – was blown apart chiefly as a result of Buscetta's evidence, and led to the trial and conviction of the leading members of New York's Mafia Commission in September 1986. The trial introduced a significant new note in Mafia cases, when the defence lawyers stated at the outset that their clients were self-confessed members of Cosa Nostra. That raised the issue of whether the Mafia was necessarily a *criminal* organization; with most of the American drug profits safely invested in legitimate gambling, construction and high finance, there was little to distinguish it from any other business cartel.

The history

The Mafia has certainly come a long way since its rustic beginnings in feudal Sicily. Although Buscetta denied that the word "Mafia" is used to describe the organization – the term preferred by its members is "Cosa Nostra" – the word has been in currency for centuries, and is thought to derive from the Arabic, *mu'afah*, meaning "protection". In 1863, a play entitled *Mafiusi della Vicaria*, based on life in a Palermo prison, was a roaring success among the high society of the island's capital, and gave the word its first extensive usage. When the city rose against its new Italian rulers three years later, the British consul described a situation where secret societies were all-powerful: "*Camorre* and *maffie*, self-elected juntas, share the earnings of the workmen, keep up intercourse with outcasts, and take malefactors under their wing and protection."

Until then, *mafiosi* had been able to pose as defenders of the poor against the tyranny of Sicily's rulers, but in the years immediately following the toppling of the Bourbon state in Italy *mafiosi* were able to entrench themselves in Sicily's new power structure, acting as intermediaries in the gradual redistribution of land and establishing a modus vivendi with the new democratic representatives. There is little or no documentary proof of the rise to power of the "Honoured Society", but most writers agree that between the 1890s and the 1920s its undisputed boss was **Don Vito Cascio Ferro**, who had close links with the American "Black Hand", a Mafia-type association of southern Italian emigrants. Despite numerous homicide charges brought against him, the only man whom Ferro admitted to shooting was an American detective, Jack Petrosino, who was killed on the same day that he docked at Palermo to investigate links between the Sicilian and American organizations.

Ferro's career ended with Mussolini's anti-Mafia purges, instigated to clear the ground for the establishment of a vigorous Fascist structure in Sicily. **Cesare Mori**, the Duce's newly appointed Prefect of Palermo, arrived in the city in 1925 with the declared aim of "clearing the ground of the nightmares, threats and dangers which are paralysing, perverting and corrupting every kind of social activity". This might have worked, but the clean sweep that Mori made of the Mafia leaders (in all, 11,000 cattle rustlers, thieves and "conspirators" were jailed during this period, often on the basis of flimsy hearsay) was annulled after World War II when the prisons were opened and Mafia leaders, seen as unjustly jailed by the Fascist regime, returned to their regular operations. In the confusion that reigned during Italy's reconstruction, crime flourished throughout the south, and criminal leagues regrouped in Naples (the Camorra) and Calabria ('ndrángheta), controlling the black market and smuggling rackets. In Sicily, men such as **Don Calógero Vizzini** were the new leaders, confirmed in their power by the brief Anglo-American postwar administration, in return for their contribution towards the smooth progress of the Allied landings and occupation. One of them, **Lucky Luciano**, a founder member of the American Commission, was even flown out from prison in America to facilitate the invasion. Later he was alleged to be responsible for setting up the Sicilian-American narcotics empire, which was taken over at his death in 1962 by **Luciano Leggio**, who subsequently manoeuvred himself into the leadership of the Corleone family (though he was jailed in 1974).

The new Mafia

The cycle was by now complete: the Mafia had lost its original role as a predominantly rural organization, and had transformed itself by its postwar "Americanization" through transferring its operations to the cities and moving into entrepreneurial activities such as construction, real estate and, ultimately, drug smuggling. The growth of the heroin industry raised the stakes immensely, as shown by the vicious feuds fought over the division of the spoils, and the struggle for control of narcotics trafficking played a key role in the consolidation of power within the Mafia. The Italian state responded with an **anti-Mafia Parliamentary Commission** that sat from 1963 to 1976, and posed enough of a threat to the underworld to provoke a change of tactics by the Mafia, who began to target important state officials in a sustained campaign of terror that continues to this day. In 1971, Palermo's chief public prosecutor, Pietro Scaglione, became the first in a long line of "**illustrious corpses**" – *cadáveri eccellenti* – which have included journalists, judges, lawyers, police chiefs and left-wing politicians. A new peak of violence was reached in 1982 with the ambush and murder in Palermo's city centre of **Pio La Torre**, Regional Secretary of the Communist Party in Sicily, who had proposed a special government dispensation to allow lawyers access to private bank accounts.

Among the mourners at La Torre's funeral was the new Sicilian prefect of police, **General Dalla Chiesa**, a veteran in the state's fight against the anarchist/terrorist Brigate Rosse, or Red Brigades. His dispatch promised new action against the Mafia. The prefect began to investigate Sicily's lucrative construction industry, which provided an efficient means of investing drug profits. His scrutiny of public records and business dealings threatened to expose one of the most enigmatic issues in the Mafia's organization: the extent of corruption and protection in high-ranking political circles, the so-called "**Third Level**". However, exactly 100 days after La Torre's death, Dalla Chiesa himself was gunned down, together with his wife, in Palermo's Via Carini. The whole country was shocked, and the murder revived questions about the depth of government commitment to the fight. In his engagement with the Mafia, Dalla Chiesa had met with little local cooperation, and had received next to no support from Rome, to the extent that Dalla Chiesa's son had accused the mandarins of the Christian Democrat party – former prime minister Andreotti among them – of isolating his father. Nando Dalla Chiesa refused to allow many local officials to his father's funeral, including Vito Ciancimino, former mayor of Palermo and a Christian Democrat. Later, Ciancimino was accused, not just of handling huge sums of drug money, but of actually being a sworn-in member of the Corleone family. Those who were present at the funeral included the Italian president and senior cabinet ministers, all of them jeered at by an angry Sicilian crowd and pelted with coins – an expression of disgust that has since been repeated at the funerals of other prominent anti-Mafia fighters.

To ward off accusations of government inertia or complicity, the law that La Torre had demanded was rushed through Parliament soon afterwards, and was used in the **super-trials**, or *maxiprocessi*, that arose from the confessions of Buscetta and the other *pentiti* (penitents) who had followed his lead. The biggest of these trials, lasting eighteen months, started in February 1986, when five hundred *mafiosi* appeared in a specially built maximum-security bunker adjoining the Ucciardone prison in the heart of Palermo. The insecurity felt by the Mafia was reflected in continuing bloodshed in Sicily throughout the proceedings, but the worst was to come after the trial closed in December 1986, starting right on the steps of the courthouse with the murder of one of the accused *mafiosi* – many of whom were freed after they had squealed on their accomplices. Of those that were convicted, 19 received life sentences, and 338 others sentences totalling 2065 years.

The fightback in the 1990s

The violence reached a new level of ferocity during the **1990s**, starting in 1992 when a wave of assassinations of high-profile figures splashed over the headlines. In March, **Salvatore Lima**, a former mayor of Palermo who later became a Euro MP, was shot dead outside his villa in Mondello. Lima didn't have police bodyguards because he didn't believe he needed them; he had, in fact, been in the Mafia's pocket throughout his political career. His "crime" was his failure to fix the Supreme Court, which had gone ahead and confirmed the convictions of scores of *mafiosi* who had been incriminated in the super-trials of the 1980s.

This murder was followed by two more atrocities in quick succession: in May, the best-known of Sicily's anti-Mafia crusaders, **Giovanni Falcone**, was blown up by half a tonne of TNT on his way into Palermo from the airport, together with his wife and three bodyguards, while two months later his colleague, **Paolo Borsellino** (and five of his police guards), was the victim of a car-bomb outside his mother's house, also in Palermo. These two were the more visible half of the so-called "four musketeers" – judges who refused to be intimidated by death threats routinely made against anti-Mafia investigators. As ever, public opinion was divided over what it all meant. There were those who claimed that these murders were public gestures, while others saw in them increasing evidence of the panic percolating through the Mafia's ranks in the face of the growing number of defections of former members who were turning *pentiti*.

The carnage certainly propelled the state into action, and a dramatic breakthrough came shortly afterwards. In January 1993, **Salvatore Riina**, the so-called Boss of all the Bosses, and the man held ultimately responsible for the murder of the anti-Mafia judges, was arrested. (For more on Riina and the Corleone connection, see p.307.) **Leoluca Bagarella**, Riina's successor and brother-in-law, and the convicted killer of the chief of the Palermo Flying

Squad in 1979, was captured in 1995 (Bagarella's hideout turned out to be a luxury apartment overlooking the heavily guarded home of two of the judges who had helped catch him). Another of the Corleone clan, **Giovanni Brusca**, was arrested in 1996 – a particularly gratifying coup for the anti-Mafia forces, as Brusca was one of the organization's most ruthless hitmen, the mastermind behind Falcone's assassination and believed to have been responsible for the strangling of an informant's 11-year-old son, whose body was then disposed of in a vat of acid. Elsewhere on the island, **Natale D'Emanuele**, alleged to be the financial wizard behind the Mafia in Catania, was arrested and charged with trafficking arms throughout Italy, using hearses and coffins to transport them in a throwback to 1930s Chicago. Two other bosses, **Vito Vitale** and **Mariano Troia**, were netted in 1998, but the tide was reversed the following year when five people were gunned down in a bar in Vittória, a town little known for Mafia violence – one of the bloodiest Mafia massacres in the last half-century.

On the political front, **Leoluca Orlando**, the mayor of Palermo who was forced out of office by his own Christian Democrat party in 1990, spent much of the decade establishing an independent power base on an anti-Mafia ticket, at the head of his Rete (Network) party. Meanwhile, the confessions of Tommaso Buscetta began to provide evidence for the first time of the postwar alliance between Italy's former leading party and organized crime. Allegations inexorably focused on the very highest levels of government, and specifically on the relationship of Mafia stooge Salvatore Lima to his protector, **Giulio Andreotti**, the Christian Democrat leader and Italy's most successful postwar politician. Formerly considered untouchable, Andreotti finally bowed to increasing pressure to relinquish the parliamentary immunity that had hitherto blocked any serious investigation into his role, and in September 1995, aged 75, went on trial in Palermo for complicity and criminal association. Much fuss was made of the famous *bacio*, a kiss he was reported to have symbolically exchanged with Riina, according to *pentiti* revelations in 1994. However, the fact that most of the charges levelled against Andreotti were based on the testimony of Mafia informers (and therefore unreliable witnesses) led to Andreotti's complete acquittal in 1999. Many saw the result as simply further evidence of the famous cunning and survival skills of this political stalwart, which have given him the nickname "the fox".

Statements by *pentiti* and others accused of Mafia associations were also at the bottom of investigations into the business dealings of the then-prime minister **Silvio Berlusconi** and his Fininvest consortium. This time they were considered serious enough to warrant a raid on Berlusconi's Milan headquarters by an elite anti-Mafia police unit in July 1998, and a hasty dash to Sicily by Berlusconi to defend himself against charges of money-laundering for Cosa Nostra. Despite these high-profile events, though, the very concept of Mafia involvement was becoming increasingly irrelevant to most Italians, as reports of political and business corruption began to dominate public life throughout the 1990s. As the mayor of Venice remarked, in response to whispers of Mafia involvement in the fire that destroyed La Fenice opera house in 1996, "claiming it was burnt by the Mafia is about as useful as saying it was attacked by alien spacecraft."

Contemporary events

Since the turn of the millennium, the violence has for the most part calmed down. While killings still occur, few political figureheads are targeted these days, perhaps because fewer are willing to take the visible risks that sealed the fate of

crusaders like Falcone and Borsellino. More Mafia bosses have been jailed –
Bernardo Provenzano, for thirteen years *capo dei capi*, was captured in 2006,
quickly followed by 52 arrest warrants against the top echelons of Cosa Nostra
in Palermo, while the man thought to be Provenzano's successor, **Salvatore Lo
Piccolo**, was arrested in 2007. Perhaps more significantly, the last decade has
seen the repossession by Palermo's anti-Mafia magistrate of over €6 billion in
assets held by *mafiosi*, largely from the real estate and construction industries.

The most important development, however, has been the growth of a new
open attitude towards the Mafia, in contrast to the previous denial and *omertà*.
One of the most watched TV programmes in Italy in recent years has been
La Piovra ("The Octopus"), a drama series along the lines of *The Sopranos*, while
in Corleone, an anti-Mafia museum has opened to educate both foreigners and
Sicilians alike. Sicilians themselves are now bolder than ever in their public
demonstrations of disgust at the killings and intimidation, and a new movement
against the **pizzo**, the protection money which some eighty percent of stores
in Catania and Palermo are estimated to pay, has gathered force throughout the
island. An increasing number of brave individuals are willing to make a stand:
people such as Rita Borsellino, sister of murdered judge Paolo Borsellino and
now an anti-Mafia figurehead, or the widow of another "illustrious" victim,
Judge Cesare Terranova (killed in 1979), who launched a women's movement
against the Mafia with the words, "If you manage to change the mentality, to
change the consent, to change the fear in which the Mafia can live – if you can
change that, you can beat them."

It is precisely that element of "consent" among ordinary Sicilians that has
always been the strongest weapon in the Mafia's armoury, indeed the very
foundation of the Mafia's existence, bolstered by an attitude that has traditionally
regarded the *mafioso* stance as a revolt against the State, justified by centuries of
oppression by foreign regimes. This historical dichotomy is perhaps best
expressed by one of Sicily's greatest writers, Leonard Sciascia, who proclaimed,
"It hurts when I denounce the Mafia because a residue of Mafia feeling stays
with me, as it does in any Sicilian. So in struggling against the Mafia I struggle
against myself. It is like a split, a laceration."

At least the problem is being confronted, and few Sicilians now hold any
illusions about the true nature of the Mafia, shorn of its one-time altruistic
ideals – if they ever existed. And crucially, the myth of the Mafia's invincibility
has been irreparably dented.

Sicilian Baroque

Most of the church and civic architecture that you'll come across in Sicily, certainly in the east of the island, is Baroque in style. More particularly, it's of a type known as Sicilian Baroque. What follows is a brief introduction to the subject, designed to serve as a handy reference for some of the more important aspects of the style mentioned in the text.

Origins

To some extent, the qualities that attract art historians to the Sicilian Baroque – its "warmth and ebullience", "gaiety", "energy", "freedom and fantasy"– typify all **Baroque** architecture. The style grew out of the excesses of Mannerism, a distorted sixteenth-century mode of painting and architecture that had flourished in Italy in reaction to the restraint of the Renaissance. The development of a full-blown, ornate Baroque style followed in the late sixteenth century, again originating in Italy, and it quickly found a niche in other countries touched by the Counter-Reformation. The Jesuits saw in Baroque art and architecture an expression of a revitalized Catholicism, its particular theatrical forms involving the congregation by portraying spiritual ecstasy in terms of physical passion.

The origin of the word "Baroque" itself is uncertain: the two most popular theories are that it comes either from the seventeenth-century Portuguese *barroco*, meaning a misshapen pearl, or the term *barocco*, used by philosophers in the Middle Ages to mean a contorted idea. Whatever its origins, it was used by contemporary critics in a derogatory sense, implying odd or extravagant shapes, as opposed to the much-vaunted Classical forms of the Renaissance.

Although Baroque was born in Rome, the vogue quickly spread throughout Europe. Everywhere, the emphasis was firmly on elaborate ornamentation and spectacle, something that reflected the growing power of the aristocracy, who had begun to challenge the established wealth and tradition of the Church. Civic architecture gained in importance, at the expense of formerly pre-eminent religious buildings. The primary motivating force behind the decoration of the buildings was the need to impress the neighbouring gentry; building to the glory of God came a poor second.

Some of the finest (though least-known) examples of Baroque architecture are to be found in Sicily, although there's some debate as to the specific origins of the **Sicilian Baroque** style. During the eighteenth century alone, Sicily was conquered and ruled in turn by the Spanish Habsburgs, the Spanish Bourbons, the House of Savoy, the Austrian Habsburgs and the Bourbons from Naples, lending a particularly exuberant flavour to its Baroque creations – which some say was borrowed from Spain. Others argue that the dominant influence was Italian: Sicilian architects tended to train and to travel in Italy, rather than Spain, and brought home what they learned on the mainland, adapting prevalent Roman Baroque ideas to complement peculiarly Sicilian architectural traditions. Both theories contain an element of the truth, though perhaps more pertinent is Sicily's unique long-term history: two and a half millennia of invasion and domination have produced a very distinct culture and society – one that is bound to have influenced, or even produced, an equally distinct architectural form.

Baroque towns

Sicily's seismic instability has profoundly affected its architectural history. The huge **earthquake of 1693** that almost flattened Catania, and completely destroyed Noto, Ragusa, Ávola and Módica, provided a fantastic opportunity for local architects, who began massive rebuilding programmes in the southeast corner of Sicily. To them, as to all contemporary Baroque planners, a **Baroque town** aspired to be, and should be seen to be, a centre of taste and sophistication. They designed their new towns to please and delight their citizens, to encourage the participation of passers-by and to impress outsiders, with long vistas contriving to focus on the facade of a church or a palace, or an unexpected view of the sea. To enhance the visual effect even more, a building was designed to offer multiple, changing views from different angles of approach. This way, a completed plan might include all the buildings in a square or series of squares, and the experience of walking from place to place through varied but harmonious spaces was considered as important as the need to arrive at a destination. Moreover, as much of eighteenth-century Sicilian town-life took place outside, the facade of a building became synonymous with the wealth and standing of its occupant. External features became increasingly elaborate and specialized, and some parts of buildings – windows and staircases, for example – were often merely there for show. Invariably, what seem to be regular stone facades have been cosmetically touched up with plaster to conceal an asymmetry or an angle of less than ninety degrees: a self-conscious approach to town planning that can sometimes give the impression of walking around a stage set. Interestingly, this approach remained confined to the south and east of Sicily; outside the earthquake zone, in the west of the island, local architectural traditions continued to dominate in towns that hadn't had the dubious benefit of being levelled and left for the planners.

Ideally, where there was scope for large-scale planning, an entire city could be constructed as an aesthetic whole. As early as 1615 the Venetian architect and theorist **Vincenzo Scamozzi** published a treatise, *Dell'Idea dell'architettura universale*, in which he stated that the architectural harmony of the ideal city should reflect the perfect relationship between the prince, the judiciary, the Church, the marketplace and the populace.

Noto is an almost perfect example of Scamozzi's ideal city. After the 1693 earthquake, the old town was so devastated that it was decided to move its site and rebuild from scratch. The plan that was eventually accepted was nearly an exact replica of Scamozzi's. Noto is constructed on a grid-plan, traversed from east to west by a wide corso crossing a main piazza, which is itself balanced by four smaller piazzas. The buildings along the corso show remarkable balance and grace, while the attention of the Baroque planners to every harmonious detail is illustrated by the use of a warm, golden stone for the churches and *palazzi*.

Neighbouring towns in the southeast were also destroyed by the earthquake and rebuilt along similar lines, utilizing wide squares and thoroughfares, designed with the possibility of future tremors in mind. Both **Ávola** and **Grammichele** were moved from their hill-top positions to the coastal plain, and their polygonal plans were similarly influenced by Scamozzi. Grammichele, particularly, retains an extraordinary hexagonal layout, unique in Sicily. **Ragusa** is more complex, surviving today as two towns: the medieval Ragusa Ibla, which the inhabitants rebuilt after the earthquake, and the Baroque upper town of Ragusa, which is built on a sloping grid-plan, rather similar to Noto. Although Ibla isn't built to any kind of Baroque pattern, it does lay claim to one of the most spectacular of Sicilian Baroque churches.

Catania, unlike the other southeastern towns, was not completely destroyed by the earthquake, and was rebuilt over its old site. New, broad streets were built to link existing monuments and to facilitate rescue operations in case of another earthquake. The city is divided into four quarters by wide streets that meet in Piazza del Duomo, and wherever possible these spaces are used to maximize the visual impact of a facade or monument. The main piazza was conceived as a uniform set piece and, although several different architects collaborated, their intention was to produce a homogenous ensemble. They also went a step further in utilizing the city's natural assets: the main street, Via Etnea, cuts a swath due north from Piazza del Duomo, always drawing the eyes to the volcano, Mount Etna, smoking in the distance.

Over on the other side of the island, Baroque **Palermo** evolved differently, without the impetus of any one great natural disaster. There's no comparable city plan, Palermo's intricate central layout owing more to the Arabs than to seventeenth- and eighteenth-century designers; what Baroque character the city possesses has almost entirely to do with its highly individual churches and palaces. These were constructed in a climate of apparent opulence but encroaching bankruptcy; as the Sicilian aristocrats were attracted to Palermo to pay court to the Spanish viceroy, they left the management of their lands to pragmatic agents, whose short-sighted policies allowed the estates to fall into neglect. This ate away at the wealth of the gentry, who responded by mortgaging their lands in order to maintain their living standards. The grandiose palaces and churches they built in the city still stand, but following the damage caused during World War II many are in a state of terrible neglect and near collapse; wild flowers grow out of the facades, and chunks of masonry frequently fall into the street below. Renovation work is hampered by the local Mafia, and minor earthquake tremors always ensure that the need for repair is one step ahead of the builders, though EU funding and the initiatives of Palermo's mayor Leoluca Orlando have made a big impact in recent years.

Specific features

Eighteenth-century aristocrats in Palermo felt the need for **summer villas** outside the city, to which they could escape in the hottest weather, and many of these still survive around Bagheria. The villas tend to be quite small and simply designed, but are bedecked with balconies and terraces for afternoon strolling, and were approached by long, impressive driveways. Above all, they are notable for their **external staircases**, leading to the main entrance on the first floor (the ground floor usually contained the kitchen and servants' quarters). It's typical of the Baroque era that an external feature should take on such significance in a building – and that they should show such a remarkable diversity, each reflecting the wealth of the individual owners. Beyond the fact that they were nearly always double staircases, symmetrical to the middle axis of the facade, each was completely different. External staircases can be found elsewhere on mainland Europe, but they rarely display such imaginative construction as in Sicily.

While **balconies** had always been a prominent feature of Sicilian domestic architecture, during the eighteenth century they became prolific. The balcony supports, or buttresses, were elaborately carved: manic heads, griffins, horses, monsters and mythical figures all featured as decoration, fine examples of which survive at Noto's **Palazzo Villadorata**, as well as in Módica and Scicli. The wrought-iron balustrades curved outwards, almost like theatre boxes, to allow room for women's billowing skirts; they still afford the best views of street processions and other festivities at Carnevale.

Church building, too, flourished during this period. Baroque architects could let their imaginations run wild: the facade of the **Duomo** at Siracusa was begun in 1728, based on designs by Andrea Palma of Palermo, and the result is highly sophisticated and exciting. Other designs adapted and modified accepted forms for church architecture, as well as inventing new ones. In Palermo especially, typically Sicilian elements – like central circular windows – were used to great effect.

It was in the church **interiors**, however, that Sicilian Baroque came into its own, with tomb sculpture ever more ostentatious and stucco decoration abundant. Inlaid marble, a technique introduced from Naples at the start of the seventeenth century, became *de rigueur* for any self-respecting church. It reached its prime during the second half of the century, when entire walls or chapels would be decorated in this way. Palermo fields some of the best examples of all these techniques, at their most impressive in the church of **San Giuseppe dei Teatini**, designed by Giacomo Besio, a Genovese who lived most of his life in Sicily. For real over-the-top detail, though, the churches of **Santa Caterina** and **Il Gesù**, also in Palermo, conceal a riot of inlaid marble decoration.

Palermo is also distinguished by a series of highly decorative **oratories**, constructed in the late seventeenth and early eighteenth centuries, when the Spanish viceroys placed much of the city's power in the hands of the local aristocrats, who could afford to endow monasteries with new funds. Much was spent on small private chapels, where local sculptors had the chance to shine. The master of the genre was Giacomo Serpotta, and his best works are in the oratories of **Santa Zita**, **San Domenico** and **San Lorenzo**, though he left his mark over much of the west of the island.

Architects and sculptors

Rosario Gagliardi was responsible for much of the rebuilding of Noto and Ragusa, and became known as one of the most important architects in southeast Sicily. Born in Siracusa in 1698, he worked in Noto as a carpenter from the age of ten, and was first acknowledged as an architect in 1726. Between 1760 and 1784 he was chief architect for the city of Noto, and during this time also worked on many different projects in Ragusa and Módica. As far as is known, he never travelled outside Sicily, let alone to Rome, yet he absorbed contemporary architectural trends from the study of books and treatises, and reproduced the ideas with some flair.

Gagliardi's prime interest was in facades, and his work achieved a sophisticated fusion of Renaissance poise, Baroque grandeur and local Sicilian ornamentation. He had no interest, however, in spatial relationships or structural innovation, and the interiors of his buildings are disappointing when compared to the elaborate nature of their exteriors. Perhaps his most significant contribution was his development of the **belfry** as a feature. Sicilian churches traditionally didn't have a separate belltower, but incorporated the bells into the main facade, revealed through a series of two or three arches – an idea handed down from Byzantine building. Gagliardi extended the central bay of the facade into a tower, a highly original compromise satisfying both the local style and the more conventional notions of design from the mainland. The belfry on the church of **San Giorgio** in Ragusa Ibla, Gagliardi's masterpiece, is an excellent example of this.

The principal architect on the design and rebuilding of Catania after the 1693 earthquake, **Giovanni Battista Vaccarini**, was born in Palermo in 1702. He trained in Rome and embraced the current idiom, working with such illustrious figures as Alessandro Specchi (who built the papal stables) and Francesco de Sanctis (designer of the Spanish Steps). In 1730 he arrived in Catania, having been appointed as city architect by the Senate, and at once began work on finishing the Municipio. The lower two floors had been designed by a local architect, but Vaccarini completely ignored the original plan and transformed the building by redesigning the *piano nobile* in the Roman style. Outside he placed a fountain, whose main feature is an obelisk supported by an elephant, the symbol of Catania – reminiscent of Bernini's elephant fountain in Rome.

Giacomo Serpotta, master of the Palermitan oratories, was born in Palermo in 1656. He cashed in on the opulence of the Church and specialized in decorating oratories with moulded plasterwork in ornamental frames. He would include life-sized figures of Saints and Virtues, surrounded by plaster draperies, trophies, swags of fruit, bouquets of flowers and other extravagances much beloved of the Baroque. Among his most remarkable works is the Oratory of the Rosary in the church of **Santa Zita**, where the end wall is a reconstruction of the Battle of Lépanto. Three-dimensional representation is taken to an extreme here, and actual wires are used as rigging.

Other Baroque architects are less well known, but influential in Sicily all the same. **Giacomo Amato** (1643–1732) was a monk, sent to Rome in 1671 to represent his Order, where he came into contact with the works of Bernini and Borromini. Dazzled by what he'd seen, he neglected his religious duties after his return to Palermo in order to design some of the city's most characteristic churches, **Sant'Ignazio all'Olivell** and **San Domenico** among them. **Vincenzo Sinatra** had a more traditional career, starting as a stonecutter before working with Gagliardi in the 1730s as his foreman. In 1745 he married Gagliardi's niece, a move which did him no harm at all, since by 1761, when Gagliardi had a stroke, Sinatra was managing all his affairs. For ten years he directed the construction of Noto's Municipio, and during the rest of his life Sinatra worked in collaboration with the other city architects on a variety of projects – a respectable career, but one that makes it difficult to trace any personal architectural method. More important, and certainly with an identifiable style, was **Giovanni Verméxio**, who was active in Siracusa at around the same time. His work graces the city's Piazza del Duomo, notably the **Palazzo Arcivescovile**, while he gets a couple of ornate-interior credits, too, in the shape of one of the Duomo's chapels, and the octagonal **Cappella di San Sepolcro** in the church of Santa Lucia in the Achradina quarter of Siracusa.

Books

Although only a few modern writers have travelled in and written about Sicily, the island has provided the inspiration for some great literature, by both Sicilians and European visitors. If you can't find what you want in your local bookshop, try Amazon (www.amazon.co.uk, www.amazon.com) or other online retailers, which can often turn up long out-of-print tiles. Translations of Italian and Sicilian classics are also often available at bookshops in major towns and resorts in Sicily.

Travel and general

Luigi Barzini *The Italians*. Outdated now, but long the most respected work on the Italian nation; Barzini leaves no stone unturned in his quest to pinpoint the real Italy.

Vincent Cronin *The Golden Honeycomb*. Disguised as a quest for the mythical golden honeycomb of Daedalus, this is a searching account of a sojourn in Sicily in the 1950s. It combines colourful descriptions of Sicily's art, architecture and folklore with a knowing and erudite commentary.

Duncan Fallowell *To Noto*. Details a trip from London to Baroque Noto in an old Ford – an erudite travelogue, seeping with wit and pithy observations on Sicily and the Sicilians.

Norman Lewis *In Sicily*. A broad contemporary portrait of the island which Lewis came to know through his wife and her family. Subjects range from reflections on Palermo's ruined *palazzi* to the impact of immigration, and there's plenty on the Mafia.

Theresa Maggio *Mattanza: Love and Death in the Sea of Sicily*. A first-hand observation and explanation – awesome, fascinating and often gruesome – of the rituals of the annual trapping and killing of bluefin tuna off the island of Favignana. See also her *The Stone Boudoir*, a lyrical

investigation of obscure Sicilian villages inspired by her American family's stories of their ancestral home.

Daphne Phelps *A House in Sicily*. An Englishwoman inherits a grand *palazzo* in Taormina, and turns it into a guesthouse to make ends meet. This allows vignettes of eminent guests – Bertrand Russell, Tennessee Williams, Roald Dahl – as well as of the locals, though her patronizing tone grates and her anglocentric, provincial style is off-putting.

Fiona Pitt-Kethley *Journeys to the Underworld*. English poet searches Italy for the Sibylline sites, a good third of her time spent in Sicily – though Pitt-Kethley's salacious appetite for sexual adventure often distracts from the real interest.

Gillian Price *Walking in Sicily*. A superb Cicerone hiking guide that details 42 walks throughout the island – along the coasts, over mountains and up Etna.

Mary Taylor Simeti *On Persephone's Island: a Sicilian Journal*. Sympathetic record of a typical year in Sicily by an American who married a Sicilian professor and has lived in the west of the island since the early 1960s. Full of keenly observed detail about flora and fauna, customs, the harvests, festivals and – above all – the Sicilians themselves. Also see "Cuisine" for her splendid book on Sicilian food.

History, politics and archeology

David Abulafia *Frederick II: a Medieval Emperor*. Definitive account of the Hohenstaufen king, greatest of the medieval European rulers, with much on his reign in Sicily as well as elsewhere in Europe. It's a reinterpretation of the usual view of Frederick, revealing a less formidable king than the omnipotent and supreme ruler usually portrayed. For more on Sicily, see the same author's *Italy, Sicily and the Mediterranean, 1100–1400*.

Brian Caven *Dionysius I: Warlord of Sicily*. The life of Dionysius I, by a historian who sees him not as a vicious tyrant but as a valiant crusader against the Carthaginians.

M.I. Finley, D. Mack Smith & C.J.H. Duggan *A History of Sicily*. An updated abridgement of the trilogy first published in 1968 by Finley and Mack Smith, this is concise but informative, skipping fast from the Stone Age to the early 1980s.

Christopher Hibbert *Garibaldi and His Enemies*. A popular treatment of the life and revolutionary works of Giuseppe Garibaldi, thrillingly detailing the exploits of "The Thousand" in their lightning campaign from Marsala to Milazzo.

R. Ross Holloway *The Archaeology of Ancient Sicily*. Accessible and comprehensive introduction to the wealth of ancient monuments and artefacts discovered in Sicily, from the Paleolithic to the later Roman period.

John Julius Norwich *The Normans in Sicily*. Published together for the first time under one title, J.J. Norwich's *The Normans in the South* and *Kingdom in the Sun* are the accessible, well-researched story of the Normans' explosive entry into the south of Italy, dealing with their creation, in Sicily, of one of the most brilliant medieval European civilizations. Full of fascinating anecdotes and background to Sicily's glittering eleventh and twelfth centuries.

Steven Runciman *The Sicilian Vespers*. The classic account of Sicily's large-scale popular uprising in the thirteenth century. More entertaining is Runciman's *A History of the Crusades: 1, 2 & 3*, complete with full details of the Norman kings of Sicily, as well as of the crusading Frederick II himself.

Gaia Servadio *Motya*. On one level, an account of Phoenician history and culture as they relate to the excavated ruins of Motya – but in truth, so much more than that, as Servadio explores the fabric of Sicily and its people in uncompromising, enlightening detail.

Crime and society

John Dickie *Cosa Nostra*. Dickie, an Italian professor at University College London, has been researching the Mafia and its role in Sicilian society for over twenty years. This highly readable work provides an in-depth look at the secret workings of the Mafia, from its early days in the mid-1800s to its current manifestation in contemporary society. His strong narrative drive is backed up by impressive research, though events since 2003 demand an appendix at the very least.

Danilo Dolci *Sicilian Lives*. Dolci's formidable record of the lives of the Sicilians he met when he moved to Trappeto in the early 1950s. Short accounts told in their own words provide at once a moving and depressing document.

Giovanni Falcone *Men of Honour*. Judge Falcone's compelling account of what he found out about the Mafia during his time as chief investigator, knowledge that ultimately led to his murder in 1992. Essential reading for those who still question the existence of the Mafia, or anyone interested in its labyrinthine organization and why the State has failed to curb it.

Norman Lewis *The Honoured Society*. Famous account of the Mafia, its origins, personalities and customs. Certainly the most enjoyable introduction to the subject available, though much of it is taken up with banditry – really a separate issue – and the lack of accredited sources leaves you wondering how much is conjecture.

Clare Longrigg *Mafia Women*. A fascinating look at the active role of women within organized crime in the 1990s, mainly in Naples and Sicily. Intimidation and fear are shown to be the oil that turns the Mafia wheels, with the supreme place of the family appearing to justify almost any outrage or degree of complicity.

Gavin Maxwell *The Ten Pains of Death*. Maxwell lived in Scopello during the 1950s, and recorded the lives of his neighbours in their own words. There's much on Sicilian small-town life and poverty, and sympathetic portraits of traditional festivals and characters. His *God Protect Me from My Friends* is a good and sympathetic biography of the notorious bandit Salvatore Giuliano, ripe with intrigue and double-dealing.

Peter Robb *Midnight in Sicily*. The Australian Robb spent fifteen years in the Italian south

tracing the contorted relations between organized crime and politics. Here, he focuses on the structure of the Mafia, the trials of the bosses in the 1980s, the high-profile assassinations that ensued, and the trial of Andreotti, in a thorough, fast-paced study that provides deep insights into the dynamics of Sicily's society and an authentic portrait of Palermo.

Tim Shawcross & Martin Young *Men of Honour: the Confessions of Tommaso Buscetta*. An account of the Sicilian and American Mafia's move into the international narcotics trade, based on the evidence of Buscetta (a former high-ranking Cosa Nostra lieutenant), which kick-started the 1990s' fightback and saw several leaders imprisoned. See also Shawcross's *The War Against the Mafia*, an informative background on the ways and workings of the Mafia and the attempts to contain it.

Renate Siebert *Secrets of Life and Death: Women and the Mafia*, translated by Liz Heron. History and analysis of the patriarchal nature of Mafia organizations, which are held to be the apotheosis of the masculine society of Italy's south. Poignant first-person narratives give background to the account, exploding the myth of the Mafia as protecting the weak and defending women, who continue to be used as drugs mules and decoys. The author is a German-born professor of sociology at the University of Calabria.

Alexander Stille *Excellent Cadavers*. An important book tracing the modern fight against the Mafia as led by Giovanni Falcone and Paolo Borsellino, both of whom were assassinated in 1992.

Novels about Sicily

Allen Andrews *Impossible Loyalties.* Fast-moving, if unevenly paced, narrative of an Anglo-Sicilian family caught up in the turmoil of World War II, containing an authentic portrait of prewar Messina society.

Tahar Ben Jelloun *State of Absence.* The French-Moroccan author visited southern Italy and Sicily in 1990, fashioning his notes about daily life into a provoking, realistic novel about the effect of the Mafia on the people of the south.

Michael Dibdin *Blood Rain.* Dibdin's Venetian detective, Aurelio Zen, is a classic and idiosyncratic loner, always up against the Italian state and society in an unequalled series of crime novels. Here, Dibdin sends him to Sicily, with dark consequences for all concerned.

Simonetta Agnello Hornby *The Marchesa.* Dealing with an aristocratic family in nineteenth-century Palermo, this has echoes of Lampedusa's *The Leopard*, but makes a great holiday read in its own right, full of subtle intrigue, voluptuous imagery and period detail. Hornby's two other Sicily-based novels are also worth seeking out.

Norman Lewis *The March of the Long Shadows.* An affectionate novel set in postwar Sicily, dealing with the Separatist movement, the bandit Giuliano and a whole cast of endearing characters. *The Sicilian Specialist* is Lewis's Mafia thriller, full of authentic Sicilian background, which flits from the island to the US to Cuba on the trail of a Mob assassin.

Dacia Maraini *The Silent Duchess.* The work of a Florence-born author, but with a Sicilian mother. Set in eighteenth-century Sicily, it's a tale of a noble family seen through the eyes of a young duchess; beautifully written and dripping with authentic detail, particularly about the lot of women in those times. Her *Bagheria* is a delightfully engaging memoir of her childhood in the town of the title, entwining criticism of local corruption with a historical awareness of events and people who figured in her earlier work.

Lily Prior *La Cucina.* Subtitled a "novel of rapture", this chronicles the romance between a spinster librarian from Castiglione and an enigmatic English chef. Drawn into the plot are the Mafia, copious recipes, and the convolutions of Sicilian family life.

Mario Puzo *The Godfather.* The New York Godfather – Don Corleone – was born in Sicily and the book touches on all things Sicilian. In Francis Ford Coppola's three-part film, the first to rehabilitate the Mafia in American eyes, Marlon Brando played an old Don Corleone. The book's a great read, even if you've seen the films (which are pretty faithful to Puzo's novel). Also by Puzo is *The Sicilian*, a novelized life of the bandit Salvatore Giuliano, and the basis of an uninspiring 1988 film starring Christopher Lambert. Better, if you're interested, is to try and catch Francesco Rosi's 1962 film, *Salvatore Giuliano*.

Ann Radcliffe *A Sicilian Romance.* Early Gothic novel, written in 1790, telling of supernatural events haunting an aristocratic family, with much purple description of the Sicilian landscape.

Peter Vansittart *A Choice of Murder.* This clever novelized account of the life of Timoleon of Siracusa, based on Plutarch's history of the same, provides a gripping view of the ancient Greek world in Sicily and beyond.

Sicilian literature

Gesualdo Bufalino *The Plague Sower, Blind Argus, The Keeper of Ruins,* and *Night's Lies.* "Discovered" by Sciascia, Bufalino arrived late on the literary scene, publishing his first novel, *The Plague Sower,* in his sixties. Subsequent publications enhanced the reputation made by this remarkable debut, notably *Night's Lies,* which won Italy's most respected literary award, the Strega Prize, in 1988. Bufalino himself – seeking to explain the Sicilian character – commented, "Don't forget that even our most obscene vices nearly always bear the seal of sullen greatness."

Andrea Camilleri *Inspector Montalbano Mysteries.* Born in Agrigento, Camilleri is one of Italy's favourite modern authors, though he writes in Sicilian dialect that not all Italians can understand. His intelligent, and often vulgar and graphic, crime novels have subsequently become hugely popular all over Europe. Inspector Montalbano delves deep into the folds of Sicilian culture in an ongoing series, starting with *The Shape of Water.*

Maria Grammatico & Mary Taylor Simeti *Bitter Almonds: Recollections and Recipes from a Sicilian Girlhood.* Maria Grammatico was raised in a convent, where she learned the pastry-cooking skills that she employs in her outlets in Érice. The book, co-authored by Mary Taylor Simeti (see "Cuisine"), relates her life with the nuns, and includes some of her famous recipes.

Giuseppe di Lampedusa *The Leopard.* The most famous Sicilian novel, written after World War II but recounting the dramatic nineteenth-century years of transition from Bourbon to Piedmontese rule from an aristocrat's point of view. A good character study and rich with incidental detail, including some nice descriptions of the Sicilian landscape, which was put to great effect in Visconti's epic 1963 film. David Gilmour's *The Last Leopard: A Life of Giuseppe di Lampedusa,* is the first biography in English of Lampedusa, a readable account of the life of an otherwise rather dull man.

Luigi Pirandello *Six Characters in Search of an Author, Henry IV, The Late Mattia Pascal, Short Stories.* His most famous and accomplished work, *Six Characters ... ,* written in 1921, and his *Henry IV,* written a year later, contain many of the themes that dogged Pirandello throughout his writing career – the idea of a multiple personality and the quality of reality. *The Late Mattia Pascal* is an early novel (1904), entertainingly written despite its stylistic shortcomings; while the collection of short stories is perhaps the best introduction to Pirandello's work: abrasive stuff, the dialogue possessing an assured comic touch.

Salvatore Quasimodo *Complete Poems, Collected Poems.* Born in Siracusa in 1901, Quasimodo was a founder of Italy's hermetic school of poets. His earliest poems were rather abstruse and metaphysical, while his later work addressed more mundane themes like sociality and mortality. He was awarded the Nobel Prize for Literature in 1959.

Carmelo Samona *Brothers.* Palermo-born author of only two novels, Samona here investigates the fraught relationship of two brothers – an eerie work.

Leonardo Sciascia, *Sicilian Uncles, The Wine-Dark Sea, Candido, The Knight and Death, Death of an Inquisitor, The Day of the*

Owl, Equal Danger. Sciasca's short stories and novellas are packed with incisive insights into the island's quirky ways, and infused with the author's humane and sympathetic view of its people. The first to describe the Mafia in Italian literature, he wrote metaphysical thrillers in which the detectives often turn out to be the hunted; the best known is *The Day of the Owl.*

Giovanni Verga *Short Sicilian Novels, Cavalleria Rusticana, Maestro Don Gesualdo, I Malavoglia* or *The House by the Medlar Tree, A Mortal Sin, La Lupa,* and *Sparrow.* Born in the nineteenth century in Catania, Verga spent several years in various European salons before coming home to write his best work. Much of it is a reaction against the pseudo-sophistication of society circles, stressing the simple lives of ordinary people, though they're occasionally bestowed with a heavy smattering of "peasant passion", with much emotion, wounded honour and feuds to the death. D.H. Lawrence's translations are suitably vibrant, with excellent introductions. *Sparrow* is a doomed love story set in cholera-ravaged mid-nineteenth-century Sicily, and filmed by Zeffirelli in 1993.

Elio Vittorini *Conversations in Sicily.* A Sicilian emigrant returns from the north of Italy after fifteen years to see his mother on her birthday. The conversations of the title are with the people he meets on the way, local villagers and his mother, and reveal a prewar Sicily that, while affectionately drawn, is ridden with poverty and disease.

▲ Visconti's opulent 1963 film version of *The Leopard*

Cuisine

Antonio Carluccio *Southern Italian Feast*. Britain's avuncular Italian master is particularly good on Sicilian fish and snacks – his *arancini* recipe is definitive.

Elizabeth David *Italian Food*. First published in 1954, this was the book that introduced Mediterranean flavours to a UK ravaged by postwar shortages. Although a learned and entertaining stroll through the whole canon of Italian cooking, there are plenty of Sicilian dishes covered.

Valentina Harris *Southern Italian Cooking*. Excellent book with a chapter on Sicilian cooking, including several of the classic recipes. Also covers the related cuisine of Calabria and other southern regions.

Anna Tasca Lanza *The Flavors of Sicily*. Sicilian summer cooking from the respected owner of a cooking school established at her family estate on the island. An anecdotal trawl through the classics and the lesser-known dishes, including several from such out-of-the-way places as Pantelleria and Strómboli. Look out too for her *Heart of Sicily*: *Recipes and Reminiscences of Regaleali, a Country Estate*.

Mary Taylor Simeti *Sicilian Food*. Everything a book on food should be: historically and culturally informed, and packed with recipes and fascinating detail about life and food on the island. Thoroughly recommended.

Wanda Tornabene, Giovanna Tornabene & Michele Evans *La Cucina Siciliana di Gangivecchio*. A collection of over two hundred sophisticated dishes, each with a *nouveau* slant on Sicilian cuisine, though there's little Arab influence and virtually no fish recipes.

Films

Though Sicily doesn't yet have its own motion picture industry, the island's stunning scenery has served as a backdrop to a number of very successful films. The Aeolian and Pélagie islands, in particular, have proved popular settings for some interesting films, a few of them now classics of Italian cinema.

Michelangelo Antonioni *L'Avventura* (1960). Shot on the barren rocks of Panarea's Lisca Bianca, this film notes the beginning of a marked change in postwar Italian social mores. When a group of friends get together for a day out in the islands, one gets lost, and the relationships between those remaining begin to fracture. Here, Antonioni focuses ingeniously on the internal responses of those affected.

Emanuele Crispalese *Il Respiro* (2002). Filmed on the southern island of Lampedusa, this is a timeless, well-constructed look at how an eccentric mother is misunderstood by other islanders. Crispalese's second film, it addresses the overwhelming patriarchy of Italian families and the sexual tension latent between family members.

Francis Ford Coppola *The Godfather* (1971). Mario Puzo's brilliant screenplay tells the story of how Don Vito Corleone, *capo* of the New York Sicilian Mafia, tries to maintain his hold on the family business and his old-world values, despite his renegade son Michael. Since the town of Corleone itself was far too developed for the period filming, much of it was shot in Savoca and Forza d'Agro, outside Taormina.

Pietro Giermi *Divorzio alla Siciliana* (1961). Proof that not all Sicilian films need be deep or cinematic, this is a hilarious and pointed satire of Italian marital conventions. Marcello Mastroianni plays a Sicilian nobleman trying to prove his wife unfaithful so he can kill her and marry his younger cousin. Known as *Divorce Italian Style* in English, it was filmed in Ispica near Ragusa, and got Giermi nominated for a Best Director Oscar.

Nanni Moretti *Dear Diary* (1994). Moretti plays himself as he tours Italy on a Vespa, visiting all the Aeolian Islands, showing how the inhabitants of each differ in mentality and lifestyle. Mostly comic, but a real downer at the end.

Michael Radford *Il Postino* (1994). An international favourite, featuring a postman who learns to love poetry after befriending Pablo Neruda, who was recently exiled to a small island. The film was shot in the town of Pollara on Salina, leading to a dramatic increase in tourists to the region.

Roberto Rossellini *Strómboli: Terra di Dio* (1949). Starring Ingrid Bergman as a tormented young refugee who marries an Italian to escape the war, this is a sad story of solitude and cynicism, that received little praise in its home country. The real star, however, is the volcano itself, whose brooding presence undermines the illusion of an idyllic, happy island.

Giuseppe Tornatore *Cinema Paradiso* (1988). Though declaimed by critics for its saccharine storyline, this Oscar-winning film by Sicilian director Tornatore received popular acclaim the world over. Shot around Cefalù, it follows the friendship between a young boy and the local cinema projectionist, and is in many ways a homage to cinema itself.

Language

Language

Italian

The ability to speak English confers enormous prestige in Sicily, and plenty of locals – particularly returned *emigrati* – are willing to show off their knowledge. Few outside the tourist resorts, however, actually know more than a few simple words and phrases, more often than not culled from pop songs or films. To get the most from your visit, therefore, you'd do well to master at least a little **Italian**.

Some tips

Attempting to speak Italian brings instant rewards; your halting efforts will often be greeted with smiles and genuine surprise that an English-speaker should stoop to learn the language. In any case, Italian is one of the easiest European languages to learn, especially if you already have a smattering of French or Spanish, both of which are extremely similar grammatically. The best **phrasebook** is Rough Guide's own *Italian Phrasebook* (Penguin), while Collins publishes a comprehensive series of **dictionaries**.

Easiest of all is the **pronunciation**, since every word is spoken exactly as it's written, and usually enunciated with exaggerated, open-mouthed clarity. The only difficulties you're likely to encounter are the few **consonants** that are different from English:

c before e or i is pronounced as in church, while ch before the same vowels is hard, as in cat.

g is soft before e and i, as in gentle; hard when followed by h, as in garlic.

gn has the ni sound of our onion.

gl in Italian is softened to something like li in English, as in vermilion.

h is not aspirated, as in hour.

sci or sce are pronounced as in sheet and shelter respectively.

When **speaking** to strangers, the third person is the polite form (ie *Lei* instead of *Tu* for "you"); using the second person is a mark of disrespect or stupidity. It's also worth remembering that Italians don't use "please" and "thank you" half as much as we do: it's all implied in the tone, though if you're in doubt, err on the polite side.

All Italian words are **stressed** on the penultimate syllable unless an **accent** denotes otherwise, although accents are often left out in practice. Note that the ending **-ia** or **-ie** counts as two syllables, hence *trattoria* is stressed on the i. We've put accents in, throughout the text and below, wherever it isn't immediately obvious how a word should be pronounced: for example, in *Maríttima*, the accent is on the first **i**; conversely *Catania* should theoretically have an accent on the second **a**. Other words where we've omitted accents are common ones (like *Isola*, stressed on the I), some names (*Domenico*, *Vittorio*), and words that are stressed similarly in English, such as *Repubblica*.

None of this will help very much if you're confronted with a particularly harsh specimen of the **Sicilian dialect**, which virtually qualifies as a separate

For political reasons, all regional languages in Italy are considered dialects of Italian. In reality, however, each has its own history and influences, and the majority of them are, linguistically speaking, separate languages. During the 600-year-long Roman occupation of Sicily, Vulgar Latin became the lingua franca for the entire island, though it was highly influenced by close contacts with Arabic, Norman and Spanish languages. The grammar, lexicon and phonology of Sicilian thus differs immensely from modern standard Italian – so much so that during the American Mafia trials of the 1980s, the FBI had to enlist special agents fluent in Sicilian to translate the conversations of *mafiosi* based in New York. The Sicilian language even has its own regional dialects (*parrati*), though in general these are understood by all Sicilians.

Today nearly all Sicilians speak and understand standard Italian, though, unlike numerous other dialects spoken throughout Europe, the language is in no danger of extinction: in most towns, the younger generation prefers Sicilian to Italian, and almost everyone speaks Sicilian at home. While Sicilians are well known for using their hands and arms as much as their vocal cords to communicate, their language is rich in idioms and sayings. Below are some favourite Sicilian proverbs:

Si vo' passari la vita cuntenti, statti luntanu di li parenti.
If you want quiet, stay away from relatives.

Sciarri di maritu e mugghieri, duranu finu a lu lettu.
Quarrels between wives and husbands always end in the bed.

Cu'arrobba pri manciari, nun fa piccatu.
He who steals to eat is no sinner.

Cu'asini caccia e fimmini cridi, faccia di paradisu nun ni vidi.
He who seeks girls and asses will never reach heaven.

Camina chi pantofuli finnu a quannu non hai i scarpi.
Walk with your slippers until you find your shoes (ie make the best of a bad situation).

Cu' va a Palermu e nun va a Murriali, si nni parti sceccu e torna maiali.
He who visits Palermo and not Monreale arrives an ass and returns a pig.

language (see above). However, television has made a huge difference, and almost every Sicilian can now communicate in something approximating standard Italian.

A language guide

Basics

Buongiorno	Good morning		Ciao (informal;	Hello/goodbye
Buonasera	Good afternoon/		when speaking to	
	evening		strangers use the	
Buonanotte	Good night		phrase above)	

Arrivederci (formal)	Goodbye	Oggi	Today
Sì	Yes	Domani	Tomorrow
No	No	Dopodomani	Day after tomorrow
Per favore	Please	Ieri	Yesterday
Grázie	Thank you	Adesso	Now
(molte/mille grazie)	(very much)	Più tardi	Later
Prego	You're welcome	Aspetta!	Wait a minute!
Va bene	Alright/that's OK	Di mattina	In the morning
Come stai/sta?	How are you? (informal/formal)	Nel pomeriggio	In the afternoon
		Di sera	In the evening
Bene	I'm fine	Stasera	Tonight
Parla inglese?	Do you speak English?	Qui/là	Here/there
Non parlo italiano	I don't speak Italian	Buono/cattivo	Good/bad
Non capisco	I don't understand	Grande/píccolo	Big/small
Non ho capito	I haven't understood	Económico/caro	Cheap/expensive
Non lo so	I don't know	Presto/ritardo	Early/late
Scusa	Excuse me/sorry (informal)	Caldo/freddo	Hot/cold
		Vicino/lontano	Near/far
Mi scusi	Excuse me/sorry (formal)	Líbero/occupato	Vacant/occupied
Permesso	Excuse me (in a crowd)	Velocemente/ lentamente	Quickly/slowly
		Piano	Slowly/quietly
Mi dispiace	I'm sorry	Con/senza	With/without
Sono qui in vacanza	I'm here on holiday	Più/meno	More/less
Abito a...	I live in...	Basta	Enough/no more
Sono inglese	I'm English	Signor...	Mr...
Sono gallese	I'm Welsh	Signora...	Mrs...
Sono scozzese	I'm Scottish	Signorina...	Miss...
Sono irlandese	I'm Irish	(il Signore, la Signora, la Signorina	
Sono americano/a (masculine/feminine)	I'm American	when speaking about someone else)	
australiano/a (masculine/feminine)	I'm Australian	Primo nome	First name
		Cognome	Surname

Accommodation

Albergo	Hotel	con una doccia/ un bagno	with a shower/bath
C'è un albergo qui vicino?	Is there a hotel nearby?	con una terrazza	with a balcony
Ha una cámera...	Do you have a room...	acqua calda/fredda	hot/cold water
per una persona, due/tre persone	for one/two/three people	Quanto costa?	How much is it?
		È caro	It's expensive
per una notte, due/tre notti	for one/two/three nights	È compresa la prima colazione?	Is breakfast included?
per una settimana, due settimane	for one/two weeks	Ha niente che costa di meno?	Do you have anything cheaper?
con un letto matrimoniale	with a double bed	Pensione completa/ mezza pensione	Full-/half-board

Posso vedere la cámera?	Can I see the room?	C'è un camping qui	Is there a campsite nearby?
La prendo	I'll take it	Tenda	Tent
Vorrei prenotare una cámera	I'd like to book a room	Cabina	Cabin
Ho una	I have a booking	Ostello per la gioventù	Youth hostel
Possiamo fare il campeggio qui?	Can we camp here?		

Questions and directions

Dove?	Where?	Può dirmi quando devo scendere?	Can you tell me when to get off?
(Dov'è/Dove sono?)	(Where is/are…?)	A che ora apre?	What time does it open?
Quando?	When?		
Cosa?	What?	A che ora chiude?	What time does it close?
(Cos'è?)	(What is it?)		
Quanto/Quanti?	How much/many?	Quanto costa?	How much does it cost?
Perché?	Why?		
È/C'è	It is/There is	(Quantocostano?)	(…do they cost?)
(È/C'è…?)	(Is it/Is there…?)	Come si chiama in italiano?	What's it called in Italian?
Che ora è?/Che ore sono?	What time is it?		
Come arrivo a…?	How do I get to…?	Sinistra/destra	Left/right
Quant'è lontano a…?	How far is it to…?	Sempre diritto	Go straight ahead
Mi può dare un passaggio a…?	Can you give me a lift to…?	Gira a destra/ sinistra	Turn to the right/left

Getting around

Aeroplano	Aeroplane	Posso prenotare un posto?	Can I book a seat?
Autobus/Pullman	Bus	A che ora parte?	What time does it leave?
Treno	Train		
Mácchina	Car	Quando parte il próssimo pullman/ treno/traghetto per…?	When is the next bus/train/ferry to…?
Taxi	Taxi		
Bicicletta	Bicycle		
Traghetto	Ferry		
Nave	Ship	Da dove parte?	Where does it leave from?
Aliscafo	Hydrofoil		
Autostop	Hitch-hiking	Da quale binario parte?	Which platform does it leave from?
A piedi	On foot		
Autostazione	Bus station	Devo cambiare?	Do I have to change?
Stazione ferroviaria	Train station	Quanti chilómetri sono?	How many kilometres is it?
Stazione maríttima	Ferry terminal		
Porto	Port	Quanto ci vuole?	How long does it take?
Un biglietto a…	A ticket to…		
Solo andata/andata e ritorno	One way/return	Que número di autobus per…?	What number bus is it to…?

Dov'è la strada a…?	Where's the road to…?	La próssima fermata, per favore	Next stop, please

Signs

Entrata/uscita	Entrance/exit	Binario	Platform
Ingresso líbero	Free entrance	Cassa	Cash desk
Signori/signore	Gentlemen/ladies	Avanti	Go/walk
Gabinetto/bagno	WC/bathroom	Alt	Stop/halt
Líbero/occupato	Vacant/engaged	Dogana	Customs
Aperto/chiuso	Open/closed	Non toccare	Do not touch
Arrivi/partenze	Arrivals/departures	Perícolo	Danger
Chiuso per restauro	Closed for restoration	Attenzione	Beware
Chiuso per ferie	Closed for holidays	Pronto soccorso	First aid
Tirare/spingere	Pull/push	Suonare il campanello	Ring the bell
Guasto	Out of order		
Acqua potabile	Drinking water	Vietato fumare	No smoking
Affítasi	To let		

Driving

Parcheggio	Parking	Strada chiusa/ guasta	Road closed/up
Divieto di sosta/ Sosta vietata	No parking	Vietato il transito	No through road
Senso único	One way street	Vietato il sorpasso	No overtaking
Ambo i lati	Both sides of the street	Incrocio	Crossroads
		Límite di velocità	Speed limit
Senso vietato	No entry	Semáforo	Traffic light
Rallentare	Slow down		

Numbers and days of the week

Uno	1	Diciassette	17
Due	2	Diciotto	18
Tre	3	Diciannove	19
Quattro	4	Venti	20
Cinque	5	Venticinque	25
Sei	6	Trenta	30
Sette	7	Quaranta	40
Otto	8	Cinquanta	50
Nove	9	Sessanta	60
Dieci	10	Settanta	70
Undici	11	Ottanta	80
Dodici	12	Novanta	90
Tredici	13	Cento	100
Quattordici	14	Mille	1000
Quindici	15	Lunedì	Monday
Sedici	16	Martedì	Tuesday

L

LANGUAGE | A language guide

463

Menu reader

Basics and snacks

Aceto	Vinegar	Pane	Bread
Aglio	Garlic	Pane integrale	Wholemeal bread
Biscotti	Biscuits	Panino	Bread roll
Burro	Butter	Patatine	Crisps/potato chips
Caramelle	Sweets	Patatine fritte	Chips/French fries
Cioccolato	Chocolate	Pepe	Pepper
Focaccia	Oven-baked snack	Pizzetta	Small cheese-and-tomato pizza
Formaggio	Cheese		
Frittata	Omelette	Riso	Rice
Gelato	Ice cream	Sale	Salt
Grissini	Bread sticks	Uova	Eggs
Maionese	Mayonnaise	Yogurt	Yoghurt
Marmellata	Jam	Zúcchero	Sugar
Olio	Oil	Zuppa	Soup
Olive	Olives		

Antipasti and starters

Antipasto misto	Mixed cold meats and cheese (plus a mix of other things in this list)	Mortadella	Salami-type cured meat with nuggets of fat, often with pistachios
Caponata	Mixed aubergine, olives and tomatoes	Pancetta	Italian bacon
Caprese	Tomato and mozzarella cheese salad	Peperonata	Grilled green, red or yellow peppers stewed in olive oil
Insalata di mare	Seafood salad (usually squid, octopus and prawn)	Pomodori ripieni	Stuffed tomatoes
		Prosciutto	Ham
Insalata di riso	Rice salad	Salame	Salami
Insalata russa	"Russian salad": diced vegetables in mayonnaise	Salmone/tonno/ pesce spada/ affumicato	Smoked salmon/tuna/ swordfish
Melanzane alla parmigiana	Fried aubergine in tomato sauce with parmesan cheese		

Pizzas

Biancaneve	"Black and white": mozzarella and oregano
Calzone	Folded pizza with cheese, ham and tomato
Capricciosa	"Capricious": topped with whatever they've got in the kitchen, usually including baby artichoke, ham and egg
Cardinale	Ham and olives
Diavolo	"Devil": spicy, with hot salami or Italian sausage
Funghi	Mushroom: tinned, sliced button mushrooms unless it specifies fresh mushrooms, either **funghi freschi** or **porcini**
Frutti di mare	Seafood: usually mussels, prawns, squid and clams
Margherita	Cheese and tomato
Marinara	Tomato and garlic
Napoli/Napoletana	Tomato, anchovy and olive oil (often mozzarella too)
Quattro formaggi	"Four cheeses": usually mozzarella, fontina, Gorgonzola and Gruyère
Quattro stagioni	"Four seasons": the toppings split into four separate sections, usually including ham, peppers, onion, mushrooms, artichokes, olives, egg etc
Rianata	Fresh tomato, oregano, garlic and anchovy; a western Sicilian speciality
Romana	Anchovy and olives

The first course (il primo): Soups

Brodo	Clear broth
Minestrina	Any light soup
Minestrone	Thick vegetable soup
Pasta e fagioli	Pasta soup with beans
Pastina in brodo	Pasta pieces in clear broth
Stracciatella	Broth with egg

Pasta

Cannelloni	Large tubes of pasta, stuffed
Farfalle	Literally "bow"-shaped pasta; the word also means "butterflies"
Fettuccine	Narrow pasta ribbons
Gnocchi	Small potato and dough dumplings
Lasagne	Lasagne
Maccheroni	Macaroni (tubular pasta)
Pappardelle	Pasta ribbons
Pasta al forno	Pasta baked with minced meat, eggs, tomato and cheese
Penne	Smaller version of rigatoni
Ravioli	Ravioli (stuffed, square-shaped pasta)
Rigatoni	Large, grooved, tubular pasta
Risotto	Cooked rice dish, with sauce
Spaghetti	Spaghetti

Spaghettini	Thin spaghetti	Vermicelli	Very thin spaghetti
Tagliatelle	Pasta ribbons, another word for **fettuccine**		(literally "little worms")
Tortellini	Small rings of pasta, stuffed with meat or cheese		

Pasta sauces (salsa)

Aglio e olio (e peperoncino)	Tossed in garlic and olive oil (and hot chillies)	Panna	Cream
		Parmigiano	Parmesan cheese
		Pesto	Ground basil, pine nut, garlic and pecorino
Amatriciana	Cubed pork and tomato sauce, with onions and hot chillies (originally from Rome)	Pomodoro	Tomato sauce
		Puttanesca	"Whorish": tomato, anchovy, olive oil and oregano
Arrabbiata	Spicy tomato sauce, with chillies	Ragù	Meat sauce
		Trápanese	Cold puréed tomato, garlic and basil
Bolognese	Meat sauce		
Burro e salvia	Butter and sage	Vóngole (veraci)	Clam and tomato sauce (fresh clams in shells, usually served with oil and herbs)
Carbonara	Cream, ham and beaten egg		
Frutta di mare	Seafood		
Funghi	Mushroom		

The second course (il secondo): Meat (carne)

Agnello	Lamb	Manzo	Beef
Bistecca	Steak	Ossobuco	Shin of veal
Cervello	Brain	Pollo	Chicken
Cinghiale	Wild boar	Polpette	Meatballs
Coniglio	Rabbit	Rognoni	Kidneys
Costolette/cotolette	Cutlets/chops	Salsiccia	Sausage
Fégatini	Chicken livers	Saltimbocca	Veal with ham
Fégato	Liver	Scaloppina	Escalope (of veal)
Involtini	Steak slices, rolled and stuffed	Spezzatino	Stew
		Tacchino	Turkey
Lepre	Hare	Trippa	Tripe
Lingua	Tongue	Vitello	Veal
Maiale	Pork		

Fish (pesce) and shellfish (crostacei)

Note that **surgelato** or **congelato** written on the menu next to a dish means "frozen" – it often applies to squid and prawns.

Acciughe	Anchovies	Baccalà	Dried salted cod
Anguilla	Eel	Calamari	Squid
Aragosta	Lobster	Céfalo	Grey mullet

Cernia	Grouper	Ricciola	Amberjack
Cozze	Mussels	Rospo	Monkfish
Dattile	Razor clams	Sampiero	John Dory
Déntice	Dentex (like sea bass)	Sarago	White bream
Gamberetti	Shrimps	Sarde	Sardines
Gámberi	Prawns	Seppie	Cuttlefish
Granchio	Crab	Sgombro	Mackerel
Merluzzo	Cod	Sógliola	Sole
Nasello	Hake	Spígola	Sea bass
Orata	Gilthead bream	Tonno	Tuna
Ostriche	Oysters	Tótani	Species of squid
Pesce spada	Swordfish	Triglie	Red mullet
Pólpo	Octopus	Trota	Trout
Ricci di mare	Sea urchins	Vóngole	Clams

Vegetables (contorni) and salad (insalata)

Asparagi	Asparagus	Finocchio	Fennel
Basílico	Basil	Funghi	Mushrooms
Broccoli	Broccoli	Insalata verde /mista	Green salad/mixed salad
Cápperi	Capers		
Carciofi	Artichokes	Melanzane	Aubergine/eggplant
Carciofini	Artichoke hearts	Orígano	Oregano
Carotte	Carrots	Patate	Potatoes
Cavolfiori	Cauliflower	Peperoni	Peppers
Cávolo	Cabbage	Piselli	Peas
Ceci	Chickpeas	Pomodori	Tomatoes
Cetriolo	Cucumber	Radicchio	Red chicory
Cipolla	Onion	Spinaci	Spinach
Fagioli	Beans	Zucca	Pumpkin
Fagiolini	Green beans	Zucchini	Courgettes

Desserts (dolci)

Amaretti	Macaroons	Torta	Cake, tart
Cassata	Ice-cream cake with candied fruit	Zabaglione	Dessert made with eggs, sugar and Marsala wine
Gelato	Ice cream		
Macedonia	Fruit salad	Zuppa Inglese	Trifle

Cheese

Caciocavallo	A type of dried, mature mozzarella	Mozzarella	Soft white cheese, traditionally made from buffalo's milk
Fontina	Northern Italian cheese used in cooking		
		Parmigiano	Parmesan cheese
Gorgonzola	Soft, strong, blue-veined cheese	Pecorino	Strong-tasting, hard sheep's cheese

| Provolone | Cheese with grooved rind, either mild or slightly piquant | Vastedda Palermitana | Similar to Caciocavallo, but tastes slightly more acidic |
| Ricotta | Soft white cheese made from ewe's milk, used in sweet or savoury dishes | | |

Fruit and nuts

Albicocche	Apricots	Limone	Lemon
Ananas	Pineapple	Mándorle	Almonds
Anguria/coccómero	Watermelon	Mele	Apples
Arance	Oranges	Melone	Melon
Banane	Bananas	Néspole	Medlars
Cacchi	Persimmons	Pere	Pears
Ciliegie	Cherries	Pesche	Peaches
Fichi	Figs	Pinoli	Pine nuts
Fichi d'India	Prickly pears	Pistacchio	Pistachio nut
Frágole	Strawberries	Uva	Grapes

Cooking terms

Affumicato	Smoked	Al Marsala	Cooked with Marsala wine
Arrosto	Roast	Milanese	Fried in egg and breadcrumbs
Ben cotto	Well done		
Bollito/lesso	Boiled	Pizzaiola	Cooked with tomato sauce
Alla brace	Barbecued		
Brasato	Cooked in wine	Ripieno	Stuffed
Cotto	Cooked (not raw)	Sangue	Rare
Crudo	Raw	Allo spiedo	On the spit
Al dente	Firm, not overcooked	Stracotto	Braised, stewed
Ferri	Grilled without oil	Surgelati	Frozen
Al forno	Baked	In úmido	Stewed
Fritto	Fried	Al vapore	Steamed
Grattugiato	Grated		
Alla griglia	Grilled		

Sicilian specialities: starters and pasta

Arancini	"Little oranges": deep-fried rice balls with minced meat, cheese and peas	Cozze pepata	Mussels in spicy tomato stock
		Crocchè di patate	Potato croquettes
		Insalata di arance	Orange salad, dressed with oil and parsley
Caponata	Sautéed aubergine, olives and tomatoes; served cold		
		Maccu	Fava-bean (like lima-bean) soup
Cozze alla marinara	Mussels in a rich wine-based soup	Panelle	Chickpea fritters

Pasta con i broccoli arriminati	Pasta cooked with broccoli, anchovy paste, pine nuts and saffron
Pasta con la mollica	Pasta with oil and toasted breadcrumbs
Pasta con le sarde	Macaroni with fresh sardines, fennel, raisins and pine kernels; a speciality of Palermo
Penne all'arrabbiata	Short tubular pasta with spicy tomato sauce made with chillies (*arrabbiata* means "angry")
Peperonata	Peppers (capsicum) sautéed in olive oil until soft and sweet, either served as antipasto or as a vegetable
Spaghetti alla carrettiera	"Carter's spaghetti", cooked with garlic, oil, pecorino and salt and pepper; a dish traditionally cooked by roving carters, common in Catania province
Spaghetti alla Norma	Spaghetti with tomato sauce topped with fried aubergine and parmesan or pecorino cheese; a speciality of Catania, named after one of Bellini's operas
Spaghetti alla Trapanese	Spaghetti tossed with cold puréed tomatoes, basil and garlic; a pungent dish from Trápani
Uova/funghi in tegame	Eggs/mushrooms fried in olive oil, served at the table in a little metal pan

Sicilian specialities: main courses

Cuscus	Couscous, usually served with fish and vegetable sauce, sometimes meat; a common dish in western Sicily and on the islands of Lampedusa and Pantelleria
Fritto misto	A standard seafood dish; deep-fried prawns and squid rings in batter
Fritto di pesce	As above but also with other fried fish, like sardines and whitebait
Involtini di pesce spada	Slices of swordfish, stuffed, rolled and fried
Pesce spada alla Ghiotta	Swordfish cooked in spicy tomato sauce with capers and olives; from Messina province
Sarde a beccafico	Sardines stuffed with breadcrumbs, nuts, dried fruit and anchovies; a Palermitan speciality
Scaloppine di maiale al Marsala	Escalopes of pork cooked in Marsala wine; the most common way of cooking meat with this Sicilian wine

| Stocca alla Messinese | Dried cod stewed with potatoes, olives, tomatoes, capers and celery; a speciality of Messina although there are other regional variations | Zuppa di cozze/ vóngole | A big dish of mussels/ clams in rich wine-based soup |
| | | Zuppa di pesce | As above but usually with pieces of cod, squid and prawns, and served with fried bread |

Sicilian specialities: desserts and festival food

Cannoli	Fried pastry stuffed with sweet ricotta and candied peel; a Carnevale speciality	Sfinci	Fried pastry stuffed with ricotta; served at the festival of St Joseph (San Giuseppe)
Cassata	Ice-cream cake with candied fruit	Torrone di mándorle	Crystallized almonds and sugar, sold at markets around All Saints' Day
Crispelle di riso	Sweet rice fritters		
Frutti di Martorana	Marzipan-based confection shaped and coloured to look like fruit, vegetables, and even fish		
Ossa dei morti	Literally "dead men's bones", a clove-flavoured, sugared pastry handed out to children on All Hallows' Eve (October 31), and almost identical to *Agnellini pasquali* (Easter lambs)		

Drinks

Acqua minerale	Mineral water	Succo di frutta	Concentrated fruit juice with sugar
Aranciata	Orangeade		
Bicchiere	Glass	Tè	Tea
Birra	Beer	Tónico	Tonic water
Bottiglia	Bottle	Vino	Wine
Caffè	Coffee	Rosso	Red
Cioccolata calda	Hot chocolate	Bianco	White
Ghiaccio	Ice	Rosato	Rosé
Granita	Iced coffee/fruit drink	Secco	Dry
Latte	Milk	Dolce	Sweet
Limonata	Lemonade	Litro	Litre
Selz	Soda water	Mezzo	Half-litre
Spremuta	Fresh fruit juice	Quarto	Quarter-litre
Spumante	Sparkling wine	Salute!	Cheers!

Glossaries

Artistic and architectural terms

Agora Square or marketplace in an ancient Greek city.

Apse Domed recess at the altar-end of a church.

Architrave The lowest part of the entablature.

Atrium Forecourt, usually of a Roman house.

Bothros A pit that contains votive offerings.

Campanile Belltower.

Capital Top of a column.

Catalan-Gothic Hybrid form of architecture, mixing elements from fifteenth-century Spanish and northern European building styles.

Cavea The seating section in a theatre.

Cella Sanctuary of a temple.

Cupola A dome.

Decumanus The main street in a Roman town.

Entablature The part of the building above the capital on a classical building.

Ex-voto Decorated tablet designed as thanksgiving to a saint.

Hellenistic period 323–30 BC (Alexander the Great to Augustus).

Hypogeum Underground vault, often used as an early Christian church.

Kouros Standing male figure of the Archaic period (700 BC to early fifth century BC).

Krater Ancient conical bowl with round base.

Loggia Roofed gallery or balcony.

Metope A panel on the frieze of a temple.

Naumachia Mock naval combat, or the deep trench in a theatre in which it took place.

Nave Central space in a church, usually flanked by aisles.

Odeon Small theatre, usually roofed, for recitals.

Orchestra Section of the main floor of a theatre, where the chorus danced.

Pantocrator Usually refers to Christ, portrayed with outstretched arms.

Pediment The triangular front part of a building, usually surmounting a portico of columns.

Polyptych Painting or carving on several joined wooden panels.

Portico The covered entrance to a building.

Punic Carthaginian/Phoenician.

Scene-building Structure holding scenery in Greek/Roman theatre.

Stelae Inscribed stone slabs.

Stereobate Visible base of any building, usually a temple.

Stoa A detached roofed porch, or portico.

Stylobate Raised base of a columned building, usually a temple.

Telamon A supporting column in the shape of a male figure.

Thermae Baths, usually elaborate buildings in Roman villas.

Triptych Painting or carving on three joined wooden panels.

Italian words

Aliscafo Hydrofoil.

Anfiteatro Amphitheatre.

Autostazione Bus station.

Autostrada Motorway.

Belvedere A lookout point.

Cappella Chapel.

Castello Castle.

Cattedrale Cathedral.

Centro Centre.

Chiesa Church (main "mother" church, Chiesa Matrice/Madre).

Comune An administrative area; also, the local council or the town hall.

Corso Avenue/boulevard.

Duomo Cathedral.

Entrata Entrance.

Faraglione Obelisk-shaped deposits of volcanic rock rising out of the sea.

Festa Festival, carnival.

Fiume River.

Fumarola Volcanic vapour emission from the ground.

Golfo Gulf.

Lago Lake.

Largo Place (like piazza).

Lungomare Seafront promenade or road.

Mare Sea.

Mercato Market.

Mongibello Sicilian name for Mount Etna.

Municipio Town hall.

Palazzo Palace, mansion or block (of flats).

Parco Park.

Passeggiata The customary early-evening walk.

Pedaggio Toll.

Piano Plain (also "slowly", "gently").

Piazza Square.

Pineta Pinewood.

Santuario Sanctuary.

Sottopassaggio Subway.

Spiaggia Beach.

Stazione Station (train station, stazione ferroviaria; bus station, autostazione; ferry terminal, stazione maríttima).

Strada Road/street.

Teatro Theatre.

Tempio Temple.

Torre Tower.

Traghetto Ferry.

Uscita Exit.

Vícolo Alley

Via Road (always used with name, as in Via Roma).

Zona Zone.

Acronyms

AAST Azienda Autonoma di Soggiorno e Turismo (local tourist office).

ACI Italian Automobile Club.

APT Azienda Provinciale di Turismo (provincial tourist office).

EPT Ente Provinciale di Turismo (provincial tourist office).

DC Democrazia Cristiana; the Christian Democrat party.

FS Italian State Railways.

IVA Imposta Valore Aggiunto (VAT).

MSI Movimento Sociale d'Italia; the Italian Neo-Fascist party, now called the Alleanza Nazionale.

PDS Partito Democratico della Sinistra; the former Italian Communist Party.

PSI Partito Socialista d'Italia; the Italian Socialist Party.

RAI The Italian state TV and radio network.

SP Strada Provinciale; a minor road, eg SP116.

SS Strada Statale; a main highway, eg SS120.

Travel
store

Small print and
Index

A Rough Guide to Rough Guides

Published in 1982, the first Rough Guide – to Greece – was a student scheme that became a publishing phenomenon. Mark Ellingham, a recent graduate in English from Bristol University, had been travelling in Greece the previous summer and couldn't find the right guidebook. With a small group of friends he wrote his own guide, combining a highly contemporary, journalistic style with a thoroughly practical approach to travellers' needs.

The immediate success of the book spawned a series that rapidly covered dozens of destinations. And, in addition to impecunious backpackers, Rough Guides soon acquired a much broader and older readership that relished the guides' wit and inquisitiveness as much as their enthusiastic, critical approach and value-for-money ethos.

These days, Rough Guides include recommendations from shoestring to luxury and cover more than 200 destinations around the globe, including almost every country in the Americas and Europe, more than half of Africa and most of Asia and Australasia. Our ever-growing team of authors and photographers is spread all over the world, particularly in Europe, the USA and Australia.

In the early 1990s, Rough Guides branched out of travel, with the publication of Rough Guides to World Music, Classical Music and the Internet. All three have become benchmark titles in their fields, spearheading the publication of a wide range of books under the Rough Guide name.

Including the travel series, Rough Guides now number more than 350 titles, covering: phrasebooks, waterproof maps, music guides from Opera to Heavy Metal, reference works as diverse as Conspiracy Theories and Shakespeare, and popular culture books from iPods to Poker. Rough Guides also produce a series of more than 120 World Music CDs in partnership with World Music Network.

Visit www.roughguides.com to see our latest publications.

Rough Guide travel images are available for commercial licensing at www.roughguidespictures.com

Rough Guide credits

Text editors: Greg Ward & Ruth Blackmore
Layout: Anita Singh
Cartography: Alakananda Bhattacharya
Picture editor: Nicole Newman
Production: Vicky Baldwin
Proofreader: Jason Freeman
Cover design: Chloë Roberts
Photographer: Jon Cunningham
Editorial: London Ruth Blackmore, Alison
Murchie, Karoline Thomas, Andy Turner, Keith
Drew, Edward Aves, Alice Park, Lucy White,
Jo Kirby, James Smart, Natasha Foges, Róisín
Cameron, Emma Traynor, Emma Gibbs, Kathryn
Lane, Christina Valhouli, Monica Woods, James
Rice, Mani Ramaswamy, Joe Staines, Peter
Buckley, Matthew Milton, Tracy Hopkins, Ruth
Tidball; **New York** Andrew Rosenberg, Steven
Horak, AnneLise Sorensen, April Isaacs, Ella
Steim, Anna Owens, Sean Mahoney, Courtney
Miller, Paula Neudorf; **Delhi** Madhavi Singh,
Karen D'Souza
Design & Pictures: London Scott Stickland, Dan
May, Diana Jarvis, Mark Thomas, Chloë Roberts,
Sarah Cummins, Emily Taylor; **Delhi** Umesh

Aggarwal, Ajay Verma, Jessica Subramanian,
Ankur Guha, Pradeep Thapliyal, Sachin Tanwar,
Nikhil Agarwal
Production: Rebecca Short,
Cartography: London Maxine Repath, Ed
Wright, Katie Lloyd-Jones; **Delhi** Jai Prakash
Mishra, Rajesh Chhibber, Ashutosh Bharti, Rajesh
Mishra, Animesh Pathak, Jasbir Sandhu, Karobi
Gogoi, Amod Singh, Swati Handoo
Online: Narender Kumar, Rakesh Kumar,
Amit Verma, Rahul Kumar, Ganesh Sharma,
Debojit Borah, Saurabh Sati, Ravi Yadav
Marketing & Publicity: London Liz Statham,
Niki Hanmer, Louise Maher, Jess Carter, Vanessa
Godden, Vivienne Watton, Anna Paynton, Rachel
Sprackett, Libby Jellie; **New York** Geoff Colquitt,
Katy Ball; **Delhi** Ragini Govind
Manager India: Punita Singh
Reference Director: Andrew Lockett
Operations Manager: Helen Phillips
PA to Publishing Director: Nicola Henderson
Publishing Director: Martin Dunford
Commercial Manager: Gino Magnotta
Managing Director: John Duhigg

Publishing information

This seventh edition published June 2008 by
Rough Guides Ltd,
80 Strand, London WC2R 0RL
345 Hudson St, 4th Floor,
New York, NY 10014, USA
14 Local Shopping Centre, Panchsheel Park,
New Delhi 110017, India
Distributed by the Penguin Group
Penguin Books Ltd,
80 Strand, London WC2R 0RL
Penguin Group (USA)
375 Hudson Street, NY 10014, USA
Penguin Group (Australia)
250 Camberwell Road, Camberwell,
Victoria 3124, Australia
Penguin Books Canada Ltd,
10 Alcorn Avenue, Toronto, Ontario,
Canada M4V 1E4
Penguin Group (NZ)
67 Apollo Drive, Mairangi Bay, Auckland 1310,
New Zealand

Cover concept by Peter Dyer.
Typeset in Bembo and Helvetica to an original
design by Henry Iles.
Printed in China
© Robert Andrews and Jules Brown 2008
No part of this book may be reproduced in any
form without permission from the publisher except
for the quotation of brief passages in reviews.
488pp includes index
A catalogue record for this book is available from
the British Library
ISBN 9-78185-828-437-8

The publishers and authors have done their
best to ensure the accuracy and currency of all
the information in **The Rough Guide to Sicily**,
however, they can accept no responsibility for
any loss, injury, or inconvenience sustained by
any traveller as a result of information or advice
contained in the guide.

1   3   5   7   9   8   6   4   2

Help us update

We've gone to a lot of effort to ensure that the
seventh edition of **The Rough Guide to Sicily** is
accurate and up to date. However, things change
– places get "discovered", opening hours are
notoriously fickle, restaurants and rooms raise
prices or lower standards. If you feel we've got it
wrong or left something out, we'd like to know,
and if you can remember the address, the price,
the hours, the phone number, so much the better.

Please send your comments with the subject
line "**Rough Guide Sicily Update**" to © mail@
roughguides.com. We'll credit all contributions
and send a copy of the next edition (or any other
Rough Guide if you prefer) for the very best
emails.
   Have your questions answered and tell others
about your trip at
® community.roughguides.com

ROUGH
GUIDES

SMALL PRINT

Acknowledgements

Robert Andrews would like to thank Uncle Arthur and Auntie Giovanna, Agata, Doriano, Jan, and Specky, a great chick. Grateful thanks are also due to Ruth Blackmore and Greg Ward for a superb edit.

Jules Brown sends his thanks to all those who helped with the research and provided assistance for this edition, notably Ros Belford, Diana Brown, Lynette Chaplin, Mario at Mamma Santina, Alfio Settembre at Hotel Roma, the Lombardo family at Villa Greta, and UNA hotels.

Readers' letters

Thanks to all the readers who took the trouble to write in with their comments and suggestions (and apologies to anyone whose name we've either transcribed incorrectly, or omitted):

Ruth Baker, Margaret Bevans, Alan Blandamer, Frank Blasi, Robert Bottomley, Ray Boyce, Amanda Briffa, Rosena Davison, Monica DeVold, Gary Elflett, Theresa Gatward, Alan and Helen Gibson, Frank Graziano, Janet Grylls, Rich Hall, Sue & Dave Hardwick, Peter Hoare, Jock Holm, Jeremy Hoult, Neil Hunter and Paula Rogers, Mark Jackobson, Colm Kenneally, Richard Lamey, June Lightfoot, Karen Mann and Kevin Marren, John Murtagh, Norma Negrete, Ann and Geoff Obee, James Owen, Terhi Pakkala, Neil Richmond, Bob & Rose Sandham, Marcello Sanucci & Pilar, Simon Sapper and Bev Fitzsimons, Robert Schick, Andreas "the great" Stegmann, Larry Steingold, David Thomas, Dave Tootell, Caroline Wright, Nagapriya Wright.

Photo credits

All photos © Rough Guides except the following:

Title page
Palace of the Normans, Palermo © Tips images

Introduction
Beach, Cefalù © The Travel Library Ltd.
A snow-covered Mount Etna at sunrise © Ellen Rooney/Robert Harding
Shop detail, Lípari Island, Aeolian © Sarah Cummins
Football in Ortigia, Siracusa © Tips images
Acrid sulphuric gas in the walls of the Gran Cratere, Vulcano © Frits Meyst/drr.net
Al fresco dining, Cefalù © Chuck Pefley/drr.net
Il Postino (1995) © Movie Store Collection

Things not to miss
Mount Etna © REUTERS/Antonio Parrinello
Ortigia, Siracusa © Hubert Stadler/CORBIS
Pantelleria © Dino Fracchia/drr.net
Trekking, Strómboli volcano © Frits Meyst/drr.net
Diving, Ustica © Tips Images

Black and whites
p.120 Caccamo, Hill Town View © Walter Bibikow/DanitaDelimont.com/drr.net
p.212 Gola di Alcántara © Sarah Cummins
p.233 Etna volcano © Getty Images/Aurora Creative
p.453 *The Leopard* (1963) © Movie Store Collection

SMALL PRINT

Selected images from our guidebooks are available for licensing from:

ROUGHGUIDESPICTURES.COM

Index

Map entries are in colour.

I

Map symbols

maps are listed in the full index using coloured text

– – –	Chapter division boundary	◊	Point of interest
▬▬	Motorway	@	Internet café
═══	Major road	ⓘ	Tourist office
══	Minor road	ℂ	Phone office
▬▬	Viaduct	⊠	Post office
⊞⊞⊞	Steps	⊞	Hospital
}·····{	Underpass or long tunnel	◉	Accommodation
▬▬	Railway	▣	Restaurant
●---●	Cable car	⚘	Campsite
- - - -	Footpath	⋮	Ruin
———	River/coastline	ⵋ	Lighthouse
— —	Ferry/hydrofoil	▮	Tower
■ ■ ■	Wall	ⵣ	Gardens
⊠—⊠	Gate	♦	Museum
)(	Bridge	ⵜ	Church (regional maps)
∧	Mountain range	⛪	Monastery
▲	Mountain peak	☐	Market
⌇	Cliff	▬	Building
⌇	Rocks	⊞	Church
⌇	Gorge	⬭	Stadium
⸜	Viewpoint	⊞	Cemetery
✈	Airport	▨	Park
★	Bus stop	⣿	Beach
P	Parking		

MAP SYMBOLS

487